Proceedings of the Seminar for Arabian Studies

Volume 40

2010

Papers from the forty-third meeting of the
Seminar for Arabian Studies
held at the British Museum, London,
23–25 July 2009

Seminar for Arabian Studies

Archaeopress
Oxford

Orders for copies of this volume of the *Proceedings* and of all back numbers should be sent to Archaeopress, Gordon House, 276 Banbury Road, Oxford OX2 7ED, UK.
Tel/Fax +44-(0)1865-311914.
e-mail bar@archaeopress.com
http://www.archaeopress.com
For the availability of back issues see the Seminar's web site: www.arabianseminar.org.uk

Seminar for Arabian Studies
c/o the Department of the Middle East, The British Museum
London, WC1B 3DG, United Kingdom
e-mail seminar.arab@durham.ac.uk

Opinions expressed in papers published in the *Proceedings* are those of the authors and are not necessarily shared by the Editorial Committee.

Typesetting, Layout and Production: Dr David Milson

The *Proceedings* is produced in the Times Semitic New font, which was designed by Paul Bibire for the Seminar for Arabian Studies.

ISSN 0308-8421
ISBN 978-1-905739-33-2

The Steering Committee of the Seminar for Arabian Studies is most grateful to the

MBI Al Jaber Foundation

for its continued generosity in making a substantial grant toward the running costs of the Seminar and the editorial expenses of producing the *Proceedings*.

Contents

Transliteration

From *PSAS* 39 onwards, the transliteration system shown below has been in operation. Authors should use this when preparing their manuscripts for submission. For further details on submission of papers, authors are requested to consult and follow the latest *Instructions for Authors* which are available on the Seminar website at http://www.arabianseminar.org.uk

Quotations, single words, and phrases from Arabic, or other languages written in non-Roman alphabets, should be transliterated according to the systems set out below.

However, unless an author insists on a particular transliteration in all circumstances, place names and words from languages written in non-Roman alphabets which have entered English or French in a particular form (e.g. Mocha, Dhofar, qadi, wadi, imam/iman), are reproduced in that form when they are part of an English or French sentence, rather than part of a quotation in the original language or of a strictly transliterated name or phrase. For example:

1. "the settlement was built in the wadi bed" BUT "the settlement in Wādī Mayfaʿah"
2. "l'iman alla à Médine" BUT "Imām ʿAlī vint de al-Madīnah al-Munawwarah"

The transliteration systems are as follows:

(a) Arabic

ء	ʾ	ج	*j*	ذ	*dh* (*dh*)	ش	*sh* (*sh*)	ظ	*ẓ*	ق	*q*	ن	*n*
ب	*b*	ح	*ḥ*	ر	*r*	ص	*ṣ*	ع	ʿ	ك	*k*	ه	*h*
ت	*t*	خ	*kh* (*kh*)	ز	*z*	ض	*ḍ*	غ	*gh* (*gh*)	ل	*l*	و	*w*
ث	*th* (*th*)	د	*d*	س	*s*	ط	*ṭ*	ف	*f*	م	*m*	ي	*y*

Vowels: **a i u ā ī ū**; Diphthongs: **aw ay**.

Initial *hamzah* is omitted.

The *lām* of the article is not assimilated before the "sun letters", thus *al-shams* not *ash-shams*.

The *hamzat al-waṣl* of the article is shown after vowels except after the preposition *li-*, as in the Arabic script, e.g. *wa-ʾl-wazīr*, *fī ʾl-bayt*, but *li-l-wazīr*. This rule applies specifically to papers on language or literature. See Guidelines for further details.

Tā' marbūṭah (ة) should be rendered *-ah*, except in a construct [*iḍāfah*]: e.g. *birkah*, *zakāh*, but *birkat al-sibāḥah*, *zakāt al-fiṭr*.

(b) Ancient North and South Arabian

ʾ	*b*	*t*	*ṯ*	*ḥ*	*g*	*ḫ*	*d*	*ḏ*	*r*	*z*	s^1	s^2	s^3	*ṣ*	*ḍ*	*ṭ*	*ẓ*	ʿ	*ġ*	*f*	*q*	*k*	*l*	*m*	*n*	*h*	*w*	*y*

(c) Other Semitic languages appear in the transliteration systems outlined in the *Bulletin of the American Schools of Oriental Research* 226 (1986), p. 3.

(d) Persian, Urdu, and Ottoman Turkish as for Arabic with the additional letters transliterated according to the system in the *Encyclopaedia of Islam* (New Edition) except that *ž* is used instead of *zh*.

Editor's Foreword

The **Seminar for Arabian Studies** is the only international academic forum which meets annually for the presentation of research in the humanities on the Arabian Peninsula. It focuses particularly on the fields of archaeology, architecture, art, epigraphy, ethnography, history, language, linguistics, literature, and numismatics from the earliest times to the present day. A wide range of papers presented at the Seminar are published in the *Proceedings* and reflect the dynamism and scope of the interdisciplinary event.

The *Proceedings* are published each spring in time for the subsequent Seminar which is held in July. Yet again, as its Editor, I have been truly impressed by the energy of the authors themselves, who have answered my comments promptly and effectively, often while undertaking fieldwork in locations where internet connections are difficult. The *Proceedings* appear on schedule as a result of effective collaboration between the production team, authors, and editors. We are particularly grateful to our marvellous copy editor, Helen Knox; to the hard work, computer enthusiasm, and cheerful energy of Dr David Milson; and to Rajka Makjanic of Archaeopress for her fine attention to detail.

As papers are subject to rigorous review in order to maintain the highest academic standards, not all the papers that are offered are accepted for publication. The *Proceedings* benefit from the support of enthusiastic and diligent editorial and steering committees, which provide an extended range of expertise and support. Thanks are due to all the members of these committees, as well as many others. Their conscientious and useful academic reviews were generally provided speedily, despite conflicting teaching, exhibition, administrative, and research commitments. Dr Ardle MacMahon and Andrew Thompson provide excellent logistical support and Dr Mark Beech kindly maintains and updates the Seminar website. Thanks are also due to Dr John Cooper for the evocative cover image on this edition.

During the summer of 2009, the *Instructions for Authors* and the *Guidelines for Editors* were rigorously revised to accommodate recent IT facilities. Robert Carter (Chair, Seminar Committee), Helen Knox, Michael Macdonald, David Milson, and Paul Starkey have been particularly rigorous in their reviews of these documents and provided the Editor with many helpful suggestions and corrections. These *Instructions* and *Guidelines* mark a significant change in the preparation of papers as authors can now opt either for the traditional slash system or for diacritics and symbols embedded in Times Semitic New. For the first time, this font and the recommended Greek font are now available online on the Seminar website at http://www.arabianseminar.org.uk/fonts.html, as are the *Instructions for Authors* (http://www.arabianseminar.org.uk/GuidelinesforPSASauthors_revised4.pdf) and *Guidelines for Editors* (http://www.arabianseminar.org.uk/PSAS40guidelinesforeditors2009.pdf). These *Instructions* and *Guidelines* will be maintained, refined, and clarified by the Editorial Committee for *Proceedings* produced in subsequent years, as necessary.

In addition, there is now a very useful online cumulative index by author surname with article titles for volumes 1 to 39 (1971 to 2009) of the *Proceedings of the Seminar for Arabian Studies* at http://www.arabianseminar.org.uk/psas-index.html. A downloadable PDF version is also available. Thanks to Dr David Milson and Dr Mark Beech for helping to produce this index. Furthermore, it is now possible to buy a CD-ROM containing the entire *Proceedings* as searchable PDF files up to 2007 on CD-ROM. For details, please contact Archaeopress at: www.archaeopress.com.

We hope you find the papers from a wide range of disciplines in this volume fascinating. The *Proceedings* present the cutting edge of new research on Arabia and includes reports of new discoveries in the Peninsula. Several papers from the focus session on Qatar at the Seminar are included in this volume, as are interesting reports from archaeological sites in Oman, Saudi Arabia, UAE, and Yemen. Other topics include an important paper on Sabaean-Ethiopian connections as discovered on a site in Tigray, Ethiopia; epigraphic studies (including irrigation management in pre-Islamic South Arabia; Sabaic inscriptions, Epigraphic South Arabian; linguistic studies on Mahri, and on the dialect of Zabīd); papers variously focusing on topography, old trade routes, and architecture in Arabia; on talismans in the Ḥaḍramawt; and on boatbuilding in Yemen, among many other topics. We also include notes in memoriam on Professor Serge Cleuziou who has done so much to encourage archaeological research in Arabia and on Dr Geraldine King, Secretary of the Seminar and Editor of the *Proceedings* between 1993 and 1996 (volumes 23 to 26). We encourage you to recommend the volume to your academic institutions and colleagues and look forward to further stimulating and informative Seminars.

Another important feature of the Seminar 2009 was a special session on "The development of Arabic as a written language", which took place on the morning and early afternoon of the second day. It was followed, later that afternoon, by a very successful informal workshop at which the morning's discussions were continued, and inscriptions, manuscripts, and other items of particular relevance to the subject of the session were presented. An introduction and background to the session was provided the evening before by the MBI Al Jaber Foundation Annual Lecture at the British Museum, which was given by Michael Macdonald on "Ancient Arabia and the written word".

A large amount of new material was presented in the Session, as well as new interpretations of the linguistic milieu and the uses of literacy in Arabia in the centuries before and just after the rise of Islam. Almost all the papers presented in the Session, plus the MBI Al Jaber lecture, are being published in a Supplement to this volume of the *Proceedings*, edited by Michael Macdonald, which is available either with this volume or separately. Together, these important contributions to the subject provide the most up-to-date assessment of how and why Arabic changed from a purely spoken to a written language.

For more information about the Seminar for Arabian Studies please contact: Dr Ardle MacMahon (Secretary), Seminar for Arabian Studies, The British Museum, c/o Department of the Middle East, Great Russell Street, London WC1B 3DG, United Kingdom. E-mail: seminar.arab@durham.ac.uk and/or visit the seminar website at: www.arabianseminar.org.uk.

Janet Starkey
Editor, Proceedings of the Seminar for Arabian Studies
Honorary Research Fellow,
Department of Archaeology,
Durham University,
South Road,
Durham DH1 3LE
UK

e-mail j.c.m.starkey@dur.ac.uk

Proceedings of the Seminar for Arabian Studies 40 (2010): ix–x

In memoriam
Serge Cleuziou

Serge Cleuziou sadly passed away on the 7 October 2009 after a long battle with illness. He was sixty-four. He was Professor of Ancient Near Eastern archaeology from 2003 at Paris 1 Panthéon-Sorbonne University and also a researcher at the CNRS (Centre National de la Recherche Scientifique) from 1972. He headed the team "Du Village à l'État au Proche et Moyen Orient" of the CNRS laboratory "Archéologies et Sciences de l'Antiquité" (ArScAn, UMR 7041). His tragic death has come as a shock to his family, friends, colleagues, and students.

It is difficult to sum up a career and a life in a few words. Both were marked with high-quality research and political commitment. Serge Cleuziou considered archaeological research could only be carried out by taking part in the methodological, epistemological, and ideological struggle that would allow archaeology to gain scientific credit and to confer it an important place among the social sciences. This is why interdisciplinarity held such an important place in his research, as he always focused on the convergence of the social sciences with the natural sciences, as well as being interested in other fields such as history, linguistics, or climatology. In the same way, even though he was a specialist in the ancient Near East, he never ceased to be interested in the archaeology of other continents in order to go beyond the orientalist clichés of which this field is still riddled. The variety of his interests, the multiplicity of his approaches, the will to work in a team, and his scientific involvement were the guidelines of Serge Cleuziou's career.

After a degree in French Language and Literature followed by a degree in History, he was a primary schoolteacher for four years, and in 1972 became a researcher at the CNRS. In 1974 he obtained his PhD in Ancient Near Eastern Archaeology at the Paris 1 University with a thesis entitled, *Les Pointes de flèche en métal au Proche et Moyen Orient des origines à la période achéménide: étude typologique.* A student of Jean Deshayes, he applied systematic descriptive methods in his thesis on the typology of arrowheads. He also employed one of the earliest technologies of data processing: perforated cards. The aim of his thesis was to show, thanks to this innovative approach, that an historical interest in archaeological data had been given little consideration by the majority of researchers at that time.

His field of research began with archaeological excavations in the north of Iran on the site of Tureng Tepe (under the direction of Jean Deshayes). He then took an interest in the archaeology of the Gulf on the "arid margin" of the Middle East, where many unknown types of remains had been discovered but which up until that time had remained under-studied. Having been appointed Director of the French Archaeological Mission to Abu Dhabi, he was one of the first archaeologists to work there. He conducted several campaigns of surveys and excavations in the Jabal Ḥafīt and in the oasis of al-ʿAyn (Hili graves, Hili 8 building), in Abu Dhabi in the UAE between 1977 and 1984. From 1985, with his Italian colleague Maurizio Tosi, he co-directed the Joint Hadd Project, a French-Italian project that focused on the study of the Jaʿalān, the easternmost area of the Sultanate of Oman. Under this project he conducted excavations on the site of Raʾs al-Jinz. From 2006, he initiated the "Adam Oasis Project", for which three campaigns were led by a French team, beginning their excavations in 2007. In thirty years of field research, Serge Cleuziou contributed in a major way to the development of archaeology in eastern Arabia.

Alongside his activities in the Middle East (in addition to the UAE and the Sultanate of Oman, he worked in Iraq, Yemen, and Turkmenistan), he was also one of the main agents for the renewal of archaeology in France, being one of the founding members, with Anick Coudart, Jean-Paul Demoule, and Alain Schnapp, of the journal *Les Nouvelles de l'Archéologie*. He also participated in the development of field methods for preventive archaeology. He was always a committed, non-conformist researcher, often deliberately provocative, but also a very warm person, a helpful tutor, and very close to his students.

The prehistory of maritime exchanges, interactions between men and their environment, and models of social evolution were at the heart of his last works. Serge Cleuziou will be deeply missed by the archaeological community, but his work and theories will no doubt contribute for a long time to the progress of research in his chosen field.

G. Gernez, J. Giraud, S. Righetti, and O. Munoz

Serge Cleuziou
1945-2009

Proceedings of the Seminar for Arabian Studies 40 (2010): xi–xii

In memoriam
Geraldine King

Geraldine Margaret Harmsworth King died on 12 October 2009 after a long and courageous battle with cancer. She was fifty-five and leaves a daughter, Ellie, who is thirteen. Geraldine served as Secretary of the Seminar and editor of the *Proceedings*, between 1992 and 1996. She organized the annual meetings in Oxford, Cambridge, Manchester, and London and all those who attended the Seminar in those days will remember her kindness, efficiency, and extremely hard work. When the news of her death was circulated to all those on the Seminar's mailing list I received an enormous number of warm messages from those who remembered her with gratitude and affection.

Geraldine was an excellent scholar who played an important part in deepening our understanding of the Ancient North Arabian inscriptions and providing a much sounder basis for their study. She undertook a number of expeditions to the deserts of Jordan and Syria and the mountains of Dhofar, recording thousands of inscriptions which she then worked on patiently and perceptively over many years.

Before she went up to the University of Durham to read Philosophy in the early 1970s, Geraldine had spent a year teaching in Ethiopia. After graduating from Durham, she spent another year teaching, this time in Sudan. While there, she began to learn spoken Arabic and on her return to the UK enrolled for a degree course in Arabic at the School of Oriental and African Studies, University of London. As part of this course, she spent a year in Amman at the University of Jordan; it was there that Annie Searight and I first got to know her and she became a life-long friend.

Having completed her SOAS degree she came to work with me at Yarmouk University on the Corpus of the Inscriptions of Jordan Project which I had set up there, at the behest of Professor Mahmud al-Ghul. Geraldine worked on the Project for almost five years, recording large numbers of Safaitic inscriptions and creating much of the academic infrastructure for the Project.

In 1986 and 1987, she single-handedly recorded over 1500 Hismaic inscriptions in the south of Jordan. She produced an edition of most of these in her doctoral thesis at SOAS, which was completed in 1990. However, her thesis was much more than an edition, for in it she undertook the first detailed analysis of every aspect of this type of Ancient North Arabian inscription, thus making it possible to separate it from the "Thamudic pending file" in which, under the name "Thamudic E", it had languished since the 1930s. Although she never published her thesis, it quickly became, and has remained, the standard reference work on the subject; photocopies of it can be found in most academic libraries dealing with ancient Jordan and Arabia.

Between January and March 1989, Geraldine and Becca Montague spent six weeks in the basalt desert of north-eastern Jordan in freezing temperatures, recording inscriptions and sites which were about to be destroyed by bulldozers clearing a network of tracks for the enormous machines searching for oil-bearing rocks. In the process, Geraldine recorded over 3700 inscriptions and a huge number of rock drawings, and Becca over 400 sites (see *PSAS* 20, 1990: 55–78). Geraldine had almost finished preparing the inscriptions for publication when she died.

In the 1980s and early 1990s, ᶜAlī Aḥmad al-Maḥāsh al-Shaḥrī discovered hundreds of painted and carved texts in the mountains of Dhofar, in a previously unknown form of the South Semitic script (see *PSAS* 21, 1991: 173–191). He asked Geraldine to mount an expedition with him to record these and in 1991 and 1992 they recorded some 900. Geraldine wrote a very full report and even designed a font to represent the letters of the inscriptions so that she could prepare a concordance, a prerequisite for any decipherment.

I am happy to say that, within the next two years, her thesis and these two other large collections of inscriptions will be published online on the website of the new *Ancient Arabia: Languages and Cultures* (AALC) project of the Khalili Research Institute, University of Oxford.

In 1995 and 1996 she joined the first two seasons of the Safaitic Epigraphic Survey Programme, which recorded over 4000 Safaitic inscriptions in southern Syria. However, in December 1996 her daughter, Ellie, was born and from then on Geraldine concentrated on the more important and rewarding role of being a mother.

Geraldine was not only an excellent scholar and an indefatigable field-worker, but also a warm, loyal, generous, and affectionate friend. She could always be relied on in any circumstances, however gruelling, and showed great courage and endurance when required. She was also gentle and funny and very kind. She will be fondly remembered by all who were lucky enough to come into contact with her.

Michael Macdonald

Geraldine King
1954-2009

Focus session: current fieldwork in Qatar

In recent years the Qatar Museums Authority has been actively encouraging archaeological research and fieldwork in Qatar. This work has taken the form of field surveys, remote sensing, and excavations and has resulted in the production of a considerable amount of new and potentially important archaeological information from an area that was, for some archaeological periods, one of the least known areas in eastern Arabia.

In recognition of this, and as a way of bringing together both new information and those responsible for retrieving and studying it, the Committee of the Seminar for Arabian Studies, in association with the Qatar Museums Authority, organized a special focus session on current fieldwork in Qatar at the Seminar on the morning of Friday, 24 July 2009.

The five papers listed below were presented at this session. They were followed by a useful discussion with an audience of around fifty people:

Rebecca Beardmore, Richard Cuttler (Birmingham University, UK), Heiko Kallweit, Eleanor Ramsey (Birmingham University, UK), Faisal Abdulla al-Naimi (Qatar Museums Authority) & Simon Fitch (Birmingham University, UK). *Reconstruction of the late Pleistocene and Holocene palaeogeography of Qatar using remotely-sensed datasets, and the implications for the integration of such data into the National Monument Record for Qatar.*

Juergen Schreiber. *Excavations at Umm al-Maa, Qatar — preliminary report on the first two campaigns.*

Alexandrine Guérin (Maison de l'Orient, Lyon) & Faisal Abdulla al-Naimi (Qatar Museums Authority). *Pottery study from an area of the Abbasid village of Murwab (ninth century — Qatar).*

Andrew Petersen (University of Wales). *Qalᶜat al-Ruwayḍah, Qatar.*

Alan Walmsley (Copenhagen University). *Al-Zubarah and its hinterland: archaeology and heritage.*

In addition the following poster was displayed:

Faisal Abdulla al-Naimi, Richard Cuttler, Hatem Arrock & Howell Roberts. *An Upper Palaeolithic and Early Holocene flint scatter at Raʾs ᶜUshayriq, western Qatar.*

The following five papers in this volume are those from this session that were submitted for publication. It is hoped that they will provide a useful overview of some of the archaeological work that is currently being undertaken in Qatar.

Dr Derek Kennet
Durham University/Seminar for Arabian Studies

Mr Faisal Abdulla al-Naimi
Qatar Museums Authority

Current Fieldwork in Qatar

Proceedings of the Seminar for Arabian Studies 40 (2010): 5–16

The Qatar National Historic Environment Record: a bespoke cultural resource management tool and the wider implications for heritage management within the region

Rebecca Beardmore, Richard Cuttler, Faisal Al-Naimi, Eleanor Ramsey, Simon Fitch & Heiko Kallweit

Summary

It is no surprise that the integration of remotely sensed data from both terrestrial and marine sources is improving our discovery and interpretation of cultural heritage. As technological advances provide the capacity to produce and utilize large spatial datasets, their integration with existing data presents new challenges for heritage managers and future researchers. In terms of large datasets, countries such as Qatar are in a unique position given the vast amounts of commercially gathered geophysical and geotechnical data. These data can be used to model past landscapes and inform future research within the region, without the major expense of large-scale geophysical survey. However, the true value of such datasets can only be achieved if this leads to the pro-active management and protection of the resource, from designation and curation to forward planning and future research.

Over the past year, Qatar has developed a new National Historic Environment Record (known as QNHER) for this purpose. This includes data standards for recording and archiving both currently known and new archaeological sites. The diversity of cultural heritage, site types, and chronology between the Arabian Peninsula and Europe meant that simply attempting to transplant Western models of historic environment records and heritage management was inappropriate. QNHER was therefore developed as a bespoke database together with staff from the Department of Antiquities and specifically geared towards regional chronologies, local environments, chronological and spatial variation, and existing data standards. This is not to say that useful aspects of data management in other regions were ignored. Data managers were extensively consulted about the most efficient way in which data should be stored to optimize retrieval. Combined with GIS, QNHER becomes a very powerful management and research tool, able to map the distribution of sites according to variable criteria and produce reports on the data from specific queries. This combined database and GIS is not simply a tool for analysis, but also facilitates a flow of data between the Department of Antiquities and the Urban Planning Development Authority, bringing heritage into the frame when planning decisions are taken. In addition, QNHER facilitates a systematic digital record of Qatar's known archaeological and built heritage in accordance with the Qatar Antiquity Law No. 2, 1980. Managing monuments in this way will empower and inform heritage custodians, while leaving a lasting legacy for future researchers.

A number of Antiquities departments within the GCC (Gulf Cooperation Council) countries are investigating models for historic environment record development and it currently seems an ideal opportunity for heritage managers across the region to meet and discuss international Arabian data standards. Such strategies impact upon education, the accessibility of heritage information to the public, and how the historic resource is managed across the Arabian Peninsula.

Keywords: Arabia, cultural resource management, historic environment record, remote sensing, data standards

Introduction and background to the project

During 2008 and 2009 the Qatar Museums Authority (QMA) and the VISTA Centre at Birmingham University collaborated on a project to analyse remotely sensed data in both the marine and terrestrial areas of Qatar. The aim was to identify not only archaeological sites, but also deposits that would provide information about changes in the environment during the late Pleistocene and early Holocene. The interpreted data was subject to verification on the ground and accessed via a Geographical Information Systems (GIS) platform. At the same time the QMA initiated the development of a historic environment record in order to be able to manage archaeological sites within Qatar effectively, and enable the Department of Antiquities to maintain effective digital records of sites as required by Article 4 of Qatar's "Law No. 2 of 1980 on Antiquities." This law states that "Registered antiquities, whether movable or immovable, shall be listed in records kept in the Department of Tourism and Antiquities" (Qatar National Law 1980: Article 4).

This paper will focus on the development of the Qatar National Historic Environment Record (QNHER), and the design and creation of the database, which forms the basis of this record. Over the coming years, as the database is used and enhanced by staff from the Department of Antiquities, QNHER will undoubtedly be subject to further refinements and changes.

The challenge was to develop a cultural resource management tool for both onshore and offshore heritage, integrating new data from remote sensing with existing records. These data were needed in a format that was accessible through GIS but compatible with existing data standards within Qatar. Qatar has an excellent Centre for GIS which links forty-four ministries and dictates how data is transferred between these ministries. While the Centre for GIS curates its own data, it also acts as a hub enabling effective communication between different ministries and data access. By adhering to data standards set by the Centre for GIS, the new QNHER produced data that was accessible to the Urban Planning Development Authority (UPDA) through the Centre for GIS, highlighting the need for a heritage response in advance of development. This effectively puts archaeology "on the map" in Qatar, affecting future planning applications and the way in which the cultural heritage is managed.

Prior to the development of QNHER a number of other options were considered, including off-the-shelf content management systems from the UK, Europe, and America. However, a bespoke database was viewed as the best option, but using universally available software (Access and ArcGIS) with a design flexible enough to enable data to be migrated into future packages, if needed. The importance that such a tool should conform to locally accepted data standards and be based on regional monument types and chronologies cannot be overstated. QNHER has been developed using regional thesauri, but taking into account advice regarding data storage from other regional data managers, in particular UK historic environment records offices.

The development of a historic environment record has wider implications than being simply a method by which to record information about archaeological sites, landscapes, and objects. The creation of the database itself is only one part of the wider process of heritage management, and the database and accompanying GIS will both affect and be affected by existing culture and protocol within the QMA in its future use. The project within which the QNHER was created is ongoing, and to date all use of the database has been by researchers from Birmingham University carrying out remote sensing work. Denis Byrne has highlighted problems caused by the insistence on what he calls the "Western model" in determining the nature of heritage management in non-Western countries through a process of "inappropriate ideology transfer" (2008: 232). An imposition of UK heritage management culture such as that illustrated by Byrne would indeed be inappropriate, and the project has sought to create a methodology and framework for recording that is not only familiar to UK researchers, but also complies with current standards and guidance in Qatar, and current practice within the QMA. As has been stated above, this is a long-term project, and use and adaptation of the QNHER database by staff at the QMA will move the historic environment record away from an "inappropriate ideology transfer" and towards a fruitful synthesis of both UK and Qatari heritage management.

Data standards

Before exploring the QNHER database in detail, the creation, implementation, and use of a data standard will be discussed. By recording data relating to the historic environment consistently, information can be searched, analysed, disseminated, and integrated with ease. Standardized data also facilitates quality control, ensuring that the information entered is meaningful to future researchers. In addition, adhering to a data standard can facilitate any future migration of the data to new systems that may be developed. A data standard can be said to assist "in the use, communication and long-term survival" of the data to which it refers (English Heritage 2007: 8).

A data standard can be defined as "a standard that meets an existing need and tells future users the information that has been recorded and why" (*ibid*: 8). The specific requirements of data capture should be identified and then formalized into a standard that is clear to those not involved in the initial stage of data capture or the decision-making process. A data standard specifies both the types of information that are recorded, and the *way* in which this information is recorded. In practice, a data standard specifies the scope of the information that should be recorded about the historic environment, for example the name, location, dating, and significant finds of a site. It then specifies how these broader themes should be recorded as individual pieces of data, e.g. the location of the site or find recorded as a national grid co-ordinate. Also specified is the minimum amount of information required for a record to be considered complete. While this may sound restrictive, it is the challenge of those creating a historic environment record to ensure that there is as much flexibility in the system as possible, and that the fine balance between data consistency and the adaptability of the recording system is maintained. The QNHER database has been designed to allow the development and refinement of thesauri in both English and Arabic, and new fields can be added to the database should they be required in the future.

Data standards are extremely important in the creation and maintenance of records relating to the historic environment, or indeed any database, and in the UK there has been much work and discussion on the deployment of data standards for use in historic environment records (see English Heritage 2007; Gilman & Newman 2007). By contrast, in the Arabian Gulf countries, management of information relating to the historic environment has lacked consistency over the years. The absence of a formal academic dialogue relating to archaeological resource management has had a negative impact on the systems currently employed in the Gulf States to manage historic environment information (Al-Belushi 2005: 28).

As a result of the lack of a data standard for historic environment records in Qatar or other Arabian Gulf countries, the overall database design follows standards set out in the English Heritage document "MIDAS Heritage: the UK Historic Environment Data Standard". This data standard was followed because it has been developed for over ten years by those working in the heritage information management sector in the UK, and provides a solid, logical data structure with which to record information relating to the historic environment. While the form has followed these guidelines, the content of the database has been tailored to suit the needs of the QMA through parallel development of a field survey recording form, created in close collaboration with the QMA, and fields and tables in the QNHER database. While some of the thesauri used in the UK were found to be appropriate for Qatar, such as different types of archaeological investigation, other thesauri which provide classifications of topography, periods, and site types have been created to be specific to Qatar. The creation and maintenance of these thesauri and the overall data standard is an ongoing process that will require revision and refinement with new developments in archaeology and heritage research in the future.

Key objectives of creating the QNHER

During the creation of the QNHER database the requirements of the QMA and the existing structure of geographic data management within Qatar formed core considerations in identifying the objectives of the project. In addition to these longer-term requirements, the remote sensing and survey project demanded a flexible and easy to use system that could function for data entry while further development of the user interface took place. The generation of data during the remote sensing and survey project — in particular, the parallel development of the survey form — shaped the decisions that were made during the creation of the database and its interoperability with GIS.

One of the initial objectives in the database project was to record physical information about new archaeological sites, monuments, and other elements of the historic environment of Qatar as they were identified during survey and remote sensing work. The remote sensing survey in particular had the potential to identify hundreds of previously unknown sites, and it became clear early on that such information would be best recorded using a database that could provide fast and simple data entry, querying of the data on a number of complex criteria, and perhaps more importantly, presentation of the data using GIS.

Further to recording information regarding the physical attributes of archaeological features, and in line with the event–monument–archive model (outlined in the "Design choices" section below), a second objective in designing the database was that bibliographic references should be recorded, as well as their relationship to the records on sites within the database. Bibliographic references can refer to a wide range of sources pertaining to the historic environment, ranging from literature such as books and journal articles, to maps, photographs, and oral testimonies. Further relating to this data model, the third objective was to record information about events (archaeological or otherwise) that affect the sites, monuments, or artefacts recorded in the database. Again, the relationship between event and site records should be recorded in the database in addition to information about the event itself.

A fourth objective, inseparable from those objectives outlined above, is that all the data in the database should be stored in such a way as to facilitate searches by various criteria, both textual and spatial. This is linked to the fifth objective, which was to create a database

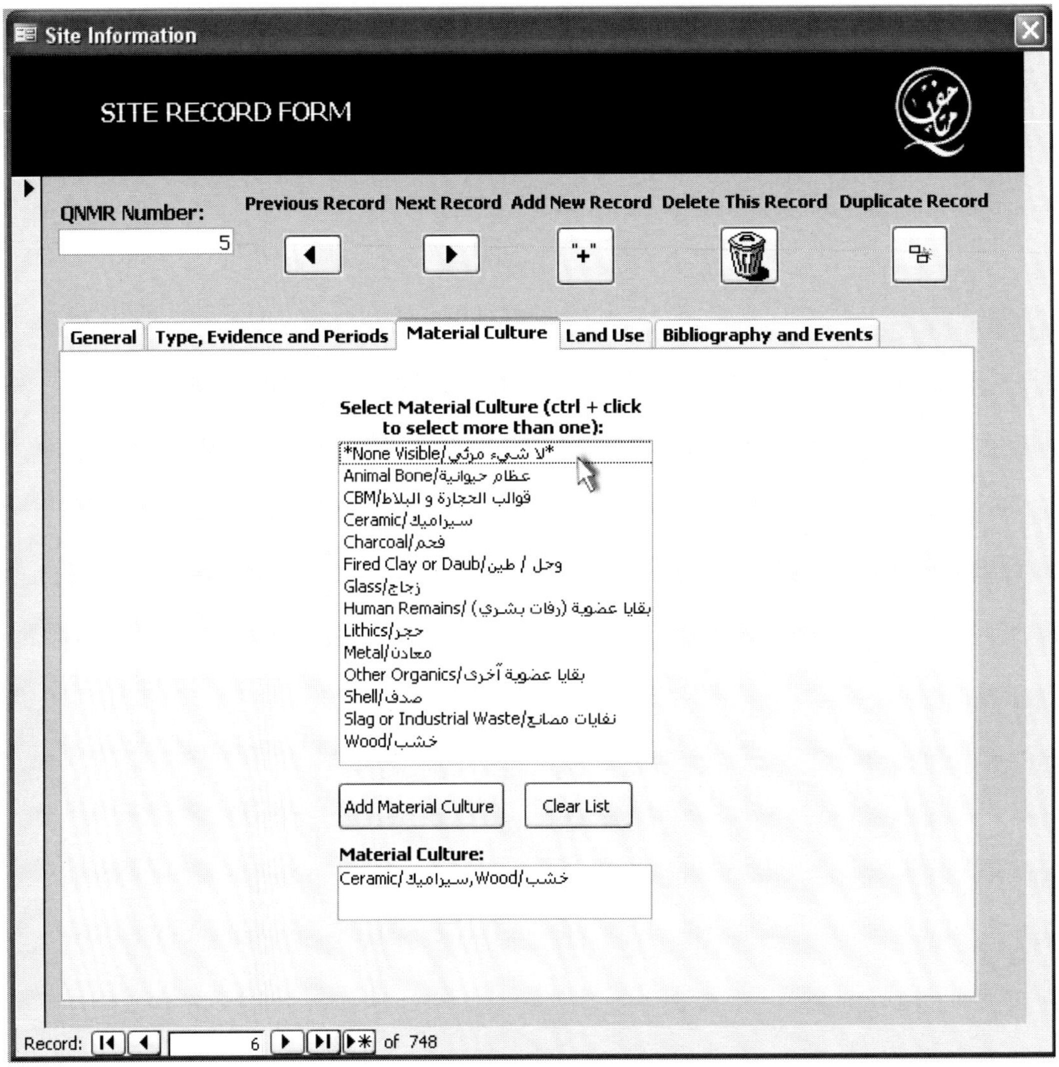

Figure 1. *The use of thesauri as lookup lists with the corresponding index numbers.*

that is compatible with GIS software (in this case ArcGIS 9.3), allowing data to be presented and queried spatially. This is particularly important in relation to dissemination of the data to the Qatar Centre for GIS, which in turn distributes spatial information to key government agencies.

The final, but perhaps most important, objective was to create a database with a user interface that could operate, as far as possible, bilingually in both English and Arabic. Having the ability to search and enter data in both languages offers the opportunity for Qatari management and maintenance of the data, and at the same time gives the opportunity for data to be disseminated more widely and presented to a variety of audiences.

Design choices

The database has been created using Microsoft Access 2003. This database management system was selected because it allows rapid database development, which was well suited to the timescale of the project. In addition, Microsoft operating systems are widely available, offering the best solution for compatibility. There is also extensive online and offline support and training available for Microsoft Access, so that should further staff training be required or technical support needed that is non-specific to the QNHER, it will be widely available from certified providers in both countries. The database was developed using Access 2003 rather than Access 2007 to ensure compatibility between all users on the project, and between the GIS and the database.

The use of Microsoft Access as the database management system allows all the above objectives to be achieved because the types of information stored in the QNHER database, the expected required capacity, and the types of relationships required between tables are all supported in Access. Access is also fully compatible with ArcGIS 9.3, which is the GIS programme utilized in both the QMA and Birmingham. The ability to split the database into front-end and back-end components means that both Arabic and English versions can be created without compromising any of the functionality of the database. This also enables a limited number of concurrent connections to the back end of the database (up to five), allowing the GIS software to be connected to the back-end database at the same time that the user interface for the database is open. Should more connections to the database be required in the future, the database has the potential to be migrated to Structured Query Language (SQL).

In order for the user interface of the database to be operable in both English and Arabic, all fields that could be logged in thesauri (for example, site type, topography, geology) were stored numerically in the main table, and a corresponding lookup list was created in which both the English and Arabic terms were listed together with their numerical index numbers. The front end of the database can then summon either the English or the Arabic term depending on the language version of the user interface (Fig. 1).

Many of the design choices in the database were in part dictated by the need to integrate with the ArcGIS 9.3 program. This has affected, to some degree, the normalization of tables, and some fields within a record are repeated with a numerical index (e.g. Period1, Period2 etc.), which would not occur in a normalized table. However to ensure compatibility with ArcGIS 9.3 the following constraints were identified:

— Field names should not exceed ten characters;

— Field names should not contain spaces;

— To make the linking, display, and sorting of the key site attributes within the GIS more straightforward, these attributes, which might — in a normalized table — be stored in separate tables with many-to-many relationships (such as site type, period, and evidence type), should in this case be stored in the main site table and limited to four entries for each attribute. While this limits the data entry for each table, it affords spatial analysis of the data, a key requirement of the project;

— Tables linked to the main sites and monuments table (tblSite) cannot link to more than one field within that table. This constraint raises the problem of identical lookup tables for key attributes, such as site type, where each of the four site type fields will have an independent lookup table associated with it. This problem has been ameliorated somewhat by providing a "master" table for each lookup list, updated through the user interface.

The database has been modelled on the event–monument–archive model, which is widely adopted in historic environment records in the UK. This model incorporates the three principal heritage themes identified in the MIDAS Heritage document, these being "Heritage Asset", "Activity", and "Information Sources", and reflects the dynamic nature of information relating to the historic environment. The "Heritage Asset" theme refers to sites, monuments, individual artefacts, and eco-facts, and geographical areas that can be identified as having archaeological or historic value. Anything which gives information relating to a heritage asset can be classified under the "Information Sources" theme, and includes, but is not limited to, references in literature such as books and fieldwork reports, photographs, historic maps, and satellite images. The "Activity" theme refers to any activity that has been carried out in relation to a heritage asset. Activities can include field survey, excavation, and remote sensing. Together, these three themes and the way that they interact with each other form the core design model of the QNHER database.

In addition to the three main themes, MIDAS also outlines three additional "supporting themes", which are "Spatial Information", "Temporal Information", and "Actor Information" (English Heritage 2007: 23). These supporting themes add additional layers of information to the main themes and the depth of information that is recorded in the historic environment record, and have been taken into consideration in the design of this database and used where appropriate.

The entities about which information is stored in the QNHER database are listed below. Each of these entities is stored as a table in the database, and the table name is given in brackets below.

— Heritage Asset (tblSite): a site, monument, find, or area that has archaeological or historical value.

— Event (tblEvent): an activity that has taken place and which affects or informs about a heritage asset.

— Bibliographic references (tblBiblio): literary references, historic maps, and historic photographs that hold information relating to heritage assets.

FIGURE 2. *The Arabic user interface with the English translation in a pop-up text box.*

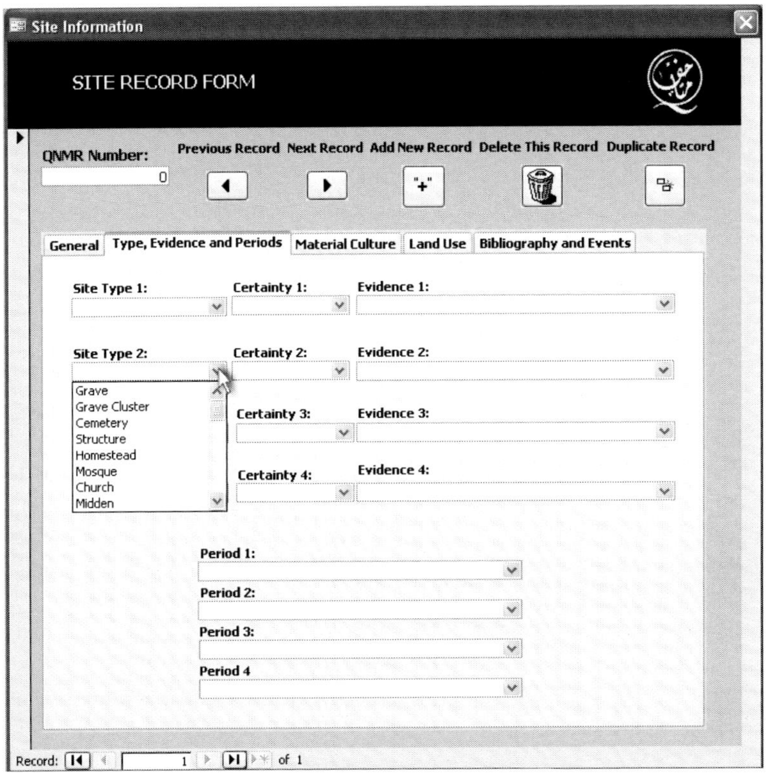

FIGURE 3. *The use of a drop-down list to facilitate data entry.*

— Survey photographs (tblPhoto): note that the photographs generated from recently conducted surveys and other work have been separated from other bibliographic references. Treating photographs as separate entities allows more specific information about a photograph to be stored in a logical way, such as the file number, the date, and the time of the photograph.

In addition to these main entities, many of the attributes stored in the database are stored as an index number with a corresponding lookup table. This is to allow the creation of thesauri for various classifications such as geology, chronology, topography etc., in both English and Arabic.

The QNHER database in practice

Having explored the design choices behind the creation of the back end of the database, we will now present some of the features of the user interface and how the QNHER works in practice. The QNHER user interface has been developed to work in both Arabic and English. While many fields are presented to the user as a list from which to select the appropriate term, there are of course some fields such as descriptions and names, which demand free text entry. These fields will be completed in the language appropriate to the user, and a translation or transliteration provided where possible. In the Arabic version, holding the mouse over an Arabic term from one of the thesauri will reveal the English translation in a pop-up box at the mouse tip (Fig. 2). This serves a dual purpose both to help clarify any nuances in terminology, and to allow those users who are not familiar with Arabic to use the Arabic version of the database when necessary.

Data entry is carried out by users through forms in the front-end user interface. Where possible, users select entries from drop-down lists to ensure data consistency (Fig. 3), and input masks have been put in place for fields such as dates, requiring a single format to be entered by the user.

The use of tabbed forms allows all the information on a site to be displayed clearly. This aids in data entry, by enabling users to view and enter data according to themes, and makes it easier to navigate around the main data entry form. It also provides a simple way of browsing through the data, allowing the user to select a particular theme and compare entries into the database.

The QNHER database can be fully searched on multiple criteria and the results can be displayed either within the database in a standard query, exported to a Microsoft Excel file (.xls), or as a pre-prepared report in a print-ready format. The search form presents the user with the option to search multiple criteria either within the entire database, or within those records that have been imported from a spatial query within the GIS. The standard query return within the database allows for record-level amendments to the data, which is displayed as a table when the query is run. Alternatively, the export function means that data can be analysed and presented in Microsoft Excel without any changes being made to the original data in the database. In contrast, a print-ready report displays the selected sites in a fixed format as a paper report. The title and any comments can be added to this report by the user, and if suitable software is installed, the report can be "printed" to PDF format for electronic distribution (Fig. 4).

Regarding the use of GIS as part of the QNHER, the spatial data created within ArcGIS and the attribute data held within the QNHER are created as separate entities, joined by the unique QNHER recorded for both datasets. The "shapefiles", relating to central points or defined areas of identified elements of the historic environment, have no additional fields other than the QNHER number, which allows a one-to-one relationship with the QNHER in the main table of the QNHER database. Additional fields can be created, such as easting and northing for points, or area and perimeter for polygons, if analysis requires. This facilitates data entry within the database environment, allows the standardization of terms, the optimization of data storage, and one-to-many and many-to-many relationships for appropriate additional datasets, and enables all the data, regardless of its spatial nature, to be accessed via queries and reports.

To enable the dissemination of this important dataset to other governmental departments, it is envisaged that shapefiles with summary attribute data from the QNHER database will be created in ArcGIS and deposited with the Qatar Centre for GIS periodically, providing updates as frequently as required.

It should be noted that Arabic text is not supported in regular shapefiles in ArcGIS, and instead the text is represented by "?" or "-". In the case of creating regular shapefiles to disseminate the data via the Centre for GIS, it would not therefore be relevant to export the Arabic text fields. However, an alternative method of exporting and storing the summary dataset is to create a personal geodatabase feature class rather than a regular shapefile. As these datasets are stored in a geodatabase, the Arabic text can both be read and queried within ArcGIS.

The database and its forms alone will not suffice to ensure that good practice in data entry and retrieval is

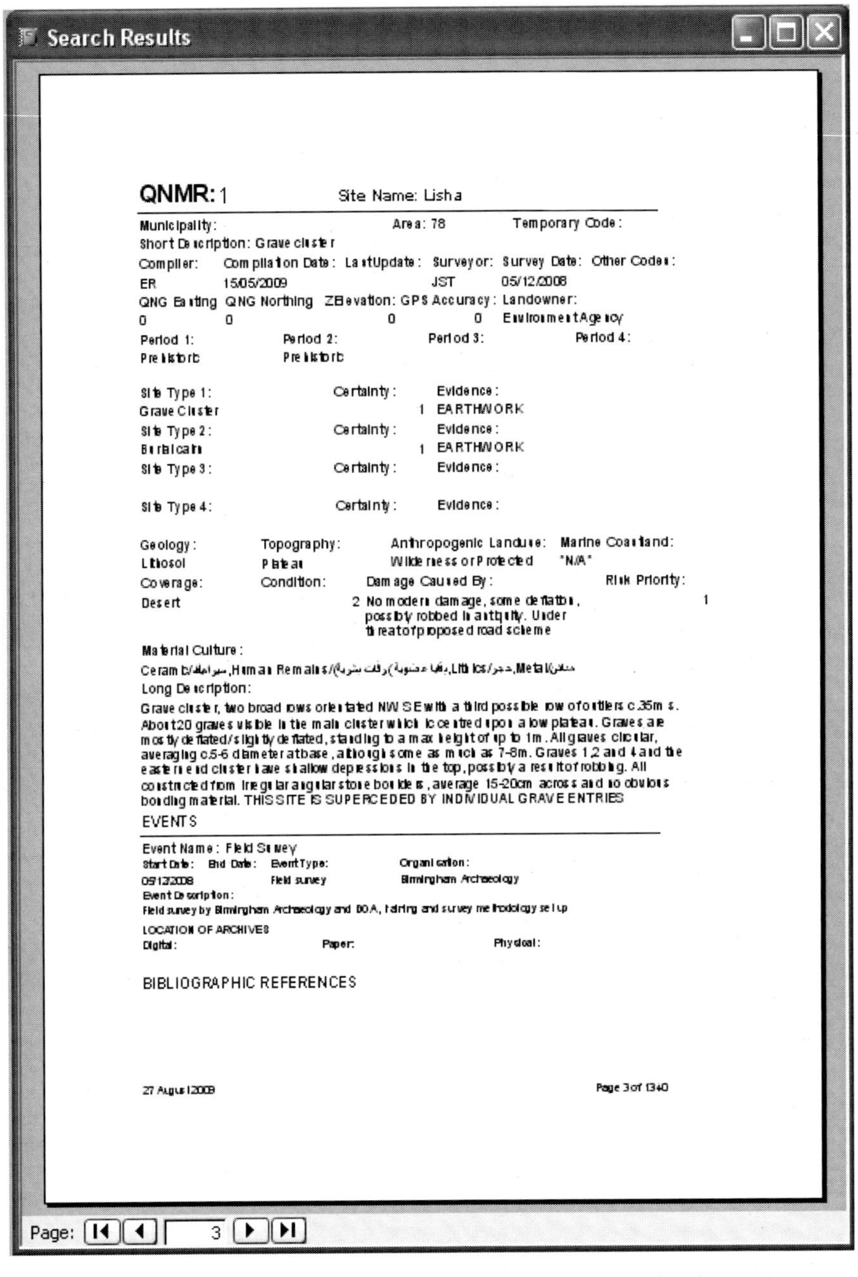

Search Results

QNMR: 1 Site Name: Lisha

Municipality: Area: 78 Temporary Code:
Short Description: Grave cluster
Compiler: Compilation Date: LastUpdate: Surveyor: Survey Date: Other Codes:
ER 15/05/2009 JST 05/12/2008
QNG Easting QNG Northing ZElevation: GPS Accuracy: Landowner:
0 0 0 0 Environment Agency
Period 1: Period 2: Period 3: Period 4:
Prehistoric Prehistoric

Site Type 1: Certainty: Evidence:
Grave Cluster 1 EARTHWORK
Site Type 2: Certainty: Evidence:
Burial cairn 1 EARTHWORK
Site Type 3: Certainty: Evidence:

Site Type 4: Certainty: Evidence:

Geology: Topography: Anthropogenic Landuse: Marine Coastland:
Lithosol Plateau Wilderness or Protected "N/A"
Coverage: Condition: Damage Caused By: Risk Priority:
Desert 2 No modern damage, some deflation, possibly robbed in antiquity. Under threat of proposed road scheme 1

Material Culture:
Ceramic/فخار, Human Remains/بقايا عظمية بشرية, Lithics/حجر, Metal/معادن
Long Description:
Grave cluster, two broad rows orientated NW SE with a third possible row of outliers c.35m s. About 20 graves visible in the main cluster which is centred upon a low plateau. Graves are mostly deflated/slightly deflated, standing to a max height of up to 1m. All graves circular, averaging c.5-6 diameter at base, although some as much as 7-8m. Graves 1,2 and 4 and the eastern end cluster have shallow depressions in the top, possibly a result of robbing. All constructed from irregular angular stone boulders, average 15-20cm across and no obvious bonding material. THIS SITE IS SUPERCEDED BY INDIVIDUAL GRAVE ENTRIES
EVENTS

Event Name: Field Survey
Start Date: End Date: Event Type: Organisation:
05/12/2008 Field survey Birmingham Archaeology
Event Description:
Field survey by Birmingham Archaeology and QOA, testing and survey methodology set up
LOCATION OF ARCHIVES
Digital: Paper: Physical:

BIBLIOGRAPHIC REFERENCES

27 August 2009 Page 3 of 1340

Page: 3

FIGURE 4. *A print-ready report from a query in the database.*

always followed, and the next stage of the project will be the writing of a user manual in collaboration with staff at the QMA. This manual will act as a practical guide and data standard guidance, specifying such standards as the minimum amount of information required for a record to be considered acceptable, and clearly outlining the roles of any staff charged with the responsibility of maintaining and managing the data.

Some limitations of the database

The main structural limitations of the database have been dictated by the need to link successfully with the GIS, and to make this linkage as simple as possible for users, but the database itself follows the structure of existing historic environment record software. Should further development of the database and the protocol regarding its use prove successful for the QMA, the database can be migrated to another, more complex system. This database should not therefore be seen as the finished product to be presented to the QMA, but is rather the "first stage" of a wider system of heritage protection and management that will be developed over the coming years.

Moving on to some more technical limitations, the database is limited to a total file size of 2GB due to the limitations in the Microsoft Access program. In reality, however, this is likely to equate to a limit of at least 1 million records if not more, and is therefore more than adequate for the current needs of both the project and the QMA over the distant future.

While the database has been created to encourage and guide consistent and logical data entry, no required fields or prescriptive input masks have been applied to the user interface as yet, and only non-required fields for input masks have been enforced. There are also currently no user security levels of access active in the database, and it may be that such a need is identified in subsequent testing stages of the database and in discussion with data managers at the QMA.

Discussion and future developments

The development of the QNHER database has played a crucial role in the remote sensing and survey project, and has enabled speedy analysis and presentation of generated data, in addition to providing a flexible and straightforward way in which to store these data. More importantly, the process of developing the database in consultation with the QMA and UK-based specialists has been invaluable in encouraging a dialogue pertaining to heritage management. It is hoped that this dialogue will continue throughout the duration of the project and beyond, engaging other states of the Arabian Peninsula.

One of the key applications of the database, and indeed of the QNHER, is that of its use in the planning process in the face of development within Qatar. As with all the Arab Gulf States, development can happen rapidly and on a grand scale, and having a comprehensive and up-to-date record of all archaeological sites and monuments that can be queried spatially will allow the QMA to monitor potentially damaging activities more closely. In addition to the use of the database within the QMA, the provision of a regularly updated GIS shapefile to the Centre for GIS will raise the profile of heritage within the planning process ahead of development.

The QNHER database, as with any dataset, requires dedicated maintenance and management, and the appointment of a historic environment records officer in charge of the upkeep of data standards will be the key to the success of the historic environment record. It is also recommended that data entry and retrieval should be carried out by a small number of trained individuals to ensure that standards are maintained and data remains consistent, manageable, and intelligible. These considerations will form part of the second stage of the project, when staff from the QMA and Birmingham will work together to create an instruction manual and data standard that will form the core operating procedures of the QNHER.

Considering the wider region

A pan-Arabian historic environment record may not be politically possible at present, but this does not preclude regional heritage managers from adopting a co-ordinated approach across the region. Clearly each country must be responsible for the enhancement, maintenance, and integrity of their own data since they will be reliant on the accuracy of these data to make informed decisions about the future of heritage in each country. However, it would be a great shame to miss the present opportunity to meet and prepare documentation relating to international Arabian heritage data standards. This really sets a vision for the future in terms of an integrated research tool that could be made possible via the Internet in the future.

An example of one issue that could be easily resolved at an early stage to facilitate improved data cohesion in the future is to be found in co-ordinate systems. An integrated search facility would not be possible without an agreed standard co-ordinate system. The Arabian Peninsula is host to four UTM (Universal Transverse Mercator) co-ordinate zones, and in addition several countries (including Qatar) have their own projection and co-ordinate systems. Of course, each historic environment record needs to conform to the locally established co-ordinate system so that these data can be integrated with existing data in each country, but there is no reason why a historic environment record cannot record two established co-ordinate standards, one local standard and one agreed international standard. With this in mind, there is now the opportunity to establish a joint historic environment record working group with representatives from each country to discuss international Arabian heritage data standards.

The creation of any historic environment record is part of a process stemming from a productive dialogue relating to issues of regional heritage management. It is necessary to avoid inappropriate impositions of ideologies, Western or otherwise, in implementing any new procedure, particularly one that can be fraught with political, cultural, and ethical pitfalls. However, radical historical, political, and cultural differences can provide a useful means by which to question the values and assumptions that each party brings to the discussion, and it has certainly encouraged a rigorous approach in the creation of the QNHER database. The consolidation of information and regionally based historic environment records within the Arabian Peninsula would be an invaluable management tool for heritage managers. It is hoped that this dialogue will continue in the future years of the project, and will engage wider participation across the Gulf in the future.

Acknowledgements

We would like to thank H.E. Sheikha Al Mayassa Bint Hamad Al Thani (Chairperson of the Board of Trustees for the Qatar Museums Authority) and H.E. Sheikh Hasan Bin Mohammed Al-Thani (Vice Chairman of the Board of Trustees for the Qatar Museums Authority), without whose support the development of the Qatar National Historic Environment Record would not have been possible. We would also like to express our gratitude to Mr Abdulla Al-Najjar (CEO of the Qatar Museums Authority) and Earl Roger Mandle (Executive Director of the Qatar Museums Authority) for their continued support. The thesauri were developed in collaboration with staff from the Department of Antiquities and foreign missions, in particular Himyan J. Al-Kuwari and Dr Monir Taha, who also translated the thesauri. We would also like to extend our thanks to Lucy Dingwall from the Herefordshire Historic Environment Record for her invaluable assistance and advice in the design and continued development of the QNHER database.

References

Al-Belushi M.A.K.
2005. Archaeological Resource Management in Oman. PhD thesis, University of Birmingham. [Unpublished].

Byrne D.
2008. Western Hegemony in Archaeological Heritage Management. Pages 229–234 in G. Fairclough, R. Harrison, J.H. Jameson Jnr & J. Schofield (eds), *The Heritage Reader*. Abingdon: Routledge.

English Heritage
2007. *MIDAS Heritage: The UK Historic Environment Data Standard.* English Heritage. Viewed September 2009. www.english-heritage.org.uk/server/show/nav.18041

Gilman P. & Newman M.
2007. *Informing the Future of the Past: Guidelines for Historic Environment Records* (Second edition). Swindon: English Heritage. Viewed September 2009. www.ifp-plus.info/contents.html

Qatar National Law.
1980. No. 2 of 1980 on Antiquities. Viewed September 2009. http://unesdoc.unesco.org/images/0006/000666/066600eo.pdf

Authors' addresses

Rebecca Beardmore, Institute of Archaeology, University College London, 31–34 Gordon Square, London WC1H 0PY, UK.

e-mail rebecca.beardmore.09@ucl.ac.uk

Richard Cuttler, Senior Project Manager, IBM VISTA, Institute of Archaeology and Antiquity, University of Birmingham, Edgbaston, Birmingham B15 2TT, UK.

e-mail r.cuttler@bham.ac.uk

Faisal Abdulla Al-Naimi, Head of Antiquities, Department of Antiquities, Qatar Museums Authority, P.O. Box 2777, Doha, Qatar.

e-mail falnaimi@qma.com.qa

Eleanor Ramsey, IBM VISTA, Institute of Archaeology and Antiquity, University of Birmingham, Edgbaston, Birmingham B15 2TT, UK.

e-mail e.ramsey@bham.ac.uk

Simon Fitch, Head of Marine Remote Sensing, IBM VISTA, Institute of Archaeology and Antiquity, University of Birmingham, Edgbaston, Birmingham B15 2TT, UK.

e-mail s.fitch@bham.ac.uk

Dr Heiko Kallweit, Honorary Research Fellow, IBM VISTA, Astrid Lindgren Straße 10, D 79100 Freiburg, Germany.

e-mail heiko_kallweit@yahoo.de

Proceedings of the Seminar for Arabian Studies 40 (2010): 17–34

Preliminary pottery study: Murwab horizon in progress, ninth century AD, Qatar

Alexandrine Guérin & Faisal Abdulla Al-Naimi

Summary
The site of Murwab in Qatar is a village made up of 220 cells, two forts, and two mosques. Stratigraphic results from excavations make it possible to give an account of two visible distinct occupations in the forts and in its domestic architecture during the ninth century. Five phases of the process of sedentarization can be identified in the domestic habitat. A study of ceramics from the site indicated intense trade between Murwab and the Arab and Iranian provinces during the early Abbasid period.

Keywords: Murwab village, sedentarization, glazed pottery, ninth century, Qatar

1. The site

1.1 Description and dating

Discovered in 1959 by a Danish team (Frifelt 1974), investigations continued for two further campaigns, first by a French team directed by C. Hardy-Guilbert (1984: 169–188) then by a second team directed by the author (Guérin 2009: 173–186).

The site of Murwab is a desert village located 5 km from the sea and comprises 220 cells, two forts, and two mosques. Stratigraphic results indicate two visible distinct occupations in the forts as in the domestic architecture, both exclusively dated to the ninth century. Five phases of sedentarization were observed in the domestic habitat. The study of ceramics reflects the intense trade between Murwab and the Arab and Iranian provinces during the early Abbasid period.[1]

1.2 Historical context

During the conversion of the Arabian tribes to Islam (632), the Prophet Muḥammad received several delegations representing "Bahrain", the provincial administrative district. The Persian geographer, Abū ʾl-Qasīm ʿUbayd Allāh ibn Khurradādbih (towards 846) and the Yemeni scholar al-Hamdānī (towards 945) described a very broad area of the Gulf under the toponym of Bahrain, which covered a geographical zone including current al-Qaṭīf, ʿUqayr, Qatar, and the island of Bahrain. Qatar is briefly mentioned and constitutes one of the stopping points on the road connecting Basra to the province of Oman. The harbour of the province of Bahrain is regarded as being the one mentioned by the authorities that served Oman, India, and China but no other information is given about the famous port of Bahrain, not even its location. For tax-collecting purposes in this area, the terms Bahrain, al-Rumaylah, and al-Khaṭṭ are indexed as districts, but no information is given concerning the geographic scope of this tax data. Al-Hamdānī includes the Qatari peninsula in a list of localities in Arabia and describes it as a stopping point on the road skirting the coast of the Arabian Peninsula. This geographer is the only one to mention "a sea is called Qatar, in the district of Bahrain". As for Ibn Ḥawql (end of the tenth century), he briefly alludes to the pirates of the province of Bahrain. Lastly, his contemporary, al-Masʿūdī (*c.*896–956), indicated that the water surrounding the peninsula contained pearls (Ibn Khurradāḍbih 1885–1939, vi: 40–41, 60, 181, 191; Serjeant 1978: 151–157; Cornu 1984: 360; 1988: 105–106; Johnstone 1978: 781–783).

It is consequently difficult to determine information relating exclusively to the current emirate of Qatar. The concept of an administrative territory with geographical limits can only have fleeting application, since during

[1] Descriptions of the site, as known from the 2007 excavations, are presented in Guérin 2009. All the pottery drawings published here are by A. Lagoutte (campaign 2007), and C. Verdellet and T. Moriceau (campaign 2009). All the photographs are by C. Gabillault and the architectural drawings are by the author.

these periods Qatar was strongly dependent upon the settled nomadic population and tribal territories, the proportions of which may have fluctuated according to the movements of the population and their rivalries.

At the beginning of the eighth century, two factions of the ᶜAbd al-Qays tribe, the Djahima ibn ᶜAwf (Jaḥīma ibn ᶜAwf) and the Banū Muḥārib (which held the harbour of ᶜUqayr), occupied this area. They divided up the province of Bahrain with a rival faction of the Banū Tamīm tribe, the Banū Saᶜd (Caskell 1975: 74–76). The latter part of the Abbasid period at the end of the eighth century was marked by political disturbances, with the emergence of various small autonomous states in most areas of the empire, generally under Ismaili influence. In the Gulf area, starting in 886, the Qarmatians rebelled against the Abbasid state and, after various battles (from 903), defeated the Abbasid governor of the area located in al-Qaṭīf and in al-Ḥasāʾ oasis in 926. The Qarmatians created permanent settlements from Bahrain to Yemen. It was only in 939 that the Qarmatians of Bahrain established agreements with the Abbasid government under the terms of which they committed themselves to protect the pilgrimage in exchange for an annual tribute and rights of protection to be paid by the pilgrims (Madelung 1978: 688). One can consider that there was a peaceful period in this area starting from the middle of the tenth century. The abandonment of Murwab at the end of the ninth century corresponds to the military rise to power of the Qarmatians. How were the Qatari tribes implicated in this regional conflict? Was there disturbance of the maritime routes, cabotage, the transport of goods or passengers between two ports in the same country, and thus the displacement of the commercial trade points? How was the displacement of the populations related to this trade? These are some of the ideas to be explored in order to explain the abandonment of the village of Murwab at the end of ninth century.

The various types of ceramics discovered in a domestic context in Murwab show an exceptional abundance of referenced and imported ceramics and give us a picture of intense trade, not only with the great Mesopotamian centres (Basra, Samarra, and Susa) but also with the Iranian provinces (Nishapour [Neyshābūr], Samarqand). These standard referents of importation also allow a relatively precise dating of the duration of occupation of the Murwab site.

2. The ceramic assemblage

2.1 Sampling

The ceramics used in this study come exclusively from the 2007 excavation of sectors 3 and 6. They are a set of 6948 sherds of which 68% are ceramics of "common" wares ("kitchen vessels": 4697 sherds) and 32% are glazed ware or vessels with specific decorations allowing them to be dated by comparison (decorated and imported ceramics, "table vessels": 2251 sherds).[2]

Wares typology. Dating markers

The macroscopic study carried out at the "Archéométrie and Archéologie — UMR 5138, Lyon" Laboratory, made it possible to differentiate the various wares present at Murwab. This study allowed us to establish a catalogue of twenty-six categories, twenty-two of which are classified as "common" ceramics and four of which are glazed or decorated ceramic wares. A petrographic study will be conducted during 2010 in order to refine and conclude this ceramological study in a more complete way. These analyses will make it possible to determine the sources of these imports and thus to propose a chart of the commercial exchanges with Murwab during the ninth century.

Four wares considered to be "referenced dating" ceramics are divided into two groups. The first consists of the wares P and K1, which are characterized by the fact that they may or may not be glazed, whereas the second group, K2 and GB2, comprises exclusively glazed ceramics (Fig. 1). The difference between P and K1 is the greater presence of inclusions (brown quartz, orange quartz, carbonate, 0.125–0.5 mm) in the first case, with concentrations from 2% to 3%, while the K1 ware has lower concentrations (< 1%) of smaller size (0.125 mm). The colour of the ware varies between rosy-white and light rosy-brown. The K1 ware has the largest number of pieces (960 sherds, 42.5% of all imports with glazes) of which 36% are not glazed and belong to the "eggshell" type (346 sherds). The P ware is the least represented: 237 sherds (10.5%) of which ninety-three sherds are not glazed (4%) and can be classified as "eggshell" type.

[2] The dating of the glazed forms from the excavation of 2009 is used. A total of 121 forms substantiate a broader range of comparisons. In the discussion of formless glazed sherds and those of common ware, the excavations of 2009/sector 6 are not included here.

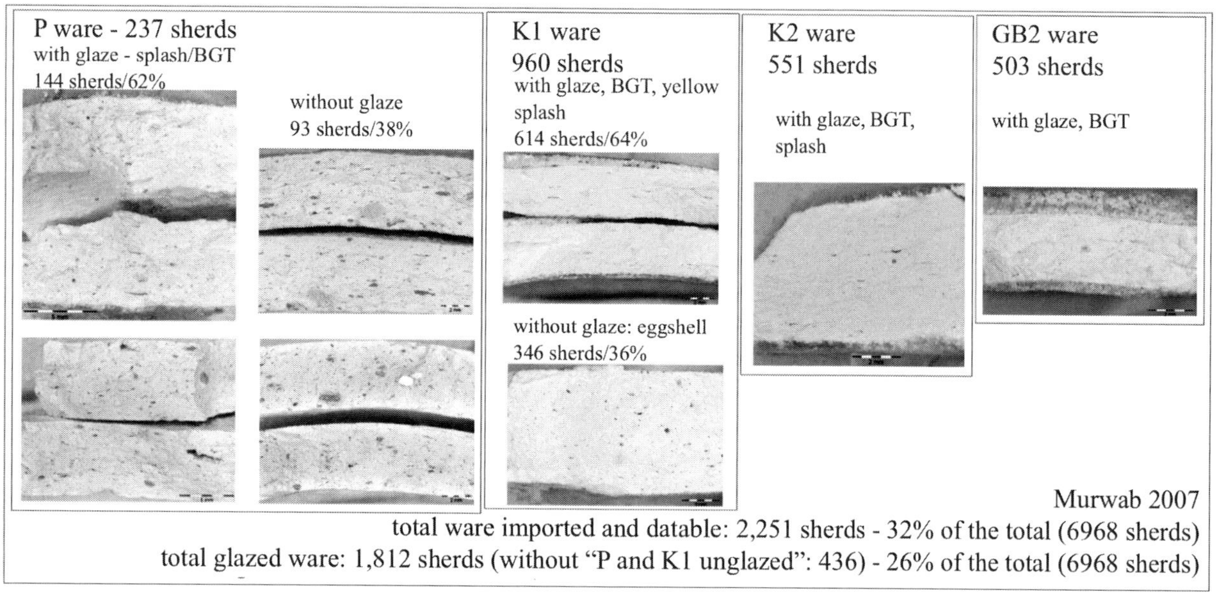

Figure 1. *Typology of various wares: photomicrographs of glazed wares.*

The wares K2 and GB2 are sometimes decorated under their glaze (moulded ceramic, appliqué strip of clay). They are similar to the K1 ware in terms of size and abundance of inclusions. The colour varies between creamy-white and rosy-white. These two wares account for almost 50% of the imported material, 24.5% for the K2 ware (551 sherds) and 22.5% for the GB2 ware (503 sherds), which is exclusively covered with blue glaze (blue/green/turquoise or BGT).

2.2 Early Abbasid wares: table vessels

The corpus present at Murwab is rich and varied and the proportion of "referenced dating" ceramics is 32% of all ceramics discovered at the time of the 2007 excavation. This figure may appear high in comparison with the results of the recent excavations carried out on comparable sites of the Gulf area. The major difficulty for a reliable quantitative comparison is the chronological breakdown obtained on these sites. For example, our principal reference relates to the site of Kush (Kennet 2004) with a level III in two phases (E-04 and E-05) and relates to ceramics classified and dated "late eighth–early ninth" century; then level IV in one phase (E-06) dated from the ninth to eleventh century.[3] In this case it is difficult to compare exclusively contemporary layers with those detected in Murwab from the ninth century. In spite of this difficulty, it is possible to take into account the reference glazes known to date from the ninth century and to obtain a presence of around 8 to 10% at Kush,[4] close to the percentage observed in the Persian port of Siraf (10%), where occupation continued into the tenth century although there was evidence of abandonment in 977 (Tampoe 1989: figs 100, 103, 106, 108). For the site of Sharmah in Yemen, which was occupied from 980 to 1140, the proportion of glazed ceramics corresponds to 6.61% (Rougeulle 2005: 226).

2.2.1 Eggshell ware

The characteristic of this unglazed ware is the smoothness of the walls as well as the scarcity of inclusions. The solidity is ensured by thorough baking. Generally represented by jugs with a high neck and straight walls but whose bodies are exclusively globular in shape, this form is present at Murwab and would correspond to level I of Susa (dated 800–850, Kervran 1977: fig. 31/2; Base Atlas 2010: MAO S. 727). There are no bodies with marked careen (Kervran 1977: fig. 30, levels I and II; Hardy-Guilbert 1984: fig. 16/7,11, level 2, dating the stratigraphy to 750–800). Certain necks have a combed

[3] Kennet 2004: 14, table 2. A Wajihid fractional dinar dated 951/2+ AD was found in this phase.

[4] Kennet 2004: 16, table 4. The following categories (imported glazed and eggshell) were taken into account for this calculation: TURQ (1, 2, 3, 4 ?) 5; EGG; YBTIN; COBALT; YSPLASH; BTIN; FRIT.F.

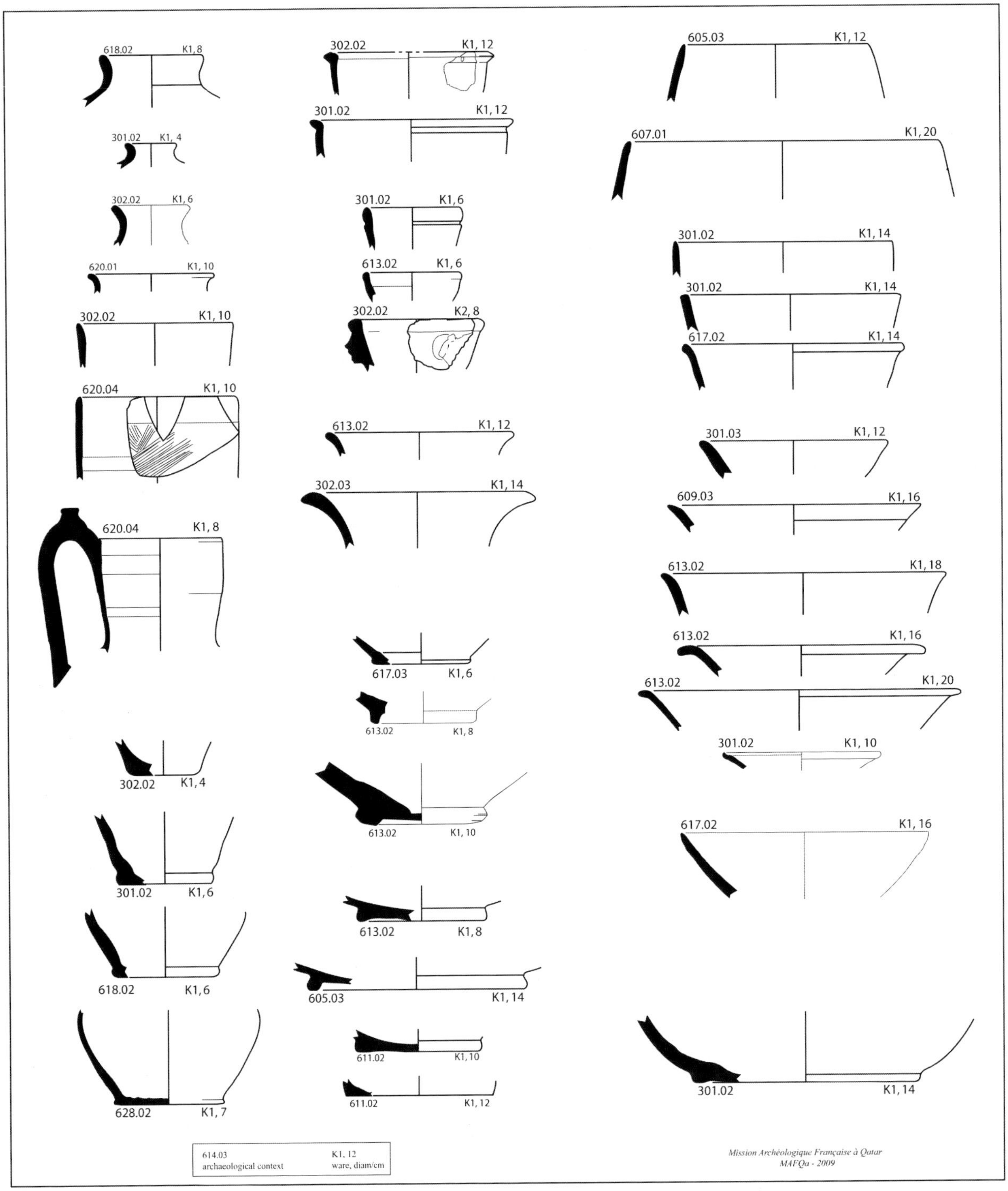

Figure 2. *Dating and importation. Eggshell without glaze category. Murwab seasons 2007–2009. Ninth century. Early Abbasid sequence.*

decoration. The forms discovered in this ware make it possible to present a varied catalogue: bowls with straight walls and slightly inverted, cups with oblique walls and simple rims (round termination, slightly everted) (Fig. 2).

2.2.2 Alkaline blue glazed ware

Known since the third century in the Gulf (Salles 1984: 248–250), this ceramic ware with a blue glaze continued to be found during the Sasanian period and is abundant until the end of tenth century (Kennet 2004: 29), but the production and the diffusion continued over the period from the eleventh to the thirteenth centuries. It is generally considered that this production came from the Basra area (Keall & Mason 1991: 52). Ceramics with blue glaze and applied decorations are found in Murwab and dated from the eighth and ninth centuries (Kennet 2004: 29, TURQ.5).

They are generally covered earthenware storage jars, with an internal and external glaze that ensures their impermeability as well as the conservation of the products inside. We have some examples of earthenware jars without necks but the category of jars and jugs with short and high necks presents the greatest number. In this category, we also have a certain number of basins and a bowl with a straight wall with an indentation at the base (Fig. 3).

2.2.3 Opaque white glazed ware

The dating of the series of the "opaque white glaze" is a little more complex when it comes to comparisons with other sites, with a high or low chronology for Susa (Kervran 1977: 152), present until the second half of the ninth century; for Samarra (Northedge 1997: 231–235), the ninth century for the latest products with monochromic lustre; or for Siraf (Whitehouse 1979: 51–56), standard type "W" is well represented in period 3 C (40%–50%). For Kush, this ceramic type appears in level IV (Kennet 2004: 32), ninth–eleventh century.

Blue cobalt glazed ware

The blue cobalt decoration was used for a short time: it appeared only from 803–804 in Samarra and then in Susa, and the production seemed to continue only until 835–836 (Kervran 1977: 89, fig. 37; Tampoe 1989: 92). It is currently assumed that its production was localized in Basra (Keall & Mason 1991). However, because of the important expansion of distribution of this type, the presence of several local centres, particularly in Iran, is to be considered (Williamson 1987: 14–16). Few objects with this blue decoration are present in Murwab and only two complete forms were discovered during the 2009 excavation.[5]

One is a bowl with a palmette decoration in blue cobalt colour on a creamy-white colour background (Fig. 4). This complete bowl shows the percussive impact that caused the break in the wall, and was discovered on the first occupation layer of house no. 619 (first half of the ninth century). A small pot with a short neck and two handles, perhaps used for the preservation of ointments, has a blue cobalt cover. This complete ceramic was discovered in a public area (no. 633), between the courtyards of houses 620 and 622 in the last layer of occupation, before the abandonment of sector 6 of the 2009 excavations.

Grey glazed ware

This grey tone is obtained either by an imperfection of manufacture or by a deterioration of the parts in a damp environment (Northedge & Falkner 1987: 218). On the other hand, at Susa, the grey enamel adheres well to the ware, and is thick and with a brilliant aspect. Many large cups with floral purple on light blue decorations were discovered in level I (enclosed spaces: well, dated 835–850, Kervran 1977: 84, 152–153; Hardy-Guilbert 1984: fig. 27/5). The Murwab discoveries are associated to this category from Susa (perhaps it was imported from Susa?). The forms are divided into two main types (Fig. 5).

All cups of large diameter (20–36 cm) with bent walls, an everted rim and a round termination, are dated against those found in Susa. One of these cups carries a grey splashed-on white decoration while another cup presents an interior stylized floral decoration (red-purple with palmettes), possibly lustred (in the course of restoration at the Laboratory of the Museum of Islamic Arts, Doha?). The second category is very evident: it has high- and straight-walled bowls, generally without a trace of specific decoration.

Pseudo-epigraphic glazed ware

This well-known particular production in Nishapour, as in Samarkand, appears between the middle and the end of the ninth century. The Murwab example is cream-coloured or light green, with manganese oxide decorations: a pseudo-

[5] I wish to thank Mr A. Al-Najjar, CEO/Qatar Museum Authority and Mr O. Watson, Chief Curator of the Museum of Islamic Art, Doha, as well as all his team in the conservation laboratory, for assuming responsibility of this archaeological material.

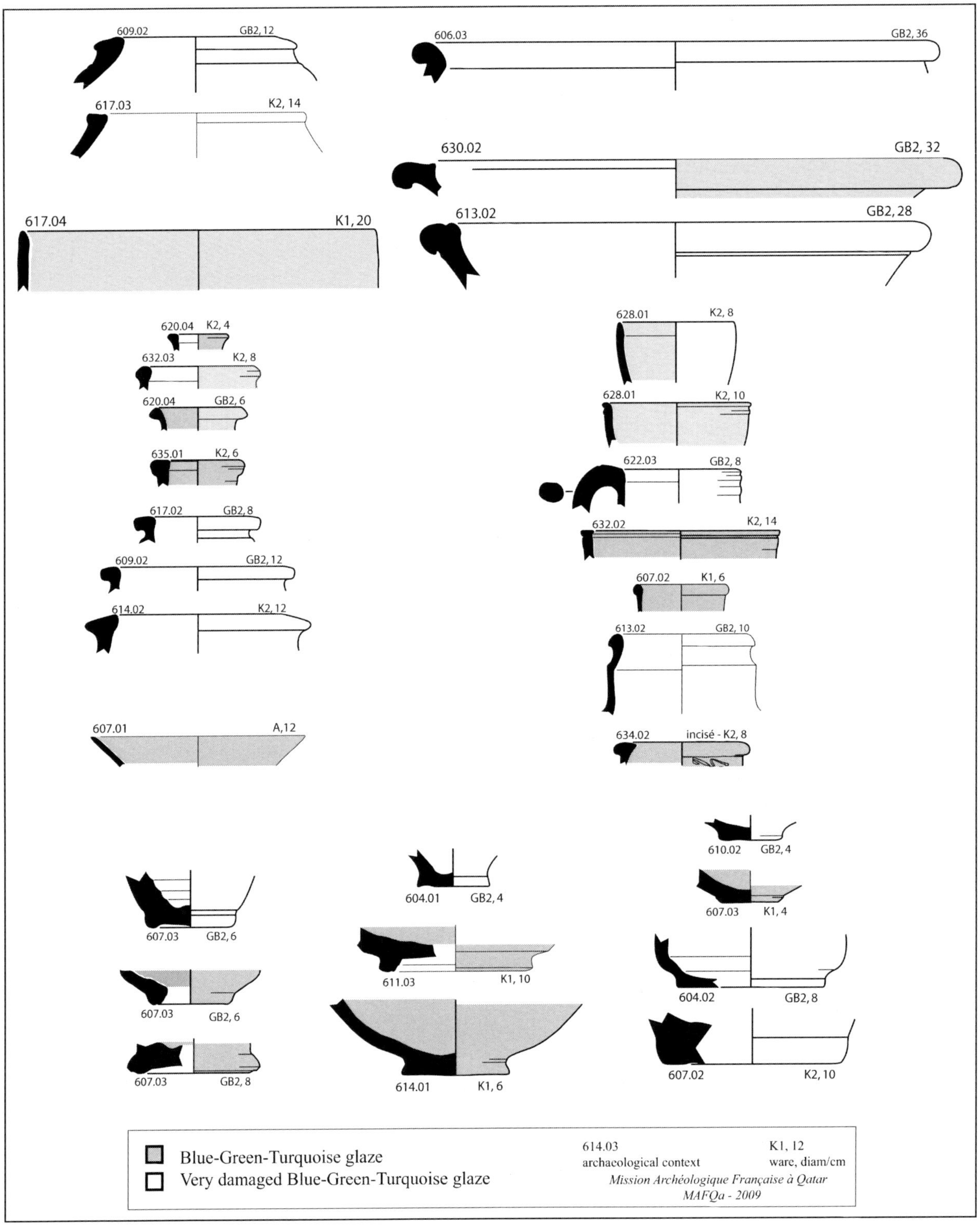

FIGURE 3. *Dating and importation. Blue-green-turquoise category. Murwab seasons 2007–2009. Ninth century. Early Abbasid sequence.*

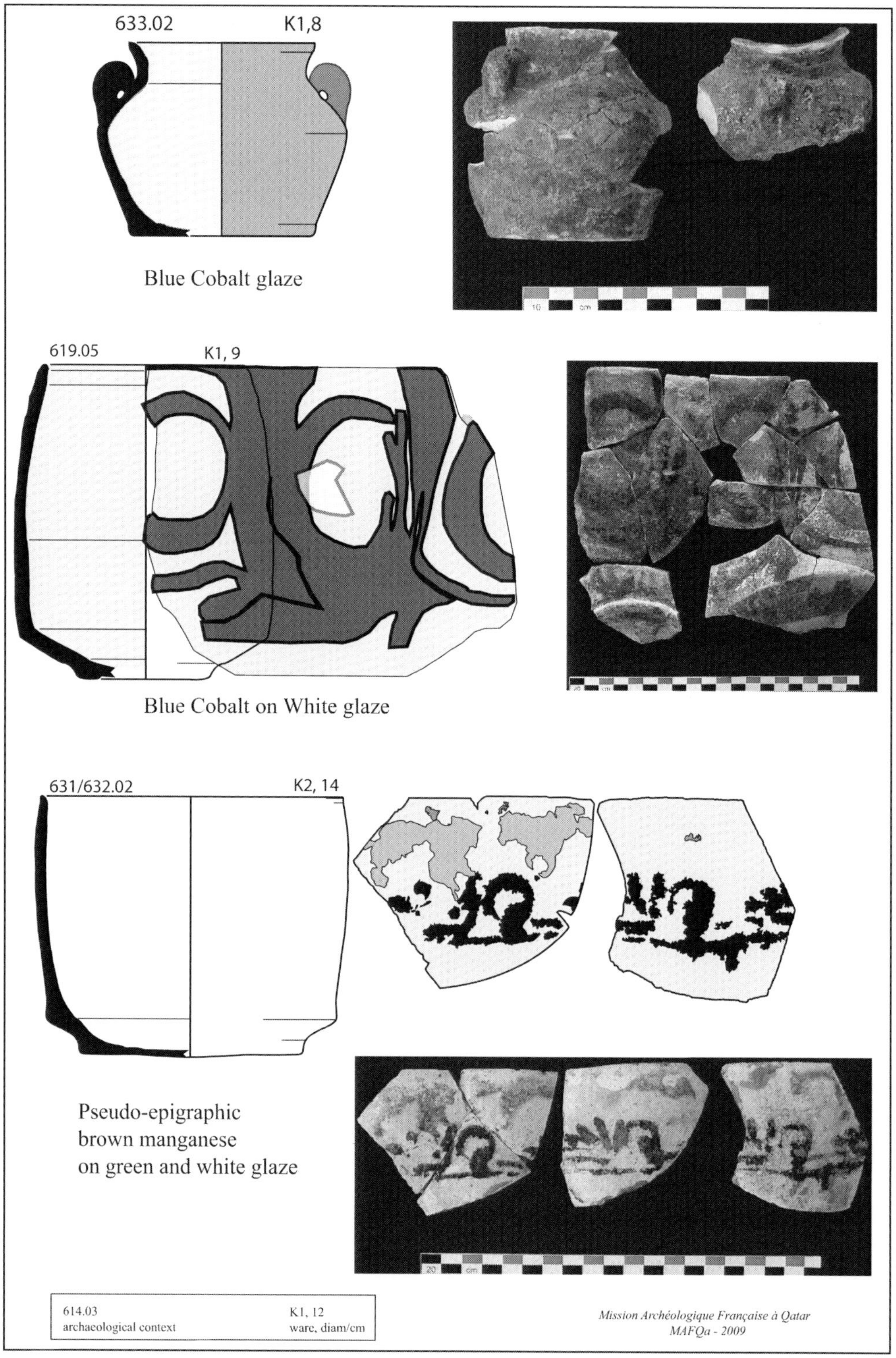

FIGURE 4. *Dating and importation. Alkaline glaze category. Murwab seasons 2007–2009. Ninth century. Early Abbasid sequence.*

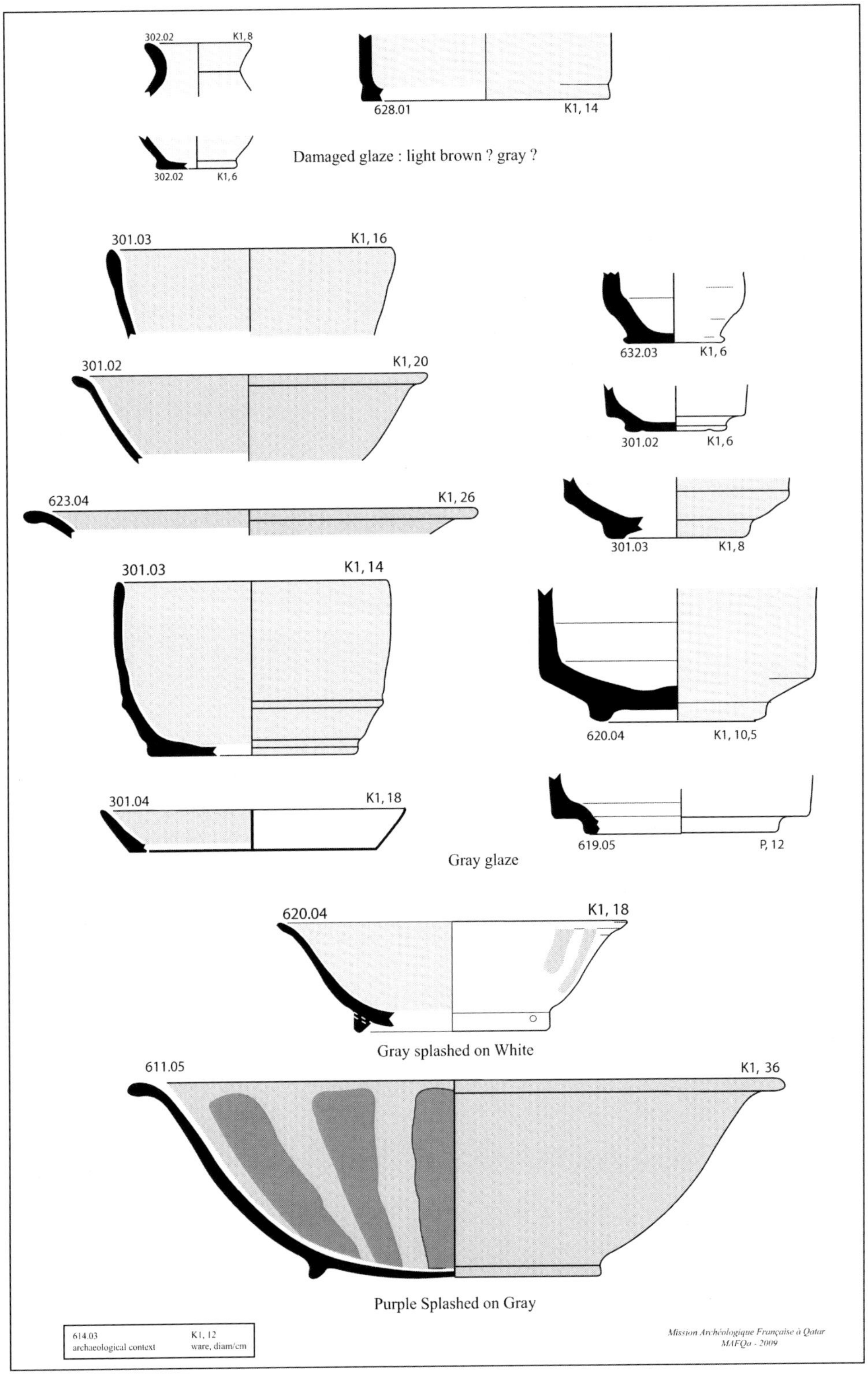

FIGURE 5. *Dating and importation. Grey glaze category. Murwab seasons 2007–2009. Ninth century. Early Abbasid sequence.*

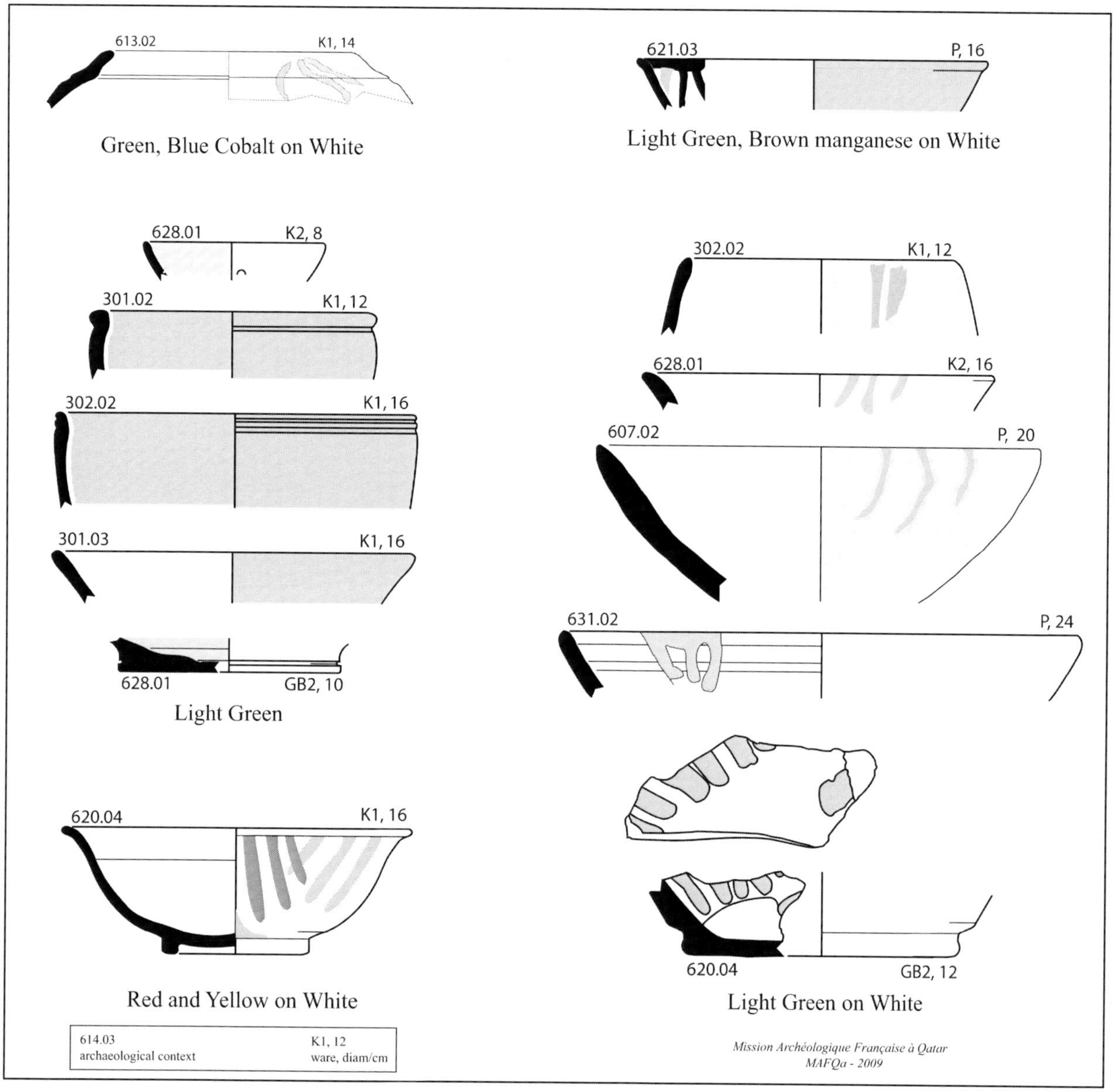

FIGURE 6. *Dating and importation. Splashed glaze category. Murwab seasons 2007–2009. Ninth century. Early Abbasid sequence.*

epigraphic line is painted in brown-black colour. The bowl with a high and straight wall is complete and is the only known specimen in Murwab (see Fig. 4).

Splashed glazed ware

Several categories are indexed in the class of the splashed glaze. A series of straight-walled bowls with a round termination are covered with a light green/acid green glaze, the colour being due to the addition of copper oxide and similar to the blue cobalt decoration of the beginning of the ninth century (Kervran 1977: 85, fig. 43/2; Base Atlas 2010: MOA S. 439; Whitehouse 1979: 52–56; Tampoe 1989: 88). This light green/acid green is splashed on white glaze on bowls with a slightly inverted wall or on cups with an oblique wall (Kervran 1977: 85, fig. 42/2, 4, 5). A cup with a red and yellow splash on white (on the exterior) completes this category (Fig. 6).

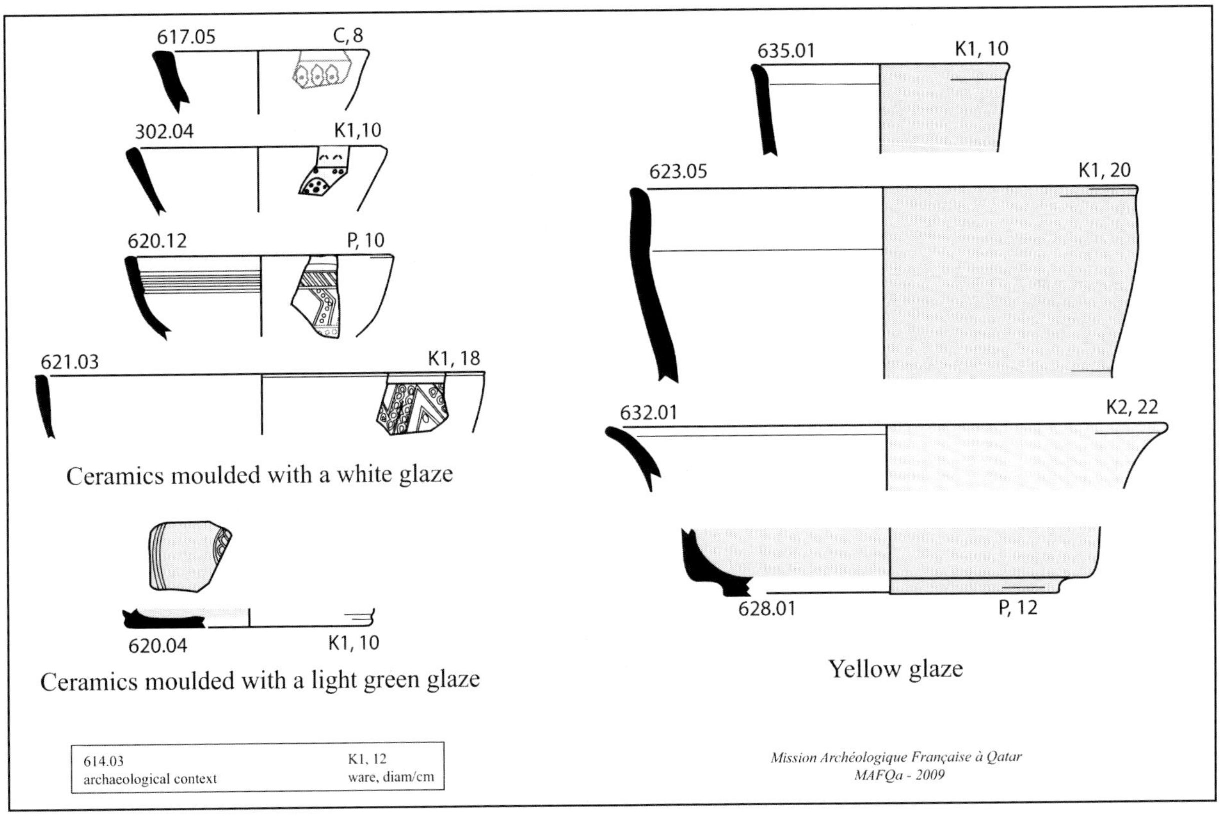

Figure 7. *Dating and importation. Moulded ceramics and yellow glaze category. Murwab seasons 2007–2009. Ninth century. Early Abbasid sequence.*

We also have a large number of fragments that do not enable the reconstruction of specific forms, and they could possibly be bottles. They have dark green, brown manganese, and blue cobalt splashed decoration (Kervran 1977: fig. 38; Base Atlas 2010: MAO S. 524). Some other cases include a complete cup with a curved wall and everted rim, with a grey decoration on a white background.

2.2.4 Moulded ceramic under monochrome glaze

This ceramic type, generally plates, is well known in Samarra (Lane 1939, ninth century) with a decoration of half-palmettes and planks of pearls under a generally yellow glaze which finds its origin in the Sasanian decorations.

At Murwab, the bowls with a curved or oblique wall are moulded and carry an opaque white glaze (Base Atlas 2010: MAO S. 376). There are also moulded plates covered with a dark green glaze (Kervran 1977: 125.19–21; Base Atlas 2010: MAO S. 384); and finally, the third category of this type is covered with a yellow glaze and relates to the earthenware jar, to everted rims cups and to straight-walled bowls (Fig. 7).

In comparison with the study of imports, the whole of the ceramic "table vessels" material is homogeneous, not only by source, i.e. Mesopotamia and Iran, but also according to the assemblies of the various known categories between the beginning of the ninth century (803–830) and the second half of the ninth century (850–885). Two types of ceramics which would allow a relatively precise dating are also absent in Murwab. These are ceramics with "sgraffiato" decoration with colours marbled under an opaque glaze, and the lustred category. These two types appear towards 870–885 at Siraf and at Susa and are attested after 885 in Samarra (Kervran 1977: 90; Whitehouse 1979: 59–60; Northedge 1985: 24).

In addition, it is necessary to mention the absence of Chinese ceramics in the excavation of Murwab and also in the survey that we carried out in the whole of the northern part of Qatar. Yet Chinese ceramics are present on all the other sites of the Gulf in stratigraphic context

(Rougeulle 1991) and they appear in the region from the end of the eighth century with the advent of caliph Hārūn al-Rashīd (763–809) whose rule stimulated international trade.

How did Murwab and the western coast of Qatar escape this trade? We can take into account the rhythm of the currents that allowed ocean navigation in the Gulf throughout the winter. The winter currents entering the Gulf skirt the Iranian coast from Siraf to Basra; then outgoing currents skirt the western coast of the Arabian Peninsula. Qatar and the village of Murwab would have benefitted from trade in products coming from the Arab and Iranian provinces at the very time of the return of the boats involved in trade with China. This possibility may be particular to Murwab, as most other harbours in the Gulf, even those of secondary importance, were involved in the networks of eastern trade in the ninth and tenth centuries. It seems that only coastal sites were supplied by China: in Samarra, capital of the Abbasid empire (836–892), only a small number of ceramics of Chinese production was discovered. Many of these eastern products were sold on the spot, in the same harbours where they were unloaded. Even though 32% of Murwab's table vessels were imported, the site does not appear to have been an entrepôt or bridgehead for trade caravans that would have enabled the diffusion of Chinese ceramics to other, more important, centres of the Arabian Peninsula, for example. In addition, future excavations of the supposed *khān* of al-Nahy (al-Nāʾih), located 12 km north-east of Murwab and dated to the ninth century by material from the surface, will make it possible to propose other hypotheses in order to answer this question (Guérin 2009: 181–183, fig. 1).

2.3 Early Abbasid wares. "Common" pottery: kitchen vessels

The dating suggested by the study of imported and referenced ceramics known as "table vessels" seems restricted to the years 805 to 885 and common ceramics ("kitchen vessels") are discovered in the context of the same layers of occupation. Twenty-four common ceramic wares were defined as part of the 4697 sherds, both forms and formless, and made up 68% of the total of the ceramic material of Murwab. Eight wares represent 84% of this "common" material. Each of the sixteen other wares is present in a lower proportion than 1%. We present three classes of "common" wares discovered at Murwab. All the sampling will be regarded as complete and reliable only after the excavation of districts 3 and 6 has been finalized, and this study is currently in progress (autumn 2009).

2.3.1 Description

In this paper we will just consider the case of three wares whose clay is supplemented by multiple inclusions of minerals.

"I ware" accounts for 14% of the total of the "common" ware; it is white-pinkish to pinkish-beige in colour and a certain number of sherds are burned (Fig. 8). Two types of carbonate are present (white and orange) as well as fragments of volcanic rocks (basalt?). The typology of the forms is varied, as follows:

— earthenware jars with short necks;

— earthenware jars with high and straight necks, allowing for gripping and transport; also large earthenware jars that could be used for storage;

— bowls with oblique walls, high walls, or straight walls with a combed and incised decoration; they include the six basin shapes.

"R ware", also relatively important (10% of the total of the "common" ware), is a term exclusively used for the short-necked pots (Kervran 1977: fig. 26/11; Hardy-Guilbert 1984: fig. 22/3) or many bowls and basins of large diameter (Fig. 9). Only one basin has a horizontal combed decoration. This ware has various inclusions: carbonate, quartz, and volcanic rock; it is a pinkish colour.

"G ware", in spite of being only a small percentage (3%) of the total ceramics at the site, is formed of mainly basins of large diameter, of which the distinctive shapes of the rims seem characteristic of ware imported from India (Fig. 10). Of red-brown colour, the ware consists of carbonate and quartz inclusions.

2.3.2 Local and imported ceramics: type of trade

A comparative study of common ceramics is in progress and will be supplemented later on with sampling extended to the whole of the common ceramics of the 2007 and 2009 excavations. We must not ignore the problem of the lack of publication of typologies of ceramics known as "common" ware coming from the great referent sites. Nevertheless, a number of questions about the "common" wares of Murwab can now be posed.

The excavation of 2009 made it possible to identify a very large number of ceramics carrying traces of repair (approximately 18% of common ceramics): many of the relevant holes indicate bitumen trace which would have been used to ensure impermeability after the repair. These repairs are also found on steatite braziers on the site: a thin bronze wire makes it possible to join together

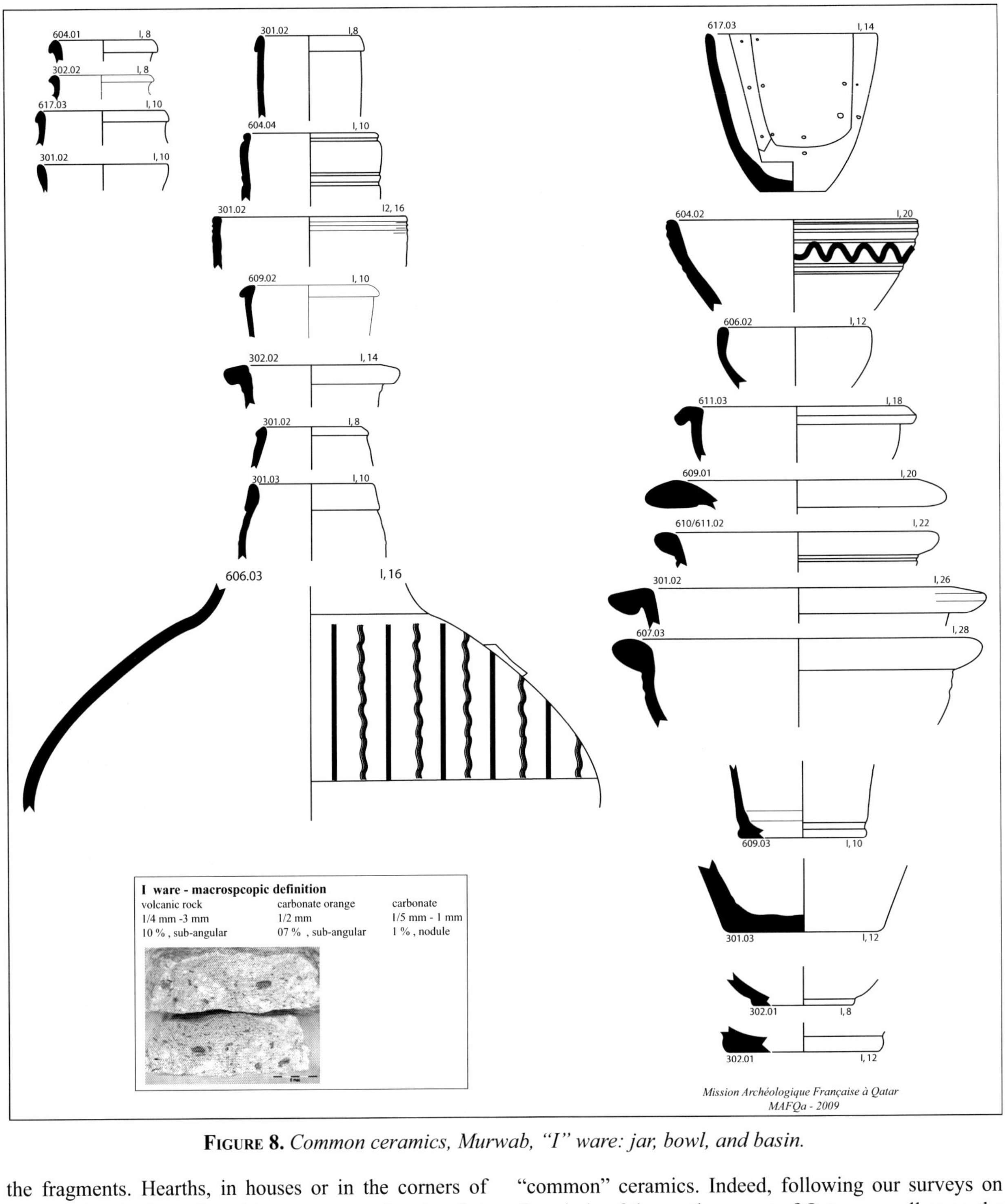

FIGURE 8. *Common ceramics, Murwab, "I" ware: jar, bowl, and basin.*

the fragments. Hearths, in houses or in the corners of courtyards, also have these bitumen traces, showing that ceramics were repaired *in situ*.

Another consideration resulting from this phenomenon of repair was a discussion on the source of these "common" ceramics. Indeed, following our surveys on the whole of the northern part of Qatar, as well as on the western coast, we found no trace of a pottery kiln, of fragments of firing failures, or of utensils used in furnaces (e.g. the *pernette* used with tripod supports). One can

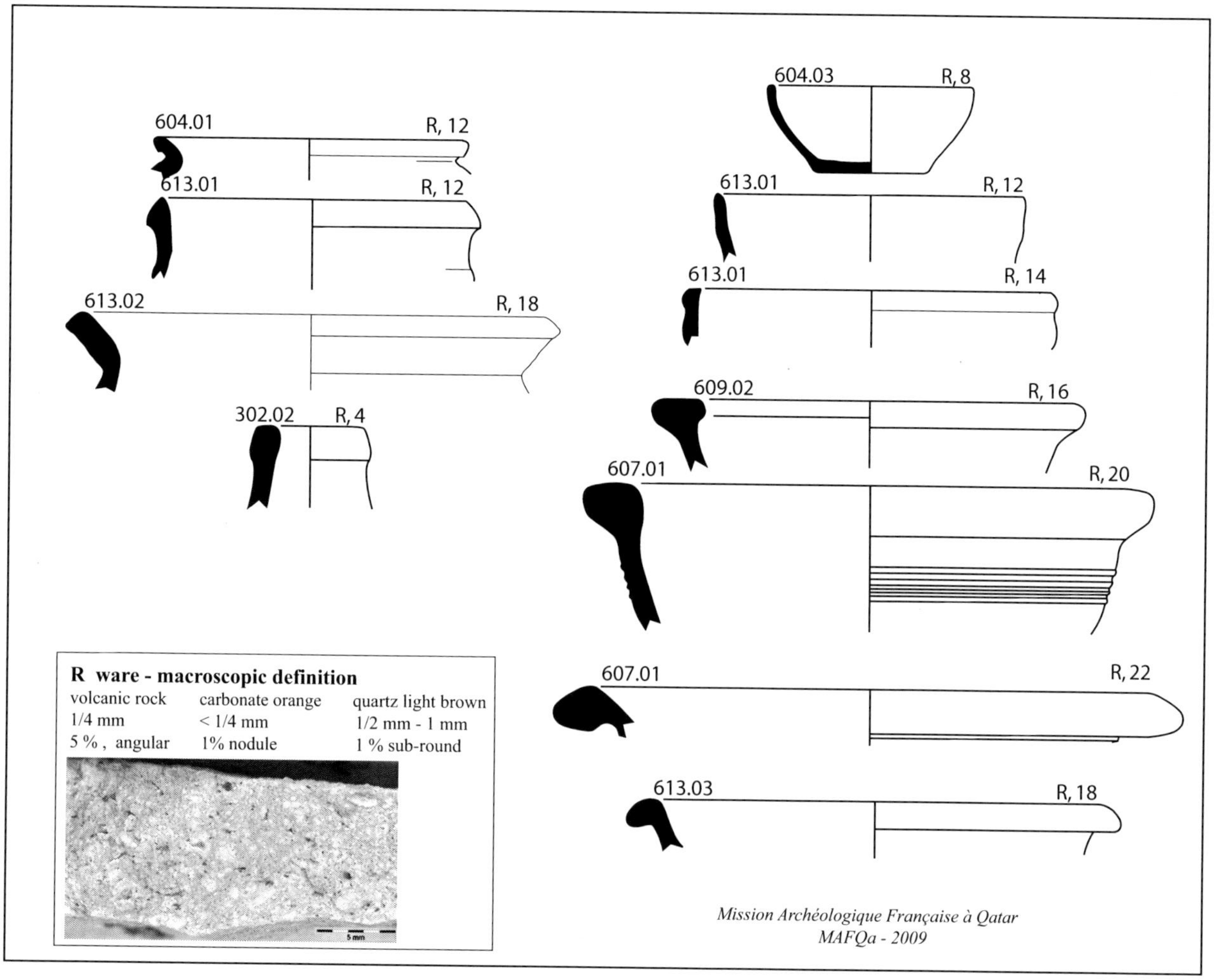

Figure 9. *Common ceramics, Murwab, "R" ware: jar, bowl, and basin.*

suppose that large basins, for example, were sun-baked or fired in a temporary hearth. If the ceramics were imported in great numbers, the population of Murwab would have been dependent on average- and long-distance trade.

The seasonal variation of the economic activities (winter: ocean navigation and trade, summer: fish and pearls) could determine phased deliveries of products, including ceramics. The current repairs discovered on the Murwab ceramics represent one of the immediate solutions to the difficulty of obtaining imported products easily all through the year.

What type of product could the inhabitants of Murwab exchange for "luxury" ceramics? There is a high proportion (32%) of these luxury items. According to Arabic sources, these imported luxury ceramics may have been exchanged for pearls and/or acquired as a result of acts of piracy, as is well known for the region of Bahrain, Qatar, and al-Hasa. Among the discoveries in the excavations, certain ceramics — jugs with three handles and small pots used for decoction or extraction of substances — have traces of red dye. Unutilized grinding stones also have these red traces. A study of this dye in the laboratory is essential in order to determine the chemical components of the red matter and its geographical and organic source. We did find shells of the *Murex* type but not in sufficient numbers to extract useful quantities of purple dye but further study will be directed towards fishing, perhaps focusing on *Murex*. Nevertheless, the process for obtaining the purple dye is likely to have taken place elsewhere rather than at Murwab or even Qatar — to date no traces of relevant shell deposits have been found anywhere on the Qatari littoral — and may have taken place in Bahrain or along the coast of Arabia.

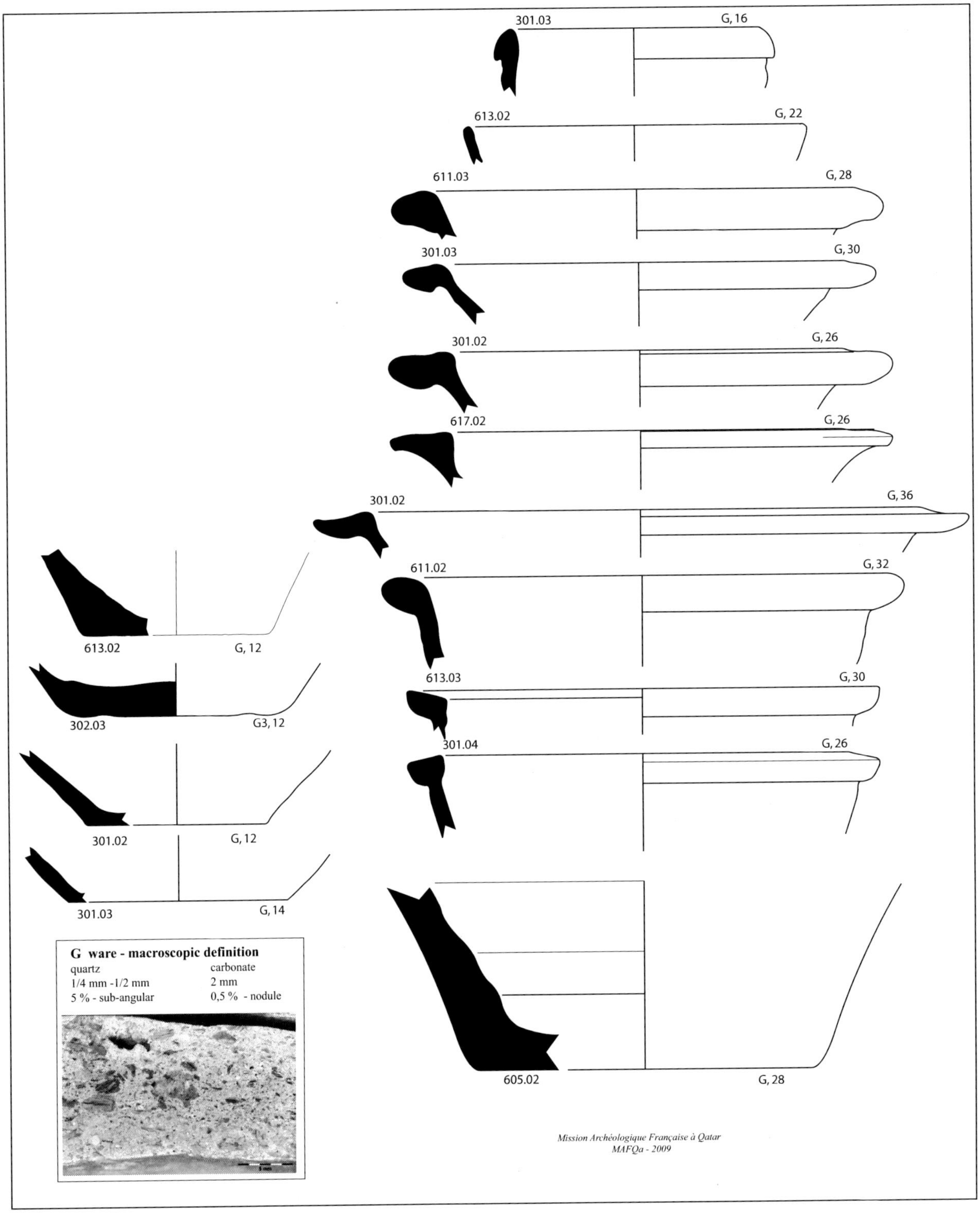

FIGURE 10. *Common ceramics, Murwab, "G" ware: jar, bowl, and basin.*

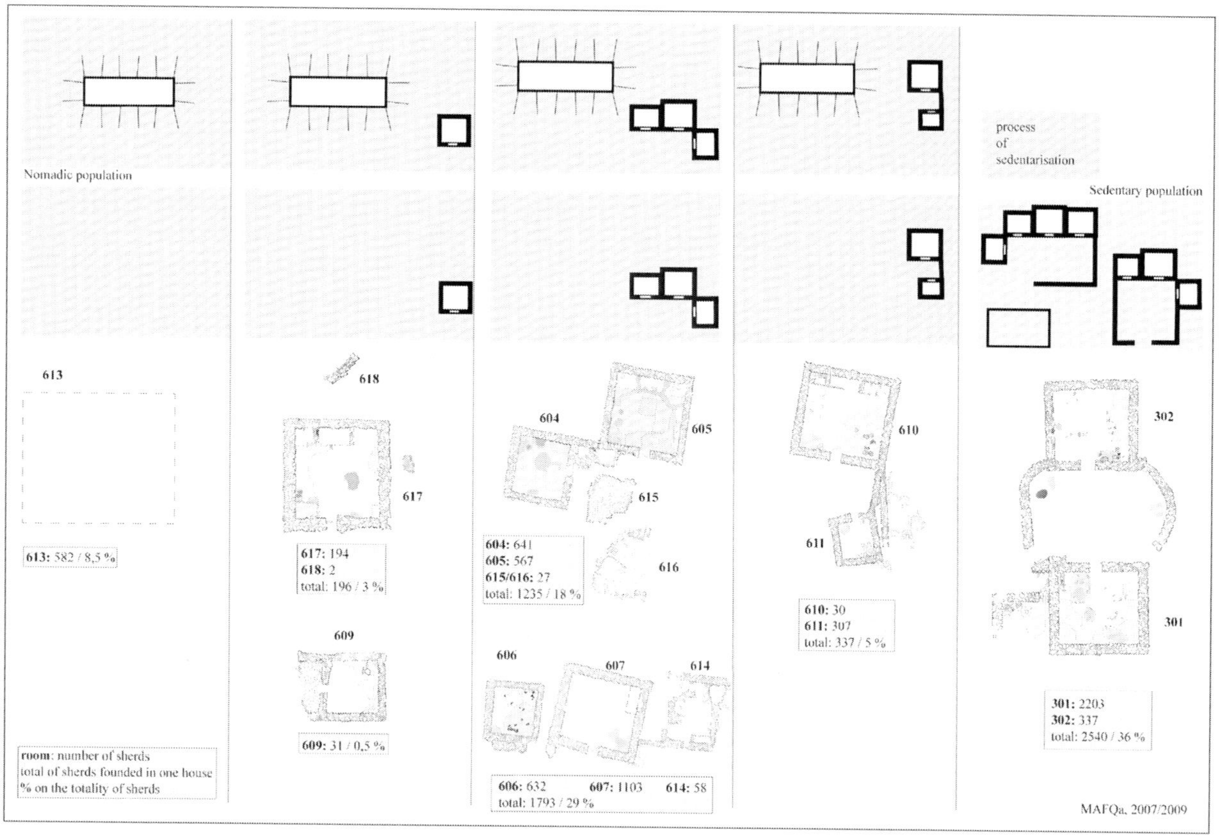

Figure 11. *Murwab sedentarization in progress. The various phases of the process of sedentarization observed in Murwab with the pottery distribution. Ninth century, early Abbasid.*

Conclusion

Ceramic distribution and phases of sedentarization

A specific classification was established with reference to the stratigraphic context. The batch of ceramics discovered was catalogued with reference to each house or cell in which it was found and allotted registration codes in the inventory *in situ*. This inventory proves that several cells associated with similar architectural and stratigraphic contexts together make up houses. This analysis is part of the model of the process of sedentarization and has been completed in Murwab: the pattern that emerges is one of several cells enclosed by a courtyard, with cells separated by a wall and only one cell near an "empty" zone (Guérin 1994: 177–197). The inventory of material is also forming a complete corpus (Fig. 11) as all the houses contained tableware jugs, vessels used for storage and transport, table vessels (glazed wares and eggshell wares), bowls, and basins.

The proportion of finds in the "isolated" cells is smaller than other parts of the site, for example, in section 617 which contained only 3% of the ceramics found, but this can be associated with the "empty" zone with a strong incidence of ceramics (8.5%). Section 609 also has few ceramics (0.5%). This section, according to the gypsum grounds discovered, was an area intended for work and was not a living space.

House no. 610–611, which is in the second phase of sedentarization, presents only one density of occupation that is much lower than the other houses (5%), but this is located on the southern part of the "empty" zone no. 613. This house was associated with the "tent" no. 613 — or is there another "empty" zone not yet excavated? On the other hand, the third stage of sedentarization exhibits prolific ceramic material: 18% for houses 604 and 605 and 29% for houses 606, 607, and 614. It should be noted that the workplace for shell processing determined in no. 614 also has a very low density of ceramics (2%), as does the workplace no. 609. Lastly, house 301–302 represents effective sedentarization (identified as the fifth stage of sedentarization), with two cells facing each other enclosed by a courtyard, and has the largest proportion of ceramics (36%).

The study of the distribution of ceramics in spaces defined within the framework of the process of sedentarization is evidence of a more or less intensive occupation of family spaces. As for the distribution, each house (defined as an association of cells) reflects a "complete sampling" that includes earthenware storage jars, glazed table cups imported from Nishapur (Neyshābūr) or Susa, not forgetting the basins and pots that were probably used for extraction of various substances: all the essential objects of daily life are present.

For a complete study, it will be necessary to take into account non-ceramic artefacts, such as steatite braziers, kohl sticks and bronze oil lamps. The results of research on Murwab lead to an account of two distinct architectural layers and the definition of two "ceramic" phases ranging between 805 and 885. This definition will make it possible to refine the ceramics typology of what was previously just called "early Abbasid–ninth century".

Acknowledgements

This project is supported by the CNRS, the "Groupe de Recherches et d'Études sur la Méditerranée et le Moyen-Orient" UMR 5195, Lyon, and the French Ministry of Foreign and European Affairs, Paris, as well as by the Qatar Museum Authority, Department of Antiquities, Doha, Qatar. The director of the French team would like to express her profound gratitude to H.E. Sheikha Al-Mayyassah b. Hamad b. Khalifa Al-Thani, Minister for the Culture of Qatar and H.E. Shaeikh Hassan b. Mohammad b. Ali Al-Thani, Vice Chairperson of Qatar Museum Authority. The French team appreciated the full support of the Department of Archaeology and is particularly grateful to Faysal Al-Naimi, Chief Director of the Department of Antiquities, for his total co-operation on the scientific field and for all administration of the excavations.

References

Base Atlas.
2010. Base des œuvres exposées Atlas. January 2010. *Musée du Louvre* Online. http://www.louvre.fr/llv/oeuvres/bdd_oeuvre.jsp?bmLocale=fr_FR#bddoeuvre.

Caskell C.
1975. ᶜAbd al-Qays. Pages 74–76 in *Encyclopédie de l'Islam.* i. Leiden: Brill.

Cornu G.
1984. Aperçu sur les toponymes de la rive arabe du Golfe chez les géographes arabes d'époque classique. Pages 359–361 in R. Boucharlat & J-F. Salles (eds), *Arabie orientale, Mésopotamie et Iran méridional, de l'âge du fer au début de la période islamique.* (Mémoire 37). Paris: Édition Recherche sur les Civilisations.
1988. La circumnavigation de l'Arabie aux IXᵉ–Xᵉ siècles. Pages 103–110 in J-F. Salles (ed.), *L'Arabie et ses mers bordières.* Lyon: Travaux de la Maison de l'Orient.

Frifelt K.
1974. Murwab. Copenhagen: Moesgaard Museum. [Unpublished circulated report.]

Guérin A.
1994. Majlis et processus de sédentarisation. Étude ethnoarchéologique au Qatar. *Archéologie Islamique* 4: 177–197.
2009. Territory and settlement patterns during the Abbasid period (ninth century AD): the village of Murwab (Qatar). *Proceedings of the Seminar for Arabian Studies* 39: 181–196.

Hardy-Guilbert C.
1984. Les niveaux islamiques du secteur Apadana-Ville Royale. Pages 121–210 in *Cahiers de la Délégation Archéologique Française en Iran.* xiv. Paris: Paléorient.

Ibn Khurradādbih/ed. M.J. de Goeje
1885–1939. *Kitāb al-masālik wa'l-mamālik.* (Bibliotheca Geographorum Arabicorum, 6). Leyden.

Johnstone T.M.
1978. Katar. Pages 781–783 in *Encyclopédie de l'Islam*. iv. Leiden: Brill.
Keall E.J. & Mason R.B.
1991. The ᶜAbbasid glazed Wares of Siraf and the Basra connection: Petrographic Analysis. *Iran* 29: 51–66.
Kennet D.
2004. *Sasanian and Islamic Pottery from Ras al-Khaimah, Classification, chronology and analysis of trade in the Western Indian Ocean*. (British Archaeological Reports, 1248). Oxford: Archaeopress.
Kervran M.
1977. Les niveaux islamiques du secteur oriental du Tépé de l'Apadana. Pages 75–160 in *Cahiers de la Délégation Archéologique Française en Iran*. iv. Paris: Paléorient.
Lane A.
1939. Glazed Relief Ware of the Ninth Century AD. *Ars Islamica* 6: 56–65.
Madelung W.
1978. Karmati. Pages 687–692 in *Encyclopédie de l'Islam*. iv. Leiden: Brill.
Northedge A.
1985. Planning Samarra: a report for 1983–1984. *Iraq* 47: 109–128.
1997. Les origines de la céramique à glaçure polychrome dans le monde islamique. Pages 213–223 in Gabielle Démians d'Archimbaud (ed.), *La Céramique médiévale en Méditerranée*. Aix-en-Provence: Actes du 6ᵉ congrès.
Northedge A. & Falkner R.
1987. The 1986 Survey season at Samarra. *Iraq* 49: 143–173.
Rougeulle A.
1991. Les importations des céramiques chinoises dans le Golfe arabo-persique (VIIIᵉ–XIᵉ siècles). *Archéologie Islamique* 2: 5–46.
2005. The Sharma Horizon. Sgraffiato Wares and other Glazed Ceramics of the Indian Ocean Trade (*c*. AD 980–1140). *Proceedings of the Seminar for Arabian Studies* 35: 223–246.
Salles J-F.
1984. Céramiques de surface à Ed-Dour, E.A.U. Pages 241–270 in R. Boucharlat & J-F. Salles (eds), *Arabie Orientale, Mésopotamie et Iran Méridional, de l'âge du fer au début de la période islamique*. (Mémoire 37). Paris: Édition Recherche sur les Civilisations.
Serjeant R.B.
1978. Historical Sketch on the Gulf in the Islamic Era from the Seventh to the Eighteenth century AD. Pages 149–163 in B. de Cardi (ed.), *Qatar Archaeological Report, excavations 1973*. Oxford: Oxford University Press.
Tampoe M.
1989. *Maritime Trade between China and the West. An Archaeological Study of the Ceramics from Siraf (Persian Gulf), 8th to 15th centuries AD*. (British Archaeological Reports, International Series, 555). Oxford: Archaeopress.
Williamson A.
1987. Regional Distribution of medieval Persian pottery in the light of recent investigations. Pages 11–22 in J.W. Allan & C. Roberts (eds), *Syria and Iran: Three studies in medieval ceramics*. Oxford: Oxford University Press for the Faculty of Oriental Studies, University of Oxford.
Whitehouse D.
1979. Islamic pottery in Iraq and the Persian Gulf: the ninth and the tenth centuries. *Annali dell' Instituto Orientale di Napoli* 39: 45–61.

Author's address
Alexandrine Guérin, 5 rue Audran, 69001 Lyon, France.

e-mail alexandrine.guerin@mom.fr

Faisal Abdulla Al-Naimi, Head of Antiquities, Department of Antiquities, Qatar Museums Authority, P.O. Box 2777, Doha, Qatar.

e-mail falnaimi@qma.com.qa

Proceedings of the Seminar for Arabian Studies 40 (2010): 35–40

A possible Upper Palaeolithic and Early Holocene flint scatter at Raʾs ᶜUshayriq, western Qatar

Faisal Abdulla Al-Naimi, Richard Cuttler, Hatem Arrock & Howell Roberts

Summary
The site of a flint scatter (Qatar National Historic Environment Record 141) thought to have been occupied in both the Upper Palaeolithic and the Late Stone Age periods was discovered during a survey to the south of the Raʾs ᶜUshayriq peninsula in north-western Qatar. The site is located on the former Early Holocene coastline at *c.*3 m above present-day sea level, to the south of the historic walled town of al-Zubārah. For most of the Upper Palaeolithic the site would have been inland, with a hyper-arid environment prevailing for much of this period. For this reason the most likely time for occupation would have been during Marine Isotope Stage 3, corresponding with a humidity maxima of *c.*35–25 ka. However, the results outlined in this paper are provisional and the exact nature and date of occupation will need to be clarified by further study.

Keywords: flint, Upper Palaeolithic, Levallois, Qatar, Ubaid

Introduction

The site (Figs 1 and 2) is located on a flat area of ground to the north of a wadi and is incised with small natural channels that drain towards the wadi. The wadi is several hundred metres across, with extensive alluvial silts that retain water for much of the year, and has abundant vegetation from late winter through to early summer. Surface inspection suggests there is good evidence for the presence of significant stratigraphy in the form of hearths and the outline of a possible stone structure. Nonetheless, the association of these features with any phase of the flint scatter is unclear. No excavation was undertaken and all the flints were recovered as part of a surface scatter, approximately 150 m across. The drawn flints represent only a small sample of the wide variety of flints from the site. Most were left *in situ* until a more comprehensive measured survey of the site can be undertaken.

The proximity of the wadi provides the potential for buried silt horizons that may be associated with the occupation of the site.

Artefact types

Diagnostic flint types (see Fig. 3) include flake cores (1), a possible Levallois point (2), end scrapers (7), discoid scrapers (3 and 8), retouched flakes (4 and 5) and denticular flakes (6). Among the other artefacts recovered

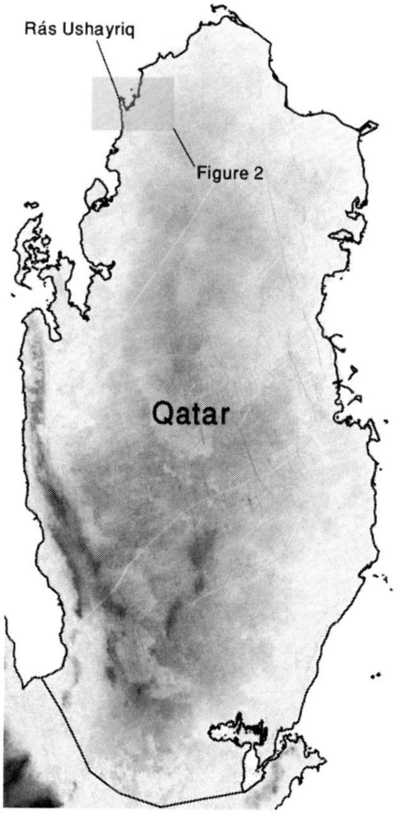

Figure 1. *The Raʾs ᶜUshayriq peninsula.*

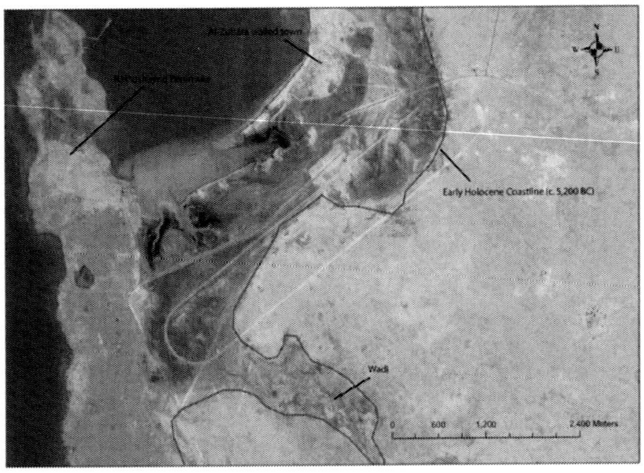

Figure 2. *Site topography.*

from a preliminary survey of the site are white quartz flakes and fragments of obsidian. Also included in the assemblage are fragments (some burnt) of Ubaid pottery. It is notable that blades are absent from this assemblage.

The drawn flints

1. Flake core: difficult to date as this form is present during most prehistoric periods. However, the extensive patina may suggest an Upper Palaeolithic date.
2. Possible Levallois point: this technique is found within the Lower Palaeolithic but is more typical of the Middle Palaeolithic. The core shows evidence of retouch (possibly during a later period) and has extensive patina across the flaked surfaces.
3. Possible disc scraper fragment.
4. Flake with evidence of rectangular retouch along one edge. Characteristic of Epi-Palaeolithic stone tool industries (*c*.20,000–14,500 BP).
5. Flake with evidence of rectangular retouch along one edge. Characteristic of Epi-Palaeolithic stone tool industries (*c*.20,000–14,500 BP).
6. Flake with denticular retouch.
7. End scraper with retouch on both the distal and proximal ends.
8. Atypical disc scraper.
9. Large end scraper, typically Late Stone Age period.

Dating the assemblage (Fig. 3)

One of the cores (1) and the Levallois point (2) suggest Upper Palaeolithic occupation (Kapel's "Qatar A").

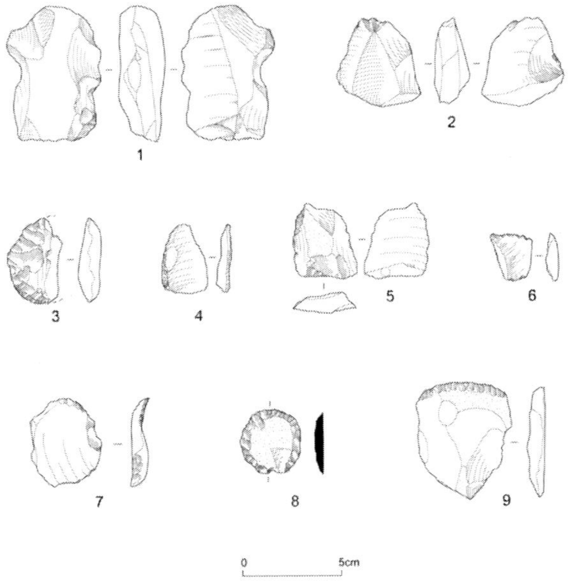

Figure 3. *Illustrated flints.*

Heavy patination across the flaked surfaces of some fragments (note in particular the Levallois point: 2) is consistent with the tools being of some antiquity, while other flints show little or no patination. Several of the tools, including the large end scraper (9) and the Ubaid pottery clearly point to Ubaid/Late Stone Age occupation. These technological differences in the assemblage appear to imply several phases of occupation, with the site abandoned as the climate changed to a hyper-arid phase and reoccupied when the climate ameliorated.

The Gulf as an open landscape

The earliest known stratified site within the Arabian Peninsula is at Jabal Fāyah 1 rock shelter in Sharjah Emirate (Uerpmann, Potts & Uerpmann 2010). This has produced Levallois points and discoidal cores (Assemblage C), provisionally dated to MIS (Marine Isotope Stage) 5 or older (approximately 85 ka). These technologies are not present in later assemblages at Jabal Fāyah (A and B). At Filī in the foothills of the Ḥajar mountains (Scott-Jackson *et al.* 2008) dense scatters of lithics were recorded with a high frequency of side scrapers and bifacial tools. Stone tools with features suggestive of the Middle Palaeolithic are also found at Jabal Barākah in Abu Dhabi Emirate as surface scatters on the Baynūnah Formation mesas and their surrounding slopes (McBrearty 1993; 1999; Wahida, Al-Tikriti & Beech 2008; Wahida *et al.* 2010). Here the core reduction strategy is a centripetal Levallois technique commonly found in Middle Palaeolithic or Middle Stone Age assemblages throughout Africa and Eurasia. The evidence for a bidirectional Levallois technique on these sites show a clear typological differences with Palaeolithic tools found in Africa and suggest an Arabian regional variation of this technology.

While the technology is suggestive of some occupation during the Upper Palaeolithic, during this period Raʾs ᶜUshayriq would have been far inland. Since the confluence of the Tigris and Euphrates would have been approximately 100 km to the east, and the Gulf could have been traversed by foot, there would be no access to marine resources. Access to sweet water, flora, and fauna would have played a key role in the occupation of the site. While there is the potential for aquifers and natural springs, it seems likely that as an inland site Upper Palaeolithic occupation at Raʾs ᶜUshayriq most likely dates to periods of increased rainfall. One such period may have been the humidity maxima during MIS 3 when lakes reached their highest levels around 37,000 years ago (Parker & Rose 2008). The onset of the hyper-arid conditions of MIS 2 (25,000 to 12,000 years ago) would likely have led to the abandonment of the site. Re-occupation of the site due to an amelioration of the climate between 10,000 and 6000 years ago would fit with several of the tool types at Raʾs ᶜUshayriq, which include disk and end-scrapers more typical of the Late Stone Age period (Charpentier 2008: 109).

The obsidian fragment and trade within the Arabian Peninsula

It is not the first time that obsidian has been reported from Qatar. It was found by the French in a grave at al-Khawr (Midant-Reynes 1985). There are no known natural sources of obsidian within Qatar, therefore this must be a traded or imported commodity. While it remains difficult to determine the age of surface artefacts, the associated flints and ceramic assemblage suggest this is likely to date to the Ubaid period. The nearest obsidian sources include the Red Sea, Central East Africa, Yemen, and the Levant, all of which imply wider trade connections with distant regions: Zarins (1989: 359) is of the opinion that the obsidian in Qatar can be sourced to western Arabia. Inductively coupled plasma mass spectrometry (ICP) should provide some indication as to the origin of the obsidian and some clues regarding this trade network.

Both quartz and obsidian were found during excavations on the Ubaid site at H3 in northern Kuwait, with preliminary analysis suggesting it originated from western Arabia or Yemen (Carter & Crawford 2009). This is indicative of a network of trade between eastern and western Arabia during the Neolithic. During this period changes in the Inner Tropical Convergence Zone (ITCZ) caused a shifting of the Indian Ocean Monsoon northwards over the Arabian Peninsula (Preusser, Radies & Matter 2002). With increased rainfall and vegetation more akin to savannah, there are potential conditions suitable for occupation across the Arabian Peninsula including areas of large deserts, as evidenced for the Rubᶜ al-Khālī (Beech *et al.* 2008; Cuttler *et al.* 2007; Parker *et al.* 2006; Parker & Rose 2008), which would have facilitated overland trade. It cannot therefore be assumed that these were maritime trade networks since the Rubᶜ al-Khālī would not have been the major geographical barrier it was later to become.

Acknowledgements

The survey around Raʾs ᶜUshayriq was undertaken under the direction of the Qatar Museums Authority and Birmingham University by Hatem Arrock, Faisal Abdulla Al-Naimi, Himyan Jassim Al-Kuwari, Howell Roberts, Richard Cuttler, and James Taylor. The flint drawings were prepared by Hatem Arrock and Nigel Dodds.

References

Beech M., Cuttler R., Moscrop D., Kallweit H. & Martin J.

2008. Excavations at the Neolithic Settlement of MR11 on Marawah Island, Abu Dhabi, United Arab Emirates: 2004 season. *Proceedings of the Second Annual Symposium on Recent Archaeological discoveries in the Emirates, Al Ain 2004* 2: 25–41.

Carter R. & Crawford H. (eds)

2009. Maritime Interactions in the Arabian Neolithic. *American School of Prehistoric Research Monograph Series*. Boston/Leiden: Brill.

Charpentier V.
2008. Hunter-gatherers of the "empty quarter of the early Holocene" to the last Neolithic societies: chronology of the late prehistory of south-eastern Arabia (8000–3100 BC). *Proceedings of the Seminar for Arabian Studies* 38: 93–116.

Cuttler R., Beech M., Zander A., Kallweit H. & Al-Tikriti W.
2007. Nomadic Communities of the Holocene Climatic Optimum: Excavation and research at Kharimat Khor al-Manahil and Khor al-Manahil in the Rub^{c} al-Khālī, Abu Dhabi, UAE. *Proceedings of the Seminar for Arabian Studies* 37: 61–78.

McBrearty S.
1993. Lithic artefacts from Abu Dhabi's Western Region. *Tribulus: Bulletin of the Emirate National History Group* 3/1: 13–14.
1999. Earliest Tools from the Emirate of Abu Dhabi, United Arab Emirates. Pages 373–388 in P. Whybrow & A. Hill (eds), *Fossil Vertebrates of Arabia — with emphasis on the Late Miocene Fauna, Geology, and Palaeoenvironments of the Emirate of Abu Dhabi, United Arab Emirates*. New Haven, CT: Yale University Press.

Midant-Reynes B.
1985. Un ensemble de sépultures en fosses sous cairn à Khor (Qatar): étude des rites funéraires. *Paléorient* 11: 129–144.

Parker A.G. & Rose J.I.
2008. Climate change and human origins in southern Arabia. *Proceedings of the Seminar for Arabian Studies* 38: 25–42.

Parker A.G., Goudie A.S., Stokes S., White K., Hodson M.J., Manning M. & Kennet D.
2006. A record of Holocene climate change from lake geochemical analyses in southern Arabia. *Quaternary Research* 66: 465–476.

Preusser F., Radies D. & Matter A.
2002. A 160,000-Year Record of Dune Development and Atmospheric Circulation in Southern Arabia. *Science* 296: 2018–2020.

Scott-Jackson J., Scott-Jackson W., Rose J.I. & Jasim S.
2008. Upper Pleistocene stone tools from Sharjah, UAE. Initial investigations: interim report. *Proceedings of the Seminar for Arabian Studies* 38: 43–54.

Uerpmann H-P., Potts D.T. & Uerpmann M.
2010. Holocene (re-)occupation of Eastern Arabia. Pages 205–214 in M. Petraglia & J.I. Rose (eds), *Evolution of Human Populations in Arabia. Paleoenvironments, Prehistory and Genetics.* London: Springer Academic Publishers.

Wahida G., Al-Tikriti Y.W. & Beech M.
2008. Barakah: A Middle Paleolithic site in Abu Dhabi Emirate. *Proceedings of the Seminar for Arabian Studies* 38: 55–64.

Wahida G., al-Tikriti W.Y., Beech M. & A. al-Muqbali.
2010. A Middle Palaeolithic Assemblage for Jabal Barakah, coastal Abu Dhabi Emirate. Pages 117–124 in M. Petraglia & J.I. Rose (eds), *Evolution of Human Populations in Arabia. Paleoenvironments, Prehistory and Genetics.* London: Springer Academic Publishers.

Zarins J.
1989. Ancient Egypt and the Red Sea Trade: the Case for Obsidian in the Predynastic and Archaic Periods. Pages 339–368 in A. Leonard & B.B. Williams (eds), *Essays in Ancient Civilization presented to Helene J. Kantor.* Chicago: The Oriental Institute of the University of Chicago.

Authors' addresses

Faisal Abdulla Al-Naimi, Head of Antiquities, Department of Antiquities, Qatar Museums Authority, P.O. Box 2777, Doha, Qatar.

e-mail falnaimi@qma.com.qa

Richard Cuttler, Senior Project Manager, IBM VISTA, Institute of Archaeology and Antiquity, University of Birmingham, Edgbaston, Birmingham B15 2TT, UK.

e-mail r.cuttler@bham.ac.uk

Hatem Arrock, Antiquities Department Qatar Museums Authority, P.O Box 2777, Doha, Qatar.

e-mail hatem.arrok@yahoo.fr

Howell Roberts, Fornleifastofnun Islands Institute of Archaeology, Bárugata 3, 101 Reykjavík, Iceland.

e-mail howell@instarch.is

Proceedings of the Seminar for Arabian Studies 40 (2010): 41–54

Excavations and survey at al-Ruwayḍah, a late Islamic site in northern Qatar

Andrew Petersen & Tony Grey
with a contribution by Catherine Rees
and drawings by Ifan Edwards

Summary
This paper discusses the results of the first season of excavations at Qalʿat al-Ruwayḍah sponsored by the Qatar Museums Authority and carried out by a team from the University of Wales, Lampeter. Al-Ruwayḍah is a large Islamic period site stretching over an area of more than 2 km along the beach of a shallow bay on the northern tip of Qatar. The site comprises at least seven discrete areas including an extensive prehistoric component. Although the site has been noted before, this is the first time it has been investigated through archaeological excavation and topographic survey. Preliminary findings indicate that the main site was inhabited from the medieval to the early modern period (*c.* eleventh–eighteenth centuries), although this dating is subject to modification based on further analysis of the finds and other dating materials. Excavation concentrated on the most visible feature of the site, which is a fortress divided into four separate courtyards. The principal aim of the 2009 excavation was to identify the building sequence of the fort and also get some idea of its foundation date. The results of the excavation are discussed within the context of other sites in northern Qatar and in relation to other maritime sites in the Gulf.

Keywords: Islamic archaeology, coastal settlement, Ottoman era, fortifications, Qatar

Introduction

The archaeological excavation and survey of al-Ruwayḍah is a joint project of the Qatar Museums Authority, Office of Antiquities, Director Faisal al-Naimi and the University of Wales, Lampeter. The Qatar Museums Authority has provided the financial resources and infrastructure for the project while the University of Wales supplied the personnel and research capacity. The fieldwork was carried out by a field team of six, which, besides the authors of this article, included Daniel Jones, Matthew Jones, and Loveday Allen. The first season took place from January to March 2009 and this article represents a report on the main results of that work set within the context of the post-medieval archaeology of the Gulf. Further seasons of excavation are planned and it is envisaged that the site will give important information about the history and culture of northern Qatar prior to the nineteenth century, as well as providing a significant heritage resource.

Location and identification

The name of the site probably derives from the Arabic term *rawḍah*, a green place or meadow. Ruwayḍah is the diminutive form of *rawḍah* and implies an area for grazing livestock. The site is first mentioned in historical documents by Lorimer (1908: 1515) who refers to the site as Dohat Ruwaydha and states that the inhabitants had left and migrated to al-Zubārah.

Al-Ruwayḍah is located in a wide bay stretching east–west for a distance of *c.*2 km between the abandoned villages of al-Jumayl and al-Khuwayr (Fig. 1). The archaeological site is defined by a series of mounds and surface pottery stretching along the coast for a distance of 1.5 km. The area of occupation does not extend more than 500 m inland and is clearly oriented towards the sea (Fig. 2). The most prominent feature of the site is a large building or fort made up of a series of enclosures with corner towers, which is located at the eastern end of the site less than 20 m from the high water mark (Figs 2–3). At this point the coast is lined by extensive mangrove plantations, which extend out to a distance of more than 400 m.

The site may be subdivided into six areas as follows:

1. The eastern area of Islamic settlement comprising the remains of buildings and surface scatters of pottery (glazed and plain wares), glass, and copper alloy fragments;

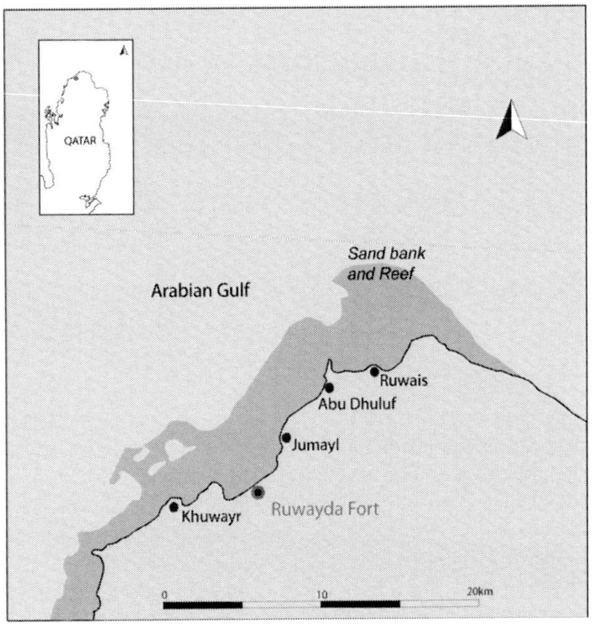

FIGURE 1. *The north coast of Qatar showing the location of al-Ruwayḍah and related settlements.*

2. Qalᶜat al-Ruwayḍah: this is the largest single structure on the site measuring 150 m per side with towers at each corner (Figs 2–3);
3. The western area of settlement: this extends for a distance of more than 1 km to the west of Qalᶜat al-Ruwayḍah and is of similar character to the eastern area;
4. The cemetery area. This is located at the western end of the western area of settlement and comprises two square walled cemetery areas (Fig. 2);
5. A deserted village and compound with walls standing to an average height of 1 m (Fig. 2).
6. An area of flint knapping spreading over an area of *c.*700 m to the south of Qalᶜat al-Ruwayḍah (Fig. 2).

The earliest documented archaeological investigation of the site was carried out by Beatrice de Cardi in 1973. The survey indicated that this was a substantial site built around a large fort made up of several enclosures (de Cardi 1978). Particular attention was paid to the surface finds, which, besides eighteenth-century material also contained some "Sasanian Islamic" and "scratched sgraffito wares" indicating "occupation from the tenth century onwards" (de Cardi 1978: 187 and pl. 30/a). After the de Cardi survey, al-Ruwayḍah was visited by a number of archaeological teams though none of these reported the presence of any material prior to the eighteenth century

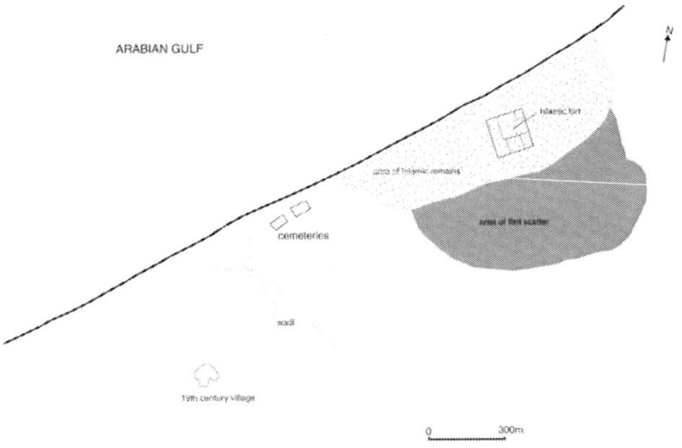

FIGURE 2. *Al-Ruwayḍah: a general site plan showing the location of the fort area of the Islamic settlement and the area of flint working.*

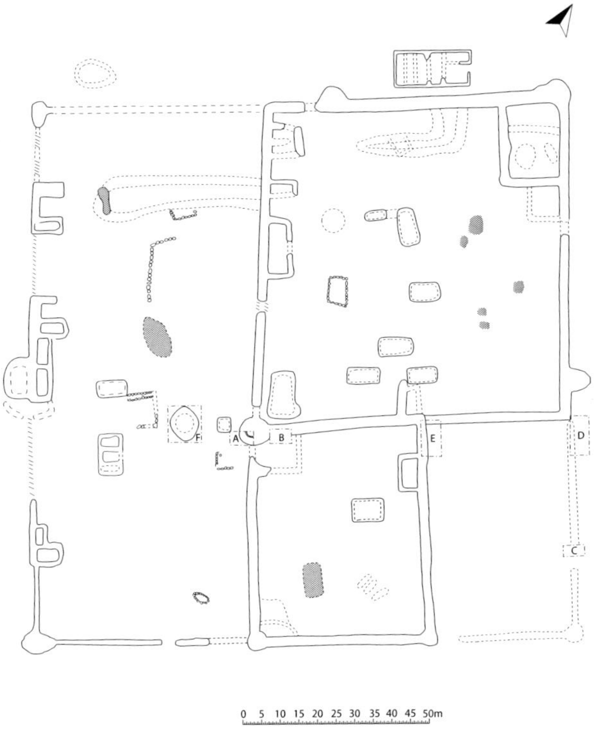

FIGURE 3. *A plan of Qalᶜat al-Ruwayḍah showing the location of the trenches and the layout of the enclosures.*

(al-Khulayfi 1996: 55; Guérin, personal communication 1.2.2009), except for Carter (2009: 267 and n. 37) who reported Chinese celadon at the site.

Based on a reading of the 1978 de Cardi report and a brief visit to the site in October 2008, the following specific research questions were formulated for the first season of work. It should be emphasized that these are

Figure 4. *Areas A (left) and B (right) from the south showing the tower in Area A and the room with installations in Area B.*

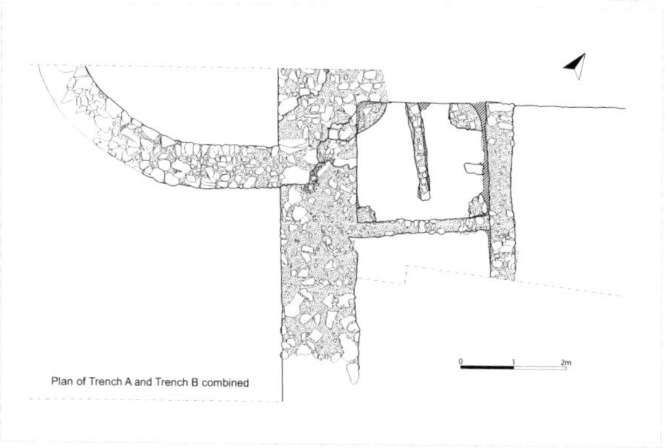

Figure 5. *A plan of Trenches A and B combined.*

preliminary questions relating to the site and should be regarded as supplemental to the wider research agenda concerned with the historical archaeology of the Gulf.

1. What is the size and composition of the site as a whole?
2. What was the period of occupation of the site?
3. What were the nature and sequence of the enclosures which make up Qalᶜat al-Ruwayḍah?
4. How does al-Ruwayḍah fit into patterns of global trade?

These questions formed the basis for the excavation strategy, which in the first season was concentrated on specific diagnostic areas within the fort. The central position of the Qalᶜat al-Ruwayḍah together with the possibility of the survival of major structural features, indicated that this was likely to yield valuable information as well as providing a focus for a future heritage display on the site. In addition, the total station was used to start a detailed survey of the whole site, which could then be used to inform strategic excavation in subsequent seasons.

Six areas of Qalᶜat al-Ruwayḍah were selected for excavation based on surface features and finds of pottery and glass (Fig. 3/A–F). The aim of the excavation was to identify the sequence of construction, which might then be used to identify the earliest structures on the site. Aerial and satellite photographs show that the fort was a large square enclosure which was subdivided into small units. Field inspection of the site showed that only the central and eastern part of the fort contained wall mounds which stood to any height, while on the western part of the fort the wall lines were only visible as low mounds or soil marks. Based on this evidence, a hypothesis for the sequence of structures at the fort suggested that there had originally been a large square enclosure with corner and interval towers which was later reduced in size by using stone from the west wall to build smaller enclosures within. However, the excavations indicate that the structural history of the fort is more complex and it seems that the large enclosure represents the last phase of construction.

Area A (Figs 3/A, 4–5)

This area (4×6 m) was laid out on the south-west side of the highest point of the site. Excavation revealed a large tower built in a distinctive pattern using alternating bands of large and small stones (Fig. 6). The inner face of the tower was lined with mud plaster suggesting that the interior was also used for occupation (i.e. it was not a tower with a solid fill). The tower was not perfectly round and seems to have a "D"-shape outline.

Area B (Figs 2/B, 4–5)

This area (4×6 m) was laid out to the east of the tower. Excavation revealed a north–south wall (104), two small dividing walls, and an installation.

Area C (Figs 2/C, 6)

This area was laid out across the presumed course of the east wall (203) in the south-east quadrant of Qalᶜat al-Ruwayḍah. Excavation revealed traces of a north–south wall one course high. The wall did not extend to the south side of the trench, suggesting either a gateway at this point or that the wall had been robbed out.

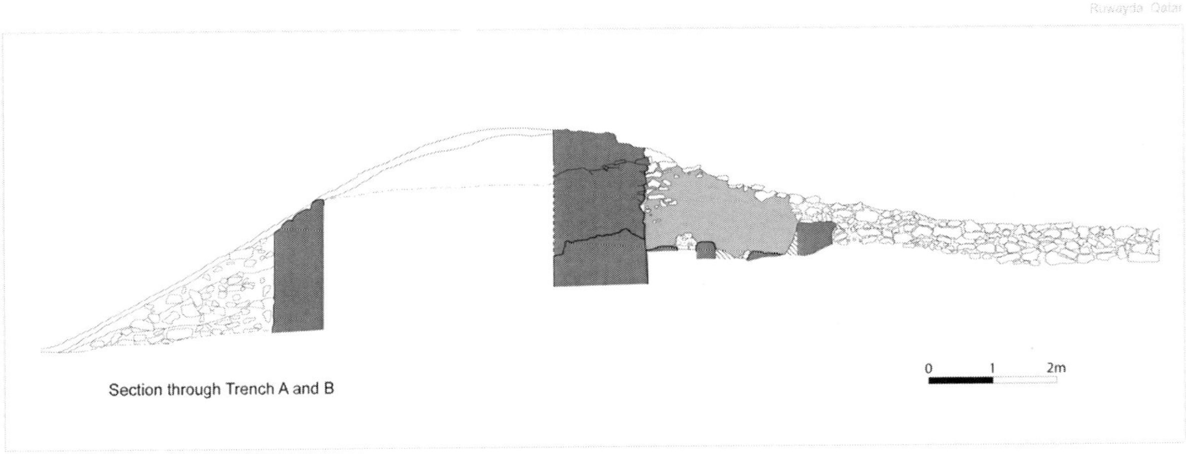

Figure 6. *A section through Trenches A and B.*

Area D (Fig. 2/D)

This area was laid out to the north of Area C to test the relationship between the south-east courtyard and the north-east courtyard. Excavation of the area outside the wall revealed large quantities of ceramics, glass, seashells, bones (fish and mammals), and some metal (copper alloy) fragments. This trench also indicates that the south-east enclosure abuts the large south enclosure.

Area E (Figs 2/E, 7)

Area E was laid out on the west side of the wall dividing the two southern enclosures. After removal of various layers of collapse it is apparent that the eastern wall of the south-west enclosure (403) was built earlier than the south wall of the northern enclosure (404).

Area F (Figs 2/F, 8–9)

Area F was located over the presumed site of a well. Several layers of wind-blown sand covered an extensive layer of rubble (603) sloping down from west to east. The sides of the excavation were bounded by limestone bedrock. Finds include fragments of buff ware water jars (e.g. Fig. 10/9).

Finds

A wide range of finds was recovered from the excavations and from a limited surface survey. Finds not mentioned in the ceramic and lithic reports below include carnelian beads, glass bangles, soft stone (chlorite schist) bowls, worked and unworked shells, metal fragments, a ceramic stamp (or possibly weight), gaming pieces, large quantities of fish bone, marine mammal bones, bitumen residues (see Insoll 2005: 324–327), and traces of textiles. The reports on the pottery and flints are preliminary, although they are indicative of the range of materials recovered.

Flint assemblage

Catherine Rees

Thirty-four flint tools were recovered from the fort and immediate surrounding area. Six flints were discovered during excavation with three recovered from Trench B and one tool each from Trenches A, D, and E. The flints from Trenches A and B were deposited among layers of wall collapse, but the flints from Trenches D and E were found within charcoal-rich possible occupation layers. The flint assemblage consists of twenty-six scrapers and eight awls/piercing tools. These tools are primarily roughly retouched natural flakes and stylistically rather crude. The tools vary in size, with width measurements ranging from 1.5 cm to 4.5 cm for scrapers and 0.7 cm to 3.5 cm for awls. The assemblage appears to be of a domestic character and the tools would appear suitable for use in food preparation. Although it is possible that the flints relate to pre-historic occupation of the site the context suggests that they are contemporary with the Islamic period occupation of the site.

Figure 7. *Area E from the south-east showing the wall of the north enclosure (404) butting against the wall of the smaller south enclosure.*

Pottery

Tony Grey

The pottery from the first season of excavation at al-Ruwayḍah totalled 3429 sherds weighing 46.8 kg (excluding surface finds). Collection was total and from six separate excavation areas/trenches. The material was counted, weighed, assessed, and recorded on pro forma sheets and on an Excel pottery register database. Diagnostic (registered) sherds were drawn and photographed. The range and variety of wares is relatively limited and reflects the seaborne trade around the Persian Gulf with attested types of coarse wares derived from Raʾs al-Khaymah, Bahrain, and possibly Oman, and fine tablewares imported from Persia (glazed frit wares/stone paste), China, and Southeast Asia (porcelain).

The fine wares

Tablewares and fine wares include imported porcelains, imported glazed Islamic stone paste from Persia, and coarser more "local" equivalents.

Porcelain

Porcelain wares include cups, bowls, and plates. Much of the clear deep cobalt blue on blue-on-white porcelain originated from the Jingdezhen kiln, which produced the best quality porcelain. Other porcelain appears as fuzzy, smoky grey-blue on blue-on-white. Some porcelain

Figure 8. *Area F from the west, during excavation, showing the rubble fill of a presumed well.*

emanated from provincial kilns such as Dehua, Swatow, or further afield from places like Annam (Vietnam). The wares include: blue-on-white Jingdezhen kiln (early fourteenth century to 1900, Kennet 2004: 67, 68); blue-on-white Chinese provincial, e.g. Dehua (fourteenth century to 1900, Kennet 2004: 67, 68); polychrome with overglaze yellow enamelling which is wearing off, dated 1730–1750 (Museum of London Archaeology); Chinese Imari ware dated 1720–1740 (class as a whole 1680–1900, Museum of London); monochrome pale green/celadon (1650–1900, Museum of London); Batavian with *café au lait* or chocolate brown ground mid-eighteenth century (class as a whole 1700–1750, Museum of London); and Japanese blue-on-white.

The porcelain was all made for export and not for domestic ("imperial") use. Some was produced especially for the Middle Eastern market. Some is of a high quality, and some of poor quality, thickly potted with poorly mixed paste producing a fairly coarse fabric. All the porcelain from al-Ruwayḍah dates from the eighteenth century, mostly before *c.*1750.

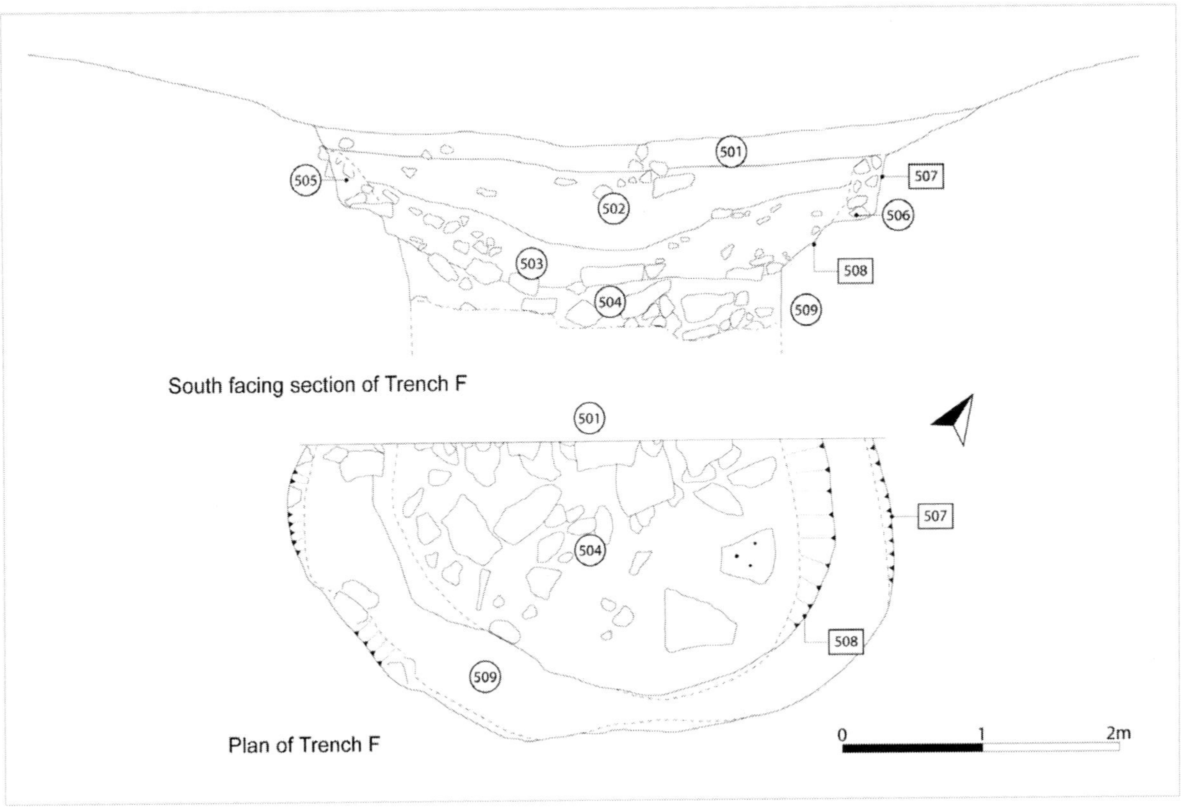

Figure 9. *A plan and section of Trench F.*

Glazed Islamic stone paste (fourteenth–nineteenth century, Kennet 2004: 51)

These sherds may have originated from Persia from sites such as Kirman. Three sherds of polychrome glazed ware including red colour are late seventeenth to eighteenth century. The body may be earthenware or frit (stone paste). Some is blue-on-white produced with cobalt and a clear alkaline glaze on a frit/soft paste body. In most cases the glaze has weathered and deteriorated. One item is a lobed cup with a clear glaze appearing white. Other products include bowls and dishes. These are influenced by Chinese styles but often with Persian inspiration.

Bowls in cream sandy ware (possibly dating to the nineteenth century)

A small rounded bowl in buff-cream sandy ware with a flared neck and everted rim (diameter 130 mm) from Trench D (308). Parallels: bowls from Raʾs Abaruk (Raʾs Abrūq) (Garlake 1973*a*: 169, fig. 2/24–28); al-Zubārah (QIAH Project, Grey, ongoing).

Rouletted glazed bowls (possibly sixteenth–eighteenth century, cf. monochrome glazed bowls of this date, Kennet 2004: 56)

All classes of glazed wares present were decorated by applying the glaze directly onto the body of the pot with no slip used. These bowls are straight-walled, steeply sloping with a bead rim and internal groove in a friable cream sandy ware, and decorated with several bands of rouletting and zones of clear mauve glaze that is very poorly adhering and usually flaking off. Only a few small sherds have survived at al-Ruwayḍah. Examples from Trench D (06): a rim sherd, diameter 170 mm; and Trench E (408): a body sherd with rouletting, clear and manganese purple glaze (Fig. 10/14).

Manganese painted bowls (sixteenth to possibly eighteenth century, Kennet 2004: 52)

One example is present from Trench C (303): a bowl base with a broad shallow ring base in a buff, fairly fine and hard-fired fabric with black manganese painted outlines of flower petals, with yellow glaze within the outlines

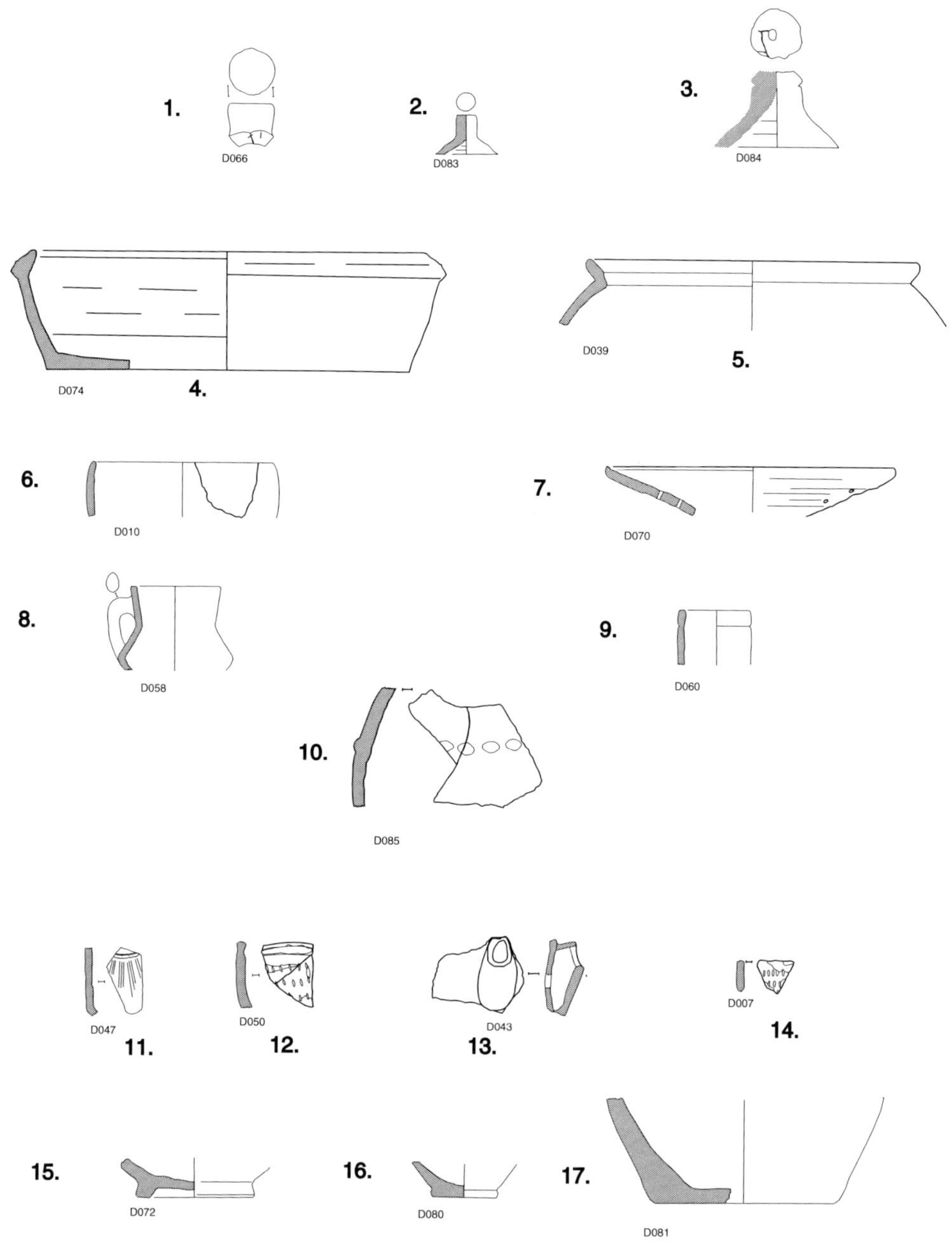

FIGURE 10. *Islamic pottery from al-Ruwayḍah (see text for a discussion).*

against a clear glaze ground. The glaze has deteriorated and is turning iridescent (Fig. 10/6). This is reported as common at Raʾs al-Khaymah (Kennet 2004 52: 139, fig. 12, Manganese painted with manganese bands 2–5 mm wide, plus green glaze, origin sixteenth–eighteenth century, possibly from Persia). This type was reported at Bahrain (Larsen 1983: 221, fig. 12) and is common at al-Zubārah (Qiah Project, Grey, ongoing).

Alkaline glazed in turquoise green/blue

Only a few small sherds of this ware were present at al-Ruwayḍah. The ware has a buff fabric with a deep turquoise-blue alkaline glaze on the exterior. Parallels are found at al-Huwaylah, which is Sasanian-Islamic, used mainly for jars: "Islamic monochrome glazed wares with transparent and olive glazes on a fine-textured cream fabric" (Garlake 1973*b*: 174); and "turquoise-glazed sherd possibly Seljuk or eighteenth-century imitation of Seljuk ware" (1973*b:* 176).

Monochrome brown glazed bowls (Khunj) (fifteenth or sixteenth–twentieth century, Kennet 2004: 54)

This ware is common at al-Ruwayḍah and present in most contexts. Referred to as Khunj and Dark Khunj Ware at Ra'̓s al-Khaymah (Kennet 2004: 54, 55, fig. 11) from a site in Persia, where this material was collected by Williamson who believed this represented the manufacturing site (Hansman 1985: 52), and as Kung Ware from Ra'̓s Abaruk (Ra'̓s Abrūq), Qatar (Garlake 1973*a*: 174, fig. 2/1–4) and at al-Huwaylah (1973*b*: 174, fig. 2/1–4). A very similar class is reported from Oman as Baḥla Ware (Whitcomb 1975: 129). This ware may also have been made at Khaṭṭ, Ra'̓s al-Khaymah (de Cardi, Kennet & Stocks 1994: 63, pl. 15). It occurs at Bahrain (Kennet 2004: 54) and on the East African coast (de Cardi 1971: 225–289) with a sixteenth- to seventeenth-century date suggested. At Ra'̓s al-Khaymah Types 101, 111, and 112 (Kennet 2004: fig. 11) are the most common. Types 101 and 102 are flanged bowls. Type 106 with a straight rim is present at al-Ruwayḍah and also at al-Zubārah.

The ware is earthenware from well-levigated clay, wheel-made, very hard and fired to colours from light grey to pinkish-red, often with colour variation present on one vessel. The clear lead glaze is often patchy with orange patches visible under the glaze. The glaze ranges in appearance from greenish or dark brown to "dirty" yellowish-brown. The bowls are plain with rims varying from a flange to straight or slightly in-turned and internally bevelled. The base is always a ring base. The bowls vary in size and some are heavy-duty. Frequently the ware is very weathered and the glaze flaked off.

Examples from al-Ruwayḍah include a rim sherd with a slightly in-turned rim with an internal groove, a ridged exterior, a steeply sloped wall with a slight concave exterior profile, and a patchy yellow-brown glaze on interior and exterior, rim diameter 300 mm, Trench A (011) (Fig. 10/12). Others include: a fairly high-footed ring base, diameter 80 mm, pinkish-grey fabric, and dark brown decayed glaze on interior and exterior, Trench B (101) (Fig. 10/15); a rim sherd with a slightly in-turned rim, diameter 250 mm, with a yellowish-brown glaze and three repair holes, Trench B (101) (Fig. 10/7).

Coarse wares

Jugs

The most common form present from al-Ruwayḍah is the water jug in a well-levigated buff-cream sandy ware recorded as CS (cream sandy ware), BCS (buff-cream sandy ware), and OCS (orange-cream sandy ware) with the colour in the section varying according to kiln firing conditions. The ware surfaces are generally cream. The same ware from Ra'̓s Abrūq, Qatar, was identified by A. Williamson as Aali ware made in Bahrain in the eighteenth century (Garlake 1973*a*: 166, 169, fig. 2/43–46). This ware was also recorded from al-Huwaylah, Qatar (Garlake 1973*b*) and al-Zubārah. Possibly the same ware is present from Ra'̓s al-Khaymah (UAE) as buff ware for jars and bowls in a well-levigated, well-fired buff fabric with an orange tint dating to the post-sixteenth century (Kennet 2004: 81).

Water jugs vary in both size and form. Most frequently the form is a rounded body tapering to a shallow ring base, with a single strap handle opposed to a handmade tubular spout luted onto the body over a roughly pierced opening (cf. Ra'̓s Abrūq [Garlake 1973*a*: fig. 2/24–26] for ring bases [Fig. 10/13]). The rim may be collared with a narrow neck (cf. al-Huwaylah, 1973*b*: 134, fig. 2/6) or thickened and rounded as in an example from Trench F (504) (Fig. 10/9). A nearly complete water jug was recovered from Trench E (408) (Fig. 10/8). The base diameter varies but 70 mm is the most common size. One example of a disk base, diameter 55 mm, was recorded in Trench D (309) (Fig. 10/16). Water jugs were abundant at the well in Area F.

Some of the water jugs bear a simple decoration on the body or shoulder panel of groups of diagonal or vertical incised lines. In some examples the lines form cross-hatching as in an example from Trench F (501) (Fig. 10/11). Similar jug types with incised and combed decoration were excavated at Ra'̓s Abrūq (1973*a*: fig. 2/18–21). Smaller water vessels from late post-medieval Yemen are decorated with paint or incised designs and cross-hatching (Posey 1994: 37).

Small jugs are present in the same ware. An example from Trench E (408) is a small carinated jug with a straight, slightly tapered rim (diameter 63 mm), slightly concave neck profile, and a ring handle from mid-neck to shoulder (Fig. 10/8).

Storage jars, water jars, and basins

1. Coarse oxidized jar ware (CoarJarO)

There may be more than one fabric type under this general heading but predominant is a pink fabric that is very sandy with frequent ill-sorted angular quartz and lime inclusions up to 4 mm in size. The fabric is porous and rather light in weight, handmade/coil-built and thick-walled at up to 18 mm with internal rilling. Flat jar bases from Trench A (011) (Fig. 10/17) and Trench B (105) are more sandy than the ware with abundant lime inclusions and pale orange in colour.

2. Coarse reduced jar ware (CoarJarR)

The ware is grey (sometimes pale grey) and very sandy with occasional lime inclusions and tempered with black fragments (some of which are platelets) up to 3 mm in size. The ware is porous, light in weight, with internal rilling and walls up to 15 mm thick. The ware may correspond with the class with black angular inclusions from Raʾs al-Khaymah (Kennet 2004: 80, 81) dated to the eighteenth century and with frequent large black angular inclusions 1–7 mm in size. Both the oxidized and reduced coarse wares are present from al-Zubārah (QIAH Project, dated up to the twentieth century, Grey, ongoing).

A basin profile from Trench D (303) has an upwardly arched, broad incurved, and externally thickened and bevelled rim, with a diameter of over 300 mm and a height of 86 mm, a straight wall that is 9–11 mm thick, and a flat base (Fig. 10/4). The vessel appears to be wheel-made with internal rilling. This heavy rim form has antecedents in eighth- to ninth-century AD Abbasid period basins.

A variant is lime-tempered, handmade, very hard, very coarse, and very sandy with frequent ill-sorted quartz and lime inclusions up to 3 mm in size and black, possibly iron-rich, fragments in this red-firing clay that is reduced to black on its internal and external margins and surfaces. A jar sherd with finger-impressed cordon with thin white wash traces on the exterior is present from Trench E (408) (Fig. 10/10).

3. Other

A neckless jar with collared rim is present from Trench B (116), diameter 105 mm, in buff-cream sandy ware.

4. Jar lids

Two examples of jar lids were encountered. A heavy-duty lid with a large circular lid knob in orange sandy ware from Trench F (504), and a large lid with roughly pinched-up lid knob in buff-cream sandy ware from Trench D (303) (Fig. 10/3).

Cooking vessels

1. Julfar (Julfār) Ware

This ware, used for cooking vessels and bowls at al-Ruwayḍah, was made at Raʾs al-Khaymah, UAE, at a site inland from Kush (Kennet 2004: 112, table 45). It is handmade, in a red ware that is frequently fired and reduced to black, coarse with ill-sorted angular quartz and lime that gives a white speckled appearance to reduced pieces. It dates from its source from the eleventh to the twentieth century (Kennet 2004: 74) and to the eighteenth century at al-Ruwayḍah. Kennet defines four variants of this ware by decoration and firing that are present from the fifteenth to twentieth century (2004: 71–72, 112, table 45) and all are present at al-Ruwayḍah (2004). It is common at al-Zubārah (QIAH Project, Grey, ongoing). The types identified are as follows:

Julfar-1: oxidized buff to orange ware with an exterior white wash with red-painted lines. Trench E (408): two body sherds in red-brown ware with a white wash exterior with red-painted stripes from a closed-form bowl with an internal ledge and plain straight rim (cf. Raʾs Abrūq, Garlake 1973*a*: 116, fig. 2/49, 53).

Julfar-2: reduced ware, often black with a purple/red-painted rim and trails or lines on both interior and exterior for a closed-form cooking pot with side lugs. From Trench D (301) a ledge-rim closed-form rounded cooking pot with a slight groove in the rim, a holed side lug in a reduced ware with blackish exterior and dark brown interior, and a red-painted rim and diagonal stripes on the exterior (cf. al-Huwaylah, Garlake 1973*b*: 175, fig. 2/7, 8 with side lug, 9 with incurved rim, 10 red-painted rim with diagonal stripes, 11 everted rim). The side lugs published by Kennet (2004: fig. 19, CPO2 and CPO3) are dated eleventh–thirteenth century.

Julfar-3: oxidized ware (buff, Kennet 2004) with red-painted decoration. A bowl fired deep orange with an orange self-slip interior with a ledge rim grooved for lid seating. Red-painted rim and stripes on the interior with a poorly finished exterior, with large lime inclusions visible and a characteristic boundary between luted rim and bowl body from Trench D (308). A flange-rim bowl of closed form in red-brown ware with a self-slip exterior and geometric red-painted repeating triangles immediately below the rim on the exterior. A ledge-rim rounded bowl in dark red-brown ware with a red-painted rim and vertical stripes on the exterior (cf. Kennet 2004: fig. 24, CP4.4 from the class of post-al-Matāf cooking pots; fig. 22 B1.4 [3] bowl from al-Matāf dated fifteenth–sixteenth century); Raʾs Abrūq (Garlake 1973*a*: 166, fig. 2/48, sherd with diagonal red stripes on tan slip). From Trench D (303) a bowl in very coarse, hard orange-brown ware with a rough poorly finished exterior, a self-slip interior with a red-painted stripe, and a disk base was found. Kennet dates these Julfar-3 bowls to the fifteenth–sixteenth century but at al-Ruwayḍah they form part of an eighteenth-century assemblage.

Julfar-4: reduced thin-walled ware vessels, fired black for cooking, with a flat base and apparently no red-painted decoration. From Trench D (303) a rounded closed-form bowl with a plain straight rim with internal ridge and exterior side lug, reduced ware with a black exterior with lime inclusions visible and an orange-brown interior in fairly thick-walled ware and no red paint visible. The characteristic luting joining the rim to the body is visible. It may be Julfar-2 (cf. Kennet 2004: fig. 24, CP5.1 [1] post al-Matāf date 1600 to 1950s).

2. Coarse Cooking Pot Ware (CCPW) (dating uncertain, but to nineteenth century)

This is a different ware to Julfar Ware and the origin is unknown. It is handmade, fairly thin-walled, very coarse with large angular quartz and lime inclusions, rough to the touch, hard-fired but friable. The ware is fired orange-brown with a self-slip. The form present at al-Ruwayḍah is that of a fairly deep closed-form cooking pot with a rounded body and a broad flange rim grooved for lid seating. The only decoration noted is a horizontal white slip-painted band around the girth of an example from Trench D (Fig. 10/5).

It is present at al-Zubārah (QIAH Project, Grey, ongoing).

3. Cooking-pot lids

A range of cooking pot lids made in buff-cream/orange-cream sandy ware is present, characterized by burning on the rim. The lids are flange-rimmed with a flat circular lid knob. Lid knobs from Trench D (301) (Fig. 10/1) and Trench D (303) (Fig. 10/2). No lids in Julfar ware or CCPW were noted. Cooking-pot lids in this ware, some with steam holes, are present at al-Zubārah (QIAH Project).

Other coarse wares

Small amounts of Coarse Hard Orange Ware (COH), Coarse Friable Orange Ware (COF), and Coarse Cream Ware (CCW) are present.

Conclusion

Architecture

Although there may well be an earlier component of the site, the main period of occupation of the fort can be dated to the seventeenth and eighteenth centuries with little or no material from the nineteenth century. The excavations indicate that the fort was developed in three phases. In Phase 1, the small enclosure to the south was built with four corner towers including the excavated tower in Area A. In Phase 2, a large enclosure without towers was added to the north of the first enclosure. In Phase 3, the area of the fort was expanded by adding a large extension to the west of the Phase 1 and Phase 2 enclosures as well as an enclosing area in the south-east corner. This huge fort had corner and interval towers, and at 150 m on each side it is the largest of its kind in Qatar. At 22,500 m^2 this makes it more than double the internal area of the fort at Huwaylah (for details, see Garlake 1973*b*), which has an internal area of approximately 10,000 m^2.

Forts are a ubiquitous feature of late Islamic settlement in Qatar, possibly indicating a lack of security or perhaps some form of communal or tribal identity. Nearby architectural comparisons for the fort at Ruwayḍah can be found at al-Thaqab and al-Rakīyah forts both located inland within 20 km of al-Ruwayḍah (al-Khulayfi 1987: 76–80, 81–84). Al-Rakīyah fort has a mixture of three rectangular towers and one round tower. Like the fort at al-Ruwayḍah, it is divided internally into two enclosures and has rooms built against the enclosure walls (cf. Area B). Al-Thaqab fort also has four corner towers (three round and one rectangular) and two rooms built against the inner face of the north wall. However, both of these forts are considerably smaller than al-Ruwayḍah (al-Rakīyah 47×30 m and al-Thaqab 30×28 m) as are the associated areas of settlement.

Context

Al-Ruwayḍah's position on the coast is the probable reason for its greater size, with access both to international maritime routes (Floor 2007), as indicated by imported pottery and opportunities for harvesting pearls from one of the world's largest pearl banks which lies less than 10 km off Qatar's coast at this point (Carter 2005). It seems likely that the harvesting of pearls was the basis of the economy of the site and it may well be that the flints found on the site are connected with the processing of the pearl oysters. The significance of pearls to this area of the Gulf has been extensively discussed by Carter (2005; 2009) and it seems that Ruwayḍah played a leading role in this activity. In addition, the fish traps in the vicinity indicate a thriving fishing industry, which would have provided a valuable subsistence base for the economy.

The pottery and other finds present at al-Ruwayḍah and historical sources relating to Qatar in the seventeenth and eighteenth century indicate that the site was part of a trading network which operated within the Gulf and beyond. Certainly the location of al-Ruwayḍah on the north coast meant that it was in an ideal situation to monitor shipping passing through the Gulf. The reason for the abandonment of the site is not clear, though it may be connected with changes to international trade patterns and local factors such as the foundation of al-Zubārah as implied by Lorimer (1908: 1515; see also Rahman 2005: 16). This also calls into question the relationship of al-Ruwayḍah with the deserted villages in the vicinity, in particular al-Khuwayr and al-Jumayl (Hardy-Guilbert 1998: 120). In any case, by the nineteenth century the site appears to have been deserted with only a small village or farmstead to the west of the fort inhabited during this period. What is clear is that more research, and excavation in particular, is needed to determine the nature of the occupation at the site, with a special emphasis on the rooms within the fort and buildings in the immediate vicinity.

In historical terms al-Ruwayḍah is important for helping to understand how Qatar fitted into the geopolitics of the Gulf in the eighteenth century. The neighbouring settlements of Furayḥah, al-Khuwayr, Jumayl, Abū Ẓulūf, Yūsufiyyah, and Ruways are all mentioned in historical documents (see e.g. Niebuhr 1792). However, al-Ruwayḍah is absent from eighteenth-century descriptions of the coast. It is probable that the site was inhabited by one of the Arab tribal groups known to be in the region at the time (e.g. Āl Musallam, Ḥuwala, ᶜUtūb), though which one is a matter of debate.

The only historical reference to the occupation of the site in the eighteenth century comes more than a century later from Lorimer (1908: 1515) who states that the inhabitants of the site moved south to al-Zubārah. Given the size of the site and the evidence for its occupation in the seventeenth and eighteenth centuries, the silence of the historical sources is surprising. It is of course possible that the site was known by another name in the eighteenth century, or that for some reason it did not attract the attention of Europeans or others who documented the coast at the time.

There may be references to the site in Ottoman sources, although these have yet to be fully investigated (e.g. Özbaran 1994: esp. 119–158). The Ottomans were certainly interested in Qatar and the earliest description of the country dates from 1555. The Defter states: "the Qatar Arabs, who are seafarers without exception, possess about 1000 boats of all sizes. They have contributed to the prosperity of the country both with respect to shipping services and as merchant tradesmen. Their Sheikh is Muhammad bin Sultan Benî Muslim. This personage has also landed property at al-Hasa with which he has close contacts" (*Rüûs Defteri* no. 213 cited in Kursun 2002: 33).

Qatar seems to have been considered part of the Ottoman province of al-Hasāh, which was occupied in the 1550s and was key to the Ottoman ambition to capture Bahrain (Kursun 2002: 33–34; Orhonulu 1967: 2–11; Özbaran 1994: 129). Within this context, it is possible that the fort at al-Ruwayḍah was first established by Ottoman forces, though at present this must be regarded as speculation. Whatever the precise historical circumstances of the fort, it is certainly essential to carry out further excavation to gain a better idea of the place of this major site in the history of northern Qatar.

Acknowledgements

The fieldwork and research on which this article is based could not have been carried out without the support of Abdullah Faisal al-Naimi, Director of the Office of Antiquities within the Qatar Museums Authority. Himyan al-Kuwari, also of the QMA, provided considerable organizational support and co-ordination within Qatar. Alexandrine Guérin (French Mission) and Jurgen Schreiber (German Team) provided help of all kinds within the field. I am also grateful to Munir Taha for his advice and Robert Carter for additional historical references and archaeological background.

References

Carter R.

2005. The History and Prehistory of pearling in the Persian Gulf. *Journal of the Economic and Social History of the Orient* 48/2: 139–209.

2009. How pearls made the modern Emirates. *Proceedings of conference on New Perspectives on Recording UAE History, 23–25 November 2008.* Abu Dhabi: Centre for Documentation and Research.

de Cardi B.

1971. Archaeological Survey in the Northern Trucial States. *East and West* 21: 225–289.

1978. *Qatar Archaeological Report. Excavations 1973.* Doha: Qatar National Museums/Oxford: Oxford University Press.

de Cardi B., Kennet D. & Stocks R.

1994. Five Thousand Years of settlement at Khatt, U.A.E. *Proceedings of the Seminar for Arabian Studies* 24: 35–95.

Floor W.

2007. *The Persian Gulf, The Rise of the Gulf Arabs; The politics of trade on the Persian Littoral 1747–1792.* Washington DC: Mage Publishers.

Garlake P.S.

1973*a*. An Encampment of the 17th to 19th centuries on Ras Abaruk Site 5. Pages 164–171 in B. de Cardi (ed.), *Qatar Archaeological Report: excavations.* Doha: Qatar National Museums/Oxford: Oxford University Press.

1973*b*. Fieldwork at al-Huwailah, Site 23. Pages 172–179 in B. de Cardi (ed.), *Qatar Archaeological Report: excavations.* Doha: Qatar National Museums/Oxford: Oxford University Press.

Hansman J.

1985. *Julfar, an Arabian Port. Its Settlement and Far Eastern Ceramic Trade from the 14th to the 18th Centuries*. (Royal Asiatic Society Prize Publications Fund 22). London: Royal Asiatic Society.

Hardy-Guilbert C.

1998. Villages côtiers abandonnés du Qatar. Pages 89–104 in C.S. Phillips, D.T. Potts & A. Searight (eds), *Arabia and its Neighbours: Essays on Prehistoric and Historical Development in Honour of Beatrice de* Cardi. Turnhout: Brepols.

Insoll T.

2005. *The Land of Enki in the Islamic Era.* London/Bahrain: Kegan Paul.

Kennet D.

2004. *Sasanian and Islamic Pottery from Ras al-Khaimah: classification, chronology and analysis of trade in the Western Indian Ocean.* (Society for Arabian Studies Monographs, 1). BAR International Series 1248. Oxford: Archaeopress.

al-Khulayfi M.J.

1987. *The Traditional Architecture in Qatar.* Doha: National Council for Arts and Heritage, Museums and Antiquities Department.

1996. *Archaeological Sites in Qatar.* Doha: Ministry of Information Office of Museums.

Kursun Z.

2002. *The Ottomans in Qatar*. Istanbul: Isis Press.

Larsen C.E.

1983. *Life and Land Use on the Bahrain Islands: the geoarchaeology of an ancient society.* Chicago: Chicago University Press.

Lorimer J.G.

1908. *Gazeteer of the Persian Gulf, 'Oman and Central Arabia.* Calcutta: Government Printing Press.

Niebuhr C./trans. R. Heron

1792. *Travels through Arabia and Other Countries in the East.* Edinburgh: R. Morison and Son.

Orhonulu C.
1967. 1559 Bahreyn Seferine ait bir Rapor. *Tarih Dergesi* 17/22: 1–16.
Özbaran S.
1994. *The Ottoman response to European expansion: Studies on Ottoman-Portuguese relations in the Indian Ocean and Ottoman administration in the Arab Lands during the sixteenth century*. Istanbul: Isis Press.
Posey S.
1994. *Yemeni Pottery: the Littlewood Collection*. London: British Museum Press.
Rahman H.
2005. *The Emergence of Qatar. The Turbulent Years 1627–1916*. London/New York: Kegan Paul.
Whitcomb D.
1975. The archaeology of Oman: a preliminary discussion of the Islamic periods. *Journal of Oman Studies* 1: 123–157.

Authors' addresses
Dr Andrew Petersen, Department of Archaeology, University of Wales, Lampeter, SA48 7ED, UK.
e-mail andrewduncanpetersen@yahoo.co.uk

Anthony Grey, Flat 2 Regency Hall, Tunbridge Wells, TN2 5QZ, UK.
e-mail a.d.grey@hotmail.co.uk

Ifan Edwards, c/o North Qatar Project, Department of Archaeology, University of Wales, Lampeter, SA48 7ED, UK.
e-mail ifanedwards@googlemail.com

Catherine Rees, c/o North Qatar Project, Department of Archaeology, University of Wales, Lampeter, SA48 7ED, UK.
e-mail catherinelrees@yahoo.co.uk

Proceedings of the Seminar for Arabian Studies 40 (2010): 55–68

Al-Zubārah and its hinterland, north Qatar: excavations and survey, spring 2009

Alan Walmsley, Hugh Barnes & Phillip Macumber

Summary

In anticipation of a major new project at the extensive walled site of al-Zubārah, which dates to the Islamic period and is located on the west coast of northern Qatar, an exploratory programme of archaeological survey work, excavations, and environmental studies was undertaken from January to May 2009. At the invitation of the Qatar Museums Authority, Antiquities Department, the University of Copenhagen fielded a team of thirteen led by Alan Walmsley (Director, Excavations) and Ingolf Thuesen (Director, Heritage) with the intention of completing a preliminary assessment, recording, and survey of al-Zubārah and its hinterland, as well as initial reconnaissance of other north Qatar sites. This paper will focus on the results of the work in and around al-Zubārah, including the mapping of the site, the geomorphological and archaeological investigation of its hinterland including associated sites, and two areas of investigative open-area excavations within the town of al-Zubārah. Overall, the extraordinary complexity of the natural and human environment encountered through this work is being revealed, and suggests that in the future many more rewarding outcomes can be expected in the study of Qatari archaeology, history, and heritage.

Keywords: Qatar, al-Zubārah, Islamic archaeology, urban plan, geomorphology

Introduction

At the invitation of, and in partnership with, the Qatar Museums Authority, new archaeological investigations were undertaken in the spring of 2009 at the large and underexplored site of al-Zubārah on the west coast of northern Qatar.[1] An investigative survey in the expansive hinterland of the site began, with an initial emphasis on water sources and settlement profiles. The programme of archaeological and heritage research at al-Zubārah, expected to continue over a five-year period, stems from a bold initiative of the Qatar Museums Authority (QMA), spearheaded by H.E. Dr Shaykh Hassan Bin Mohammad Bin Ali Al-Thani, Vice Chairman of the Board of Trustees of the Qatar Museums Authority. As Shaykh Hassan has stated, this programme "forms part of the core for our long term strategy for the protection of our historic environment" (Huda N.V. 28 July 2009).

The agreement between QMA and the Department of Cross-Cultural and Regional Studies at the University of Copenhagen calls for a fully inclusive research and field programme, labelled the Qatar Islamic Archaeology and Heritage Project (QIAH), into all aspects of the archaeological and heritage value of north Qatar, with a focus on the Islamic history of the region. The intention is to reveal, document, and explain the full range of settlement, economic, and social structures in north Qatar since the arrival of Islam up to the twentieth century, thereby forging a more complete connection between contemporary Qatar and its formative Islamic past.

The Project is overseen by the Archaeology Section of QMA under the direction of Mr Faisal al-Naʾimi, with the support of Himyan Jassim al-Kuwari, Saif al-Nuaimi, and Mohammed al-Obeidy. We sincerely thank all our Qatar colleagues for their unflinching support for the Project. The fieldwork, team logistics, daily running, and scientific aims of the Project were fully delegated to Professors Ingolf Thuesen and Alan Walmsley of the University of Copenhagen. The Deputy Director of the Project, charged with overseeing all aspects of the daily running of the work, was Mikkel Bille. Much of the fieldwork was assigned to a number of field co-ordinators in charge of excavations (Louise Blanke and Daniel Eddisford), mapping (Hugh Barnes), and a survey of the geomorphology and hydrology of the region (Phillip Macumber). This paper represents a summary of the comprehensive end-of-season reports written by these

[1] Site names are spelled in accordance with the 1986 *Gazetteer of Qatar* (United States Board on Geographic Names 1986).

and other team members, which have been compiled into a two-volume work submitted in paper and electronically to the Qatar Museums Authority (Bille 2009; Macumber 2009).

Background

Al-Zubārah, located along the eastern edge of a broad bay on the west coast of the Qatar Peninsula (Fig. 1), is Qatar's largest and most significant archaeological zone, gaining entry on UNESCO's tentative list in March 2008 (see http://whc.unesco.org/en/tentativelists/5316/). The archaeological town site of al-Zubārah is situated on the coastline on top of low rocky platforms, separated from the rising hinterland to the east by large *sibākh* flats (sg. *sabkhah*) (Fig. 2), a natural landscape that emerged in stages during the mid-Holocene transgression "variously put at between 7,000 to 4,000 yr BP" (Macumber 2009: 9). The al-Zubārah townscape today is typified by extensive stone-built features, notably circuit walls, gateways, towers, mosques, large residential units, and food-processing installations, currently all in a very dilapidated state and threatened by natural (sea and wind) and human (unrestrained access) factors. Lining the top of the scarp some 1.65 km to the east of the town site, and linked to it by northern and southern screening walls, are two forts (Qalᶜat Zubārah, constructed in its current form in 1938, and the largely destroyed Qalᶜat Murayr), associated settlements and their cemeteries, a number of dug water wells, and extensive field systems. Together the town site, forts, settlements, cemeteries, and agricultural systems constitute a coherent, interrelated archaeological zone that cannot be studied piecemeal and, furthermore, has strong ties with other sites in the northern region, both along the coast and deeper inland.

Historically, emphasis has habitually focused on the lively political events that unfolded in al-Zubārah during the seventeenth to nineteenth centuries and the ongoing dispute over ownership of the Zubārah region, a question not formally determined until 2001 (Al-Arayed 2003; Al-Khalifa & Rice 1993; Belgrave 1960: 152–159; 1966; Higgins 2009; Nonneman 2002). The causes and implications of these events have been vigorously contested, and it is not the intention of this paper to revisit these. Although any history prior to the seventeenth century can only be surmised, yet may not be impossible (e.g. Potts 1990: 317, n. 239), the presence of a settlement of some note is first attested in Arabic sources dating to the seventeenth century CE. In the eighteenth century al-Zubārah achieved historical prominence in the Gulf following the arrival in the 1760s of tribal elements from Kuwait belonging to the ʿUtūb and a concomitant expansion of the settlement, perhaps reaching 3000 inhabitants. Other groups followed, especially from Basra in the 1770s. The traditional activities of Gulf trade, pearling, and primary industry were likewise relocated in al-Zubārah by settlers, resulting in a greatly expanded economic and political role in the region. To protect the new-found wealth and influence of al-Zubārah, later sources record the building of a fort called Murayr (1768), a canal from the sea to supply it (by 1794; see below), and towered circuit walls on the land side of the town. Yet success was accompanied by a reciprocal increase in calamitous events, from famine to raids and attack, including the devastating sack of al-Zubārah in 1811. While, at times, these events were turbulent and violent, it is unlikely they were the only — even the main — reason for the town's demise and eventual abandonment. A new, smaller settlement grew among the ruins, mostly consisting of members belonging to al-Nuᶜaym, but the economic focus of the middle Gulf had already shifted to Bahrain, limiting any chance of a significant revival of al-Zubārah as a major player in the region.

A different historical perspective can be expected from archaeology, one that will elucidate social processes, economic activity, religious behaviour, subsistence patterns, and intra-site and hinterland relations over the full spectrum of settlement in the Zubārah Archaeological Zone (ZAZ). In addition, the Project promises to illustrate Zubārah's — and Qatar's — relations with the wider world, both at the level of the Gulf and as far afield as East Asia, East Africa, and Europe. Furthermore, as the chronological period under study leads into the twentieth century, the Project also provides a key to understanding the character of socio-cultural relations between Qatar and its neighbours during the formation of the modern State of Qatar (see, for instance, the excellent study on the formation of contemporary Jordan in Rogan & Tell 1994).

Previous archaeological work at the al-Zubārah town site has been largely limited to investigations by Mohammad Jassim Al-Kholaifi in 1983–1984, and more recently of some residential units, the clearance of a section of the outer circuit wall and, by the shoreline, the excavation of structures commonly known as "the souq" (*sūq*) (Area J5) by Munir Taha (Al-Kholaifi 1987). The stone architecture exposed by this work was consolidated but is in need of attention, a task that has been allocated to the QIAH Project.

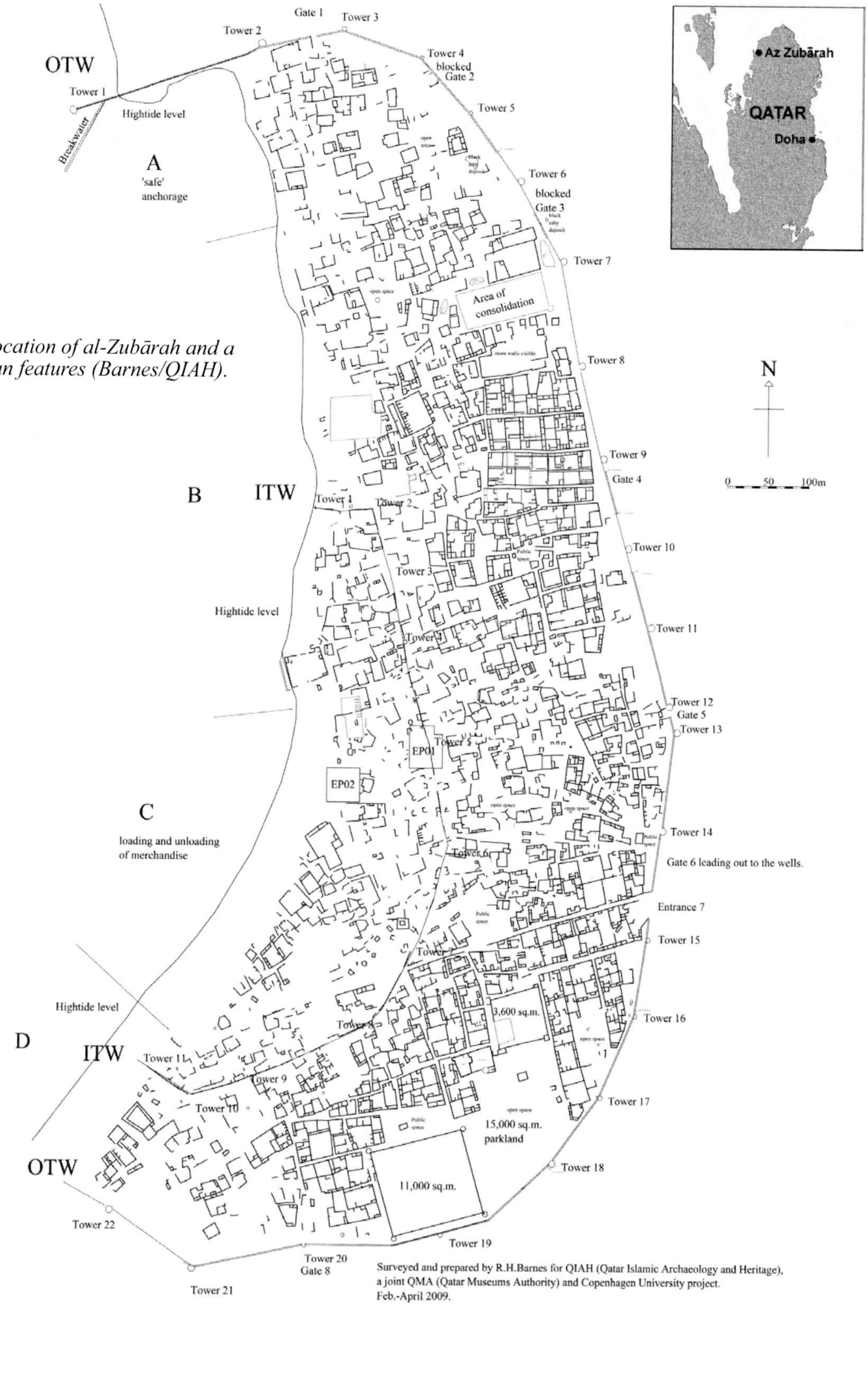

FIGURE 1. *The location of al-Zubārah and a plan of the urban features (Barnes/QIAH).*

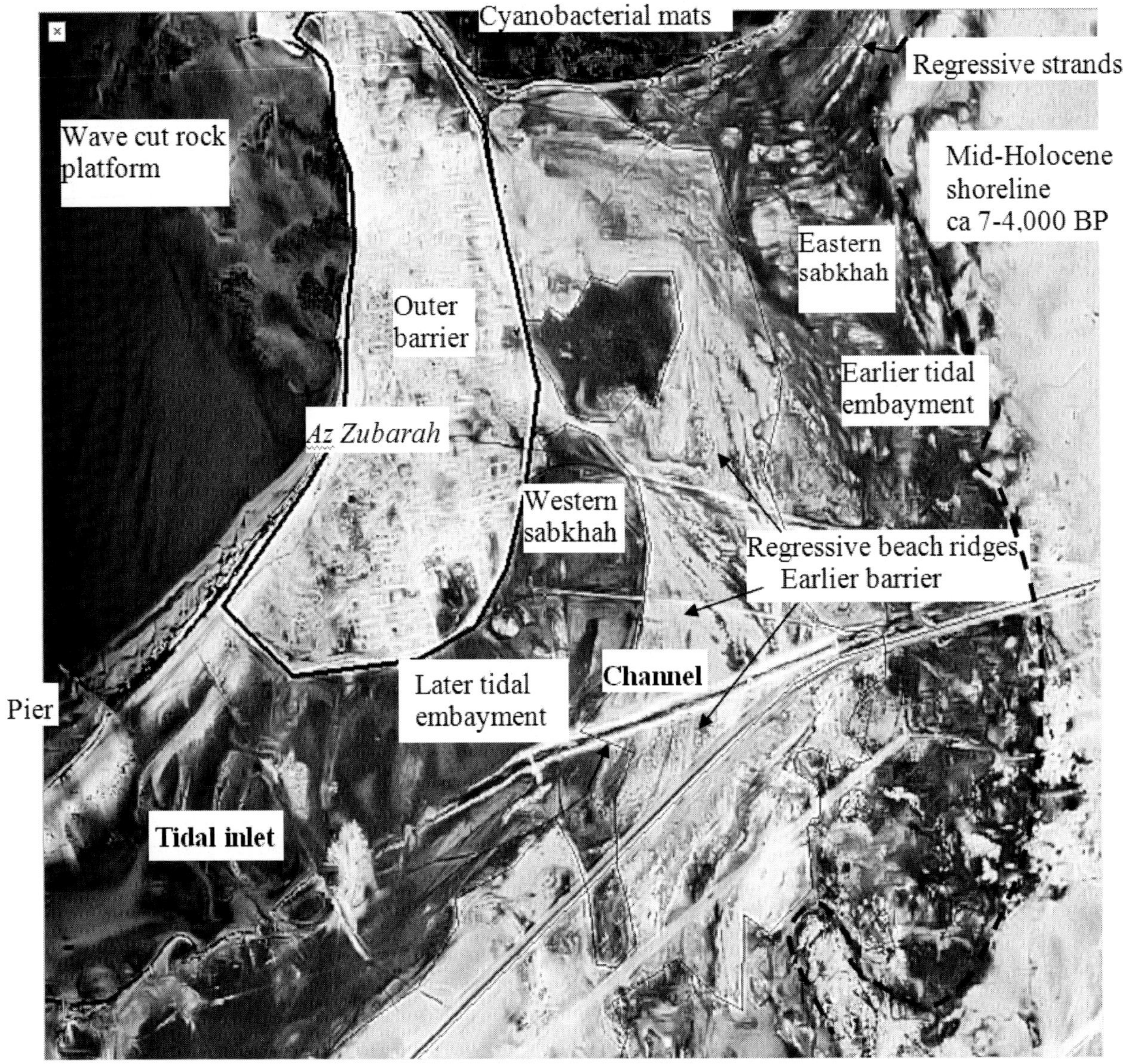

Figure 2. *The al-Zubārah zone showing the mid-Holocene shoreline, eastern and western sabkha, beach ridges, and earlier barrier (Macumber).*

Objectives

The objectives of the survey and excavation work in the al-Zubārah Archaeological Zone between 1 February and 30 April 2009 were threefold:

1. to create a comprehensive plan of the site, incorporating earlier survey and excavation work;
2. to undertake an initial hinterland survey, with a focus on the geomorphology and hydrology of the zone;
3. to commence new investigative, systematic archaeological excavations at al-Zubārah, focusing on two areas (called Excavation Points — EP) identified as potentially important because of their location within the townscape.

These aims were successfully met, with significant results. The following sections present in a summarized form the results of each of these three objectives.[2]

[2] The material presented in the following is largely extracted from

Figure 3. *The sea foundations for OTW-Tower 1. Note the black tar deposit from the 1990s crude oil discharge in the Gulf (QIAH image 4127).*

The survey of al-Zubārah

Hugh Barnes

A new ground survey of standing remains at al-Zubārah and its immediate hinterland was undertaken by Hugh Barnes. As well as documenting in detail the existing topography and surface remains at the site, the intention was also to produce a useful public presentation tool and a basic resource for future site planning and research strategies. The superb preliminary work carried out over the last few years by the QMA in terms of two third-generation geodetic points with Qatar National Grid (QNG) co-ordinates and numerous cemented points around the site, giving complete visual coverage, allowed the quick and easy establishment of a project site grid based on the QNG and meant that ground mapping of the site could begin almost immediately.

Using a two-step process of interpretative scaled sketches followed by a detailed digital survey using a total station, a map of the town with the various types of buildings identified was created (see Fig. 1). Two circuit walls were recorded in detail: a substantial outer wall and an inner one, both with towers. The outer town wall (OTW) has twenty-two round towers, entered from within the town, with eleven towers on the inner town wall (ITW). Both the inner and outer circuit walls are firmly anchored in the north: the inner town wall by a tower (ITW-Tower 1) on the high-water tide line; the outer town wall by a tower (OTW-Tower 1) once located on foundations built in the sea 25 m out from the shoreline (Fig. 3). The southern termini of the walls are considerably less distinct, petering out 30 m (ITW) and 90 m (OTW) away from the shoreline. The prime area for landing boats — the curved shoreline (Fig. 1, area C)

the end of season reports (Bille 2009; Macumber 2009). Author contributions are acknowledged where relevant.

with a shelf of soft sand on which shallow-draft vessels could beach — was enclosed by the inner town wall, further emphasizing the importance of this facility.

The inner town wall is approximately 70–80 cm wide and built entirely from stone and reused building fragments (plasterwork), with only rough coursing. This wall was probably meant to be a method of securing the waterfront area and setting it off from the rest of the town. The wall, then, did not serve the same military function as the outer town wall, but had more of a policing and second-defence role, especially as the ramps of the circular towers were accessible from both sides of the ITW. The outer town wall measures some 2.5 km in length and is, where measurable, *c.*1.4 m wide (sections of the wall have been cleared and consolidated). It was constructed with inner and outer faces with the thickness of two stones (*c.*40 cm) with a 60 cm-wide packing of stone and sand, with no obvious reused building materials. Generally, the wall runs in straight-line sections between clearly defensive circular towers, which segment the wall at just over 100 m apart or at each change of direction of the wall. There are eight identifiable entrances through the outer town wall.

Within the walls, four major groups of structures were identified. The first group comprises non-linear structures, primarily located in the western third of the town within the inner wall. These consist of rectangular-roomed structures connected by very coarse walling to create a common, roughly rectangular-shaped, courtyard unit. The irregularity of the walls is produced by reusing wall lines from preceding structures as foundations. One such structure was excavated in EP02 (see below; see also Al-Kholaifi 1987: 50–51). The second group comprises courtyard structures, typically compact, neatly built courtyard houses of rectangular rooms along one to three sides of a square central open courtyard. They mainly occupy the central town area, but the style continues into the regular grid pattern part of the town. The third group comprises compound structures, consisting of blocks of houses, commonly two houses deep and up to seven houses long, belonging to one construction phase (for an example see Al-Kholaifi 1987: 30–46). The entire central eastern third of the town seems to have been laid out in this fashion, probably when the outer town wall was still in use. The last group comprises rectangular structures, measuring roughly 9×4 m and spread throughout the site. Relatively well preserved, their location, orientation, and condition suggest a late date.

Other important features were recorded as part of the survey, including cemeteries, rubbish heaps, and mounds of recent beach flotsam. The heaps of town refuse are composed of very humus-rich sand, sherds, bones, and a high proportion of charcoal fragments. They have been deposited outside OTW gates 8 (a very large amount), 6 (a large amount), 4 (a medium amount), 3 (a large amount) and 2 (a small amount). Ridges in the deposits indicate tip lines. In addition to the extramural deposits, there is an enormous mound 3 m high in an open area west of OTW-Tower 11 and several other heaps around the town. These certainly require detailed investigation. Scattered around the site are numerous beach clearance deposits, probably of 1990s date. These are legitimate archaeological deposits and will require recording before any removal.

At least from the surface details recorded in the survey, two phases of town development are discernible. The earliest development is characterized by a high density of civic structures in the centre of the town, and an organic building and street pattern evident between the inner town wall and the outer wall from Gate 6 northwards. The later phase is characterized by: (a) the deconstruction of screening walls that extended towards al-Murayr and its water sources (see above); (b) the blocking of the outer town gates; and (c) the construction of the inner town wall (on this latter event, see further below).

The geomorphology of the al-Zubārah Archaeological Zone

Phillip Macumber

The landscape in the vicinity of al-Zubārah has its origins in the mid-Holocene marine transgression, which lasted from perhaps 7000 to 4000 years BP, probably peaking at *c.*5500 BP. At that time the sea level was 1–2 m above that at present. The mid-Holocene shoreline is now marked by a low, 2–4 m scarp where the coastal plain gives way to the mid-Tertiary Dammām limestone in the vicinity of al-Zubārah fort (see Fig. 2). The mid-Holocene transgression pre-dated the establishment of the high ground on which al-Zubārah town was later constructed, and this area only came into existence during the latter parts of the transgression and during the subsequent sea-level fall (regression) to its present position. During the high sea-level stand and leading into the initial stages of regression, a shallow near-shore sandbar formed a barrier, which separated the then existing open marine regime to the west from a tidal embayment or *khawr* (now the eastern *sabkhah*) that developed between the barrier and scarp. Today the eastern *sabkhah* is several metres above sea level and is rarely flooded. As sea levels fell, regressive beach strand lines formed; these are clearly visible on the satellite imagery. With the ongoing regression, a second outer barrier developed seawards of the first barrier, and this too became exposed as the sea level fell before stabilizing at the present level. This second barrier was to become the higher ground on which al-Zubārah was built. A tidal embayment also formed landwards of the new barrier; however, unlike the earlier case, this embayment remains linked to sea level and is still active today. A gradual filling of the embayment since the regression has led to the development of an intertidal flat linked to the sea: a supra-tidal flat inundated to a shallow depth at times of high tide and/or strong *shamāl* winds, and the western *sabkhah*, now divided into a northern isolated component and a main southern *sabkhah*.

The respective depositional environments during the mid-Holocene transgression and regression in the al-Zubārah embayment are reflected in the lithology and faunal composition exposed in the spoil heaps of a channel cut south-east of al-Zubārah (see below). This cutting dissects the higher areas of the inner barrier and the western *sabkhah*, which was a tidal inlet at the time. Apparent here is the light-brownish marine rock used for the construction of al-Zubārah, which features a partial gypseous (Ca SO4 2H2O) cement derived from rising groundwater. When exposed in hot, arid environments, the gypsum may dehydrate to white anhydrite (Ca SO4), which is powdery and readily deflated.

The cove to the north of al-Zubārah has a zone of cyanobacterial mats, while to the north-west are wave-cut rock platforms, mostly relating to the present sea level. The distribution of the rock platforms probably affected the town plan at al-Zubārah, in that the off-shore platforms mute any significant storm impact by dissipating wave energy. The platforms are best developed north of the beachfront tower (ITW-Tower 1) and wall. South of this tower the platforms are discontinuous and less well developed, and are unlikely to dampen storm impacts. This is reflected in beach development, whereby south of the tower the beach widens markedly and the town retreats further back from the shoreline. It seems likely that this was to allow space for the beach to disperse strong wave energy whipped up by the strong *shamāl* winds. The location of a pier 300 m south of the town probably reflects the nearest point of safe navigable access from the sea, unimpeded by rock platforms. A prior phase of pier development may be presupposed before that indicated by twentieth-century reinforced concrete additions to the upper parts of the construction. The only path for a road from the pier runs directly north towards the town, before which a major road strikes eastwards just beyond the western end of the channel. This is the only route to bypass al-Zubārah.

Nearby, the cut channel starts at the far end of the tidal flat some 1.6 km from the coast and extends 1.2 km eastwards to end at the eastern *sabkhah*, stopping 480 m west of Qalᶜat al-Murayr at the edge of the eastern *sabkhah*. It is cut through a lightly cemented shelly shoreline or near-shore sediments for much of its length, and then passes eastward into denser fossiliferous limestone and dense cryptocrystalline Eocene dolomite. The faunal and facies variation in the bank passing westward along the channel length reflects the probable passage from a strand line to an environment of tidal embayment. The pattern formed by regular heaps of channel spoil suggests that the current channel is the result of a mechanical rather than a hand-dug process. While historical sources propose that the channel once served as a seawater canal to link Qalᶜat al-Murayr with the sea, such a function was eventually impractical. At its coastward end the channel today terminates in an area beyond which the land to the sea consists of saturated sand and pelletal muds of the tidal flat; it would have been very difficult, if not impossible, to maintain a sea canal over such a flat. While the tidal flats and the end of the channel are submerged under high tides and strong *shamāl* winds, the depth of the water is, mostly, only 5–10 cm deep. For most of the time, however, there is little or no direct water connection from the existing channel end to the coast, some 1.6 km distant.

Without groundwater there could be no settlement, and the history of settlement in Qatar is therefore reflected in the history of its wells. This was the situation at al-Zubārah, where the principal water supply came from the many large, shallow wells dug at Qalᶜat Murayr and other localities on the Eocene limestone beyond the *sabkhah*-dominated coastal plain, about 1.5 km east of al-Zubārah. Apart from their clear use as a domestic water supply, the wells are associated with agricultural systems, confirming that they were once fresh.

The *sabkhah* in the vicinity of al-Zubārah are saline zones of regional groundwater discharge with salt crusts and polygons on the surface. The underlying groundwater is most probably hypersaline. On the higher ground to the east, inflowing fresh groundwater will be underlain at shallow depth by a ghyben-herzberg interface with fresh water giving way to brackish then saline water. The fresh groundwater occurs as a lens overlying more saline water; it is probably mostly fossil water recharged in the past during wetter conditions than at present. Because of the underlying saline water, wells on the edge of the *sabkhah* would have been necessarily shallow, with fresh water "skimmed" from the top. The shape and size of the wells, commonly some 6×6 m, suggest that in some cases they were essentially large pits that could be entered at one end. A shallow well 1.8 km east of al-Zubārah and another in the abandoned town of Ḥalwān, 2.8 km from al-Zubārah, still hold water. Bailed samples of these wells gave salinities of 3700 mg/l and 4200 mg/l respectively, indicating salinities now higher than previously, assuming that they were originally used for domestic purposes including drinking water. A pumped sample from a small irrigation bore, one of a number on a farm located 10 km east of al-Zubārah, had a salinity of 3000 mg/l. Hydrogeological studies including groundwater modelling in the late 1970s and early–mid-1980s showed that, prior to 1958, the aquifer was in equilibrium, with groundwater outflow equalling inflow. However, there were gradually increasing abstractions between 1958 and 1979. The consequences were a reduction in the size of the freshwater lens as extractions exceeded recharge. Falling groundwater levels led to coastal seawater intrusion and upconing of saline water. The impact would have been greatest at the coast, with the groundwater modelling suggesting seawater intrusion rates of between 90 to 1000 mm/yr. Hence, there is overwhelming evidence that a rise in groundwater salinity played a central part in the decline of the coastal towns and nearby farms of northern Qatar after 1958.

Excavations in al-Zubārah

Two central localities in the town of al-Zubārah were selected for detailed archaeological investigation. Within a built-up site that measures about 1.4 km north–south by 300 to 500 m east–west, there was plenty of choice, but the final selection of areas had specific objectives: to investigate the chronology, purpose, and function of the inner wall, and to elucidate further the characteristics and development of the seaside zone adjacent to the curved shoreline (see Fig. 1, area C) that probably served as a boat beaching area.

Excavation Point 01 (EP01)

EP01 gave considerable insight into the development of the town. The aim was to expose what appeared to be a large compound, a section of the inner town wall, and an associated tower, the latter standing as a prominent landmark before excavation. EP01 measured 40×40 m, with the south-west corner located at the grid point of 0960E/9240N. Subsequently the area was extended 10 m northwards in

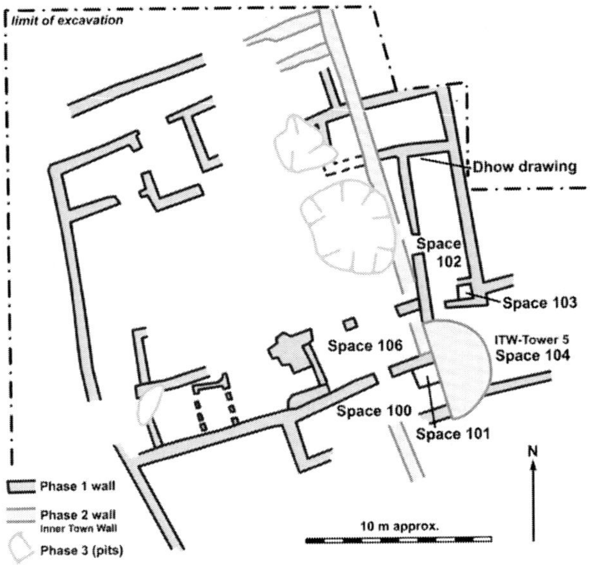

Figure 4. *A general phased sketch plan of EP01.*

order to incorporate the northern part of the Phase 1 building complex. The excavations revealed at least two mains phases in this area, and a third phase characterized by later digging into the collapsed architecture.

Phase 1

Only partially exposed to date, Phase 1 represents a relatively long period of occupation, judging from the complexity of the architecture and the considerable depth of floor deposits, the latter exposed by later pitting.[3] Encountered were a series of walls, surfaces, and features, which appear to be associated with one or more courtyard units and, to the north, an east–west road (Fig. 4).

The main structure exposed featured a number of smallish rooms positioned on at least three sides of a central courtyard, and entered by doors in their long walls. Walls were constructed of stone bonded by a pale green slightly sandy mortar. Significant is Space 106, a rectangular area measuring approximately 5×7.62 m, which probably served as a veranda to the room represented by Space 100 and another room to the east, subsequently buried by the tower of Phase 2, both connected by doorways. Removal of stone and rubble collapse revealed a light-brown compact surface with white inclusions. In the eastern part several potsherds were uncovered *in situ*. These showed a variation in types and styles of ceramic, but the

[3] Summarized from the report by Dan Eddisford and Anne Mette Harpelund in Bille 2009: 8–28.

Figure 5. *An overview of ITW-Tower 5 with Phase 1 building, looking south. Note the ramp on the left (east), inner ring, and core, all overlaying an earlier building. On the right: part of Space 106 with sherds in situ; in the foreground: the south section of Space 102 with the hammam, Space 103 (QIAH image 1275).*

majority came from a very large, thick-walled, coarse-tempered dark-brown/black vessel (Fig. 5). The related Space 100 and Space 101 revealed a similar sequence of tumble above occupational surfaces.[4] The surface levels produced numerous artefacts, such as large lightly (sun-?) baked clay storage jars, each with three feet (Fig. 6), numerous iron nails, bone pieces, and sherds from diverse ceramic vessels. Space 101 turned out to be a hammam (bathhouse) with hard-plastered walls and floor, the latter sloping towards two drainage holes in the north wall. These exited into the veranda area (Space 106).

To the east another long room was excavated, designated Space 102, also with a corner hammam (Space 103).[5] Below stone tumble and fill, a 3–5 cm occupational deposit of dark-brown colour was exposed. Excavation produced three coins and revealed an underlying surface. The walls of Space 102 are covered with a pinkish-coloured plaster, sometimes with moulded geometric designs such as dogtooth. Deeply incised on the north wall (see Fig. 4), positioned some 10 cm from the floor level, is a bold depiction of a dhow measuring 158×65 cm (Figs 7 and 8). Skilfully manufactured with great confidence, the image depicts in detail the appearance of these dhows as they were some 200 years or so ago.

Phase 2

Phase 2 of EP01 suggests that a planned reconfiguration of the town took place, apparently after an occupational hiatus. This phase is characterized by the construction of a long wall with an associated semi-circular tower (ITW-Tower 5). The tower butted and overlaid the plastered walls of the Phase 1 structure, demonstrating its later date (see Fig. 5). The tower core was made of sand and stones, contained

[4] Summarized from the report by Benjamin Fabre in Bille 2009: 29–45.

[5] Summarized from the report by Mette Low W. Sørensen in Bille 2009: 52–60.

Figure 6. *Three-footed lightly (sun-?)baked clay storage jars in Space 100, with a step into Space 101 (hammam) behind (QIAH image 0446).*

Figure 7. *The incised dhow on the north wall of Space 102 (QIAH image 1116).*

Figure 8. *A line drawing of the incised dhow image.*

by two rings of beach stone packed with grey and green mortar, faced with a hard plaster. The outer ring, some 85 cm in width, turned out to be a ramp that ascended from the south to the top of the tower around the east side, a style reflected, on a larger scale, in the ninth-century Sāmarrā minarets as well as the contemporary Islamic Cultural Centre (Fanar) in Doha. Hence the tower and its associated wall appear to be designed as a second line of protection, securing the largely undefended compounds that lay within the ITW (as noted above). Thus the excavation revealed that, contrary to expectations, the inner town wall and accompanying tower post-dated the associated compound. Rather than the town expanding from a smaller core area within ITW, it seems that it either became increasingly divided into separate areas, or simply contracted.

Phase 3

This was a late phase, represented by several large pits, which truncated the architecture and floor surfaces associated with earlier phases; no architecture was apparent. Above the pits were mixed layers from which a wooden compartmented pearler's box, minus its lid, was recovered.

Excavation Point 02 (EP02)

EP02 revealed details about occupation at the beach area of the town, with work focusing on a large compound and an associated street.[6] The excavation revealed at least four phases of development, of which Phase 2 has the most substantial architectural remains to date.

Phase 1

Phase 1 is mostly apparent in the street area located north of the compound. This area revealed a street running east–west towards the sea, with a multi-layered surface flanked by walls. To the south a line of rooms was identified, perhaps shops. Walls were well constructed of beach stone with extensive use of a grey-green clay mortar, and coated with a pinkish plaster. Similar rooms were also identified east of the later compound. A period of abandonment separated this phase from that which followed.

Phase 2

Phase 2 visually dominated the layout of the area at the commencement of excavations, and featured an irregular compound consisting of a large central courtyard, with a room in the north-east corner, three rooms on the western side, and co-joining units to the east and south, all accessed through doorways from the courtyard. The south unit was initially part of a larger configuration of rooms around a central courtyard, but subsequently was transformed into a smaller self-contained building, similar to changes observed in the eastern unit, a process commonly associated with inheritance. Found in the north-east corner room were the charred remains of the roof, consisting of large wooden beams, smaller pieces of wood, and woven palm leaves (Fig. 9).

Based on the size of the fibres, the roof comprised at least two different types of wood. Directly lying on the surface of the room were many porcelain sherds from several different vessels. In addition to ceramics, bones, coins, clay-pipe bowls, and iron nails were found in this phase. Prominent was a broken bowl manufactured in Maastricht, a major centre of ceramic production from the mid-nineteenth century noted for its decorated porcelains with transfer-printed patterns depicting natural and romantic scenes. The Zubārah bowl, dating to the early decades of the twentieth century, is decorated with a reddish-brown abstract floral design above a rosetted band (Fig. 10). Written under the ring-base is "Made in Holland" with the name of the factory, "Société Céramique", and the place of production around the rampant lion trademark. Below this is the name of the pattern, known as JOKO.[7]

Phase 3

This phase represents a period of abandonment, which allowed for a build-up of wind-blown sand on which a

[6] Summarized from the reports by Louise Blanke, Alexis Pantos, Philip Woltz, and Sandra Rosendahl in Bille 2009: 61–135.

[7] The pattern on the bowl is recorded in the archives of the Sociaal Historisch Centrum voor Limburg, available online.

Figure 9. *Charred roof remains as found in the north-east corner room (QIAH image 1714).*

rough wall was constructed, perhaps to prevent further sand intrusion into the building (Phase 3). The final discernible phase (Phase 4) consisted of a post hole and pits in one area, perhaps associated activity with the late wall of Phase 3.

Post-excavation

At the end of the excavation season, both EP01 and EP02 were backfilled in order to ensure the preservation of the architecture and remaining archaeological deposits. Hessian was used to cover and protect the more delicate architecture and surfaces prior to backfilling. Excavated spoil was used to backfill the trenches and sandbags were used where appropriate. Our intention is to reopen both excavation points in the autumn 2009–spring 2010 season, as well as commencing new investigations into a third component in the urban plan of al-Zubārah.

Figure 10. *Decorated porcelain with JOKO transfer-printed pattern from the "Société Céramique" factory, Maastricht, Holland (QIAH images 3532, 3533).*

Conclusions

It is very early days in the renewed archaeological investigation of al-Zubārah, but a few preliminary, tentative comments on the significance of the finds may be in order. The overall trend in the urban arrangement of the settlement, starting with the earliest levels exposed so far (EP01, Phase 1; EP02, Phase 1), was from a well-built and intentionally planned town primarily oriented towards the coast to a less methodical arrangement of compounds separated by unevenly configured open space. This change may reflect the reduced state of the town after the 1811 sacking, when al-Zubārah contracted to a smaller settlement largely occupied by al-Nuᶜaym and economically in the shadow of a flourishing Bahrain, although great care has to be taken in making possibly simplistic historical equations, especially in the early years of a project. EP02 has revealed a reasonably long period of use of the Phase 2 compound, including alterations to structures, their final destruction, and ceramics extending into the early decades of the twentieth century, thus spanning the final documented years of long-term occupation of al-Zubārah by al-Nuʿaym. Evidence for subsequent occupation (EP01, Phase 3 and EP02, phases 3 and 4, consisting of rough structures, pits, post holes) reveals transient and probably seasonal use of the site, a tradition that extends up until the present day.

References

Al-Arayed J.S.
2003. *A Line in the Sea: the Qatar versus Bahrain border dispute in the World Court.* Berkeley, CA: North Atlantic Books.

Belgrave C.D.
1960. *Personal Column*. London: Hutchinson.
1966. *The Pirate Coast*. London: Bell.

Bille M.
2009. Qatar Islamic Archaeology and Heritage Project. End of Season Report, 2009. Archaeological Excavations and Survey at Az-Zubarah, Qatar. i. Doha: The Qatar Museums Authority/Copenhagen: The University of Copenhagen. [Unpublished report].

Higgins R.
2009. *Themes and Theories: selected essays, speeches, and writings in international law*. ii. Oxford: Oxford University Press.

Al-Khalifa A.B.K. & Rice M. (eds)
1993. *Bahrain through the Ages: the history*. London: Kegan Paul International.

Al-Kholaifi M.J.
1987. *Athar. al-Zubarah and Marwab*. Doha: Ministry of Information, Department of Tourism and Antiquities. [In Arabic].

Macumber P.G.
2009. Qatar Islamic Archaeology and Heritage Project. End of Season Report, 2009. Preliminary Report on the Geomorphology and Hydrology of the Al Zubarah Region, Northern Qatar. ii. Doha: The Qatar Museums Authority/Copenhagen: The University of Copenhagen. [Unpublished report].

Nonneman G.
2002. al-Zubāra. Page 547 in *The Encyclopaedia of Islam*. (Second edition). xi. Leiden: Brill.

Potts D.T.
1990. *The Arabian Gulf in Antiquity*. ii. Oxford: Clarendon.

Rogan E.L. & Tell T.
1994. *Village, Steppe and State. The Social Origins of Modern Jordan*. London: British Academic Press.

United States Board on Geographic Names.
1986. *Gazetteer of Qatar: names approved by the United States Board on Geographic Names*. Washington, DC: Defense Mapping Agency.

V. Huda N.
28 July 2009. Archaeological digs uncover Qatar's past. *The Peninsula*. 10 October 2009. www.thepeninsulaqatar.com/Display_news.asp?section=local_news&month=july2009&file=local_news2009072815420.xml

Authors' addresses
Alan Walmsley, Department of Cross-Cultural and Regional Studies, University of Copenhagen, Snorresgade 17–19, DK-2300 Copenhagen S, Denmark.

e-mail walmsley@hum.ku.dk

Hugh Barnes, Department of Cross-Cultural and Regional Studies, University of Copenhagen, Snorresgade 17–19, DK-2300 Copenhagen S, Denmark.

e-mail rhbarnes@gmx.de

Phillip Macumber, Phillip Macumber Consulting Services, 20 Rangeview Rd, Donvale 3111 Victoria, Australia.

e-mail pmacumber@optusnet.com.au

Proceedings of the Seminar for Arabian Studies

Plenary Session

Proceedings of the Seminar for Arabian Studies 40 (2010): 71–84

The dhow's last redoubt? Vestiges of wooden boatbuilding traditions in Yemen

Dionisius A. Agius, John P. Cooper, Chiara Zazzaro & Julian Jansen van Rensburg

Summary

Researchers from the MARES Project visited Yemen in February 2009 in order to investigate the building and use of traditional wooden boats ("dhows" in English) in the country. The survey covered the coastline from Aden to al-Salīf in the Red Sea, and visited centres of dhow building and use, including Ghurayrah (Ghureira), al-Mukhā (Mocha), and al-Khawkhah (Khokha). The project's aim was to assess the state of the industry, establish a vessel typology, understand construction processes, learn about the use of these vessels, and compile a lexicon of boatbuilding and nautical terms. This article offers the preliminary findings of the survey, pending more comprehensive publication in the future. The survey found that, in all locations visited, the building of new vessels had rapidly diminished in the preceding decade, and has now all but ceased. The only ongoing activity witnessed during the survey was repairs to existing wooden craft. In formerly large boatbuilding centres, builders of wooden boats, mostly elderly, have ceased work, while younger men were building fishing craft using fibreglass — the material used in the great majority of vessels in Yemen today. A preliminary typology of surviving vessels was established. The double-ended cargo-carrying *zaʿāyim* (sg. *zāʿīmah*) and *zawārīk* (sg. *zārūk*) were recorded only as abandoned hulks. Double-ended *ʿabārī* (sg. *ʿobrī*) and the transom-sterned "large *hūrī*" (pl. *hawārī*), with its stern-quarter "fins", continued to be used in small numbers for seine fishing and transporting livestock. Again, most examples were abandoned. Various forms of small log and plank *hūrī* "canoes" were observed, few still in use, while the log-raft *ramas* survives on the Red Sea coast. The terms used for these vessel types form part of a linguistic survey of dhow activity in Yemen.

Keywords: Yemen, dhow typology, boatbuilding, maritime, ethnography

Introduction

The wooden dhow-building traditions of Arabia have suffered a series of blows since the mid-twentieth century, not least with the end of pearling in the Arabian-Persian Gulf, and the onset of oil-driven economic development. In the oil states, in particular, traditional ways of life have been set aside, and on the maritime front, boatyards and harbours have been subsumed under rapid urban and industrial development. Between 1990 and 2000, Agius (2002; 2005; 2008) investigated boat typologies, boatbuilding practices, and maritime traditions of the Gulf States and Oman, but most of these traditions have since been swept aside. Dhow building has survived longest in areas least affected by the oil boom, namely coastal Yemen. Even here, however, the practice of building a variety of wooden boats for fishing and transportation is coming to a rapid end. Even a decade ago wooden boatbuilding was thriving, but boatbuilders have now abandoned constructing wooden boats entirely, as fibreglass boatbuilding takes over.

The MARES Project is currently investigating surviving wooden boatbuilding traditions in the Gulf of Aden and southern Red Sea. The work is, in some respects, a continuation of Agius's previous ethnographic work in the Arabian-Persian Gulf and Oman, while an expanded team enables a more diverse methodological approach, including the systematic survey of boat distribution, architecture, and construction methods.

The fieldwork

Field research was carried out along the Gulf of Aden and Red Sea coasts of the Republic of Yemen over a three-week period in February 2009. Yemen was chosen in part because the country was a region not yet covered by Agius's research, and also in the knowledge, based on previous fieldwork along parts of the Yemeni coast in 2007,[1] that large wooden vessels and residual boatbuilding activities were extant.

[1] This work, a survey of *hūrī* (pl. *hawārī*) fishing canoes, was conducted as part of the University of Southampton Huri Project, directed by Dr Lucy Blue, in which Cooper participated.

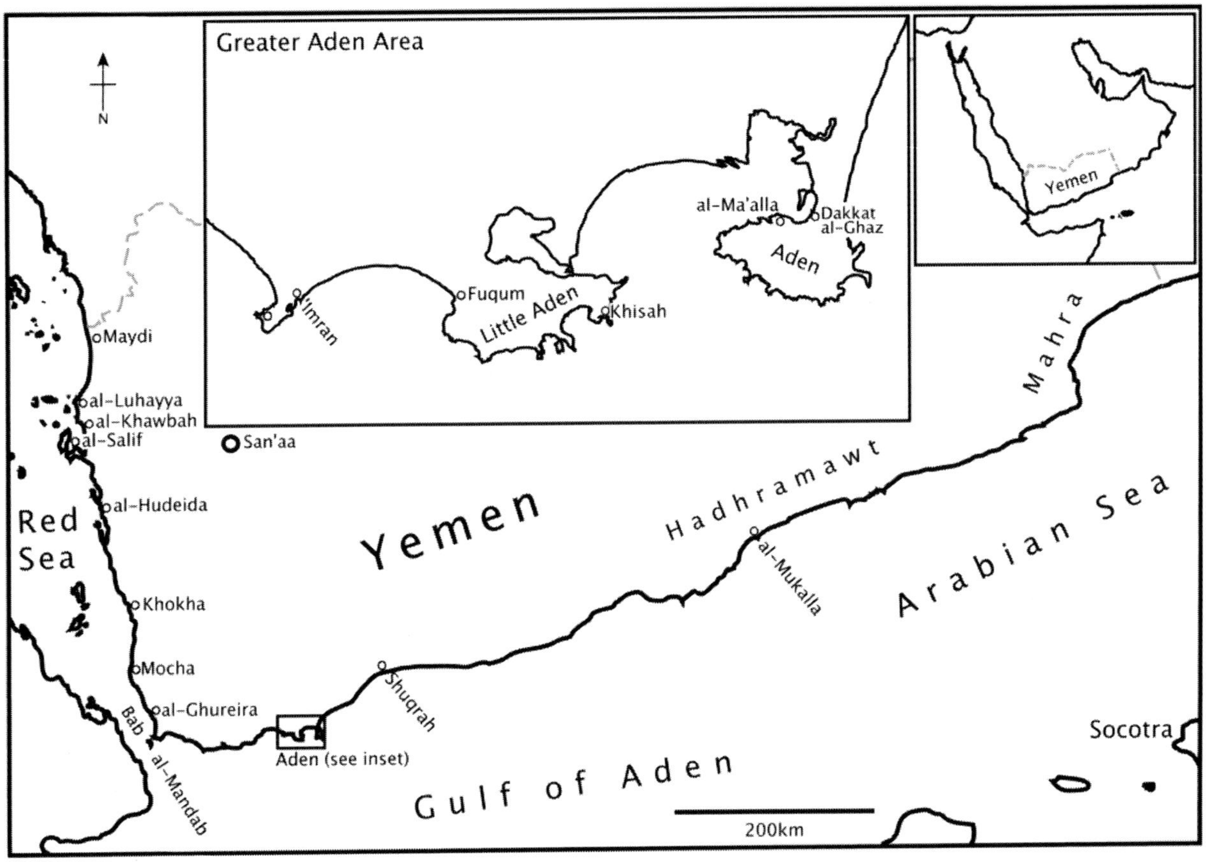

FIGURE 1. *A map of Yemen, showing the sites discussed in the text (MARES/J.P. Cooper).*

Yemen's rich natural fisheries support a large and growing fishing population. Indeed, the Yemeni government regards the industry as an important component in Yemen's future economic development. However, growth in population and fishing is putting pressure on marine reserves, a situation that has contributed to Yemen's shift away from wooden boatbuilding and towards fibreglass manufacture. Meanwhile, the use of traditional cargo "dhows" has diminished sharply amid competition from modern freighters and land and air transport, as well as the effects of changing trade patterns. The few remaining cargo vessels in use in Yemen are largely used to transport livestock and foodstuffs, as well as contraband and refugees from the African coast. In the mid-90s, Prados (1998*a*: 195) was able to say that, "… wooden boatbuilding … remains an integral and essential part of everyday commerce." This is no longer the case. Such a decline argues for detailed documentation of traditional boats and ethnographic interviews of the people who built and operated them before both disappear. Yemen's scarce fiscal resources, particularly for cultural programmes, mean that the chances of these boats being preserved in any other way are slim indeed.

Given the relatively limited time available, the MARES survey could cover only part of Yemen's 1900 km coastline. For reasons of insurance limitations and ease of access the survey concentrated on the section of the Gulf of Aden and the Red Sea coast between Aden and al-Salīf — a section of coastline that was known to include sites containing vestiges of wooden boats and boatbuilding (Fig. 1). While the main survey continued on the Yemeni mainland, Julian Jansen van Rensburg pursued research into traditional vessels on the island of Socotra.

The Survey began in Aden, and in particular in the part of Maᶜallah (today called Dakkat al-Ghāz), which was formerly Aden's dhow harbour. It also took in Little Aden and especially the fishing villages of K͟hīsah and Fuqum.

The survey then headed west, passing through ʿImrān, and along a largely empty and exposed coast to the Bāb al-Mandab. From there it proceeded north up the Red Sea coast, taking in the village of Ghurayrah (Ghureira) and its eponymous creek, the former coffee port of al-Mukhā (Mocha), the fishing and former boatbuilding town of al-Khawkhah (Khokha), the city of al-Ḥudaydah (Hudeida), and finally the fishing town of al-Salīf.

Methodology

The fieldwork aimed to survey the distribution of traditional vessels; to observe and record the vessel types found; to investigate construction techniques; and to assess the state of traditional boatbuilding and usage by location. Equally, a linguistic survey aimed to gather terms for the various boat types and parts, as well as the broader material culture and activities associated with them. This was achieved through direct observation and survey techniques — note taking, photography, sketching, and scale drawing — as well as through ethnographic interview.

At each site, the team surveyed the vessels present. At minimum, this involved photography and the noting of basic features. In some cases, the team took the principal measurements, such as the maximum length, height, and width amidships of the relevant vessels. For selected vessels, the team endeavoured to make line drawings of the hull, and in one case — an incomplete and abandoned "large *hūrī*" (pl. *hawārī*, see below) — the team recorded the fine detail of the hull construction. The team also collected wood samples from different elements of various vessels in order to establish the type and provenance of the timbers used in boat construction, and to corroborate the contributions obtained from ethnographic interviewees.

At each site, the team sought out local boatbuilders and mariners. Interviews were conducted in Arabic, and were open, rather than being based on a questionnaire, since it was believed that a more formalized approach might deter informants or impose an agenda. In fact, interviewees were found to be almost always amenable to interview. Team members took field notes of interviews, made rough sketches, and voice-recorded interviewees where appropriate. In addition, digital video recording was used to document boat repair and maintenance activity where this continued.

One approach to handling this diverse data has been to create a computer database comprising photographs, measurements, terminologies, and field observations of the individual vessels recorded in Yemen. This database will allow the team to manage and interpret the data, while creating a legacy for future researchers. In addition to the data collected through fieldwork in Yemen, the MARES team has also initiated a survey of archival resources, investigating in particular photographic archives and models held by museums and private individuals in the hope of better understanding the recent history of vessel typologies in Yemen. These results will be published in the final field report.

FIGURE 2. *Relics of dhow building at Dakkat al-G͟hāz, Aden (MARES/J.P. Cooper).*

Preliminary outcomes

The fieldwork yielded preliminary insights into the state of wooden boatbuilding and use at various locations in Yemen, a typology of the main dhow types to be found at those sites, and a lexical dataset related to those types. An overview of these findings is presented here.

FIGURE 3. *The creek at Ghurayrah, with abandoned vessels (MARES/J.P. Cooper).*

1. Boatbuilding activity and boat use

The MARES survey indicated a wide variation in activity between the major boatbuilding sites visited:

Aden and environs

A thriving hub of the British imperial maritime network, the port of Aden went into decline following independence in 1967. The remains of the traditional dhow harbour and boatyard can be found at Dakkat al-Ghāz (Fig. 2). However, much of the inter-tidal area that constituted the harbour has been reclaimed, and is now a lorry park. This appears to have happened after 1990, when Cooper visited Maᶜallah and photographed the site. Wooden boat activity is today limited. The team recorded two wooden dhows — an *ᶜobrī* (pl. *ᶜabārī*) and a *bōt* (pl. *abwāt*) (see below for a discussion of boat typologies) — that had been hauled out and abandoned. A pile of wooden masts was also recorded. Local informants said that a large quantity of undressed timber at the site comprised locally grown woods known as *damas* (*Conocarpus lancifolius Engl* [Bilaidi 1978: 3]) and *muraymira* (*Melia azaderach L.* [Awadh Ali *et al.* 2001: 175]). These timbers formed natural crooks used to make futtock and floor timbers, and are indicative of an extensive former boatbuilding industry at the site.

The small modern dock at Dakkat al-Ghāz is still used by occasional traditional vessels: a moored *ᶜobrī* at the time of our visit was from al-Khawkhah, and vessels sometimes bring livestock to Dakkat al-Ghāz from Somalia.[2] The few other vessels in Maᶜallah were fibreglass. Across the harbour, dhows could also be seen abandoned on the inaccessible island of Qulfatayn. Other abandoned examples of *ᶜabārī* and large *hawārī* were recorded at the Little Aden villages of Fuqum and al-Khaysah (Khīsah). In addition, small wooden dugout and plank "canoes" (also called *hawārī*) were observed abandoned, and occasionally still in use, at various fishing settlements in greater Aden.

Ghurayrah

The lagoon at Ghurayrah, some 5 km north of the Bāb al-Mandab on the Red Sea coast, contained a remarkable assemblage of dhow types. To its north lies the associated fishing and former shipbuilding village, where a vessel was seen under construction as recently as 2007, as observed by Blue and Cooper. The lagoon's southern shore contained an assemblage of thirteen large cargo vessels including double-ended *zawārīk* (sg. *zārūk*),[3] *zaᶜāyim* (sg. *zāᶜīmah*), and *ᶜabārī*, and a large transom vessel of unknown type, almost all of which were clearly abandoned and in a highly dilapidated state (Fig. 3). These were interspersed with a number of large *hawārī*, some still in use. On the north bank of the lagoon, fringing the village, a number of other vessels, mostly large *hawārī*, were also hauled up. The village's boatbuilding yard stood idle, in it an incomplete *ᶜobrī* that had been abandoned early in the construction process.

Mocha

Evidence of wooden boats at Mocha was limited to four large *hūrī* vessels abandoned on the beach of the town's

[2] Blue and Cooper observed such a vessel at Dakkat al-Ghāz in 2007.

[3] Or *zāwārīq* (sg. *zārūq*) final "k", a voiceless velar stop, and "q", a uvular occlusive, are often interchangeable.

FIGURE 4. *An abandoned boatyard in al-Khawkhah (MARES/J.P. Cooper).*

southern bay; a number of dugout *hawārī*, none of which appeared to be still in use; and various ships' timbers incorporated into beach huts. There was no wooden boatbuilding yard remaining in the town. Fibreglass boats dominated the fishing fleet.

Al-Khawkhah

Further north, the town of al-Khawkhah contained the largest number of wooden vessels found anywhere on our itinerary — over 100 in total. The overwhelming majority of completed vessels were large *hawāri*. However, all but one, which was anchored offshore, had been hauled up and abandoned, or at least "mothballed", on the shores of the town's lagoon. Small fishing vessels at al-Khawkhah included a number of abandoned dugout *hawāri* and the lashed log-rafts (known as *ramas* in the singular, the plural form probably being *ramasāt*), the latter being used for inshore reef fishing. Most working boats were open fibreglass fishing "canoes".

Wooden boatbuilding had ceased at al-Khawkhah within the last decade, and the presence of several vessels abandoned in mid-construction suggests that the process happened rapidly (Fig. 4). Prados in the mid-90s had observed over sixty boats under construction in the town during his fieldwork: he described it as Yemen's largest boatbuilding centre (1996: 51).

There were two centres of former wooden boatbuilding activity. The smaller of the two, south of the fish market, comprised at least three boatyards containing four large *hawārī* and an *ᶜobrī* that had been abandoned during construction. One former boatbuilder said he had not built a wooden vessel there in eight years. Instead, younger men were building fibreglass fishing boats in the same location.

Some 1.5 km up the coast from the fish market was a second, larger, boatyard site. There were at least eight individual yards, each comprising a small concrete hut and open shelter, alongside the boatbuilding area. Once again, the team observed a large number of unfinished boats — *hawārī* and an *ᶜobrī* — that had been abandoned at different stages of construction. There was no evidence of ongoing construction or repair anywhere in the town.

Ḥudaydah

Ḥudaydah is Yemen's largest Red Sea port. Wooden boat construction and use appears in recent years to have been concentrated on the modern fishing harbour and market. The marina in the northern part of the market site contained dozens of fibreglass fishing vessels, and a small number — less than ten — of double-ended *ᶜabārī* still in use as fishing vessels. The area south of the main market buildings comprised a "graveyard" of some seventy abandoned wooden vessels, chiefly large *hawārī* and *ᶜabārī*, and one *bōt*. A group of men was breaking up one of these vessels for wood to produce charcoal.

Within the central cluster of buildings at the site was a surviving and active boatyard and ships' chandlers, the latter selling boatbuilding supplies including planking and hull preservatives. The former was the only boatyard in the survey where structural work on traditional boats was under way during the survey. The team observed a rudder being repaired, hull planking being replaced and caulked, and hull preservative being applied — all to an *ᶜobrī*. Another *ᶜobrī*, newly refurbished, was being prepared for launch. However the master builder overseeing the work said that no new vessels had been built at the site for some years.

al-Salīf

The most northerly site visited during the survey, al-Salīf is a relatively large fishing village located alongside an oil-exporting terminal. The bays around the village contained numerous wooden fishing *ᶜabārī* and large *hawārī* that were still in use — indeed this was by far the largest number of wooden vessels still in use anywhere in the survey area. However, as elsewhere on the survey route, the local boatbuilding yard had been abandoned, with three vessels — a *zārūk* and two large *hawārī* — abandoned and unfinished. The family associated with the yard said that they continued to carry out repairs, but that new boats were not being built. An old boat was being broken up for its timber.

FIGURE 5. *Three types of double-ended* sanbūq *found in Yemen — the* ʿobrī *(top) in Aden, and the* zārūq *(centre) and* zāʿīmah *(bottom), in Ghurayrah (MARES/J.P. Cooper, C. Zazzaro).*

As elsewhere, fibreglass boat construction had started in al-Salīf, but here fibreglass construction followed a practice not observed elsewhere. In al-Khawkhah and the Ḥaḍramawt, for example, fibreglass boatyards specialize in the production of the familiar "canoe"-type fishing boats with an outboard motor seen throughout the Yemen coast. However, fibreglass boats seen under construction at the al-Salīf fishing association building were clearly modelled on the double-ended wooden *ʿobrī*, and used an inboard motor.

Socotra

Due its isolated position, Socotra has until recently retained many dugout *hawārī*. Other traditional vessels found on the island include a sewn planked vessel known as a *shirkah* (Socotran Arabic), all surviving examples of which are abandoned, as well as a number of planked vessels from Oman and elsewhere that have been brought to the island and abandoned. However, it is the log-boat *hūrī* that has been the primary means of accessing the rich fishing grounds around the island. The log-boat *hawārī* of Socotra, like those on the mainland, originate in India (Jansen van Rensburg 2005*a*; 2005*b*; 2006; 2009). However modifications and repairs are undertaken locally by fishermen using an array of techniques, including sewing, to prevent further splitting of the hull. This technique was also used previously to maintain the *shiṛkah*. With the gradual increase in the import of fibreglass vessels the *hawārī* and other vessels are being abandoned, and few remain in use. With increasing economic development on Socotra, abandoned wooden vessels are being used to fuel lime kilns. Thankfully, with the opening of a craft museum on Socotra and the actions of several individuals, a few *hawārī* have been saved.

FIGURE 6. *A* bōt *at Ḥudaydah (MARES/J.P. Cooper).*

2. The vessels

The survey encountered a range of double-ended and transom-sterned vessels. The larger "dhows" varied in length from 16–24 m and in width from 3–7 m. All had motors, either inboard or outboard. Planks were fastened with cleated nails to crook timbers, and floor timbers were bolted to the keel.

Three main dhow-types were recognized during our survey. These included double-ended boats of different shape, powered by inboard motors, and sometimes with an extant mast or mast step. These were generically referred to as *sanābīk* (sg. *sanbūk*),[4] although specific hull shapes attracted more precise names, such as *ʿobrī*, *zārūk*, and *zāʿīmah*. The general shape and structure of these hulls was quite similar from type to type, the main difference being in the bow and stern profiles, and overall hull size.

[4] Or *sanābīq* (sg. *sanbūq*): final "k", a voiceless velar stop, and "q", a uvular occlusive, are often interchangeable.

Figure 7. *A "large* hūrī *" at al-Khawkhah (MARES/J.P. Cooper).*

Figure 8. *A* galbah/jalbah *at Fuqum, Little Aden (MARES/J.P. Cooper).*

ᶜObrī

The *ᶜobrī* is a double-ended vessel with an inboard motor, characterized by a straight, raking prow and a stem-post that terminates at or slightly above the sheer line. The largest recorded was at Dakkat al-Ghaz: it was 22.8 m long, 5.8 m wide, and 2.6 m high amidships (Fig. 5).

Zārūk

Another double-ended vessel, the *zārūk*, is characterized by straight but foreshortened stern- and stem-posts, which end approximately two-thirds of the way up the bow (Fig. 5). A *zārūk* observed at Ghurayrah was the largest vessel of any the team surveyed. It was 24 m long and 6.2 m wide. One informant said the *zārūk* had a typical capacity of 300 tons.[5]

Zāᶜīmah

The term *zāᶜīmah* refers to a double-ended vessel with inboard motor, characterized by a curving bow profile. Informants who used this term or sketched this type were interviewed in locations where the *zāᶜīmah* no longer existed. However, vessels matching their description were recorded at Ghurayrah (Fig. 5). A former builder of *zaᶜāyim* living at Fuqum said the *zāᶜīmah* had a capacity of up to 500 tons and a keel length of 15–24 m.[6]

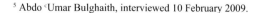

Figure 9. *A fibreglass* galbah *under construction at al-Salīf. The hull form retains that of the wooden* ᶜobrī *(MARES/J.P. Cooper).*

Bōt

Two examples of the *bōt* were observed, in Aden and Ḥudaydah. These were transom-sterned vessels with a box-like cross-section and blunt bow profile, having an inboard motor (Fig. 6). Informants unanimously identified this vessel as "not Yemeni", and variously attributed its origins to Oman or India. The MARES team subsequently observed similar craft in use in Djibouti.

---

[5] Abdo ᶜUmar Bulghaith, interviewed 10 February 2009.

[6] Muhammad ᶜAlī Najjār, a boatbuilder, interviewed 10 February 2009.

Figure 10. *A* ramas *at al-Khawkhah (MARES/C. Zazzaro).*

The "large hūrī"

The most common of the larger vessels of the Yemeni Red Sea coast, the "large *hūrī*" is transom-sterned and powered by two outboard motors, or occasionally one (Fig. 7). While its bow is almost identical to that of an *ᶜobrī*, it is distinguished by having two sweeping "fins" at its stern quarters, these being a continuation of the hull planking. The opening above the low transom and between the fins was used to pay out and gather in seine nets. The type varies in length from 14 to 20 m and in width from 2.5 to 4.5 m. The term "large *hūrī*" was used by the team to distinguish it from the various forms of smaller fishing canoes that were also called *hūrī*.[7] Interviewees referred to it simply as a *hūrī*, unless likewise distinguishing it.

Transom "sanbūk"

A large dhow was recorded at Ghurayrah that was similar in its hull shape to the *ᶜobrī*, except that it had a transom stern. The vessel measured 23.5 m in length and was 7.1 m wide. We tentatively associate this type of boat with the description of a *sāᶜiyah* that informants outlined elsewhere, but the identification is by no means certain.

Galbah[8]

In the Aden area, the *galbah* was a plank fishing vessel around 11 m in length, characterized by small transom stern and an outboard motor (Fig. 8). In the Red Sea, however, the term applied exclusively to fibreglass vessels of various forms (Fig. 9).

Ramas

The *ramas* is a small punted log-raft made with logs lashed together and onto two cross-timbers with rope (today synthetic). Although most were abandoned, some were still being used for inshore fishing (Fig. 10).

3. Boatbuilding

Although the survey did not record boatbuilding in progress, ethnographic interview, the presence of numerous abandoned boatyards, and a large number of unfinished *hawārī* and *ᶜabārī* enabled the construction sequence of these craft to be established. Indeed, the survey encountered remarkable variations in the approach to building wooden vessels, even within the same boatyard. In one boatyard at al-Khawkhah, the team found the construction of *ᶜabārī* followed a sequence familiar to vessels in other areas of the Red Sea. The first piece to be laid is the keel, followed by stem- and sternpost timbers and the *samakah* timber through which the propeller shaft is fitted. The hull shape is then established by building up futtocks and planks in parallel, i.e. the approach is neither shell- first nor frame-first, but a mixed method.[9] In contrast, yet in the same boatyard, the "large *hūrī*" was built in a quite different sequence, in that the keel and stem- and sternposts are added at the very end of the hull construction sequence. Having built the hull up from its garboard strakes, including all planks and framing timbers, the builders roll the hull to one side, and affix the prepared keel by bolting it to the floor timbers.

Within the same vessel type, the team noted variations in the construction sequence between locations. In al-Khawkhah, the planking of the large *hūrī* was applied in an upward direction, starting with the garboard strake (see also Prados 1998*a*: 199–201). However, in al-Salīf builders of the *hūrī* preferred to attach the sheer strakes immediately after the garboard strakes and initial shape-giving futtocks.[10] The intermediate strakes and framing timbers were added afterwards. Even though the outcomes

[7] The 2007 Southampton University survey had focused on recording these smaller *hawāri* — either dugout or plank-built vessels. The MARES survey retained a complimentary focus on other types of boat, most of which were larger.

[8] Alternatively, the initial voiced velar stop /g/ is pronounced as the voiced alveolar affricate /j/.

[9] For a definition of the mixed construction technique see McGrail (2004: 7–9) and Pomey & Rieth (2005: 33–34). In maritime archaeology the discussion of the sequences of boat construction and preconception methods was first introduced by Olof Hasslöf (1963) and Lucien Bash (1972), both using ethnographical and archaeological data.

[10] See also boatbuilding methods recorded by Prados at Luḥayyah (1998*a*: 201–205).

are entirely similar, the variation in approach at different yards on the same coast perhaps reflects concomitant variations in the paths of transmission of the underlying boatbuilding skills.

Linguistic enquiry

The survey identified a range of names applied to different Yemeni vessel types. Of these, *sanbūk* is today applied quite generically, covering the vessels also known as *zawārīk*, *zaᶜāyim*, and *ᶜabārī*: none of these vessels resemble the large transom-ended, curved-prow *sanābīk* that plied Yemeni waters during British rule in the south (Howarth 1977: 36), which are no longer found, nor do they resemble the *sanābīq* of the Gulf or Oman (Howarth 1977: 36; Agius 2005: 18). Even more generically applied was the term *hūrī*, historically referring to dugout fishing canoes, but today referring to fibreglass vessels, and also to the "large *hūrī*" discussed above. Linguistic informants also provided other names for vessel types that no longer exist in Yemen. These names, and their historical usage, are discussed below. Of course vessels referred to historically are unlikely to correlate in precise form to modern vessels given the same name.

Sanbūq (pl. *sanābīq*)

The word *sanbūq* (in Yemen, also *sanbūk* (pl. *sanābīk))* has been applied to a diverse set of vessels in a wide variety of Western Indian Ocean locations for almost a millennium. It has been commonly known over the centuries, with cognates in Mehri, Ḥaḍramī, and Amharic (de Landberg 1920–1942, iii: 1985–1986, n. 1; Glidden 1942: 71). It is also found in Greek *sambúke* (σαμβύκε), which seemingly came about because of the Greek presence in Egypt and the Red Sea before the Christian era. An attempt has also been made to derive the word from Persian, through Middle Persian **sambūk* (al-Jawālīqī 1969: 177–179; Tabrīzī 1982, ii: 1170; Glidden 1942: 71; Agius 2002: 85–86). This is possible, but there is a greater possibility that the nomenclature derives from Sanskrit *çambuka*, and there may also be links with Malay *sampan* (Kindermann 1934: 43) or Chinese *sanpan* (Yajima 1976: 24).

The earliest mention of *sanbūq* in Arabic sources comes from the mariners' tales recounted by the captain, Buzurg b. Shahriyār (*d.* 1009), who reports a cargo *sanbūq* sailing to China (al-Rāmhurmuzī 1883–1886: 190). The Moroccan traveller, Ibn Baṭṭūṭah (1368–1389 or 1377) speaks of a *sanbūq* functioning as a coastal ferry (1968, ii: 17, 181, 183, 198, 251). The Egyptian historian, al-Maqrīzī (1441–1442), mentions the name in the context of a war fleet in the Red Sea during the Ṭulūnid period (868–884) (1853, ii: 180). We also find the name in sixteenth-century Portuguese sources: Afonzo de Albuquerque (*d.* 1515), Duarte Barbosa (*d.* 1521) (1918–1921, i: 7, 9), and Vasco da Gama (*d.* 1524) (1869: 75–76, 79, 80, 109) often mention the *sambucho* or *zambuco*.[11] De Albuquerque notes that Portuguese caravels "were guided by small or large vessels called *sanbūq*[s]." He also remarks that they were undecked, and describes them moreover as "having no nails" (1875–1884, iv: 206), a probable reference to the former Indian Ocean practice of stitching hull planks (Agius 2008: 161–167). In the same period, the Italian Ludovico di Varthema, who lived in Yemen for some time, reports a type of "flat-bottomed" *sanbūq* (1863: 154).

In the nineteenth century, Karl Klunzinger (*d.* 1861), classifies the *sanbūq* as the most common Red Sea type (2000: 295), while Richard Burton (*d.* 1890) sailed on a two-masted, 50-ton pilgrim *sanbūq* from Suez to Jeddah, which carried ninety-seven pilgrims (1964, i: 188).

ᶜObrī (pl. *ᶜabārī* or *ᶜobriyyāt*)

The name *ᶜobrī* comes from Arabic *ᶜabara* "to cross over (the sea)", by extension a boat which journeys from one point to another (Lane 1984, ii: 1936). Given the meaning, one would expect to find a boat term in classical Arabic sources related to this verb-root but none has been found (Agius 2002: 46–47). Hunter (1877: 83) mentions an *ᶜabra*, which he says is a small boat of 5 to 15 tons from al-Mukalla. More recently, Hawkins uses *ᶜabra* generically to refer to "all manner of small craft which can be anything from decrepit all-purpose boats in Aden to the sleek ferries of Dubai Creek" (1977: 81). Moore (1925: 123) is a little more specific: he says an *ᶜabra* had a lowered bow and elevated stern, while Serjeant (1974: 134) speaks of a Mehri *ᶜabriyya sambūk*, which might or might not be similar to the *ᶜobrī* encountered during the MARES fieldwork.

Zārūk (pl. *zarārīk* or *zārūkāt*)

In classical Arabic, the verb-root *zariqa* carries the meaning of "piercing with a spear" and *zarūqah* is the word for "spear"; by extension this root gave the word *zawraq* "a skiff; a small boat" (Lane 1984, i: 1227–1228)

[11] For reports on the *sanbūq* from the Ḥaḍramī chronicles, see Serjeant 1974: 58, 69; see also Agius 2008: 141–170.

with the meaning of light and fast; it is mentioned by Ibn Jubayr (*d.* 1217) (1952: 64). The Yemeni term *zārūk* seems to be related to this. At the turn of the twentieth century, de Monfreid (*d.* 1976) often speaks of *zarārīk* in the southern Red Sea (1934: 14, 106, 220); he gives the impression that it was the most common vessel of his times, but this could be a generic term for various boat types.

Zaᶜīmah (pl. *zaᶜāyim*)

The name seems to be associated with one of the meanings of the verb-root *zaᶜama* "(the camel that) conveys (someone to a desired place)"; hence *zaᶜīmah* is the "conveyor" with reference to the laden camel (Lane 1984, i: 1232). That would perhaps explain the Yemeni application of the name to a type of cargo boat.

Our informants sketched a double-ended vessel with a curved bow profile and spoke of its large size — descriptions which correspond to a drawing by Hawkins (1977: 79). The MARES team identified an abandoned vessel at Ghurayrah as such.

Sāᶜiyah (pl. *sāᶜiyāt*)

Informants in Yemen referred to a type of large transom-sterned vessel of this name, but the MARES team identified no such actual vessel with certainty.[12] The name may have come from the verb-root *saᶜā* meaning "to go along with vigorousness" and the word *sāᶜi* signifies "a messenger that journeys with haste", which would fit well with the nomenclature *sāᶜiyah* (Lane 1984, i: 1367). Yemenis have adopted the feminine usage, as several names of vessels in Arabic do. Johann Ludwig Burckhardt (*d.* 1829) describes a *sāᶜiyah* as the smallest type of dhow "only nine feet [2.7 m] across the beam" (1822: 8–9).

Jalbah or *Galbah* (pl. *jilab/gilab* or *jalbāt/galbāt*)

The name *jalbah* does not occur in classical and medieval lexica. From the verb-root *jalaba* we have "to transport things, such as camels, sheep ... slaves or any merchandise" (Lane 1984, i: 438, 440); hence, it might be said that the ship that carried them was called *jalbah*. The *jalbah* was a well-known Red Sea vessel; it is first mentioned by Buzurg ibn Shahriyār (*d.* 1009) with reference to a journey from Oman to Jeddah (al-Rāmhurmuzī 1883–1886: 93–94). Cargo *jilab* were used to trade goods from Egypt to Aden and return, according to the Genizah letters (tenth–thirteenth centuries) (Agius 2008: 116–117). Ibn Jubayr says that a *jalbah* was a pilgrim-cargo boat with sewn planks (1952: 63). Some were large enough to carry camels from Jeddah to Yemen, says Ibn Baṭṭūṭah (1968, i: 158). Portuguese diaries report a type that was a small sailing or rowing vessel used on the southern Red Sea coast. In the greater Aden area, *galbah* is a term applied to a relatively small transom-ended wooden fishing boat (*c.*11 m). However, on the Red Sea coast the term was invariably used to refer to fibreglass vessels, whatever their form.

Hūrī (pl. *hawārī*)

The origin of the name *hūrī* stems from Hindi *hōrī* and ultimately from Sanskrit *hoḍa* (Agius 2002: 119–121; 2008: 123, n. 73). Other than the dugout "canoe" this is perhaps the most familiar vessel of that name and the term also applies to a wide range of small plank-built fishing vessels found in every place we surveyed. In many locations it is also applied to the type of fibreglass fishing vessels mainly manufactured in the Ḥaḍramawt area, and found throughout Yemen. The name is also applied to the much bigger "large *hūrī*" described above.

Ramas (pl. *ramasāt*)

Ramas is a name of Demotic origin (from the root r.m.s.) (Agius 2008: 122). It appears in Hieratic, and is also a cognate term with Somali *ramsi* and its variant, Ethiopic. It has survived in the Red Sea, the Horn of Africa, and the Ḥaḍramawt area. The classical Arabic term is *ramath*.

The earliest mention of the term in classical Arabic sources is a verse from a pre-Islamic ode of Abū Ṣakhr al-Hudhalī (second half of the seventh century AD) (Montgomery 1997: 195); also found in a Ḥadīth, sometime after the seventh century; the Andalusian lexicographer Ibn Sīda (1007–1066) sets a definition of *ramath*, describing it at some length. We have then no sources mentioning this name until the nineteenth century: Burckhardt sailed in Nubia on a *rāmūs* "a small raft of reeds", though elsewhere he described it as constructed of four trunks of date-trees, worked by a paddle 4 feet long (1.2 m) (Agius 2002: 128–130; 2008: 120–121). Barrett Miles (1994: 414) reports that in the early twentieth century he saw Socotrans sailing from the island to Muscat on a *ramas* made of "three logs about six feet [1.82 m] long, the central one being the longest". Moore (1925: 138) came across a three- to four-log *ramas* in Massawa, Eritrea.

[12] Prados (1998*b*: fig. 3) identified such a vessel preserved as a monument in al-Ḥamī (Ḥaḍramawt).

Conclusion

As recently as 1996, Prados was able to write that, "…wooden boatbuilding continues to thrive in Yemen." (1996: 50). The situation has changed radically in the intervening time. The MARES fieldwork suggests that the building of new wooden dhows in Yemen may now have ceased, and that the only work currently conducted in traditional boatyards is repair work on existing vessels. Reports from the Ḥaḍramawt and Maḥra, to which this survey did not extend, suggest that this was the first area of Yemen to start the transition to fibreglass boatbuilding, and hence there are few vestiges of the wooden tradition. The area north of al-Salīf remains an unknown quantity. Prados noted boatbuilding activity at al-Luḥayyah and al-Khawbah in the mid-90s (1996: 51; 1998*a*: 199–206), and local informants told us that wooden vessels continue to be used at Maydī. Future research along this coast north of al-Salīf is therefore warranted.

Oral accounts obtained from Yemenis in Aden and on the Red Sea relate that fibreglass boatbuilding in Yemen took off in the aftermath of the 1990 Iraqi invasion of Kuwait, when over a million resident Yemenis were expelled from member states of the Gulf Co-operation Council. Many of these Yemenis were Ḥaḍramīs, some of whom returned to their home province and invested their savings in establishing fibreglass boatyards. Fibreglass fishing "canoes" throughout Yemen, and also in Djibouti, carry makers' marks from Ḥaḍramī yards. Fibreglass boatyards are now to be found in the major Red Sea fishing centres of al-Khawkhah and al-Salīf, and fibreglass boats have been observed carrying the name of a builder in Mocha.

The uptake of fibreglass boats in Yemen appears to be the product of raw economics. Fibreglass boats are robust, require less maintenance (and associated downtime), and can be repaired by unskilled hands using low-cost materials at a time when skilled workers are disappearing. Fishermen say that fibreglass boats are uncomfortable compared to wooden fishing vessels, but they travel faster and therefore further, allowing more distant fishing grounds to be reached at a time of falling fish stocks and rapid population growth.

It appears that Yemenis are witnessing the end of the practices of wooden boatbuilding, and the maritime traditions associated with it. In the Arabian-Persian Gulf and Oman, the wealth of the state and of individuals has enabled the preservation of some traditional vessels, either in museums or as hobby craft, and the archiving of documentary information on maritime activity in research centres. However, Yemen's relative poverty means that none of the surviving wooden dhows are likely to be preserved in a cultural-heritage context, a fact that argues for assiduous recording of these vessel types and their associated oral and craft traditions before they are lost entirely.

Acknowledgements

This research was conducted as part of the MARES Project, a three-year programme investigating the maritime past and heritage of the Red Sea and Arabian-Persian Gulf. MARES is based at the Institute of Arab and Islamic Studies at the University of Exeter (http://projects.exeter.ac.uk/mares). The programme is funded by the Golden Web Foundation, an educational charity registered in the UK (www.goldenweb.org), to which our gratitude is due. Thanks are also due to the Seven Pillars of Wisdom Trust, which provided additional financial support for the fieldwork. In addition, the MARES team would like to thank the following people for their assistance: Dr Abdulla M. Bawazir, President of Yemen's General Organization of Antiquities and Museums (GOAM); Dr Muhammad Taha al-Asbahi, General Director of Antiquities at GOAM; Dr Raja Batawil, head of GOAM in Aden; our GOAM-appointed field companion, Salah al-Mansuri; Mr Hasan Saleh Shihab; Emily Allardyce, Fuad Mazid al-Matairi, and their colleagues at the British Yemeni Language Institute; our driver and guide Muhammad al-Matairi; Edward Prados, Director of Amideast; Chris Evens; the British Council; and the British Embassy. Last but not least, the team wishes to thank the many individual informants along Yemen's coast who gave their assistance to its research.

References

Agius D.A.

2002. *In the Wake of the Dhow: The Arabian Gulf and Oman*. Reading: Ithaca.

2005. *Seafaring in the Arabian Gulf and Oman*. London/New York: Kegan Paul.

2008. *Classic Ships of Islam: From Mesopotamia to the Indian Ocean*. Leiden: E.J. Brill.

Awadh Ali N.A., Jülich W.D., Kusnick C. & Lindequist U.

2001. Screening of Yemeni medicinal plants for antibacterial and cytotoxic activities. *Journal of Ethnopharmacology* 74/2: 173–179.

Barbosa D./trans. M.L. Dames.

1918–1921. *The Book of Duarte Barbosa*. (2 volumes). London: The Hakluyt Society.

Basch L.

1972. Ancient wrecks and the archaeology of ships. *The International Journal of Nautical Archaeology and Underwater Exploration* 1: 1–58.

Bilaidi A.S.

1978. *Silviculture in the People's Democratic Republic of Yemen*. 10 March 2009. Rome: Food and Agriculture Organisation. www.fao.org/docrep/12680e/12680e05.htm

Burckhardt J.L.

1822. *Travels in Nubia*. London: J. Murray.

Burton R.

1964. *Personal Narrative of a Pilgrimage to Al-Madinah and Meccah*. (ed. I. Burton). (2 volumes). New York: Dover. [First published 1893].

da Gama V./trans. H.E.J. Stanley

1869. *Three Voyages of Vasco da Gama and his Viceroyalty. From the Lendas da India of Gaspar Correa*. London: The Hakluyt Society.

de Albuquerque A./trans. W. De Gray Birch.

1875–1884. *The Commentaries of the Great Afonso Dalboquerque*. (4 volumes). London: The Hakluyt Society.

di Varthema L./trans. J.W. Jones & ed. G.P. Badger.

1863. *The Travels of Ludovico di Varthema*. London: The Hakluyt Society.

Glidden H.W.

1942. A comparative study of the Arabic nautical vocabulary from al-ᶜAqabah, Transjordan. *Journal of the American Oriental Society* 62: 68–72.

Hasslöf O.

1963. Wrecks, Archives and Living Traditions. *The Mariner's Mirror* 49/3: 162–177.

Hawkins C.W.

1977. *The Dhow*. Lymington: Nautical Publishing/London: George G. Harrap.

Howarth D.

1977. *Dhows*. London: Quartet Books.

Hunter F.M.

1877. *An Account of the British Settlement at Aden, in Arabia*. London: Trübner.

Ibn Baṭṭūṭah, Abū ʿAbdallāh Muḥammad/trans. C. Derfrémery & B.R. Sanguinetti.

1968. *Voyages d'Ibn Battûta, Arabic text with translation*. (4 volumes). Paris: Anthropos. [First published 1853–1858].

Ibn Jubayr, Abū al-Ḥasan Muḥammad/trans. R.J.C. Broadhurst.

1952. *Riḥla, The Travels of Ibn Jubayr*. London: Jonathan Cape.

Jansen van Rensburg J.

2005*a*. An Ethno-technical study of the *hawari* on Soqotra. *Tayf — the Soqotra Newsletter* 2: 17.

2005*b*. Soqotra Hawari Expedition — an Ethno-Technical study of the *hawari* on Soqotra. *Bulletin of the Society of Arabian Studies* 10: 33.

2006. Hawari — Socotra's unique fishing boats. Pages 316–319 in C. Cheung, L. De Vantier & K. Van Damme (eds), *Socotra: a Natural History of the Islands and their People*. Hong Kong: Odyssey Books & Guides.

2009. The Hawārī of Socotra, Yemen. *International Journal of Nautical Archaeology*. 5 December 2009. DOI: 10.1111/j.1095-9270.2009.00234.x

Al-Jawālīqī, Abū Manṣūr Mawhūb b. Aḥmad b. Muḥammad/ed. A.M. Shākir.

1969. *Kitāb al-muʿarrab min al-kalām al-aʿjamī ʿalā ḥurūf al-muʿjam*. Tehran: Dār al-Kutub.

Kindermann H.

1934. *"Schiff" im Arabischen. Untersuchung über Vorkommen und Bedeutung der Termini*. Bonn: Zwickau.

Klunzinger C.B.

2000. *Upper Egypt: Its People and its Products*. London: Darf. [First published 1878].

Landberg, Comte de

1920–1942. *Glossaire Daṭînois*. (3 volumes). Leiden: E.J. Brill.

Lane E.W.

1984. *Arabic-English Lexicon*. (2 volumes). Cambridge: Islamic Texts Society Trust. [First published 1863–1893].

McGrail S.

2004. *Boats of the World*. Oxford: Oxford University Press.

Al-Maqrīzī, Taqī al-Dīn / ed. M.Q. al-ʿAdawī

1853. *Al-mawāʿiẓ wa l-iʿtibār fī dhikr al-khiṭaṭ wa l-āthār*. (2 volumes). Bulaq.

Miles S.B.

1994. *The Countries and Tribes of the Persian Gulf*. Reading: Garnet. (2 volumes). [First published 1919; reprinted 1920].

Monfreid H. de/trans. H.B. Bell.

1934. *Secrets of the Red Sea*. London: Faber & Faber.

Montgomery J.E.

1997. *The Vagaries of the Qaṣīdah. The Tradition and Practice of Early Arabic Poetry*. (Gibb Literary Studies, 1). Warminster: Aris Phillips.

Moore A.

1925. *Last Days of Mast and Sail*. Oxford: Clarendon Press.

Pomey P. & Rieth E.

2005. *L'Archéologie navale*. Paris: Éditions Errance.

Prados E.

1996. Traditional Fishing Craft of the Tihamah and Southwestern Arabian Coast. *The American Neptune* 56: 89–115.

1998*a*. Wooden Boats of the Yemeni Tihamah. *Nautical Research Journal* 43/4: 195–209.

1998*b*. Contemporary Wooden Fishing Craft of Yemen. *Yemen Update* 40. 5 December 2009. www.aiys.org/webdate/prados.html

Al-Rāmhurmuzī, Buzurg b. Shahriyār/ed. P.A. Van der Lith & trans. L. Marcel Devic.

1883–1886. *Kitāb ʿajāʾib al-hind (Livre des merveilles de l'Inde)*. Leiden: E.J. Brill.

Serjeant R.B.

1974. *The Portuguese off the South Arabian Coast*. Beirut: Librairie du Liban.

Tabrīzī M.Ḥ.

1982. *Burhān-e qāṭeʿ*. (4 volumes). Tehran: Amīr Kabīr.

Yajima H.

1976. *The Arab Dhow Trade in the Indian Ocean* (Studia Culturae Islamicae, 3). Tokyo: Institute for the Study of Languages and Cultures of Asia and Africa.

Authors' addresses

The MARES Project, Institute of Arab and Islamic Studies, University of Exeter, Stocker Road, Exeter, EX4 4ND, UK.

Prof Dionisius A. Agius
e-mail d.a.agius@exeter.ac.uk

John P. Cooper
e-mail j.p.cooper@exeter.ac.uk

Julian Jansen van Rensburg
e-mail jj243@exeter.ac.uk

Chiara Zazzaro
e-mail c.zazzaro@exeter.ac.uk

Proceedings of the Seminar for Arabian Studies 40 (2010): 85–98

Building materials in South Arabian inscriptions: observations on some problems concerning the study of architectural lexicography

ALESSIO AGOSTINI

Summary

Among the South Arabian inscriptions are many that relate to construction activities. A complete understanding of them is far from being achieved, in particular as regards the technical terminology connected with architectonic structures. A more reliable and accurate methodology can help to clarify the semantic values of many words which are of great interest, not only from an epigraphical point of view but also for the archaeological study of the ancient South Arabian civilization. Apart from some comments on the methodology required for this demanding task, this paper presents a survey on a particular aspect of this technical lexicography: building materials and their finishing processes.

The most common vocabulary is analysed in order to show which materials were involved and recorded in these texts, and in what way they were refined according to the structures involved. The analysis of these lexical data within South Arabian documentation can reveal a certain degree of uniformity and also, in some cases, linguistic differentiations depending on the area, chronology, and the monument concerned. We will also attempt to demonstrate that an examination of these terms, together with the archaeological records at our disposal, can reveal some nuances in their semantic value, i.e. distinguishing between words indicating raw materials, the combination of different materials, and different work processes. Continuous comparison with the archaeological data can also establish how this terminology was adapted to indicate the different natural resources available in the geographical and cultural areas of southern Arabia.

Keywords: ancient South Arabia, architecture, materials, epigraphy, lexicography

The study of the lexicon connected with architecture, as revealed in ancient South Arabian construction inscriptions (Agostini 2008), leads us to consider some general problems concerning those words which are somehow connected with the real world, but which are for the most part still largely obscure as regards their actual meaning. These problems are not only connected with South Arabia, of course, as they are also common to disciplines in other domains, but the characteristics of South Arabian documentation contribute to emphasize some of them.

Methodological observations

The first stage is to give more importance to the internal linguistic evidence. This is to say, to study every single word within the most complete texts in which it has been found. Consequently, grammatical and syntactic characteristics are the first ones to be isolated and taken into account. To consider some examples, the number (singulars, duals, plurals) is very important because it allows us to distinguish the actual quantity of the objects; the connections of the substantive with other words in the sentence (first of all, the genitive) can also help to clarify the function of the object which is expressed by that particular word. The identification of a term denoting an architectural object (which is not always so immediate) can be made by first taking into account those terms that are the object of a verb clearly expressing a construction activity. This will also help to gain a better understanding of those contexts in which that same word is the object of another type of action (e.g. dedications to a divinity). Some extra-textual aspects should also be stressed, in particular those connected with the distribution of the documentation in its diachronic and synchronic perspectives, but in both cases also paying attention to geographical variations.

The external linguistic evidence should be investigated only at a later stage, and only when this documentation has become clearer in its internal dynamics. Comparisons with other Semitic languages is by no means essential in the historical linguistic perspective, and the lexicon, more than other linguistic aspects, is of great importance in the historical approach, but it loses most of its value when we come to the field of linguistic classification, which is subject — more than phonetics and morphology — to external influence and diffusion. This approach, in the case of a technical lexicon such as the architectonic one, must in no case be neglected, since the discovery of its origin and later diffusion is certainly of the greatest importance for interpreting the origins of these techniques. A new technique usually goes hand in hand with its nomenclature. It is clear, then, that the consequences of this study bring us to etymology, which in turn could lead us astray where semantic problems are concerned. To repeat the words of James Barr, the great scholar of biblical semantics: "a word has its meaning only in its own language at its own time and in relation of proximity and opposition to other words in that same language at that same time" (1968: 55).[1]

The study of this kind of lexicon leads us also to take into account concrete archaeological evidence. Naturally one has to look at the archaeological data in order to get input and confirmation of our theories. Every idea on the semantic clarification of an obscure word must first of all be consistent with the reality that it probably contributed to define, but we have to bear in mind other problems.

First of all, epigraphical data and archaeological evidence are two different aspects of the study and should be treated separately, especially considering the incompleteness of these forms of documentation. In the case of texts we only have what was intentionally transmitted and in the case of archaeology we only have what has been preserved or discovered. The joining up of these two disciplines is without a doubt necessary, but the difficulty is that the incomplete evidence left by epigraphy and by archaeology does not always coincide. In the best scenario, the archaeological data is confirmed by the epigraphic data, and vice versa. This rarely happens, and more often we are given two different aspects of a more complex reality.

This problem is aggravated if we consider that the categories, which nowadays we use to define things (in other words and in our case, what seems to us important and evident in a given monument) were not necessarily felt important enough to be recorded in ancient times by those who commissioned both the building and its commemorating inscription. These texts are not, in fact, expected to provide in-depth technical information, being intended only as a public record of the construction activity and its client. Moreover, the fixed patterns in which these texts are written add to the impression that the lexical content they reveal is derived from a textual tradition rather than being strictly connected with the monument they describe. Finally, we must bear in mind that such a lexicon presents evolutions and differentiations, both in time and space, thus making the lexical documentation scarcer than it actually is, because it cannot be taken as entirely representative of the same building tradition in a given historical period.

Looking at the documentation that is most closely linked with the ancient remains can simplify this task, since the *in situ* texts can provide more reliable elements connected with the original archaeological setting of both the text and the monument itself.[2]

Building materials

Ancient and modern Yemen has always been labelled as a "land of builders", and this is certainly true if we think of the extraordinary architecture that is still admired by visitors and archaeologists. The building capability of ancient South Arabians is particularly evident in the great skill in which stone was worked and how it was used with other materials, above all wood and mud brick.

Looking at the construction inscriptions, the first impression is that the mention of building materials was not frequent in the texts. This reveals that this kind of specification was not used as a fixed pattern in the phraseology of construction inscriptions, as it was for some formulas of building dedication or for the completion of works (Agostini 2009; Avanzini 1987).

First, it is important to recognize and divide those terms that identify simple building materials from other words, which denote a finishing process. We will leave out for the moment those terms which can scarcely be attested and whose contexts do not help us to find out their original function or meaning, and for this reason remain obscure. For every lexical root that is at the origin of this kind of terminology we can infer some general descriptions of the single words produced and observe how they were used and recorded in texts. The tables (Figs 1–8) will help to organize this documentation, putting particular emphasis on the most complete attestations where evidence is given of a combination of

[1] He also says: "Semitic studies have been bedevilled by an over-etymological sense in semantics, which appears to suggest that a word in one language is *prima facie* likely to mean what its cognate means in another language" (Barr 1968: 54).

[2] This kind of approach proved to be very useful for the interpretation of some fundamental words connected with the structures of the Barāqish walls (Robin 1979).

Language	Other materials combined	Attestations	Chronology	Archaeological context	Monument type
Sabaic	*ḥs*^{3}*s*^{3}	CIH 448/2	281 AD	Hakir	Hydraulic
	gyr (plaster)	CIH 540/30	450 AD	Maʾrib Dam	
Minaic	*ᶜḍ*	Maᶜīn 7/3	third century BC	Maᶜīn East Gate	Defensive
		M 283/4	third century BC	Barāqish walls	
	ᶜḍ + blq	M 164/2	?	Barāqish walls	
Qatabanic	*ᶜḍ + blq*	Ḥuwaydar 1/5	third century BC	Ḥuwaydar walls	Defensive
	ᶜḍ + blq + mrt	CIAS 47.11/b2/2	second century BC	Tamnaᶜ South Gate	
	ᶜḍ + blq + mrt + mwgl	Timnaᶜ-MAFYS 1/4	third century BC	Tamnaᶜ North Gate	
	ᶜḍ + blq + mrt + ᶜwt (?)	RES 3880/6	third century BC	Tamnaᶜ (Gate?)	
Hadramitic	*ᶜḍ + ftl*	Naqb al-Hajar 2/1	first century BC	Naqb al-Hajar walls	Defensive
		RES 3869/3	first century BC ?	Naqb al-Hajar walls	

Figure 1. *ʾbn*

different materials: this will constitute a good basis for the description of the building techniques in inscriptions and create a point of departure for a comparison with the archaeological record, which is still at its beginning.

Types of material

As far as the use of stones is concerned, we can identify at least three terms that define them (Sima 2000: 289–305). Root ʾBN (Fig. 1) indicates stone in general, and this is also proven by the fact that this term appears both alone and in contexts of a different nature. It frequently appears in texts concerning defensive or hydraulic works. In Minaic and Qatabanic it is listed first even when other materials are recorded. In Hadramitic it was used in a defensive context and in Qatabanic it was most probably related, for example, to the massive structure of the south-west gate of Tamnaᶜ, thus also indicating that this term has a secondary association with the massive granite blocks of which this gate was made.

Its generic semantic content is also confirmed by the fact that this root belongs to common Semitic, in which it simply means "stone".[3] Furthermore, this is indirectly corroborated by Ethiopic (Geᶜez) where it is always used in combination with other more specific terms to identify, with more precision, some kind of precious stone.

Two more specific kinds of stone are indicated by the terms based on the roots BLQ and WGL, and they are commonly associated with limestone and a sort of alabaster respectively.

BLQ (Fig. 2) is cited in all areas of South Arabian.[4] In Sabaic it indicates the material used both in religious and hydraulic structures. The sacral context is also shared by Minaic but it usually uses *blq* in the context of defensive works. The first problem arises when we look at the Qatabanic textual documentation, especially that connected with a known archaeological context, as in the defensive works of Tamnaᶜ and in particular its main city gate. Here, as stated above, the remaining structures reveal that granite was the preferred material, because of its abundance in the region.[5] Limestone was of course also used, but only in some selected structures, generally where a more malleable or refined material was needed (de Maigret & Robin 2006: 26, 33, 47).[6] Since

[3] Arabic does not have this term as a common noun but it maintains it as a proper name for the town of Petra (Cohen 1970: 4).

[4] A recent Hadramitic text has given the first occurrence of *blq* in this language (RAMRY/94-al-Zālif 1 no. 1/2). The text is very fragmentary and the possible restitution of the term *ᶜḍ* as "wood", before *blq*, is too uncertain: for this reason it has not been included in the figures concerning the combination of different materials.

[5] This is an intrusive rock from the pre-Cambrian era, which is found in North Yemen (Najrān region) and also in the southern part of Sabaʾ, from Wādī al-Jubā to Wādī Beyḥān.

[6] In Tamnaᶜ it has been used for the Athirat temple well, and for the lateral staircase in TT1 and its basin. It was probably also used for the monolithic pillars, which were not found on their plinths, as in the Athirat temple, TT1, and in the Rṣfm temple of the necropolis. BLQ also denotes limestone in the case of small objects, like those named *bḥt*,

Language	Other materials combined	Attestations	Chronology	Archaeological context	Monument type
Sabaic	*ʿḍ*	Ja 557/1	fourth–third century BC	Maʾrib ʾAwwām wall	Temple
Minaic	*ʿḍ +ʾ bn*	M 164/2	?	Barāqish walls	Defensive
	ʿḍ + tqr	M 185/2	fourth–third century BC	Barāqish walls	
		M 236/3	third century BC	Barāqish walls	
		M 252/1	?	Barāqish walls	
	mʿrbt	Maʿīn 51/1	?	Maʿīn walls	
	ʿḍ	M 203/3	fourth century BC	Barāqish, Nakraḥ Temple	Temple
Qatabanic	*ʾbn + ʿḍ*	Ḥuwaydar 1/5	third century BC	Ḥuwaydar walls	Defensive
	ʾbn + ʿḍ + mrt	CIAS 47.11/b2/2	second century BC	Tamnaʿ South Gate	
	ʾbn + ʿḍ + mrt + mwgl	Timnaʿ-MAFYS 1/4	third century BC	Tamnaʿ North Gate	
	ʾbn + ʿḍ + mrt + ʿwt (?)	RES 3880/6	third century BC	Tamnaʿ (Gate?)	

Figure 2. *blq*

the term *blq* is clearly stated in the inscriptions connected with these structures, we can deduce that it was used as a finishing element, which has not been preserved (and probably disappeared after the town was plundered).[7] We can, on the other hand, rule out that in this case the term *blq* denotes granite since, in all probability, this material was already mentioned under the general term *ʾbn*.

The Minaic documentation, moreover, extensively uses this term in connection with defensive and religious buildings. Here, however, we are dealing with different kinds of limestone, which was specifically used in different kinds of buildings. At Barāqish, for example, the particular "lumachelle" type, so defined by the fossils visible in it, was used inside the town, in particular for the monolithic pillars of temples (Darles 2009: 105), but when we come to the city walls, a more compact and solid sort of limestone is noted, such as the oolitic (Bessac 1998*a*: 174–176; Breton 1994: 23). The same use of the term *blq* in both monuments (temples and walls) leads us to rule out that this differentiation was also expressed in the terminology. The conscious choice of the materials by ancient South Arabians can also be recognized archaeologically in the Sabaean region (Brunner 1989: 1–3; 2002), and this tendency seems to be more frequent in the recent phase of Sabaean architecture when the specific use of stones of different quality is more perceivable (Wright 1987: 71–72).

The term *mwgl* (root WGL) (Fig. 3) is less problematic and indicates the material which has been usually defined as "alabaster", but which recent investigations reveal more precisely to be "calcite-alabaster" (Weiss *et al.* 2009; St John Simpson 2002: 191). The attestations are moreover limited to Sabaic and Qatabanic and this may reflect the actual availability of this kind of stone in these two regions. The absence of the word in Minaic, by contrast, is totally consistent with the near absence of this kind of material in the Minaean area. One need only think of the funerary stelae. In Qatabān and Sabaʾ they were preferably made using this sort of alabaster, while in Maʿīn these stelae, besides having stylistic and formal differences, are of limestone, which was easily obtainable in this area and therefore less expensive.[8]

which probably had an apotropaic function (see Sima 2000: 298–299).

[7] As happened to some blocks of the monumental fountain in the Athirat temple of Tamnaʿ (de Maigret 2003: 135–136).

[8] Jabal Maḫdarah is the quarry of calcite-alabaster closest to the Minaean region. Some funerary stelae from the Jawf region are in fact made in calcite-alabaster, but their scarcity suggests that in such cases non-endogenous material was used. The study of exogenous materials in a given area, at least for small objects, is a topic of great interest, but

Language	Other materials combined	Attestations	Chronology	Archaeological context	Monument type
Sabaic	*(g)rb* + *rbᶜt*	CIH 325/1	554 AD	?	Domestic
	nhmt	Bayt al-Ašwal 4/7	504 AD	?	
Qatabanic	*ʾbn* + *ᶜḏ* + *blq* + *mrt*	Timnaᶜ-MAFYS 1/4	third century BC	Tamnaᶜ North Gate	Defensive

FIGURE 3. *mwgl*

This term usually appears at the end of a list of materials. It is most likely, then, that the mention of alabaster in architectural structures, because of its precious nature, probably refers to the decorative fittings included in the external masonry — especially in Sabaʾ and Qatabān — such as false windows or little "shutters"[9] (Loreto 2008).

Types of stone work

Nomenclature connected with types of stone has proved to be quite scarce, but we should expect more precise definitions of stone working and finishing, in view of the great accuracy with which these techniques were utilized in ancient South Arabia. We have, at present, at least four words that have been identified as such.

For example, some of the terminology (verbal and nominal forms), which is created with the root GRB "body" (Fig. 4), is linked with building. It should also be remembered that the important class of "stonemasons" was indicated by the name *grby* in Hadramitic and in South Arabian inscriptions from Ethiopia (Frantsouzoff 2001, with its useful bibliography on previous works published on this subject). The verbal forms seem to be used especially in an agricultural context, where they probably indicated the walling of fields, both for enclosures and terraces. This usage suggests that this term was connected particularly with rough stone. In the late Sabaic documentation, from the fifth and sixth centuries AD, the term *grb* was used in connection with domestic architecture and in the works involving the Maʾrib dam (CIH 540; CIH 541; DAI GDN 2002-20).

As the mention of "stonemasons" suggests, Hadramitic offers several texts with this term, and this is particularly striking in view of the numerical scarcity of this epigraphical documentation. Here it appears mostly in connection with hydraulic and funerary monuments. The term *grb* is not attested in Minaic, and Qatabanic keeps it as a verb to describe agricultural activities.

All this data leads us to think that *grb* is the stonework that was linked with the rough material used in the foundation of buildings or in cases where a particular finish on the surface of the stone was not needed.

The nominal forms realized with root ᶜRB, in particular *mᶜrb* and *mᶜrbt* (pl.) (Fig. 5), have been generally associated with dressed stones. For this reason this terminology was readily identified archaeologically with those blocks hewn in a perfect parallelepiped shape (isodomic).

Minaic gives little evidence of these expressions, and then only in a defensive context. One example is, however, significant because it proves that this term indicated a particular type of technique: it is in fact in genitival link with the word for limestone material (*mᶜrbt blq*: Maᶜīn 51/1 from Qarnaw).

Sabaic has attestations concentrated in the late period (i.e. from the fifth century AD) and in the specialized domain of hydraulic constructions. In fact, RES 4069 mentions a restoration of the Maʾrib dam, which started off from this kind of stone (*bn mᶜrbt*), and for this reason it probably indicates those blocks in the lower part of the structure for which precise adherence between them guaranteed its solidity, being vital also for the good functioning of the construction (e.g. no water dispersion).

Hadramitic presents attestations related to both defensive and hydraulic contexts. Together with these, the text from Shaᶜab al-Layl, near Shabwa, allows us to identify the quarry from which the stone was extracted and from which it was later moved to the site itself, an operation expressed

it has yet to be adequately and extensively investigated. In the case of "alabaster", however, we have information from an Assyrian text from Suhu and, later, from the *Periplus Maris Erythraei*, that Southern Arabia was exporting this material even outside its geographical borders (Liverani 1992: 111–114).

[9] In the case of the Barʾān temple in Maʾrib, calcite-alabaster has also been used to construct monolithic benches (i.e. horizontal monolithic pillars for each row of seats: long rows can be constructed by interlocking more than one piece of stone). We should also differentiate between the two references to materials in the gate of Tamnaᶜ as follows: *blq* indicating the small decoration panels which represent a portion of masonry and *mwgl* the more elaborate decoration for false windows and shutters.

Language	Other materials combined	Attestations	Chronology	Archaeological context	Monument type
Sabaic	*mnhmt*	CIH 325/9	554 AD	?	Domestic
		CIH 537/4	467 AD	?	
		Fa 74 a+b/1	499 AD	?	
	lbt (bricks?) + *ʾzyy frzn* (iron clamps) + *brr* (?)	CIH 540/11-12	450 AD	Maʾrib Dam	
	gyr	DAI GDN 2002-20/29	494 AD	Maʾrib Dam	
	nhmt + *ṣhr* (plaster?) + *ḫfg* (?)	CIH 541/58–59	543 AD	Maʾrib Dam	
	gyr + *nhm*	Ja 2354/2–3	fifth century AD	Jabal Mġānīmeh	
Hadramitic	*nhmt*	Khor Rori 1/3	60 AD	Khor Rori Gate	Defensive
		RES 2687/2–3	second century BC ?	Al-Bināʾ Gate	

FIGURE 4. *grb*

Language	Other materials combined	Attestations	Chronology	Archaeological context	Monument type
Sabaic	*grb*	CIH 540/77	450 AD	Maʾrib Dam	Hydraulic
	mrt + *ṣhr* (plaster?)	Fa 90/2	?	?	
Hadramitic	*qṣ* (gypsum?)	CT 4/9	?	Ḥurayḍa Sʾyn Temple	Hydraulic

FIGURE 5. *mʿrb/mʿrbt*

by the verb *nql* (Shaʿab al-Layl/3: *nql mʿrb h-mbny*). The rough stone was probably later finished in the building area itself (Bessac 1998*b*: 231–232, 260–262).

Qatabanic, on the other hand, indirectly confirms this datum because until now, no proof of the use of such terminology has been found. In Qatabān, as stated above, the preferred material was granite, for which a precise geometrical finish was very hard to obtain. Again, one need only be reminded of the "cyclopic" blocks, which constitute the still visible foundation of both the main city gate (south-west) and the building TT1 in Tamnaʿ. A more precise shaping was attempted using smaller granite blocks, like those for some of the houses in the Market Square in Tamnaʿ (i.e. houses G and I). This isodomic finishing was certainly known about in Qatabān but it was connected with those few structures which were made of limestone and for which, at the moment, we have no Qatabanic textual evidence that could contribute to a clarification of the original lexical definition (see above).

Terms such as *mnhm*, *mnhmt*, and *nhmt* (from the root NHM) (Fig. 6) are usually found in opposition to *grb* both in Sabaic and Hadramitic, thus suggesting that they indicated a different stone working in respect to "rough stone". The old translations, like those in CIH, which rendered this antonym with "white and red stones", have now been completely abandoned since they did not take into consideration the actual archaeological context to which they referred. This words connection rather suggests that this root (NHM) indicates a more accurate working of the stone, which was very often realized for the blocks of the upper walls in contrast with those used for the base and foundations. This semantic content can also be sustained by the early Islamic attestation in the al-Hamdānī language (Al-Selwi 1987: 209). This terminology often appears in Sabaic inscriptions of the fifth and sixth centuries AD, which refer more often to domestic structures. In Hadramitic they are found especially in a defensive context. Minaic, on the other hand, has revealed only one example connected to this root, but the reading of it is very uncertain.[10]

[10] Maʿīn 7/4: *w-ywm* s^3*lʾ Wdm b-ṣrḥm ms*^{3}*nd ṭyb w-ʾfẓ[ḥ] w-ḏhb mwṯ b-n(h)mn* : "he dedicated to Wd in the curtain an inscription made in gold, silver and bronze fixed on the wall (?)" (Bron 1998: 45–48).

Language	Other materials combined	Attestations	Chronology	Archaeological context	Monument type
Sabaic	*mwgl*	Bayt al-Ašwal 4/7	504 AD	?	Domestic
	grb	CIH 325/9	554 AD	?	
		CIH 537/4	467 AD	?	
		Fa 74 a+b/1	499 AD	?	
	grb + *gyr*	Ja 2354/2–3	fifth century AD	Jabal Mġānīmeh	Hydraulic
	grb+ *ṣhr* (plaster?) + *ḫfg* (?)	CIH 541/58–59	543 AD	Maʾrib Dam	
Hadramitic	*grb*	Khor Rori 1/3	60 AD	Khor Rori Gate	Defensive
		RES 2687/2–3	second century BC ?	Al-Bināʾ Gate	

FIGURE 6. *nhm/nhmt/mnhmt*

Language	Other materials combined	Attestations	Chronology	Archaeological context	Monument type
Minaic	*ʿḍ*	M 169/1	?	Barāqish walls	Defensive
		M 247/1	fourth century BC	Barāqish walls	
		M 268/1	?	Barāqish walls	
		M 347/1	fourth century BC	Barāqish walls	
		Maʿīn 1/2	fourth century BC	Maʿīn Gate	
		Maʿīn 6/2	second century BC	Maʿīn Gate	
		Maʿīn 24/1	?	Maʿīn walls	
	ʿḍ + *ʾbn*	M 236/3	third century BC	Barāqish walls	
	ʿḍ + *blq*	M 185/2	fourth–third century BC	Barāqish walls	
		M 252/2	?	Barāqish walls	
	ʿḍ	Maʿīn 13/2	third century BC	Maʿīn walls	Domestic

FIGURE 7. *tqr*

The term *tqr* (Fig. 7) is proper to Minaic where it often describes the masonry of city walls. Minaic examples can be interpreted as a nominal form *ta*-, with prefix, from the root *WQR (with the loss of the first weak radical), which is also present in Sabaic but with a different usage.[11] This term in Minaic deserves a very central position within the sentences that named different building materials, here in a particularly specific way. As stated above, in Minaean defensive works only one kind of stone was used, i.e. limestone identified by the name *blq*. It is quite natural then to see in this terminology a reference not only to the type of stone but also the technique of finishing the ashlar masonry, a technique that was used particularly for blocks on the façade that were more visible and on the surfaces of which were lateral plain bands and a central pecking. This decoration shows different degrees of accuracy depending on the position of the rows of stone (more refined in the most visible and central blocks).

[11] CIH 438/1; CIH 601/14; CIH 947/4 (*wqr*); YMN 13/5 (*mwqrt*). The attestation of *tqr* in the Sabaean text RES 3918/2 is difficult as the text is not entirely legible. The attestation is therefore based on the perceptions of the first editor, so we cannot be totally sure of its presence here. Other attestations, like those from Ḥaṣī, could be also considered as homographs of the term we are dealing with, since their use is far removed from that observed in Minaic construction inscriptions (cf. MAFRAY-Ḥaṣī 1/9, 10). Note also the Hadramitic *mwqrt* "sculpted object ?" (RES 3512/3).

Other materials

In Minaic and Qatabanic inscriptions, especially those concerning defence, the term based on the root ʿḌ is mentioned among building materials. It has been

	Sabaic	Minaic	Qatabanic	Hadramitic
Types of stone	*ʾbn; blq; mwgl*	*ʾbn; blq*	*ʾbn; blq; mwgl*	*ʾbn; blq*
Stone working	*grb; mʿrb; mnhm*	*mʿrb; (nhm?); tqr*	–	*grb; mʿrb; nhm*
Other materials	*ʿḍ; ḥ*s^3s^3*; (lbn ?)*	*ʿḍ*	*ʿḍ; mrt*	*ʿḍ; ftl; (lbn ?)*

FIGURE 8. *The linguistic distribution of the materials cited.*

associated with "wood" thanks mainly to linguistic external comparisons. This material was certainly used in the ancient Yemen building tradition, especially to sustain structures in mud brick behind the wall façade, as in the case of the well-preserved Minaean city walls (Breton 1994: 27, 30–31). It is, however, only rarely found in archaeological contexts probably because of its scarce preservation but, although it is difficult to prove, the possibility of its reuse even in ancient times should also be considered, precisely because of its scarce availability, if we consider the present geographical conditions of the region (on this matter see Darles, this volume). The Minaic text M 203, for instance, clearly mentions this material just before *blq*, both being used during restoration works, which involved the hypostyle hall of the Nakraḥ temple. We cannot confirm at the moment that wood was used inside this area, but we cannot at the same time rule it out since it could have been inserted in some structure near the cellae, probably as some kind of finishing element, and then destroyed or removed.[12] We could also suppose that the mention of this term in this text follows the model of the city walls texts, but we should also remember that this word indicated something other than wood, which we cannot clarify at present.[13]

The last essential component in South Arabian building technique, mud bricks, is not very well defined and is linguistically scarce in the documentation. It should be stressed, firstly, that South Arabian does not have a word indicating this material common to all dialects. Hadramitic probably uses the term *ftl*, where Sabaic has *ḥ*s^3s^3, for which the etymological meaning of "straw" has been proposed, i.e. together with mud, one of the two components of brick (Garbini 1971: 306). The meaning of *mrt*, which seems to be typical of the Qatabanian region, is not clear at all, since it could be either a sort of plastering or clay (Avanzini 2004: 54). It is also attested in Minaic to indicate the material used in the manufacture of small objects (i.e. incense burners), which are likely to have been in pottery (Sima 2000: 299–301). Moreover, Minaic has not yet given us a word that could reasonably indicate mud bricks. We have, finally, some attestations of the term *lbn* in both Hadramitic and Sabaic, which is particularly fascinating since this same root indicates mud bricks in Arabic, but at present the two texts we have are not of great help in clarifying its meaning.[14]

Conclusions (Fig. 8)

Sabaic provides information about materials, especially the finishing processes, concentrated in texts of the late period, between the fourth and sixth centuries AD. We may conclude that this terminology entered the textual patterns only at this stage and consequently we lack lexical data to compare with the remains showing the Ancient Sabaean building tradition (Buffa 1996).

We can observe a consistency between the terminology used in one of the Ancient South Arabian languages with the materials actually present in the corresponding areas, as is evident in

[12] The situation concerning the Awwām temple in Maʾrib, to which text Ja 557/1 refers, has been recently clarified by the discovery of wood beam traces (Ibrahim 2006: 202).

[13] On the problems concerning this term, in particular those connected with the archaeological remains, see the remarks of Beeston (1979: 96–97) and Sima (2000: 290, n. 6).

[14] The sentence *lbn* s^2ms^1 (RES 2687/5) has been interpreted as "mud brick dried in the sun" (Breton 1994: 22, following Rhodokanakis), but this translation is highly dubious, because it could also be rendered as "for the grace of S^{2}ms^1" (see Avanzini 2008: 632). Avanzini (2008: 626) has also been followed concerning the chronological placement of this text (see Figures). The *lbt* seen in CIH 540 should be interpreted as a plural form of the root LBN with the final *nun* assimilated; it is cited in this hydraulic context alongside other materials, but here it seems somehow linked with a sort of "iron clamps" (*ʾzyym frznm*), so here again interpreting "mud bricks" is difficult (see the list of inscriptions below).

the lexicon concerning stone types in South Arabian documentation. Leaving apart *ʾbn*, also because it is shared by the entire Semitic world, both *blq* and *mwgl* seem mostly attested where the materials so defined were effectively available and used in constructions. Firstly, this kind of terminology needs to be analysed with extreme care with reference to the particular geological condition in a given area. Further discoveries of stone quarries may clarify the actual origin of the stones used in monuments. Secondly, the detection of some of the routes used for the supply of material will also help to gain a better understanding of the differences in building traditions and techniques. This aspect seems less well defined in the analysis of stone-finishing processes, which could be, at least hypothetically, applicable to stones of a different origin. Nevertheless, the terminology that seems to express working with stone is less homogeneous, and we can furthermore identify some isogloss in its distribution. A stronger lexical continuity seems to unite Sabaic with Hadramitic, as can be seen in the case of a pair of terms, *grb* and *mnhm*, that are frequently used in combination only in Sabaic and Hadramitic. In these two linguistic areas we also have the most widespread use of the term *mʿrb*, even if in Sabaic its use seems to be more specialized (for hydraulic structures) than it is in Hadramitic.

The few attestations we have for *mʿrb* do not at this stage allow us to establish its archaeological identification and its actual difference from the term *mnhm*. Identification would be of great value since these two terms seem to have a sort of semantic closeness, as revealed by their usage and the contexts available.

Minaic seems to show a greater originality in recording the materials employed, using a lexicon peculiar to this language, as the frequent use of the term *tqr* demonstrates. This term could also be seen as the counterpart of the Sabaic/Hadramitic *mnhm* in indicating ashlar masonry, which is one of the most typical features of South Arabian stonework (van Beek 1958; Wright 1987).

The great architectonic tradition of ancient South Arabia is revealed by imposing remains and by a strong survival even in the more recent Yemenite constructions. The epigraphical documentation we have at the moment allows only a limited reconstruction of the ancient lexicography used for building materials and their use: this must almost certainly have been more complex, as is always the case when a technique achieves such a stage of development.

List of inscriptions cited in the figures (listed alphabetically)

Bayt al-Ašwal 4 (4–7): ... *brʾw w-hqs^{2}bn w-ṯwbn byt-hmw S^{2}bʿn bn mwṯr-hw ʿdy ṯfrʿ-hw w-hqs^{2}bw b-hw mbhʾtm b-m* ***nhmtm*** *w-**mwglm*** ...

CIAS 47.11/b2 (1–2): ... *bny w-s^{1}ḥdṯ kl mbny w-mhlk [ḫ](lf)n (ḏ-S^3)dw w-nmr-s^{1}ww Ḥmrr w-S^{2}ḫb* ***ʾbn**-s^1 w-**blq**-s^1 w-**ʿḍ**-s^1 w-**mr(t)**[-s^1 ...]*

CIH 325 (1–3): *[... g]**rbm** w-**rbʿtm mwg(l)m** w-(fṯḥm) [...](ṣ)lt-hw ḏ-s^{1}n ms^{3}wdn ʿlyn w-wzʾw ʿḏ[b ...] wlm l-gyrmw ṯfrʿ-hw w-hwʿbw kl qh yr[...]* (8-9): ... *w-qṣʿw ḥṣm-hw lb(ḫ)[...]ḏ ḫgrm w-wṯn ʿkm w-kl qh-hw **mnhmtm** w-**(grb)m** ḫb[...]*

CIH 448 (1–2): *[...] w-hdb w-hqs^2[b ...] gnʾ w-ṣwbt w-mḥfdt hgr-hmw Hkrm w-hdbw-hw w-brʾ w-ḥẓyn mbrʾ [...] mbrʾm **ḥs^{3}s^{3}m** w-**ʾbnm** [...]*

CIH 537 [+RES 4919] (3-5): ... *br(ʾ)[w] [w- ... by]t-hmw Rymn ʾḫrm ʾs^{1}q(f)m **grbm** w-**mnhmtm** bn mwṯ[r-hw ...] ... w-ʿrbw w-s^{1}tqfw* ...

CIH 540 (11–13): ... *w- ʿḏbw mḏʾbn bn s^{1}fl-hw w-ẓr-hw mbrʾm **grbm** w-**lbtm** w-ʾzyym frznm w-brrm mhbḏlm b-**lbt** ʾzyyn* ...(24-25): ... *w-ʿḏbw ʿwdn ḏ-mbrʾn w-**gyrn** ḏ-s^{3}n wdyn* ...(28-30): ... *hs^{2}qr-hw w-zlw ms^{1}rn w-s^{2}ṣnn b-s^{1}bʿt w-ʿs^{2}ry ymtm w-tqh-hw w-fqḥ mḏrft ḏ-[ʾ]fn **ʾbnm** w-**gyrm*** ...(62-63): ... *w-nmryn w-ʿwdn w-ʿrmn w-ḏʾfn bn mwṯr-hw mbrʾn w-**grbn*** ... (73-79): ... *w-s^{2}ṣnm b-ʾʾ**bnm** w-s^{2}mw **ʿrḍ** rʾs^1-hw s^{1}ṯ ʾmm w-brʾw ʿglmn w-nmryn ḥrṣm b-**grbm** w-**lbtm** w-ʾzyym frznm w-ʿwdn brʾw b-**mʿrbtm** w-**[grbm]** w-k-lmdw kl ʿglmn w-nmryn w-ʿwdn b-**gyrm*** ...

CIH 541 (55–61): ... *w-mlkn ḏky ʿẓtm ʿly ʾs^{2}ʿbn l-ḥrrtm w-ms^{1}rm w-**grbtm** w-brʾm w-**ḫfgm** w-**nhmt** w-**ṣhrm** l-ʿḏbn ʿrmn w-ʿwdn w-mṯbrtn ḏ-b-Mrb* ...

CT 4 (5–9): ... *w-s^{1}ḥds^3 w-gs^{1}m b-ʾmnt-s^{1}mn bʾrhn S^{2}ʿbt w-s^{1}ʿqb-s^3 rḥhtm w-mdrr w-mqld w-ʾʿtbm w-b-**(qṣ)m** w-**mʿrb*** ...

DAI GDN 2002-20 (27–30): ... *w-hs^{2}qr-hw b-ʿḏr-hw mbrʾm b-**grbm** w-**gyrm** mbrʾm* ...

Fa 74 a+b (1): ... *w-brʾw kl **grb** w-**mnhmt** byt-hmw Ykrb* ...

Fa 90 (2): *[... **mʿ**]**rbt** (w-)s^{3}ftn **mrtn** w-**ṣhr**[**n** ...]*

Ḥuwaydar 1 (4–6): ... *bny w-gnʾ w-ṣyr w-s^{1}ḥdṯ gnʾ w-m(ḥ)fd hgrn ʿbr glm **ʾbnm** w-**ʿḍm** w-**blqm** bn s^{2}rs^{1}m ʿd frʿm*

Ja 557 (1): ... *w-bny w-mlʾ tmlʾ nṯʿ hmlʾn w-hws^{3}qn gnʾ ʾwm ln ḏn ʾwdn ḏ-sṭrn w-rymm kl **blq**-hw w-**ʿḍ**-hw* ...

Ja 2354 (2–4): ... *kbr **nhmn** w-brʾn w-**mgyrtn** w-**grbtn** w-tqdm ʾrḍ-hw b-ḏn mʾgln Bnʾ* ...

Khor Rori 1 (2–4): ... *qtdm hgrhn S^{1}mrm* ***grbt-ṯ*** *w-****nhmt-ṯ*** *w-hyʿ-ṯ bn rbbm ʾd s^{2}qrm* ...

M 164 (2): ... ***ʾbnm*** *w-****ʿḏm*** *w-****blqm*** *qdmm w-mʿ[...] mbny mḥfdn* ...

M 169 (1): *[... ʿ]****ḏm*** *w-****tqrm*** *bn ʾs^{2}rs^1 ʿd s^{2}qrn* ...

M 185 (1–2): ... *bny w-s^{3}lʾ w-s^{1}ḥdṯ b-gnʾ hgrn Yṯl kl tẓwrt mḥfdn ḏ-Bqrn w-tẓwr ṣḥft S^{1}lfʾlhn ḏt ḏ-Ndbn w-tẓwr ṣḥfth ḏ-S^{2}ftn qdmm w-mʿḏrm* ***ʿḏm*** *w-****tqrm*** *w-****blqm*** ...

M 203 (1–4): ... *s^{3}lʾ w-bny w-s^{1}ḥdṯ k-Nkrḥ s^{2}ymh-s^{1}m kl s^{1}qf w-bynt ʾtḥn w-ʿ(l)ly w-s^{1}ʿḏb kl ḏ-ḫḫbl b-mknt s^{2}ymn [...] gwn b-gwbn* ***ʿḏm*** *w-****blqm*** *w-mṣrby w-(t) wṭbt w-zlty mkntn w-ʾtḥn w-qbly ḫbl b-s^{1}qfh qr(q)r b-(m) gwbn* ...

M 236 (2–3): *[... ʿ]****ḏ*** *w-mʿḏr-s^1* ***ʾbnm*** *bn w(s^1)[ṯ] hgrn w-kl* ***ʿḏ****-s^{1}w w-****t[qr-****s^1 ... bn ʾ]s^{2}rs^1 ʿd s^{2}rqn* ...

M 247 (1): ... *s^{3}lʾ w-bny w-s^{1}qny k-ʿṯtr ḏ-Qbḍm ṣḥftn Tnʿm ʾnf mws^{1}m* ***ʿḏ*** *w-****tqrm*** *bn ʾs^{2}rs^1 ʿd s^{2}qrn w-mʿḏr-s^1* ***ʾbnm*** *kl ṣḥft byn mḥfdnyhn Ẓrbn w-Lbʾn* ...

M 252 (1–3): *[...](qw)d w-mʿḏrm [...](n)m bn w(s^1)ṯ[...] rdʿm* ***blqm*** *w-****ʿḏm*** *w-****tqrm*** *w-[...]w w-ʾḥṭb-s^1 s^{2}ʾml-s^1* ...

M 268 (1): *[...] ṣ(ḥ)ftn Ts^2(b)m* ***ʿḏm (w-t)qrm*** *[...]*

M 283 (3–4): ... *s^{3}lʾ w-s^{1}qny ... kl mbny ṣḥftn Ddn* ***ʾbnm*** *w-****ʿḏm*** *qdmm w-mʿḏrm bn ʾs^{2}rs^1 ʿd s^{2}qrn* ...

M 347 (1): ... *kl mbny ṣḥftn Mḏb bn ʾs^{2}rs^1 ʿd s^{2}qrn ʾnf mws^{1}m qdm w-mʿḏr* ***ʿḏm*** *w-****tqr*** ...

Maʿīn 1 (1–2): ... *s^{3}lʾ w-bny w-s^{1}qny ... kl tʿly w-tẓwr s^{1}dṯ ṣḥfm w-s^{1}dṯt mḥfdt b-gnʾ hgrn Qrnw b-qlḥ rbʿn Rms^{3}w bn mḥfd bny ḥfy nfs^1 ʿd s^{2}lwṯ hgrn ḏ-bny w-ʿlly ḏ-Ẓll* ***ʿḏm*** *w-****tqrm*** *w-(ḫb)zt mʿḏrh-s^{1}m bn mbny qdmn ʿd s^{2}qrn* ...

Maʿīn 6 (2, 4): ... *s^{3}lʾ w-s^{1}qny ... kl mbny mḥfdn Yhr w-ṣḥft-s^1 Rtʿ* ***ʿḏm*** *w-****tqrm*** *bn ʾs^{2}rs^1 ʿd s^{2}qrn ... w-ywm bny w-s^{3}lʾ ... s^{2}lṯy ʾmhm b-gnʾ Yṯl* ***tqrm*** *bn ʾs^{2}rs^1 ʿd s^{2}qrn* ...

Maʿīn 7 (2-3): ... *s^{3}lʾ ʿ(t)tr ḏ-Qbḍm kl mbny mḥfdn Yhr* ***ʾbnm*** *w-****ʿḏm*** *ʿd s^{2}qrn* ...

Maʿīn 13 (2–3): ... *ʿs^{1}y w-bny* ***ʿḏ*** *w-****tqr*** *byt-s^1 Yfs^2 w-ṣrḥt-s^1 w-mṣbḥ-s^1 w-mnḫl-s^1 w-kl mhn qny bytn bn rmdn ʿd ṣnqn b-ʾs^{3}nnh-s^1* ...

Maʿīn 24 (1): *[... ʾn]f mws^{1}mm w-****ʿḏm*** *w-****tqrm*** *qdmm w-m(ʿḏrm)[...]*

Maʿīn 51 (10): ... *b-mbny ḏt ṣḥftn* ***mʿrbt blq*** *ʾnf* ...

Naqb al-Hajar 2 (1–2): ... *q(t)dm mbny gnʾ Myfʿt w-ḫ(l)f-ṯ* ***ʾbnm*** *(w-ʿ)****ḏm*** *w-****ftlm*** *(w-)mbny ʾbyt ʿl(ʾ)hy gnʾ-ṯ hn (ʿ)s^{1}nm ʾd (m)nʿym* ...

RES 2687 (2–5): ... *h-b(n)ʾ ʿqbthn Qlt w-ʿqb Ḥgr ʿlhtyhn bn bḥrhn qdmm ʿlhy* ***grbt*** *w-****(nh)mt*** *w-gs^{1}mhy gnʾ Qlt w-ʿqb(h)n (m)t ḥḏrw ... w-bny w-yʿr ʿqb Ḍyfthn w-bny gnʾhn w-mḥfdyhn Yḏʾn w-Yḏtʾn w-ḫlfhn Ykn b-****mʿrb*** *ws^{3}dm w-ḍwym [...] w-ʾbry bn-mw rbbm ʾd s^{2}qrm bn-mw lbn S^{2}ms^1* ...

RES 3869 (2–3): ... *qtdm w-gs^{1}m gnʾ Myfʿt* ***ʾbnm*** *w-****ʿḏm*** *w-****ftlm*** ...

RES 3880 (5–7): ... *bny w-s^{1}ḥd[ṯ kl mhl]k w-mbny* ***ʾbnw*** *w-****ʿḏ*** *w-****blq*** *w-****mrt*** *w-****ʿwt*** *mʿs^{2}q ms^{2}mn* ...

Timnaʿ MAFYS 1 (3–5): ... *bny w-s^1[ḥdṯ](S^1)qrw w-nmr-s^{1}ww w-mḏqnt-s^1* ***ʾbn****-s^1* *w-****ʿḏ****-s^1* *w-****mwgl****-s^1* *w-****mrt****-s^1* *w-****blq****-s^1* *w-kl ḏ-[...] (w-)ts^{2}rʿ-s^1* ...

Acknowledgements

I wish to thank in particular Alessandro de Maigret, Christian Darles, Zaydoon Zayd, and Alexandra Porter, whose advice and suggestions on archaeological matters contributed to improve the present paper. Any error or inaccuracy is of course my own responsibility.

Sigla[15]

Bayt al-Aświal 4	Garbini 1970: 545–547, pls 43–44.
CIAS 47.11.b2	Pirenne 1977: 109–116.
CIH	*Corpus Inscriptionum Semiticarum. Pars IV. Inscriptiones Ḥimyariticas et Sabaeas continens*. Paris: Imprimerie nationale, 1889–1932.
CT 4	Caton Thompson 1944: 158–160, pl. 63.
DAI GDN 2002–20	Nebes 2004: 221–225, figs 2 a–b.
Fa 74a+b, 90	Fakhry 1952: 46–49, 59.
Ḥuwaydar 1	Pirenne 1981: 226–227, pl. 12 (see also Avanzini 2004: 67–68).
Ja 557	Jamme 1962: 22–23.
Ja 2354	Jamme 1971: 88.
Khor Rori 1	The most recent edition of this text is in Avanzini 2002: 128–130, figs 3–4 (as KR2).
M	Garbini 1974.
Maʿīn	Bron 1998.
MAFRAY-Ḥaṣī 1	Robin 2001: 182–191, figs 2–14, 30.

[15] For other bibliographical references, concerning each text cited, see Kitchen 2000 who has also been followed for the chronology of inscriptions, although in many cases this is still a matter of debate.

Naqb al-Hajar 2	Robin 1987: 18–19, fig. 9.
RAMRY/94-al-Zālif 1 no.1	Frantsouzoff 2005: 196–198, pl. 48.
RES	*Répertoire d'épigraphie sémitique.* Paris: Imprimerie nationale, 1900–1968.
Shaʿab al-Layl	Pirenne 1990: 49–50, fig. 15.
Timnaʿ-MAFYS 1	Bron 1999.
YMN 13	ʿAbdallāh 1979: 45–50, fig. on p. 59.

References

ʿAbdallāh Y.M.

1979. Mudawwanat an-nuqūsh als-yaminiyya al-qadīma. *Dirāsāt Yamaniyya* 3: 29–72.

Agostini A.

2008. Le iscrizioni di costruzione sudarabiche. Lessico, archeologia, società. PhD thesis, Università degli Studi di Firenze, Dipartimento di Linguistica, Florence. [Unpublished].

2009. Il "costruire" nelle iscrizioni sudarabiche. A proposito dei verbi *bny* e *brʾ*. *Quaderni del Dipartimento di Linguistica. Università di Firenze* 19: 1–20.

Avanzini A.

1987. For a Study on the Formulary of Construction Inscriptions. Pages 11–20 in C. Robin & M. Bāfaqīh (eds), *Ṣayhadica. Recherches sur les inscriptions de l'Arabie préislamique offertes par ses collègues au Professeur A.F.L. Beeston*. Paris: Geuthner.

2002. The construction inscriptions on the gate complex. Pages 125–140 in A. Avanzini (ed.), *Khor Rori Report* 1. Pisa: Edizioni Plus/Università di Pisa.

2004. *Corpus of South Arabian Inscriptions I–III.* Pisa: Edizioni Plus/Università di Pisa.

2008. Notes for a history of Sumhuram and a new inscription of Yashhurʾil. Pages 609–641 in A. Avanzini (ed.), *A port in Arabia between Rome and the Indian Ocean (3rd C. BC–5th C. AD)*. (Khor Rori Report, 2). Rome: "L'Erma" di Bretschneider.

Barr J.

1968. The ancient Semitic languages — The conflict between philology and linguistics. *Transactions of the Philological Society* 67: 37–55.

Beeston A.F.L.

1979. Studies in Sabaic Lexicography I. *Raydān* 2: 89–100.

Bessac J-C.

1998*a*. Techniques de construction, de gravure et d'ornementation en pierre dans le Jawf. Pages 173–230 in J-F. Breton (ed.), *Fouilles de Shabwa III. Architecture et techniques de construction.* Beirut: Institut Français d'Archéologie du Proche Orient.

1998*b*. Le travail de la pierre à Shabwa. Pages 231–282 in J-F. Breton (ed.), *Fouilles de Shabwa III. Architecture et techniques de construction.* Beirut: Institut Français d'Archéologie du Proche Orient.

Breton J-F.

1994. *Les Fortifications d'Arabie méridionale du 7e au 1er siècle avant notre ère.* (= Archäologische Berichte aus dem Yemen, 8). Mainz: Phillip von Zabern.

Bron F.

1998. *Inventaire des Inscriptions sudarabiques.* iii. *Maʿīn.* Paris: Académie des Inscriptions et Belles Lettres/ Rome: IsIAO.

1999. L'inscription qatabanite de la porte nord de Tamnaʿ. Pages 69–74 in Y. Avishur & R. Deutsch (eds), *Michael. Historical, Epigraphical and Biblical Studies in Honor of Prof. Michael Heltzer.* Tel Aviv/ Jaffa: Archaeological Center Publications.

Brunner U.

1989. Bausteine der Sabäer. *Sonderdruck aus Münchner Beiträge zur Völkerkunde* 2: 27–42.

2002. The Geography and Economy of the Sabaean Homeland. *Archaölogische Berichte aus dem Yemen* 10: 1–6.

Buffa V.
1996. Note per una tipologia delle tecniche costruttive del periodo sudarabico antico. Pages 165–177 in C. Robin & I. Gajda (eds), *Arabia Antiqua. Early Origins of South Arabian States.* Rome: IsMEO.

Caton Thompson G.
1944. *The Tombs and Moon Temple of Hureidha (Ḥaḍramawt).* (Reports of the Research Committee of the Society of Antiquaries of London, 13). Oxford: University Press.

Cohen D.
1970. *Dictionnaire des racines sémitiques ou attestées dans les langues sémitiques. Comprenant un fichier comparatif de Jean Cantineau.* (With the collaboration of F. Bron and A. Lonnet from fasc. 3. i [1970]; ii [1996]). Paris: Leuven/Mouton: Peeters.

Darles C.
2009. Les monolithes dans l'architecture monumentale de l'Arabie du Sud antique. *Proceedings of the Seminar for Arabian Studies* 39: 95–110.
(in this volume). L'emploi du bois dans l'architecture du Yémen antique. *Proceedings of the Seminar for Arabian Studies* 40

de Maigret A.
2003. Tamnaᶜ, ancient capital of the Yemeni desert. Information about the first two excavation campaigns (1999, 2000). Pages 135–140 in M. Liverani (ed.), *"Arid Lands in Roman Times". Papers from the International Conference (Rome, July 9th–10th 2001).* (Arid Zone Archaeology, Monographs 4). Florence: All'insegna del giglio.

de Maigret A. & Robin C.
2006. *Tamnaᶜ, antica capitale di Qatabān/Tamnaᶜ, capitale antique de Qatabān.* Ṣanᶜāʾ: Yemeni-Italian Centre for Archaeological Research.

Fakhry A.
1952. *An archaeological Journey to Yemen (March–May 1947).* Part II. G. Ryckmans, *Epigraphical Texts.* Cairo: Goverment Press.

Frantsouzoff S.
2001. La mention du "tailleur de pierre" (*grby-n/hn*) dans les inscriptions sudarabiques. *Raydān* 7: 125–143.
2005. Epigraphic documentation from Ḥaḍramawt. Pages 193–216 in A.V. Sedov, *Temples of Ancient Ḥaḍramawt.* Pisa: Edizioni Plus/Università di Pisa.

Garbini G.
1970. Antichità yemenite II. *Annali dell'Istituto Orientale di Napoli* 30 [N.S. 20]: 537–548.
1971. Iscrizioni sabee da Hakir. *Annali dell'Istituto Orientale di Napoli* 31 [N.S. 21]: 303–311.
1974. *Iscrizioni sudarabiche I. Iscrizioni minee.* (Publicazioni del Seminario di Semitistica, Istituto Orientale di Napoli. Ricerche, 10). Naples: Istituto Orientale.

Ibrahim M.M.
2006. Report in the 2005 AFSM excavations in the Ovoid Precinct at Maḥram Bilqīs Mārib: preliminary report. *Proceedings of the Seminar for Arabian Studies* 36: 199–216.

Jamme A.
1962. *Sabaean Inscriptions from Maḥram Bilqīs (Mārib).* (Publication of the American Foundation for the Study of Man, 3). Baltimore, MD: Johns Hopkins Press.
1971. *Miscellanées d'ancient (sic) arabe.* II. Washington D.C. [Privately printed].

Kitchen K.A.
2000. *Documentation for Ancient Arabia. Part II: A Bibliographical Catalogue of Texts.* Liverpool: Liverpool University Press.

Liverani M.
1992. Early Caravan Trade between South Arabia and Mesopotamia. *Yemen: Studi archeologici, storici e filologici sull'Arabia Meridionale*: 1: 111–115.

Loreto R.
2008. Architectural decorations from the private buildings in the Market Square at Tamnaᶜ. *Arabian Archaeology and Epigraphy* 19: 22–47.

Nebes N.
2004. A new ʾAbraha inscription from the Great Dam of Mārib. *Proceedings of the Seminar for Arabian Studies* 34: 221–230.

Pirenne J.
1977. *Corpus des inscriptions et antiquités sud-arabes*. Louvain: Peeters.
1981. Deux prospections historiques au sud-Yémen. *Raydān* 4: 205–240.
1990. *Fouilles de Shabwa I. Les témoins écrits de la région de Shabwa et l'histoire*. Paris: Geuthner.

Robin C.
1979. À propos des inscriptions *in situ* de Barāqish, l'antique Yṯl (Nord-Yémen). *Proceedings of the Seminar for Arabian Studies* 9: 102–112.
1987. Naqab al-Hajar. Les inscriptions. *Syria* 64: 17–20.
2001. Les inscriptions de Ḥaṣī. *Raydān* 7: 179–206.

Al-Selwi I.
1987. *Jemenitische Wörter in den Werken von al-Hamdānī und Našwān und ihre Parallelen in den semitischen Sprachen*. (Marburger Studien zur Africa- und Asienkunde). Berlin: Dietrich Reimer.

Sima A.
2000. *Tiere, Pflanzen, Steine und Metalle in den altsüdarabischen Inschriften. Eine lexikalische und realienkundliche Untersuchung*. Wiesbaden: Harrassowitz.

Simpson StJ. (ed.).
2002. *Queen of Sheba. Treasures from Ancient Yemen*. London: British Museum Press.

van Beek G.
1958. Marginally Drafted, Pecked Masonry. Pages 287–295 in L. Bowen & F.B. Albright (eds), *Archaeological Discoveries in South Arabia*. Baltimore, MD: American Foundation for the Study of Man.

Weiss C., O'Neill D.A., Koch R. & Gerlach I.
2009. Petrological characterisation of "alabaster" from the Marib province in Yemen and its use as an ornamental stone in Sabaean culture. *Arabian Archaeology and Epigraphy*, 20: 54–63.

Wright G.R.H.
1987. Some Preliminary Observations on the Masonry Work at Mārib. *Archäologische Berichte aus dem Yemen* 4: 63–78.

Author's address

Dr Alessio Agostini, c/o Università degli Studi di Firenze, Dipartimento di Linguistica, Piazza Brunelleschi 3-4, 50121, Florence, Italy.

e-mail ale.agostini@inwind.it

Proceedings of the Seminar for Arabian Studies 40 (2010): 99–110

Conflation of celestial and physical topographies in the Omani decorated *miḥrāb*

Soumyen Bandyopadhyay

Summary

This paper discusses the role and overlapping meaning of two key themes persistent within the Omani decorative tradition, stars and date palms, by focusing on the decorated prayer niches (*maḥārīb*, sg. *miḥrāb*) of Oman. It also addresses the close connection between conceptions of topography in Omani culture and the articulation of thresholds, both sacred and domestic. The paper argues that an attempt to connect the celestial and physical topographic conceptions that is at the heart of the complex water distribution strategy of the *aflāj* irrigation system also prevails in the *miḥrāb*. The Ibadī artisan of Oman integrated representations of both continuous and instantaneous time employing the endless knot and stellar motifs. Emphasizing the sacred nature of time and light as divine attributes or essence of God, the *miḥrāb* sought to represent a celestial topography, which was made possible through Ibadī analogical interpretations of anthropomorphism in the Qurʾān and an expanding influence of mysticism amongst Omani scholars. Omani *miḥrāb* and door decoration shows a close affinity between stellar and date-palm representations, the latter also held in sacred esteem in Oman. The *aflāj* irrigation system once depended significantly on the position of stars in the night sky to ensure the distribution of water. The interchangeable representation suggests a conflation of the terrestrial topography of the oasis and the celestial topography. The horizon mediated this relationship, acting as a threshold through which the celestial bodies had to pass to be meaningfully associated with the terrestrial topography. Appearing as woven tapestries or bounded spatial representations, both the *miḥrāb* and the Omani doorway decoration mark a threshold in the sacred and secular passage.

Keywords: *miḥrāb*, Oman, Ibadī, topography, threshold

Introduction

This paper aims to discuss two key themes persistent within the decorative tradition of Omani architecture, stars and date palms. It is an attempt to understand the role and overlapping meaning of these motifs within the traditional architectural context by focusing on the decorated prayer niches (*maḥārīb*) of central Oman. The sudden appearance in 1252 of such a decorative *miḥrāb* tradition in Saʿāl, Nizwah, its disappearance immediately thereafter, and its subsequent equally surprising revival in Manaḥ in the early sixteenth century, unique in many respects in the Arabian Peninsula, raises many questions, especially in view of the prevalent Ibāḍī ideals of asceticism, for they strove for simplicity and austerity in their mosques. The paper attempts to connect the celestial and physical topographic conceptions that are at the heart of the complex water distribution strategy of the *aflāj* irrigation system with those that prevail in the *miḥrāb*. The paper also aims to study the close connection between these topographic conceptions and the articulation of thresholds — both sacred and domestic.

Likely influences

The sudden appearance of these motifs could suggest the importation of foreign artisans who delivered the first *miḥrāb* in its finished and highly developed form under local Omani patronage, or it could well be that all previous attempts to refine the motifs were lost during the period of extreme turmoil that characterized central Oman in the thirteenth and fourteenth centuries.[1] Kervran has suggested that the sixteenth-century Omani artisans were employing "out-of-date" Saljūq and Mongol Iranian models of the tenth to fourteenth centuries (1996: 109), making the influence contemporaneous with thirteenth-century Saʿāl. It is likely that the first *miḥrāb* at Saʿāl was a result of patronage of the Nabāhinah rulers of central Oman, who were well established in Nizwah during its

[1] J.C. Wilkinson (1987) has discussed the chaos and political complexity that prevailed in central Oman from the thirteenth until the fifteenth centuries, as Ibāḍī imamate power collapsed and the Nabāhinah and various local rulers vied for control over Omani towns and villages. The Ibāḍī historians have tended to describe this interregnum of 250 years as the "dark age" of Omani history.

execution (Bandyopadhyay 2008). As vassals under the Buyid occupying forces in the Ṣuḥārī hinterland, it is people from the early Nabāhinah period who appear to have first come into contact with the Persian tradition of *miḥrāb* decoration, exemplified by al-Muqaddasī's description of the striking metal polychrome faïence lustre decoration in Ṣuḥār's grand mosque (Kervran 1996: 112).

Kanaᶜan, on the other hand, has suggested a possible Yemeni Ṣulayḥid (1038–1138) and Rasūlid (1229–1454) influence, especially on the Saᶜāl *miḥrāb* and the intrusion of Fatimid Shīᶜī and Ayyubid artistic traditions by proxy (Kanaᶜan 2008). While both claims require further careful examination and substantiation,[2] these nevertheless suggest a wider Shīᶜī influence in the region to which the al-Dākhiliyyah and al-Sharqiyyah regions of Oman were subjected. Given the nature of Ibāḍī theological traditions that prevailed, it is probable that the Shīᶜī influence remained largely limited to a formal and aesthetic one, although it is difficult to accept a complete divorce between theological trajectories and their artistic manifestations. The later attempts at concealing (by painting over in green), damaging, or even removing early sixteenth-century ceramic bowl insertions suggest at least an implicit understanding among Ibāḍīs of what these artistic moves might have connoted. Broadly following the foreign schema, the Omani artisans conflated expressive and representative aspects of indigenous agricultural traditions at hand.

Two important factors could have contributed to the acceptance of this unique art form into the Omani mosque in the mid-thirteenth century. The first factor was the theological debate concerning the allegation of dynastic succession of the Yaḥmad tribe to the office of the imam. This debate split the Ibāḍī community in Oman into an extremist "Rustāq School" of ascetic ᶜ*ulamā*ᵓ, opposed by a moderate "Nizwah School", characterized by flexibility and pragmatism. The "Nizwah School" received support from the early Nabāhinah *umarā*ᵓ (sg. *amīr*) or *mulūk* (sg. *malik*) of Nizwah, who were busy establishing themselves politically, and in opposition to the Yaḥmadī dominance of the imamate (Bandyopadhyay 2008: 374).

The second factor was the development of mystical traditions in Islam from the mid-ninth century onwards and their subsequent rapid extension across Arabia and Persia in the eleventh and twelfth centuries following al-Junayd's (830–910) development of a new language of "sobriety" (*ṣaḥw*) to describe mystical experience, which eventually made such traditions acceptable to the puritanical ascetics and traditionalists (Melchert 1996: 66–70).[3] Celestial imagery became associated with the appearance of the Kaᶜbah, especially in the mystical poetry of the Arabs and the Persians from the tenth century onwards, where the Kaᶜbah was often treated as a female or a bride surrounded by her companions, the days and nights, and the stars and the planets (Beelaert 1988–1989).[4] For example, Beelaert, quoting Burton, cites the eleventh-century minor Arab poet, ᶜAbd al-Raḥīm al-Buraᶜī: "And Meccah's bride (i.e. the Kaᶜabah) is displayed with (miraculous) signs" (1988–1989: 109). This mystical poetic strand appears to persist into the early thirteenth-century Arabic poetry concerned with pilgrimage to Mecca. Ibn Jubayr (1145–1217) in his *Riḥlah* makes allusions not only to the idea of the Kaᶜbah being a bride but the Black Stone being a beloved with attractive sensual properties (1988–1989: 109). That the medieval Omani Ibāḍīs might have been influenced by such mystical thoughts, could be suggested as a possibility from parallel influences among contemporary Maghribi Ibāḍī scholars (Hoffman, personal communication, 2005)

[2] Largely due to the Ibāḍī historians' depiction of Nabāhinah rulers as tyrants and characterization of the period as the "dark ages" of Omani history, much of Nabāhinah history and its details still remains unclear. The evidence of the influence of Ḥaḍramī and Yemeni theological and architectural thoughts on Omani Ibāḍīs during the period in question is equally difficult to ascertain (Hoffman, personal communication, 2005). Hoffman, however, noted that the modern Ibāḍīs and Shāfiᶜīs in Zanzibar intermingled, the latter with strong links to Ḥaḍramawt. She also found a nineteenth-century Ibāḍī scholar's commentary on a poem by an important Ṣūfī Sayyid of the Ḥaḍramawt.

[3] As Hoffman mentions, "the type of Sufism that appeals most to the Omani Ibāḍīs is that of al-Junayd, ᶜAbd al-Qādir al-Jīlānī [1077/8–1166], and al-Ghazālī [1058–1111], but they also read and enjoy Ibn al-Fāriḍ's [1181–1235] poetry" (Hoffman, personal communication, 2005).

[4] Beelaert (1988–1989: 112) cites a *qaṣīda* from the Persian poet Khāqānī Shirwānī (1127–1199) in this regard:

The Kaᶜbah is the queen of the two worlds, see how for her in this green tent/
the seven women came as chambermaids.
Morning and evening are two slaves for her, named "Pearl" and "Amber"/
Although they came as commanding officers, this one from Abyssinia, that one from Byzantium.
Her slaves are her Atabegs for her two children/
for one of these children the cradle is Babylon, for the other the cradle is Khurasan.
The musk-coloured mole on the wheat-coloured face of the Arabian queen/
grants the lovers their desires and conquers their hearts.

He interprets "the seven women came as chambermaids" as the seven planets and "her two children" as the moon and the sun (Beelaert 1988–1989: 122; nn. 29 & 30).

Figure 1. *The earliest extant* miḥrāb *in Oman at the Masjid al-Jāmaᶜ in Saᶜāl, Nizwa dated to 1252 and recently restored.*

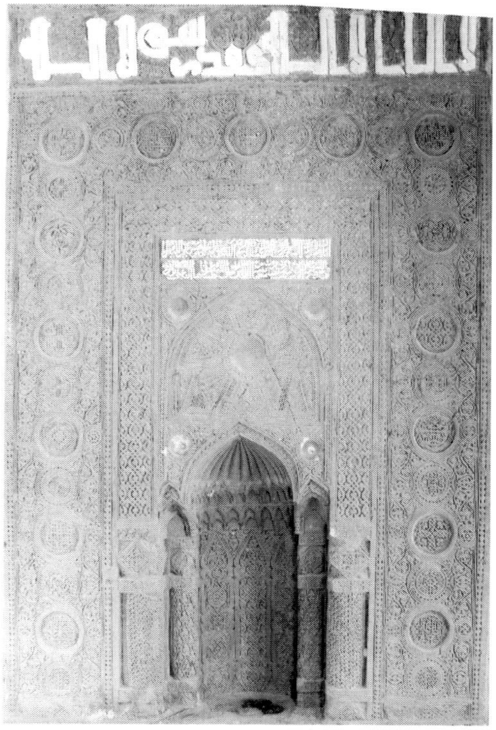

Figure 2. *The* miḥrāb *of Masjid al-Sharah, Ḥārat al-Bilād, Manaḥ showing an early sixteenth-century decorated prayer niche. Note the missing porcelain bowl inserts and the later application of green paint.*

and more overt mystical leanings among modern Ibāḍī scholars from the eighteenth century onwards (Hoffman 2004), which I discuss later.

The Omani decorated *miḥrāb*

While the characteristics of the decorated *maḥārīb* of central Oman (Fig. 1) have been discussed elsewhere in some detail (e.g. Baldissira 1994; Kervran 1996; Bandyopadhyay 1998; Costa 2001; Kanaᶜan 2008), the main features could be summarized here from the earliest examples from Saᶜāl in Nizwah (mid-thirteenth century) and those thereafter from Manaḥ (early sixteenth century). Just over two and a half centuries separate the first example at Nizwah (Friday Mosque [*masjid al-jāmiᶜ*], Saᶜāl) and the next at Manaḥ (*masjid* al-ᶜAlī). The other three decorated *maḥārīb* of Manaḥ, in al-ᶜAyn, al-Shārah, and al-Manḥiyyah mosques, appeared in close succession. The decorated *maḥārīb* are rectangular in their overall form; from the first to the second, the height had increased and the width had reduced so that the width to height ratio moved from roughly 1:1 to 1:1.6. However, the overall compositional schema and the major decorative elements had remained almost unchanged.

The centrepiece, a low-arched niche with a simple shallow alcove (which in the later examples appears heavily scalloped) is supported on two sets of half-columns progressively receding from the surface of the *miḥrāb*. In Saᶜāl, the inner sets of columns are much shorter in comparison, a difference that seems to have evened out by the time of al-ᶜAlī. It is worth noting that in the *maḥārīb* in the tenth-century Iranian mosque at Nayīn, and the many others that followed, much taller columns were a consistent feature (Pope 1968), calling into question any unmediated importation of the design schema. The niches in al-ᶜAyn and al-ᶜAlī have triple and quadruple recessed arches of diminishing size, with alternate arches corresponding to the columns. However, in al-Sharāʾ, al-Manḥiyyah mosques they are made up of a large central arch flanked by two half arches joining to create a pendentive on either side. The niche arch is surmounted by a decorative arch in a shallow recess with a rosette; the circular medallion at its centre later gave way to a porcelain bowl inset (Fig. 2). While in al-ᶜAlī

Figure 3. *Part of the outer band of decoration in Masjid al-ᶜAlī, Ḥārat al-Bilād, Manaḥ showing the alternate large and smaller medallions set within an "endless knot" motif.*

and al-ᶜAyn the decorative arches were separated by a horizontal band, in the other two cases from Manaḥ the decorative arches were sitting immediately above the niche arch.

These arches are surrounded by a rectangular band that appears to be supported by the outer set of columns. In al-ᶜAyn, this band is broken into a narrow band going around the niche and two decorative panels flanking the upper arched recess, terminated by circular impressions. This band is surrounded by a wider band extending all the way down to the ground with impressed or recessed decorations of alternating small and large circles ensconced in a complex closed pattern, all set within intricate foliage motifs (Fig. 3). In al-ᶜAlī and al-Manḥiyyah mosques, this outer band is further divided into a wider middle section containing the circular decorations with two narrower bands on either side.

The inscriptions on the *miḥrāb* have a standard format: at the top, above the outer band, the Profession of Faith (*shahādah*) is inscribed in very bold Kufic script, which in Saᶜāl runs across the *qiblah* wall. The name of the sponsor(s), the date of construction, the name of the artist (*naqqāsh*, pl. *naqqashūn*), and other details are inscribed in a much more fluid and interlocking script immediately above the shallow recessed arch over the niche. In al-ᶜAlī, however, these details appear between the two bands, and at Saᶜāl this forms a thin band wrapping around the medallion band. The decoration is in fine gypsum (*jiṣṣ jamīl*), which was either left in its natural state, whitewashed or, as in Manaḥ, painted green, perhaps at a later date. From the sixteenth century onwards (i.e. from al-ᶜAlī), Omani *maḥārīb* incorporate glazed ceramic bowls, either of Chinese origin or in their Persian imitation.

The origin of the term *miḥrāb*

The extension of South Arabian presence and cultural influence along the southern and eastern shores of the Arabian Peninsula is now well known (e.g. Wilkinson 1977; Potts 1990; Bhacker & Bhacker 2004). The distinctive formal characteristics of the central Omani mosque suggest a continuation of an older sacred architecture consistent with Serjeant's Ḥaḍramī mosque (Serjeant 1959), which interacted with the more localized culture to incorporate the domical *būmah* into the schema (Bandyopadhyay 2000; Bandyopadhyay & Sibley 2003). This regional origin of the Omani mosque architecture, largely independent of developments in the northern Islamic heartland, acquires further substantiation as we consider the origin of the term *miḥrāb*.

While the use of the term *miḥrāb* denoting the prayer niche is entirely Islamic, the earliest mosques did not contain a *miḥrāb*. In the Qurʾān, the word *miḥrāb* is mentioned only five times, but in no instance does it suggest a prayer niche.

Quoting Ibn Manẓūr's *Lisān al-ᶜArab*, Khoury suggests that it might have denoted a range of disparate entities, "The *miḥrāb* is the central-most location of the main room (or residence; *bayt*), and the most honoured (*akramu*) area in it . . . It is also the elevated chamber (*ghurfa*)" (Khoury 1998: 7).

Earlier, Serjeant and Mahmud ᶜAlī Ghul had shown how, during the time of the Prophet and in early Arabic commentary, it variously meant, "a covered place where the people sat", a chamber (*ghurfah*), and the highest or most prominent place, probably derived from southern Arabia, where it appears in South Arabian inscriptions on at least two occasions, and meant "a row of columns with intervening space . . . erected upon a plinth or a courtyard" (Serjeant 1959: 450). In a slightly derivative sense of a covered portico supported by columns, it was still in use in the mosques of Ḥaḍramawt (*maḥārīb*) and had precedents in the pre-Islamic temples in Yemen (Serjeant 1959; Ghul 1960).

Thus the *miḥrāb*, which in South Arabian temples denoted a portico or a hall-like space or a court, in other words, a transitory space, a threshold of no clear sacred intentions, and also perhaps, an elevated, lofty room with possible feminine connotations, was shifted along the spatial hierarchy and elevated in status to become the sacred focus of Islamic prayer. Kanaᶜan suggests that the concentrically arched Ibāḍī *maḥārīb*, set entirely within the depth of the wall, as opposed to the projecting alternative within the Sunni realm, is perhaps an independent tradition (Kanaᶜan 2008: 232), to which the stucco version was adapted, as I would suggest. It is tempting to read in this the compacted depth of the pillared portico originally denoted by the term *miḥrāb*.

Stellar representation

The earliest extant *miḥrāb* at Saᶜāl from 1252 and many of the subsequent ones display ample examples of stellar representation, interspersed with vegetal motifs (Fig. 4/a–c). Although the use of a six-pointed star or the radial motifs are prevalent, in many cases stellar and floral motifs could be read in conjunction — one subsumed into another, interchangeably or as a date-palm motif seen from above, i.e. as planimetric representations. In earlier examples, such as at al-ᶜAlī in Manaḥ, the radiating variant is articulated further as a geometric construction derived from the master grid of the hexagonal star, examples of which are found in many classical Islamic monuments (e.g. the eleventh-century Chehel Dukhtaran, Isfahan; El-Said & Parman 1976: 70–71, pl. 27 and fig. 50). At Saᶜāl the central rosette bears a close resemblance to a certain Cairene depiction of a keel arch associated with the seven-pointed astral/floral motif (Kanaᶜan 2008: 241).

Stars have played an important role in South Arabian agricultural practices. Varisco (1993) described the limited but continued use of the traditional Yemeni star-calendar in highland Yemen to define the seasons and timings of agricultural activities, which consists of twenty-eight distinct star periods defined by their own marker stars. Yemeni farmers refer to this calendar as the *maᶜālim al-zirāᶜah*, the "agricultural markers". This contemporary form of the star calendar linked to the well-known

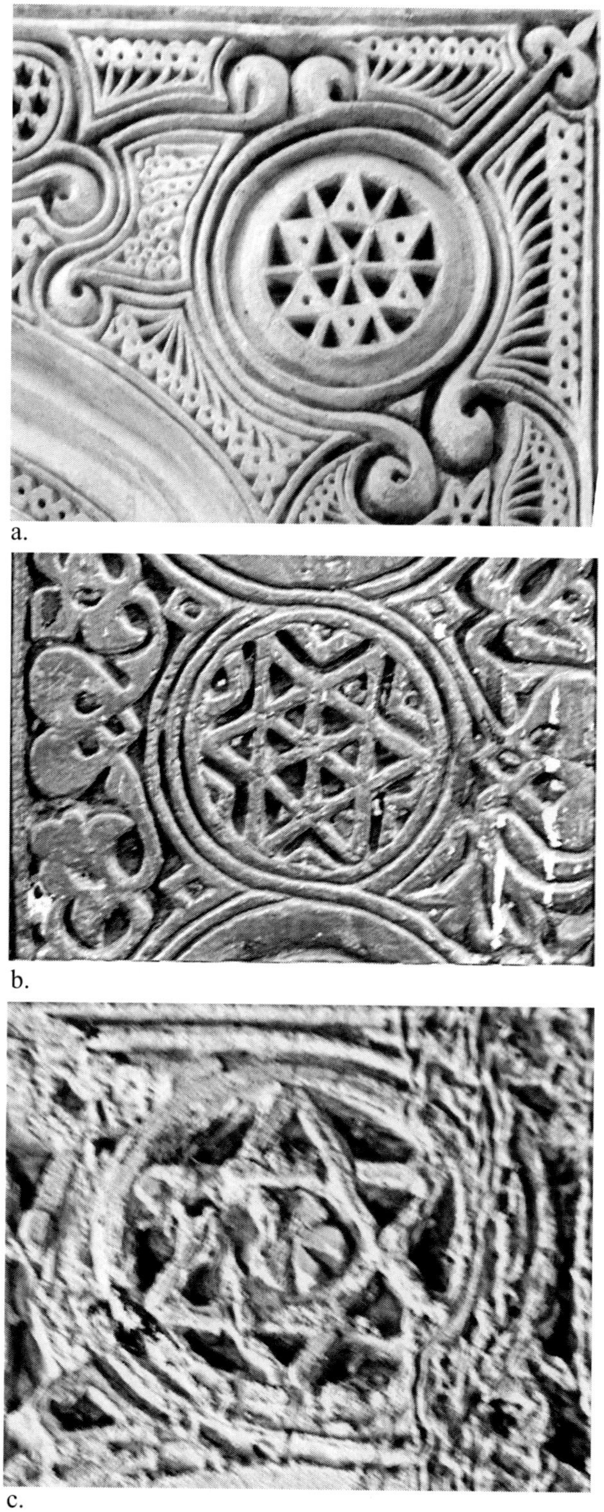

a.

b.

c.

Figure 4. *Examples of stellar representations on Omani mahārib:* **a.** *Masjid al-Jāmaᶜ, Saᶜāl;* **b.** *Masjid al-ᶜAyn, Manaḥ;* **c.** *Masjid al-Sharjah, Nizwa.*

manāzil al-qamar, "lunar stations" of Arabian astrology, as Varisco points out, appears to be a more recent variant of numerous localized star lists: "There were several ways to divide up the natural seasons of a particular locality, but the simplest was use of a natural sky clock established by the local farmers through repeated observation of star positions and movements. Even those who were ignorant of formal astronomical knowledge, a science of great importance in the courts of medieval Yemen, could create such simple clocks to define the seasonal round for a particular location" (1993: 121).

Although the main purpose of these systems was to focus the farmers' attention on the arrival of the rains, "early Islamic scholars combined the Indian lunar zodiac with indigenous Arab folklore on certain stars used to mark seasons and rainfall" (1993: 121–122), in reality these were more of academic value as analogous astronomical systems than as practical methods for ascertaining agricultural time. Many of the earlier marker star systems in Yemen relied on the solar year instead. In both cases, as the asterisms used were unevenly spaced along the path of the moon or the sun, the systems were only approximate in nature setting up an arbitrary grid, which in the case of the lunar system, divided the year into twenty-eight thirteen-day periods (1993: 124). The two formalized systems represent scholarly constructs attempting to integrate local star names into the formal lunar and solar zodiacs.

While in Yemen the stars have been used to establish the most propitious time for harvesting based on the arrival of the rains, in Oman these have been used to ascertain the time at night. The *aflāj* irrigation system, at the heart of the Omani oasis, relies heavily on the sun during the day and the stars at night to tell the time to ensure the distribution of allocated water.[5] The system differs from village to village in terms of the methods of stellar observation, the name and number of main and divider stars used for keeping time. The Omani star names often differ from those found in classical Arabic and to make things complicated, the same name is used for different stars, which are not always employed in the observation system according to their brightness either. While some stars are distinguished due to their brightness, size, or colour, the dividers often remain unnamed, known only as dividers of the main stars. The localized nature of the stellar system is highlighted by the fact that when a stargazer from al-Ḥamrah was taken to Muscat, there he failed to recognize the stars used in the village (Nash 2007: 159–160). Nash notes the observational system in Qaryat Banī Ṣubḥ:

> In Qaryah Benī Ṣubḥ stars are watched rising above the horizon. In other villages, walls, palm trees, and posts attached to buildings are used to mark the rising, setting, or zenith of stars.
>
> In Qaryah Benī Ṣubḥ, twenty-one main stars are used with dividers and other stars, totalling approximately fifty. In the Muḍaybī area and beyond, twenty-four stars are used, but there are minor differences in the twenty-four stars used in different villages. (2007: 165)

Important parallels could be observed in the number of stellar roundels in the decorative schemes of Omani prayer niches. The earliest *miḥrāb* at Saᶜāl employs twenty-two roundels in the outer band, made prominent through their diameter and edge detail, interspersed with smaller roundels, which also flank these. At Saᶜāl these smaller roundels contained three different motifs: overt stellar motifs, miniature depictions of the "endless-knot", and a quartered-circle, similar to the one-star calendar from Muḍayrib published by Nash (2007: 167, fig. 12). In the sixteenth-century *maḥārīb*, prominence is given to fifteen roundels by recessing those with interstitial roundels larger than those at Saᶜāl, and between three and five roundels or circular depressions around the central rosette. The *maḥārīb* at al-ᶜAlī (1504) and al-ᶜAyn (1505) mosques in Manaḥ both contain twenty-one on the outer band with three at the centre; al-Shawādinah mosque in Nizwah has fifteen with five at its centre; while Bahlah has twenty. The outer band of the *miḥrāb* in Rustāq contains twenty-eight roundels.

The horizon as threshold

This broad agreement between the number of stars used in ascertaining spans of time and the major and minor roundels employed on the *miḥrāb* — irrespective of the size and proportion of the decorative project — brings the conception of the latter closer to the reality of the oasis. In asking how this might have happened, I suggest that we remind ourselves of the quasi-real nature of the *miḥrāb*, in that it is a threshold that mediates, and always indicates something beyond itself, something it is not. It is this imbued virtuality — analogous to our understanding of the

---

[5] The *aflāj* water distribution system has been discussed in great detail by Wilkinson, especially in his seminal work of 1977. Nash has discussed the use of star systems that ensure appropriate distribution of *aflāj* water (2007).

FIGURE 5. *The landscape east of Manaḥ oasis. The horizon, its profile resulting from natural topography and architectonic features, has played an important role in the understanding of negotiated relationships with the wider society, nature, and the celestial order by those who live in Omani oasis settlements.*

continually receding horizon as a threshold — that makes the acceptance of the mediated stellar selection possible. Leatherbarrow (2001: 3) demonstrates how the Renaissance scholar and architect Leon Battista Alberti (1404–1472) devised an instrument he called the "horizon" — a circular disc marked with equally divided and marked segments and concentric rings with a movable arm or "radius" — to measure the city, which anticipated the theodolite. This was also an instrument that measured and located body contours; in both cases rays were projected back or forth on to a virtual edge, the "horizon", underscoring the horizon's encoding or recording role in the process of "conveyance" or of "transfer" (2001: 9).

The engagement of the horizon, either as the line where the ground met the sky or its substitution through parts of the settlement — date palm, walls, lanes, edges of buildings, and mosque courtyards — aligns the celestial topography with the immediate landscape of the oasis through the measuring of time. It is also a threshold through which the "agricultural marker" stars are required to pass to come into the realms of the physical landscape, firstly by establishing terrestrial markers through the position of the stargazer, and secondly by initiating and partaking in the process of measuring time and water flow. In Misfat al-ᶜAbriyīn, architectonic features articulate this horizon as threshold; as Nash notes, "four small towers were built on a ridge forming the horizon to mark some of the main stars, to assist people with poor eyesight" (2007: 168). Employing an anthropomorphic analogy, many stars' names in Arabia are for parts of the body (e.g. al-Janb, the side or flank; al-Buṭayn, the little belly; al-Qalb, the heart) (2007: 163), drawing curious parallels with the names of geographical regions (e.g. Jawf, belly), suggesting alignment of celestial and physical topographies on an even larger scale. The notion of territoriality embedded among the settled (*ḥaḍar*) Omani population, centred on the oasis, addressed horizon as thresholds to negotiate the complex relationships with the nomads (*badw*) and the semi-nomadic population of the mountains (*shawāwī*) (Wilkinson 1983) (Figs 5 and 6).

The unattainability of the horizon as threshold appears to be a feature of the Omani *miḥrāb*, distinguished through its inaccessible shallow, and especially, low niche, mainly as a result of Ibāḍī doctrinal proscription against the imam to be separated from his congregation. By emphasizing concentration on God and directing towards the Kaᶜbah, it acts as a threshold between the temporal existence and the transcendental experience of the essence of God.

This notion of the threshold is further strengthened at Saᶜāl by the placement of the Qurᵓānic verse, "[God] will be sufficient for you against them"; this or similar Qurᵓānic verses are often used as talismans on doors to ward off evil from Omani dwellings (Kanaᶜan 2008: 241). The Saljūq monument of Mama Hatun Kumbed in Tercan, eastern Anatolia, employs the "endless knot" motif and the star at its entrance (Rogers 1975: fig. 7), reminding us of this combination on Omani *maḥārīb*. The horizon, the surrounding landscape, and the date palm also feature in Omani dwelling thresholds and are associated with representations on Omani doors and windows (Fig. 7).

Figure 6. *The horizon as seen from the Qal^{c}at al-Fayqayn, Manaḥ. The main settlement quarter, Ḥārat al-Bilād, lies where the date-palm plantation meets the sky, its now ruined distinctive square tower, Burj al-Juṣṣ, barely visible on the horizon.*

Figure 7. *The date-palm and "endless knot" motif on Omani door decoration from Ḥārat al-Bilād, Manaḥ. Note both the curvilinear and the sharp angular form of the "endless knot", the latter imitating the braided matting techniques of traditional basketry.*

The "endless knot" motif

One of the main motifs used in the *miḥrāb* is the so-called "endless knot", which, as Parpola describes, is "a complex, maze-like closed pattern" (1994: 56–57) often employed to represent endless or continuous space or time. This motif, found from the Middle East to India from prehistoric to modern contexts, could be traced back to third-millennium BCE Mesopotamia. The introduction into the Omani *miḥrāb*, however, appears to have happened from Iran where, by the tenth century, similar motifs were being used in the *maḥārīb*. In its simplest form it appears on the rectilinear elements of the column base and capital; however, it features heavily on the *miḥrāb* decorative scheme (Fig. 8). A sharp angular version of the motif could be found on many Omani doors. In its more complex version the "endless knot" can be read in the uninterrupted curvilinear form weaving around the alternating small and large medallions of the outer band, which extends outwards to incorporate the smaller flanking roundels.

In his extensive study of the Islamic ideas of time, and especially in Persian Sufism, Böwering (1992) explains how Islam modified the pre-Islamic Arab concept of time expressed in the idea of *dahr*. Punctuated only by the Days of the Arab (*ayyām al-^{c}Arab*), i.e. the days of vengeance and brilliance in combat that took their permanent place in Arab memory, folklore, and poetry, the *dahr* was characterized by an endless, fathomless continuity of time, often paralleled with the experience of the desert nights. In countering the fatalistic view of time expressed in the *jāhiliyyah*, Islam introduced the transcendental

FIGURE 8. *Detail of a niche in the* miḥrāb *of Masjid al-ᶜAyn, Manaḥ. The stellar medallions are held within the curvilinear "endless knot" in the outer band of the decoration scheme.*

dimension of the promise of paradise and the idea of the Day of God (*ayyām Allāh*), and stressed the importance of the "instant" or "moment" in man's life, emphasized by such crucial instants as the point of origin of a person's life and the "hour" of revelation.

An imagery of illumination or enlightenment often associates such moments and can be seen, for example, in expressions in connection with the perfect moment of revelation, "the twinkling of an eye" (*lamḥ al-baṣar*). Extending the Qurʾānic view that Allāh is the Lord of the instant, an important *ḥadīth* (*ḥadīth qudsī*) later amplified this divine determination by identifying time (*dahr*) with God through his own proclamation: I am time (*anā al-dahr*) (Böwering 1992: 77–78). Following this elevation of time to a divine status, the "law followed the Qurʾānic summons to give witness (*shahādah*) to the divine signs (*āyāt*) that established events in time" (1992: 79), making possible the representation of time on the Omani *miḥrāb*, always favouring, however, observation over precise calculation as a testimony to the transcendental essence of God. The Qurʾān explicitly confirmed the moon as the measurer of time; the day began with nightfall and the month began with the sighting of the new moon.

Acceptance

The method of allegorical interpretation developed in early Ibāḍīsm of anthropomorphism (*tashbīh*) present in Qurʾānic expressions describing God through aspects of the human body, and its later explanation through the expanded and less austere principle of Unity (*tawḥīd*), I would argue, provided the Ibāḍī artisans the basis for representing notions of time on their *maḥārīb*. The founder of the Ibāḍī school, Jābir b. Zayd, acquired his views from a number of the Companions of the Prophet, especially Ibn ᶜAbbās, which contributed to the intellectual foundation of the movement (al-Nāmī 2007: 106). Some of the exegeses in early Ibāḍī theology addressed such issues of anthropomorphism including *qabḍah* (handful), *al-yad* (hand), *ᶜayn* (eye), *nūr* (light), *wajh* (face), *al-ṣāq* (leg), and *al-nafs* (soul). The *ᶜayn* (in suras 20, v. 39; 11, v. 37; 23, v. 27; 52, v. 48; and 54, v. 14) for example, was interpreted as knowledge and protection; *nūr* (in Sura 24, v. 35) as "the Guide of the inhabitants of heavens and earth"; and *al-nafs* (sura 5, v. 116) as knowledge (2007: 106–107).

In later Ibāḍī theological discussions on the Unity with God (*tawḥīd*) and regarding the rules and premises of association and friendship (*al-walāyah*), a more mystical tendency could be noticed within a continued asceticism; as Hoffman notes, "the emphasis is on purifying the soul, [on] asceticism, the defects of the soul and how to replace them with virtues — and receiving direct knowledge of God through the light of His love; a lot of emphasis on God's light and mystical insight, on nearness to God, His intimacy and His presence, but not union with God or the oneness of being. There is also emphasis on love of the Prophet and the friends of God, though not to the extent of saint shrine veneration" (Hoffman, personal communication, 2005).

In Hoffman's view, Ibāḍism in Oman challenges the assumption that puritanism and mysticism are an unlikely juxtaposition in Islam (2004: 203). Mysticism, she suggests, has deep roots in Oman, exemplified by the presence of much Ibāḍī mystical poetry. A number of modern Ibāḍī scholars — from at least the eighteenth century onwards — embraced mysticism as part of their lives,[6] skilfully integrating discussions on the way of love and conceptualization of knowledge in terms of ideas of illumination (2004: 209).

[6] Hoffman lists the following modern Ibāḍī scholars as having mysticism as part of their lives (2004: 204): Jaᶜid "Abū Nabhān" b. Khamīs al-Kharūṣī (1734/5–1822); his son, Nāṣir b. Abī Nabhān (1778–1847); Saᶜīd b. Khalfan al-Khalīlī (1811–1871); ᶜAbdullāh "Nūr al-Dīn" al-Sālimī (1869–1914); and Nāṣir "Abū Muslim" b. Sālim al-Bahlānī al-Rawwāhī (1860–1920).

Sanctity of the date palm

In Bahlah, as Limbert noticed, dates and date palm were regarded as sacred, mainly as a miraculous gift from God that sustained life to the fullest:

> Sacredness … is nothing, if it is not also about visiting and social responsibility, survival, respect for common property, and good governance. Indeed . . . dates are considered sacred precisely because the relevant qualities of sweetness, portability, and nutrition are embodied in a material object that is also critical for these everyday ideals, ideals that are themselves understood to be what a 'good' person does and is. Sacredness is not simply one regime of value in and out of which dates move and which belongs solely to a domain beyond the 'profane,' but emerges out of, and yet is clearly also part of, the combination of their multiple roles in everyday life. (Limbert 2008: 362)

However, judging by the anthropomorphic date palm widely worn as a pendant for its talismanic qualities, its perceived supernatural powers could not be disregarded either. Perhaps this anthropomorphism could be seen as representing one end of the spectrum of how the date palm — its location, distribution, and harvesting — becomes spatial and temporal markers within oasis settlements, as Limbert notes. The "hot" quality of date is balanced by the "cold" quality of coffee during Omani ritual coffee sessions (Limbert 2008: 365). One could read a similar balance between the "coldness" of *falaj* water and the "hotness" of the date palm, represented in simple curvilinear and floral motifs on Omani doors.

This theme, in its more complex manifestation as the "endless knot", complete with the star/date-palm motifs, could be found on Omani doors, either forming a circular pattern or inscribed within an arched motif, which probably represented the horizon. The outer bands of such decorations closely resemble the more angular version found on Omani doors and is close in expression to the palm-leaf matting or braiding still in vogue. This woven tapestry — defining territory through bounded space — brings to mind yet another tapestry employed in many central Omani homes, that of painted ceilings depicting celestial objects (Figs 9 and 10).

FIGURE 9. *Omani door decoration from Ḥārat al-Bilād, Manaḥ.*

Conclusion

Thus the Ibāḍī artisan of Oman managed to integrate in the decorated *miḥrāb* representations of both continuous and instantaneous time employing the endless knot and stellar motifs. Emphasizing the sacred nature of time and light as divine attributes or essence of God, the *miḥrāb* sought to represent a celestial topography, which was made possible through Ibāḍī analogical interpretations of anthropomorphism in the Qurʾān and an expanding influence of mysticism amongst Omani scholars. Omani *miḥrāb* and door decoration shows a close affinity between stellar and date-palm representations, the latter held in sacred esteem across Omani oasis settlements. The *aflāj* irrigation system at the heart of date-palm cultivation once depended significantly on the position of stars in the night sky to ensure appropriate distribution of water. The interchangeable representation suggests a conflation

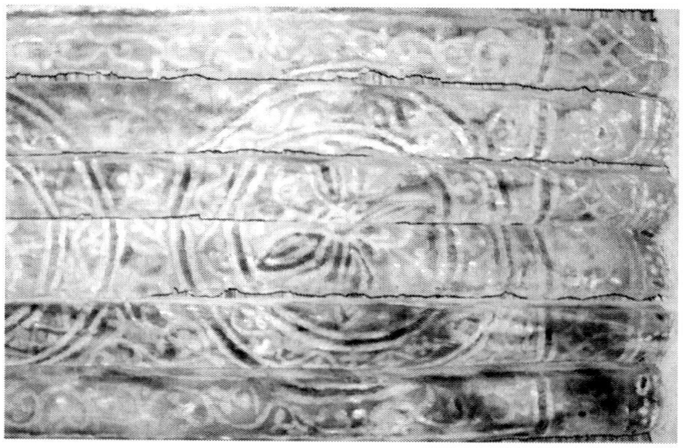

Figure 10. *Painted ceiling decoration on date-palm beams from Ḥārat al-ᶜAqr, Nizwa.*

of the terrestrial topography of the oasis and the celestial topography. The horizon mediated this relationship — acting as a threshold through which the celestial bodies had to pass to be meaningfully associated with the terrestrial topography. Appearing as woven tapestries or bounded spatial representations, both the *miḥrāb* and the Omani doorway decoration seem to mark a threshold in the sacred passage. However, in mystical thought, while space was perceived as "an accident of the body", time was regarded as "proceeding from the soul". This led Abū Ḥayyān Tawḥīdī (d. 1023) to answer the question, "Which is better, space or time?" with "Time is better, for space is of the senses but time is spiritual; space is in the world but time surrounds it" (Böwering 1992: 81). It is not my intention to suggest that the Omani artisans and scholars were consciously working in unison to make such ideas tangible. What I have sketched out however is a plausible and likely cultural environment that would have contributed towards the development of an unconscious (and perhaps conscious) aesthetic language.

References

Baldissira E.

1994. *Al-Kitābāt fī l-masājid al-ᶜumāniyyah al-qadīmah.* Muscat: Ministry of Heritage and Culture.

Bandyopadhyay S.

1998. Manḥ: The Architecture, Archaeology and Social History of a Deserted Omani Settlement. PhD thesis, University of Liverpool. [Unpublished].

2000. From the twilight of cultural memory: the *būmah* in the mosques of central Oman. *Proceedings of the Seminar for Arabian Studies* 30: 13–25.

2008. From another world! A possible Būyid origin of the decorated *miḥrāb* of Central Oman? Pages 372–382 in E. Olijdam & R.H. Spoor (eds), *Intercultural Relations between South and southwest Asia, Studies in Commemoration of E.C.L. During Caspers (1934–1966).* Oxford: Archaeopress.

Bandyopadhyay S. & Sibley M.

2003. The distinctive typology of central Omani mosques: its nature and antecedents. *Proceedings of the Seminar for Arabian Studies* 33: 99–116.

Beelaert A.L.F.A.

1988–1989. The Kaᶜba as a woman: a topos in classical Persian literature. *Persica* 13: 107–123.

Bhacker M.R. & Bhacker B.

2004. Qalhāt in Arabian history: context and chronicles. *Journal of Oman Studies* 13: 11–56.

Böwering G.

1992. Ideas of time in Persian Sufism. *Iran: Journal of the British Institute of Persian Studies* 30: 77–89.

Costa P.M.

2001. *Historic Mosques and Shrines of Oman.* (British Archaeological Reports, International Series, 938). Oxford: Archaeopress.

Ghul M.A.

1960. Was the ancient South Arabian *MD/-QNT* the Islamic *Mihrab*? *Bulletin of the School of Oriental and African Studies* 23: 331–335.

Hoffman V.J.

2004. The articulation of Ibādī identity in modern Oman and Zanzibar. *The Muslim World*: 94: 201–216.

Kanaᶜan R.
2008. The carved-stucco *mihrabs* of Oman: form, style and influences. Pages 230–259 in A. al-Salimi, H. Gaube & L. Korn (eds), *Islamic Art in Oman*. Muscat: Ministry of Heritage and Culture & Ministry of Endowment and Religious Affairs.

Kervran M.
1996. Miḥrāb(s) omanais du 16e siècle: un curieux exemple de conservatisme de l'art du stuc iranien des époques seldjouqide et mongole. *Archéologie Islamique* 6: 109–156.

Khoury N.N.N.
1998. The *miḥrāb*: from text to form. *International Journal of Middle Eastern Studies* 30: 1–27.

Limbert M.E.
2008. The sacred date: gifts of God in an Omani town. *Ethnos* 73/3: 361–376.

Leatherbarrow D.
2001. *Uncommon Ground: Architecture, Technology and Topography*. Cambridge, MA: Massachusetts Institute of Technology Press.

Melchert C.
1996. The transition from asceticism to mysticism at the middle of the ninth century CE. *Studia Islamica*: 83: 51–70.

al-Nāmī A.K.
2007. *Studies in Ibadhism*. 8 April 2010. Online at Open Mind. http://open-books.blogspot.com/

Nash H.
2007. Stargazing in traditional water management: a case study in northern Oman. *Proceedings of the Seminar for Arabian Studies* 37: 157–170.

Parpola A.
1994. *Deciphering the Indus Script*. Cambridge: Cambridge University Press.

Pope A.U.
1968. *A Survey of Persian Art from Prehistoric Times to the Present*. London: Oxford University Press.

Potts D.T.
1990. *The Arabian Gulf in Antiquity*. Oxford: Clarendon Press.

Rogers J.M.
1975. Saljūq architectural decoration at Sivās. Pages 13–27 in W. Watson (ed.), *The Art of Iran and Anatolia from the 11th to the 13th Century AD*. (Colloquies on Art & Archaeology in Asia, 4). London: Percival David Foundation of Chinese Art.

El-Said I. & Parman A.
1976. *Geometric Concepts in Islamic Art*. London: World of Islam Festival Publishing.

Serjeant R.B.
1959. Miḥrāb. *Bulletin of the School of Oriental and African Studies* 22/3: 439–453.

Varisco D.M.
1993. The Agricultural Marker Stars in Yemeni Folklore. *Asian Folklore Studies* 52/1: 119–142.

Wilkinson J.C.
1977. *Water and Tribal Settlement in South East Arabia: The Study of the* Aflaj *of Oman*. Oxford: Clarendon Press.
1983. Traditional concepts of territory in southeast Arabia. *The Geographical Journal* 149/3: 301–315.
1987. *The Imamate Tradition of Oman*. Cambridge: Cambridge University Press.

Author's address
Professor Soumyen Bandyopadhyay, School of Architecture, Design and the Built Environment, Nottingham Trent University, Nottingham NG1 4BU, UK.

e-mail soumyenb@ntu.ac.uk

Proceedings of the Seminar for Arabian Studies 40 (2010): 111–118

Al-Balīd ship timbers: preliminary overview and comparisons

Luca Belfioretti & Tom Vosmer

Summary
The discovery of a number of planks, beams and frames from sewn boats at the site of al-Balīd in southern Oman has offered new information about ship construction during the period from the tenth to the fifteenth centuries AD. Structural elements from ships were discovered during excavations of the citadel and a mosque on the site, where they were being reused as lintels, shelving, and ceiling beams, etc. Some of the planks showed remains of the stitching that held them together. The plank-stitching patterns display a variety of forms, perhaps indicating different origins or differences in chronology of construction. Identification of some botanical species of the materials used yielded possible origins. Taken together, the data from these discoveries advance our knowledge about ship construction in the Islamic period.

Keywords: al-Balīd, sewn planks, Belitung, Arab shipping, ship construction

Introduction

During several archaeological campaigns since 2004 in al-Balīd, a settlement site with an Islamic citadel in Dhofar, Oman (Fig. 1), various timbers recognizable as parts of boats were discovered. We know they are boat timbers because they retain scarf joints typical of boat construction, oblique dowels in planks, as well as planks sewn together, some with the stitching still preserved.

Having come to the end of their useful life in boats, these timbers were reused for building construction in the citadel as shelves, lintels, or roof beams.

All the techniques used in these timbers — carpentry, joinery, and stitching — look very similar to those in use today in traditional sewn-boat construction. Even the repairs adopted are exactly the same as those used in the present day. The cordage used in all the observed sewn timbers also seems to be the same material used today: coir (*Cocos nucifera*), as is the wadding under the stitching.

There are several places along the coasts of this region where we can observe the unique testimony of sewn-boat construction and compare it with the archaeological recoveries. In the Kerala region of India there are examples of all the processes needed for a sewn boat: from gathering the fibres of coconut husks to making the ropes and to hand carpentry with basic tools such as chisel, adze, saw, and hammer. This unquestioned skill comes from a remote past.

In Oman there are only a few people with this particular sewing skill, in the Musandam region of northern Oman. The last Omani of Dhofar (southern Oman) who could sew boats together died in the 1990s. The last few possessors of the ancient tradition are also found in Tanzania. We can observe the last remains of this sewn-boat tradition in vessels abandoned and almost destroyed by weather conditions, by the passing years, and by natural disasters, as in Sri Lanka where sewn boats are no longer built since the 2004 tsunami, which destroyed the wooden boat industry.

Identification and dating of the al-Balīd timbers

To provide a context for the study, some wood and cordage samples were sent to laboratories for species identification and dating. The cordage used in the timbers seemed to be all of the same material and samples of the cordage were identified by the Department of Materials Conservation at the Western Australian Maritime Museum as "very likely" to be coconut fibre (Godfrey, personal communication, 2007).

Examination of macro- and microscopic features of the timbers provided the identification of some of the woods used, as follows:

BA 0604172.69 — *Terminalia* sp. (Commonwealth Scientific and Industrial Research Organisation (CSIRO),

Figure 1. *A map of the western Indian Ocean, showing the location of al-Balīd.*

Figure 2. *Plank BA0604172.69, the outside surface of the hull.*

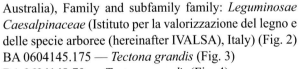

Figure 3. *Plank BA0604175.145, the outside surface of the hull. Note the frame-lashing holes with cordage* in situ.

Australia), Family and subfamily family: *Leguminosae Caesalpinaceae* (Istituto per la valorizzazione del legno e delle specie arboree (hereinafter IVALSA), Italy) (Fig. 2)
BA 0604145.175 — *Tectona grandis* (Fig. 3)
BA 0604148.70 — *Tectona grandis* (Fig. 4)
BA 0604159.263 — Family and subfamily family: *Leguminosae Caesalpinaceae* (IVALSA, Italy). No genus or species was identified.
A fourth sample, BA 0604128.73 (Figs 5 and 6) cannot be positively identified because of its advanced state of degradation. The closest match with a known specimen was with an *Estribeiro* sp., which is indigenous to Brazil. It is interesting to speculate that this timber may have been brought from Brazil during visits of Portuguese ships to al-Balīd.

Three samples of the al-Balīd timber, BA0604148.70, BA 0604128.69, and BA0604128.74 were tested at the Beta Analytic Radiocarbon Dating Laboratory, Miami, Florida. The results are tabulated in Figure 7.

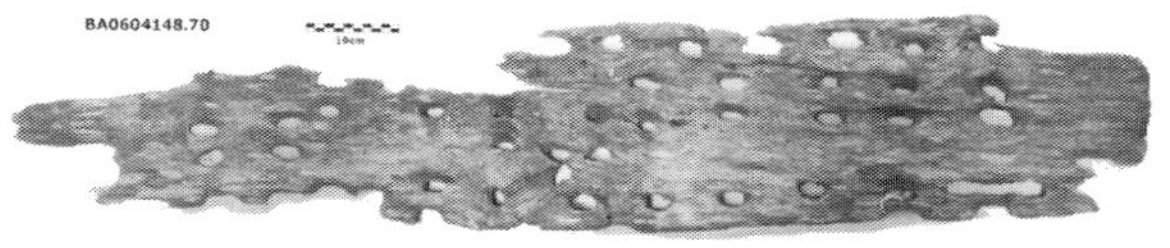

Figure 4. *Plank BA0604148.70, the oldest of the timbers (1020 CE ±50 years).*

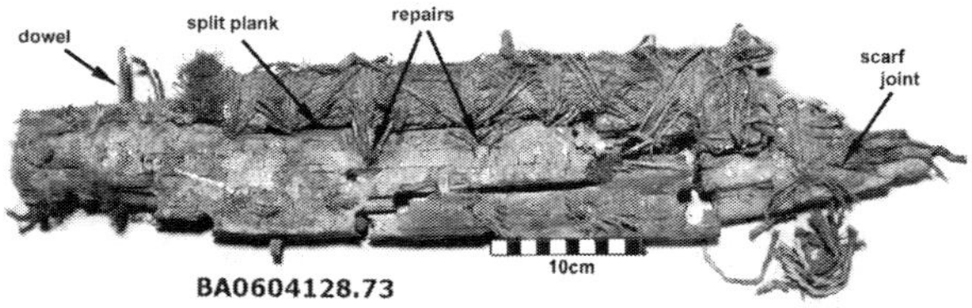

Figure 6. *Plank BA0604128.73, the inner face showing stitching over wadding, scarf joint, and repaired seam.*

Timber description

BA0604172.69 and BA0604159.263

This artefact comprises two wooden planks that fit together (BA0604172.69 and BA0604159.263) (Fig. 8). Together they are 1 m long overall, 21 cm wide and 5 cm thick. There are traces of a black substance on one faying surface, a substance that would have served as luting between adjacent planks. Identification of the substance is pending, but it might be *dammar,* a varnish resin, or copal resin and fish oil (the same as that used today), or bitumen.

BA0604128.74

Timber BA0604128.74 (Fig. 9) is a composite of four pieces of plank, with the stitching still *in situ*. They present the typical and most common stitching of western Indian Ocean technology, with wadding under the stitching only on the inside of the planking and vertical stitches on the outside. The main stitching runs from one end to the other along the midsection. A second stitching in the lower right corner, about 17 cm long, is a repair of the damaged plank, the plank having split along the original line of stitching holes. Additional holes were drilled in the plank and new stitching added.

On the opposite (presumably outside) face of the plank the stitching is recessed in rebates from 5 to 10 mm wide and 4 to 5 mm deep. There are oblique dowels, from 7 to 11 mm in diameter, running from the face of the plank into the centre of the faying edge of the next plank.

Figure 5. *Plank BA0604128.73* in situ.

The wood and the fibres of the stitching are fragile, the timber is split along the grain, and the stitching is disintegrating due to degradation of the rope fibre. It is impossible to verify the presence of dowels between the planks, although no oblique dowels are evident on the outside. The upper left corner has a white layer on the surface; the substance has not been analysed, but it could possibly be the remains of a natural antifouling, such as the lime/animal fat composition commonly used in the region, or a lime-based putty. Also on the surface of the plank was a dark substance identified as bitumen, which originated from southern Iran (Connan, personal communication, 2008).

BA0604148.70

BA0604148.70 (Fig. 4) is the oldest of the three dated pieces and is fashioned from teak (*Tectona grandis*). It is heavily degraded, the stitching holes eroded and elongated in the direction of the grain. The piece has holes running along the edge with a certain consistency, the holes approximately 8 cm centre to centre. Those

Sample data	Measured radiocarbon age	13C/12C ratio	Conventional radiocarbon age
Beta–218106			
Sample: BA0604128.74	480±40 BP	-24.1	490±40 BP
Analysis: AMS-standard delivery			
Pre-treatment	acid/alkali/acid		
2 Sigma calibration	Cal AD 1400 to 1460		
1 Sigma calibration	Cal AD 1420 to 1440		
Beta–218107			
Sample: BA0604148.70	950±50 BP	-26.2	930±50 BP
Analysis: radiometric standard delivery			
Pre-treatment	acid/alkali/acid		
2 Sigma calibration	Cal AD 1010 to 1220		
1 Sigma calibration	Cal AD 1030 to 1180		
Beta–218108			
Sample: BA0604172.69	670±50 BP	-23.8	690±50 BP
Analysis: radiometric standard delivery			
Pre-treatment	acid/alkali/acid		
2 Sigma calibration	Cal AD 1260 to 1400		
1 Sigma calibration	Cal AD 1280 to 1440		

Figure 7. *Tables of radiocarbon analyses for three of the al-Balīd ship timbers.*

holes were used to sew this plank to its adjacent planks on either side. The plank has holes in the midsection as well; their spacing indicating the placement of frames, which had been lashed to the planks.

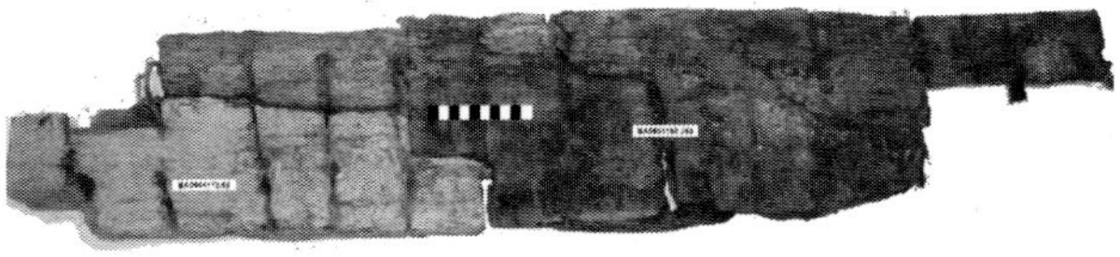

Figure 8. *Planks BA0604172.69 and BA0604159.263 together, the outside surface of the hull.*

BA 0604128.73

BA 0604128.73 is perhaps the most interesting of all the pieces, as it preserves a great deal of stitching, numerous dowels, an angled scarf, and repairs to split planks (Figs 5 and 6). It displays the most common stitching pattern of western Indian Ocean sewn boats, with alternating "X" and "I" stitches over wadding on the inside of the planks and vertical "I" stitches on the outside. The planking is only 2.5 cm thick, indicating it probably came from a small boat. Perhaps because of the relative thinness, no rebates have been cut on the outside of the planks to accommodate the vertical stitching. The stitching is therefore proud of the outside plank surface.

In general appearance, this closely resembles BA0604128.74 and may be from the same vessel. The two pieces share many similarities: dimensions of plank width and thickness, stitching pattern, the inside surface

Figure 9. *Plank BA0604128.74, the inner face showing stitching and repair of split plank.*

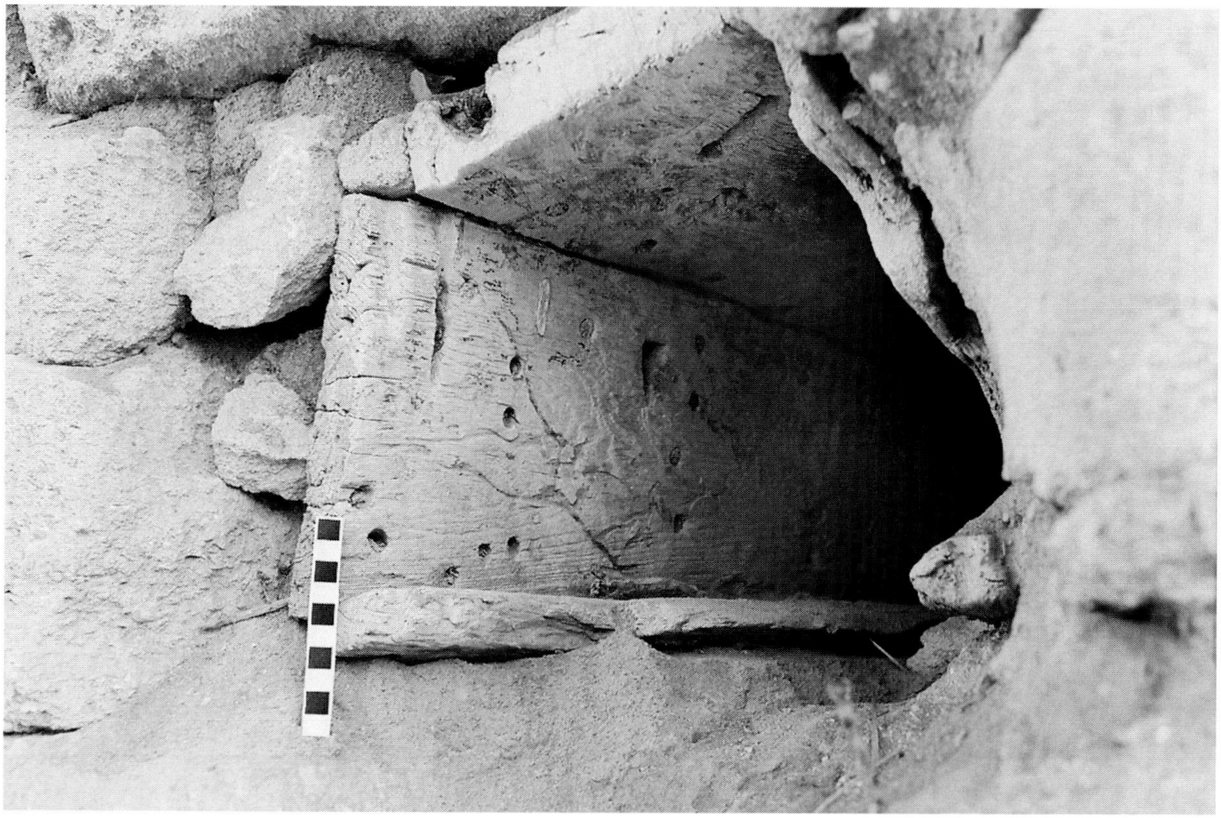

Figure 10. *A recess in the citadel wall lined with planks from boats. Note the triangular notches, frame-lashing holes, edge-sewing holes, and oblique dowel.*

coated with a dark brown substance — perhaps fish oil — holding inclusions of sand and dirt, and in similar states of degradation.

Species identification was not successful on either of these fragments.

In one section of wall near the citadel gate is a deep (3.4 m) recess, approximately 22 cm^2. This recess housed the heavy sliding timber that was used to secure the gate, and the recess is lined with timbers recycled from boats. One plank (unlabelled, Fig. 10) is of particular interest as it displays elements of the plank sewing system common to the Mediterranean, i.e. it appears to have stitches locked by wooden pegs set in V-shaped notches. But it also shows characteristics of Indian Ocean shipbuilding practice (oblique dowels, holes for frame lashings, edge sewing), and therefore may be a hybrid.

Beams

Some of the timbers used as lintels had been previously used as beams in boats. They display the notching where the planks met the beams (Fig. 11). The angle and width of the notching can provide very useful information, such as the thickness of the planking, the angle it meets the beam (and thus the hull shape at that point) or the possible position of the beam in the boat.

Figure 11. *A beam from a ship, with rebates cut for the planking.*

Bearing in mind that beams in any one vessel may be of a variety of different sizes depending on their use and position within the vessel, the beams may also provide an indication of the size of the vessel from which they came. A piece of teak excavated by Professor Paolo Costa from the largest mosque at al-Balīd (Costa 1979: 146 and pl. 76/a–c) almost certainly had a previous life as a beam in a boat. The angled rebates cut on the faces of the beam, which would have accommodated the planking of the vessel, are the best evidence of this.

Observations

Most of the timbers have dowels in between the planks, usually fitted obliquely from the side of a plank into the faying surface of the adjacent plank. They are used to reinforce joints or in our specific case to assist the cohesion and alignment of the planks, helping to keep the planks aligned during the process of stitching and to decrease the stress on the sewing cordage.

The ropes used in the timbers observed seem to be of the same material: coir; the wadding, also coir, is no different from the modern material commonly used today.

Planking thickness may provide an indication of ship size. For instance, we can compare the Belitung wreck with the reconstruction of Tim Severin's sewn boat *Sohar* (Severin 1982: 235). The Belitung wreck is a ninth-century shipwreck found in the Java Sea off Belitung Island in Indonesia (Flecker 2000). In the Belitung wreck, which we believe represents a vessel around 18 m long displacing about 50 tons, the planking ranges from 2.6 to 4 cm thick. The planking on Tim Severin's *Sohar*, a vessel 23 m long displacing about 75 tons, was 6 to 7.5 cm thick (Severin 1982: 235). The sewn *sanābīq* (sg. *sambūq*)[1] of southern Oman, ranging up to 11 m long have planking 1.8 to 2 cm thick. One can easily see how plank thickness roughly parallels vessel size. Thus the thickness of planking of the al-Balīd timbers can provide a rough estimate of the size of those ships from which they came.

The Belitung wreck appears to have a similar construction to the common western Indian Ocean sewn boat, but with some important differences. In comparison to the dominant modern sewing pattern in the western Indian Ocean, the primary difference is the presence of wadding under the stitching on both sides of the planking. This technique, however, is historically known in Sri Lanka. Whether it was more widespread in ancient times is not yet known.

It may be possible to recognize the approximate region or origin from the pattern of the stitching and the material used. Identification of some samples of the wood in the Belitung wreck includes: teak (*Tectona grandis*), *Afzelia africana*, *Juniperus* sp., and palm wood). Teak grows in India and south-east Asia and is very well known in many cultures as an excellent timber for naval construction. As its name implies, *Afzelia africana* is indigenous to Africa and is probably not the wood used, as it is not usually utilized in Asia, while *Juniperus* species are found throughout the region. The eclectic nature of the construction materials and the fact that they are not Asian timbers suggest that the ship was probably built in Arabia or East Africa. The methods and material used to build and sew the vessel clearly belong to the western Indian Ocean.

In addition to the al-Balīd timbers, the modern Dhofari *kambārīs*, and the Beltitung wreck, we have the sewn boat timbers of Quseir Qadim (al-Quṣayr al-Qadīm) on the Red Sea coast of Egypt which have been dated to the Islamic period, and exhibit a similar technique to the ones found in the citadel. These similarities can be integrated as a comparison and a confirmation of familiar methodology in boat-building construction in this region.

Conclusion

Comparing recent modern construction with the ancient evidence in our hands we can say that they have not changed substantially in at least 1000 years. With the relative paucity of direct archaeological evidence, it is clear that at present ethnographic studies can offer much towards the understanding of early Indian Ocean shipbuilding methodology and ship structure. The similarities among recent practices — stitching patterns, joinery, and materials — and those of the past as revealed by the al-Balīd ship timbers, the al-Quṣayr al-Qadīm timbers, and the ninth-century Belitung shipwreck timbers are remarkable.

Acknowledgements

We would like to thank H.E. Abdul Aziz bin Mohammad al-Rowas, Advisor to H.M. the Sultan for Cultural Affairs in Oman, for his interest and support for the excavations and research; Dr Juris Zarins and Dr Lynne Newton for their assistance and generosity in sharing their data and research; and we would also like to thank J. Connan and I. Godfrey for the useful information they provided on this project.

[1] Elsewhere called *sanbūq (*pl. *sanābīq*), also called sg. *kambārī.* Note that *sanbūq/sambūq* is a common mutual variant.

References

Costa P.
1979. The study of the city of Zafar. *Journal of Oman Studies* 5: 111–150.

Flecker M.
2000. A ninth-century Arab or Indian shipwreck in Indonesian waters. *International Journal of Nautical Archaeology* 29/2: 199–217.

Severin T.
1982. *The Sindbad Voyage*. London: Hutchinson.

Authors' addresses
Mr Luca Belfioretti, *Jewel of Muscat* Project, PO Box 812, Postal Code 100, Muscat, Sultanate of Oman.
e-mail belfiorettiluca@hotmail.com

Dr Tom Vosmer, *Jewel of Muscat* Project, PO Box 812, Postal Code 100, Muscat, Sultanate of Oman.
e-mail foxlake@omantel.net.om

Proceedings of the Seminar for Arabian Studies 40 (2010): 119–130

Fouilles à Masāfī-3 en 2009 (Émirat de Fujayrah, Émirats Arabes Unis): premières observations à propos d'un espace cultuel de l'Âge du Fer nouvellement découvert en Arabie orientale

Anne Benoist

Summary
Between 2000 and 2004, excavations at Bithnah-44 (Biṭnah) revealed a cultic area that acted as the focus for meetings and festivities during the Iron Age II period (*c.*1100–600 BC). Since 2006 new excavations by Anne Benoist at the site of Masāfī have revealed another cultic area (Masāfī-3), which is set in the vicinity of another meeting place (Masāfī-1). On the basis of the data from these two sites, this paper reconsiders some aspects of territorial organization, religion, and collective life during the Iron Age II period in eastern Arabia.

Keywords: Iron Age, eastern Arabia, snake, religion, cultic material
Âge du Fer, Arabie orientale, serpent, religion, mobilier cultuel

Introduction

Le symbole du serpent se rencontre dans de nombreuses régions du Proche et Moyen Orient depuis des périodes très anciennes. Symbole de danger pour son venin toxique, symbole des forces chtoniennes, des énergies primaires et des ressources émanant de la terre, étroitement associé au feu et à l'eau, le serpent semble avoir acquis une connotation nettement positive au fur et à mesure que s'affirmait la maîtrise d'un certain nombre de techniques d'exploitation et de transformation des ressources naturelles, dispensatrices de bienfaits et de profits: médecine, arts du feu (métallurgie, céramique), techniques d'irrigation. Le serpent apparaît ainsi comme un symbole de fertilité lié à la végétation et au monde des eaux souterraines, un symbole de longévité lié au renouveau et à la guérison, un symbole de prospérité lié à la maîtrise de connaissances élaborées, dispensatrices de richesses et de pouvoir (Dhorme 1949: 121; de Miroschedji 1981: 16; Antonini 2004: 88; Root 2002; Benoist, Pillaut & Skorupka, sous presse: notes 48–53).

En Arabie orientale, on connaît des représentations de serpents dès le troisième millénaire av. J.C., à Bidyah-2 par exemple (al-Tikriti 1989: pl. 80/A), mais on ignore s'il jouait ou non un rôle particulier dans les religions locales dès cette période. En revanche les recherches récentes permettent d'affirmer que le serpent tenait une place prépondérante dans l'imagerie cultuelle de cette région au cours du premier millénaire av. J.C. En 1982, sur le «monticule aux serpents» d'al-Qusays, des figurines en bronze en forme de serpents et des récipients en céramique décorés de serpents en relief furent recueillis au cours de fouilles dirigées par M.Y. Taha dans et autour d'un petit bâtiment rectangulaire installé à l'écart de la zone d'habitat (1983; 2009: 90–93). Le matériel recueilli permettait de dater le site du premier millénaire av. J.C., les figurines en bronze furent interprétées comme des objets votifs, et l'endroit comme un sanctuaire.[1]

Entre 2000 et 2004 des fouilles menées à Biṭnah (Émirat de Fujayrah, Émirats Arabes Unis) sous la direction de l'auteur[2] révélèrent un autre site cultuel, daté de la même période (Benoist *et al.* 2004; Benoist 2005; 2007; Benoist, Pillaut & Skorupka, sous presse). Constitué dans un premier temps d'un bâtiment unique, muni d'un autel et ouvert au nord sur une zone sacrée dans laquelle étaient enfouies des offrandes alimentaires, le sanctuaire s'étoffa au cours d'une deuxième puis d'une

[1] L'opération Biṭnah était l'un des volets des recherches menées aux Émirats Arabes Unis par la Mission Archéologique Française aux Émirats Arabes Unis sous la direction générale de S. Méry (CNRS, ArScan, Nanterre), en collaboration avec le Département des Antiquités de Fujayrah. Ces travaux sont financés conjointement par le Ministère des Affaires Étrangères et le Département des Antiquités de Fujayrah.
[2] Je tiens ici à remercier le Département des Antiquités de Fujayrah pour l'aide logistique et financière apportée au projet.

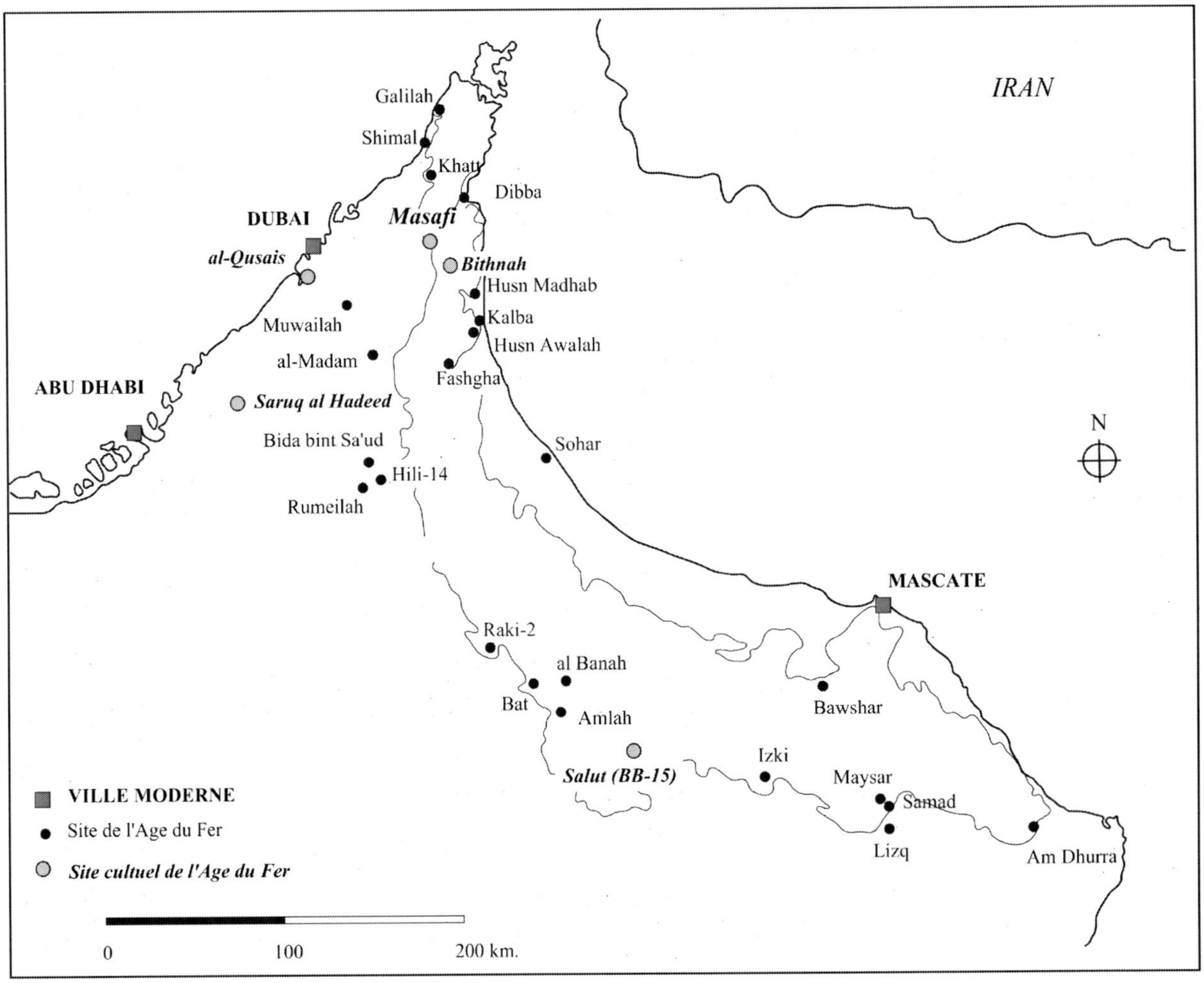

Figure 1. *Localisation de Masāfī.*

troisième phase de construction: le bâtiment d'origine perdit son autel et fut fermé au nord, des autels furent érigés à l'extérieur, dans de petits bâtiments ouverts ou en plein air, tout autour de la zone centrale où demeurait une aire d'offrandes alimentaires entourée d'une bordure. Deux bassins alimentés en eau par un canal furent installés au nord-ouest du site, dans lesquels se pratiquaient vraisemblablement des ablutions en relation avec le culte.

Aucun décor de serpent n'avait pu être mis en évidence dans l'architecture religieuse proprement dite, à l'exception d'un hypothétique décor en pierres qui dessinait peut-être un serpent au sommet d'un autel à ciel ouvert (autel L). Mais le serpent figurait sur une cinquantaine de récipients en céramique, vraisemblablement tous des produits d'une industrie peu lointaine et qui ne se distinguaient pas, par leur pâte ou leur qualité, des céramiques à vocation domestique également présentes sur le site (bols, grands récipients ouverts, jarres de stockage ou jarres à col).

En 2004, de nouvelles recherches furent mises en place par une équipe italienne dirigée par A. Avanzini sur le site de Salūt (BB–15) dans le Wādī Bahlāʾ, au Sultanat d'Oman. Y fut dégagée une plate-forme monumentale de plus de 25 m de haut, qui dominait la plaine environnante et à laquelle on accédait par une série de rampes. Ce site livra à son tour un mobilier se démarquant par un grand nombre d'objets en céramique ou en métal avec des représentations de serpents (Avanzini *et al.* 2007: figs 18, 19).

Durant la même période une autre découverte surprenante était faite à la faveur d'une prospection dans l'émirat d'Abu Dhabi par une équipe jordanienne

Figure 2. *Vue de Masāfī-1.*

dirigée par Hussein Qandil: à Sārūq al-Hadīd à plusieurs centaines de kilomètres de toute source de minerai, un épandage de scories de bronze s'étendait sur plusieurs hectares en plein cœur de la zone dunaire (Qandil 2003: 126). Des fouilles réalisées sur le site livrèrent un matériel d'une exceptionnelle richesse, qui incluait là encore des céramiques à décor de serpents en relief et des figurines en bronze en forme de serpents dans un secteur qui cependant ne semblait receler aucune architecture construite.[3]

Nous présentons dans cet article les premières observations effectuées sur un cinquième site découvert durant la campagne 2009 dans l'oasis de Masāfī, sur lequel des représentations de serpents ont également été recueillies en grand nombre. Les premières fouilles nous incitent à y voir un temple, qui paraît s'insérer dans l'habitat environnant selon un modèle un peu différent de celui qui semble avoir prédominé à Biṭnah.

[3] La plus grande partie du matériel est inédite. Quelques représentations de serpents sont illustrées dans Qandil 2003: figs 10/5, 14/2.

Masāfī: le site

Masāfī se localise dans la partie occidentale des montagnes d'Oman, dans une zone de confluence entre deux grands wadis, Wādī Ham (Wādī 'l-Ḥāmī) et Wādī Abadilah (Wādī ᶜAbādilah), qui relient la plaine du piémont occidental à la côte orientale des Émirats, à hauteur de Dibba (Dibā) au nord et à hauteur de Fujayrah au sud (Fig. 1). C'est un axe de circulation transversal majeur, l'un des rares passages à travers les montagnes et sans conteste le plus large entre le Musandam au nord et Wādī Jizzi (Wādī al-Jizī) au sud. Une aire stratégique entre deux zones de peuplement distinctes, qui furent occupées pendant l'Âge du Fer.

Des recherches sont menées dans cette région depuis 2006 par la Mission Archéologique Française en collaboration avec le Département des Antiquités de Fujayrah, et avec l'accord du Département des Antiquités de Ra's al-Khaymah. La prospection de l'oasis de Masāfī a permis de circonscrire très grossièrement une zone de 600×200 m localisée dans la partie sud de l'oasis, au

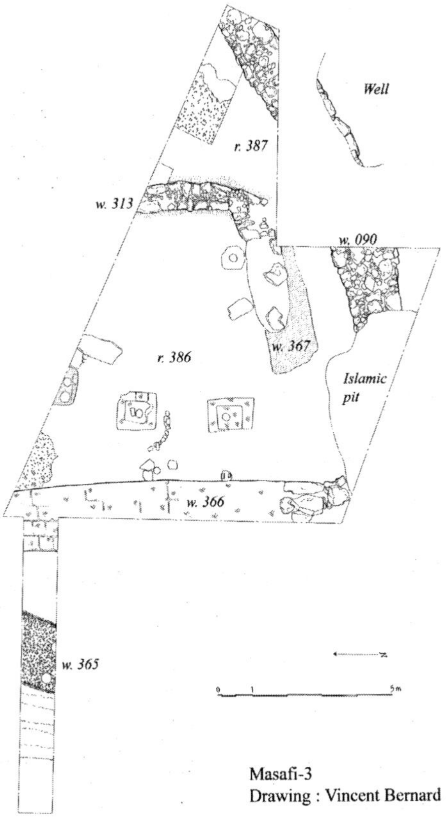

Figure 3. *Plan de Masāfī-3.*

nord-ouest du grand rond-point de Masāfī, et sur laquelle de la céramique de l'Âge du Fer se rencontre en surface.

Un premier chantier ouvert en 2006 à Masāfī-1 dans la partie occidentale du village, en bordure de la palmeraie, a permis de mettre au jour une succession de trois bâtiments munis chacun d'une grande salle à piliers (Fig. 2).

Dans le niveau le plus ancien il s'agit d'un bâtiment construit en briques crues blanchâtres, contenant une salle de 6×6 m munie de trois, sans doute quatre, bases de piliers rectangulaires, et entourée au nord, à l'ouest et à l'est de plusieurs salles oblongues. Dans le niveau suivant, un nouveau bâtiment est construit au dessus du précédent. C'est toujours une architecture en brique crues, mais en briques crues jaunâtres, faites d'une argile plus grasse, et c'est une architecture plus opportuniste, avec des bouchages, des murs parfois épais et peu réguliers, un plan moins symétrique. Le bâtiment n'est préservé qu'en partie, mais il intègre toujours une salle à piliers de 7×8 m avec cinq bases de piliers en terre à brique grossièrement circulaires, munies de dalles sur lesquelles étaient implantés des poteaux en bois. Enfin, au cours d'une troisième phase de construction un troisième bâtiment, en pierres, remplace le précédent, avec une salle similaire munie non pas de bases de piliers mais de trous de poteaux de 20 cm de diamètre en moyenne, qui se distribuent grossièrement sur trois rangées parallèles.

Le mobilier des niveaux 2 et 3 forment un assemblage comparable à celui qui caractérise d'autres bâtiments collectifs munis d'une salle à piliers de la région (Bâtiment G à Rumailah, Bâtiment II à Muwayliḥ): il comporte une proportion élevée de récipients à becs pontés, de petits bols peints ou portant un graffito gravé et de grandes jarres de stockage, et inclut des braseros vraisemblablement utilisés à maintes reprises, dont quelques-uns portent un décor de serpent en relief. On y trouve encore des objets et des fragments de bronze, ainsi que plusieurs fragments de fonds de creusets.

La fonction des bâtiments munis d'une salle à piliers a été débattue à plusieurs reprises par différents chercheurs (Boucharlat & Lombard 2001; al-Tikriti 2002; Magee 2003; Benoist, sous presse), qui y voient pour l'essentiel des lieux de rencontres et de cérémonies à caractère officiel et prestigieux et des lieux de stockage ou de management d'un certain nombre de ressources de la communauté: eau du système d'irrigation, produits de l'agriculture, produits de l'artisanat (métallurgie) et du commerce. À Biṭnah, le bâtiment central des second et troisième niveaux du sanctuaire avait été comparé par sa forme et son matériel à ces bâtiments collectifs et nous avions proposé de lui attribuer une fonction analogue, en dépit du contexte religieux dans lequel il s'insérait.

L'exemple de Biṭnah où il nous apparaissait qu'un espace de ce genre avait pu se développer au sein d'un sanctuaire nous conduisit à Masāfī à nous interroger sur l'environnement immédiat des trois bâtiments à piliers successifs mis en évidence, et à entreprendre une exploration systématique des alentours. C'est au cours de cette exploration que fut découvert le bâtiment de Masāfī-3.

Il se localise à 65 m environ au sud-ouest de Masāfī-1, dans la zone de palmeraie, sous une ancienne maison en briques crues de type traditionnel. Le site n'était pas visible en surface, mais de très grosses pierres émergeaient de la paroi d'un puits signalant une ancienne construction à environ 1 m de profondeur. Un sondage mené tout près révéla un mur épais associé à un sol qui livra une surprenante quantité de matériel du Fer II, et parmi ce dernier plusieurs tessons décorés d'un serpent en relief.

Une aire de 15×9 m fut ouverte en 2009 avec l'autorisation du propriétaire de la ferme, son Altesse Cheikh Hamad ben Mohammed al-Sharqi, l'Émir de Fujayrah. La fouille nous permit de dégager une partie d'un bâtiment en pierres et en briques crues, qui parait être un bâtiment de grande taille, de forme irrégulière. Il est limité au sud-est par un mur de 1,70 m d'épaisseur construit en blocs bruts de grand calibre (Fig. 3/mur 090). Ce mur, dégagé sur une dizaine de mètres de long, semble avoir eu une trajectoire légèrement courbe et non rectiligne. Il est en partie détruit au sud par une grande fosse d'époque islamique (Fig. 3/cour 302). À l'ouest, il pourrait être limité par un second ouvrage, un mur bas constitué d'une sorte de conglomérat de petites pierres et de graviers, pris dans une matrice argileuse compacte et bordé à l'ouest par un canal peu profond (Fig. 3/mur 365). Ce mur pourrait n'avoir été que la base d'un ouvrage aujourd'hui disparu. Nous ignorons encore s'il constitue la limite du site religieux ou s'il séparait simplement deux espaces à l'intérieur du sanctuaire. Il forme avec le mur m. 090 un angle aigu.

À l'intérieur de l'espace limité au sud-est et à l'ouest par ces deux murs, a été partiellement dégagé un espace quadrangulaire assez grand (Fig. 3/pièce ou cour 386), qui mesure au moins 10 m du nord au sud pour 7,50 m d'est en ouest. Il est bordé à l'ouest par un mur de briques crues de 1,20 m d'épaisseur (Fig. 3/mur 366), à l'est par un mur de pierres de 65 cm d'épaisseur (Fig. 3/mur 313), et au sud par un mur de 70 cm d'épaisseur incluant une partie en pierres au sud-est et une autre en briques crues au sud-ouest (Fig. 3/mur 367), le tout endommagé par une fosse de récupération. A l'extrémité ouest de ce mur existait vraisemblablement une entrée, à laquelle on accédait par un passage depuis un autre espace aménagé à l'est (Fig. 3/pièce 387).

Nous n'expliquons pas encore clairement le caractère composite de cette architecture de pierres et de briques crues. En l'état actuel des fouilles, il n'est pas encore possible d'identifier avec certitude deux phases de construction distinctes qui se seraient succédé, l'une en pierres, l'autre en briques, bien qu'une telle hypothèse ne soit pas tout à fait exclue. Un épais niveau de destruction exclusivement constitué de briques crues s'étendait au-dessus des niveaux de sols sur l'ensemble de la zone fouillée: il nous conduit à penser que l'ensemble des murs était bâti en briques crues en partie haute, les pierres n'étant utilisées qu'en partie basse de certains murs, peut-être pour pallier à des problèmes d'érosion ou d'humidité. Des traces d'argile blanchâtre relevées le long de la face des murs indiquent que ceux-ci étaient uniformément recouverts d'un enduit blanchâtre, et que leur caractère hétéroclite n'était pas visible.

En l'état actuel des données, rien ne permet d'affirmer avec certitude que l'espace 386 était couvert. Deux trous de poteaux ont été trouvés dans la partie ouest à environ 1,50 m du mur. Tous deux sont entourés d'un petit massif de briques rectangulaires, d'environ 1 m de côté. Au sud-est, un troisième trou de poteau également entouré d'un petit massif de terre à brique a été trouvé contre le mur. Un quatrième pourrait avoir existé au nord-est: dans ce secteur une fosse islamique a en partie détruit les niveaux de sols, et une structure de ce type pourrait avoir disparu. Cinq mètres séparent cependant les poteaux situés à l'ouest de l'espace 386 de ceux de la partie est, une distance inhabituelle pour la région: si couverture il y a eu, il faut envisager une charpente en bois d'un type inhabituel. On peut aussi s'interroger sur une couverture partielle de l'espace (en galerie le long des murs), ou bien considérer ces trous de poteaux comme la base d'installations dont la forme reste à préciser (podiums?). Dans la partie nord du chantier, une structure en briques blanches et une grande dalle plate signalent la présence d'une autre structure encore mal définie (podium? cloison ou mur? seuil?). Le sol de la pièce semble avoir été installé sur une couche de briques crues.

Le mobilier de Masāfī-3

Le sol était recouvert d'un abondant mobilier, en grande partie constitué de récipients complets piégés sous la destruction. Ce mobilier forme un assemblage original incluant de petits ex-voto en bronze en forme de serpent, des armes en bronze, des braseros et de petites jarres décorées de serpents en céramique.

Les serpents en bronze, trente-quatre pièces au total, se concentraient pour la plupart à l'extrémité nord-est de la zone fouillée, et nous sommes tentés de restituer dans ce secteur au nord-est de la zone ouverte, une partie importante du lieu cultuel (autel?). La plupart d'entre eux sont réalisés dans une feuille de bronze découpée, enroulée sur elle-même et bien souvent ré-aplatie. Tous représentent des serpents en train de ramper en «zigzag». Nombre d'entre eux ne semblent pas décorés et rares sont les détails anatomiques qui sont clairement indiqués: la langue du serpent apparaît dans un cas, un décor de petits cercles sur l'ensemble du serpent dans un autre cas. La tête est souvent clairement individualisée, et parfois redressée au dessus du corps (Fig. 4). Ces serpents forgés trouvent des parallèles à al-Qusays (Taha 2009: pl. 53), Salūt (Avanzini *et al.* 2007: fig. 18/1), et Saruq al Hadeed

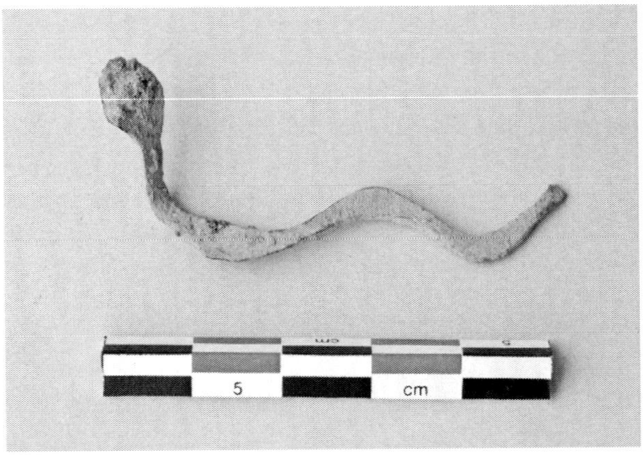

Figure 4. *Masāfī-3: serpent en bronze forgé.*

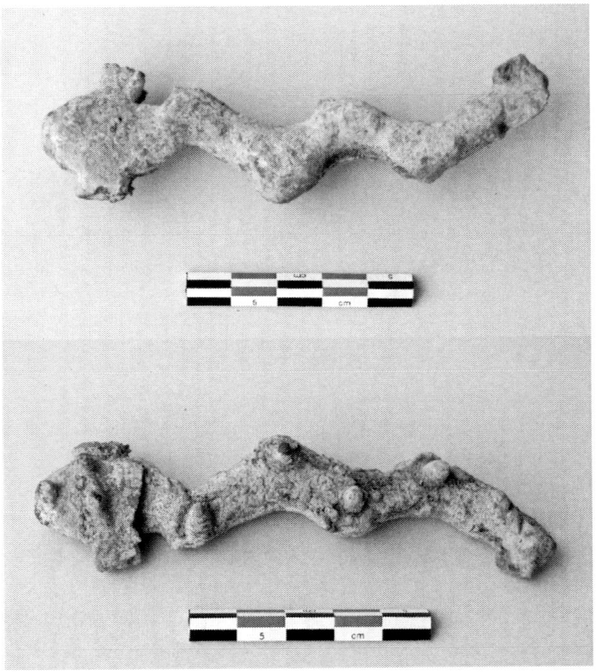

Figure 5. *Masāfī-3: serpent en bronze moulé.*

(Sārūq al-Hadīd) (Qandil 2003: fig. 14/2).

On trouve également quatre serpents plus massifs, en bronze moulé, qui pourraient tous les quatre provenir d'un même objet, élément de décor d'un coffre, d'un podium ou d'une porte (Fig. 5). Ce sont quatre serpents rampant en «zigzag», avec sur le ventre de petites tiges pointues qui constituent vraisemblablement des éléments de fixation, et de part et d'autre de la tête et de la queue, le départ d'une tige plate, peut-être un élément du décor qui réunissait tous ces serpents. Nous ignorons si ces serpents moulés faisaient partie d'un décor en place ou

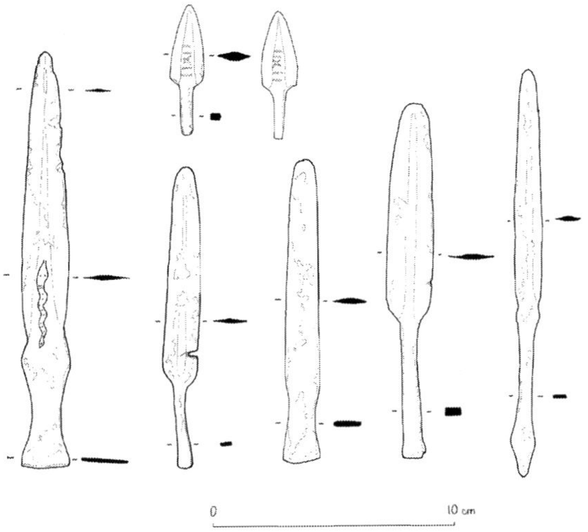

Figure 6. *Masāfī-3: armement en bronze.*

s'ils ont été récupérés pour être offerts en ex-voto. Tous se localisaient au même point, à l'extrémité nord-est du chantier. À Salūt des serpents en bronze moulés ont également été découverts (Avanzini *et al.* 2007: fig. 19/3). Ce sont cependant des objets plus massifs (25 cm de long environ contre 8 cm ici), et chaque serpent constitue un objet à part entière.

Les objets en bronze comprennent également quelques armes, une dizaine environ (Fig. 6). À l'exception de deux pointes de flèches triangulaires à soie d'un type courant dont une porte des signes gravés, toutes les armes peuvent s'interpréter comme des objets votifs et non comme des armes fonctionnelles: on trouve ainsi des pointes de lances à extrémité arrondie, des couteaux miniatures dont un porte un petit serpent gravé sur la lame et une pointe à extrémité distale en forme de tête de serpent. À al-Qusays, M. Taha affirme avoir découvert sur l'emprise du monticule aux serpents pas moins de 622 pointes de flèches de types divers, qui vraisemblablement faisaient partie des offrandes déposées dans la zone sacrée (2009: 95) et mentionne deux épées miniatures parmi le mobilier (2009: 93). À Biṭnah nous avons comptabilisé sur le site cultuel une dizaine de pointes, dont trois clairement déposées dans une fosse avec un brûle-encens à proximité de l'autel L (Benoist *et al.* 2004: 13). Toutes cependant étaient d'un type commun.

La céramique recueillie sur le sol est abondante (785 formes dont près d'une centaine complètes). La plus grande partie semble constituée de productions locales (céramiques à pâte rouge, à inclusions rouges

FIGURE 7. *Masāfī-3: récipient à pied cylindrique avec perforation.*

et blanches), que l'on rencontre également sur les sites voisins (Masāfī-1 et Masāfī-2). L'éventail des formes est réduit et très spécialisé: on trouve principalement des bols à manche latéral, des récipients à pied cylindrique, de petites jarres et un couvercle décorés de serpents en relief et quelques jarres à bec ponté. Ce sont des formes que l'on rencontre également sur d'autres sites cultuels comme Biṭnah (Benoist 2007: figs 14, 15) où cependant elles côtoient un abondant mobilier domestique (bols, bassins, jarres de stockage; 2007: fig. 13), rare ici (quelques jarres incomplètes, sur lesquelles aucun décor de serpent n'a été identifié).

Les bols à manche latéral et les récipients à pied cylindrique plein ou ajouré constituent un peu plus de 60% du corpus et trouvent de nombreux parallèles à Biṭnah, al-Qusays ou Salūt.

À Biṭnah, tous les récipients à manche latéral ou à pied cylindrique montraient des traces de brulé importantes et marquées à l'intérieur. Ces traces nous ont conduits à interpréter ces récipients comme des braseros, sans doute destinés à brûler des produits aromatiques, et il est vraisemblable étant donné l'état des vases, qu'ils ont été utilisés à maintes reprises. La distribution de ces deux types de formes sur le site nous avait incités à attribuer à chacune une fonction distincte: les braseros à pied cylindrique, trouvés près des podiums, apparaissaient comme des récipients destinés à être posés sur les autels et les produits brûlés à l'intérieur pouvaient être interprétés comme des offrandes. Les récipients à manche latéral apparaissaient comme des objets qui pouvaient être transportés avec soi, et nous y avons vu des lampes ou bien des récipients destinés à des fumigations de la personne au cours de rituels de purification en relation avec le culte (Benoist, Pillaut & Skorupka, sous presse).

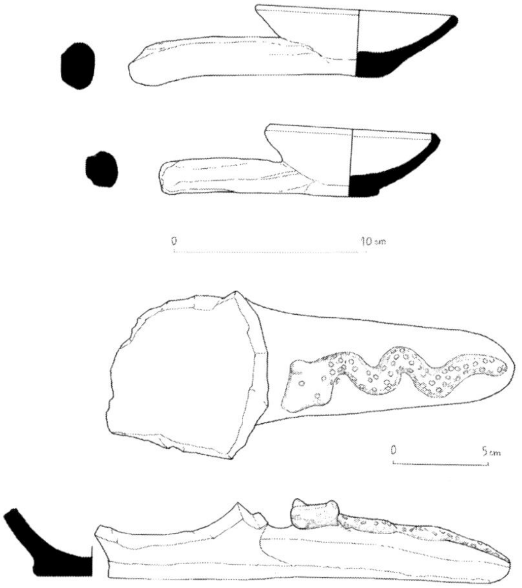

FIGURE 8. *Masāfī-3: bols à manche latéral.*

On trouve également des traces de brûlé au fond des récipients de Masāfī. Quelques récipients à pied cylindrique sont même percés d'un trou au fond, un trou qui traverse tout le pied et désigne clairement le vase comme un brasero plutôt qu'un récipient à boire (Fig. 7). Mais les récipients de Masāfī-3 semblent avoir été peu utilisés au contraire de ceux de Biṭnah, et certains pourraient n'avoir pas été utilisés du tout. Une partie du mobilier recueilli était peut-être sur place pour être vendue à des particuliers désireux de faire une offrande et n'avaient pas encore trouvé de preneur. Dans cette perspective, le vase apparaît comme partie intégrante de l'offrande faite à la divinité, ce qui ne transparaissait pas dans le mobilier de Biṭnah.

À la différence de Biṭnah où les braseros à pied cylindrique ou à manche horizontal constituaient deux classes homogènes du point de vue de la taille, on distingue à Masāfī-3 dans chaque groupe deux sous-ensembles: des bols à manche horizontal de petite taille, simples et au décor limité (incisions ou décor peint seulement), se distinguent de bols similaires plus grands, souvent décorés de serpents en relief (Fig. 8). Il en est de même des récipients à pied cylindrique plein, qui comportent également une sous-classe simple, de petite taille, et une autre un peu plus grande, plus fréquemment décorée (Fig. 9). Faut-il y voir la coexistence d'offrandes «simples» et d'offrandes plus élaborées et sans doute un peu plus chères? Ou bien des usages un peu différents, chaque ensemble étant destiné à

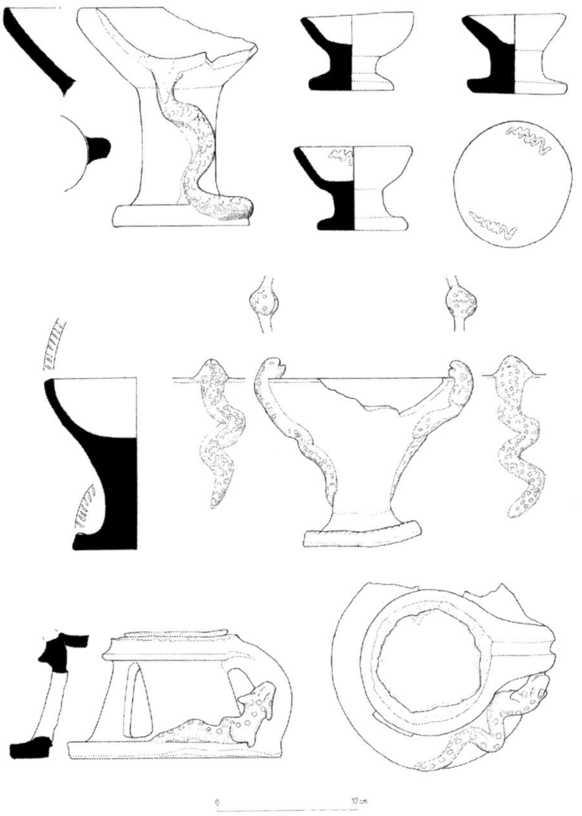

Figure 9. *Masāfī-3: récipients à pied cylindrique.*

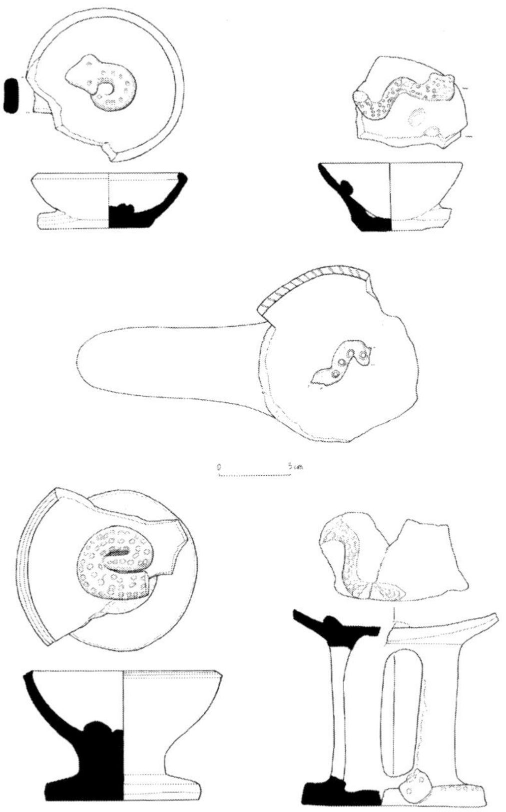

Figure 10. *Masāfī-3: récipients à manche ou à pied avec un serpent à l'intérieur.*

contenir un produit particulier? Nous n'avons pu établir de relation directe entre taille du récipient et plus ou moins grande fréquence ou la plus ou moins grande intensité des traces de brûlé présentes à l'intérieur, et seules des analyses chimiques de la paroi des vases seraient susceptibles de fournir un élément de réponse.

Le site a également livré un petit ensemble de récipients à manche latéral ou à pied cylindrique absent à Biṭnah, et qui se distingue par un décor de serpent en relief figurant à l'intérieur de la coupelle (Fig. 10). Ces récipients ne portent aucune trace de combustion et peut-être ont-ils été utilisés d'une façon différente. Ils évoquent curieusement un autre rituel, connu dans un bâtiment cultuel de l'île de Bahreïn un peu plus tard, au sixième siècle av. J.C., et qui consistait à enterrer des serpents dans des sacs placés dans des bols. Ce rituel a été mis en relation par G. Bibby avec la légende mésopotamienne de Gilgamesh, dans laquelle le serpent devient le détenteur de l'immortalité (1969: 174), et plus récemment par D.T. Potts avec des pratiques d'origine indienne (rituels védiques) et sans aucun lien ni avec la Mésopotamie, ni avec l'Arabie (2007).

Or quelques vases à pied cylindrique ornés d'un serpent placé à l'intérieur de la coupelle se distinguent à Masāfī-3 par leur pâte, caractérisée par un abondant dégraissant constitué de petites inclusions qui ont explosé à la cuisson, formant de petites cavités rondes tapissées de blanc (Fig. 11). C'est un dégraissant particulier, connu pour caractériser la céramique de Bahreïn. Des analyses récemment effectuées par P. Magee, F. Højlund et S. Zambelli (2009) sur des fragments de céramique «à explosions blanches» (bols et jarres) trouvés en petite quantité sur des sites de la frange occidentale des EAU tels que Muwayliḥ, suggèrent leur importation depuis cette région. À Masāfī-3, la présence parmi le mobilier cultuel d'exemplaires issus de Bahreïn permettrait de mettre en évidence pour la première fois des échanges induisant une communauté de culte entre les deux régions, et mettrait en lumière une communauté interrégionale de pratiques cultuelles, un phénomène habituellement peu visible. Elle doit toutefois être confirmée par des analyses pétrographiques et chimiques.

Figure 11. *Masāfī-3: récipient à pied cylindrique en céramique à explosions blanches.*

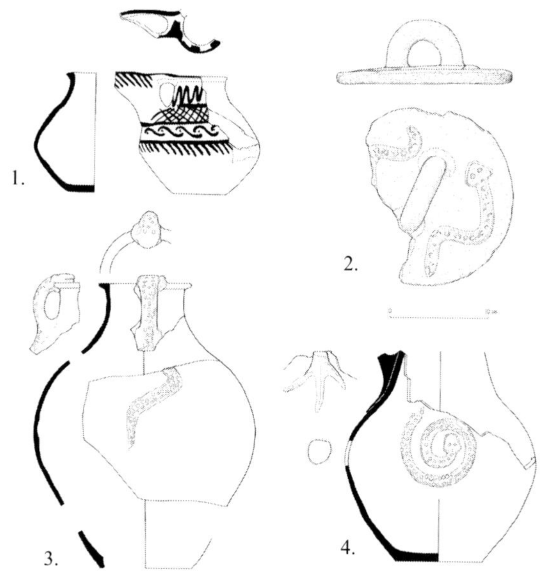

Figure 12. *Masāfī-3: jarres et couvercle.*

Des jarres sans col décorées de serpents, des cruches munies d'une anse en forme de serpent et un couvercle avec deux serpents disposés de part et d'autre de la poignée trouvent également des parallèles sur d'autres sites cultuels de la région (Biṭnah et al-Qusays) (Fig. 12/2–4). Pour la plupart ce sont de petits vases, et on remarque ici l'absence des très grandes jarres de stockage décorées de serpents, qui se rencontrent par exemple à Biṭnah (Benoist 2007: fig. 15/11) ou Saruq al-Hadeed (inédites).

Le site cultuel a également livré un peu de céramique fine rouge peinte, une catégorie que l'on retrouve en faible quantité sur de nombreux sites de l'Âge du Fer, et qui apparaît comme un ensemble homogène ayant circulé dans toute la région (Benoist 2000: 393; Magee *et al.* 1998). Elle a livré ici deux récipients à bec ponté (Fig. 12/1) qui sont parmi les rares objets présents sur le site dont on retrouve des équivalents exacts sur des sites à vocation domestique (Rumaylah: Boucharlat & Lombard 1985: pl. 50/1–3) ou funéraire (Dadnā: Benoist & Ali Hassan, sous presse: fig. 5/11) et qui pour cette raison, n'apparaissent pas comme des objets à vocation exclusivement cultuelle. Ce sont cependant des céramiques de prestige.

Enfin le site de Masāfī-3 a livré une figurine qui représente un animal composite avec quatre sabots fendus et une courte queue de mouton, un long cou flexible de chameau et une tête plate rappelant le profil des selles

Figure 13. *Masāfī-3: figurine animale avec serpents.*

que portent les figurines de chameaux de Muwayliḥ (Fig. 13). Sur son dos rampent deux serpents, dont l'un a de petites boules rondes dans la gueule (œufs? perles? objets précieux?). Un serpent en relief rampe autour du cou et un autre entre ses pattes. Plusieurs serpents sont peints sur son corps. De petits cercles sont imprimés sur son cou et sur ses pattes, identiques aux petits cercles imprimés sur le corps de nombreux serpents en relief recueillis sur le site. Dans le bâtiment voisin de Masāfī-1, un brûle-encens constitué d'un gobelet porté par deux chameaux avec des serpents en relief sur les côtés semble de la même veine (Benoist, sous presse: fig. 7).

Conclusion

Masāfī-3 apparaît comme un temple dédié à une ou plusieurs divinités représentées sous forme de serpents, qui s'inscrit dans une tradition régionale maintenant documentée sur plusieurs sites d'Arabie orientale au cours de l'Âge du Fer (Biṭnah, al-Qusays, Salūt, Sārūq al-Ḥadīd). Sa forme et son architecture sont encore mal comprises, dans la mesure où nous ignorons quelle proportion du bâtiment la zone dégagée représente et où nous ne disposons d'aucun modèle architectural standard qui puisse nous servir de référence pour tenter de le préciser: il semble que l'architecture religieuse d'Arabie orientale ait réuni des structures de forme et de taille diverses, du petit temple de 5 m de long d'al-Qusays à la plate-forme monumentale de Salūt de plus de 25 m de haut dominant la plaine.

En dépit des nombreux points communs qu'il offre avec le site de Biṭnah, le site cultuel de Masāfī-3 nous paraît de nature bien différente. À Biṭnah, nous avions pu mettre au jour un site cultuel établi dehors, dans un espace ouvert, avec au centre un bâtiment qui était devenu un bâtiment à piliers comparable à ceux de Masāfī-1, et une aire sacrée où étaient soigneusement enterrés des offrandes alimentaires et des résidus de banquets, avec aussi de petites constructions ou des autels en plein air, sur lesquelles des fumigations étaient pratiquées, ou devant lesquelles des offrandes étaient enfouies. À Biṭnah, le mobilier regroupait des vases décorés de serpents mais également des céramiques de type domestique, et la vaisselle paraissait abondamment utilisée. À Masāfī, on se trouve dans un bâtiment hyperspécialisé, un espace fermé nettement séparé des bâtiments à piliers voisins, avec un mobilier entièrement spécifique, et cependant aucune structure encore qui puisse être clairement comparée à celles qui ont été mises en évidence autour de Biṭnah (le podium trouvé sous la berme nord du chantier pourrait être un autel mais cela doit être confirmé). On pourrait tout aussi bien se trouver devant un simple entrepôt d'objets cultuels, et seule l'évidente qualité de l'architecture (en dépit de son mauvais état de préservation et de son caractère hétéroclite) invite à y voir avant tout un espace solennel.

C'est là une situation intéressante car susceptible de nous permettre d'affiner notre analyse des relations unissant le domaine cultuel proprement dit et ce qui relève davantage du domaine festif, et d'approfondir notre typologie des sites religieux régionaux en distinguant des ensembles cultuels ouverts comme celui de Biṭnah, de portée peut-être essentiellement locale, dans lesquels pratiques cultuelles et vie publique ont pu s'interpénétrer fortement, de lieux cultuels plus spécialisés, davantage isolés du tissu villageois, mais dont l'influence a pu s'étendre paradoxalement davantage et qui ont pu avoir aussi des répercussions économiques plus importantes: Masāfī-3 pourrait appartenir à ce second ensemble, que nous espérons pouvoir documenter davantage au cours des prochaines campagnes.

Références

Antonini S.

2004. *I motivi figurativi delle Banāt 'Ad nei templi sudarabico. Repertorio Iconografico Sudarabico.* ii. Paris: Académie des inscriptions et belles lettres/Rome: Instituto Italiano per l'Africa et l'Oriente.

Avanzini A., Phillips C., al-Jahfali M., Condoluci C., Cremaschi M., Iamoni M. & Santoni R.

2007. *Salut. Preliminary Report (February–March 2007).* IMTO — Italian Mission to Oman — University of Pisa. (Rapport de fouilles remis au département des Antiquités, Mascate/Salalah, Mars 2007). Pisa: IMTO.

Benoist A.

2000. La céramique de l'Âge du Fer en Péninsule d'Oman. Thèse de doctorat, Université de Paris I. [Inédit].

2005. Excavations at Bithna — Fujairah. First and second seasons. Pages 70–87 in P. Hellyer & M. Ziolkowski (eds), *Emirates Heritage I. Proceedings of the First Annual Symposium on recent Paleontological and Archaeological discoveries in the Emirates.* Al Aïn: Zayed Center for Heritage and History.

2007. An Iron Age II snake cult in the Oman Peninsula: evidence from Bithnah (Emirate of Fujairah). *Arabian archaeology and epigraphy* 18: 34–54.

(sous presse). Authority and religion in eastern Arabia during the Iron Age (1150–250 BC). In A. Avanzini (ed.), *Settlements and Society in Eastern Arabia during the Iron Age. Acts of the Symposium on Eastern Arabia, University of Pisa, 12–13 May 2008.*

Benoist A. & Ali Hassan S.

(sous presse). An inventory of the objects collected in a collective burial in Dadna (Emirate of Fujairah). In L. Weeks & A. Porter A. (eds), *Proceedings of the Conference Death, Burial and the Transition to the Afterlife in Arabia (London, 27–29 November 2008*). Oxford: Archaeopress.

Benoist A., Pillaut S. & Skorupka M.

(sous presse). Rituels associés au symbole du serpent en Arabie orientale au cours de l'Age du Fer (1200–300 av. J.C.): l'exemple de Bithnah (Emirat de Fujairah). In C. Robin & I. Sachet (eds), *Dieux et déesses d'Arabie: images et représentations. Compte rendu de la table ronde tenue au Collège de France les 2 et 3 octobre 2007.*

Benoist A., Bernard V., Hamel A., Saint-Genez F., Schiettecatte J. & Skorupka M.

2004. L'Age du Fer à Bithnah (Emirat de Fujairah): campagnes 2001–2002. *Proceedings of the Seminar for Arabian Studies* 34: 17–34.

Bibby G.

1969. *Looking for Dilmoun*. New York: Alfred Knopf.

Boucharlat R. & Lombard P.

1985. The oasis of al Aïn in the Iron Age. Excavations at Rumeilah 1981–1983. Survey at Hili-14. *Archaeology in the U.A.E.* 4: 44–73.

2001. Le bâtiment G de Rumeilah: remarques sur les salles à poteaux de l'Age du Fer en péninsule d'Oman. *Iranica Antiqua* 36: 213–238.

de Cardi B., Kenneth D. & Stocks R.

1994. Five thousand years of Settlement at Khatt. *Proceedings of the Seminar for Arabian Studies* 24: 35–96.

Dhorme E.

1949. *Les religions de Babylonie et d'Assyrie. Les anciennes religions orientales II.* Paris: Presses Universitaires de France.

Humphries J.H.

1974. Harvard Archaeological Survey in Oman II: Some later prehistoric sites. *Proceedings of the Seminar for Arabian Studies* 4: 49–76.

Magee P.

2003. Columned Halls, Power and Legitimisation in the South-East Arabian Iron Age. Pages 182–191 in D. Potts, H. Al Nabooda & P. Hellyer (eds), *Archaeology of the U.A.E. Proceedings of the first international Conference on the archaeology of the U.A.E.* London: Trident Press.

Magee P., Grave P., Al-Tikriti W.Y., Barbetti M., Yu Z. & Bailey G.

1998. New Evidences for specialized ceramic production and exchange in the Southeast Arabian Iron Age. *Arabian archaeology and epigraphy* 9/2: 236–245.

Magee P., Højlund F. & Zambelli A.

2009. A mysterious barrier or just business as usual? First Millennium BC trade in the Arabian Gulf. Paper delivered at the Seminar for Arabian Studies, July 2009. [Inédit].

Miroschedji P. de

1981. Le Dieu élamite aux serpents et aux eaux jaillissantes. *Iranica Antiqua* 16/2: 1–25.

Potts D.T.

2007. Revisiting the snake burials of the Late Dilmun building complex on Bahrain. *Arabian archaeology and epigraphy* 18: 55–74.

Qandil H.

2003. Survey and Excavation at Saruq al Hadeed 2002–2003. Pages 121–139 in P. Hellyer & M. Ziolkowski (eds), *Emirates Heritage*. i. *Proceedings of the first annual Symposium on Recent Palaeontological and archaeological discoveries in the Emirates*. Al Aïn: Zayed Center for Heritage and History.

Root M.C.
2002. Animals in the Art of ancient Iran. Pages 169–211 in B.J. Collins (ed.), *A History of the animal world in the Ancient Near East*. Leiden/Boston: Brill.

Taha M.Y.
1983. The Archaeology of the Arabian Gulf during the first Millennium B.C. *Al-Rafidan* 3–4: 75–87.
2009. *The Discovery of the Iron Age in the United Arab Emirates*. Abu Dhabi: Ministry of Culture, Youth and Community Development.

Al-Tikriti W.Y.
1989. The excavations at Bidya, Fujairah: the 3rd and 2nd millennia BC cultures. *Archaeology in the U.A.E.* 5: 101–114.
2002. The south-east Arabian origin of the *falaj* system. *Proceedings of the Seminar for Arabian Studies* 32: 117–138.

Adresse de l'auteur

Anne Benoist, CNRS (Centre National de la Recherche Scientifique), UMR 5133 – Archéorient, Maison de l'Orient, 7 Rue Raulin, 69007 Lyon, France.

e-mail Anne.benoist@mom.fr

Proceedings of the Seminar for Arabian Studies 40 (2010): 131–134

First investigations at the Wādī al-ᶜAyn tombs, Oman (poster)

Manfred Böhme

Summary
The "beehive tombs" from Wādī al-ᶜAyn (Wādī ʾl-ᶜAyn) W are a well-known part of a UNESCO World Heritage Monument site in Oman. Despite the popularity of the tombs, detailed records are rare. The "Bat Research & Restoration Project" has now begun the documentation as preparatory work for urgent preservation treatment. This preliminary report provides helpful information in order to develop a chronology for this assemblage of tombs.

Keywords: tomb construction, Ḥafīt period, Umm an-Nar period, Wādī al-ᶜAyn, Oman

Wādī al-ᶜAyn (Wādī ʾl-ᶜAyn) is situated in the western Ḥajar region of Oman, in Wilāyat ᶜIbrī.

The ensemble of tombs near al-ᶜAyn village has been part of the "Bāt, al-ᶜAyn, al-Khutum" UNESCO World Heritage Monument since 1988. The impressive scenery is well known to everybody: the tombs are aligned on a rocky crest at Wādī al-ᶜAyn, the Jabal Mishṭ is in the background. The first records concerning Wādī al-ᶜAyn were published as site 47 in connection with field research by teams directed by Beatrice de Cardi in the wider environs of ᶜAmlaḥ (de Cardi, Collier & Doe 1976). From that time, the terms "Wādī al-ᶜAyn" and "beehive tombs" have been synonymous. We can often find illustrations of Wādī al-ᶜAyn tombs as references for typical Ḥafīt grave architecture (Cleuziou & Tosi 2007: figs 93, 97, 98). Despite the popularity of the tombs, further detailed records are rare. There was only one attempt at splitting up the group into several construction types. This was undertaken by Paul Yule and Gerd Weisgerber (1998).

In general and so far, the dating of the tombs ensemble into the Ḥafīt period has not been contradictory. In particular, if we accept the definition of "beehive tomb" (Frifelt 1975), the monuments consequently belong to a later horizon of the Ḥafīt period. Due to their uniform shape, which can be seen from afar, the chronology seems clear, but the investigation, tomb by tomb, reveals unexpected details.

For our analysis, we initially separated the ensemble into seven groups. Only tombs nos. 1–19 (group A–C) on the ridge are visible from a distance (see Fig. 1, left to right). The tombs of the other groups are partially or fully dismantled. These tombs probably generally indicate an older Ḥafīt horizon. The detailed description and registration of the tombs included features of the construction (i.e. both the concept and the technology); the building material (the exploited stones varied in size, colour, and other petrographic qualities); the situation (a microanalysis of the morphology of the terrain and the distance and proximity of the tombs nearby); and the preservation (as a result of decay and stone robbery interacting with each other). By doing this, we can integrate most of the constructions into a sequence, without using any real stratigraphic links or excavated finds.

One contributing aspect that is helpful in establishing a method is the discovery that stone robbery for subsequent construction activities was considered normal behaviour in the Ḥafīt and Umm an-Nar cultures. A percentage of stones was partially circulated inside a "closed system" of construction–dismantling–reuse. If we rule out modern stone robbery, the preservation status and the occurrence of material in secondary use (*spolia*) can provide evidence for the sequence analysis. This approach derives from the studies made at the Bat necropolis. In the case of the al-ᶜAyn ensemble, the robbery and reuse does not apply to all stages. Because our investigations have only just begun, this presentation of a chronological proposal of Wādī al-ᶜAyn stages should be understood as provisional, to serve as a basis for future discussions.

Stage I: the first stage is indicated by dismantled tombs, especially in group E (Fig. 4). A small flat plateau on the ridge was initially studied and the

FIGURE 1. *The ensemble of the tombs at Wādī al-ᶜAyn. A view from the south. Visible are tombs 1–19, group A–C.*

FIGURE 2. *Tomb no. 15. After the outer skin collapsed, the core construction became visible. The upper part was previously combined together with the outer skin. This is the reason for the break in the masonry structure. It should be emphasized that this kind of "cap" was originally covered and hence invisible.*

monuments were exposed on the southern edge of this terrain. Because the destruction of tombs was a gradual process, fully dismantled constructions indicate an earlier stage of partially dismantled monuments in general. Inside the chamber of tomb no. 1 we discovered the remains of a base belonging to a previous construction: one example of real stratigraphic evidence. This older tomb was fully dismantled and could be representative of stage I.

Stage IIa: in the next phase, the northern edge of the small plateau was used.

The best position was certainly occupied by tomb no. 3. Accordingly, it is the construction with the largest diameter. The tomb positions are indicated only by minor differences in the morphology. The height of the ground level is important, although the differences are only of 0.5 m or less, created by protruding bedrock for example. These small details cannot be seen from a distance, as is shown in Figure 1.

Stage IIb: we found tombs in less advantageous positions near the slightly saddled parts on the ridge, although located higher up. With two circular walls, the constructions are relatively large in diameter.

Stage IIc: the remaining spaces between tombs of stages IIa and IIb were used for further buildings. The distance between neighbouring tombs was thus reduced.

Stage III: tomb no. 1 is representative of stage III. The change in the building material used to one of another colour and size becomes distinctive. In contrast to the earlier tombs, its structure with only one ring wall is remarkable.

Stage IV: these are tombs with one circular wall (nos. 2, 4 and 5). The change of stone exploitation areas has resulted in a greyish building material. All the available surface stones had already been used by that time. The occupation of the remaining spaces on the mountain crest has led to a dense monument assemblage. Two technological aspects offer chronological evidence: the high threshold on the entrance passage and traces of stone trimming (Fig. 3), leading to the hypothesis that stage IV belongs to the Umm an-Nar culture. For the present, an elaborate stone preparation is positive identification of an Umm an-Nar culture construction (Yule & Weisgerber 1998).

Stage V: two smaller tombs are in a disadvantageous position. They consist of an inhomogeneous stone mixture, built up with robbed stones only (nos 7 and 8). The construction consists of one ring wall. To sum up, these examples could be the final horizon of tomb construction at al-ᶜAyn.

With regard to burial practices and beliefs, it should be noted that a flint workshop beside tomb no. 1 has been documented. It is possible that tool production was supposed to benefit from the power of the ancestors. A *terminus post quem* for the date is inferred by the location on a surface that was previously exploited for the construction of the tomb.

The monuments are representative of a much wider range of construction varieties than the so-called "beehive" type. The "Wādī al-ᶜAyn" assemblage was developed by construction activities over more than five successive horizons. A later stage of the "Wādī al-ᶜAyn" sequence possibly belongs to the Umm an-Nar period. The "Bat Research & Restoration Project" has now started the documentation as preparatory work for very urgent preservation treatment.

FIGURE 3. *Tomb no. 5, detail of the entrance. A high threshold and traces of stone trimming are indications of an Umm an-Nar culture construction. (Scale 0.5 m).*

References

Cleuziou S. & Tosi M.

2007. *In the shadow of the ancestors: The prehistoric foundations of the early Arabian civilization in Oman.* Muscat: Ministry of Heritage & Culture.

de Cardi B., Collier S. & Doe B.

1976. Excavations and Survey in Oman, 1974–75. *Journal of Omani Studies* 2: 101–187.

Figure 4. *Tomb group A–H. Satellite image overlay.*

Frifelt K.
1975. On prehistoric settlement and chronology of the Oman Peninsula. *East and West* 25/3–4: 359–424.
Yule P. & Weisgerber G.
1998. Prehistoric tower tombs at Shir/Jaylah, Sultanate of Oman. *Beiträge zur allgemeinen und vergleichenden Archäologie* 18: 183–241.

Author's address

Manfred Böhme, M.A. State Office for Heritage Management and Archaeology Saxony-Anhalt (Halle/Saale), Richard-Wagner-Str. 9, 06114 Halle, Germany.

e-mail bat_restoration@yahoo.de

Proceedings of the Seminar for Arabian Studies 40 (2010): 135–148

Glass bangles of al-Shiḥr, Ḥaḍramawt (fourteenth–nineteenth centuries), a corpus of new data for the understanding of glass bangle manufacture in Yemen

Stéphanie Boulogne & Claire Hardy-Guilbert

Summary

This article on glass bangles from al-Shiḥr, Ḥaḍramawt, presents a corpus of new data (fourteenth–nineteenth centuries) leading to an understanding of the manufacture of glass bangles in Yemen. The paper discusses the case for local production versus glass imports in south Yemen, using archaeological, textual, and ethnographic data to support the argument. This is the result of a glass study made in October 2007 at al-Shiḥr.

Keywords: glass bangles, al-Shiḥr, Ḥaḍramawt, imports, local manufacture

Introduction

Al-Shiḥr (Fig. 1) is mentioned as a well-known harbour of medieval and later Yemen in texts such as Sulaymān al-Mahrī b. Aḥmad b. Sulaymān's (1480–1550), *Al-ᶜumdah al-mahriyyah fī ḍabt al-ᶜulūm al-baḥriyyah*.

Investigations undertaken between 1995 and 2002, and in 2007, under the direction of C. Hardy-Guilbert (CNRS, Paris) (Hardy-Guilbert 2007), have produced an interesting corpus of ceramic and glass that mixes imports from Iran, Iraq, Asia, Africa, and India with local Yemeni manufactured material (Hardy-Guilbert 2002: 39–53). The investigations focused on material from Tell al-Qaryah, one of the ancient quarters of the city, 60 m from the shoreline. As a result, fifteen levels of occupation were defined, dating from *c.* AD 780 to 1996,[1] which could be identified with ten phases.[2] In the 2007 season, a full study of the large corpus of glass from the 1996–2002 excavations was made. We registered several samples of decorated vessels, as well as undecorated glass and many coloured bangles: a total of about 500 bangle fragments, from which we selected 185 in good condition for closer study. The corpus is generally later than the fourteenth century. Glass bangles have also been discovered in Kawd am-Saylāᵓ, around the seventeenth century in the Gulf of Aden, 600 km from al-Shiḥr (Monod 1978: 110–124), as well as in India, the Near East, and the Red Sea region.

This article intends to demonstrate how the study of al-Shiḥr bangles is important for the understanding of glass manufacture in Arabia. The paper is in three parts: the first is on the archaeological corpus; the second provides comparative data on styles and techniques; and the third focuses on the question of local production versus the importation of glass.

[1] APIM (Atlas des Ports et Itinéraires Maritimes de l'Islam Médiéval) resources.

[2] From Phase 1, the first occupation (to 4.30 m), to Phase 4, the fill of the last Abbasid structures (i.e. eighth century to the beginning of the thirteenth century), no glass bangle was recovered. Phase 5 is an open-air platform (from 6.30/6.50 to 7.00) on which huts were erected and numerous pits and ovens containing deposits of ash and fish bones were found. These structures are included inside a thick layer of ash (0.50 m thick) clearly visible throughout Tell al-Qaryah. Mustard ware and late sgraffiati associated with Longquan stoneware were found, datable to between the latter half of the thirteenth and the first half of the fourteenth century. Phase 6 (fifteenth century) is a domestic occupation of mud-brick and stone houses based on earthen floors (from 7.30 m) with other types of Tihāmah ceramics that replaced Mustard ware and with blue and white Chinese porcelain. During Phase 7 (sixteenth century) a level of mud-brick houses was built with wall foundations of stone. A glass workshop (from 7.90 m) with its hearth and crucibles (SHR 99 2345–2) belongs to this phase. In Phase 8 (seventeenth century) a part of the site was abandoned, but mud-brick dwelling rooms were built in the southern area associated with Haysī ceramics and Persian cups in frit ware imitating Chinese porcelain. At the end of the eighteenth or in the nineteenth century, during Phase 9, stone houses stood on the top of the tell. They were already destroyed when the site was discovered in 1995; a surface deposit 1 m thick, cut into by rubbish pits down to the level of Phase 8, belongs to Phase 9. In Phase 10 (twentieth century) part of the site was covered by a platform for drying fish, made of a thick layer of mud and fish oil above a bed of pebbles (from 8.95/9.10 m).

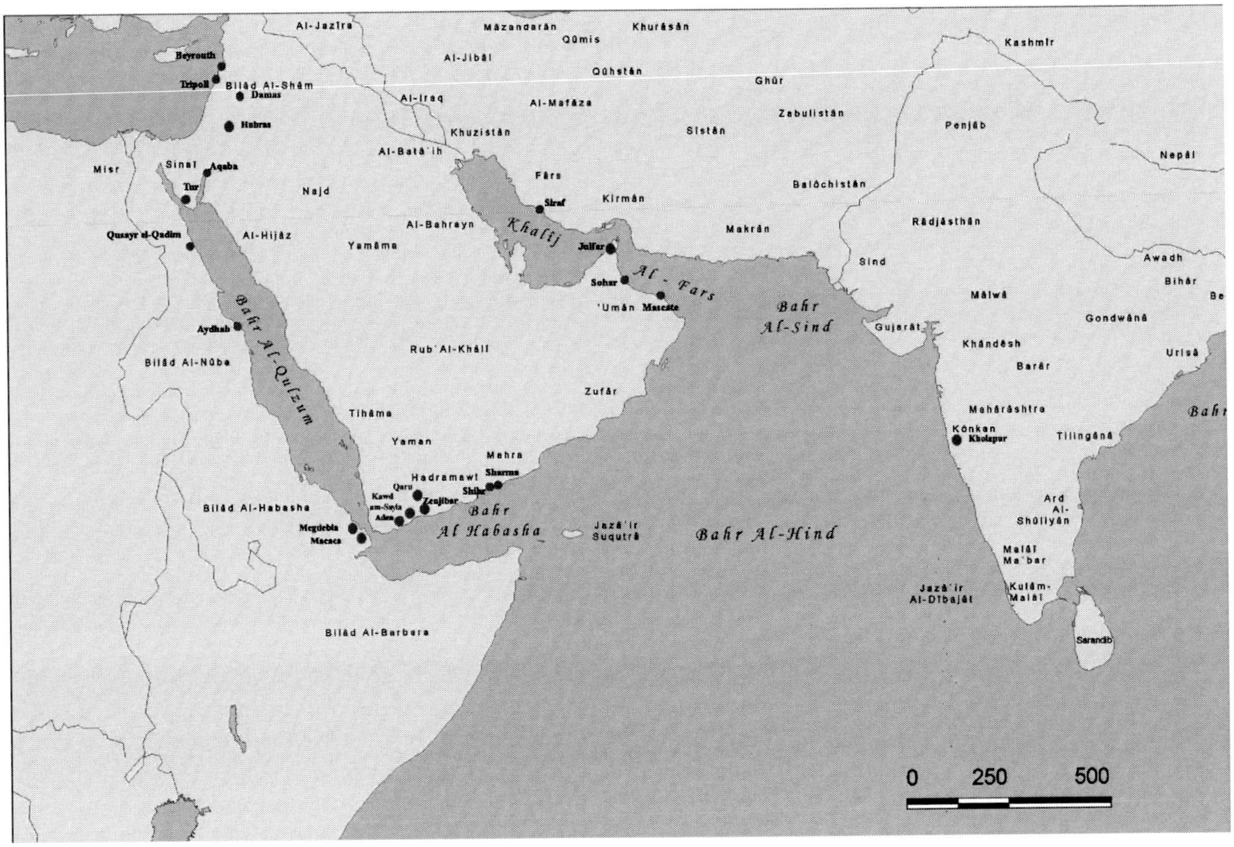

Figure 1. *A map of the location of al-Shiḥr.*

The archaeological corpus

This chapter introduces the contextual archaeological data and the material used to develop a classification.

Archaeological levels and the classification used (Figs 2 and 3)

Glass bangles were recovered only in the southern part of the tell (the site under investigation) and often from levels that also contained numerous ceramic sherds. The bangles were never found below 7.00 m, which is above the layer of ash that has been dated to the fourteenth century. The only exception was SHR 99 2301, which was found in the latest level (to 6.88/6.77 m) in test trench G52.

The classification that we used separates polychrome and monochrome bangles, as is normally done in the analysis of Indian bangles (see Sankalia & Dikshit 1952: 115–118; Dikshit 1969: 69–71) and sometimes of Near Eastern coloured bracelets (Shindo 1996; 2009). By using this methodology, polychrome (57%) and monochrome (43%) glass types were identified, among which were several sub-groups. Generally each sub-group includes many of the same type of bangles and some single unique specimens.

The polychrome bangles (Figs 4 & 5)

Polychrome bangles (105 samples) make up 57% of the finds. Of this group, 85% (ninety samples) can be grouped into six patterns with similar designs, while only 14% are of a unique pattern. They are nearly all made of light or

a. Monochrome and polychrome bangles	
Polychrome	57%
Monochrome	43%
b. Polychrome bangles	
In batches	85%
Others	15%
c. Monochromes bangles	
In batches: plain green	89%
Others	11%

Figure 2. *Classification table.*

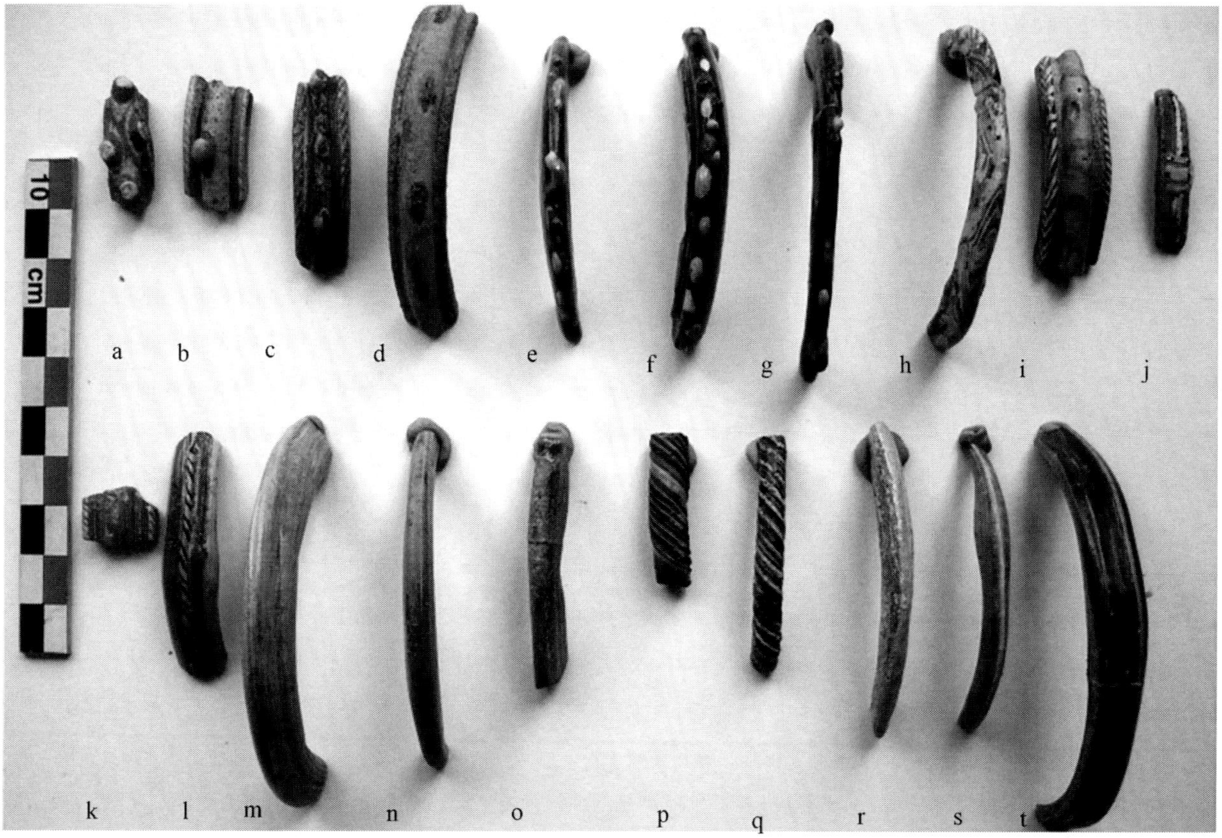

FIGURE 3. *The polychrome bangles: an overview.*
a. *SHR 97 2079-1: L 2.7 cm, W 1 cm; green core, coloured layers, flowers decoration, half flat section;* **b.** *SHR 99 2321-1: L 2.5 cm, W 1.2 cm; green core, coloured layers, prunts decoration, flat section;* **c.** *SHR 99 2370-1: L 3.6 cm, W 1 cm; green core, yellow layers, prunts decoration, flat section;* **d.** *SHR 97 2064-1: L 6.3 cm, W 1 cm; green core, coloured layers, prunts decoration, flat section;* **e.** *SHR 97 2068-1: L 5.9 cm, W 0.8 cm; green core, coloured layers, prunts decoration, triangular section;* **f.** *SHR 99 2365-18: L 5.8 cm, W 0.8 cm; green core, coloured layers, prunts decoration, triangular section;* **g.** *SHR 99 2365-10: L 6.4 cm, W 0.4 cm; green core, coloured layers, prunts decoration, triangular section;* **h.** *SHR 99 2353-12: L 5.8 cm, W 0.8 cm; green-blue core, coloured layers, marvered decoration, triangular section;* **i.** *SHR 3029-1: L 4.2 cm, W 1.2 cm; green core, coloured layers, marvered decoration, flat section;* **j.** *SHR 97 2072-4: L 3 cm, W 0.7 cm green core, coloured layers, eyes decoration, flat section;* **k.** *SHR 99 2420: L 1.4 cm, W1.2 cm; green core, coloured layers, trip decoration, flat section;* **l.** *SHR 99 2292: L 4.8 cm, W 0.5 cm; green core, coloured layers, trip decoration, flat section;* **m.** *SHR 97 2071: L 7.4 cm, W 0.7 cm; green core, bi-chrome decoration, ogival section;* **n.** *SHR 99 2366: L 6.3 cm, W 0.5 cm; green core, bi-chrome decoration, pointed section;* **o.** *SHR 97 2085: L 4.5 cm, W 0.3 cm; green core, bi-chrome decoration, ogival section;* **p.** *SHR 99 2375: L 2.5 cm, W 0.9 cm; dark core, twisted decoration, round section;* **q.** *SHR 99 2402: L 4.2 cm, W 0.5 cm; dark core, twisted decoration, round section;* **r.** *SHR 97 2073: L 5.7 cm, W 0.7 cm; green core, bi-chrome decoration, flat section;* **s.** *SHR 99 2283: L 5.4 cm, W 0.6 cm; green core, bi-chrome decoration, pointed section;* **t.** *SHR 97 2089: L 7.3 cm, W 1 cm; green core, bi-chrome decoration, flat section.*

dark green paste. Of the bangles, 85% (Fig. 4) can be dated by their context to the sixteenth to seventeenth centuries (Phases 7 and 8), although a few were found in the levels of earlier Phases 5 to 6, and can be dated from the thirteenth to fourteenth centuries. Their diameters are between 0.5 cm and 0.9 cm, with one exception of 1.2 cm.

Two sub-groups are identified. Firstly, prunts (i.e. small blobs of glass that are fused to another piece of glass) on triangular-section bangles (sixty-six examples) (Fig. 4/a, b) have two variants: a single band of prunt on a triangular section and a "crumbly decoration" on a triangular section, both variants having mostly yellow, green, or red layers on each side.

Secondly, a bi-chrome decoration (twenty-five

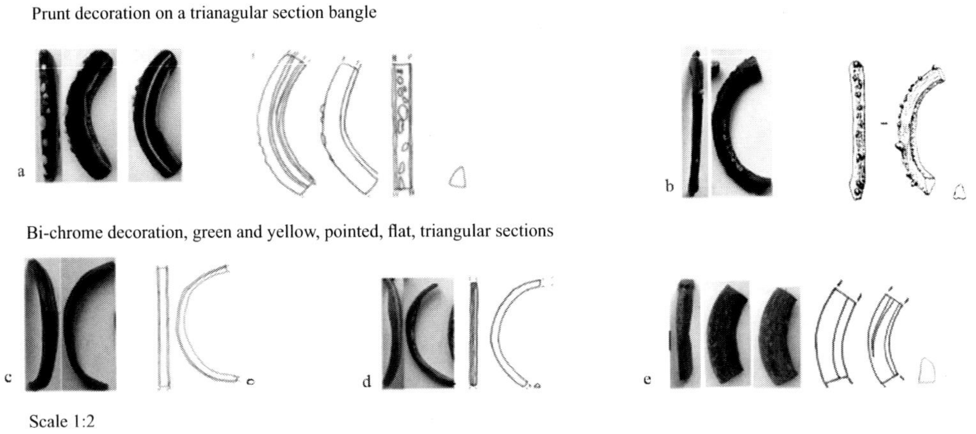

Figure 4. *Common polychrome bangles (sixteenth–seventeenth centuries).*
a. *SHR 99 2365-18: L 5.8 cm, W 0.8 cm; description as above: Fig. 3/f;* **b.** *SHR 99 2365-10: L 6.4 cm, W 0.4 cm; description as above: Fig. 3/g;* **c.** *SHR 97 2089: L 7.3 cm, W 0.6 cm; description as above: Fig. 3/t;* **d.** *SHR 99 2283-7: L 5.6 cm, W 0.4 cm; description as above: Fig. 3/s;* **e.** *SHR 97 2085: L 4.8 cm, W 1.3 cm; description as above: Fig. 3/o.*

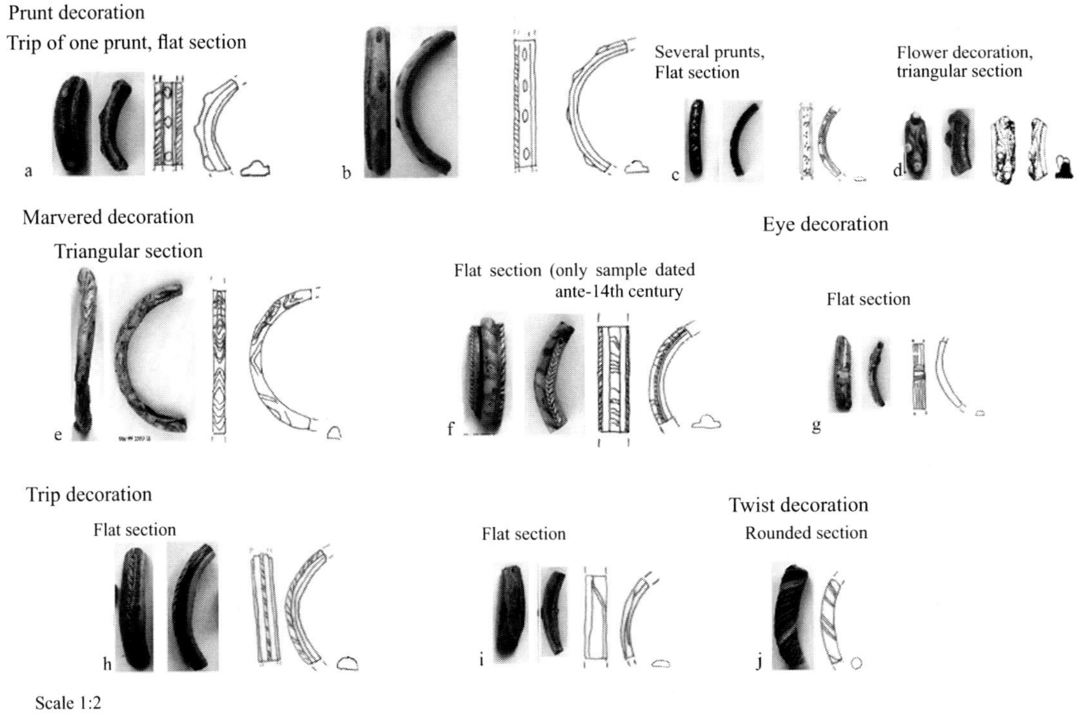

Figure 5. *Single polychrome samples (sixteenth–seventeenth centuries).*
a. *SHR 99 2370-1: L 3.8 cm, W 0.9 cm; description as above: Fig. 3/c;* **b.** *SHR 97 2064-1: L 6.3 cm, W 1 cm; description as above: Fig. 3/d;* **c.** *SHR 99 2370-3: L 3.8 cm, W 0.9 cm; blue glass, white decoration, flat section;* **d.** *SHR 97 2079-1: L 2.7 cm, W 1 cm; description as above: Fig. 3/a;* **e.** *SHR 99 2353-12: L 6.3 cm, W 0.5 cm; description as above: Fig. 3/h;* **f.** *SHR 3029-1: L 4.2 cm, W 1.2 cm; description as above: Fig. 3/i;* **g.** *SHR 99 2072: L 3.3 cm, W 0.5 cm; description as above: Fig. 3/j;* **h**. *SHR 99 2292-1: L 4.8 cm, W 0.5 cm; description as above: Fig. 3/l;* **i.** *SHR 99 2420: L 2.6 cm, W 2.5 cm; green glass, trip of glass applied, flat section;* **j.** *SHR 99 2375: L 3.1 cm, W 0.4 cm; description as above: Fig. 3/p.*

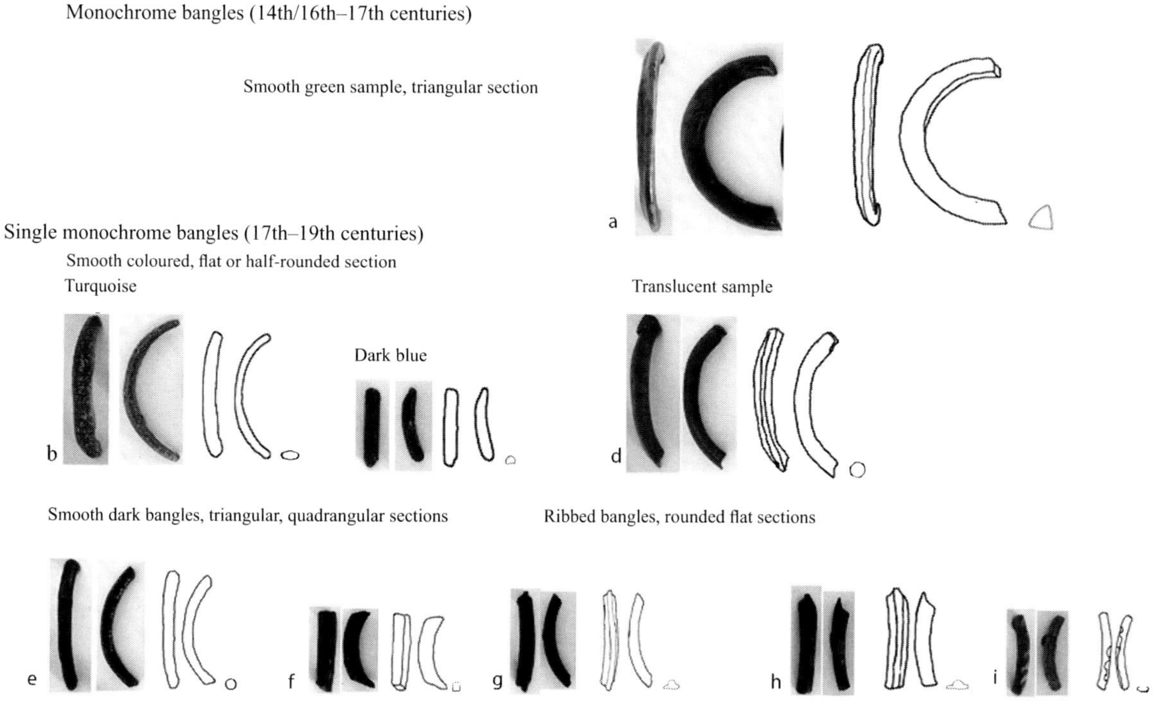

FIGURE 6. *Monochrome bangles (fourteenth–nineteenth centuries).*
a. *SHR 97 2023-1: L 8 cm, W 0.9 cm; green glass, ogival section;* **b.** *SHR 99 2417: L 6.2 cm, W 0.7 cm; blue turquoise glass, flat section;* **c.** *SHR 97 2023-3: L 2.5 cm, W 0.4 cm; marine blue glass, flat section;* **d.** *SHR 99 2282: L 4.5 cm, W 0.3 cm; translucent brown glass, flat section;* **e.** *SHR 97 2130: L 5.2 cm, W 0.2 cm; dark glass, flat section;* **f.** *SHR 99 2246: L 3.8 cm, W 1.9 cm; dark glass, quadrangular section;* **g.** *SHR 99 2297-2: L 4.2 cm, W 2.1 cm; dark glass, flat section;* **h.** *SHR 99 2292-9: L 3.3 cm, W 1.6 cm; dark glass, flat section;* **i.** *SHR 97 2088-2: L 3.4 cm, W 1.6 cm; blue light, vertical ribs, flat section.*

examples) displaying at least three variants, with a range of colours between a green core and layers of yellow glass (Fig. 4/c–e), is found on a range of thick or thin bangles. They are flat and pointed, with a triangular section. Fifteen per cent (sixteen samples) (Fig. 5/a–c) of the polychrome bangles are what we call "single" types, i.e. unique, with no more than one example of each type. These can be dated to the sixteenth to nineteenth centuries (Phases 7 to 9). Five different patterns have been identified: first, with prunt decoration on a flat or triangular section, including variants such as crumbly or flower decoration (Fig. 5/c, d); second, marvered decoration (i.e. hot decoration caused by coloured glass threads/trails fused in glass) (Fig. 5/e, f); third, eye decoration (one sample); the fourth style has a band/strip of glass (Fig. 5/g, h) decoration; the fifth and last group consists of twisted bangles. The polychrome bangles are large, around 0.8 cm in diameter and 1.4 cm thick.

The monochrome bangles (42%, eighty samples) (Fig. 6)

The majority, 89% (seventy-one samples), are smooth, thick, plain green bangles, with a large triangular section of 0.9 cm (Fig. 6/a). They can generally be dated to the seventeenth century, although a few can be attributed, by their context, to the fourteenth century. We also found a group of eight very thin bangles (Fig. 6/b–i) some of which could be dated to the sixteenth century and the majority to the seventeenth to nineteenth centuries. One is dark blue with a round section, another turquoise with a flat section, a third is translucent brown with a half-rounded section, and five are of dark paste of which two show vertical ribs on the surface.

This corpus of bangles reflects different stylistic schools, but the various styles do not reflect different dates. This is clear in the examples (Fig. 7) for the finds from inventory groups 2370, 2292, and 2023, where we find

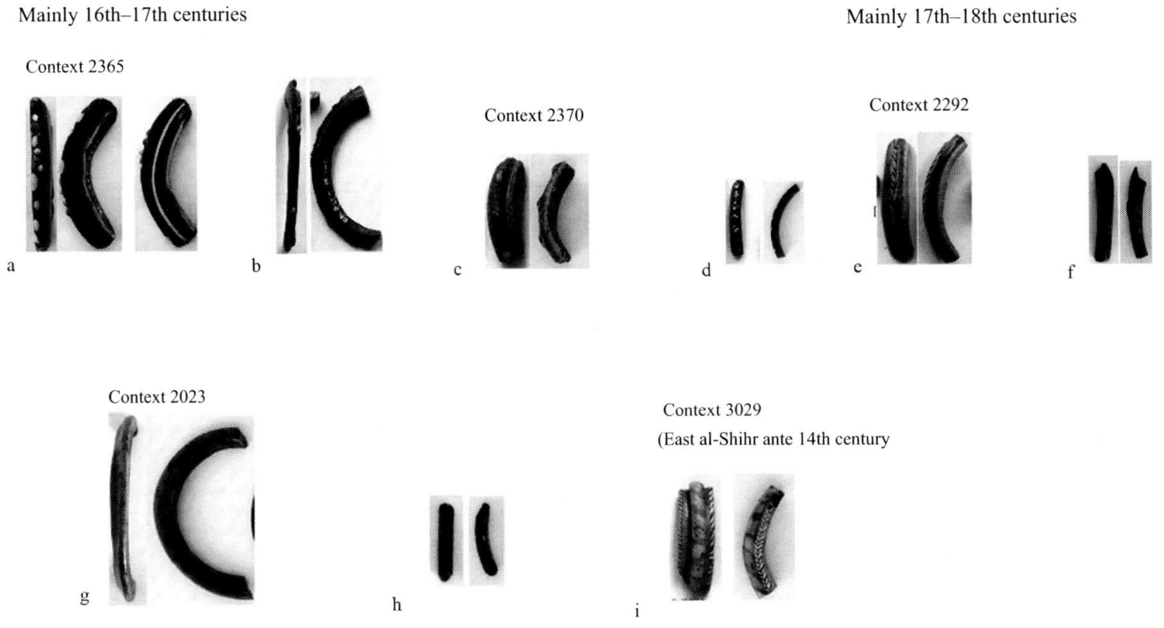

FIGURE 7. *Some bangles classified by context.*
a. *SHR 99 2365-18: L 5.8 cm, W 0.8 cm; description as above: Fig. 3/f;* **b.** *SHR 99 2365-10: L 6.4 cm, W 0.4 cm; description as above: Fig. 3/g;* **c.** *SHR 99 2370-1: L 3.8 cm, W 0.9 cm; description as above: Fig. 3/c;* **d.** *SHR 99 2370-3: L 3.7 cm, W 0.3 cm; description as above: Fig. 5/c;* **e.** *SHR 99 2292-1: L 4.8 cm, W 0.5 cm description as above: Fig. 3/l;* **f.** *SHR 99 2292-2: L 3.3 cm, W 1.6 cm; dark paste, flat section;* **g.** *SHR 97 2023-1: L 8.5 cm, W 0.4 cm; green core, description as above: Fig. 6/a;* **h.** *SHR 97 2023-3: L 2.5 cm, W 0.2 cm; blue core, round section; description as above: Fig. 6/c;* **i.** *SHR 3029-1: L 4.2 cm, W 1.2 cm; description as above: Fig. 3/i.*

different typological groups in the same archaeological context and levels.

Comparative data on style and technique

Some parallels may be established with bangles found in medieval and later levels of archaeological sites of Yemen and India, the Near East, and the Red Sea region that provide interesting comparative data.

Kawd am-Saylāʾ, al-Qarū (Abyan area oasis), Yemen, Gulf of Aden (seventeenth century) (Fig. 8)

Kawd am-Saylāʾ is located near Aden, between Shaykh ʿUthmān and Laḥj. It has been the focus of many investigations since the 1940s: by A. Lane & R.B. Serjeant (1948: 108–133); D.B. Doe (1963: 150–162); T. Monod (1978: 110–124); D. Whitcomb (1988: fig. 21); and C. Hardy-Guilbert & A. Rougeulle (1997: 147–196). Much pottery and glass vessel sherds, as well as slag and glass bangles have been found. Monod registered 156 bangles and proposed a *terminus ad quem* of the seventeenth century, at the latest. The production is very similar to that identified at al-Shiḥr, especially the prunts, bi-chrome bangles, and the plain green collection (Fig. 8/a–c), as well as single polychrome and dark monochrome smooth and ribbed bangles.

Kholāpur (fourteenth–seventeenth centuries)

Kholāpur is located in the western part of south India, near the sixteenth meridian. This site was investigated by H.D. Sankalia and M.B. Dikshit who published a report in 1952 with a small section on bangles (1952: 1–8, 115–121). Some of the items assigned to the Bahmani period (*aka* Bahmanid empire) (fourteenth–sixteenth centuries) are very similar to our corpus. The Bahmani empire was founded in 1347 by ʿAlāʾ al-Dīn Ḥasan, Bahman Shāh (Wolseley 1924: 73–80).

We can thus compare both corpuses for their prunts and coloured layers on both sides, and for the green and yellow bi-chrome examples, as well as the green monochrome bangles. All the Bahmani period bangles are said to be the work of Muslim Bahmani glassmakers,

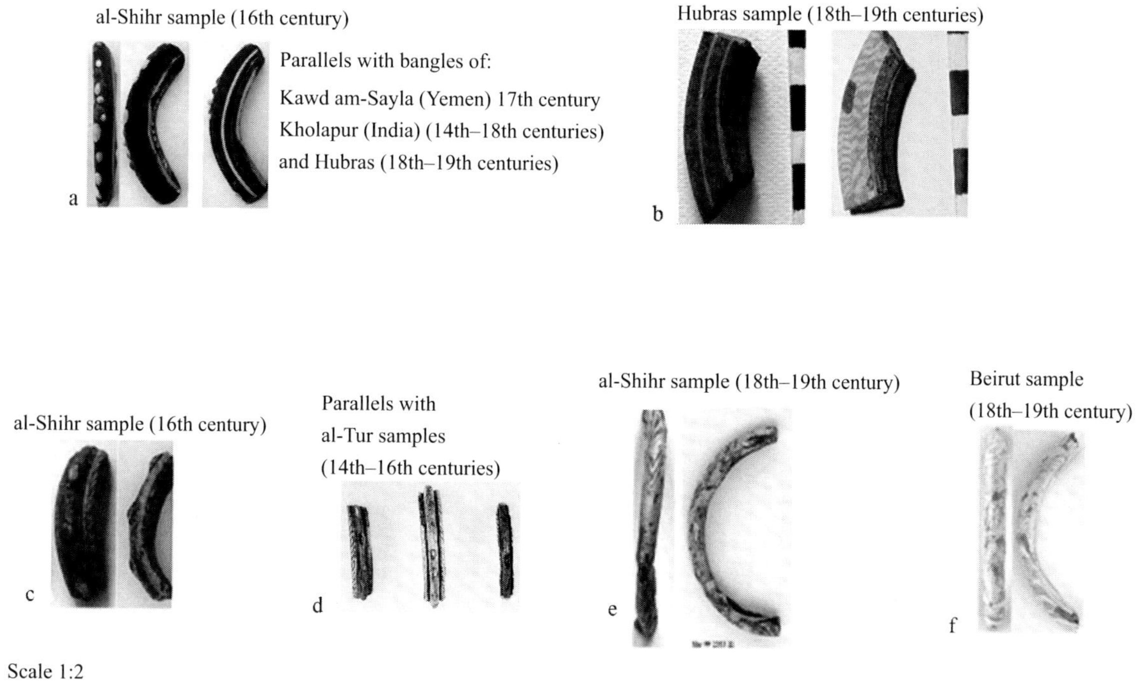

Figure 8. *Polychrome bangles parallel data.*
a. *SHR 97 2088-2: L 3.4 cm, W 1.6 cm; description as above: Fig. 6/i;* **b.** *HUBRAS: HM.06.A3.1.2. L 4.5 cm, W 1.3 cm; black core, triangular in section;* **c.** *SHR 99 2370-1: L 3.6 cm, W 1 cm; description as above: Fig. 3/c;* **d.** *TUR: TO 161, TO 1146, TO 1804 (Shindo 2009: pl. 30);* **e.** *SHR 99 2353-12: L 5.8 cm, W 0.8 cm; description as above: Fig. 3/h;* **f.** *BEYROUTH no. 32: Boulogne 2007, 097 004 008; L 5.1 cm, W 0.5 cm.*

and some remains of a workshop area were found (Sankalia & Dikshit 1952). The excavators explained that the techniques of superposed coloured glass layers were introduced by the Muslims (1952; Sankalia 1947: 252–259). This type was also found at Julfār, in the Emirates and has been attributed to India or Iran (Hardy-Guilbert 1991: 161–203; Hansman 1985: 76–83). Otherwise, items from Kholāpur (Brahmapuri) are described as different from other Indian bangles discovered, mainly because of the layer technique. Monochrome bracelets were excavated: dark coloured, light brown translucent; and turquoise bangles were registered. Such bangles are common in many levels in different Indian archaeological sites; we know, for example, of an interesting corpus from Kopia (Kanungo & Brill 2009: 11–25).

Near East: Ḥubrāṣ (Jordan), Beirut, and Damascus, late Ottoman period (eighteenth–nineteenth centuries)

The same decorative technique of coloured layers on a triangular section bangle is found on one of ten bangles discovered at Ḥubrāṣ, in northern Jordan (excavated by B. Walker, studied by S. Boulogne, 2007), that can be dated to late Ottoman times (Fig. 8/b).[3] Other comparative data may be found for the marvered white and yellow bangle of triangular section in our assemblage (sample SHR 2353–12). An almost identical example was discovered in a trading area in the upper archaeological levels of the Ottoman *sūq* in the Beirut excavations (Curvurs & Stuart 1998–1999: 167–205 and unpublished material) (Fig. 8/f). From the same levels came some amber and translucent brown twisted glass bangles, smooth dark turquoise blue ones, and a ribbed example. Some turquoise and black examples were also found in the Damascus citadel (Boulogne 2008: 127–154) (excavation report by S. Berthier [in preparation]; study by S. Boulogne [2007; 2008], and in Masyāf castle in Syria, mainly of later date (Boulogne 2007; 2008); excavations under the direction of Hathan, Direction Générale des Antiquités et Musées syriens) (Fig. 9/b, c).

[3] The Ḥubrāṣ bangles are published by S. Boulogne (Walker *et al.* 2007: 429–470).

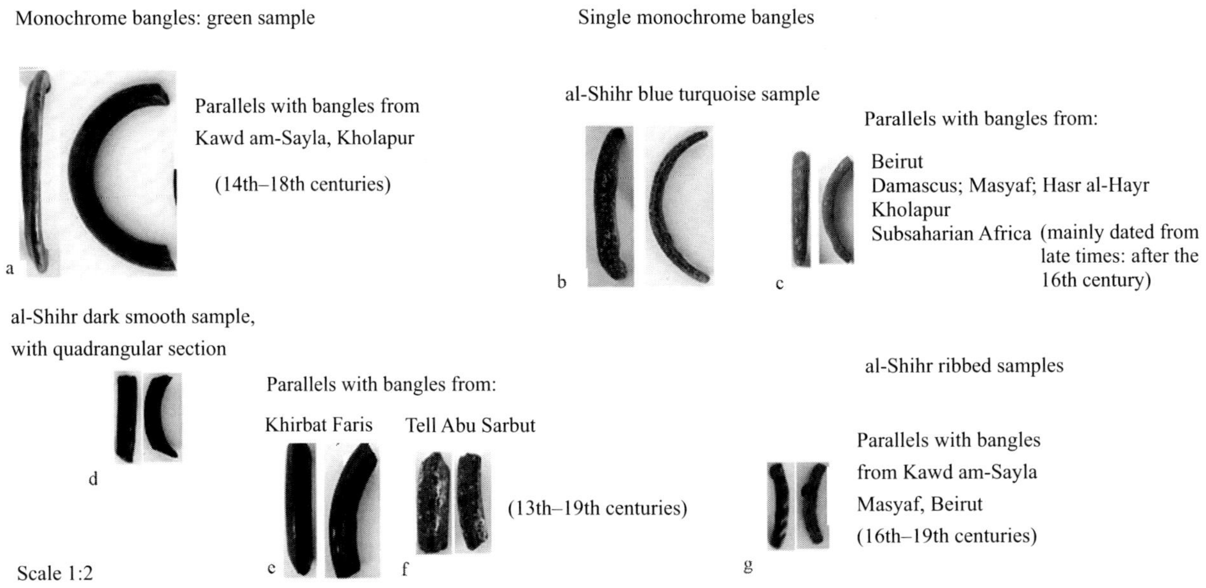

Figure 9. *Monochrome bangles parallel data.*
a. *SHR 97 2023-1: L 8 cm, W 0.2 cm; description as above: Fig. 6/a;* **b.** *SHR 99 2417: L 5.2 cm, W 0.7 cm; description as above: Fig. 6/b;* **c.** *BEY 097 004 008: L 5.1 cm, W 0.3 cm; blue glass, flat section;* **d.** *SHR 99 2246: L 3.9 cm, W 1.9 cm; description as above: Fig. 6/f;* **e.** *KHIRBAT FARIS no. 418:Boulogne 2007; 150 1 SG 1045 P19; 3.5 cm, 0.7 cm;* **f.** *TELL ABU SARBUT no. 326: Boulogne 2007; L 3.9 cm W 0.4 cm;* **g.** *SHR 97 2088-2: L 3.4 cm W 1.6 cm; description as above: Fig. 6/i.*

An interesting corpus of dark, smooth bangles was discovered in central Jordan, at Khirbat Fāris and at Tell Abū Sarbūṭ. Chemical analysis of these has revealed an interesting component that suggests an Indian or south-east Asian provenance, mixed with local elements (Boulogne & Henderson 2009: 53–75).

Red Sea region: al-Ṭūr, ᶜAydhāb, Quṣayr al-Qadīm, Mērgēbla, and Mekaᵓika (twelfth–eighteenth centuries)

A few parallels can be drawn to Red Sea region examples. A kind of bangle with a band of prunt is clearly identified in the finds from al-Ṭūr (Sinai) where a total of 3000 bangles were uncovered. These can be dated to the Mamlūk and Ottoman periods (Fig. 8/d) (Shindo 2001: 73–100; 2009: pl. 30). Others come from ᶜAydhāb, where sixty-two bangles were found (Shindo 1996), and Quṣayr al-Qadīm (Meyer 1983; 1992).

Similar samples to those of SHR 3029–1 (Fig. 5/f), dated to the thirteenth and fourteenth centuries were noted among the discoveries in Mērgēbla and Mekaᵓika near Assab in Eritrea; one is dated to the eighteenth century and from the Eritrean coast (Monod 1975: 703–718). Smooth, dark turquoise bangles were also found at al-Ṭūr.

The comparative data shows us that many of the al-Shiḥr bangles are similar to those from Kawd am-Saylāᵓ (Yemen, seventeenth century), and both have a large group of decorative elements that are like those found at Kholāpur, India (fourteenth–sixteenth century). We also found some interesting comparisons with other decorative elements from the Bilād al-Shām, but very few with those from the Red Sea region.

The question of local production versus glass imports

Medieval textual sources and ethnographic data will be used to discuss the question of local production in Shiḥr and Kawd am-Saylāᵓ versus imports from India, the Near East, and Europe, alongside previously outlined parallels, as mentioned above.

Local manufacturing at al-Shiḥr and Kawd am-Saylāᵓ mixed with Indian imports from the thirteenth to seventeenth centuries (Fig. 10)

At Kawd am-Saylāᵓ, the authors suggest that there was local glass-working. This was based on the discovery of slag and finds of glass vessels. There are numerous

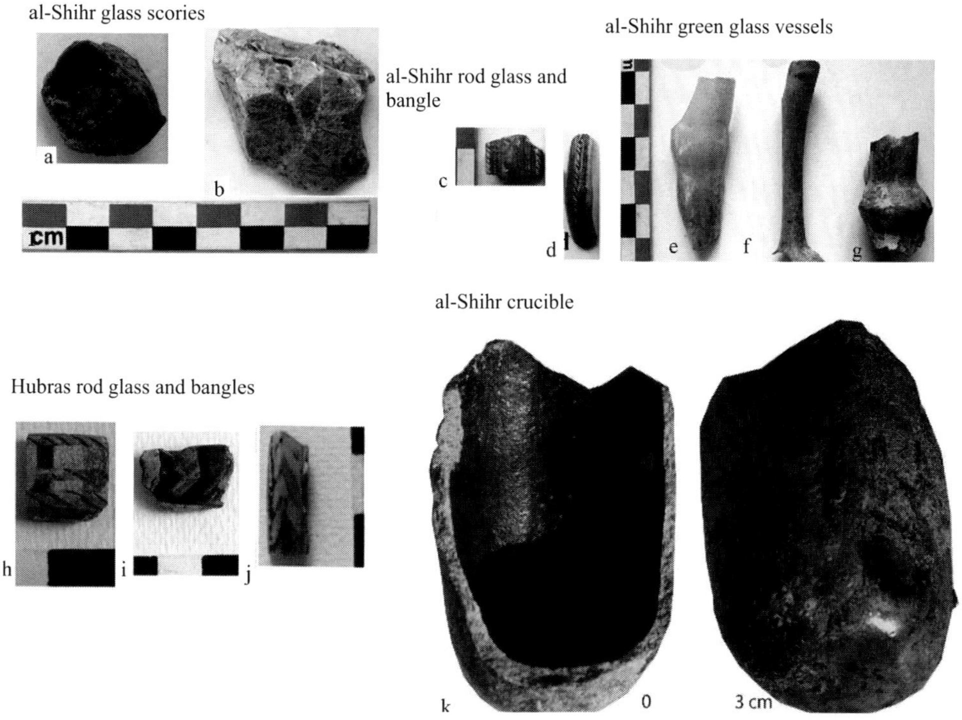

FIGURE 10. *Archaeological evidence of local manufacturing at al-Shiḥr.*
a. *SHR 97 2130: blue slag, L 2.9 cm, W 3.5 cm;* **b.** *SHR 99 2260: purple and green slag, L 2.4 cm, W 2.2 cm;* **c.** *SHR 99 2420: rod glass, L 1.5 cm, W 1.1 cm; green paste, yellow, red, black, and white layers, flat section;* **d.** *SHR 99 2292: glass bangle, L 4.7 cm, W 0.6 cm; description as above;* **e.** *SHR 99 2366: L 4.9 cm, W 1.1 cm; neck of green opaque glass;* **f.** *SHR 99 2362: l. 5.6 cm, W 0.7 cm; neck of green opaque glass;* **g.** *SHR 99 2283: 3.2 cm, 2.5 cm; neck of green opaque glass;* **h.** *HUBRAS: R1, rod glass, L 1.4 cm, W 1.5 cm; translucent core, coloured layers;* **i.** *HUBRAS: R.39, L 2 cm, W 0.6 cm; translucent core, coloured layers;* **j.** *HUBRAS: R16, L 2.7 cm, W 0.7 cm; translucent core, coloured layers;* **k.** *SHR 99 2345: crucible, L 9.2 cm, W6.4 cm.*

parallels between the bangles from both sites (al-Shiḥr and Kawd am-Saylāʾ, as explained above). Monod's investigations described the activity of workshops at Kawd am-Saylāʾ. In her work on Aden, and on the basis of the study of the thirteenth-century manuscripts of Ibn al-Mujāwir (*Taʾrīkh al-mustabṣir* i: 148) and of the sixteenth-century al-Ṭayyib Bā (Abū) Makhrama (*Taʾrīkh taghr ʿadan* i: 21), R.E. Margariti explains (2007: 60–63) that al-Lakhaba, near Aden, had been the main location of glass production for a long time. She adds that, "Kawd Am Sayla lies about nine kilometres from Aden, a distance that roughly corresponds to Abu Makhrama's 1.75 farsakh" (2007: 67). As for glass paste known as "Malipa", it is mentioned in the thirteenth century in the Chu Fan Shi among the products from Ḥaḍramawt (Chu Ju Kua 1912). At al-Shiḥr, a workshop was discovered in Phase 7 (sixteenth century), containing two samples of glass slag (Fig. 10/a, b) and numerous crucibles[4] (Fig. 10/k) (SHR 99 2345–2; Hardy-Guilbert 2005: 71, 73; Hardy-Guibert & Ducatez 2004: 128–130, 142). Another element which supports the hypothesis of a local production of glass bangles at al-Shiḥr is a rod of glass with the same patterns as a single polychrome bangle (Fig. 10/c, d; SHR 2420, 2292) discovered in Eritrea (Monod 1975). This kind of decorated glass rod was also found among the finds of Ḥubrāṣ in Jordan (Fig. 10/h–j). This may suggest an itinerant secondary workshop or a trade in decorated rod glass, which would then be reworked and the object completed at

[4] We would like to thank Aude Mongiatti, science curator at the British Museum, and Andrew Meek, scientist at the British Museum and PhD student under Professor J. Henderson at Nottingham University, for their interest in the scientific analyses of vitreous material from crucibles.

its destination. The use of the same green paste for bangles as for undecorated and decorated vessels may suggest a single provenance for all the al-Shiḥr material, either from the site of al-Qarū or of Kawd am-Saylāʾ (Doe 1963; Lane & Serjeant 1948).

Interpretation of parallels with India, imports or stylistic influences from the fourteenth to seventeenth centuries

The exchanges between India and Yemen are verified by primary sources from the Ayyubid period (1171–1250). Beads are mentioned in export registers from Sind and Daybul stating that they were exported to al-Shiḥr (Smith 1995: 127–140; Fiorani Piacentini 2003: 95–97). However, we do not have any details about the bead quality and many scholars mention the export of glass from Yemen. In the twelfth century we know of a request for glass from Aden by someone on the Malabar Coast in India (Goitein 1974: 18–35). Our dating is rather later. With regard to closely dating and comparing the many similarities between the material from al-Shiḥr and Kholāpur, we should probably think in terms of more than just imports, and perhaps in terms of the movement of craftsmen. The caste of the Indian pedlar specialized in the sale of glass bangles, known from medieval times and mentioned in a thirteenth-century manuscript,[5] may confirm this hypothesis.

Near East and Europe: Venetian imports to Yemen from the fourteenth to nineteenth centuries

The glass trade between Venice, Egypt, and the Syrian coast was very important from Ayyubid to late Ottoman times and included the raw material, vessels, and jewellery. The Portuguese presence in the Red Sea, from the beginning of the sixteenth century, should be highlighted (Chaudhuri 1985: 63–79) and may explain the presence of Venetian imports at al-Shiḥr. The white and yellow marvered example, with gold reflections found in an excavation in the Beirut suq may be related to the famous sixteenth-century gold paste mentioned by Tomé Pires: "...from Cairo ... the merchandise brought by the galleasses of Venice, to wit, many arms, scarlet-in-grain, coloured woollen cloths, coral, copper, quicksilver, vermilion, nails, silver, glass and other beads, and golden glassware" (1944: 269).

[5] The bangles are known in India from thirteenth-century primary sources (1253): Somesvara, *Surathotsava* vi, verse 165, is mentioned by Dikshit (1969: 66).

Origin of the Red Sea samples: Near East and African coast, thirteenth to nineteenth centuries

The Red Sea bangles might come from the Near East especially from the al-Khalil (Hebron) workshops in Palestine, well known from the fourteenth century for glass bangles manufacturing, or from Fusṭāṭ in Egypt (Spaer 1992: 44–62; Boulogne 2008). The importance of commercial trade in the Gulf of Aden and the Red Sea from Ayyubid times is particularly well illustrated by the Karīmī merchants (Fishel 1958: 157–174). Furthermore, the connection between the harbour of al-Shiḥr and the east coast of Africa from the eleventh century is well known through archaeological material in the form of African pottery, and the site of al-Shiḥr is also mentioned in some manuscripts as being a transit port between Asia and Africa (Hardy-Guilbert 2002: 39–53). Tuchscherer (2004: 157–163) wrote: "À la fin du 17ème siècle, les pays riverains de l'ensemble mer Rouge-golfe d'Aden commençaient à être intégrés dans leurs profondeurs dans un système complexe d'échanges qui liaient entre elles non seulement les deux rives arabe et africaine, mais aussi celles-ci avec l'Inde et la Méditerranée."

Conclusion

The main aim of this paper was to understand the manufacture of glass bangles in south Yemen through the study of a surprisingly large bangle corpus. South Yemen might well have been an important place for the manufacturing of glass and al-Shiḥr was certainly one of the centres of that manufacture. R.B. Serjeant wrote about glass bangles from al-Shiḥr in his article "The Ports of Aden and Shihr" (based on the study of the fifteenth-century primary source *Mulakhkhaṣ al-fiṭan* by al-Ḥusan b. ʿAlī al-Sharīf al-Ḥusaynī): "glass, especially polychrome bangles was manufactured in some places on the Tihāmah coast but there seems to be no allusion to these factories in the *Mulakhkhaṣ al-fiṭan* though one of them is quite near Aden" (1974: 207–224). The bangles from al-Shiḥr, like those from Kawd am-Saylāʾ, were discovered with much blue and white Asian pottery and Chinese stoneware. Al-Shiḥr is located on the South Sea Silk Road, which remained one of the most-used trade routes for glass exchange from antiquity (Brill 1993: 70–79; 2009: 109–147; Glover 1996: 57–94). No data has been found to confirm that there were any imports from Asia, and only a few parallels have been drawn with dark bangles similar to those of central Jordan. Henderson's analysis suggests that these contain some Indian and south-east Asian components (Boulogne & Henderson 2009). Whatever else, it is clear that, with regard to glass bangles, the cultural link between south Yemen and India seems much stronger than with Bilād al-Shām or Egypt.

Some clues may lie in a study of the various colours: green in the case of glass from al-Shiḥr and Ḥaḍramawt indicates further clues as to the provenance. Connections between economic aspects and social practices are introduced: the meanings of the colours are really significant during Islamic times in the Maghreb and Near East especially in the context of textiles (Mansouri 2007). Ongoing studies on Ḥaḍramawt by M. Rodionov (2007: 19–29, 98–101, 105–106, 126–134) propose that dress varies according to traditional social strata. Are there similar parallels in the colours used for glass?

In the case of the use of green glass from al-Shiḥr and in Ḥaḍramawt, can we speak of an attempt to imitate Chinese celadon, as it is often suggested, or is there a connection with Islamic rules and traditions? This topic is the focus of another article, *Les bracelets de verre coloré d'Orient médiéval et tardif: modèles et couleurs, des marqueurs identitaires* (Boulogne, in preparation).

Acknowledgements

We are grateful to the General Organization for Antiquities, Manuscripts and Museums of Yemen (GOAM) directed by Abdullah Mohammad Bawazir in Sanaa and by Dr ᶜAbd al-ᶜAziz b. ᶜAqil in Mukalla, and to the French Centre of Archaeological and Social Studies in Sanaa (CEFAS) directed by Drs F. Mermier, F. Burgat, and J. Lambert. The archaeological project of al-Shiḥr was supported by the French Ministry of Foreign Affairs and National Centre for Scientific Research (CNRS), UMR 8167, "Orient Méditerranée", Islam médiéval. The authors thank the Committee of the Seminar for Arabian Studies for their invitation to the London Seminar and for the publication of this article. The seasons of excavations (1996–2002 and 2007) were carried out with the participation of K. Badhafari, I. Al-Amiri, B. Baharama, S. Muhammad ᶜAli, A. Albari, A. al-K. al-Barakani (GOAM representatives); D. Parent, D. Guimard, and S. Dalle (topographers of AFAN [Association française d'archéologie nationale]); N. Férault de Falandre (architecte DPLG: diplômé par le gouvernement); P. Philippe, S. Eliës, and S. Vatteoni (draughtsmen); E. Allouin, S. Labroche, and V. Monaco (conservators); A. d'Arcangues (archivist); P. Baty (archaeologist of AFAN /INRAP [Institut National de recherche et d'archéologie préventive]); T. Creissen, N. Gilles, S. Guichou, R. Halaoui, A. Joyard, St. Le Maguer, A. Masson, H. Morel, G. Plisson, P. Siméon, and D. Willems (students in archaeology or history in the Universities of Nanterre, and Sorbonne (Paris I & Paris IV, and Aix-Marseille I). Dr S. Boulogne is grateful to IFPO (Institut Français du Proche-Orient), in particular to Dr F. Burgat; to ACOR (American Center of Oriental Research library in Amman); and to Dr. H. Amouric at Lamm (Laboratoire d'Archéologie Méditerranéenne Médiévale, Aix-en-Provence). She would also like to extend her special thanks to her friends A. and K.H.

References

Bā (Abū) Makhrama al-Ṭ./ed. O. Löfgren.
1936–1950. *Taʾrīkh thaghr ᶜadan*. Arabische Texte zur Kenntnis der Stadt Aden im Mittelalter. Uppsala: Almqvist & Niksells Boktryckeri.

Berthier S.
(in preparation). Rapport des fouilles de la Citadelle de Damas, Mission franco-syrienne, conduite sous la direction de S. Berthier.

Boulogne S.
2007. Reflet d'un art populaire: les bracelets de verre coloré du Bilad al-Sham médiéval et ottoman. Thèse de doctorat, Université de Paris-IV (Panthéon-Sorbonne). [Unpublished].
2008. Les bracelets de verre coloré polychromes des sites de Damas, Masyaf, Tell Abû Sarbût et Hirbat fâris au Bilâd al-Châm mamelouk et ottoman: essai de synthèse. *Bulletin d'Études Orientales* 17: 127–154.
(in preparation). *Les bracelets de verre coloré d'Orient médiéval et tardif: modèles et couleurs, des marqueurs identitaires.*

Boulogne S & Henderson J.
2009. Indian Glass in the Near-East? Medieval and Ottoman Glass Bangles from Central Jordan. *Journal of Glass Studies* 51: 53–75.

Brill R.H.
1993. Scientific Investigations of ancient Asian Glass. Pages 70–79 in UNESCO, *Maritime Route of Silk Roads. Nara Symposium '91 Report.* Nara: Nara International Foundation.
2009. Opening remarks and setting the stage: lecture at the 2005 Shanghai International Workshop on the Archaeology of Glass along the Silk Road. Pages 109–147 in G. Fuxi, R.H. Brill & T. Shouyoun (eds), *Ancient Glass Research along the Silk Road.* Hackensack, NJ: World Scientific.

Chaudhuri K.N.
1985. *Trade and Civilisation in the Indian Ocean: An Economic History from the Rise of Islam to 1750.* Cambridge/New York: Cambridge University Press.

Chu Ju Kua
1912. *His work on the Chinese and Arab Trade in the twelfth and thirteenth Centuries entitled Chu-fan-chï 1911*. Translated from the Chinese and annotated by F. Hieth & W. Rockhill. St Petersburg: Printing Office of the Imperial Academy of Sciences.

Curvurs H. & Stuart B.
1998–1999. The BCD Archaeology Project 1996–1999. *Baal* 3: 13–30.

Dikshit G.
1969. *History of Indian Glass.* Mumbai: University of Bombay.

Doe D.
1963. Pottery sites near Aden. *Journal of the Royal Asiatic Society* 63: 150–162.

Fiorani Piacentini V.
2003. *Baluchistan: Terra Incognita: a new archaeological approach combining archaeological, historical, anthropological and architecture studies*. Oxford: Archaeopress.

Fishel W.
1958. The spice trade in Mamluk Egypt. *Journal of the Economic and Social History of the Orient* 1: 157–174.

Glover I.C.
1996. The Southern Silk Road: Archaeological Evidence for early trade between India and Southeast Asia. Pages 57–94 in A. Srisuchat (ed.), *Ancient Trades and Cultural Contacts in Southeast Asia.* Bangkok: The Office of the National Culture Commission.

Goitein S.D.
1974. The Medieval Glass Industry as reflected in the Cairo Genizah. Pages 18–35 in A. Engle (ed.), *Readings in Glass History.* ii. Jerusalem: Phoenix Publications.

Hansman J.
1985. Julfar, an Arabian port, its settlement and Far Eastern ceramic trade from the 14th to the 18th centuries. *Royal Asiatic Society of Great Britain and Ireland* 22: 76–83.

Hardy-Guilbert. C.
1991. Julfar, cité portuaire du Golfe Arabo-persique à la période islamique. *Archéologie Islamique* 2: 161–203.
2002. Al-Shihr, un port d'Arabie face à l'Afrique. *Journal des Africanistes* 72: 39–53.
2005. The harbour of al-Shiḥr, Ḥaḍramawt, Yemen: sources and archaeological data on trade. *Proceedings of the Seminar for Arabian Studies* 35: 71–85.
2007. Mission archéologique de al-Shihr, Hadramaout, Yemen. Rapport sur la campagne 2007. [Unpublished report].

Hardy-Guilbert C. & Ducatez G.
2004. Al-Shihr, porte du Hadramawt sur l'océan Indien. Sources et Archéologie. *Annales Islamologiques* 38: 95–157.

Hardy-Guilbert C. & Rougeulle A.
1997. Al-Shihr and the southern coast of the Yemen: preliminary notes on the French archaeological expedition, 1995–1997. *Proceedings of the Seminar for Arabian Studies* 27: 129–140.
Ibn al-Mujāwir/ed. O. Löfgren
1936–1950. *Taʾrīkh al-mustabṣir*. Arabische Texte zur Kenntnis der Stadt Aden im Mittelalter. Uppsala: Almqvist & Niksells Boktryckeri.
Kanungo A.K. & Brill R.H.
2009. Kopia. India's First Glassmaking Site: dating and chemical analysis. *Journal of Glass Studies* 51: 11–25.
Lane A. & Serjeant R.B.
1948. Pottery and Glass Fragments from the Aden Littoral with Historical Notes. *Journal of the Royal Asiatic Society* 1–2: 108–133.
Mansouri T.
2007. *Du Voile et du Zunnar, Du code vestimentaire en pays d'Islam.* (Collection Palimpseste "Lectures historiques"). Tunis: L'or du temps.
Margariti R.E.
2007. *Aden the Indian Ocean Trade: 150 Years in the Life of a Medieval Arabian Port.* Chapel Hill, NC: University of North Carolina Press.
Meyer C.
1983. Islamic Glass from al-Qadim, Egypt. *Journal of Glass Studies* 25: 101–108.
1992. *Glass from Quseir el-Qadim and the Indian Ocean Trade.* Chicago: The Oriental Institute of the University of Chicago.
Monod T.
1975. À propos des bracelets de verre sahariens. *Bulletin de l'Institut Français d'Afrique Noire* 34: 703–718.
1978. Sur un site à bracelets de verre des environs d'Aden. *Raydan* (*Journal of Ancient Yemeni, Antiquities and Epigraphy*) 1: 111–125.
Pires T./ed. A. Cortaseo
1944. *The Suma Oriental of Tomé Pires: an account of the East, from the Red Sea to Japan, written in Malacca and India in 1512–1515.* ii. London: The Hakluyt Society.
Rodionov M.
2007. *The Western Hadramawt: Ethnographic Field Research, 1983–91.* Halle am Saale: Orientwissenschaftliche, Helfte/Halle-Wittenberg, Martin-Luther Universität.
Sankalia H.D.
1947. The Antiquity of Glass Bangles in India. *Bulletin of the Deccan College Research Institute* 8: 252–259.
Sankalia H.D. & Dikshit M.B.
1952. *Excavations at Brahmapuri (Kolhapur) 1945–1946.* Poona: Deccan College.
Serjeant R.B.
1974. The Ports of Aden and Shihr. Medieval Period. *Recueils Société Jean Bodin* 32: 207–224.
Shindo Y.
1996. Islamic Glass Bracelets found in the Red Sea region. Pages 269–276 in *Annales du 13e Congrès de l'Association Internationale pour l'Histoire du Verre (AIHV).* Lochem: AIHV.
2001. The Classification and Chronology of The Islamic Glass Bracelets from al-Ṭur, Sinai. Pages 73–100 in *Senri Ethnological Studies, 55. Cultural Change in the Arab World.* Osaka: National Museum of Ethnology.
2009. Glazed pottery and Glass Unearthed in the Rāya/al-Ṭūr Area. Pages 23–35 in M. Kawatoko & Y. Shindo (eds), *Artefacts of the Islamic Period Excavated in the Rāya/al-Ṭūr Area, South Sinai, Egypt. Ceramics/Glass/Painted Plaster.* (Joint Usage/Research Center for Islamic Area Studies, Waseda University). Tokyo: Organization for Islamic Area Studies.

Smith G.R.
1995. Have you anything to declare? Maritime trade and commerce in Ayyubid Aden Practices and Taxes. *Proceedings of the Seminar for Arabian Studies* 25: 127–140.

Spaer M.
1992. The Islamic bracelets of Palestine: Preliminary Findings. *Journal of Glass Studies* 34: 44–62.

Sulaymān al-Mahrī b. Aḥmad b. Sulaymān/ed. I. Khoury
1970. *Al-ᶜumdah al-mahriyyah fī ḍabt al-ᶜulūm al-baḥriyyah.* (4 volumes). (Collection Sciences Nautiques). Damascus: Maison des Sciences.

Tuchscherer M.
2004. Les échanges commerciaux entre les rives africaine et arabe de l'espace mer Rouge-Golfe d'Aden aux XVIe et XVIIe siècles. Pages 157–163 in P. Lunde & A. Porter (eds), *Trade and Travel in the Red Sea Region. Proceedings of Red Sea Project 1.* (Society for Arabian Studies Monographs, 2) (British Archaeological Reports, International Series). Oxford: Archaeopress.

Walker B.J., Kenney E., Holzweg L., Carroll L., Boulogne S. & Lucke B.
2007. Village life in Mamluk and Ottoman Ḥubrāṣ and Saḥam: Northern Jordan Project, Report on the 2006 Season. *Annual of the Department of Antiquities of Jordan* 52: 429–470.

Whitcomb D.
1988. Islamic Archaeology in Aden and the Hadramaut. Pages 177–204 in D.T. Potts (ed.), *Araby the Blest.* (Studies in Arabian Archaeology, 7). Copenhagen: Carsten Niehbuhr Institute.

Wolseley H.
1924. The religion of Ahmad Shah Bahmani. *Royal Asiatic Society of Great Britain and Ireland* 1: 73–80.

Authors' addresses
Stéphanie Boulogne, 1180 avenue de Beausoleil, 82000 Montauban, France.

e-mail stephaniekarine.boulogne@gmail.com

Claire Hardy-Guilbert, 157 Boulevard de Magenta, 75010 Paris, France.

e-mail claire.hardy-guilbert@wanadoo.fr

Proceedings of the Seminar for Arabian Studies 40 (2010): 149–160

L'emploi du bois dans l'architecture du Yémen antique

Christian Darles

Summary
Les recherches archéologiques menées au Yémen depuis plus de vingt-cinq ans permettent de comprendre de mieux en mieux l'art des bâtisseurs de l'Antiquité. Chaque nouvelle campagne de fouille permet de recueillir de nouveaux témoignages sur les modes constructifs mis en œuvre entre le 8e s. av. notre ère et le 5e s. de notre ère. Peu visibles car fragiles ou détruits, les éléments d'architecture en bois ont pendant longtemps été ignorés par les premiers archéologues qui attachèrent leurs regards plus aux édifices sacrés et aux fortifications que leur caractère monumental et leurs matériaux choisis avaient bien conservé, qu'à l'habitat modeste enfoui sous ses propres ruines. Ce travail entre dans une série de recherches menées sur les techniques constructives en Arabie du Sud durant l'Antiquité. L'étude des procédés constructifs permet de mieux aborder d'une part la spécificité locale de la chaîne opératoire qui mène du projet au chantier et, d'autre part, les principes de la restitution et de la reconstitution d'édifices architecturaux et d'ensembles urbains.

Keywords : Arabie du Sud antique, Yémen, architecture, construction en bois, habitat

Si l'architecture monumentale, comme celle des sanctuaires par exemple, souvent très bien conservée, a été parfaitement analysée et a fait l'objet de nombreuses publications, il n'en va pas de même pour l'architecture civile destinée principalement à l'habitat résidentiel, constitué par des maisons édifiées au-dessus de hauts soubassements massifs maçonnés.[1] Cette architecture est caractérisée par un usage important, dans les parois (éléments planaires verticaux), de pièces de bois qui constituaient une ossature tridimensionnelle dont le contreventement était assuré, dans les basses terres, par un remplissage composé généralement de briques crues. D'autres utilisations du bois sont attestées dans différentes configurations constructives: des planchers (éléments planaires horizontaux), des poutres (éléments linéaires horizontaux) et des poteaux (éléments linéaires verticaux) confectionnés en bois ont été découverts lors des différentes fouilles. Les éléments de décors qui nous sont parvenus, en nombre limité, peuvent être comparés aux panneaux en dalle de calcaire dont les motifs stéréotypés figurent entre des assemblages de menuiserie (Fig. 1). Cette « pétrification du bois » nous donne également de multiples informations sur les encadrements et les systèmes de fermeture des portes et fenêtres de ces édifices.

Nous tenons à rattacher cette étude matérielle aux apports des nombreuses dédicaces gravées sur les parois maçonnées des constructions. Les progrès réalisés dans l'interprétation du vocabulaire constructif utilisé dans les inscriptions permettent aussi de mieux comprendre l'art de bâtir, constructif et décoratif, des habitants de l'Arabie du Sud antique (Agostini, dans ce volume).

Les données sont de plusieurs types mais, à ce jour, les plus importantes sont d'ordre archéologique. Les recherches menées depuis plus de trente ans ont permis la découverte de nombreuses structures constructives en ossature de bois; elles ont été mises en évidence la première fois dans la vallée du Wādī Ḥaḍramawt à Masghra (Fig. 2) où des travaux agricoles avaient sectionné trois édifices mitoyens (Seigne 1982). Les conditions climatiques ont autorisé une bonne conservation des vestiges calcinés ou non des pièces de bois, à la fois dans des couches de destruction et également en connexion *in situ*. Bien souvent les édifices ont été enfouis sous les ruines de leurs superstructures. Ainsi à Shabwa (Shabwah), à Raybūn, à Tamnaᶜ, mais aussi à Sirwah et à Hajar am-Dhaybiya (Adh Dhāʾibiyyah) (Breton, McMahon & Warburton 1998), les archéologues ont pu découvrir intacts les premiers niveaux d'occupation au-dessus des

[1] La seule synthèse effectuée n'a pas encore été publiée, même si elle est actuellement disponible; il s'agit de la Thèse d'État par J-F. Breton sur l'architecture domestique (Breton 1997) dont les conclusions ont été partiellement reprises dans le volume III des Fouilles de Shabwa (Breton 1998*a*). Le volume IV de cette même collection aborde les influences extérieures que cette architecture a pu recevoir et interpréter (Breton 2009*a*).

Figure 1. *Ce type de dalle décorée ornait la façade du palais royal de Shabwa. Elles étaient situées entre les poteaux de bois laissés apparents et servaient de coffrage perdu pour le remplissage en terre. (Crédit Ch. Darles.)*

socles maçonnés, caractéristiques de l'architecture des basses terres de l'Arabie méridionale antique. À Tamna[c], par exemple, l'équipe italienne a découvert soixante-six fragments de bois dans les ruines d'une des maisons qui bordaient la place du marché. À Shabwa, la fouille du palais royal a permis de retrouver plusieurs centaines de pièces de bois calcinées parfois en connexion entre eux; ainsi des restitutions de certaines parties de la superstructure de l'édifice ont pu être réalisées avec une très grande précision.

À Sirwah et à Maʾrib les recherches archéologiques ont récemment abouti à la découverte des montants de dispositifs d'accès en bois, en parfait état de conservation, qui ne font que valider les restitutions qui avaient été proposées par notre équipe pour le portail monumental du bâtiment A du palais royal de Shabwa (Darles 2005).

Le bois a parfois été utilisé comme élément de construction sous forme brute, un tronc d'arbre est alors taillé à ses extrémités, horizontalement il servira de poutre, verticalement de colonne. Sous une forme travaillée il est transformé en matériau de construction. Il est taillé à la demande près du bâtiment en construction. La plupart du temps il entre dans une architecture composite qui fait également appel à la terre et à la pierre. Les données sont nombreuses, tant les vestiges eux-mêmes (bois préservés ou empreintes) que les représentations du bois ou les références au bois dans les sources écrites, et cependant ce matériau périssable n'est souvent que partiellement conservé, calciné ou non.

En dépit des vicissitudes du temps et quelquefois de l'action des hommes, certains éléments remarquables ont été conservés dont le classement et l'interprétation permettent de mieux comprendre la chaîne opératoire qui mène de la pensée à la réalisation du projet, en restituant le temps du chantier.

Les éléments linéaires en bois

La taille du tronc d'arbre permet de tirer un certain nombre de pièces linéaires de différentes sections. La longueur des pièces est fonction de la forme du tronc d'arbre et force est de constater que les bâtisseurs ont eu du mal à trouver de grandes pièces afin de franchir des portées importantes ou de soutenir des poutres avec une hauteur sous plafond de plusieurs mètres. Ces pièces de bois ont l'avantage de bien répartir les efforts de flexion et de cisaillement. Elles travaillent plus à la tension et à la traction qu'à la compression où les risques de flambement sont nombreux obligeant les constructeurs à surdimensionner des poteaux. Nous ne connaissons que les niveaux inférieurs des bâtiments, là où les portées sont les plus faibles. Dans les étages supérieurs les pièces ont pu être plus vastes et les portées plus importantes. Aujourd'hui, les édifices de Shibām acceptent des portées de 4 m, longueur qui ne semble pas avoir été dépassée dans l'Antiquité.

Ces éléments peuvent être verticaux. Il s'agit alors de poteaux comme ceux, de section octogonale, du portique au rez-de-chaussée du bâtiment B dans le palais royal de Shabwa. Seules les traces calcinées nous prouvent

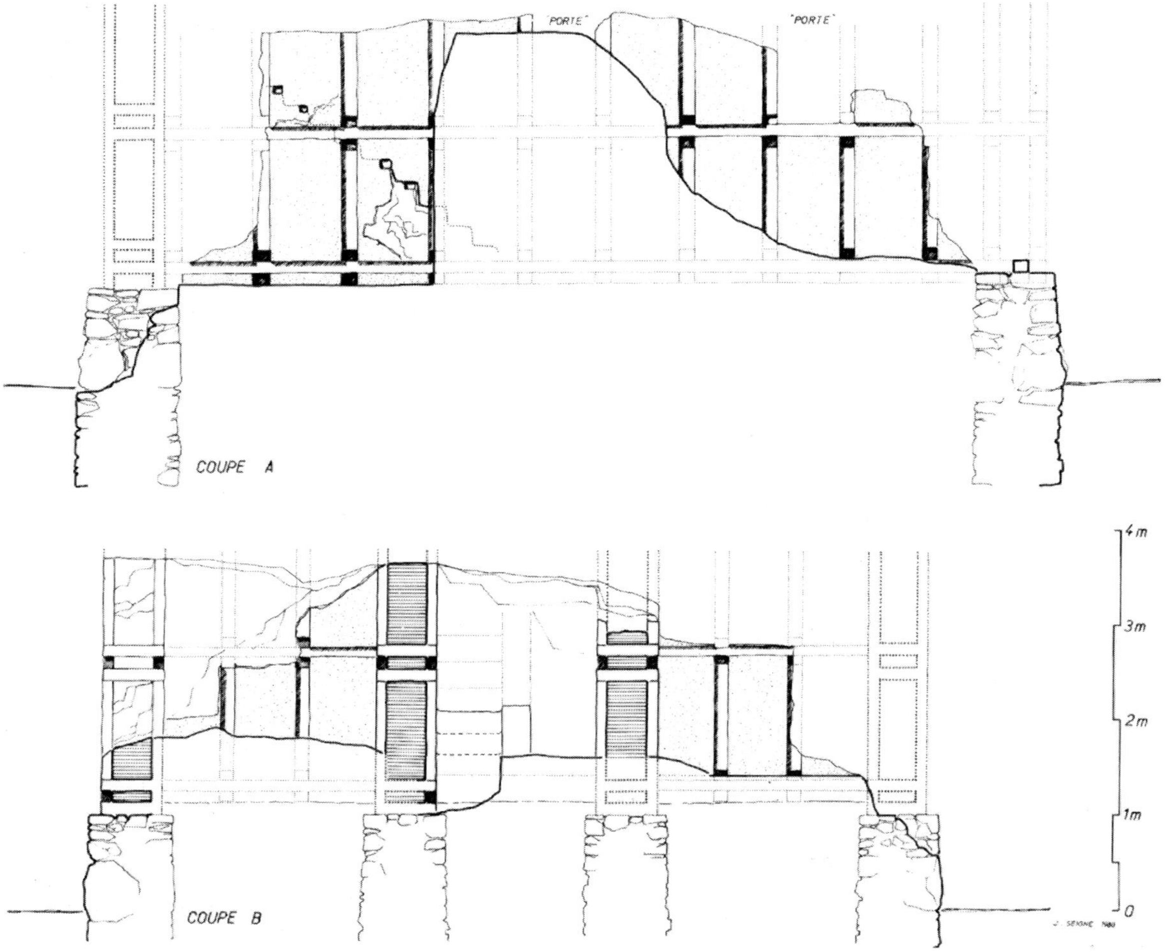

Figure 2. *L'arrachement par des engins mécaniques d'une partie des alluvions recouvrant le site de Masghra a permis aux archéologues français de découvrir, en 1979, la nature des superstructures des bâtiments d'habitation de cette région durant l'Antiquité (Seigne 1982). (Crédit Mission Archéologique Française en République Populaire et Démocratique du Yémen.)*

leur existence mais nous connaissons leurs dimensions: 3,90 m de haut pour une section de 35 cm. Ces poteaux en bois sont le plus souvent posés sur des dais de pierre alors que les colonnes en pierre sont engagées de quelques centimètres dans des mortaises réservées dans les socles. Ces dais de pierre sont fréquents dans l'architecture religieuse du royaume de Ḥaḍramawt, plus particulièrement à Raybūn (Sedov 2005) ou Bā-Qutayfah (Breton 1979). La mission italienne en Oman a également découvert de telles traces dans le sanctuaire extra-muros et le temple intra-muros oriental de Sumhuram (Khor Rôri [Khawr Rawrī]) (Sedov 2008*a*; 2008*b*). L'architecture mineure des petits villages de la vallée du Wādī Surban utilise fréquemment ce type de poteau de 15 à 20 cm de diamètre afin de tenir la charpente des maisons (Breton & Darles 1994).

La mise en œuvre horizontale d'éléments linéaires est peu connue directement dans les données archéologiques. L'existence de telles poutres est souvent déduite de l'étude des procédés constructifs et des restitutions auxquelles ils ont donné lieu (Fig. 3). On peut ainsi admettre que certaines traverses des parois se transforment au niveau du plancher en poutres et en solives. Dans plusieurs circonstances quand un niveau entier de l'édifice a été recouvert par la ruine des étages supérieurs, c'est le cas à Shabwa dans le palais royal, de nombreuses pièces de bois découvertes sont manifestement des architraves ou des linteaux.

Figure 3. *Les superstructures d'un édifice dégagé par la Mission Archéologique Soviétique en République Populaire et Démocratique du Yémen. L'incendie de l'édifice a permis la cuisson de la terre qui a conservé les traces de l'ossature en bois aujourd'hui disparue. (Crédit Ch. Darles.)*

Figure 4. *Une maquette réalisée par la Mission Archéologique Française en République Populaire et Démocratique du Yémen suite aux découvertes faites durant la mission de prospection dans le Wādī Ḥaḍramawt en 1979. Cette restitution est aujourd'hui confortée par de nombreuses découvertes réalisées sur de nombreux sites par toutes les missions archéologiques présentes au Yémen. (Crédit Mission Archéologique Française en République Populaire et Démocratique du Yémen.)*

Les éléments planaires

Les pièces de bois entrent en grand nombre dans la composition d'éléments planaires composites, verticaux comme les parois ou horizontaux comme les planchers et les toitures. Cette architecture aux parois à ossature de bois et remplissage en terre est aujourd'hui bien connue (Seigne 1992; Darles 1998; Loreto 2006) (Fig. 4). Elle fait appel à trois types de pièces de bois: des traverses dont la longueur correspond à l'épaisseur du mur, des longrines ou sablières longitudinales et des poteaux qui correspondent à des troncs coupés en deux et sont souvent semi-circulaires. L'ordre de pose est le suivant: tout d'abord des traverses sont disposées à intervalles réguliers sur le soubassement maçonné, puis des sablières basses sont installées de part et d'autre de la paroi, des traverses sont à nouveau posées qui soutiennent des poteaux sur lesquels se répète la même opération (Fig. 5). Ces trois types de pièces pouvaient varier en dimensions suivant l'épaisseur des murs ou suivant les percements des parois (Fig. 6). Nous avons à Shabwa par exemple, mais également à Tamna[c], le témoignage d'une tentative de standardisation de leur fabrication. Les assemblages par emboîtements sont de deux types, par tenons et mortaises ou par l'usage de deux mortaises et d'une cheville intermédiaire.[2] Dans le cas des pièces verticales,

[2] On trouve ce type d'assemblage sur la totalité du site de Shabwa, par exemple dans les parois du bâtiment no. 44 (Breton 1998*b*).

Figure 5. *Les éléments de l'ossature en bois du bâtiment B du palais royal de Shabwa. Au-dessus des traverses disposées à intervalles réguliers sur le socle en pierre, des longrines liées par un assemblage à mi-bois supportent de nouvelles traverses puis des poteaux en bois. (Crédit Mission Archéologique Française en République Populaire et Démocratique du Yémen.)*

les tenons sont de section trapézoïdale, les mortaises correspondantes, sur les traverses, le sont également. Les mortaises de section rectangulaire ne correspondent qu'aux assemblages des pièces horizontales (Fig. 7). Le remplissage de cette ossature était réalisé au fur et à mesure avec des fragments de briques liées avec un coulis de terre retenu parfois par des parements en pierre qui servaient de coffrage perdu. Ces dalles de parement ont été découvertes en grand nombre sur la plupart des sites de l'Arabie du Sud antique, parfois *in situ* comme au premier niveau du bâtiment A du palais royal de Shabwa. Leur épaisseur indique bien que ces panneaux étaient encastrés dans l'ossature de bois, suggérant de ce fait que

Figure 6. *Ossature de la superstructure du bâtiment no. 44 de Shabwa (Breton 1998b). Ces pièces en connexion n'étaient pas brûlées et leur étude a permis de comprendre les différents types de clavetages et de liaisons déjà entrevus lors du dégagement des ruines du palais royal. (Crédit Ch. Darles.)*

Figure 7. *Les éléments d'une pièce horizontale calcinée de l'ossature du bâtiment A du palais royal de Shabwa. Cette pièce possède une mortaise carrée. (Crédit Mission Archéologique Française en République Populaire et Démocratique du Yémen.)*

les trois types de pièces de bois étaient laissées visibles. Ce principe constructif est non seulement attesté dans la représentation de ce type d'architecture comme sur les stèles monumentales d'Aksum (Krencker 1913; Buxton & Matthews 1972; Seigne 1992; Darles 1998) mais se retrouve encore appliqué dans l'architecture de certains pays du Proche-Orient et de l'Afrique de l'Est.[3]

Il a été répondu à la nécessité de chaîner l'ensemble par l'assemblage de pièces de longueur modeste réalisé

[3] La présence de bois est déjà attestée dans le monde anatolien à l'époque hittite (Naumann 1955). Aujourd'hui nous retrouvons ces principes constructifs au Kurdistan, en Érythrée ou en Éthiopie, par exemple, certes dans des architectures composites bâties majoritairement avec une maçonnerie en pierres sèches. Les pièces de bois horizontales qui servent de chaînages sont visibles et peuvent dépasser à l'extérieur de manière significative (Breton 2009b; Libsekal & Schebat 2007).

Figure 8. *Les archéologues soviétiques ont dégagé des fragments de murs internes, en terre, qui comportent les traces d'une ossature de bois dense dont les dispositions permettent de comprendre les assemblages mis en œuvre par les bâtisseurs de la ville de Raybūn. (Crédit Ch. Darles.)*

à mi-bois et clavetées (Fig. 8). Ce type de liaison permettait d'assurer la continuité d'efforts de traction importants. Les architraves sont assemblées par queue d'aronde et sont également clavetées avec une large cheville trapézoïdale (Fig. 9). Certaines sablières basses au passage des ouvertures étaient transformées en seuils de bois, principe que l'on retrouve régulièrement dans l'architecture yéménite d'aujourd'hui.

Des pièces de bois horizontales, non continues, étaient également utilisées comme chaînages horizontaux partiels, ainsi dans le bâtiment no. 72 de Shabwa (Breton 1998*c*). Ce type de pièces se retrouve dans l'architecture actuelle des constructions sur les hauts plateaux yéménites.

L'étude des techniques de cette architecture nous informe sur plusieurs points. Les modes d'assemblage à mi-bois étaient connus. Ils n'étaient employés que lorsqu'il était nécessaire d'assurer la continuité de certaines pièces horizontales. L'absence de ce type de liaison dans les angles des bâtiments nous semble traduire la volonté de rigidifier l'édifice en utilisant les planchers intermédiaires dont l'ossature correspond à la prolongation des traverses et des longrines des parois. Les angles, en effet, ne sont pas conçus comme un coude à 90° de la paroi mais comme la rencontre de deux murs dont les structures orthogonales sont décalées d'une hauteur de bois, les traverses devenant longrines et réciproquement.

La fouille du palais royal de Shabwa a permis de découvrir les restes de la toiture de l'étage du bâtiment B. Majoritairement en bois, le plafond était composé de pièces empilées transversalement puis longitudinalement de manière à créer, par encorbellement, un caisson dont le sommet était fermé par des planches et des plaques d'albâtre alternées. Le tout était scellé puis revêtu avec un enduit étanche à gravillons. L'acrotère était construit avec

Figure 9. *Cet assemblage d'architrave permet de garantir la transmission des forces de traction dans les pièces horizontales de grandes dimensions. Un fragment découvert lors du dégagement du palais royal de Shabwa. (Crédit Mission Archéologique Française en République Populaire et Démocratique du Yémen.)*

Figure 10. *La stèle d'Aksum déplacée par Mussolini, près du Ministère des Colonies (aujourd'hui FAO) à Rome, a été depuis restituée au gouvernement éthiopien. On distingue les trois types de percements dont les éléments constructifs ont été sculptés dans la masse du monolithe. (Crédit Ch. Darles.)*

des planches décorées de denticules qui alternaient, à l'aplomb de chaque poteau, avec des gargouilles en pierre à tête de taureau dont certaines n'étaient que décoratives.

Les menuiseries comportaient d'importantes serrures en bronze. Elles sont également connues par leurs représentations en pierre, et par la conservation de leurs empreintes, notamment dans les parois en briques cuites calcinées et, plus récemment, par leur découverte *in situ* à Sirwah et à Maʾrib.

La première connaissance de ces menuiseries est due à l'analyse des stèles d'Aksum, en Éthiopie. Ces grands obélisques ont, très tôt, été considérés comme la représentation d'édifices d'habitation. Outre des données sur le système constructif en ossature de bois laissée partiellement apparente en façade, ils nous donnent plusieurs types d'information sur les menuiseries des différents percements, les portes, les ouvertures du premier niveau et les fenêtres supérieures. Les ouvertures des étages courants apparaissent comme toutes identiques; dans le cas de la grande stèle d'Aksum publiée par D. Krencker au début du 20e siècle (Krencker 1913), neuf niveaux répétitifs sont sculptés dans la pierre (Fig. 10). Seul le deuxième niveau montre des fenêtres plus petites, carrées, avec un croisillon de bois. Ces ouvertures doivent, selon nos hypothèses, correspondre à un étage consacré aux réserves ou aux animaux. Les autres niveaux, tous identiques, pourraient selon les comparaisons qui peuvent être faites avec l'architecture de l'habitat actuel de l'Arabie du Sud, être des niveaux d'habitation. En partie haute un percement serait destiné à la ventilation, en partie basse deux percements verticaux, sans nul doute destinés à être occultés, pourraient servir à l'éclairement et aux regards sur l'extérieur. La porte principale était manifestement élaborée avec soin. Elle était entourée d'une série d'encadrements, en retrait les uns par rapport aux autres, dont la structure menuisée, avec des pièces de bois de section importante, permettait de passer de l'épaisseur du mur à celle du franchissement par l'intermédiaire de pièces de bois transversales en légère saillie. Par la mise en œuvre de cadres charpentés successifs, l'épaisseur de la paroi était ainsi diminuée afin de fournir un cadre menuisé dormant susceptible de recevoir l'ouvrant nécessaire à l'accès à l'édifice. L'ensemble des ouvertures, fenêtres et portes, était sans doute intimement lié à la structure constructive en bois de ce haut édifice, dont la rigidité devait garantir la stabilité. De nombreux éléments architecturaux lapidaires ont été trouvés durant les multiples fouilles menées en Arabie du Sud. Il s'agit souvent de plaques de parement décorées avec ce que nous pouvons interpréter comme des représentations architecturales d'éléments menuisés, il s'agit également d'autels ou de brûle-parfums qui représentent sous forme de maquettes des maisons et bâtiments — réels ou imaginaires. Les décors que nous pouvons analyser sont remarquables par l'homogénéité de leurs représentations. Les portes et fenêtres représentées en Arabie du Sud évoquent par leur forme les portes et fenêtres connues dans l'architecture pharaonique égyptienne. Leur répétition fournit matière à réflexion.

La répétition des motifs suggère la fabrication standardisée des menuiseries et une interaction fine entre maçons chargés du gros œuvre et ouvriers chargés de la pose des fenêtres en bois. La multiplication d'ouvertures identiques pourrait refléter non seulement la volonté des décideurs mais également une réalité sociale.[4]

Il est habituellement admis que les variantes typologiques des décors, des menuiseries et des formes bâties sont l'expression d'une identité politique et sociale par l'ensemble d'une population urbaine (Loreto 2006; Seigne 1992). En milieu urbain, l'individu ne cherche pas à se distinguer à travers les décors de son habitat mais s'exprime à travers son appartenance au tissu urbain, sa localisation là où il faut être.

Les panneaux de pierre quelles que soient leur dimensions, la plupart du temps adaptées à la structure du bâtiment (Seigne 1992; Loreto 2006), témoignent d'une très grande homogénéité au sein de l'Arabie du Sud. Nous pouvons les interpréter comme une représentation de menuiseries ajourées de type du moucharabieh avec une partie haute comprenant une ouverture fermée par des éléments horizontaux en bois et une partie basse plus ouverte qui aurait pu être occultée à l'intérieur par des volets en bois. Ces représentations de fenêtres en pierre représentent sûrement les types de fenêtres les plus courants, les édifices de l'Antiquité de cette région étaient résolument ouverts sur l'extérieur.

Les traces d'ossature de bois ont été, dans un premier temps, particulièrement étudiées afin de comprendre le fonctionnement des parois en tant qu'éléments porteurs. Ainsi à Shabwa, certains murs externes et internes montrent bien qu'au lieu de deux rangées parallèles de poteaux verticaux, il était nécessaire, au premier niveau, de renforcer les parois — plus épaisses — et de créer ainsi une ossature avec trois rangées d'éléments linéaires verticaux dans l'épaisseur du mur. Il s'agit de variantes constructives liées à des configurations architecturales précises et conjoncturelles. Ces empreintes visibles aujourd'hui dans les massifs de remplissage d'argile calcinés et parfois même vitrifiés, qui représentent les deux tiers du volume de la maçonnerie, donnent de nombreuses informations sur la nature des parois, sur les assemblages mis en œuvre et sur le soin mis à les édifier. Par delà ces données riches en informations sur les modes de construction des bâtisseurs de cette région durant l'Antiquité, notre attention s'est portée sur les dispositifs d'entrée dont celui du palais royal de Shabwa (Darles 2005). Les hypothèses de restitution élaborées sur la base des traces en négatif, découvertes lors du dégagement du bâtiment A, ont déjà été publiées (Darles 1992; 1998; Seigne 1992), et il est nécessaire de revenir sur le principe constructif mis en œuvre. Il s'agit de cadres gigognes en bois dont les pièces possèdent les mêmes sections que l'ossature générale de l'édifice. Le système constructif fait appel à la notion d'empilement avec des principes de liaison à tenons et mortaises. La stabilité des cadres qui forment la structure d'ouverture dépend donc de la solidité des parois et de leur remplissage. Les deux contraintes techniques sont, d'une part, celle de garantir les descentes de charges à travers un empilement de linteaux qui permet de répartir les poussées verticales, d'autre part de renvoyer les forces qui recouvrent plusieurs décimètres de largeur sur un cadre de moins de 20 cm de large. Nous devons également insister

[4] À Shibam en 1980 il existe environ 500 maisons, trois types de fenêtres et un seul type de porte (Breton & Darles 1980).

sur les volontés, non pas simplement constructives et fonctionnelles, mais aussi sur l'aspect emblématique et symbolique que peut représenter l'entrée d'une demeure quelle que soit son statut social (Breton & Darles 1980; Darles 2005). Dans les restitutions que nous avons pu proposer les empilages de bois et leurs sections s'avèrent très comparables aux représentations des stèles d'Aksum ou des tombeaux de Lycie, en Anatolie (Darles 2009*a*). Ce principe d'assemblage témoigne d'une volonté générale de rigidifier l'ensemble de l'ossature par le remplissage de terre. Le seuil devient dans ce principe constructif une pièce fondamentale pour la rigidité de l'ensemble, il n'est pas simplement le lieu symbolique du franchissement entre un extérieur ouvert et un intérieur privé mais aussi un élément de la structuration architectonique d'un ensemble bâti.

Les découvertes récentes à Maʾrib, dans le temple de « Marḥam Bilqīs » par l'équipe américaine de l'American Foundation for the Study of Man dirigée par Marilyn Phillips et, à Sirwah, dans le « Five Pillars Building » par l'équipe du Deutsches Archäologisches Institut de Sanaa dirigée par le Dr Iris Gerlach, ne font que confirmer nos hypothèses. Elles complètent, de manière exceptionnelle, nos connaissances sur les menuiseries en bois. Dans les deux cas les recherches ont permis de mettre au jour des ensembles menuisés de portails calcinés partiellement conservés.[5]

Il est difficile, dans l'état de nos connaissances, d'avancer des hypothèses sur la tenue du chantier et de son déroulement. Nous savons grâce à J-C. Bessac (1998) que le ravalement se faisait de haut en bas et qu'il a donc nécessité de nombreux échafaudages en bois. Des trous de boulins, appelés opes, parsèment les élévations des fortifications comme à Maïn (Maʿīn) ou Barāqish et témoignent de la présence d'échafaudages. Qu'il ne reste que peu ou pas de vestiges de ces éléments qui puissent être aisément identifiés et seules leurs traces d'encastrement dans les parois témoignent encore de leur existence. Nous tenons à signaler que les pièces de bois destinées à de tels usages n'étaient pas pour autant banalisées et qu'elles devaient, comme de nos jours, être l'objet de réemplois successifs. La découverte, au pied du grand monolithe — que les archéologues français, à Shabwa, considèrent comme la base d'une statue monumentale encadrant l'accès au temple monumental de la ville — d'un massif maçonné qui comporte des empreintes et des vestiges d'une ossature complexe en bois, particulièrement dense, peut nous amener à envisager l'existence d'une plateforme qui servait d'échafaudage à un système de levage pour l'édification de la statue en bronze (Breton & Darles 1998). Le bois a du être considéré avant tout de manière utilitaire afin d'aider la construction des édifices et leur tenue statique; ses capacités d'isolation thermique le rendaient également propre à assurer l'interface entre un espace intérieur privé, sombre, protégé et réservé et un extérieur lumineux, chaud et parfois hostile.

Cette contribution n'abordera pas l'épigraphie. Plusieurs chercheurs se penchent depuis de nombreuses années sur les termes liés à la construction dans les langues sud-arabiques. Les progrès sont notoires et permettent lentement de relier, à travers l'étude des inscriptions, les actes de la construction à ceux des projets et, parallèlement, à ceux des options politiques et économiques des groupes humains qui contrôlaient l'Arabie du Sud antique. Les chercheurs réfléchissent depuis plusieurs années sur ces termes consacrés au bâtiment et nous considérons que leur apport à la compréhension de l'acte de bâtir, à l'entretien des édifices et à leur mutation, proposera, d'ici peu de temps, de nouvelles pistes de recherche que les archéologues pourront évaluer sur le terrain. Les inscriptions de Tamnaʿ, Barāqish et Maïn (Maʿīn) sont à ce jour les plus riches et les plus signifiantes mais nombre d'entre elles, ailleurs, méritent d'être revisitées.

Avant d'aborder la nécessaire étude des procédés constructifs et son apport à la restitution des comportements humains lors de l'édification de leur cadre bâti, nous tenons à souligner l'importance que peut avoir en Arabie du Sud l'étude des décors et des figurations. Comme a pu le souligner Ahmed Baṭayāʾ en 1986, le décor n'est pas simplement une image mais bien plutôt une représentation culturelle et politique d'un environnement bâti partagé par une communauté homogène (Baṭayāʾ 1986). L'accumulation dans les musées de la République du Yémen et du Sultanat d'Oman d'objets significatifs et représentatifs permet de classer, de rapprocher, et de confronter de nombreux éléments de décors architectoniques qui nous aident à mieux comprendre les procédés constructifs de cette époque. Parmi eux apparaissent, de plus en plus, des objets en bois qui, comme les fragments de linteaux inscrits conservés au musée national de Sanaa, permettent d'avancer de nouvelles hypothèses (Arbach & Schiettecatte 2008).

Nous tenons à mettre en avant deux pistes de travail que nous comptons exploiter prochainement. La première porte les représentations architecturales en pierre dont l'Arabie du Sud antique use à profusion, le deuxième porte sur la prise en compte des méthodes de construction dans l'étude

[5] Nous tenons à remercier les archéologues allemands, américains et yéménites pour les indications qu'ils ont pu nous donner à propos de cette problématique.

des vestiges archéologiques et l'importance de la restitution comme base scientifique d'un débat archéologique.

La représentation en pierre de l'architecture en bois est à la naissance, en 2800 av. J.-C., de l'architecture monumentale égyptienne. Imhotep, grand prêtre, architecte et chambellan, crée le complexe de Saqqarah consacré à la sépulture et au rayonnement de Djoser, pharaon de l'ancien empire. Toute son architecture représente des constructions en roseaux et en bois. Les civilisations de l'Arabie du Sud, celles de l'Anatolie, du monde Perse et bien d'autres, vont s'approprier ces leçons. Au Yémen, aujourd'hui, nous pouvons encore voir dans le Jawf et aux alentours de Maʾrib, des temples du 8ᵉ siècle av. J.-C. dont l'ossature mégalithique utilise des procédés constructifs issus des réalisations et des techniques de charpente des bâtisseurs antiques (Darles 2009*b*: 100–101). Ce type de construction mégalithique n'est pas sans rappeler différents principes égyptiens sans que l'on puisse à ce jour assurer un véritable lien entre ces civilisations. Les stèles d'Aksum témoignent de l'importance de cette volonté d'inscrire dans la pierre les actes des bâtisseurs (Buxton & Matthews 1972). Par delà leurs qualités esthétiques et plastiques, elles inscrivent matériellement un respect pour des procédés trop souvent considérés comme ordinaires ou vulgaires mais qui constituaient une culture constructive unanimement vécue et parfaitement acceptée.

L'analyse archéologique et constructive de l'architecture du sud de la Péninsule arabique durant l'Antiquité est permise grâce aux nombreux vestiges régulièrement mis au jour depuis plusieurs décennies. Elle est complétée par une approche pertinente des techniques encore utilisées aujourd'hui et par des études des typologies architecturales du patrimoine bâti. Le croisement de l'ensemble des données, complété par l'étude des inscriptions et du vocabulaire consacré à la construction, permet de proposer des hypothèses sur la nature même de l'architecture antique. La confrontation de ces hypothèses avec les nouvelles données issues des fouilles permet d'ajuster en permanence les restitutions. L'étude des influences et des échanges avec l'Afrique de l'Est, la Perse et le Proche-Orient, par exemple, a été peu abordée, elle ouvre de nouvelles voies pour la compréhension des morphologies urbaines, des typologies architecturales et des comportements constructifs des habitants de l'Arabie du Sud antique (Darles 2009*a*). L'approche thématique comme celle que nous menons à propos du matériau de construction tel le bois permet également d'approfondir et de dresser un bilan de nos connaissances.

Le bois rare et précieux, difficile à transformer, n'a pas été seulement du combustible pour le chauffage ou la cuisson. Sa transformation en matériau de construction a nécessité une opération intellectuelle et sa mise en œuvre lors de multiples opérations artisanales et techniques a permis à une civilisation des confins du désert, dans un cadre semi-aride, de l'utiliser de manière extensive. Si plus de 25 % des matériaux utilisés dans la construction des édifices construits que nous découvrons dans les villes occupées par des habitants aisés ou fortunés sont du bois, nous devons considérer qu'à cette ressource naturelle étaient rattachées des valeurs, difficiles aujourd'hui à cerner. L'étude des textes antiques consacrés à la construction paraît ainsi particulièrement prometteuse.

Références

Agostini A.

2010. Building materials in South Arabian construction inscriptions. *Proceedings of the Seminar for Arabian Studies* 40.

Arbach M. & Schiettecatte J.

2008. *Publications des collections du Musée National de Sanaa.* iii. Sanaa: Social Foundation of Development/ Centre Français d'Archéologie et de Sciences Sociales.

Baṭayāʾ A.b.A.

1986. Origine et évolution du décor architectural préislamique en Arabie méridionale, Ve siècle av. J.-C.–Ve siècle ap. J.-C. Thèse de doctorat, Paris. [Non publié].

Bessac J-C.

1998. Techniques de construction, de gravure et d'ornementation en pierre dans le Jawf (Yémen). Pages 173–230 in J-F. Breton (éd.). *Fouilles de Shabwa III. Architecture et techniques de construction.* (Bibliothèque archéologique et historique, 154). Beirut: Institut Français d'Archéologie du Proche-Orient.

Breton J-F.

1979. Le temple de Syn dhu-hlsm à Bâ-Qutfah (RDPY). *Raydan* 2: 185–241, pls 1–21.

1997. L'Architecture domestique en Arabie méridionale du VIIe s. av. J.-C. au IVe s. ap. Thèse d'État de l'Université de Paris I (Panthéon-Sorbonne). [Non publié].

1998*a*. L'habitat à Shabwa: originalité et traditions régionales. Pages 67–75 in J-F. Breton (éd.), *Fouilles de Shabwa III. Architecture et techniques de construction.* (Bibliothèque archéologique et historique, 154). Beirut: Institut Français d'Archéologie du Proche-Orient.

1998*b*. Le bâtiment 44. Pages 153–156 in J-F. Breton (éd.). *Fouilles de Shabwa III. Architecture et techniques de construction.* (Bibliothèque archéologique et historique, 154). Beirut: Institut Français d'Archéologie du Proche-Orient.

1998*c*. Les bâtiments 72 et 73. Pages 39–48 in J-F. Breton (éd.). *Fouilles de Shabwa III. Architecture et techniques de construction.* (Bibliothèque archéologique et historique, 154). Beirut: Institut Français d'Archéologie du Proche-Orient.

2009*a*. *Fouilles de Shabwa IV: Shabwa et son contexte architectural et artistique (du Ier siècle avant J.-C. au IVe siècle après J.-C.).* Sanaa/Beirut: Centre Français d'Archéologie et de Sciences Sociales/Institut Français du Proche Orient.

2009*b*. *Monastères d'Erythrée.* Asmara/Paris: Collection Cultures et Patrimoines d'Érythrée.

Breton J-F. & Darles C.

1980. Shibam. *Storia della Città* 14: 63–86.

1994. Hagar Surban 1 et 2: Villages du Gabal al-Nisiyin. Pages 46–61 in N. Nebes (éd.), *Arabia Felix, Beiträge zur Sprache und Kultur des vorislamischen Arabien, Festschrift Walter W. Müller zum 60. Geburtstag.* Wiesbaden: Harrassowitz.

1998. Le grand temple. Pages 95–152 in J-F. Breton (éd.), *Fouilles de Shabwa III. Architecture et techniques de construction.* (Bibliothèque archéologique et historique, 154). Beirut: Institut Français d'Archéologie du Proche-Orient.

Breton J-F., McMahon A.M. & Warburton D.A.

1998. Two seasons At Hajar Am-Dhaybiyya, Yemen. *Arabian archaeology and epigraphy* 9: 90–111.

Buxton D.R. & Matthews D.

1972. The reconstruction of a vanished Aksumite building. *Rassegna di Studi Etiopici* 25: 53–77.

Darles C.

1992. L'architecture civile à Shabwa. Pages 77–110 in J-F. Breton (éd.), *Fouilles de Shabwa II, Rapports préliminaires.* Extrait de *Syria* 68 (1991): 77–110. (Institut Français d'Archéologie du Proche-Orient, 19). Paris: Librairie Orientaliste Paul Geuthner.

1998. Étude typologique de l'architecture civile intra-muros. Pages 3–26 in J-F. Breton (éd.), *Fouilles de Shabwa III. Architecture et techniques de construction.* (Bibliothèque archéologique et historique, 154). Beirut: Institut Français d'Archéologie du Proche-Orient.

2005. Hypothèses de restitution du dispositif d'entrée du Palais de Shabwa. Pages 151–172 in A. Sholan, S. Antonini & M. Arbach (éds), *Sabaean studies; Archaeological, epigraphical and historical studies in honour of Yusuf M. Abdallah, Alessandro de Maigret et Christian J. Robin on the occasion of their sixtieth birthdays.* Naples/Sanaa: University of Sanaa/Yemeni Italian Centre for Archaeological Researches/Centre français d'archéologie et de sciences sociales de Sanaa.

2009*a*. Des formes et des formules architecturales originales. Pages 36–65 in J-F. Breton (éd.), *Fouilles de Shabwa IV: Shabwa et son contexte architectural et artistique (du Ier siècle avant J.-C. au IVe siècle après J.-C.).* Sanaa/Beirut: Centre Français d'Archéologie et de Sciences Sociales/Institut Français du Proche Orient.

2009*b*. Les monolithes dans l'architecture monumentale de l'Arabie du Sud antique. *Proceedings of the Seminar for Arabian Studies* 39: 95–109.

Krencker D.
1913. *Ältere Denkmäler NordAbessiniens.* ii. *Deutsche Aksum Expedition.* Ed. by E. Littman & D. Krencker. Berlin: Reimer.

Liebsekal Y. & Schebat T.
2007. *Art Erythréen, l'église Kidane Mehret à Matara.* (Collection Cultures et Patrimoines d'Érythrée). Perpignan/Asmara: Alliance française d'Asmara.

Loreto R.
2006. A hypothetical reconstruction of the small palace (Baytân Khamrân) in the Market Square in Tamna. *Arabia* 3: 161–170.

Naumann R.
1955. *Architektur Kleinasiens von ihren Anfängen bis zum Ende der hethitischen Zeit.* Tübingen: E. Wasmuth.

Sedov A.V.
2005. *Temples of Ancient Hadramaut.* (Arabia Antica Series, 3). Pisa: PLUS-Pisa University Press.
2008*a*. The cultural quarter: Area F. Pages 183–260 in A. Avanzini (ed.), *A port in Arabia between Rome and the Indian Ocean (3rd C. BC–5th C. AD). Khor Rori Report 2.* Rome: « L'Erma » di Bretschneider.
2008*b*. Religious architecture in Sumhuram: the extra muros temple. Pages 261–276 in A. Avanzini (ed.), *A port in Arabia between Rome and the Indian Ocean (3rd C. BC–5th C. AD). Khor Rori Report 2.* Rome: « L'Erma » di Bretschneider.

Seigne J.
1982. Les maisons I, J et K de Masghra. Pages 22–32 in J-F. Breton, L. Badre, R. Audouin & J. Seigne (éds), *Le wâdî Hadramawt, Prospections 1978–1979.* [Aden]: Centre Culturel et de Recherches Archéologiques.
1992. Le château royal de Shawba. Le bâtiment, architecture, technique de construction et restitution. Pages 111–164 in J-F. Breton (éd.), *Fouilles de Shabwa II, Rapports préliminaires.* Extrait de *Syria* 68 (1991). (Institut Français d'Archéologie du Proche-Orient, 19). Paris: Librairie Orientaliste Paul Geuthner.

Adresse de l'auteur
Prof. Christian Darles, École nationale supérieure d'architecture de Toulouse, 83, rue Aristide Maillol, BP 10629, 31106 Toulouse Cedex 1, France.

e-mail christian.darles@toulouse.archi.fr

Proceedings of the Seminar for Arabian Studies 40 (2010): 161–170

Once more on the interpretation of *mṯl* in Epigraphic South Arabian (a new expiatory inscription on irrigation from Kamna)

Serge A. Frantsouzoff

Summary

In her contribution to the Seminar of Arabian Studies of 2008 A. Multhoff tried to demonstrate that the term *mṯl* in several contexts of Sabaic, Minaic (originating in Kamna), and Hadramitic inscriptions should be interpreted as "similar". However, an unpublished inscription from Kamna kept in the stores of the Military Museum at Ṣanʿāʾ under no. 148 proves that at least in the case of Minaic her conclusion was incorrect.

This expiatory text, dated from the third to second century BC on the basis of palaeographic criteria, was compiled by the previously unknown king of Kaminahū Dhamarkarib Riyām, son of Ilīsami^c, and his commune (*s*^{2c}*b-s*^{1}) Kaminahū (ll. 1–3). One of the acts, of which they did penance to the god Dhū Madahwū, is rendered as follows: *w-b-hn / yḡw / b-s*^{1} | *wl / yṯ*^{c}*d-s*^{1} */ mṯl* "and because they misdirected the stream, which the document allotted (for them)" (ll. 6–7). Therefore in the final formula *f-ḥmy* | *n / bn / ʾrẖ / mṯl-s*^{1}*n* (ll. 11–12) this term should have the same meaning: "and may the defence be assured against the (corresponding) provision of the document on them" (i.e. on the cultivated lands [*mwfr*^{n}] mentioned in l. 11).

Keywords: Minaic inscriptions, Military Museum of Sanaa, site of Kamna (ancient Kaminahū), expiatory texts, the god dhū Madahwū

The corpus of the edited inscriptions originating in Kamna still remains scarce. For the most part, they are either short (Kamna 1–4, 9, 11, 13, 15–17; Ṣanʿāʾ MM 3630; al-Jawf 04.5 A–B, 04.6; YM 23208) or fragmentary (Kamna 5–8, 10, 12, 14, 18–22; YM 8871; al-Jawf 04.7).[1] The only exception to that regrettable regulation is the expiatory inscription YM 10886 published by C.J. Robin. On the 27th October 1998, during my first visit to the Military Museum of Ṣanʿāʾ, I paid attention to another text of the same category represented in the permanent exhibition. Eleven years later, on 19 November 2009, I rediscovered this epigraphic document in the stores of this museum and was kindly allowed to edit it.

Fr–Ṣanʿāʾ 5 = Military Museum of Sanaa, no. 148 (Figs 1–4)

Provenance

The royal title, the name of the *shaʿb* and that of the deity, to whom the text is addressed, leave no doubt about the origin of this inscribed stela from Kamna.

Description

The text, complete and well preserved, is engraved on a vertical surface of a rectangular limestone stela (Height: 54 cm; Width: 27 cm; Thickness: 12 cm); its upper right corner is broken. The average height of the lines is 3 cm and the characters are rather large.

Palaeography

The open *m*, the sharp *r*, slightly thickened in its middle, the sharp inclination of the intermediate bar in *n* and *ẖ* as well as the stalks of *y*, *h*, and *ḥ*, the apex of *s*^{1} and the inclined bar of *k* with considerable bulges at their ends correspond to the third to second century BC.

Text

1. *Ḏmrkrb / Rym / bn[/ ʾ]=*
2. *ls*^{1}*m*^{c} */ mlk / Kmnhw*
3. *w-s*^{2c}*b-s*^{1} */ Kmnhw / ntẖy*
4. *w-ntḏr / k-ḏ-Mdhww / b-*
5. *hn / l-ys*^{1}*twffy / b-ḡy=*

[1] Sometimes their readings are based exclusively on rather poor copies of Joseph Halévy, full of inaccuracies and mistakes (especially in the two cases, Kamna 13 and 20).

Figure 1. *The inscription Fr–Ṣanʿāʾ 5 = Military Museum of Sanaa, no. 148. (Photograph by the author).*

Figure 2. *The upper part of the inscription Fr–Ṣan^{c}ā^ʾ 5 (ll. 1–5). (Photograph by the author).*

Figure 3. *The middle of the inscription Fr–Ṣan^{c}ā^ʾ 5 (ll. 4–10). (Photograph by the author.*

Figure 4. *The lower part of the inscription Fr–Ṣan^{c}ā^ʾ 5 (ll. 7–12). (Photograph by the author).*

6. *l- < s^1 > m / w-b-hn / yḡw / b-s^1=*
7. *wl < / > yṯ^{c}d-s^1 / mṯl / w-b-*
8. *hn / l-ykyl / ḏ-krb / b-y=*
9. *wmh / s^{1}dn / b-ywm / ṯmr*
10. *w-b-hn / l-yft < ḥ > / ḏ-ymt=*
11. *ẖḍ / b-mwfr^n / f-ḥmy=*
12. *n / bn / ʾrẖ / mṯl-s^{1}n*

Translation

1. Dhamarkarib Riyām, son of
2. [I]līsami^c, king of Kaminahū,
3. and his commune of Kaminahū confessed
4. and did penance to dhū Madahwū, be-
5. cause they had to be surely protected by means of
6. their water-course and because they misdirected the
7. stream, which the document allotted (for them), and be-
8. cause they had to measure what they offered on the
9. day of performing service (for the god), on the day of (collecting) crops,
10. and because they had to give judgement on what was appro-
11. priated among the cultivated lands; and may the defence
12. be assured against the (corresponding) provision of the document on them (i.e. on the above-mentioned cultivated lands).

Commentary

Lines 1–2:

Ḏmrkrb / Rym / bn[/ ʾ] | ls^{1}m^c / mlk / Kmnhw. The personal noun of this ruler is attested in Sabaic, Minaic (Harding 1971: 257; Al-Said 1995: 30), and Qatabanic (Hayajneh 1998: 314). His epithet *Rym* is of very frequent usage in the Minaic anthroponomastics (Harding 1971: 292). The proper noun *ʾls^{1}m^c*, which occurs in all the Epigraphic South Arabian languages (Harding 1971: 67; Al-Said 1995: 19–20; Hayajneh 1998: 301), was borne by at least three kings of Kamna (Robin 2002: 198–199).[2]

Lines 3–4:

ntẖy | w-ntḏr / k-ḏ-Mdhww. The occurrence of this

[2] Apart from this, the patronymic *[ʾ]ls^{1}m^c* belongs to a king of Kaminahū, mentioned in al-Jawf 04.7/1, whose personal name and epithet are not preserved. The palaeography of this text is much more archaic than that of the inscription published here and for that reason the two texts could not have been compiled by the same person.

formula is typical for Minaic expiatory texts. As to the translation of both verbs, it should be remarked that in Minaic the verbal termination *-w* hardly occurs at all, so that the plural is usually a homograph of the singular (Beeston 1984: 60, § M 5: 4). The name of Madahwū, the principal deity of Kaminahū, with the preceding relative pronoun *ḏ-* has been already attested in YM 10886/4–5.

Lines 4–6:
b- | hn / l-ys^1*twffy / b-ḡy | l-* < *s*^{1} > *m*. On the causal usage of *b-hn*, see Beeston (1962: 65, § 55: 14). In contrast to that text the finite verbal forms in perfect are attested after this conjunction in the expiatory inscriptions from Haram (Haram 34/2–3, 35/3–5, 36/5, 40/2–3), from the temple dhū Yaghrū localized in Wādī Shuḍayf in the north of al-Jawf (Ṣilwī–Wādī Shuḍayf 1/3–4; FB – Wādī Shuḍayf 2/3) and even from Kamna (YM 10886/5, 8).

It appears that the addition of the particle *l-* to *b-hn* would impart a modal sense of duty or obligation to the following verb.

As for the interpretation of the *s*^{1}*t*-prefix stem of *WFY*, Peter Stein has the merit of introducing a correction to the *Sabaic Dictionary* (Beeston *et al.* 1982: 158) demonstrating that in all the Sabaic contexts the verb *s*^{1}*twfy* is intransitive and conforms to a passive meaning "bewahrt werden" (Stein 2003: 160, n. 29). The reduplication of the second radical is a phenomenon attested in several Minaic verbs (Beeston 1984: 60, § M 4:2) and an attempt to explain it as a marker of a lengthened consonant (1984: 7, n. 10) is to be taken into account. If such an interpretation is correct, this verbal form would represent a strict morphological equivalent of the causative-reflexive derivative of the intensive stem in classical Ethiopic (*astäfä*^{cc}*alä*). However, it is not excluded that every reduplicated consonant was followed by a vowel, as in *alḥosasa* "whisper gently" (cf. *laḥasa* "murmur") also attested in classical Ethiopic (Leslau 1987: 311).

One of the distinctive features of Minaic consists in the lack of any graphic differentiation between the masculine singular and plural forms in the so-called simple imperfect (i.e. without the final *-n*) as in the perfect (Beeston 1984: 60, § M 5: 5).

The instrumental usage of *b-* corresponds well to that context.

Lines 6–7:
w-b-hn / yḡw / b-s^1 *| wl*. The present interpretation of *yḡw* is based on the general sense of the Arabic verb *ḡawā* (imperfect *yaḡwī*) "he erred, deviated from the right way or course, or from that which was right: and was disappointed; or failed of attaining his desire: and he laboured, and persisted, in that which was vain, or false, or in ignorant conduct: or he acted ignorantly from misbelief" (Lane 1863–1893, i/6: 2304) as well as on a meaning "mislead" presumably ascribed to *ḡwy* in Sabaic (Ja 570/6; cf. Biella 1982: 391–392).

The use of the imperfect for rendering actions in the past has already been examined in detail in the rich material of Hadramitic epigraphic documents from Raybūn.

As for *s*^{1}*wl*, the context suggests its comparison with *sayl* "flood, stream" in Arabic in consideration for the alternation between *w* and *y* frequently attested in the Epigraphic South Arabian languages (Beeston 1962: 16, § 12: 1).

Line 7:
yṯ^c*d-s*^{1} */ mṯl*. The subject of this relative clause linked to the antecedent substantive *s*^{1}*wl* asyndetically is *mṯl*. Therefore any interpretation of this common noun as "the like of *s.t.*" "similar, same", "something like (that)" (Multhoff 2009: 296–298) is completely excluded, while the sense "copy, exemplar *of document*" (Beeston *et al.* 1982: 88) seems appropriate to the contents of this passage. The attached pronoun *-s*^{1} undoubtedly relates to *s*^{1}*wl*.

Although the *t*-infix stem of this verb *ṯ*^{c}*d* in Sabaic was translated as "use *s.t.* for irrigation" (Beeston *et al.* 1982: 149), A.G. Lundin succeeded in demonstrating that semantically the derivatives from this root have more general meanings connected with rights in landed property which only in some specific cases could be reduced to rights to irrigation: "part, share, allotment, parcel", "use (as an allotment)", "allot", "divide into shares" (Lundin 1987: 53–55).

The first two passages introduced with *b-hn* deal with the same subject. The first of them states that the well-being of Kaminahū depends on the irrigation system, while the second concretizes that the misdirection of a stream caused damage.

Lines 7–8:
w-b- | hn / l-ykyl / ḏ-krb. For the translation of *ykyl* see *klt* "measurement" in Sabaic (Beeston *et al.* 1982: 81) and *kāla* (*yakīlu*), *kayyala* "to measure" in Standard Arabic (Wehr 1971: 850).

The verb *kyl* and the noun having the same spelling are attested in two Minaic inscriptions from Ma^{c}īn (ancient Qarnaw), but in an obscure context (YM 28488 ɐ3–5:

w-k | yl / kyl / ʾlʾlt / Mʿn / w-kyl | s^{2}*ym / ḏ-Qbḍ / k-mlk / Mʿn*; YM 28488 B/3–5: *w- | kyl / ky l/ ʾlʾlt / Mʿn / w-kyl | s*^{2}*ym / Wd / k-s*^{2}*wʿy / Wd*^{m}). The meanings "to decorate" and "decorations" proposed for them seem dubious, but it is clear that these words describe something made for the deities by their worshippers. In both texts the verb *kyl* can be translated "to measure" and in that case the expressions *kyl / ʾlʾlt / Mʿn, kyl | s*^{2}*ym / ḏ-Qbḍ* and *ky l| s*^{2}*ym / Wd* appear to designate certain measures used for determining volumes or weights of the offerings presented to the "deities of Maʿīn", to ʿAthtar dhū Qabḍ and to Wadd.

Although the semantic connection of the Epigraphic South Arabian root *KRB* with "dedication" or "offering" was called into question (Beeston 1981: 24–30), in the Minaic inscription LuBM 2/2 the noun *krb* is translated with certainty as "offering" and in some Qatabanic contexts the verb *tkrb* can be interpreted as "to dedicate, set apart" (Ricks 1989: 86).

Lines 8–9:
b-y | wmh / s^{1}*dn / b-ywm / ṯmr*. In *s*^{1}*dn* all the three characters appear to be radical, since in the parallel expression *b-ywm / ṯmr* as well as in all the nouns of this inscription, with the only exception of *mwfr*^{n}, no determinate ending, or mīmation,[3] are attested. Thus it is to be compared with *sadana* "he acted as minister, or servant, of the Kaabeh, and of the temple of idols" and *sidāna* "ministry, or service [and particularly the ministry, or service, and superintendence, of a temple of idols; and afterwards, of the Kaabeh]" in classical Arabic (Lane 1863–1893, i / 4: 1335).

The *-h* at the end of *b-y|wmh* is a Minaic marker of the genitive case which, however, can be sporadically absent (Beeston 1962: 37–38, § 33: 2), as in *b-ywm / ṯmr*.

In all probability, a feast of harvest, which envisaged special ceremonies of worship to (dhū) Madahwū, is implied here.

Lines 10–11:
w-b-hn / l-yft < ḥ > / ḏ-ymt | ḥḏ / b-mwfr^{n}. The ground-stem of the verb *ftḥ* in Minaic is translated as "décréter" (Arbach 1993, i: 34). The similar meanings are proper to it in Qatabanic (RÉS 3566/11, 14–15: "to give (make) judgement"; see Korotayev 1997: 141, 142) and in Hadramatic (Rb I/84 no. 198 a–f = SOYCE 706/5, 6: "to impose (regulation)"; see Frantsouzoff 1997: 122).

The interpretation of *ymtḫḍ* proposed here is deduced by analogy with *s*^{1}*tmḫḍ* "appropriate *property*" in Sabaic (Beeston *et al.* 1982: 84).

The sense of all the derivatives from the root *WFR*, including *mwfr*, is examined in detail in Lundin (1987: 55–56). It is preferable to consider *mwfr*^{n} as a plural form (of the type *mfʿl* derived from the singular *mfʿlt*; see Stein 2003: 78),[4] since the feminine plural attached pronoun[5] in l. 12 seems to relate to this noun.

Lines 11–12:
f-ḥmy | n / bn / ʾrḫ / mṯl-s^{1}*n*. This formula in a slightly different shape (with the *t*-infix stem and the masculine singular attached pronoun *-s*^{1}) is attested in YM 10886/10–11: *f-ḥtmyn | bn / ʾrḫ / mṯl-s*^{1}, but unfortunately its translation proposed by the editor, "puis (les auteurs – *S.F.*) se sont prémunis contre le verdict (?) de sa statue" (Robin 2002: 198, 201), cannot be accepted. Last year in her paper delivered at the Seminar, A. Multhoff reinterpreted it as "and they will keep themselves away from doing (things) similar to those (aforementioned affairs)" (2009: 296).

However, in the present inscription *mṯl* occurs twice and there are good reasons for concluding that in l. 12 this term should have the same meaning as in l. 7, i.e. "document". Thus *mṯl-s*^{1}*n* should be interpreted as *mṯl/mwfr*^{n} "the document on the cultivated lands", i.e. a sort of decree that regulated their usage and the rights of property on them. The last two passages of the text appear to be closely connected. In ll. 10–11 the authors recognized their connivance towards the appropriation of some plots of land and then expressed their hope that such negligence would not entail judicial consequences stipulated by a clause of some specific document.

The *n*-marked infinitives are not typical at all for Minaic,[6] and at first sight a certain Sabaic influence would not be excluded. A similar formula seems to be found in two texts from the Awwām temple (FB – Maḥram Bilqīs 1/17–18: *w-ḥtmyn / bn / mṯl | ʾlt / ʾʾrḫ*^{n}; MB 2002 I-28/33: *w-ḥtmyn / bn / mṯl / hnt / ʾʾrḫ*^{n}) which go back to the late

[3] The use of the mīmation in Minaic "is so erratic that we must conclude that it has virtually no semantic or syntactic value, but is purely an ornament of diction" (Beeston 1984: 61, § M: 14: 1). Very rare contexts of the inscriptions from Kamna, in which it occurs, like *bn / ʾs*^{2}*rs*^{1} */ ʿd / s*^{1}*mh*^{m} "depuis la fondation jusqu'au faîte" in al-Jawf 04.7/2, confirm the present statement.

[4] Both forms, *mwfr* and *mwfrt*, occur in Sabaic as well as in Minaic, but it is not completely clear which of them is the plural one (see Lundin 1987: 55; Arbach 1993, i: 102; and especially Maʿīn 1/5, 88/5–6).

[5] The suffix *-s*^{1}*n* is hypothetically interpreted in this way in Beeston (1984: 63, § M 23: 2).

[6] According to A.F.L. Beeston, they "do not seem to occur" in this language (1984: 61, § 8: 1).

fourth to early third century AD and to the third quarter of the third century AD respectively.

However, the expressions *ʾrẖ / mṯl-s*^{1} (*ʾrẖ / mṯl-s*^{1}*n*) and *mṯl / ʾlt(hnt) / ʾʾrẖ*^{n} are semantically different. In the second case the term *mṯl* has the same meaning "similar", "like something" as *miṯl*, *miṯāl* in Arabic. In FB – Maḥram Bilqīs 1/17–18 this formula is translated as "et de s'abstenir de choses semblables à ces affaires" (Bron & Ryckmans 1999: 164; cf. Multhoff 2009: 296: "and to keep themselves away from [what is] similar to these [aforementioned] affairs") and in MB 2002 I–28/33 its interpretation remains the same: "and (to) protect themselves against such judicial cases (i.e. crimes)" (Maraqten 2006: 61, 63; cf. Multhoff 2009: 296: "and to keep himself away from [what is] similar to those affairs"). It is well known that by its vocabulary and use of words Sabaic bears the closest resemblance to Arabic among the Epigraphic South Arabian languages.

* * *

The interpretation of the Minaic term *mṯl* as "document" substantiated in the course of the analysis of Fr–Ṣanʿāʾ 5 and the elucidation of a modal sense proper to the conjunction *b-hn / l-* gives an opportunity to reconsider the translation of YM 10886:

Text

1. *ʾls*^{1}*m*^{c} */ Ḏrẖ*^{n}
2. *mlk / Kmnhw / w-s*^{2}*=*
3. *ʿb-s*^{1} */ Kmnhw / nt=*
4. *ẖy / w-ntḏr / k-ḏ-Md=*
5. *hww / b-hn / l-ḏbḥ / m=*
6. *ḏbḥ / twwr / s*^{2}*ty / m=*
7. *ḏbḥ / twrt / b-ʿbr-s*^{1}
8. *w-bn-hn / s*^{1}*fnw / ḡyl*^{n}
9. *b-s*^{2}*ty / s*^{2ʾ}*mt / blty*
10. *ḏ-Mdhww / f-ḥtmyn*
11. *bn / ʾrẖ / mṯl-s*^{1}

Translation

1. Ilīsami^c Dharḥān,
2. king of Kaminahū, and his com-
3. mune of Kaminahū con-
4. fessed and did penance to dhū Mada-
5. hwū, because they had to make a sa-
6. crifice of bulls instead of a sa-
7. crifice of cows to Him
8. and because they directed the water-course
9. not to the north in discord with
10. dhū Madahwū; and may the defence be assured
11. against the (corresponding) provision of His document.

From the historical point of view, YM 10886 and Fr–Ṣanʿāʾ 5, dated respectively from the fifth century BC and from the third to second century BC, to a certain degree fill a large lacuna between the mid-sixth and mid-second century BC inside the column reserved for the kingdom of Kaminahū in the chronological scheme compiled for the catalogue of the first folio of the famous Yemen exhibition (Robin 1997*a*: 228). It seems quite possible that this small state of al-Jawf maintained its independence through the first millennium BC without interruption.

Acknowledgements

I have the honour to express my deepest gratitude to Lieutenant-Colonel Sharaf Ghālib Luqmān, Chief of the Military Museum of Ṣanʿāʾ, for his kind permission to publish the inscription kept in its stores under no. 148 and to Dr Mounir Arbach who helped me to establish contact with him.

Sigla

FB – Maḥram Bilqīs 1	Inscription in Bron & Ryckmans 1999.
FB – Wādī Shuḍayf 2	Inscription in Bron 1997: 77, 78 (fig. 3), 79.
Haram 34, 35, 36, 40	Inscriptions in Robin 1992: 102–105, 109–111; pls 11b, 12a–b, 15a.
Ja 570	Inscription in Jamme 1962: 55–57; pl. 4.
al-Jawf 04.5 A–B, 04.6, 04.7	Inscriptions in Arbach & Schiettecatte 2006: 18–20; pl. 3 (figs 6, 7), 4 (fig. 8).
LuBM 2	Inscription in Frantsouzoff 2006.
Maʿīn 1, 88	Inscriptions in Bron 1998, A: 37–40, 97–98; B: pls 4–7, 34/a.
MB 2002 I–28	Inscription in Maraqten 2006: 54–64; figs 3–6.
Rb I/84 no. 198a–f = SOYCE 706	Inscription in Frantsouzoff 1997: 118–122, 125–126 & nn. 21–28; figs 3–6.
RÉS	Inscriptions in *Répertoire d'épigraphie sémitique*. V–VIII. Paris: Imprimerie nationale, 1929–1968.

Ṣanᶜāʾ MM 3630	Inscription in Robin 2002: 194–197, 210–212 (figs 3–7).	YM 10886	Inscription in Robin 2002: 197–201, 213 (fig. 8); Robin 1997*b*: 232.
Ṣilwī–Wādī Shuḏayf 1	Inscription in Bron 1997: 75, 76 (fig. 2), 77.	YM 23208	Inscription in Arbach & Audouin 2007: 39.
YM 8871	Inscription in Robin 2002: 191–194, 209 (fig. 2).	YM 28488 A, B	Inscriptions in Arbach & Audouin 2007: 58–59.

References

Arbach M.

1993. Le maḏābien: Lexique — Onomastique et Grammaire d'une langue de l'Arabie mériodionale préislamique. (3 volumes). Thèse de doctorat — Nouveau régime. Sous la direction de Monsieur Ch. Robin, Aix-en-Provence. [Unpublished].

Arbach M. & Audouin R.

2007. *Ṣanᶜâʾ National Museum. Collection of Epigraphic and Archaeological Artifacts from al-Jawf Sites.* Part II. Ṣanᶜāʾ: UNESCO-SFD — Ṣanᶜaʾ National Museum.

Arbach M. & Schiettecatte J.

2006. *Catalogue des pièces archéologiques & épigraphiques du Jawf au musée national de Ṣanᶜâʾ*. Part I. Ṣanᶜaʾ: Centre français d'archéologie et de sciences sociales de Ṣanᶜaʾ.

Beeston A.F.L.

1962. *A Descriptive Grammar of Epigraphic South Arabian*. London: Luzac.

1981. Two Epigraphic South Arabian Roots: HYᶜ and KRB. Pages 21–34 in R. Stiegner (ed.), *Al-Hudhud. Festschrift Maria Höfner zum 80. Geburtstag*. Graz: RM-Druck & Verlagsgesellschaft mbH.

1984. *Sabaic Grammar*. (Journal of Semitic Studies, Monograph 6). Manchester: University of Manchester.

Beeston A.F.L., Ghul M.A., Müller W.W. & Ryckmans J.

1982. *Sabaic Dictionary (English–French–Arabic)*. (Publications of the University of Sanaa, YAR). Louvain-la-Neuve: Peeters/Beirut: Librairie du Liban.

Biella J.C.

1982. *Dictionary of Old South Arabic. Sabaean Dialect.* (Harvard Semitic Studies, 25). Chico, CA: Scholars Press.

Bron F.

1997. Quatre inscriptions sabéennes provenant d'un temple de dhū-Samawī. *Syria* 74: 73–80.

1998. *Maᶜīn*. Fasc. A: *Les documents*. Fasc. B: *Les planches*. (Inventaire des inscriptions sudarabiques, 3). Paris: Diffusion de Boccard/Rome: Diffusion Herder.

Bron F. & Ryckmans J.

1999. Une inscription sabéenne sur bronze provenant du Maḥram Bilqîs à Mārib. *Semitica* 49: 161–169.

Frantsouzoff S.A.

1997. Regulation of conjugal relations in ancient Raybūn. *Proceedings of the Seminar for Arabian Studies* 27: 113–127.

2006. A Minaic inscription on the pedestal of an ibex figurine from the British Museum. *Proceedings of the Seminar for Arabian Studies* 36: 69–77.

Harding G.L.

1971. *An Index and Concordance of Pre-Islamic Arabian Names and Inscriptions*. (Near and Middle Eastern Series, 8). Toronto/Buffalo: University of Toronto Press.

Hayajneh H.

1998. *Die Personennamen in den qatabānischen Inschriften. Lexikalische und grammatische Analyse im Kontext der semitischen Anthroponomastik*. (Texte und Studien zur Orientalistik, 10). Hildesheim/New York: Georg Olms Verlag.

Jamme A.
1962. *Sabaean Inscriptions from Maḥram Bilqîs (Mârib)*. (Publications of the American Foundation for the Study of Man, iii). Baltimore, MD: The Johns Hopkins Press.

Korotayev A.V.
1997. A socio-political conflict in the Qatabanian kingdom? (A preliminary re-interpretation of the Qatabanic inscription RÉS 3566). *Proceedings of the Seminar for Arabian Studies* 27: 141–158.

Lane E.W.
1863–1893. *An Arabic-English Lexicon*. i/1–8. London/Edinburgh: Williams & Norgate.

Leslau W.
1987. *Comparative Dictionary of Geʿez (Classical Ethiopic). Geʿez–English/English–Geʿez with an index of Semitic roots*. Wiesbaden: Otto Harrassowitz.

Lundin A.G.
1987. Sabaean Dictionary. Some Lexical Notes. Pages 49– 56 in C. Robin & M. Bâfaqîh (eds), *Ṣayhadica. Recherches sur les inscriptions de l'Arabie préislamique offertes par ses collègues au Professeur A.F.L. Beeston*. (L'Arabie préislamique, 1). Paris: Librairie Orientaliste Paul Geuthner S.A.

Maraqten M.
2006. Legal documents recently discovered by the AFSM at Maḥram Bilqīs, near Mārib, Yemen. *Proceedings of the Seminar for Arabian Studies* 36: 53–67.

Multhoff A.
2009. *"A parallel to the Second Commandment…"* revisited. *Proceedings of the Seminar for Arabian Studies* 39: 295–301.

Ricks St.D.
1989. *Lexicon of Inscriptional Qatabanian*. (Studia Pohl. Dissertationes scientificae de rebus Orientis antiqui, 14). Rome: Editrice Pontificio Istituto Biblico.

Robin C.J.
1992. *Inabbaʾ, Haram, al-Kāfir, Kamna et al-Ḥarāshif*. Fasc. A: *Les documents*. Fasc. B: *Les planches*. (Inventaire des inscriptions sudarabiques, 1). Paris: Diffusion de Boccard/Rome: Diffusion Herder.
1997*a*. La périodisation. Pages 228–229 in C.J. Robin & B. Vogt (eds), *Yémen, au pays de la reine de Sabaʾ. Exposition présentée à l'Institut du monde arabe du 25 octobre 1997 au 28 février 1998*. Paris: Flammarion.
1997*b*. Liste des pièces exposées. Pages 230–235 in C.J. Robin & B. Vogt (eds), *Yémen, au pays de la reine de Sabaʾ. Exposition présentée à l'Institut du monde arabe du 25 octobre 1997 au 28 février 1998*. Paris: Flammarion.
2002. Vers une meilleure connaissance de l'histoire politique et religieuse de Kaminahū (Jawf du Yémen). Pages 191–213 in J.H. Healey & V. Porter (eds), *Studies on Arabia in Honour of Professor G. Rex Smith*. (Journal of Semitic Studies, Supplement 14). Oxford: Oxford University Press.

Al-Said S.F.
1995. *Die Personennamen in den minäischen Inschriften. Eine etymologische und lexikalische Studie im Bereich der semitischen Sprachen*. (Akademie der Wissenschaften und der Literatur zu Mainz, Veröffentlichungen der Orientalischen Kommission, hrsg. von W.W. Müller, 41). Wiesbaden: Harrassowitz Verlag.

Stein P.
2003. *Untersuchungen zur Phonologie und Morphologie des Sabäischen*. (Epigraphische Forschungen auf der Arabischen Halbinsel, 3). Rahden/Westf.: Verlag Marie Leidorf GmbH.

Wehr H.
1971. *A Dictionary of Modern Written Arabic*. (ed. J. Milton Cowan). Wiesbaden: Otto Harrassowitz.

Author's address
Serge A. Frantsouzoff, Institute of Oriental Manuscripts, 18, Dvortsovaya embankment, 191186 St Petersburg, Russia.
e-mail frants@spios.nw.ru

Proceedings of the Seminar for Arabian Studies 40 (2010): 171–174

New evidence on the use of implements in al-Madām area, Sharjah, UAE (poster)

ALEJANDRO GALLEGO LÓPEZ

Summary
During the last archaeological campaigns at the Iron Age site of al-Madām (Sharjah, UAE) special attention was paid to several interconnected issues. One focus has been the study of implements and ways of treating materials before building at a previously reported mud-brick working area (MWA). During the last campaign, remarkably well-preserved tool marks were unearthed. A comparison of their shape and appearance with other tool marks of the same type is made, together with an examination of possible chronological and geographical correlations, which leads us to propose an interpretation of the usage and typology of the implements.

Keywords: al-Madām, implements, traces, hoe, pickaxe

The discovery of implements and the study of building techniques

The site of al-Madām is well known in Gulf Archaeology. It has been excavated in recent years by the Spanish Archaeological Mission from the Universidad Autónoma in Madrid. In the course of the excavations, three major structures were unearthed: in a mud-brick working area where there is a building (MWA), a *falaj* and a deep well. In all three of them traces of implements were discovered that may serve as the basis for understanding the building techniques that were developed in this area, and also for the archaeological, historical, and cultural interpretation of the traces of implements unearthed.

Regarding the structures and specifically the MWA (Fig. 1), as far as they are relevant to this paper, traces of what seems to be the imprints of some kind of tools or implements were unearthed and clearly identified, together with footprints on basins and fingerprints on mud bricks. These traces were found mainly in places where rocky material was extracted clearly for building purposes. The soil at the site, due to its hardness and resistance, was exploited by the inhabitants of al-Madām for construction purposes. The special composition of the soil led peoples from this area to adapt the shapes of their implements to take advantage of what the environment had to offer in an optimal way. Thanks to the close examination of the traces and their corresponding measurements, we came to the conclusion that the extraction of the material was done using a similar procedure (Córdoba 2003).

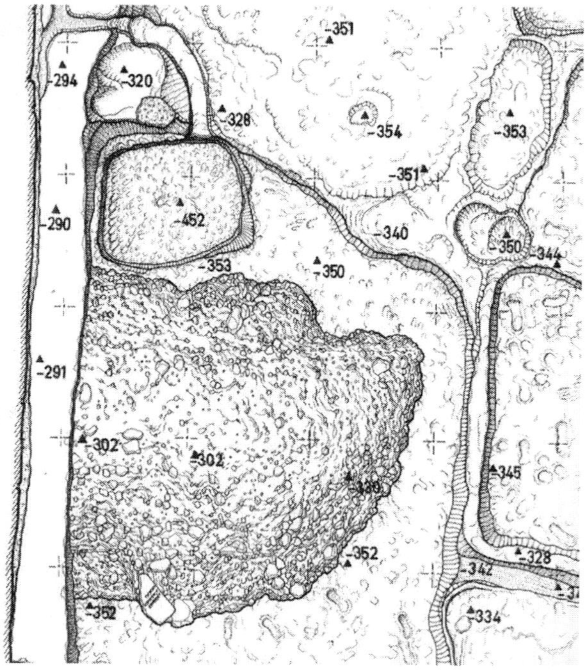

FIGURE 1. *A detailed view of MWA. Footprints and hoe traces can be seen in the basins (M.A. Núñez Villanueva).*

The excavation of the MWA was extended in the 2008 campaign (Fig. 2), when new implement marks were unearthed and carefully measured and studied. These traces were concentrated in the south of the area and specifically next to an area for the extraction of material

Figure 2. *View of part of the southern extension in MWA in 2008, with traces of the use of implements (Spanish Archaeological Mission).*

a.

b.

Figure 3a and 3b. *Detailed views of traces found during the MWA 2008 Campaign (Spanish Archaeological Mission).*

that had already been excavated in 2003. The shape and orientation of the marks clearly show they were made by a shafted hoe and not by a pickaxe, which is ubiquitous at the site. An obvious parallel is the hoe from al-Rumaylah or even the third-millennium hoes from Saar.

Given that in the case of al-Madām no metal tools have so far been found, a comparative study of the traces at other sites in the UAE — even within different chronological profiles — is necessary in order to understand the function and usage of the implements. Thanks to analogies having been established and to the exhaustive observation of the traces and hardness of the natural bedrock, we can state that the implements used in al-Madām in the Late Iron Age must have been bronze or — less likely — stone or iron.

In the very last 2008 campaign, as mentioned above, new evidence of hoe marks was discovered. The shape of the marks corresponds in depth and size to some kind of bronze hoe, perhaps of the type from al-ᶜAyn. Nevertheless, once again, we lack physical evidence.

Identification of the artefacts

Historiographers of Gulf Archaeology have recently been trying to establish the different kinds of implements used in the region, mostly by studying the material evidence, specifically artefacts, and more rarely by examining the traces left by such implements (Potts 1994). The latter analysis should be introduced at least for those sites where, as in al-Madām, numerous traces of implements can be found, while no actual implements related to them have been discovered. This type of analysis is starting to be useful mainly as an aid to understanding the usage of the tools. Therefore, what seemed to be a problem in al-Madām, i.e. the presence of numerous traces but not the implements related to them, has become a unique and novel approach to the study of tools and its functions.

So far several attempts to reconstruct the chronological and functional landscape of the tools and implements used in the Gulf in the Iron Age have been made. However, most of them have focused on agricultural tools and sometimes infer that such implements could have been used for building purposes as well (Briand *et al.* 1992; Pozo , Casas de Pedro & Rubi 1999: 608; Magee 1998; 2001). It can now be demonstrated that, at least for al-Madām area, the marks left on the bedrock were made by special construction tools. It should be noted that this is due to the special composition of the local soil.

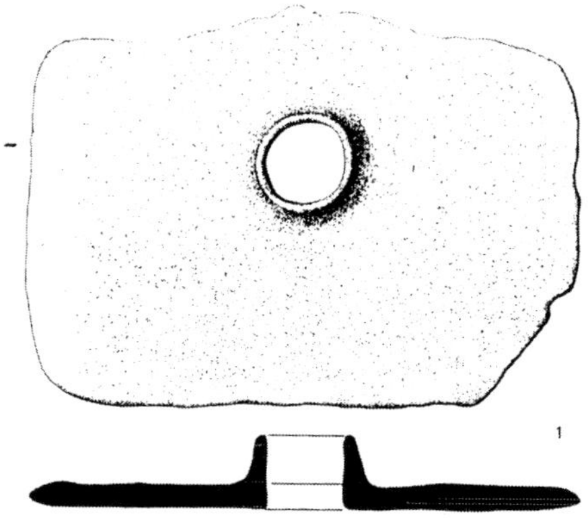

FIGURE 4. *A drawing of the hoe from al-Rumailah (Boucharlat & Lombard 1985).*

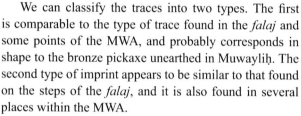

FIGURE 5. *A bronze pick from Muwayliḥ (courtesy of the Directorate of Antiquities of Sharjah, Dr Sabah Jasim, Dr Peter Magee and Dr Emma Thompson).*

We can classify the traces into two types. The first is comparable to the type of trace found in the *falaj* and some points of the MWA, and probably corresponds in shape to the bronze pickaxe unearthed in Muwayliḥ. The second type of imprint appears to be similar to that found on the steps of the *falaj*, and it is also found in several places within the MWA.

The new traces unearthed in the last campaign (Fig 3/a, b) must be classified together with the second group of imprints found on the steps of the *falaj* and in MWA in the area dug in 2008 (as pointed out by the author in the sixth ICAANE in Rome). Taking into account the average length of the traces (10 cm), and comparing this information with some bronze hoes known to us, it can be inferred that the same kind of implement, perhaps smaller but very similar in shape, was used.

Traces belonging to the first group, which are vertical marks, were also found in the 2008 campaign, specifically in the northern extension of MWA, right next to a platform containing post holes for the installation of a tent. This year we paid more attention to the traces left in the foundations of this tent. These traces were exactly the same as those discovered in the above-mentioned area used for the extraction of material, as well as those in the carving of the *falaj* alleyways and in the well unearthed in 2003 (Córdoba & Del Cerro 2005).

Again, taking into account the shape and orientation of the marks, we concluded that the implement used must have been a massive bronze pickaxe, similar to that discovered in Muwayliḥ: the parallel is indeed of importance because, as with the structures of al-Madām, it dates back to Iron Age II (Figs 4–5).

Conclusion

The site of al-Madām provides us with a piece of outstanding and important information that might improve our knowledge of Iron Age construction and building techniques in the Gulf. This data should be compared with the examination of actual metal artefacts discovered in the area, such as the hoe from al-Rumailah and pickaxe from Muwayliḥ. These two separate implements, from different sites and with their own features, share chronological and typological features with the traces found in al-Madām and, in combination, offer a new perspective on the study of the implements in the Gulf area in their use in construction, apart from observations already made with reference to agriculture. The traces from al-Madām are, in our opinion, far from being indications of agricultural practice and might instead be connected with construction enterprises, especially with reference to the contexts in which they are concentrated and the features of the implements. This is quite clear in the case of the *falaj* and its tunnels. Thus, while we look forward to further results that may be obtained in forthcoming campaigns, bearing in mind the analyses of the parallels and the search for others within Arabia, we may conclude that the site of al-Madām still has a considerable volume of information to offer.

Acknowledgements

I would like to thank the Organizing Committee of the Seminar for Arabian Studies for the chance to publish this paper. The paper presented would have not been possible without the help, advice, and support of Professor Joaquín

Córdoba, Director of the Spanish Archaeological Mission in al-Madām (UAE). I am also indebted to the Directorate of Antiquities of Sharjah, especially to Dr Sabah Jasim, Director of the Sharjah Archaeological Museum. Finally, I would also like to thank Dr Peter Magee and Dr Emma Thompson for their support.

References

Boucharlat R. & Lombard P.

1985. The Oasis of Al Ain in the Iron Age: Excavations at Rumeilah 1981–1983. Survey at Hili 14. *UAE Archaeology* 4: 44–111.

Briand B., Dalongeville R. & Ploquin A.

1992. The industries of Mleiha mineralogical and archaeological data recovered from the site and its environment. Pages 45–48 in R. Boucharlat (ed.), *Archaeological Surveys and Excavations in the Sharjah Emirate, 1990 and 1992. A sixth interim report.* Lyon.

Córdoba J.M.

2003. Villages of Shepherds in the Iron Age. The Evidence of Al Madam. Pages 173–180 in D.T. Potts (ed.), *Proceedings of the First Archaeological Conference on the UAE.* Abu Dhabi: Trident Press.

Córdoba J.M. & Del Cerro C.

2005. Archéologie de l'eau dans Al Madam (Sharjah, Emirats Arabes Unis). Puits, *aflaj* et sécheresse pendant l'âge de Fer. *Iranica Antiqua* 40: 515–532.

Magee P.

1998. New evidence for the initial appearance of iron in southeastern Arabia. *Arabian archaeology and epigraphy* 9: 112–117.

2001. Excavations at Muweilah 1997–2000. *Proceedings of the Seminar for Arabian Studies* 31: 115–130.

Pozo R.M., Casas de Pedro J.A. & Rubi J.A.M.

1999. Estudio mineralógico, químico y textural de materiales y elementos arqueológicos en asentamientos de la Edad del Hierro del oasis de al-Madam (Emirato de Sharjah, E.A.U.). *Isimu* 2: 605–634.

Potts D.T.

1994. Contribution to the agrarian history of Eastern Arabia. I. Implements and cultivation techniques. *Arabian archaeology and epigraphy* 5: 158–168.

Author's address

Mr Alejandro Gallego López, Centro Superior de Estudios de Oriente Próximo y Egipto, Universidad Autónoma de Madrid, Edif. Facultad de Filosofía y Letras, Módulo VII/Despacho 9, Campus de Cantoblanco, C/Fco. Tomás y Valiente 1, Madrid E–28049, Spain.

e-mail alejandro.gallegolopez@uam.es

Proceedings of the Seminar for Arabian Studies 40 (2010): 175–184

The first three campaigns (2007–2009) of the survey at Ādam (Sultanate of Oman) (poster)

Jessica Giraud, Ali Hamood Saif al-Mahrooqi, Guillaume Gernez, Sabrina Righetti, Émilie Portat Sévin-Allouet, Christophe Sévin-Allouet, Marion Lemée & †Serge Cleuziou

We would like to dedicate this article to Professor Serge Cleuziou, without whom we would never have had the chance of leading the research in the Ādam region.

Summary
After the discovery in 2006 of an engraved stone near Ādam, dated by Serge Cleuziou to the third millennium BC, the Ministry of Heritage and Culture in the Sultanate of Oman allowed and assisted the team to set up an archaeological study of the region of Ādam, which is the last oasis north of the Umm al-Samīm and Rub^c al-Khālī deserts. For centuries, this area has been the final shelter before travellers crossed the desert, thus it is both the last oasis and the last crossroad on the desert routes. During the first three campaigns from 2007 to 2009, survey of the area by the French team has exposed the rich archaeological potential of the area, with 1155 structures already found. These sites can be dated from the Early Bronze Age to the Islamic period. Discoveries include a large Hafit necropolis at Jabal al-Qarā^ɔ, Bronze Age graves and possible settlements in the north of Jabal Mouḍmār (Maḍmār), an Iron Age graveyard at Jabal Ḥamrā^ɔ Kahf, and two buildings of Iron Age in the east of Jabal Mouḍmār.

Keywords: Oman, Ādam, surveys, Bronze Age, Iron Age

Introduction

In the vicinity of Ādam (Figs 1 & 2), in al-Quṭaynah, 50 km to west of Ādam, the discovery in 2006 of an engraved stone representing two humans — one of them wears a dress while the other appears naked (Cleuziou & Tosi 2007: 243, fig. 261) — dated by Serge Cleuziou to the third millennium BC, Umm an-Nar period, led him to believe that the Ādam region was important during the Bronze Age.

Ādam is the southernmost oasis within the piedmonts of the Jabal A<u>kh</u>ḍar range in northern Oman. It is also the last town on the only road going to Dhofar through the Rub^c al-Khālī. At the edge of the desert, far from the large piedmont oases, Ādam is located between two small mountains: Jabal Mouḍmār and Jabal Ḥandalī (Jabal al-Ḥandalī) (Fig. 2). Such a location makes this area particularly relevant for an archaeological study, especially of the proto-historic periods. Despite being far from the central piedmonts, the Ādam region has an abundance of sites from the Bronze Age to the Iron Age. These archaeological resources remain comparatively unknown as there has never been a comprehensive survey of the region.

In 2007, we started a systematic survey. Brief survey work followed by three campaigns revealed more than 1000 structures dating to the Bronze and Iron Ages. All data was recorded so as to create a precise archaeological map of the region. In this paper we present some of the sites identified during the first three campaigns: two Bronze Age sites and two Iron Age sites.

The archaeological map of Ādam

The main objective of the three campaigns was to establish the archaeological potential of the Ādam region. The archaeological resources are so prolific that we have already been able to locate around 1000 structures.

For the first time we have been able to construct an archaeological map of the region (Fig. 2). This map will be completed in subsequent surveys, and its construction is one of the aims of this project. The map will be a major management tool for the Department of Heritage and Culture, Sultanate of Oman. It will be an exhaustive document indicating the location of all relevant archaeological structures, and this will facilitate their protection from the ever-growing urbanization of the oasis. This map, which is also the basis of our future work in the region, will allow us to make a thorough analysis of the visible settlement systems. It will be constructed using GIS and a spatial

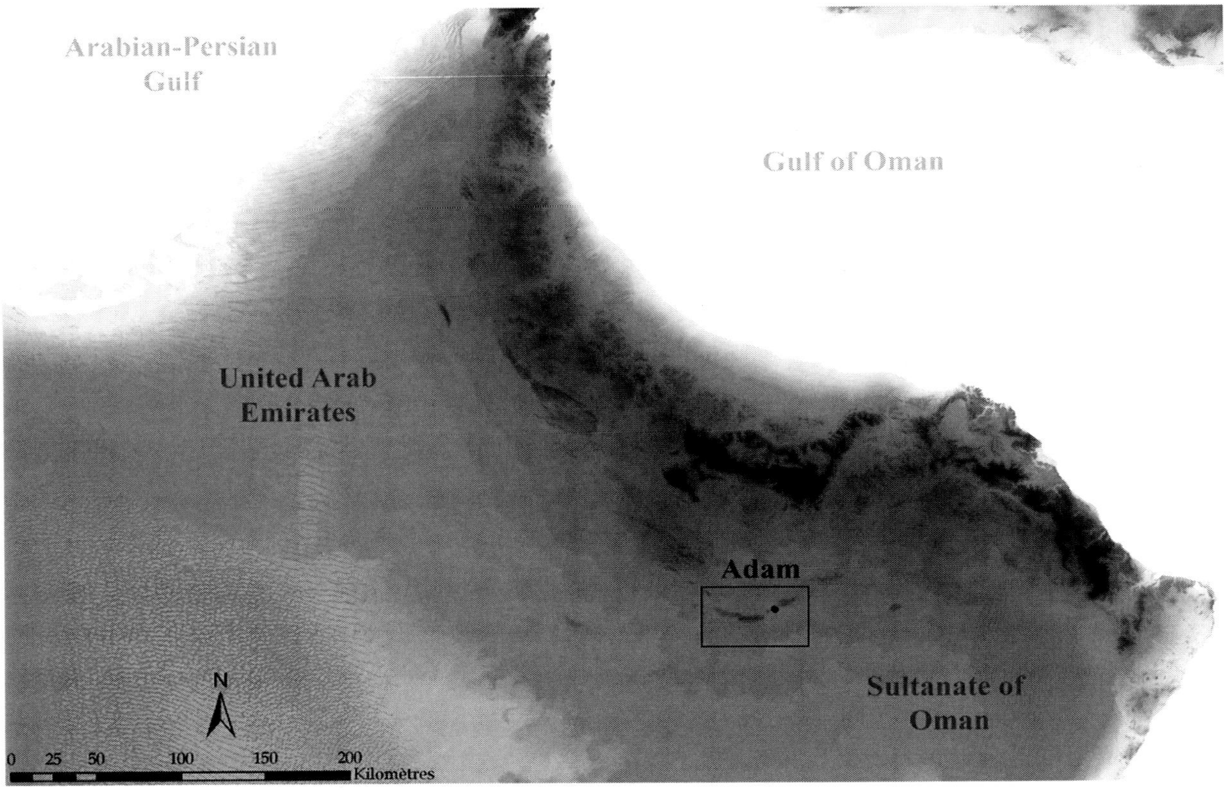

Figure 1. *The location of the region of Ādam:* **a.** *Ādam is located in central Oman (J. Giraud);* **b.** *its location between three small mountains (J. Giraud);* **c.** *an engraved stela found at al-Quṭaynah (A. al-Mahrooqi).*

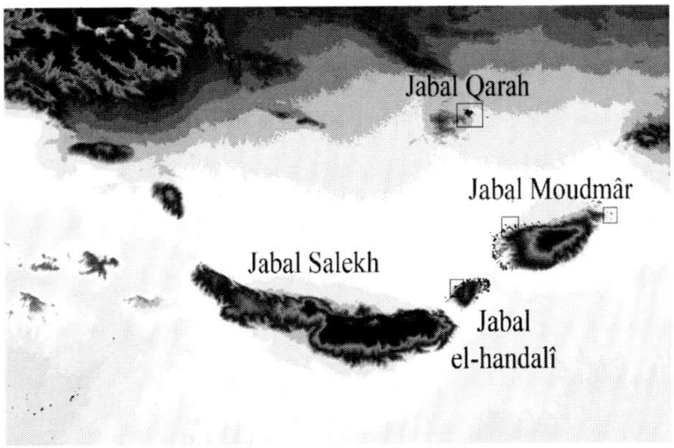

Figure 2. *An archaeological map of the region of Ādam (J. Giraud).*

reference database that we have already used in the Jaᶜalān (Giraud 2007), and has therefore been proven and tested with regard to the analysis of settlement systems (Giraud & Cleuziou 2009).

In order to create this map, we used a systematic method of survey based on our knowledge and understanding of the arid landscape of Oman, as well as on what we learnt about models of implantation of archaeological features. For instance, Hafit (Ḥafīt) necropolises are often found on hilly areas whereas Umm an-Nar necropolises are found on valley floors, wadi terraces, lower foothills, and lower flatter agricultural areas, which tend to be fringed by Hafit cemeteries on higher ground, and therefore at the centre of the individual Hafit tomb clusters (Giraud 2007). The dataset is regularly updated through systematic surveys of the whole region. Thanks to GIS, we identified areas that had not been prospected. As far as our future studies are concerned, the absence of sites is as important as their existence (Giraud & Gernez 2006).

To date, we have placed 1155 archaeological structures on the map. More than 70% of these are cairns. Three per cent of all structures were identified as dwellings. Of the ones we could identify, there were about twenty hearths (1.1% of all structures), six areas of lithic concentrations (0.5% of all structures), and one trilith (0.08% of all structures). Twenty per cent of all structures are of undetermined function (Fig. 3/a).

The 851 cairns include structures attributed to three different periods: Early Bronze Age, Middle Bronze Age, and Iron Age (Fig. 3/b). The tombs from the first half of the third millennium BC are the most numerous and account for 50% of all cairns. These tower-tombs, with a single chamber, can be found at high points of the landscape. From ceramic finds we were able to date some of them to the Hafit period. Twenty-two per cent of the tombs belong to the second part of the third millennium BC, the Umm an-Nar period. These tombs were found on the piedmonts of the Jabal Ḥandalī and Jabal Mouḍmār and were not well preserved. We were able to identify these structures as tombs as they had multiple chambers, one of the characteristics of tombs from this period. Beads (Brunet 2009) and sherds confirm this date. Seven per cent of the tombs date to the Iron Age and had single rectangular or oval chamber cairns. Systematic survey revealed numerous iron fragments scattered in and around the tombs.

As for settlement features, we found numerous types, from rectangular structures with walls that had external and internal facings, to oblong stone structures reminiscent of tent rings. All these settlements were located in the plains but, unfortunately, no artefacts were retrieved, and we therefore cannot date the structures more precisely.

The Bronze Age period

Numerous sites are dated to the Bronze Age but we have singled out two examples (Fig. 2). The first is a very large necropolis dating to the Hafit period, on the Jabal al-Qarāʾ, of which only a tenth of the surface area was covered by survey (Fig. 4). The second is a necropolis located to the north of Jabal Mouḍmār, which spatially links the two main periods of the Bronze Age (Hafit and Umm an-Nar) and which also contains later graves (Iron Age) in a narrow valley (Fig. 5).

The Early Bronze Age necropolis of al-Qarāʾ

Ali Hamood Saif al-Mahrooqi found numerous well-preserved tombs from the Hafīt period 15 km to the north of Ādam, on Jabal al-Qarāʾ (Fig. 4/a). After a few days, survey revealed a very large necropolis with a high density of structures. More than 159 tombs from the Hafit period were plotted after only surveying a tenth of the surface of the mountain. These structures are all extremely well preserved, with some of them still 2 or 3 m high (Fig. 4/b). Walls, slab roofs, and trapezoidal doors are still preserved on most of the tombs. They are all located on

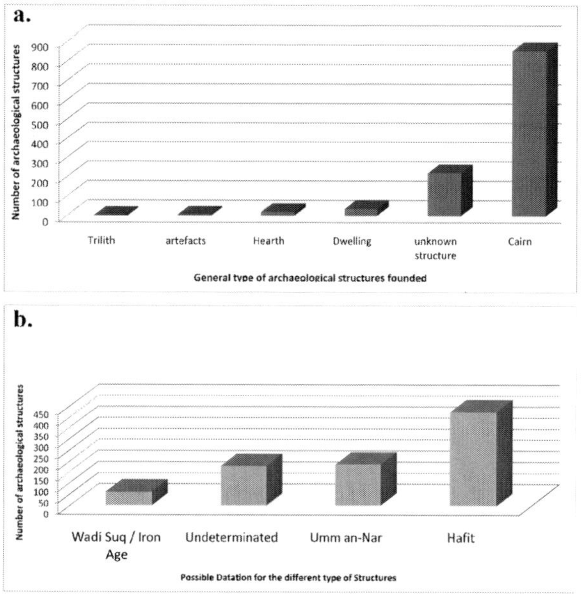

FIGURE 3. *Results of the surveys:* **a.** *the number of the different types of structures found in the region of Ādam;* **b.** *the dates assigned to the different cairns found in Ādam.*

the top of hills (Fig. 4/c). Bones were found in several funerary chambers and beads were found on the surface of the tombs, E235, E244, E250, and E1152 (Fig. 4/d). This exceptional site is interesting not only because of the variety and preservation of the structures but also because an important settlement is probably located nearby (Giraud & Cleuziou 2009). Future campaigns will aim to find this settlement.

A diachronic graveyard at north Jabal Mouḍmār

Along the Jabal Mouḍmār, numerous necropolises were found, especially to the west of the mountain, overhanging the oasis of Ādam (Fig. 2). To the north of the mountain, other tombs were also identified, allowing us to define several necropolises (Fig. 5/a). In particular, a small one was discovered in the embankment of a valley, comprising thirty-seven structures of which twenty are tombs and seventeen are still unidentified. Nine of the tombs can be dated to the Hafit period and are all located on the slope above the valley (Fig. 5/b). In the plain, we found eleven cairns, only four of which could be approximately dated (Fig. 5/c). One of the tombs is thought to be from the Umm an-Nar period since its funerary chamber had six separate rooms. Three other tombs were thought to be from a later period (Wadi Suq [Wādī Sūq] or Iron Age). They are small

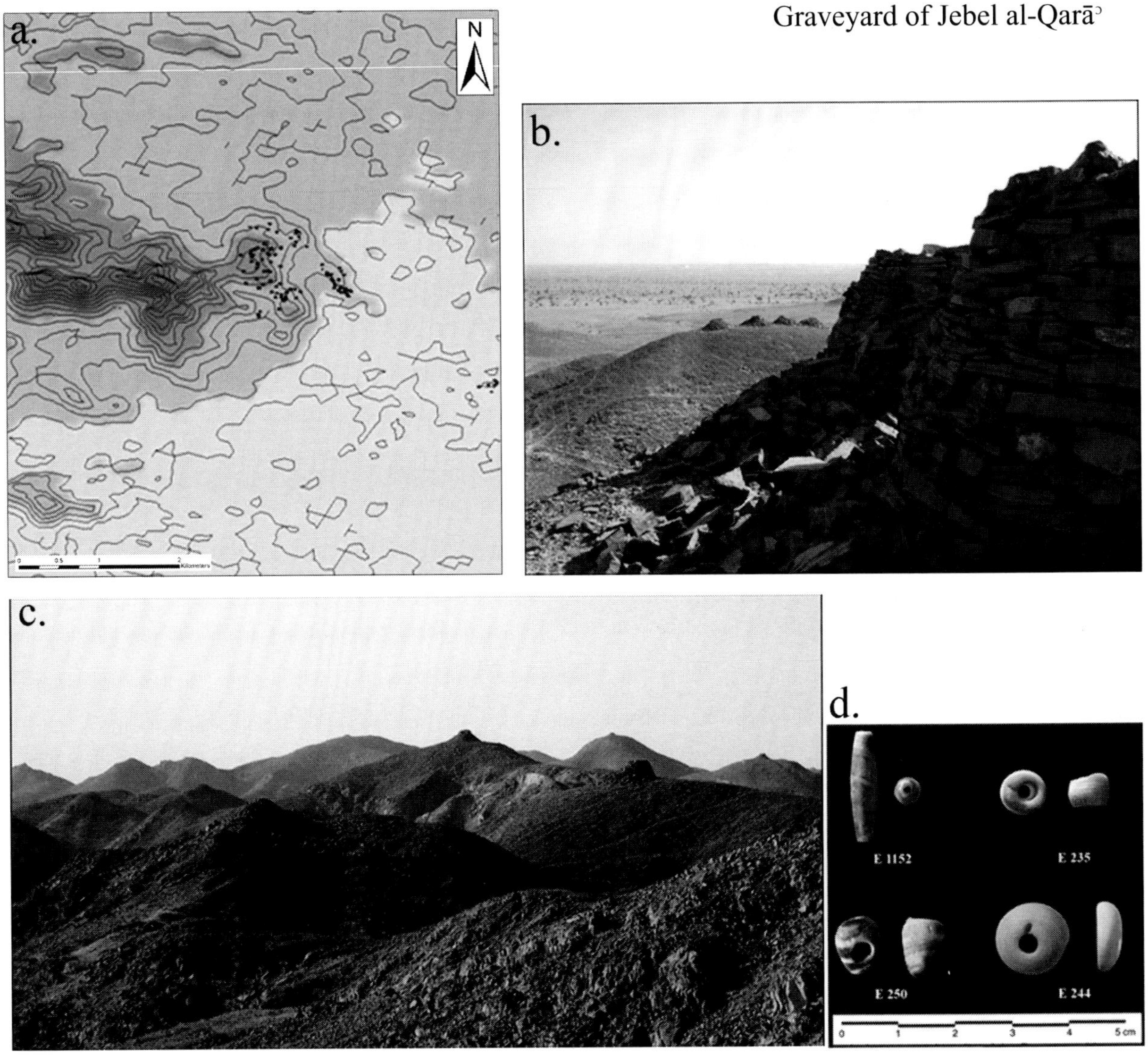

FIGURE 4. *Bronze Age settlements. The graveyard at Jabal al-Qarā᾽* (**a–d**)*:* **a.** *the location of the graveyard in Jabal al-Qarā᾽ (J. Giraud);* **b.** *the Hafit graves in this location (photograph by the French mission at Ādam);* **c.** *the hills with Hafit graves (photograph by the French mission at Ādam);* **d.** *beads found in some Hafit graves — agate, shell (photograph by G. Gernez).*

circular mounds with a rectangular chamber constructed of vertical flat stones. In one of them (E1040) we found a bronze arrowhead of a form already known at Bahlah fort (Fig. 5/d) (Weisgerber 2007: 302, fig. 327), and fragments of iron were found in a second structure. Seventeen unidentified stone structures have been found and could be in spatial relation with the small circular mounds, previously mentioned. They consist of oblong structures delimited by large boulders and filled with gravel (Fig. 5/c). This necropolis should certainly be studied more closely, but it already suggests a funerary occupation of more than 2000 years. It is probably linked to a settlement, located further in the plain, where stone structures and a concentration of lithic materials have been observed.

Iron Age sites

We have identified several sites that belong to the Iron Age period (see Fig. 2). A necropolis (Fig. 6) was located to the north of the small Jabal Ḥandalī and to the west

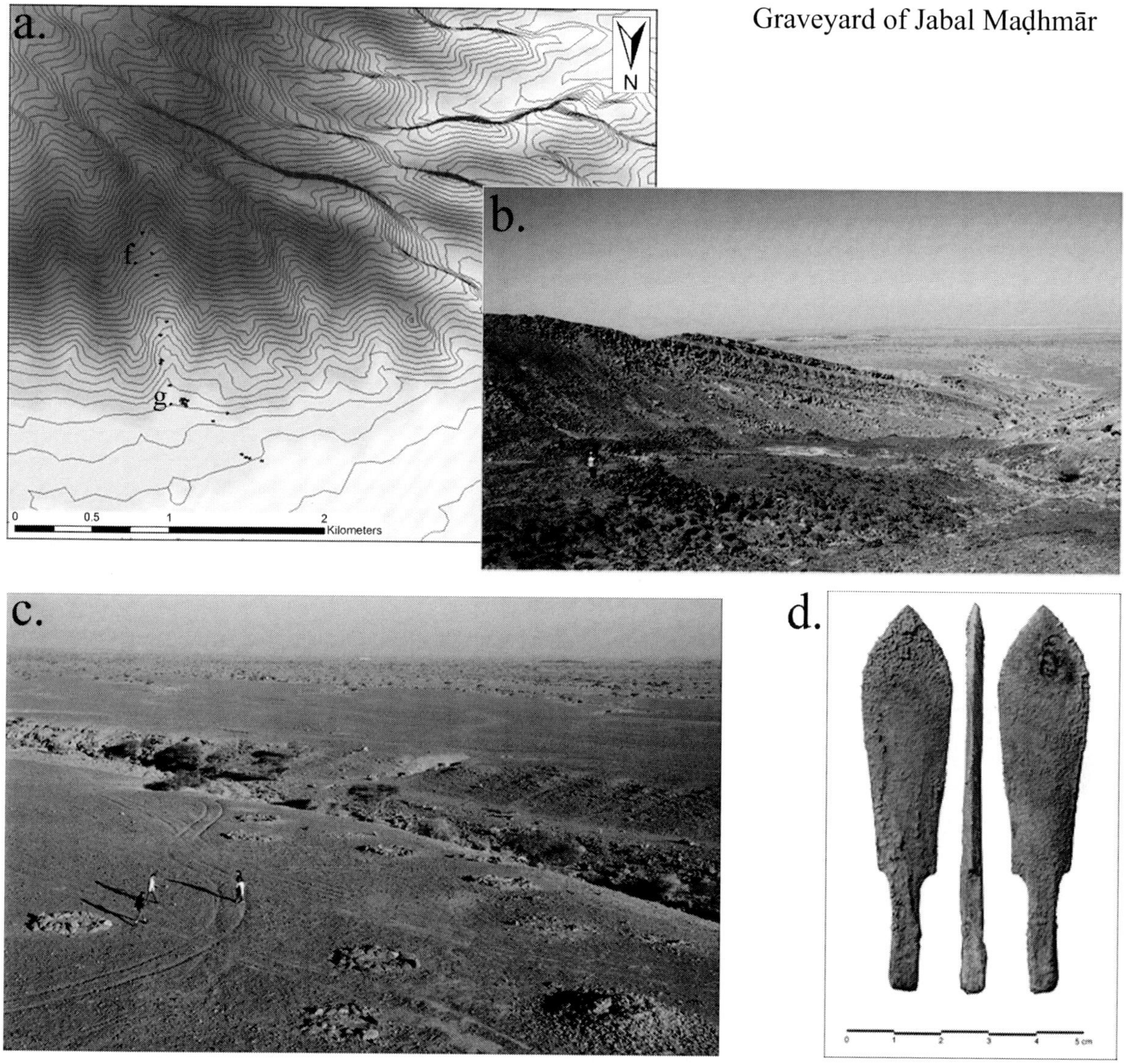

Figure 5. *The settlement north of Jabal Mouḍmār* (**a–d**)*:* **a.** *the location of the settlement (J. Giraud);* **b.** *Hafit graves in the slope of the valley (photograph by the French mission at Ādam);* **c.** *the structure on the plain (photograph by the French mission at Ādam);* **d.** *Wadi Suq bronze arrowheads (G. Gernez).*

of Ādam. We surveyed the area systematically and excavated one of the funerary structures. The second Iron Age site was found to the east of Jabal Mouḍmār (Fig. 7). It has two large rectangular buildings linked with one circular structure.

The Iron Age necropolis of Jabal Ḥandalī

To the north of Jabal Ḥandalī, some wadis have cut the slopes of the mountain into very deep valleys (Fig. 6/a). Seventeen cairns were found at the bottom of one of these valleys. One of the best-preserved structures was chosen to be cleaned and excavated (Fig. 6/b). The excavation allowed us to draw a precise diagram of this grave but neither artefacts nor bones were found in it. This structure has a rectangular chamber (1.30×0.80 m) made of limestone slabs with some blocks around forming the oval/circular structure of the cairn (Fig. 6/c). As no artefacts were found inside, we prospected the area and the other structures in order to date the site. Several iron fragments as well as bone splinters were found, which led us to assume that the necropolis dates to the Iron Age.

Graveyard in Jabal Hamrāʾ Kahf

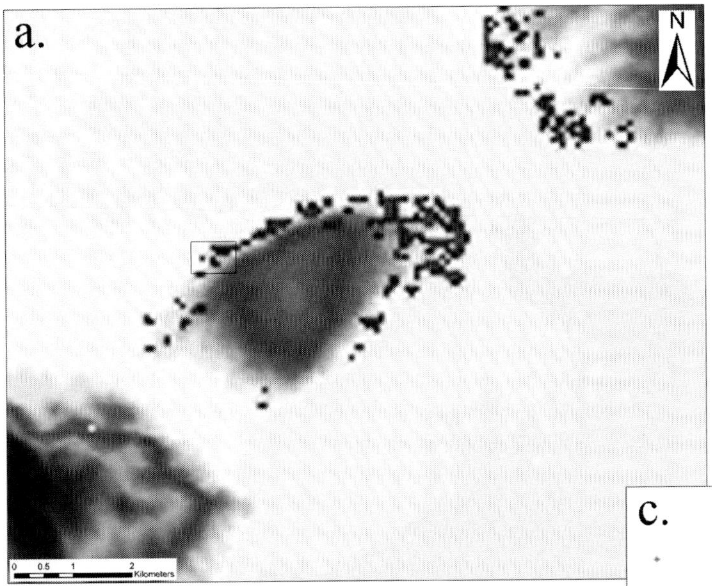

b.

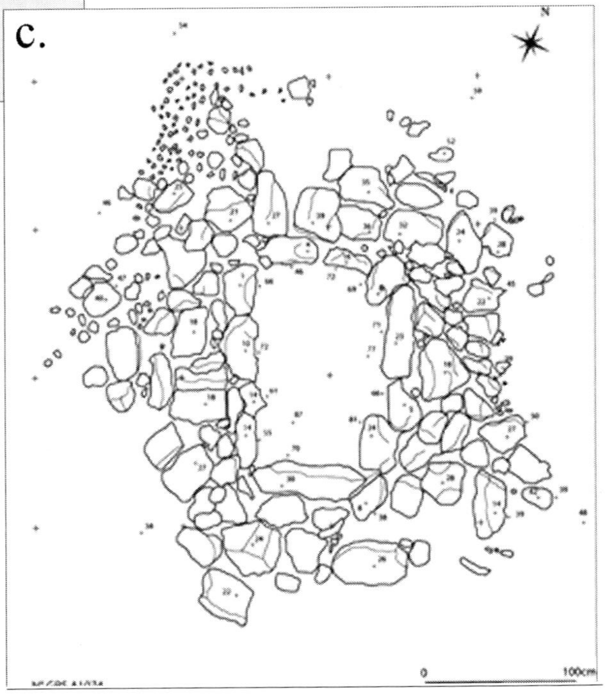

Figure 6. *Iron Age settlements. The graveyard at Jabal Ḥamrāʾ Kahf* (**a–c**)*:* **a.** *the location of the graveyard (J. Giraud);* **b.** *the excavated grave (photograph by the French mission at Ādam);* **c.** *a plan of the excavated Iron Age grave (C. Sévin-Allouet).*

East Jabal Mouḍmār

This site is located to the east of Jabal Mouḍmār (Fig. 7/a). It is made of two rectangular buildings (Fig. 7/b). The first is composed of two parallel walls and a small, enclosed courtyard surrounded by another wall. In this building, we discovered sherds of red and grey common ware, a bronze coin, and several small bronze arrowheads (Fig. 7/c, d). The second was built with a wall made of large blocks of white limestone, in which sherds of the same type were found. A circular mound constructed of large blocks of white limestone placed in a vertical setting, possibly a grave, was situated near these two buildings. The location of these two important buildings near an actual road between two big mountains and the link with the artefacts found in it, especially the large amount of bronze arrowheads and bronze objects, led us to hypothesize that these buildings could have had a

Iron Age in Jabal Maḍhmār

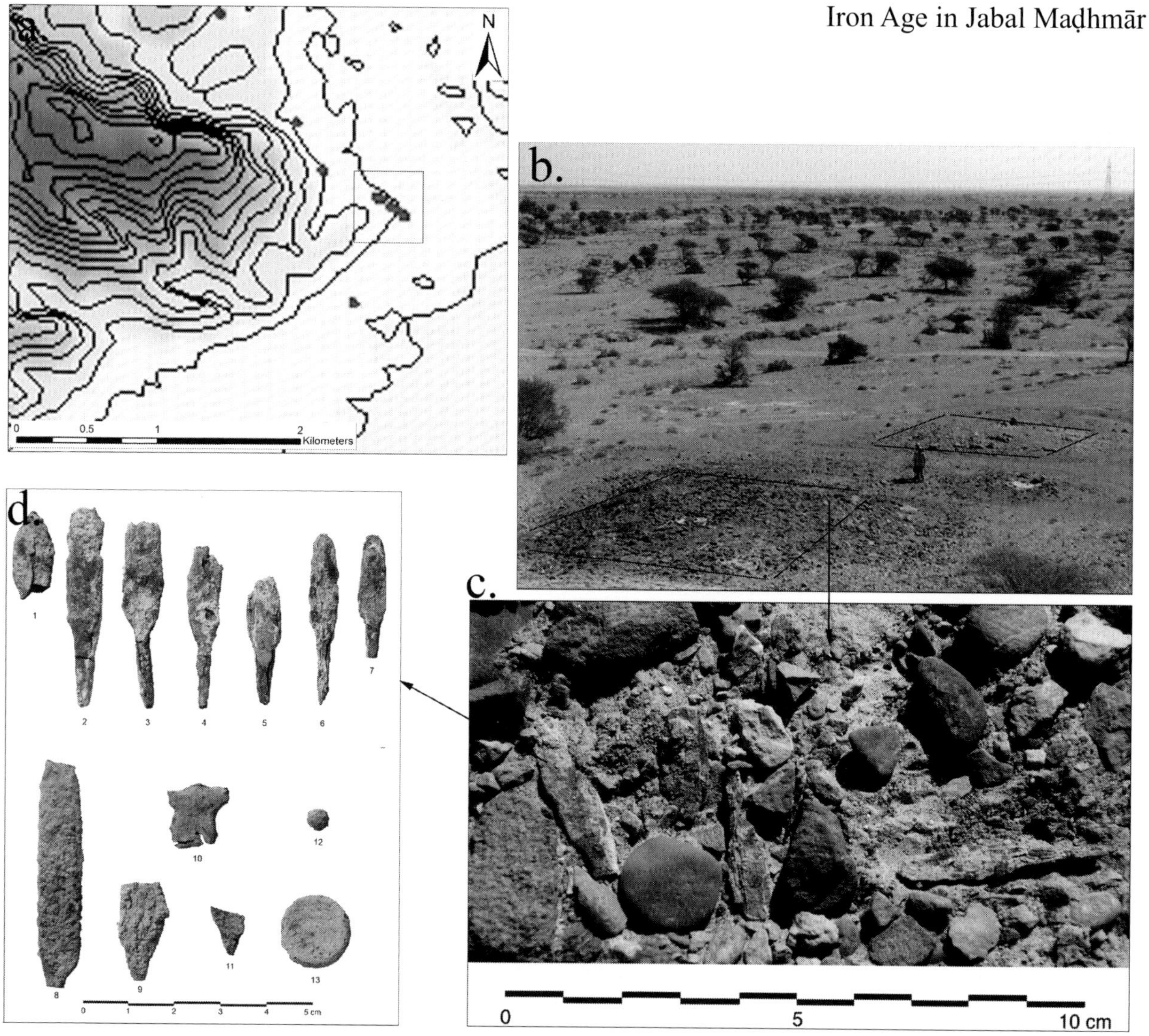

FIGURE 7. *The settlement at Jabal Mouḍmār* (**a–d**)*:* **a.** *the location of the settlement (J. Giraud);* **b.** *the two buildings that were discovered (photograph by the French mission at Ādam);* **c.** *bronze arrowheads in situ (photograph by the French mission at Ādam);* **d.** *bronze artefacts found in the large building (G. Gernez).*

particular function. Further cleaning and excavations of these unusual buildings may well confirm that possibility.

Conclusions

The first three brief surveys have confirmed the archaeological potential of the area of Ādam, especially for the proto-historic periods. A precise archaeological map of the region is being constructed and it will be updated as the research proceeds further. The map will enable us to undertake a detailed spatial analysis that will be used to develop a model of settlement patterns for the different periods of occupation. These analyses will be then compared to the situation in the Ja^{c}alān (Giraud 2007) and in the piedmonts (Gentelle & Frifelt 1989; Wilkinson JC 1977) in order to try to work out the settlement patterns that correspond to each proto-historic period. Any sites with multiple occupations will also be located and excavated to help us understand the transitional periods, especially between the Bronze and

Iron Ages. Studying the region of Ādam thoroughly will allow us to access a period that has yet to be fully explored (Wilkinson 2003; Giraud 2007).

Acknowledgements

We would like to thank the Ministry of Heritage and Culture, which made this study possible and, in particular, Mrs Biuwba al-Sabri and Mrs Rahma Alfarsi of the Sultanate of Oman for their help and support. We would also like to thank Khamis al-Asmi who accompanied us in the field during the whole campaign, and all the families in Adām for their hospitality and their warm welcome. Last but not least, our thanks also go to everyone who helped during the surveys in Adām: Olivier Blin, Claire Bernard, Julien Charbonnier, Julie Delmotte, Marie Grousset, Vincent Le Quellec, Laetitia Munduteguy, and Aude Simony, without whom the work would not have progressed so quickly.

References

Brunet O.
2009. Bronze and Iron Age carnelian bead production in the UAE and Armenia: new perspectives. *Proceedings of the Seminar for Arabian Studies* 39: 57–68.

Cleuziou S. & Tosi M.
2007. *In the Shadow of the Ancestors, the Prehistoric foundations of the Early Arabian Civilization in Oman.* Muscat: Ministry of Heritage and Culture.

Gentelle P. & Frifelt K.
1989. About the distribution of the third millennium graves and settlements in the Ibri area of Oman. Pages 119–126 in P.M. Costa & M. Tosi (eds), *Oman Studies: Papers on the archaeology and history of Oman.* Rome: Istituto italiano per il Medio ed Estremo Oriente.

Giraud J.
2007. Restitution d'un espace géographique ancien: la province du Jaʾalan à l'Âge du Bronze (Sultanat d'Oman). Thèse de Doctorat, Université de Paris I (Panthéon-Sorbonne). [Unpublished].

Giraud J. & Cleuziou S.
2009. Funerary landscape as part of the social landscape and its perceptions: three thousand early Bronze Age burials in the eastern Jaʿalān (Sultanate of Oman). *Proceedings of the Seminar for Arabian Studies* 39: 163–180.

Giraud J. & Gernez G.
2006. Les prospections dans la province du Ja'alan (Sultanat d'Oman): d'un terrain désertique à l'analyse du système d'habitat au IIIe millénaire av. J.-C. *Table ronde: prospection archéologique en milieux désertiques et tropicaux. Cahier des thèmes transversaux* 7: 38–46.

Weisgerber G.
2007. Iron Age Mining and Smelting (Lizq Peroid). Pages 302–303 in S. Cleuziou & M. Tosi (eds), *In the Shadow of the Ancestors, the Prehistoric foundations of the Early Arabian Civilization in Oman.* Muscat: Ministry of Heritage and Culture.

Wilkinson J.C.
1977. *Water and Tribal settlement in South-East Arabia: a study of* aflaj *of Oman.* Oxford: Clarendon Press.

Wilkinson T.J.
2003. *Archaeological landscapes of the Near East.* Tucson, AZ: The University of Arizona Press.

Authors' addresses
Dr Jessica Giraud, Maison de l'archéologie et de l'ethnologie, UMR 7041/ArScan, Bate 14, 21 allée de l'Université, 92023 Nanterre Cedex, France.

e-mail giraud.jessica@gmail.com

Ali Hamood Saif al-Mahrooqi, Department of Research, Studies and Translation, Ministry of Heritage and Culture, PO Box 668, Muscat, 113, Sultanate of Oman.

e-mail almahroqi999@hotmail.com

Dr Guillaume Gernez, Institut Français du Proche-Orient, BP 11-1424, Beirut, Lebanon.

e-mail g.gernez@ifporient.org

Sabrina Righetti, Maison de l'archéologie et de l'ethnologie, UMR 7041/ArScan, Bate 14, 21 allée de l'Université, 92023 Nanterre Cedex, France.

e-mail sabrina.righetti@gmail.com

Émilie Portat Sévin-Allouet, Attachée de Conservation du Patrimoine — Anthropologue, Service archéologique de la ville de Chartres, 35, rue Saint-Michel, 28000 Chartres, France.

e-mail eportat@ville-chartres.fr

Christophe Sévin-Allouet, 3 rue Michelet, 75006 Paris, France.

e-mail christophesevin@yahoo.fr

Marion Lemée, Institut national de recherches archéologiques préventives, 13 rue d'Anjou, 35150 Piré-sur-Seiche, France.

e-mail lemeemarion@gmail.com

Proceedings of the Seminar for Arabian Studies 40 (2010): 185–200

A new approach to central Omani prehistory

Reto Jagher & Christine Pümpin

Summary

The Central Oman Palaeolithic Survey (COPS), initiated by the Institute for Prehistory and Archaeological Science (IPAS), University of Basel (Switzerland), and carried out in the al-Ḥuqf–al-Ḥawshī area (Central Oman) in 2007 and 2008, focused on the earliest human occupation in the southern Arabian Peninsula. A total of 1445 locations were surveyed and 816 archaeological sites recorded. Among them, 609 held flint artefacts; these showed ample evidence of a significant and diversified prehistoric legacy.

The rich cultural history known from the Levant during the Pleistocene shows no evident exchange with its southern neighbours. This is in sharp contrast with palaeo-zoological observations that demonstrate a steady replacement across the Arabian subcontinent from the south to the north and vice versa, during the same period. Palaeo-climatic data from Oman clearly show the presence of several periods with increased rainfall during the last 400,000 years, facilitating the passage for animals and humans across the Arabian Peninsula.

Contrary to expectations, people obviously did not follow these migrations. The COPS survey demonstrated a strong cultural boundary, separating southern and northern Arabia, over a long period. This separation cannot be explained by natural constraints. At least during the later Pleistocene, southern Arabia witnessed an independent cultural history, with no evident influence from outside. Several techno-cultural lithic entities with characteristic tool sets endemic to the southern part of the subcontinent were observed by the COPS survey. Comparable traditions in stone-tool technology are at that time completely unknown in the Levant.

Furthermore, the COPS fieldwork revealed an important settlement activity in the southern part of al-Ḥuqf during the late prehistory (i.e. the Bronze and Iron Ages), a surprising discovery as it dates from a period of deteriorating climate with increased aridity, when humans withdrew to areas that are currently inhabited.

Keywords: Palaeolithic, Arabia, Pleistocene, prehistory, flint technology

Introduction

Although the history of Arabia has been proved to be old and long, Palaeolithic archaeology in the Arabian Peninsula is still in its infancy. Despite the proximity of adjacent regions with a long-standing tradition of intensive research of the Palaeolithic era in the Fertile Crescent, and the Bilād al-Shām in particular, the major part of the Arabian Peninsula has not profited from this impetus. In fact, research on the beginnings of human history on the peninsula has been intermittent. One of the main obstacles, until recently, was the remoteness and accessibility of most areas throughout Arabia, requiring considerable logistics for research and, as a result, limiting surveys.

Despite the long-standing confirmation of the high potential of a rich, early Stone Age heritage throughout the Arabian subcontinent, the interest of research, being highly active in the Levant, was hardly concerned with its southern neighbours. Only a few investigators active in the Bilād al-Shām have ventured out, albeit sporadically, of their familiar terrain. The Institute of Prehistory and Archaeological Science of the University of Basel, having a long-standing tradition of excavating Lower and Middle Palaeolithic sites in Syria for more than twenty-five years, was one of the first archaeological institutions to bridge this gap. The Central Oman Palaeolithic Survey (COPS) is a planned offshoot, trying to complete our understanding of early prehistory in the Middle East beyond the traditional realm of the Levant.

The rich legacy of Palaeolithic cultures, reaching back nearly 2 million years along the Fertile Crescent, indicates relationships or differences with their contemporaneous neighbours to the north in Anatolia and the Zagros and Caucasus Mountains. Links to northern Africa and to Europe can be drawn or rejected. However, the immediate neighbours to the south remain unidentified, and how far Levantine groups ventured into the Arabian subcontinent remains undiscovered.

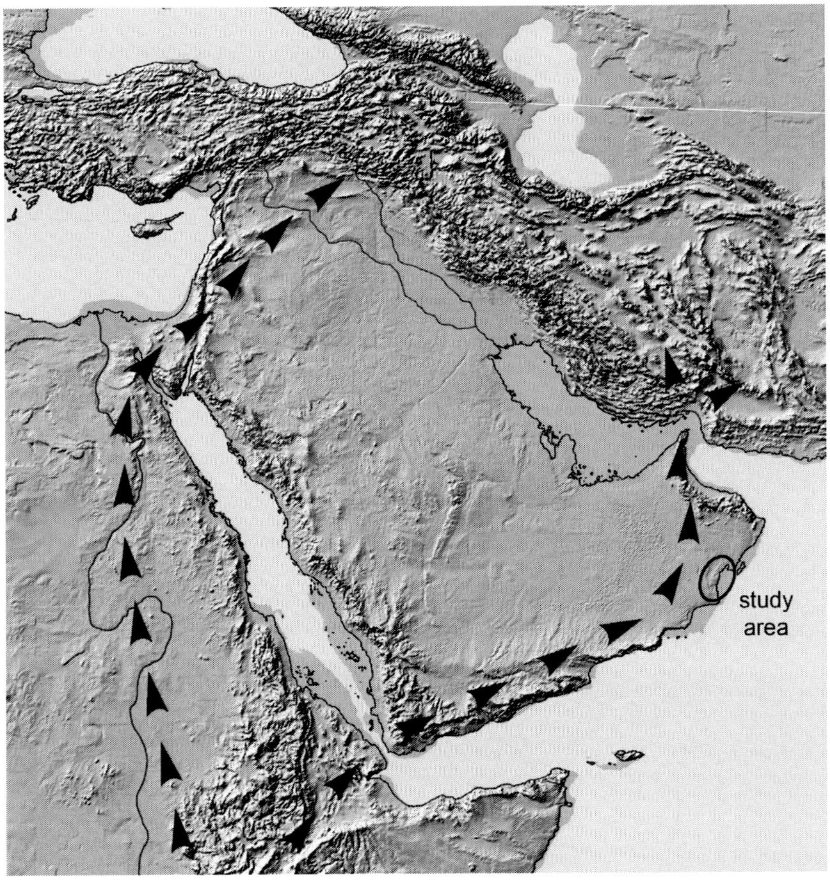

Figure 1. *The location of the COPS study area within the scheme of early human migration routes from Africa across the Arabian subcontinent and exposed land at low sea levels during the Pleistocene ice ages.*

Even if there is a considerable wealth of publications about Pleistocene archaeology in Arabia, most of it consists of preliminary observations and short notes. Even now, soundings and excavations of Palaeolithic sites on the Arabian Peninsula are rare, as are regional reports (Petraglia 2003; Petraglia & al-Sharekh 2003; Rose 2006; Rose & Usik 2009; Crassard 2009). Well-stratified sites that were extensively investigated and published in detail are largely missing. However, ongoing promising excavations on several sites will fill this gap in the near future.

The contemporary emptiness of the Arabian deserts provides an incomplete picture. In the past, climatic changes modified the landscapes extensively, alternating between drier situations than today to much better conditions, when the climate was wetter and the desert turned into a steppe. Excavations of Palaeolithic sites in Palestine and Syria showed that animals took advantage of these episodes, when African species moved north and, to a lesser extent, Eurasian animals migrated southwards (Thomas *et al.* 1998; Griggo 2000). These shifting conditions impacted on the human groups present in Arabia, seizing the opportunity to extend their range accordingly. However, because of the lack of concise information about the Arabian Palaeolithic era, such movements have remained in the realm of academic deduction.

During the Pleistocene, the global climate was subdued to steady shifts with alternating periods of warmer and cooler temperatures, setting off an increase of polar ice sheets, subsequently lowering the sea level, and exposing the inundated areas of today (Fig. 1). For Arabia, this implied a dry Arabian Gulf for more than half of the last 500,000 years, resulting in completely different migration routes from those of today (Waelbroeck *et al.* 2002). Cooler temperatures imply a reduced evaporation, thus leaving more moisture available for plant growth (Haude 1969). This is attested, for example, by thin palaeosoils dated to OIS 6 in the sand sheets underlying the Āl Wahībah sands in Oman (Preusser *et al.* 2002).

The changing climate in Arabia during the past 500,000 years is particularly well documented from its southern margins. Periods of increased rainfall are observed in dripstones in caves from the Ḥajar and Dhofar Mountains in Oman, and from Yemen (Fleitmann *et al.* 2003; 2004; Preusser 2009). Additional information comes from the inland alluvial fans in the Sultanate, corroborating and completing our knowledge of precipitation from the caves (Blechschmidt *et al.* 2009). All these palaeoclimatic data hint at extended periods of favourable conditions for an early human settlement in today's arid areas of southern Arabia. Furthermore, during times of apparently arid conditions, there were repeated spells of increased rainfall over southern Arabia, contrary to what is suggested by global palaeoclimatic models.

Despite their apparent uniformity, the wide expanses of the Rubᶜ al-Khālī exhibit complex formations with an intricate history (Warren & Allison 1998; Preusser *et al.* 2005). The emergence of these formations extends over a long period and they are in continuous and asynchronous shift (Goudie *et al.* 2000; Bray & Stokes 2003; Radies *et al.* 2004). Rather than global climatic changes, local phenomena, such as the supply of sand and persistence of winds, are decisive for the accretion of massive dunes (Kocurek & Lancaster 1999; O'Connor & Thomas 1999).

Our actual perception of the Arabian Desert is biased by substantial constraints. Human pressure has destroyed much of its natural resources. For instance, indigenous game were wiped out for food or as competition to livestock, while intensive use of pastures during the last few millennia destroyed the plant cover beyond recovery and people abandoned the exploited areas as the desert expanded. What is left today is only a poor image of the original potential, providing few clues about the possibilities for hunter-gatherer subsistence.

The COPS survey

The rich and variegated background of the Palaeolithic era in the Levant over the last 500,000 years was taken as a starting point for the COPS project, giving an idea of what could be expected in the Arabian Peninsula. Being familiar with the various lithic technologies and cultural assemblages present in the Bilād al-Shām, the COPS team was open to discoveries in the field without any preconceived expectations.

The general design of the survey focused on an impartial approach without any preconceptions. Lithic materials were classified according to their basic morphology. The adopted terminology refrained from any cultural a priori or chronological allusions. To understand which elements are frequent and which ones are exceptions, a basic precondition for the research project was a high number of surveyed places, in order to obtain a statistically significant number of observations. Instead of a premature cultural attribution for each site, the presence of different elements was recorded, as was the absence of specific elements. Furthermore, the absence or presence, as well as the quality of raw material for stone tools, was described for each site, together with its topographic setting and geological background. Within the surveyed sectors, locations without archaeological finds were also entered into the general database with regard to a positive estimate of the relative density of archaeological sites across the landscape. Furthermore, a GIS tool was designed for processing the data, in order to obtain accurate distribution maps. The visualization was based on a three-dimensional terrain model, combined with remote sensing data and conventional cartography (Fig. 2). This tool proved to be extremely valuable in the field, as the daily progress of the survey could be checked continuously for consistency.

The COPS team also profited from personal experience of surveying semi-arid areas in the Levant (Le Tensorer, Jagher & Muhesen 2001). Although the project concentrates on early prehistory, all archaeological observations, such as stone circles, tumuli, shell middens, or triliths were recorded with the same accuracy as lithic artefacts. Although it was not the prime objective of the survey, these later elements contributed to the compilation of a comprehensive archaeological map of the al-Ḥuqf area, one of the basic targets of the project.

Geographical setting

The location for the COPS project was selected based on criteria such as a topographically structured environment offering a broad spectrum of ecological niches (being attractive for a hunter-gatherer subsistence), access to fresh water, and availability of raw material for stone tools. As precipitation patterns were subject to considerable changes during the Paleolithic period, today's aridity was not considered an argument for ruling out specific areas. Based on the above criteria, the al-Ḥuqf–Ḥawshī region in central Oman was identified as a promising survey area.

Al-Ḥuqf is characterized by low hills with a rich geological setting, comprising different landscapes and

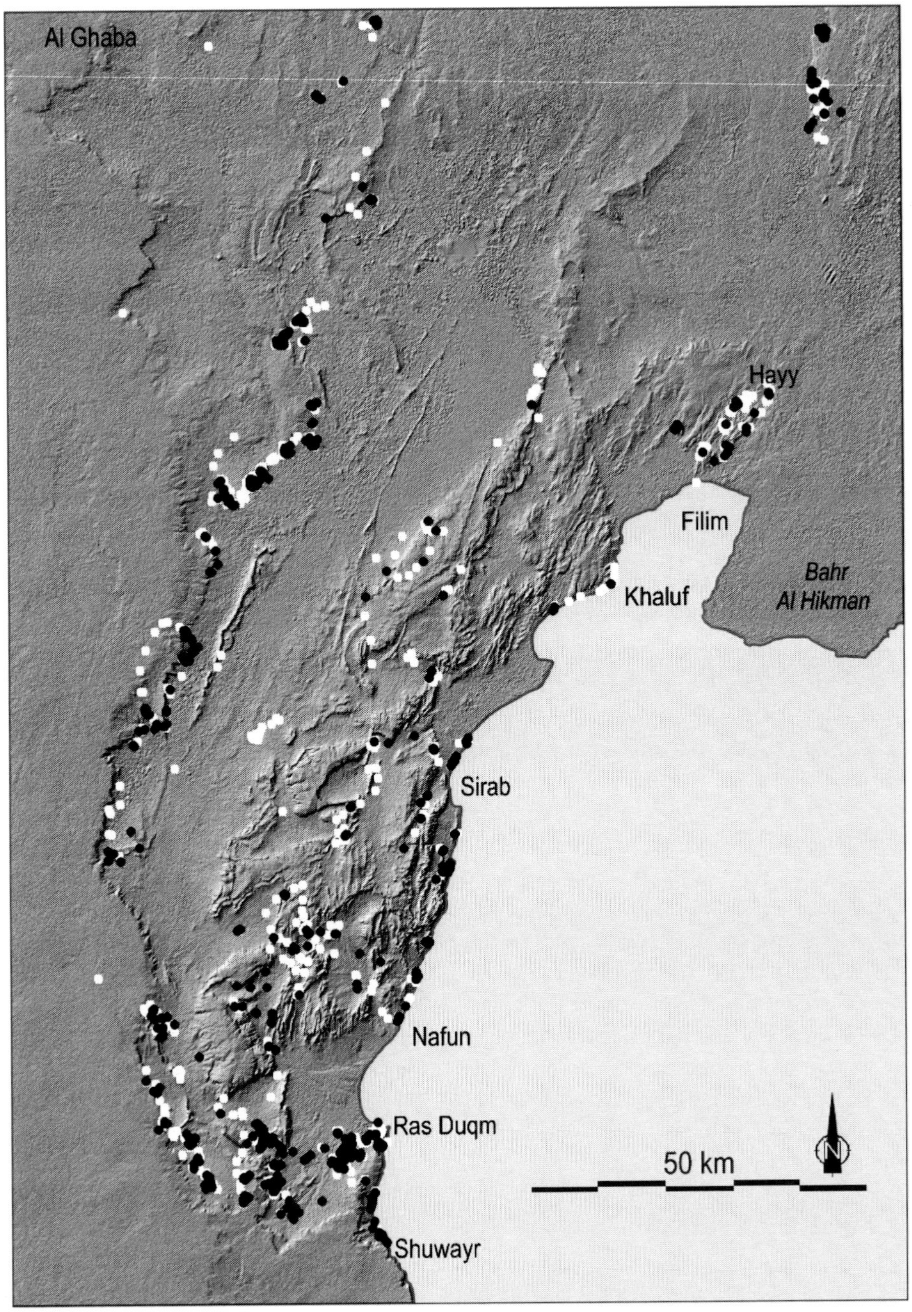

Figure 2. *A digital elevation model of the al-Ḥuqf area with the location of the COPS discoveries (black dots indicate archaeological sites, white dots indicate negative observations).*

a broad variety of bedrocks, supporting a great diversity of ecological habitats and permitting various modes of subsistence. Moreover, the area is at the pivotal point of vast territories: to the west and south, al-Ḥuqf is delimited by the huge plateau of the Jiddat al-Ḥarāsīs. Despite its topographic monotony, the Jiddat offers a big potential for grazing animals, thus making it an interesting hunting ground. To the east, al-Ḥuqf faces the Indian Ocean. The proximity of the sea is a major factor, as marine subsistence allowed the survival of early humans even

FIGURE 3. *A typical landscape in the al-Ḥuqf hills with a modest oasis fed by the runoff of a small wadi.*

FIGURE 4. *A low-density factory site (dark area in the centre) in the southern Ḥuqf (site 1068).*

during periods of extremely harsh climatic conditions. During glaciations, the coast receded 30–35 km at most, leaving the al-Ḥuqf hills always near the shore. The situation at the intersection of different ecotypes and the many ecological niches within the area, have been attractive for hunter-gatherers throughout time.

Today the entire area is only slightly covered by dunes (both fossil and active), thus allowing a perfect observation of the ground. The selected survey area is delimited by the towns of al-Ghaba and Filim in the north, Duqm in the south, al-ᶜAjāʾiz in the south, and the Jiddat al-Ḥarāsīs plateau comprising the Jaaluni Oryx-station to the west. The defined sector extends about 200 km from north to south and approximately 40–60 km from the coast into the interior (Fig. 3).

The COPS 2007 and 2008 surveys

During the two seasons, the COPS team spent a total of sixty days in the field documenting 1445 locations, compiling a database of over 10,000 individual observations. A total of 816 archaeological sites, 609 of which contained flint artefacts, were recorded. It was not only the number of sites but also, in many cases, the extension and abundance of finds exceeding by far the boldest anticipations, clearly demonstrating the archaeological potential of the al-Ḥuqf area. The two years of investigations in al-Ḥuqf revealed an unexpectedly rich and varied legacy of Stone Age archaeology (Fig. 4).

During fieldwork, lithic artefacts were divided into debitage and retouched tools. Based on general experience and observations made in the course of the survey, the debitage was eventually subdivided into four categories. The presence of cores was noted but no further details were added, as the evaluation of cores in the field was rather difficult and time-consuming. As a first approach, the observation of the products is much more rewarding than a detailed study of the cores themselves. Retouched artefacts were divided into five main groups. Typological conditions were noted simply as qualitative statements, as no comprehensive counts were carried out (Fig. 5).

Small debitage

This group is characterized by a predominance of small flakes 3–4 cm long, being occasionally laminar. They must have been a deliberate choice, as the size of local raw material would have permitted much bigger artefacts. Despite its distinctiveness, this group is quite rare, as only 8% (27 out of 311 diagnostic sites) were recorded. The association of small debitage with other lithic groups is undecided. Half of the sites with small debitage were major factory sites, with no further diagnostic elements. Among the remainder, there is a strong correlation with small foliated tools, but a conclusive cultural attribution is difficult, as the statistical base is rather small.

Light blades

These comprise elongated flakes of around 5–8 cm in length, with thin sections. They show quite regular, but not strictly, parallel edges and, in most cases, the

		flint sites						
	survey	site size	artefacts	misc.	structures	raw mat.	geology	chronology
surveyed places	1445							
archaeological sites	816							
arch. sites w/o flints	207							
arch. sites with flints	609							
locations w/o flints	835							
no archaeology	629							
misc. observations	228		397					
stray finds		208						
small sites		237						
big sites		117						
very big sites		47						
undiagnostic flint sites			298					
diagnostic sites			311					
small debitage			27					
light blades			27					
heavy blades			182					
cores			128					
heavy bifacials			113					
small bifacials			21					
foliates			84					
arrow heads			17					
retouched flakes			29					
combined categories			313					
ceramics				21				
triliths					39			
stone circles					80			
tumuli					127			
midden					30			
other					36			
no raw material						932		
good raw material						227		
bad raw material						246		
quarzite						55		
geological observation							112	
rockshelter							40	
hydrology (spring/well)							43	
undated								298
early periods								177
mixed								41
late periods								93
late Holocene (structures)								312

Figure 5. *Summary of field observations during the 2007 and 2008 seasons.*

dorsal ridges are sinuous. Formal as well as metric standardization is poor. Occasionally, individual blades are more regular, but never achieve an outstanding level and show no affinity at all to the Upper Palaeolithic or the Neolithic of the Levant. The production of these blades follows a rather basic procedure. The striking platforms are plain and only exceptionally retouched, and the flaking angle is clearly acute. The manufacture of these blades was usually unidirectional, with exceptional, opposite-striking platforms, as can be seen on the blades themselves and on the cores. Despite their distinctiveness, light blades are an infrequent phenomenon in al-Ḥuqf. They were present in 8% (27 out of 311 potential sites). With no particular tool-type associated with them, their age is difficult to estimate.

Heavy blades

This category of blanks can be considered a principal characteristic of al-Ḥuqf's prehistory, not only for their wide distribution, but also for their distinctiveness. In fact, heavy blades are the most common lithic group in al-Ḥuqf, recorded at 182 locations, i.e. more than half (58%) of the diagnostic sites.

In the field heavy blades are easily recognized by their highly standardized shapes. The well-elongated blades, 8–12 cm but sometimes up to 15 cm long, show perfectly parallel edges and dorsal ridges, and the ubiquitous thick section. In most cases, the section is trapezoidal, but triangular shapes are common. Despite their impressive dimensions, these blades present a surprisingly low longitudinal curvature, a feature rarely seen elsewhere in blade technology of this size.

The heavy blades were produced using a basic, albeit highly efficient procedure, without much preparation of the core. A prospective core was chosen from naturally broken blocks, presenting an existing striking platform adjacent to an existing face, allowing for the production of blades with little or no preparation. The striking angle between platform and flaking surface is around 75°. With very few exceptions, the striking platform of these blades is plain and production was strictly unidirectional.

This method of blade production is in sharp contrast to Neolithic and Upper Palaeolithic techniques known from northern Arabia. These follow completely different procedures, resulting in morphologically unequal products. Technologically, the best-fitting analogies to the heavy blades are found in the Levantine Amudian/Pre-Aurignacian and Hummalian ("Tabun-D") cultures, dating back to around 300,000 and 180,000 years (Mercier & Valladas 2003; Mercier *et al.* 2007). However, the associated tool sets in the Levant do not match the al-Ḥuqf finds.

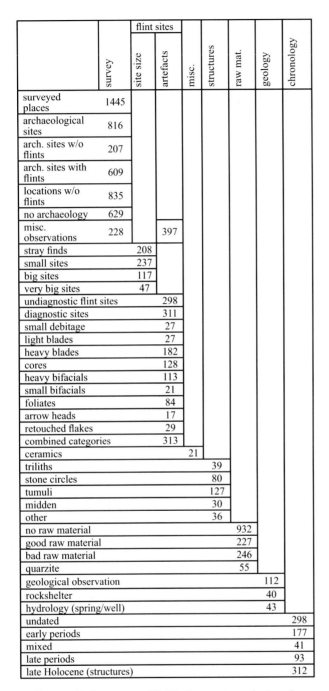

FIGURE 6. *A sample of heavy bifacials from different sites.*

Flake tools

In relation to the number of discovered Stone Age sites, the scarcity of retouched flake tools is striking throughout the survey area. Retouched flakes occurred at a mere twenty-nine sites out of 613 potential locations, where they never occurred in great numbers. Naturally, secondary retouch of flakes did not play the same role as in the Levant. It appears to be a particular trait of the South Arabian flint traditions, which preferred raw flakes, as demonstrated in the excavated sites. From many Neolithic coastal settlements in particular, chisel- or perforator-like tools were reported in substantial numbers (e.g. Maggi & Gebel 1990; Uerpmann M 1992; Charpentier 2001; Uerpmann & Uerpmann 2003; Usai 2005), but in al-Ḥuqf, no such tool was discovered along the coast or in the interior.

Heavy bifacials

These artefacts can be considered a type of hand axe made from blocks or exceptionally from very massive flakes. They are heavy tools of around 10–20 cm in length, worked over on both faces. Morphological variety is important and typological standardization is low. In general, the outline of the heavy bifacials is bipolar, with no well-defined base or tip. The sections are usually massive. Like the shapes, the style of the retouch covers a wide spectrum, being mostly heavy retouches leaving large and deep scars, which give rather an archaic appearance to these tools. Secondary retouch is largely absent.

At first glance, these tools evoke the classical hand axes of the Lower Palaeolithic, i.e. the Acheulean. Technologically comparable tools to al-Ḥuqf's heavy bifacials were produced in the Levant between 900,000 and 600,000 years ago (Copeland & Hours 1993; Bar-Yosef 1994; Goren-Inbar & Saragusti 1996; Rollefson *et al.* 1997; Jagher 2000). The peculiarities of al-Ḥuqf bifacials, i.e. a high morphological variability, their schematic execution in hard hammer technique with little or no secondary retouch, the pronounced bipolarity, and the lack of standardized shapes clearly distinguish them from the classical hand axes found commonly in the Acheulean and in the subsequent Early Middle Palaeolithic in the Levant and beyond (Le Tensorer 2006; Jagher 2000). Despite the rather archaic aspect of the heavy bifacials, it is difficult to attribute them to the Middle Acheulean (*Acheuléen moyen*) of the Levant. From that period, about a dozen sites are known from the whole Fertile Crescent, compared to 113 observations in al-Ḥuqf. The numbers and states of preservation on exposed open-air sites clearly suggest a much younger age for the Omani heavy bifacials, but it is difficult to give precise age estimates. Repeated geomorphologic observations, however, hint at a relatively old age, estimated at some 10,000 to well over 100,000 years old.

Heavy bifacials (Fig. 6) were among the most common discoveries during the COPS survey, occurring at 113 places out of 311 diagnostic sites. Identical tools have been described by Biagi (1994) from Saiwan in the

Ḥawshī depression. More recently, Rose specified similar discoveries within 25 km from Biagi's (Rose 2006: 307–317). As for the COPS sites, these are all open-air finds without stratigraphic context. Both authors compare the heavy bifacials with hand axes from the Acheulean of the Levant. Their chronological deductions can no longer be supported, as the cultural attribution is not consistent with lower Palaeolithic entities of the Fertile Crescent. In fact, the heavy bifacials belong to a cultural group unknown in the Bilād al-Shām.

Small bifacials

Like the heavy bifacials, the small bifacials are completely retouched on both sides. The size varies from 6 cm to approximately 8 cm. Small bifacials are distinct from the heavy bifacials not only by the diminutive size, but also by being more elaborate. The style of manufacture, broader proportions, and markedly thicker sections clearly distinguish them from foliates of the same size. Small bifacials were found in only twenty-one out of 609 potential sites. In several sites, small bifacials occur in substantial numbers, showing a surprising standardization in size and manufacture. A clear cultural assignment is difficult, as no clear association to other artefact categories has been identified.

Foliates

Foliates are, again, tools that are completely retouched on both faces of the artefact. Compared with the width, the section is thin. The original proportions can only occasionally be determined for certain, as most pieces found were broken. The few complete foliates or those restored from fragments indicate a length to width ratio ranging from less than 1:2 up to 1:3. The outline is usually pointed at both ends, and any clear difference between butt and tip is exceptional. With eighty-four sites, foliates were among the most frequent tools found during the al-Ḥuqf survey. Approximately a quarter (27%) of all sites with diagnostic artefacts included foliates albeit in highly different numbers, usually present with less than half a dozen pieces.

The quality of retouch never reaches the perfection typical of such artefacts attributed to the Arabian Bifacial Tradition (ABT) (e.g. Kapel 1967; Kallweit 2003; Crassard 2007). The typical pressure retouch was never observed on foliates from al-Ḥuqf. As their morphology is rather variable, they elude any exhaustive typology. Sites with analogous tools have been mentioned in the sultanate on several occasions (e.g. Sarūq, Biʾr Khafsah, Ḥabarūt, etc. in Pullar & Jäckli 1978; Pullar 1985; Charpentier 1999; Rose 2006: 321–326). Their age is controversial as the Sarūq finds are dated to *c.*7500 years ago (Uerpmann & Uerpmann 2003), whereas recent investigations in the Dhofar indicate an significantly older age, pointing to a much longer history for these artefacts (Rose & Usik 2009). During the COPS survey, exceptionally large foliates 15–25 cm long, 6–9 cm wide, and just 1.5–2.5 cm thick, were repeatedly observed (Fig. 7). Tools of this kind were regularly produced in the al-Ḥuqf area, as has been observed in several factory sites with unfinished artefacts, or pieces broken in their final stage of elaboration. Comparable objects, most of them fragmentary, have occasionally been published as remarkable artefacts (Crowfoot Payne & Hawkins 1963; Smith 1977; Gotoh 1980; Crassard 2007). Discoveries in al-Ḥuqf show that such artefacts must have been common in their time. It is likely that these tools went through different cycles of re-sharpening, thus reducing their size and their apparent numbers.

Arrowheads

An unexpected outcome of the COPS survey was the small number of sites with pressure-flaked arrowheads, the hallmark of the Arabian Neolithic, which were discovered at a mere seventeen out of 609 potential sites. Whenever found, arrowheads occurred in extremely small assemblages of just one or two pieces. One single site produced more than half a dozen leaf-shaped arrowheads. Fasad points were found in two isolated instances; trihedrals of any kind were completely absent.

Chronology

Currently, there are no absolute dates for any of the al-Ḥuqf finds as all are unburied open-air sites. Even the basic procedures for a relative chronology are difficult to apply. The main approach under the given conditions would be the examination of the preservation of artefacts, permitting us to separate materials of different ages from the same site. The patina of flint tools from sites in al-Ḥuqf is generally uniform and differences of distinct artefact series on the same site are non-existent. Patination of flint is a complex process, depending on a number of factors, such as soil chemistry and exposition to sunlight, among many others. Patina of flint is an

Figure 7. *A selection of large foliates from site 1341 near Saiwan at the margin of the al-Ḥawshi depression.*

alteration that proceeds until a natural equilibrium with its surroundings is reached. It is not a gradual change that develops indefinitely over time. Weathering as such happens in a relatively short time, geologically speaking. Consequently, prehistoric artefacts of different periods from the same site show an identical state of weathering.

Even today, a concise chronological framework of the Arabian Palaeolithic is unavailable, as are dated sites. The peculiarities of the Arabian materials hinder explicit comparisons with the well-established chronology of the Levant or adjacent areas. Conclusions about the antiquity of the Omani materials, as well as the relative succession of the different stages, are hampered by the lack of stratigraphies and are, to a large extent, academic guesswork. Age estimation for archaeological sites in al-Ḥuqf can be proposed based only on the morphology of artefacts.

In a basic and tentative model, the distinction between an older and younger stage can be drawn. The older phase comprises heavy blades and heavy bifacials, whereas the artefacts of the younger period consist of light blades, small debitage, foliates, and arrowheads. Even on such a simplified scale, some interesting observations are possible: sites with mixed materials of both stages are surprisingly rare, i.e. only 13% (41) out of 311 sites. Sites from the older phase account for 57% (177) of the locations, whereas the younger series comprise 30% (95). This indicates clearly only a minor mix of different periods, an unexpected result in open-air sites, where an amalgamation of different periods is a permanent hazard. Recent excavations on the Najd plateau in the Dhofar provided significant results on the age of foliated points assigned to the younger group in the COPS model. In al-Ḥaṭab rock-shelter dating indicates a minimal age between 13,000 and 19,000 years (Rose 2009). The old age for heavy blades and bifacials of the earlier period is supported by geomorphologic observations. At sites with artefacts of this preceding period, active erosional gullies repeatedly cut deep into the earlier surfaces, partially destroying the sites (Fig. 8). This observation is not absolute proof, but is strongly indicative of an old age.

Results

The number and quality of finds indicate a substantial human presence in the area over a considerable time span since the Middle Pleistocene. Despite a meagre chronological resolution, such a conclusion is surprising considering the arid conditions prevailing during most of that time. The quantity and density of finds challenge models of human occupation during the Pleistocene in South Arabia, occupation that proliferated only during periods of climatically favourable conditions.

Figure 8. *A heavily eroded factory site for heavy blades and heavy bifacials (site 103) at the escarpment of the Jiddat al-Ḥarāsīs.*

Locally available flint deposits were exploited with an unusual intensity. As there was no shortage of suitable materials throughout the surveyed area, extremely prolific workshops, in many cases directly adjoining each other, regularly covered many thousands of square metres, producing perhaps millions of artefacts, and often production waste (Fig. 9). Surprisingly, such factory areas did not accumulate over different prehistoric periods, but usually resulted from a single period. Amalgamation of different periods on such sites is normally insignificant. Production of whatever period in a single workshop area was usual. Either these sites supplied a substantial local population or were exported over an extended territory, but neither appears plausible for Pleistocene hunter-gatherers. More likely there was a steady exploitation of these places over an extended period. This implies long-lasting and highly conservative traditions with little change in their lithic technologies.

Considering the surveyed area as a whole, the different categories of flint artefacts show noticeable differences in their spatial distribution. Whereas heavy blades and, to a lesser extent, heavy bifacials, were produced in many manufacturing centres all over the survey area wherever the flint deposits permitted, the production of foliates or light blades occurred in fewer and more select places. Nevertheless, their production was massive in a way that is difficult to explain. At times it was an extreme, even obsessional, frenzy of flint knapping, with each available block of suitable flint material being exploited.

By looking at production from the sites and what was found throughout the surveyed area, there is a surprisingly narrow repertoire of technologies and formal variety. In fact, beyond the main categories described above, little more has been found. Anything beyond the mentioned spectrum was exceptional and was noted in just a few rare instances. Compared with the variegated lithic legacy of the Levant during the late Middle and Upper Pleistocene al-Ḥuqf materials show a completely different picture.

One of these peculiarities is the prevalence of *façonnage*, i.e. the shaping of a single block of raw material, rather than using prefabricated flakes or blades, for the manufacture of tools. This applies not only to the heavy and light bifacials, but also for most of the foliates. In some way, this even applies to Neolithic arrowheads, which are also completely worked over their two faces. The prevalence and stability of this concept seems to be a leitmotif in southern Arabian prehistory.

The rich and varied Palaeolithic legacy of the Levant has, so far, left no trace in southern Arabia. Nothing comparable with the many Stone Age cultures from the Bilād al-Shām was discovered during the COPS survey. This observation is all the more unexpected, as the Arabian subcontinent is not divided by natural barriers, and palaeocological data from the northern part has proved that during favourable conditions animals migrated regularly through the Arabian Desert in both directions. Human migration is irregular and for diverse reasons.

Heavy bifacials are alien to potential counterparts from the Levant. In fact, the postulated affinity of such tools to hand-axe traditions of the Levant can, clearly, be denied.

Aside from a few excavations dispersed all over the subcontinent, the vast majority of early Stone Age discoveries in Arabia are surface collections with poor chronological control. Cultural resolution is low, as palimpsests are a common hazard and the definition of the alleged cultural stages is limited. In the last few years, more and more Palaeolithic sites have been reported from southern Arabia (e.g. Whalen 2003; Rose 2006; Crassard 2007; Scott-Jackson *et al.* 2007; 2009; Wahida, Al-Tikriti & Beech 2008). However, most of these publications are short communications presenting a preliminary assessment of discoveries in ongoing projects. Many claims need further confirmation, as the statistical base is limited or the argumentation is based only on selected artefact categories. Cultural and technological labels are adopted in a somewhat random way with little attempt to match any original definition. Thus, in a strange way, model building in Arabian Stone Age archaeology is growing faster than the appropriate archaeological evidence.

On a regional scale in this context, the issue of the Sibakhan has to be considered. Proposed by Rose (2006) based upon surface materials, this "culture" was characterized by bifaces, a dominating blade production, and some Levallois debitage. Apart from two sites, the

Figure 9. *A small section of the highly concentrated waste of an extensive workshop for heavy blades (site 543).*

discoveries of Saiwan (Biagi 1994) were integrated in this cultural entity, all located in the Ḥawshi depression. Compared to the those of the COPS investigations, the bifaces noted by Rose and Biagi fit perfectly within the "heavy bifacials". The blades mentioned by both authors match the "heavy blades". A personal assessment of Biagi's original discoveries from Saiwan clearly showed the presence of heavy blades and bifacials, as defined in the COPS specifications.

As heavy blades and heavy bifacials are among the most frequent discoveries during the COPS fieldwork, further conclusions are possible. Considering the available information (210 sites), the combination of heavy blades and bifacials was affirmed in 37% of the observations. Of the remainder, 50% produced only heavy blades and 13% only heavy bifacials. An evident Levallois debitage is absent at all these discoveries. The distribution of all these sites shows no geographic preferences, as they occur regularly in every possible setting. Compared to initial models (Rose 2006) the "Sibakhan" elements from al-Ḥuqf are not in any way related to sabkhas. Furthermore, the relationship between blades and bifacials is not established, as all discoveries so far are open-air sites with no stratigraphic control. One should therefore be careful when using the label "Sibakhan". While the cultural and chronological circumstances are not better understood, we need to refrain from attributing any of al-Ḥuqf's materials to that cultural group.

The rarity of finds associated to the ABT was unexpected since such sites are among those regularly mentioned in the profile of Arabia's archaeology. ABT-associated arrowheads are also rare in coastal sites of the Omani Neolithic. The absence from these sites was explained by a subsistence economy that concentrated on marine resources which, unlike settlements of the interior, did not need hunting weaponry (Cleuziou & Tosi 2007). Surprisingly, however, the al-Ḥuqf survey showed an almost complete absence of such hunting camps in the inland areas.

Late Holocene archaeology was barely touched on in this paper, as it is not basically part of the SCOP project. However, a third of all archaeological features recorded during the survey, such as triliths, tumuli, stone circles, or shell middens can be dated to that period. In contrast to the earlier periods, which are generally equally distributed in the landscape, the most recent prehistory of al-Ḥuqf is clearly concentrated in its southern half. Contrary to expectations, these sites are not clustered along the coast but are regularly distributed up to 30–35 km from the sea, reflecting a steady human presence and exploitation of the hinterland throughout the late Holocene.

Conclusions

Palaeolithic archaeology in Oman and eastern Arabia is still in its infancy. There is a dire need for a well-established chronological-cultural framework. Tentative models struggle with the lack of well-excavated and published data from significant, especially stratified, sites. Furthermore, available information is at present dispersed over a huge geographic area. The COPS survey can contribute some local observations to these issues.

Compared with the Levant with its rich legacy of distinct and varied Palaeolithic cultures in al-Ḥuqf and southern Arabia there is very little perceptible cultural variability. Even though absolute dating is not available, nonetheless circumstantial evidence indicates long-standing traditions that change little over considerable periods of time. All materials observed in al-Ḥuqf are profoundly different to the known cultural entities from the Levant. No Levantine element was recognized in Oman, despite a long personal experience with the Levantine Palaeolithic amongst members of the team. On the other hand, no influence from eastern Africa could be demonstrated. Despite selective appearances, existing information points to a different history (Clark 1954; Pleurdeau 2003), having no explicit influence on that of southern Arabia. Available arguments, instead, point to regional cultures distinct from the southern part of the Arabian subcontinent. Potential influences from the Zagros Mountains across a dry Gulf, as it was for roughly half of the time in the last 500,000 years, remain an open issue, as comparable data from that area are almost completely lacking.

Supplementary to the original intentions of the COPS survey, there was a substantial contribution to the Omani prehistory of the late Holocene period. Numerous observations of that period, including the Bronze and Iron Ages, point to sizable populations, not only along the coasts but also in the hinterland, during a period of rapidly deteriorating climate with increasing aridity. Evidently, al-Ḥuqf profited from conditions that allowed a considerable settlement within an area that today is considered too arid for human subsistence. Al-Ḥuqf finds fill an important geographic gap between the Dhofar and the Ḥajar mountains as people at that time withdrew to what became inhabited areas.

Acknowledgements

The results presented in this paper would not have been possible without the unswerving dedication of the field team's members Ines Winet, Fabio Wegmüller, and Matthias Bolliger. The COPS project is much obliged to H.E. Sultan bin Hamdoon al-Harty, Mayor of Muscat and former Under-Secretary of the Ministry of Culture and Heritage, for issuing the excavation permit. Biuwa Ali al-Sabri should also be thanked for her support in all administrative matters and Petroleum Development of Oman, along with Bank Muscat, for sponsoring the fieldwork. Last, but not least, our gratitude goes to Youcef Fartas, Consul-General of Switzerland in Oman, and Dr Barbara Stäuble, Muscat. Without their enthusiasm and support, the COPS project never would have come into being.

References

Bar-Yosef O.
1994. The Lower Palaeolithic of the Near East. *Journal of World Prehistory* 8/3: 211–265.

Biagi P.

1994. An Early Palaeolithic site near Saiwan (Sultanate of Oman). *Arabian archaeology and epigraphy* 5: 81–88.

Blechschmidt I., Matter A., Preusser F. & Riek-Zapp D.

2009. Monsoon triggered formation of Quaternary alluvial megafans in the interior of Oman. *Geomorphology* 110/3–4: 128–139.

Bray H.E. & Stokes S.

2003. Chronologies for Late Quaternary barchan dune reactivation in the southeastern Arabian Peninsula. *Quaternary Science Reviews* 22: 1027–1033.

Charpentier V.

1999. Industries bifaciales holocènes d'Arabie orientale, un exemple: Ra's al-Jinz. *Proceedings of the Seminar for Arabian Studies* 29: 29–43.

2001. Les industries lithiques de Ra's al-Hadd. *Proceedings of the Seminar for Arabian Studies* 31: 31–45.

Cleuziou S. & Tosi M.

2007. *In the Shadows of the Ancestors, the Prehistoric Foundations of the Early Arabian Civilisation in Oman*. Muscat: Ministry of Heritage & Culture.

Clark J.D.

1954. *The Prehistoric Cultures of the Horn of Africa, An Analysis of the Stone Age Cultural and Climatic Succession in the Somalilands and Eastern Parts of Abyssinia*. Cambridge: Cambridge University Press.

Copeland L. & Hours F.

1993. The Middle Orontes Paleolithic Flint Industries. *BAR International Series* 587: 63–144.

Crassard R.

2007. Apport de la technologie lithique à la définition de la préhistoire du Hadramawt, dans le contexte du Yémen et de l'Arabie du Sud. Thèse de Doctorat, Université de Paris 1 (Panthéon-Sorbonne). [Unpublished].

2009. The Middle Palaeolithic of Arabia: The View from the Hadramawt Region, Yemen. Pages 151–168 in M. Petraglia & J. Rose (eds), *The Evolution of Human Populations in Arabia: Paleoenvironments, Prehistory and Genetics*. Heidelberg/London: Springer.

Crowfoot Payne J. & Hawkins S.

1963. A Surface Collection of Flints from Habarut in Southern Arabia. *Man* 240: 185–188.

Fleitmann D., Matter A., Pint J.J. & Al-Shanti M.A.

2004. *The speleothem record of climate change in Saudi Arabia*. SGS-OF-2004-8, Saudi Geological Survey. [Open-file report].

Fleitmann D., Burns S.J., Neff U., Mangini A. & Matter A.

2003. Changing moisture sources over the last 330,000 years in Northern Oman from fluid-inclusion evidence in speleothems. *Quaternary Research* 60: 223–232.

Goren-Inbar N. & Saragusti I.

1996. An Acheulian Biface Assemblage from the Site of Gesher Benot Ya'aqov, Israel: Indications of African Affinities. *Journal of Field Archaeology* 23: 15–30.

Gotoh T.

1980. A Stone Age collection from the Rub^c al-Khali desert. *Bulletin of the Ancient Orient Museum* 2: 1–15.

Goudie A.S., Coll A., Stokes S., Parker A., White K. & Al-Farra A.

2000. Latest Pleistocene and Holocene dune construction at the north-eastern edge of the Rub Al Khali, United Arab Emirates. *Sedimentology* 47: 1011–1021.

Griggo C.

2000. Adaptations environnementales et activités de subsistence au Paléolithique moyen en Syrie. *Annales de la Fondation Fyssen* 15: 49–62.

Haude W.

1969. Erfordern die Hochstände des Toten Meeres die Annahme von Pluvial-Zeiten während des Pleistozäns? *Meteorologische Rundschau* 22/2: 29–40.

Jagher R.
2000. Nadaouiyeh Aïn Askar, Entwicklung der Faustkeiltraditionen und der Stratigraphie an einer Quelle in der syrischen Wüstensteppe. PhD thesis, University of Basel. [Unpublished].

Kallweit H.
2003. Remarks on the Late Stone Age in the UAE. Pages 55–64 in D.T. Potts, H. Naboodah & P. Hellyer (eds), *Proceedings of the First International Conference on the Archaeology of the United Arabian Emirates (Abu Dhabi 15–18 April)*. London: Trident Press.

Kapel H.
1967. Atlas of the Stone-Age Cultures of Qatar. Reports of the Danish Archaeological Expedition to the Arabian Gulf. *Jutland Archaeological Society Publications* 6: 5–43.

Kocurek G. & Lancaster N.
1999. Aeolian system sediment state: theory and Mojave Desert Kelso Dune field example. *Sedimentology* 99: 505–515.

Le Tensorer J-M.
2006. Les cultures acheuléennes et la question de l'émergence de la pensée symbolique chez Homo erectus à partir des données relatives à la forme symétrique et harmonique des bifaces. *Comptes Rendus Palevol* 5: 127–135.

Le Tensorer J-M., Jagher R. & Muhesen S.
2001. Paleolithic Settlement Dynamics in the El Kowm Area (Central Syria). Pages 101–122 in N. Conard (ed.), *Settlement Dynamics of the Middle Paleolithic and Middle Stone Age*. Tübingen: Kerns.

Maggi R. & Gebel H.G.
1990. A preliminary report on the chipped stone industries of the mid-Holocene shell-midden communities of Ra's al-Hamra 5, layer 1 (Muscat — Sultanate of Oman). *Rivista di Archeologia* 14: 5–24.

Mercier N. & Valladas H.
2003. Reassessment of TL age estimates of burnt flints from the Palaeolithic site of Tabun Cave, Israel. *Journal of Human Evolution* 45: 401–409.

Mercier N., Valladas H., Froget L., Reyss J-L., Weiner S., Goldberg P., Meignen L., Bar-Yosef O., Chech M., Kuhn S.L., Stiner M.C., Tillier A-M., Arensburg B. & Vandermeersch B.
2007. Hayonim Cave: A TL-based chronology for this Levantine Mousterian sequence. *Journal of Archaeological Science* 34: 1064–1077.

O'Connor P.W. & Thomas D.S.
1999. The timing and environmental significance of Late Quaternary linear dune Development in Western Zambia. *Quaternary Research* 52: 44–55.

Petraglia M.
2003. The Lower Palaeolithic of the Arabian Peninsula: Occupations, Adaptations and Dispersals. *Journal of World Prehistory* 17: 141–179.

Petraglia M. & al-Sharekh A.
2003. The Middle Palaeolithic of Arabia: Implications for Human Origins, Behaviour and Dispersals. *Antiquity* 77: 671–684.

Pleurdeau D.
2003. Le Middle Stone Age de la grotte du Porc-Epic (Dire Dawa, Éthiopie): gestion des matières premières et comportements techniques. *L'Anthropologie* 107: 15–48.

Preusser F.
2009. Chronology of the impact of Quaternary climate change on continental environments in the Arabian Peninsula. *Comptes Rendus Geoscience* 341/8–9: 621–632.

Preusser F., Radies D. & Matter A.
2002. A 160,000 Year Record of Dune Development and Atmospheric Circulation in Southern Arabia. *Science* 296: 2018–2020.

Preusser F., Radies D., Driehorst F. & Matter A.

2005. Late Quaternary history of the coastal Wahiba Sands, Sultanate of Oman. *Journal of Quaternary Science* 20/4: 395–405.

Pullar J.

1985. A Selection of Aceramic Sites in the Sultanate of Oman. *The Journal of Oman Studies* 7: 49–87.

Pullar J. & Jäckli B.

1978. Some aceramic sites in Oman. *The Journal of Oman Studies* 4: 53–73.

Radies D., Preusser F., Matter A. & Mange M.

2004. Eustatic and climatic controls of the development of the Wahiba Sand Sea, Sultanate of Oman. *Sedimentology* 51: 1359–1385.

Rollefson G.O., Schnurrenberger D., Quintero L.A., Watson R.P. & Low R.

1997. ᶜAin Soda and ᶜAin Qasiya: New Late Pleistocene and Early Holocene Sites in the Azraq Shishan Area, Eastern Jordan. *Studies in Early Near Eastern Production, Subsistence and Environment* 4: 45–58.

Rose J.

2006. Among Arabian Sands: Defining the Palaeolithic of Southern Arabia. PhD thesis, Southern Methodist University, University Park, Texas. [Unpublished].

Rose J. & Usik V.

2009. The "Upper Paleolithic" of South Arabia. Pages 169–186 in M. Petraglia & J. Rose (eds), *The Evolution of Human Populations in Arabia: Paleoenvironments, Prehistory and Genetics*. Heidelberg/London: Springer.

Scott-Jackson J., Scott Jackson W. & Jasim S.

2007. Middle Palaeolithic or what? New sites in Sarjah (UAE). *Proceedings of the Seminar for Arabian Studies* 37: 277–279.

Smith G.H.

1977. New Prehistoric Sites in Oman. *The Journal of Oman Studies* 3: 71–81.

Thomas H., Geraards D., Janjou D., Vaslet D., Mesmeh A., Billiou D., Bochrens H., Dobigny G., Eisenmann V., Gayet M., Lapparent de Broin F. de, Petter G. & Halawani M.

1998. First Pleistocene faunas from the Arabian Peninsula: An Nafud desert, Saudi Arabia. *Comptes Rendus de l'Académie des Sciences, Sciences de la Terre et des planètes* 326: 145–152.

Uerpmann M.

1992. Structuring the Late Stone Age of Southeastern Arabia. *Arabian archaeology and epigraphy* 3: 65–109.

Uerpmann H-P. & Uerpmann M.

2003. *Stone Age Sites and their Natural Environment — The Capital Area of Northern Oman.* Part III. (Beihefte zum Tübinger Atlas des vorderen Orients, Reihe A, Naturwissenschaften 31/3). Wiesbaden: Reichert.

Usai D.

2005. Chisels or perforators? The lithic industry of Ras al-Hamra (Muscat, Oman). *Proceedings of the Seminar for Arabian Studies* 35: 293–301.

Waelbroeck C., Labeyrie L., Michel E., Duplessy J.C., McManus J.F., Lambeck K., Balbon E. & Labracherie M.

2002. Sea-level and deep water temperature changes derived from benthic foraminifera isotopic records. *Quaternary Science Reviews* 21: 295–305.

Wahida G., Al-Tikriti W.Y. & Beech M.
2008. Barakah: a Middle Palaeolithic site in Abu Dhabi Emirate. *Proceedings of the Seminar for Arabian Studies* 38: 55–64.

Warren A. & Allison D.
1998. The palaeoenvironmental significance of dune size hierarchies. *Palaeogeography, Palaeoclimatology, Palaeoecology* 137: 289–303.

Whalen N.
2003. Lower Palaeolithic Sites in the Huqf Area of Central Oman. *The Journal of Oman Studies* 13: 175–182.

Authors' addresses
Dr Reto Jagher, Institute for Prehistory and Archaeological Science, University of Basel, Spalenring 145, 4055 Basel, Switzerland.

e-mail reto.jagher@unibas.ch

Christine Pümpin, Institute for Prehistory and Archaeological Science, University of Basel, Spalenring 145, 4055 Basel, Switzerland.

e-mail christine.puempin@unibas.ch

Proceedings of the Seminar for Arabian Studies 40 (2010): 201–212

Umm an-Nar settlement in the Wādī Andam (Sultanate of Oman)

Nasser al-Jahwari & Derek Kennet

Summary
This paper describes a number of archaeological sites of different sizes dating to the Umm an-Nar period (2500–2000 BC), which were discovered or investigated during the course of a systematic archaeological survey of the Wādī Andam in the al-Sharqīyah region of northern Oman. The first, al-Khashbah, is a very large site with a number of round towers and other structures. The second is a smaller but very well preserved site, al-Ghoryeen (al-Gharīyān), with a single round tower, a tomb field, and traces of domestic structures. A number of much smaller sites are also described that have no structural remains. The existence of these sites was detected by the employment of systematic, large-scale pottery collection in small wadi villages, a technique that has not previously been widely employed by archaeological projects in the region. These sites therefore represent an aspect of Umm an-Nar rural settlement that has not received due scholarly consideration. Having described the various sites, the paper discusses the possibility that they represent three different tiers of an Umm an-Nar settlement hierarchy.

Keywords: Oman, eastern Arabia, Umm an-Nar, Bronze Age, settlement

This paper describes two significant sites of the Umm an-Nar period that are located in the al-Sharqīyah region of northern Oman, and attempts to place them within their period and regional contexts.

One of the sites, al-Khashbah, is a very large site that has been mentioned briefly a number of times in the literature but has never been fully described, and its importance and size are not generally appreciated by the academic community. The other, al-Ghoryeen, is a smaller site that has never been mentioned in the literature; it represents a very well preserved, middle-sized Umm an-Nar site that throws useful light on the nature of Umm an-Nar settlement more generally.

The area within which these two sites are located is known as the Wādī Andam region in al-Mudhaybi (Fig. 1). It is located to the east of Izkī and south of Samāʾil. It formed the basis of the doctoral dissertation of one of the present authors (al-Jahwari 2008), who carried out a survey during the course of two field seasons from December 2004 to April 2005, and from November 2005 to February 2006.

The main focus of the survey was to use a field survey technique specifically adapted for local conditions. This involves the large-scale collection of surface scatter pottery from across modern occupation areas, which allows the recording of occupation that has left no trace other than low numbers of redeposited pottery mixed with large quantities of more recent material (al-Jahwari 2008: 108–114; al-Jahwari & Kennet 2008). This technique was applied to a range of locations including a sample of six small "wadi villages" — by which is meant locations on wadi banks suitable for agriculture and the areas surrounding them — plus a number of randomly located control surveys and a variety of other sites and collection areas. By employing this technique, it was possible to produce quantified evidence on settlement history as well as to locate tombs, structures, and other archaeological finds in the normal way.

Among the larger sites recorded during this survey were al-Khashbah and al-Ghoryeen. These two sites were also revisited and more fully documented and studied during the period from January to March 2009, at which time all visible structures and related features were recorded and mapped.

A number of Umm an-Nar sites of various types and sizes are already known from this area. These include the sites recorded by the Harvard Archaeological Expedition at Wādī Ṣamad, such as the settlements of Wādī Ṣamad 4 and 5, Samad 50 (Maysar 1), and Wādī Andam sites 1, 16, 19, and 28 (Meadow, Humphries & Hastings 1976:

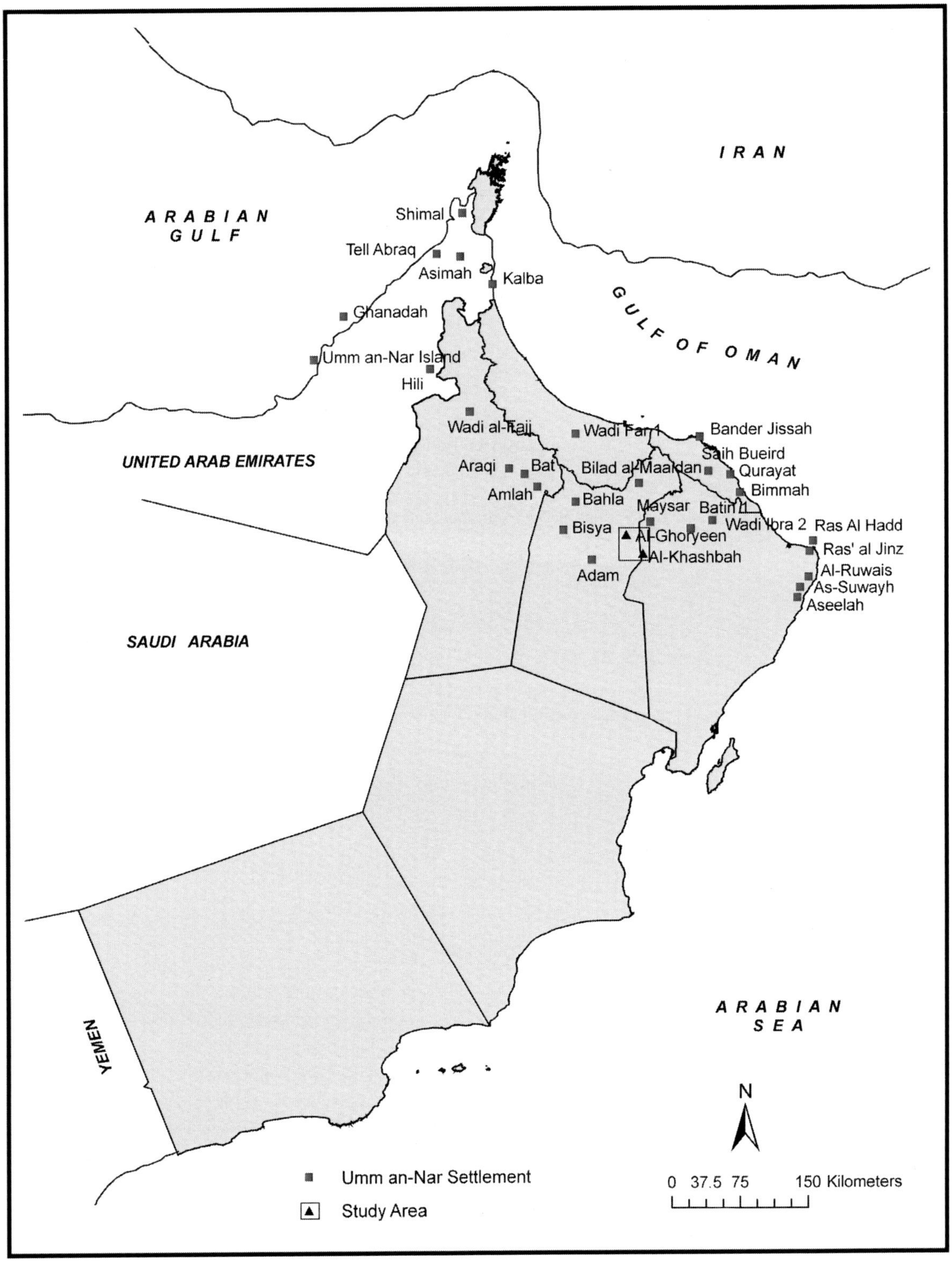

Figure 1. *A map of Oman showing the sites mentioned in the text. The small square shows the extent of the present study area.*

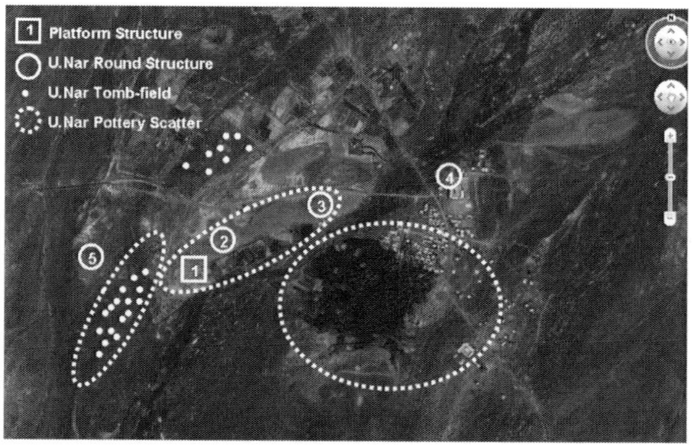

Figure 2. *A plan of al-Khashbah showing the towers, tomb fields, and Umm an-Nar pottery scatters.*

112–114). There are also the sites recorded by the British Archaeological Mission, including al-Wāṣil, Sharīʾah (Khuḍar), and Samad 15 (de Cardi, Collier & Doe 1976: 156; de Cardi 1977: 61). Finally, there are other Umm an-Nar sites found by the German Archaeological Mission. Among these are Maysar M25 (round Umm an-Nar tower surrounded by traces of domestic structures), M2, M6, M7, M16, M29, M31, and M49; and Mullaq and al-Hind (al-Khashbah) (Weisgerber 1978: 27; 1981: 174–263).

Al-Khashbah

Al-Khashbah is located halfway between the village of Khaḍrāʾ Banī Dafaʾa and the town of Sinaw, along the main road connecting Izkī with Sinaw (Fig. 1) (GPS co-ordinates: Oman WGS 1984: 0606930/2506528). It is a widely dispersed site spread over an area of about 912.5 ha (Fig. 2).

The core of the site is an area of modern date-palm groves measuring around 1.5×1.5 km located close to the Wādī Ṣamad channel. The area surrounding the date palms on both sides of the wadi contains a considerable amount of evidence of multi-period settlement located on the gravel plain and on the tops of small rocky outcrops.

As stated above, the site has already been mentioned in the literature a number of times (Weisgerber 1980: 99–100; Cleuziou 1984: 380; Potts 1990, i: 102; Yule 1993: 143–144, fig. 2/a, b; 2001: 384, pl. 511, 590; Orchard & Stanger 1994: 145–146, fig. 1; 1999: 90–91, fig. 1; Cleuziou & Tosi 2007: 243–244, fig. 262), although it has never been fully described and its size and significance are not generally recognized.

Figure 2 shows the later third-millennium (Umm an-Nar) components of the site; they consist of the remains

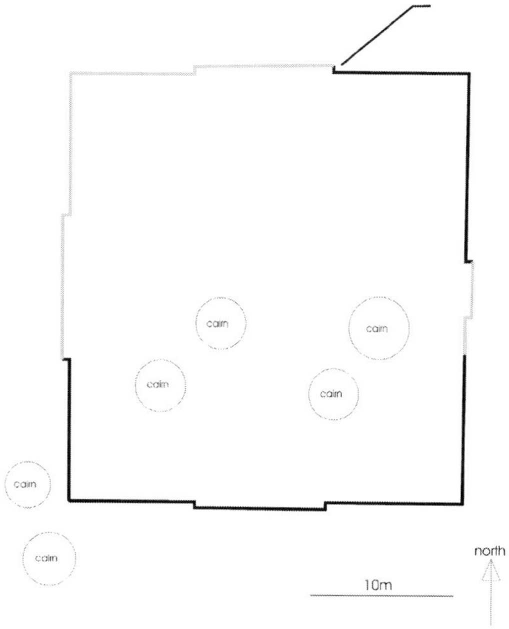

Figure 3. *A plan of Structure 1 at al-Khashbah. The black lines indicate where the wall is visible on the ground, the grey lines indicate where the wall is covered by rubble, and its location has been estimated based on the parts that are visible.*

of four or five structures — three or four round towers and one which is better described as a platform — two tomb fields, and a number of areas of Umm an-Nar pottery scatter. It can be seen that the site is widely dispersed and the monuments and pottery scatters are separated by wide areas that contain no evidence and were apparently empty of occupation. Rather than being a single, unified complex it appears to be a conglomeration of different elements scattered quite widely around a core agricultural area.

Structure 1 (0605803/2506363)

This remarkable structure is a large, square stone-built platform, which is located on a small rocky outcrop to the north-west of the site (Figs 3–6). Brief descriptions of this structure have already been given by Weisgerber (1980: 100, fig. 66), Yule (1993: 143–144, fig. 2/a, b; 2001: 384, pl. 511) and Orchard & Stanger (1994: 82), who repeat some of Weisgerber's observations.[1]

The structure is constructed with a retaining wall of large, roughly-dressed stone blocks that measure up to

[1] Yule (2001: 384) and Wiesgerber (1980: 100) refer to Structure 1 or its vicinity as "Hind" or "al-Hind".

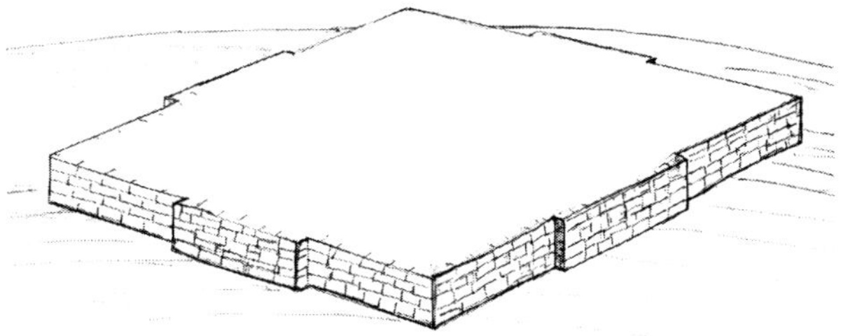

Figure 4. *A sketch reconstruction of Structure 1 at al-Khashbah from the south-west.*

Figure 5. *Structure 1 at al-Khashbah from the east.*

Figure 6. *The offset in the east wall of Structure 1 at al-Khashbah.*

2.7 m in length, up to 90 cm in width and are on average about 45 cm in height (Fig. 6). Up to six visible courses are preserved in some places, the lowest of which is mostly buried in the ground, giving the presently standing wall a maximum height of 2.3 m. There is no evidence of any mortar, but in some places thin stones have been inserted between the courses, apparently to stabilize them. It is, of course, possible that mud mortar was originally used, but if so it has entirely eroded away. The outer face of the wall is clearly visible in many places as a regular line of dressed stones, but a regular inner face was not seen anywhere. It therefore seems likely that the wall was constructed as a retaining wall and never had an exposed inner face.

The structure is square, measuring between 27.5 and 28.9 m along each side and is oriented towards magnetic north (Fig. 3). It is only possible to measure the length of the east and south walls precisely because the outer face of the north-west corner is covered by rubble. In the middle of each side the walls are offset outwards by 40 to 50 cm for a distance of about 9.5 m (shorter on the east face), effectively dividing the walls into three roughly equal sections (Figs 3, 6). At least one end of an offset is visible on all four walls but only on the south wall are both ends of the central offset visible. Here the length of each section of the wall is roughly the same; actually the western third is about 70 cm shorter than the other two. The offsets that are visible indicate that the south, north, and west walls were laid out in roughly the same way but, as mentioned, the offset on the east wall is considerably shorter. Here, assuming that the wall is symmetrical, the length of the central offset is just under 4 m (compared to 9.44 m on the south side). This means that the building was only symmetrical about the east–west axis and that the east wall was deliberately constructed differently from the other three.[2]

The interior of the structure appears to have been a raised platform, standing at least 2 m above the level of the surrounding hilltop. A sketch reconstruction of what the structure may have looked like is shown in Figure 4. No internal surfaces, walls or other features such as wells are now visible on the ground, although they may, of course, be revealed upon excavation. However, what appear to be six small burial cairns are associated with the structure, four on the interior and two just outside the south-west corner (Fig. 3). These are thought to post-date the original use of the structure. Weisgerber (1980: 100) notes that a stone block, with a worn hole resulting from its use as a door-hinge, was found in the vicinity of this structure.

The date of the structure is suggested by the dense

[2] A sketch-plan of this structure has previously been published (Yule 1993: 143–144, fig. 2/a, b; 2001: pl. 511) but it has the following errors, which have been corrected in the present plan: the orientation is shown as *c.*45° from the magnetic north; the walls are shown as having a defined inner face; no offset is shown on the north wall; the offset on the east wall is shown as being the same size as those on other walls. In addition, a series of internal walls and rooms are shown which were not observed on the ground in 2009 and have either been destroyed after 1993 or are mis-interpretations.

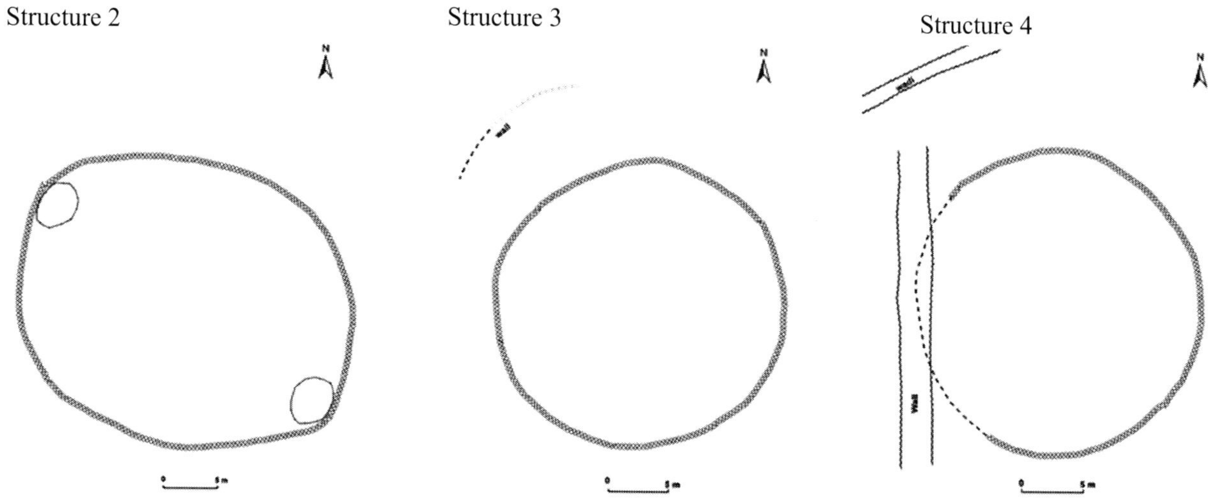

Figure 7. *Sketch plans of Structures 2, 3, and 4 at al-Khashbah.*

scatter of Umm an-Nar pottery that lies outside and below it. A number of petroglyphs can be seen on the outer face of the north-east corner of the structure showing what appear to be camels and horses with riders. These may have been cut after the abandonment of the building or during its original period of use.

The function of the structure is unknown and there is little evidence to provide any indications of its role. It may have had a ritual, defensive, domestic, or social function, although the fact that the east wall is marked out by a shorter offset might be taken to suggest that a ritual function of some sort is the most probable. The structure is much more deliberately square than any known Umm an-Nar tower and this makes it unique in the Umm an-Nar architectural repertoire. In terms of function it might perhaps be most usefully compared with the hilltop monuments that are referred to by the Orchards as "tiered structures" at Jabal Sulayman ᶜAlī and Qarn Qanṭarat Nizwā at Bisyā (Bisyah) (Orchard & Stanger 1994: figs 2, 7; Orchard 2000: 170–174; Orchard & Orchard 2002: 229–232). Even if one does not agree with the Orchards' interpretation of the date and context of these monuments, there do appear to be similarities in so far as the structures are all located on low hilltops, have similar masonry, and appear likely to be predominantly ritual (although there is no evidence of terraced walls around the lower slopes of the hill at al-Khashbah as there appear to be around the structures at Bisyā). These points appear to distinguish these monuments from the majority of Umm an-Nar round (or sub-round) towers that are well known from sites such as Bāt, Ḥili, and Maysar.

Structure 2 (0605822/2506570)

Structure 2 is a badly preserved, circular structure with a diameter of *c.*30 m (Fig. 7). It is situated on the flat plain below the mound where Structure 1 is located. Structure 2 consists of a circular wall of large and medium-sized, crudely dressed stone blocks, measuring up to 2 m surrounding a low earth and gravel mound. Although the structure is badly preserved, the circular stone wall can be distinguished standing up to three courses high in some places, particularly on the northern side. No internal walls or structures are presently visible. During the survey, Umm an-Nar pottery sherds were found and collected from the surface in and around the structure. This must be the circular structure mentioned by Yule (2001: 384) as lying roughly 100 m north-north-east of Structure 1 (Fig. 7) although, curiously, Weisgerber (1980) appears not to have noted it.

Structure 3 (0606698/2506686)

All that remains of this circular structure are parts of a circular wall consisting of one course of large, crudely dressed stones, around 40 cm high and up to 2 m long (Fig. 7). The diameter of the structure is *c.*25 m. It is situated on a low rise close to the channel of the Wādī Ṣamad. A few Umm an-Nar sherds were picked up within the structure, but there is very little material. This and Structure 4 (below) appear to be the "zwei weiterer Ruinen" (two further ruins) mentioned by Yule (2001: 384) and is probably the southernmost of the two circular structures described by Weisgerber (1980: 99–100) where only the foundations were preserved.

Structure 4 (0607221/2506844)

A third probable Umm an-Nar circular structure is found in the north-eastern part of al-Khashbah on the opposite bank of the Wādī Ṣamad channel to Structure 3 (Fig. 7). The 23 m-diameter structure is built of large and medium stone blocks, up to 2 m long. Only one or two courses of stones are still preserved, although Weisgerber notes that the structure stood up to 1.8 m high some thirty years ago (1980: 99–100). The structure appears to have been recently damaged by the deliberate removal of stone blocks so that they can be piled up along the wadi bank to prevent erosion. In addition, the western part of the structure has been damaged by the construction of a modern wall. No Umm an-Nar pottery sherds were found associated with this structure, but a few Early Iron Age sherds were collected.[3]

Structure 5 (0605085/2506327)

A further possible Umm an-Nar circular structure was found during a last visit to the area in March 2009. Due to its very bad state of preservation, it is difficult to define its original boundaries. In general, as in the other structures, this construction was built using medium and large stone blocks that were cut from the same low rocky hill of which the structure is part. The dimensions of the structure are not clear.

Tomb fields

Although it was previously believed that no Umm an-Nar tombs existed at this site (e.g. Orchard & Stanger 1999: 90), systematic survey has revealed that two large Umm an-Nar tomb fields are in fact present, one to the north of the site and one to the west (Fig. 2).

Northern Tomb field (0606181/2507367)

A number of circular Umm an-Nar tombs were located in a tomb field just *c.*800 m north of al-Khashbah village (Fig. 2). The tomb field area has now been converted into small date-palm gardens around which the tombs are now distributed. The tombs are built of flat, dressed limestone blocks with an average size of *c.*35 cm. Two or more concentric walls can clearly be distinguished on a number of the tombs with a thickness of *c.*30 cm for each wall. There are also typical walls sub-dividing the inside of the tombs to form several burial chambers. The diameters of the tombs vary between 4 and 8 m, while the highest of the best-preserved mound is almost 2 m. The survey yielded only a few surface finds, including human bone fragments, one bead, and three pottery sherds of possible Islamic date.

Western tomb field (0605251/2506155)

Another Umm an-Nar tomb field was located in the western part of the village, extending over an area of *c.*32.5 ha (Fig. 2). The shape and size of the tombs are similar to those found in the north-western tomb field described above. They are circular and consist of two, perhaps more, concentric walls *c.*50 cm thick with possible internal walls dividing the tomb into several chambers. The tombs measure between 4 and 8 m in diameter. Some of the tombs are preserved to only one course of stone wall (*c.*30 cm high), while others are preserved as mounds with a height of between 1 and 2 m. As many of the tombs have been heavily disturbed, large amounts of surface Umm an-Nar sherds and fragmentary human bones were encountered.

Ḥafīt tomb fields

It is also worth mentioning that there are other tomb fields located in different areas surrounding the village. Briefly, they consist of a large number of Ḥafīt and beehive tombs similar in shape and characteristics to those found in other parts of the Oman peninsula. They are found on rocky and gravel hills as well as flat gravel terraces. Some of these tombs were located in close proximity to the Umm an-Nar structures described above, particularly on the low rocky hill between Structures 1, 2, and 3. However, the majority are located away from the centre of the modern village area. The occurrence of tombs of this period suggests that the area within and around al-Khashbah has been attractive to settlement for some time, perhaps from as early as the late fourth millennium BC.

Pottery scatters and settlement areas

Possible traces of Umm an-Nar occupation in the form of surface pottery scatters were recovered from the area around the modern village and date-palm groves (Fig. 2). The surface pottery collection analysis showed that these

[3] Yule (2001: 384) notes that the largest of the three round structures is known locally as "Tauer Ḥanthel", without making clear which structure is meant, while Wiesgerber (1980: 99–100) must refer to Structure 4 when he notes that the northernmost of the two structures on either side of the wadi is known locally as "Tamr Hansel".

areas yielded 405 sherds of Umm an-Nar pottery unrelated to surviving tomb or other structures (al-Jahwari 2008: 115–118). These sherds are thought to be the remains of buried occupation that has since been disturbed and brought to the surface by agricultural activities (al-Jahwari & Kennet 2008). Interestingly, this evidence also demonstrates that there is more Umm an-Nar pottery in this area than any other pre-Islamic period giving, perhaps, some indication of the comparative level of intensity of occupation of this area through time. Relatively high levels of Umm an-Nar activity are also suggested by the recovery of Umm an-Nar remains within the village, such as in low mounds and cut sections where large numbers of pottery sherds are exposed. Additionally, Umm an-Nar sherds were also found scattered within an Islamic cemetery. As stated above, quite dense scatters of pottery were also observed on the low hill between Structures 1, 2 and 3. Surface collection in these areas yielded a total of 424 Umm an-Nar sherds.

al-Ghoryeen (0604445/2532515)

Al-Ghoryeen is a much smaller settlement than al-Khashbah. It extends over an area of about 15 ha on the western bank of the Wādī Maḥram, at the point where that wadi meets the Wādī Andam, close to the modern village of al-Ghoryeen south of the village of Mahleya (Fig. 1).

The site consists of a small mound thought to be the remains of an Umm an-Nar round tower, a cemetery of forty-nine tombs and, most importantly, an almost completely preserved domestic occupation area, which is visible on the surface as stone alignments marking the location and layout of walls and buildings (Fig. 8). The north-eastern and north-western parts of the site are occupied by Late Iron Age/Samad period tombs that seem to overlie earlier Umm an-Nar remains.

The site can be roughly divided into four parts, of which the round tower is the focal point being at the centre of the site. The tower mound has a diameter of between 25 and 30 m, and its height is about 5 m. Its walls are constructed of flat limestone blocks of medium size. There is no evidence on the surface of internal structures but on top of the tower there is a pile of stones, which is perhaps a later burial cairn. The south-western part of the site is where domestic occupation was located, as is suggested by the remains of more than fifty structures distributed over an area of around 200×150 m. Although it has not yet been possible to map these in detail, it is clear that they represent the remains of buildings of a variety of different sizes and plans (Fig. 9). A large number of Umm an-Nar sherds were found scattered within and around these structures. The south-eastern part of the site along the wadi bank includes a tomb field with forty-nine Umm an-Nar round tombs that appear to be quite badly preserved. Their diameters range between 4 and 12 m. They are built of local stone with deliberately selected orange rock from the other side of the wadi used as facing stones. By contrast, the north-eastern and north-western parts of the site consist of a large number of Late Iron Age/Samad period tombs. Around 200 such tombs were counted. They appear to be built on top of earlier Umm an-Nar structures.

Small village sites

In a recent paper, we described a method of field survey that is based on large-scale pottery collection and allows the systematic detection of settlement evidence in the small wadi villages that are typical of this area as well as many other parts of the Oman peninsula (al-Jahwari & Kennet 2008). Crucially, this method uses an understanding of the dynamics of more recent wadi agriculture to allow the detection of occupation evidence at sites where architectural remains such as tombs and round towers are no longer present, and where ancient surface pottery scatters are mixed with much greater densities of more recent pottery.

The technique was applied to a sample of six wadi villages in the Wādī Andam study area during two seasons from December 2004 to April 2004, and November 2005 to February 2006 (Fig. 10). There were no traces of Umm an-Nar round towers or tombs visible on the surface in any of these six villages nor were any reported in the literature. Despite this, the surface pottery provides clear evidence that there was significant occupation at five out of the six sites during the Umm an-Nar period (Figs 11, 12).

Obviously, the actual nature of this occupation is unknown, as is its precise extent and density. More information could be extracted by more precise surface survey or by excavation. It is not known whether Umm an-Nar round towers were originally present and have since been destroyed, or whether the Umm an-Nar occupation at some or all of these sites never included a round tower. It would be very difficult to determine this archaeologically at any one site but if a large enough number of such sites were to be located without evidence of a tower, it might be possible to suggest that there were Umm an-Nar settlements of this scale that did not normally include a round tower.

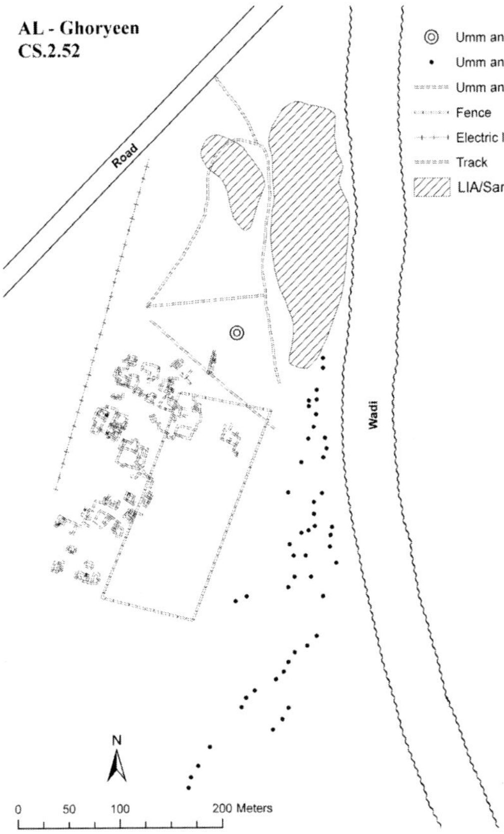

FIGURE 8. *A plan of al-Ghoryeen.*

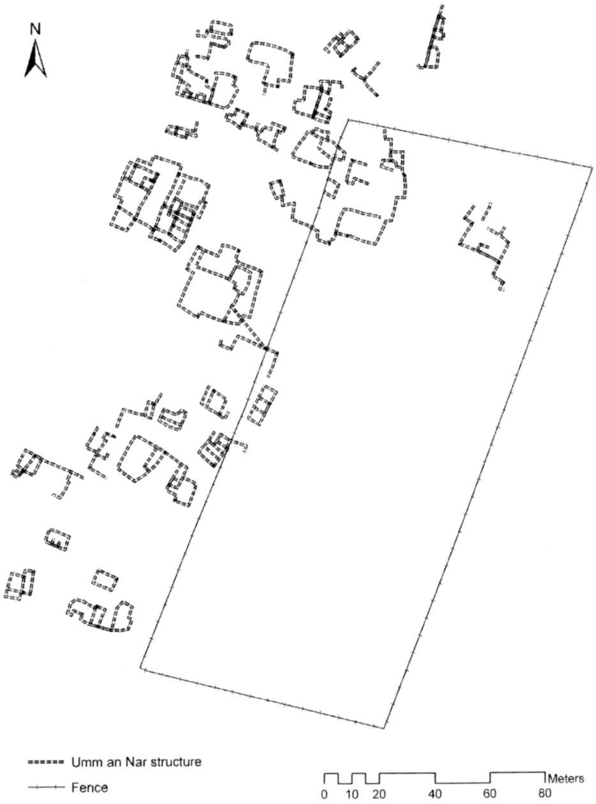

FIGURE 9. *An interpretive sketch plan of the domestic settlement area at al-Ghoryeen.*

Discussion: three tiers of Umm an-Nar settlement?

This paper has described a number of aspects of Umm an-Nar settlement in the Wādī Andam region of Oman that were previously either unknown or only partially known. Together they provide an insight into the complexity of Umm an-Nar settlement in this area. Obviously, the considerable difference in the size and nature of these sites might suggest that they represent different tiers of settlement and it is this idea that will be explored below.

The site of al-Khashbah is clearly important. First, the square platform (Structure 1) is, as Yule has observed (2001: 384), one of the largest known Umm an-Nar structures. It is certainly one of the most impressive and is unique in its monumentality, concept, and layout.[4] Secondly, in terms of its size and the number of preserved monuments which are located there, al-Khashbah is among the largest Umm an-Nar sites known from anywhere in the peninsula and is, alongside Ḥilī, Bāt, Bisyā (and perhaps Firq), one of only a few sites where four or more Umm an-Nar towers have been reported. Although the apparently low density of occupation at these large, multi-towered sites (along with the limited range of activities that are known to have taken place at them) would argue against considering them properly urban (*contra* Orchard & Stanger 1994), it seems quite likely that they represent significant regional centres of power and cultural focus.

A number of smaller multi-towered sites are known in the peninsula, such as al-Safri, al-Dreez (al-Darīz) (Frifelt 1985: 91–92), Firq (Sites 24 & 25) (de Cardi, Collier

[4] It is difficult to be certain which is actually the largest Umm an-Nar building as they are of different shapes. Basing the comparison on area would therefore seem to be the most sensible. Most round towers have reported diameters between 20 and 25 m but would need to have a diameter of about 32 m in order to exceed the area of Structure 1 at al-Khashbah. The round tower at Tell Abraq is estimated to have a diameter of 40 m (Potts 1991: 22), which, if correct, would give it an internal area of over 1200 m^2 (compared to the 784 m^2 of Structure 1 at al-Khashbah) and would make it the largest known Umm an-Nar structure by a considerable margin.

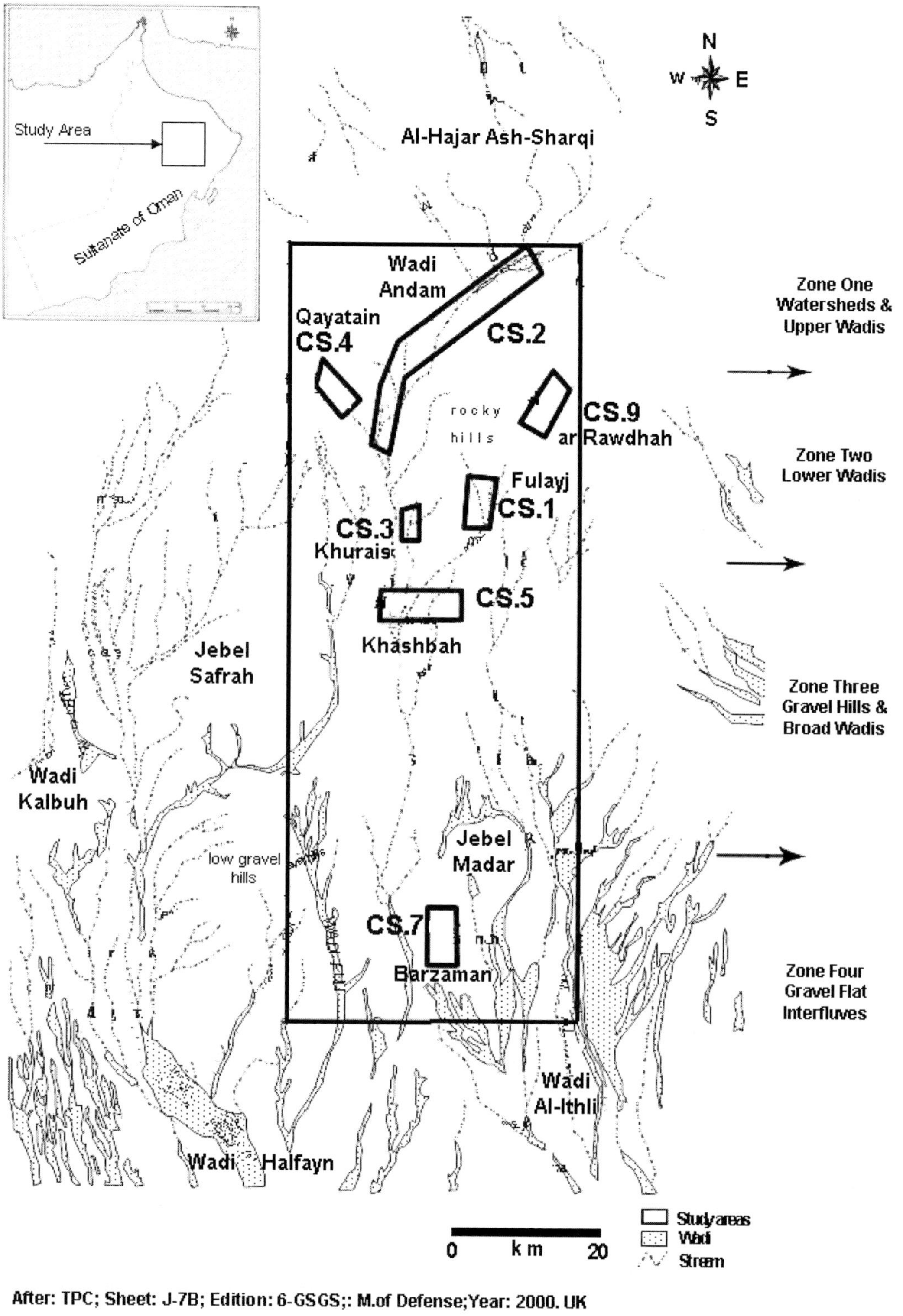

FIGURE 10. *A map of the study area showing the location of the six wadi villages where pottery collection was undertaken.*

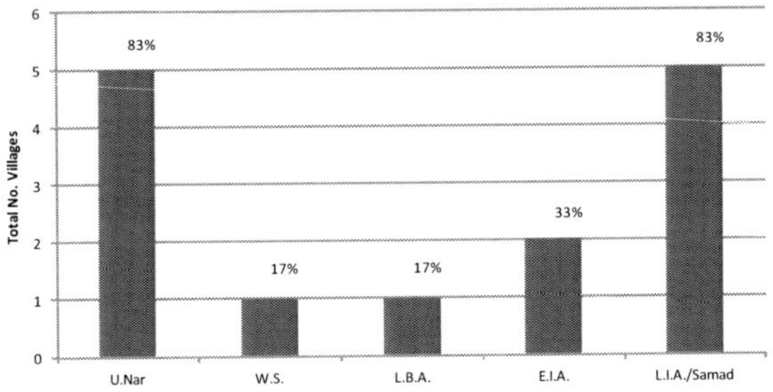

FIGURE 11. *A graph showing a ubiquity analysis of pottery from different periods in the six wadi villages.*

Period	Number of wadi villages yielding pottery (Total 6)	Number of survey areas yielding pottery (Total 69)
U.Nar	5 (83%)	14 (20%)
W.S.	1 (17%)	3 (4%)
W.S.?	0 (0%)	3 (4%)
L.B.A.	1 (17%)	0 (0%)
E.I.A.	2 (33%)	13 (19%)
L.I.A./Samad	5 (83%)	23 (33%)

FIGURE 12. *A table of the ubiquity analysis of pottery from villages and survey collection areas showing the number of villages and survey areas where pottery of different periods was retrieved.*

& Doe 1976: 159–160, 184, fig. 33, pl. 19; Orchard & Stanger 1999: 91–93, fig. 3; Orchard & Orchard 2002: 228–229), Rawḍah (Sites 28 & 29) (de Cardi, Collier & Doe 1976: 160–161, fig. 34) and Bidyah (al-Tikriti 1989: 107–109, pls 78, 83, 90), where only two or three Umm an-Nar towers have been reported.[5] Of course, it is possible that some of these sites might originally have had more towers and that they have since been destroyed, but in either case it seems quite likely that they represent similar, or perhaps slightly smaller, regional centres as the larger sites noted above. At the present time no site of this size is known from the Wādī Andam area.

Further sites are known where only one Umm an-Nar round tower has been reported; examples of such sites are Tell Abraq (Potts 1991: 21–25), Maysar (Weisgerber 1981: 198–200, Abbs. 24–27, 29), Amlah Site 2 (de Cardi, Collier & Doe 1976: 111–112, fig. 10), Kalba (Carter 1997: 91–94), and about six others. Al-Ghoryeen makes a useful contribution to this list as it is, along with Maysar, probably the best preserved of these sites. As has been noted above, many of the remains at the site are easily visible on the surface allowing a clear understanding of the size, layout, and organization of the site without excavation. This presents an excellent archaeological opportunity to explore the spatial organization of such a site in some detail.

It is tempting to consider the single-towered sites as a second, lower level in the settlement hierarchy of the Umm an-Nar period. The size and layout of al-Ghoryeen seems to argue for this as it is clearly a site of limited dimensions — much smaller than al-Khashbah — with only one cemetery, and one, or perhaps two, occupation areas of relatively limited extent. Arguing against such an interpretation would be the fact that, at present, there appear to be fewer single-towered sites than there are multi-towered sites. The reason for this is not clear and might relate to the nature of archaeological preservation and discovery, but it might also argue against a hierarchical relationship between single and multi-towered sites.

Five of the six wadi villages explored in the course of the Wādī Andam survey by al-Jahwari (2008: 111–124) present significant questions about the nature of Umm an-Nar settlement. These sites appear to suggest that there were large numbers of small Umm an-Nar agricultural villages scattered across the landscape that did not have an Umm an-Nar round tower at all. Clearly, this is a difficult, if not impossible, issue to resolve with certainty. This is because it is possible that many round towers might have been completely destroyed by later activity such as agriculture and stone robbing. Nonetheless, the level of preservation of monuments and surface remains at the five wadi villages visited by the survey suggests that there has not been undue destruction and robbing and there is therefore a good chance that many, if not all, of these sites never possessed a round tower.

If this is the case, what does it tell us? Does it perhaps suggest that Umm an-Nar round towers were themselves relatively rare symbols of local or regional power that extended some distance from the sites where the towers were actually located and incorporated possibly quite large numbers of smaller village sites? This is certainly the interpretation that seems, at present, most likely based on the data collected by the Wādī Andam survey. It must also be remembered that very few small sites have been visited and investigated so far. As further work progresses, the density, distribution, and nature of these smaller sites should become clearer.

[5] Four towers are reported at Firq by Orchard and Orchard (2002: 228–229), but there appears to be some doubt over the identification of one or two of these.

In summary, the evidence from the Wādī Andam survey, when considered in its regional context, might be interpreted as pointing towards a three-tier hierarchical Umm an-Nar settlement structure, with perhaps relatively few, large multi-towered sites at the apex above a second tier of smaller sites with one tower, which were themselves situated above a third and lowest tier of small agricultural villages with no round towers.

Of course there are many sites that cannot be fitted into this simple schema, most obviously the site of Umm an-Nar island itself, the site of Raʾs al-Jinz being another. These coastal sites may have had a specific function or range of functions — perhaps related to their coastal locations — that set them outside the normal hierarchy of rural settlement.

This model is clearly very simplistic and tentative. It is presented here simply as a working hypothesis, intended to focus debate on a number of issues related to the full range of Umm an-Nar settlement that has not, thus far, been widely considered. It is important that further investigation continues into all levels of Umm an-Nar settlement, including the lowest, if our understanding of the structure and nature of settlement in this period is to advance.

Acknowledgements

Nasser al-Hinaei is thanked for his assistance with drawing the figures in this paper.

References

Carter R.
1997. The Wadi Suq period in south-east Arabia: a reappraisal in the light of excavations at Kalba, UAE. *Proceedings of the Seminar for Arabian Studies* 27: 87–98.

Cleuziou S.
1984. Oman Peninsula and its Relations Eastward during the Third Millennium. Pages 371–394 in B.B. Lal & S.P. Gupta (eds), *Frontiers of the Indus Civilization*. New Delhi: Books & Books for the Indian Archaeological Society and the Indian History & Culture Society.

Cleuziou S. & Tosi M.
2007. *In the Shadow of the Ancestors: the Prehistoric Foundations of the Early Arabian Civilization in Oman*. Muscat: Ministry of Heritage and Culture.

de Cardi B.
1977. Surface Collections from the Oman Survey, 1976. *Journal of Oman Studies* 3/1: 59–70.

de Cardi B., Collier S. & Doe D.B.
1976. Excavations and Survey in Oman, 1974–1975. *Journal of Oman Studies* 2: 101–199.

Frifelt K.
1985. Further Evidence of the Third Millennium B.C. Town at Bāt in Oman. *Journal of Oman Studies* 7: 89–104.

al-Jahwari N.S.
2008. Settlement Patterns, Development and Cultural Change in Northern Oman Peninsula: A multi-tiered approach to the analysis of long-term settlement trends. PhD thesis, Durham University. [Unpublished].

al-Jahwari N.S. & Kennet D.
2008. A field methodology for the quantification of ancient settlement in an Arabian context. *Proceedings of the Seminar for Arabian Studies* 38: 203–214.

Meadow R.H., Humphries J.H. & Hastings A.
1976. Exploration in Oman, 1973 and 1975: Prehistoric Settlements and Ancient Copper Smelting with its Comparative Aspects in Iran. Pages 110–129 in F. Bagherzadeh (ed.), *Proceedings of the IV Annual Symposium of Archaeological Research in Iran, 3–8 November, 1975*. Tehran: Iranian Center for Archaeological Research.

Orchard J.
2000. Oasis town or tower hamlets? Bisya and the al-Hajar period. *Proceedings of the Seminar for Arabian Studies* 30: 165–175.
Orchard J. & Orchard J.
2002. The Work of the Al Hajar project in Oman. *Journal of Oman Studies* 12: 227–234.
Orchard J. & Stanger G.
1994. Third millennium oasis towns and the environmental constraints on settlement in the al-Hajar region. *Iraq* 56: 63–100.
1999. Al-Hajar oasis towns again. *Iraq* 61: 89–119.
Potts D.T.
1990. *The Arabian Gulf in Antiquity*. i. Oxford: Clarendon Press.
1991. *Further excavations at Tell Abraq: the 1990 season*. Copenhagen: Munksgaard.
al-Tikriti W.Y.
1989. The Excavations at Bidya, Fujairah: The 3rd and 2nd Millennia BC Culture. *Archaeology of the United Arab Emirates* 5: 101–114.
Weisgerber G.
1978. Evidence of Ancient Mining Sites in Oman: a Preliminary Report. *Journal of Oman Studies* 4: 15–28.
1980. "...und Kupfer in Oman" — Das Oman-Projekt des Deutschen Bergbau-Museums. *Der Anschnitt* 32/2–3: 62–110.
1981. Mehr als Kupfer in Oman: Ergebnisse der Expedition 1981. *Der Anschnitt* 33/5–6: 174–263.
Yule P.
1993. Excavations at Samad Al Shan 1987–1991, Summary. *Proceedings of the Seminar for Arabian Studies* 23: 141–153.
2001. *Die Gräberfelder in Samad al-Shān (Sultanat Oman) — Materialien zu einer Kulturgesichte*. (Deutsches Archäologisches Institut Orient-Abteilung. Orient-Archäologie, Band 4). Rahden: Verlag Marie Leidorf.

Authors' addressses
Nasser al-Jahwari, Department of Archaeology, College of Arts and Social Sciences, Sultan Qaboos University, PO Box 42, 123 Al-Khod, Sultanate of Oman.

e-mail jahwari@squ.edu.om

Derek Kennet, Department of Archaeology, Durham University, Durham DH1 3LE, UK.

e-mail derek.kennet@durham.ac.uk

Proceedings of the Seminar for Arabian Studies 40 (2010): 213–226

Mapping Maṣnaᶜat Māryah: using GIS to reconstruct the development of a multi-period site in the highlands of Yemen

Krista Lewis, Lamya Khalidi, William Isenberger & Ali Sanabani

Summary

The 2008 field season of the University of Arkansas at Little Rock (UALR) Māryah Archaeological Project was dedicated to creating a detailed, three-dimensional map of the 40.4 ha highland site of Maṣnaᶜat Māryah. This site was occupied from the Neolithic to the Himyarite period. In addition to precise mapping of the topography, buildings, streets, water cisterns, and other cultural features visible on the surface, we conducted a comprehensive assessment of the distribution of cultural artefacts across the site's surface. This work has also clarified Maṣnaᶜat Māryah's cultural chronology as it developed from a town with a focus on ceremonial space in the Bronze and Iron Ages, to a strategic elite urban production centre in the Himyarite period. The artefact densities and distributions systematically mapped out across the site reflect a number of processes that allow us to understand the use of space through time. We have identified evident access routes for local obsidian procurement and trade, specialized areas for ironworking, drainage patterns, and water management strategies, as well as areas currently heavily affected by, and prone to, erosion. This paper explains the mapping strategy developed for Maṣnaᶜat Māryah and presents the implications of the data for the spatial, socio-political, and economic transformation of this site over several millennia.

Keywords: Yemen highlands, GIS, mapping, Late Prehistoric, Himyarite

As a unique site with urban proportions and well-preserved remains, Maṣnaᶜat Māryah (DS3) ranks among the most important cultural heritage sites in Yemen. The site is well known for the published fourteen-line inscription located on one of the town's major gates (Müller 1978), but little archaeological research has previously been undertaken there. Although the peak of occupation at this mountain-top site was during the late pre-Islamic Himyarite period, our work at the site has shown that the area was in use as early as the Neolithic period (Lewis & Khalidi 2008: 224). This research is a part of the larger Dhamar Survey Project, which has been operating in the Yemeni highlands since 1994 (Edens, Wilkinson & Barratt 2000; Gibson & Wilkinson 1995; Wilkinson & Edens 1999; Wilkinson, Edens & Barratt 2001; Wilkinson, Edens & Gibson 1997; Wilkinson 1997; 2003).

In previous field seasons we completed intensive archaeological survey of an 18 km^2 area surrounding the central site of Maṣnaᶜat Māryah. We recorded an array of ancient sites and features covering all periods from the Neolithic onwards (Lewis & Khalidi 2008: 217–220). The findings of these surveys allowed us to place this major Himyarite centre within its wider regional, chronological, and landscape context. This having been accomplished, we focused our work more firmly on the main site itself. The UALR Archaeological Mission's 2008 field season was primarily dedicated to the major goal of creating a detailed, three-dimensional map of the main site. Documentation and mapping of significant archaeological sites such as Maṣnaᶜat Māryah both provide essential direct information about life in ancient towns and serve as the keystone for all future research there.

The map created during the 2008 season (Fig. 1) records in fine detail the topography of Maṣnaᶜat Māryah and the precise locations of all the buildings, streets, water cisterns, and other cultural features visible on the surface of this impressive 40.4 ha plateau site. In addition, we carried out a comprehensive survey assessment of the distribution of cultural artefacts across the site's surface. Artefacts recorded included ceramics, lithics, iron slag, shell, bone, grinding stones, and decorated architectural fragments.

This paper explains the methodologies used for the mapping and systematic surface examination of the site of Maṣnaᶜat Māryah and the results of these endeavours. The data collected during this fieldwork were processed and displayed using ArcGIS and AutoCad and serve

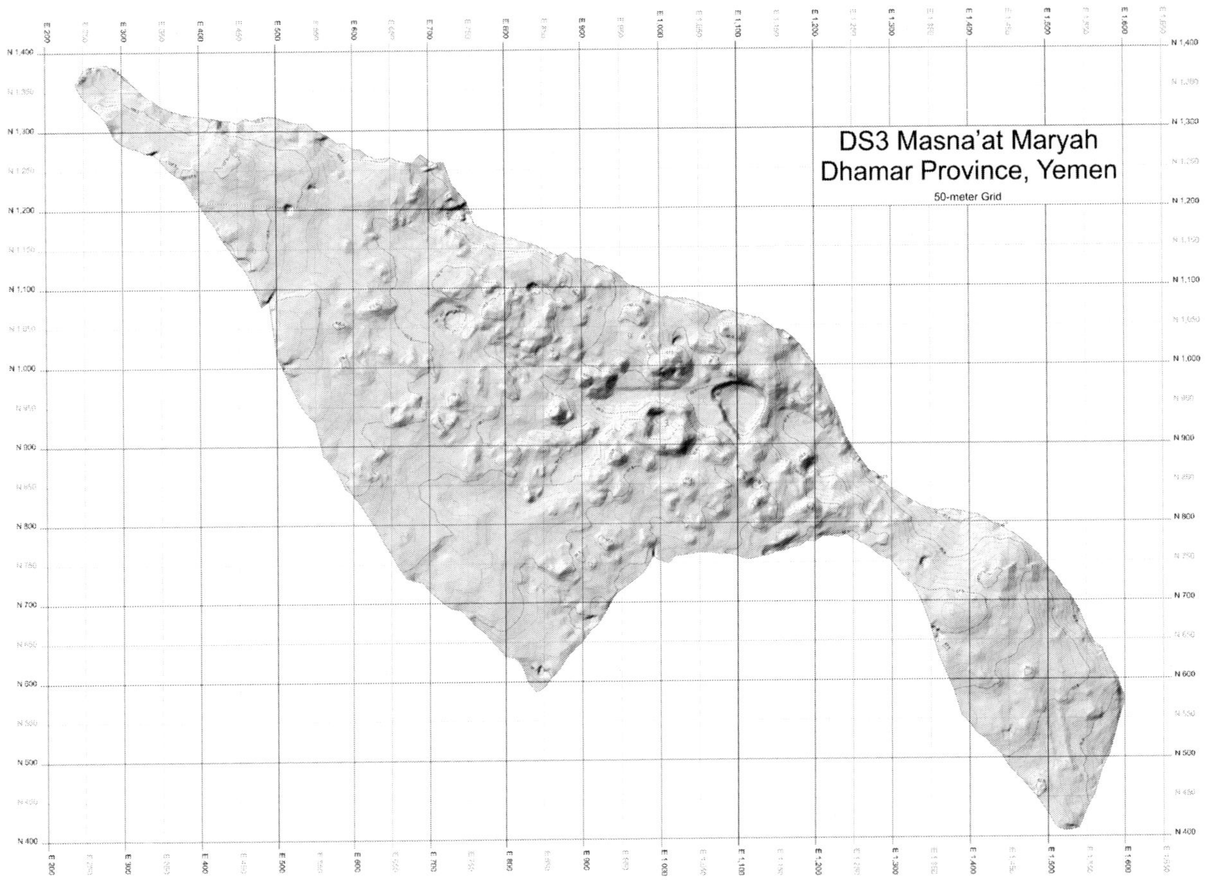

Figure 1. *A map of Maṣnaᶜat Māryah with shaded relief, 50 cm contour lines, and permanent site grid.*

to illustrate spatial patterns in the settlement, ancient activity areas, and taphonomic processes at the site. The methodological strategies employed serve as a non-destructive means of establishing the dynamics of ancient occupation, providing us with data for reconstructing the major economic and cultural strategies that persisted or changed throughout the occupation cycle of this multi-period site.

Mapping methodology

The topographic and geographic data for the site was mainly collected with a Topcon Odyssey-E RTK GPS system. The "RTK GPS" produces data with sub-centimetre accuracy and was used to establish permanent site data and a grid system, to map the topography of the site, and to record the site's cultural features. Additional data collection was acquired using a total station.

Fieldwork for the Maṣnaᶜat Māryah map took approximately four weeks, with over 10,000 points recorded with the RTK GPS alone. Although the data collection was extremely fast paced, care was also taken to note critical cultural and architectural features, and information pertaining to every geographical point recorded.

The RTK GPS was initially used to record an array of points across the site at 10 m spacing, which formed the base for the topographic modelling. Additional points were then taken along topographic and cultural break lines to allow us better to define the limits, elevation, and location of each structure, street, or feature and ensure that all cultural features could be sharply and accurately depicted. The resulting data allow us to produce topographic maps with fine contour intervals as accurate as 20 cm, as well as shaded topographic reliefs of the site.

Following the completion of the base topographic map, we mapped additional key layers of spatial data for the site such as roads, megaliths, cisterns, buildings, and other archaeological features (Fig. 2). We also began a

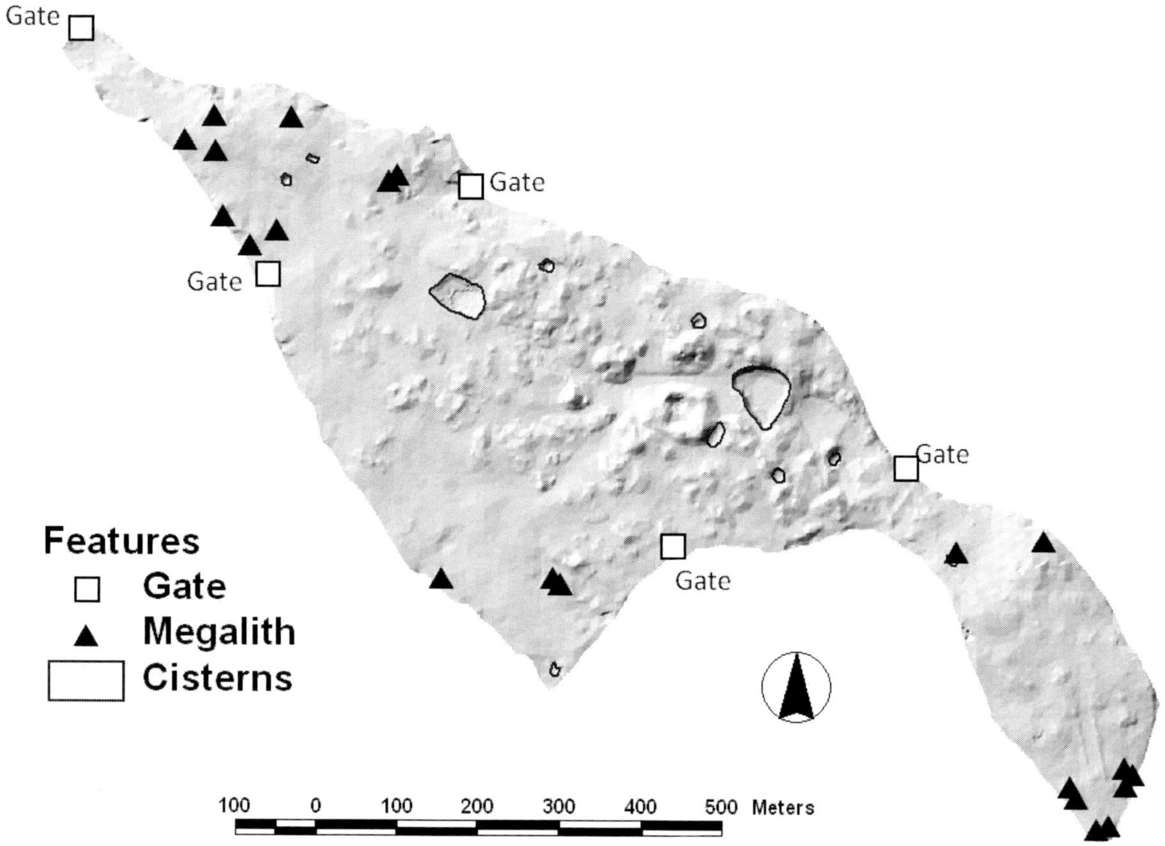

Figure 2. *A map of Maṣnaᶜat Māryah showing the locations of water cisterns, major city gates, and megalithic features.*

programme of photogrammetric recording at Maṣnaᶜat Māryah. Dramatic features on the site, including the inscription gate, the Sedd al-Kabir (al-Sadd al-Kabīr) dam and selected megalithic elements were modelled in three dimensions using high-resolution digital images taken with an SLR camera and spatially fixed with photo targets and the reflector-less total station.

Results of the mapping project

The results of this mapping project are dynamic, multi-layered datasets which enable us to manipulate and display the varied physical and cultural elements that make up the site of Maṣnaᶜat Māryah. The fully digital nature of the data means that not only can we generate a wide range of specialized maps as needed for analyses, we will also continue to add to and develop this spatial database as research questions evolve over time and with future seasons of fieldwork at the site.

On the topographic map, the most monumental buildings and mounds are clearly visible in the central area of the site and are divided into several major complexes partitioned by wide roadways running between them. This area is characterized by extremely high rubble mounds often strewn with large hewn stones, which are sometimes inscribed. The mounds often have visible wall alignments, formal stepped entranceways or courtyards, and have a distinct cultural signature that clearly belongs to the Himyarite period. These structures and spaces are the main locus of Himyarite occupation on the site and are likely related to administrative and/or religious functions.

The shaded relief and contour maps confirm that the architectural dynamic in the south-east appendix of the plateau strongly diverges from the central downtown area. In this part of the site the mounding is lower, the buildings are less densely spaced, and the visible structural remains are primarily composed of massive upright stone slabs that bound large spaces with minimal amounts of associated rubble. The most dramatic feature in this part of Maṣnaᶜat Māryah is visible on the map as two long parallel raised mounds bisecting this section of the plateau lengthwise. On the ground, this is a long, double upright stone slab "processional" that runs most of the length of the appendix and was accessed through two formal entrances to the south and to the north. On either side of this 20 m wide and 145 m long route are a series of widely spaced buildings also built of large stone slabs. Its unique placement and characteristics suggest that it served as a ceremonial street. It leads to the southernmost tip of the site where the remains of two prominent megalithic features stand perched at the edge of the plateau.

Although excavation will be required for absolute verification, the architectural style, surface artefact distribution, and taphonomic condition of the remains in this part of the site have led us to hypothesize that many of the features and buildings are pre-Himyarite and probably Bronze or Early Iron Age in date. However, judging by the fact that it remained intact even after the site reached its peak occupation under the kingdom's rule, the ceremonial use of this area of the site appears to have persisted into the Himyarite period.

The mapping programme also allowed us to gain a better understanding of and document Maṣnaᶜat Māryah holistically, including the open areas of the site without visible structural remains and other key town features such as the city wall and its gates. Equally impressive on the maps are the topographic depressions dotting the site, which acted as water reservoirs (*birak*, sing. *birkah*) for occupants of the plateau. The inhabitants of the site used a combination of natural topography and decisive engineering to secure and preserve precious water resources. Many of these, including the largest main *birkah*, Sedd al-Kabir, had monumental walls and other features built around them during the Himyarite period.

Surface collection

An additional advantage of the rapid and comprehensive mapping methods employed at Maṣnaᶜat Māryah in 2008, was the ability to conduct an assessment of surface artefact distributions simultaneously with the topographic mapping. In order to gain a systematic picture of material culture across the site, we designated collection units every 50 m along the same north–south transects used to collect the topographic data. These units were circular in shape and 2 m in diameter. Within each collection unit all cultural material was documented, including ceramics, bone, lithics, shell, iron slag, and distinctive architectural fragments. Most of the artefacts were recorded on site and returned to their original provenance rather than collected. Identifications of diagnostic pottery sherds, for instance, were made in the field according to a coded ceramic typology. However, samples of selected artefact classes, such as obsidian and iron slag, were collected for laboratory analyses. Special finds such as worked metal fragments, animal figurines, beads, and architectural fragments were also collected for photography, drawing, and curating in the Dhamar Museum.

All surface collection data was entered into a specially created database and plotted into a site GIS along with the spatial map data. As a result, we are now able to visually analyse the distribution patterns of the various artefact categories, which allow us better to understand the ancient function of archaeological structures, features, and spaces as well as the effects of stone robbing and erosion. We can use this data to identify places where specific production or consumption activities were taking place as well as to gain a better understanding of the chronology and taphonomy of the site. In the following sections, we briefly present some preliminary findings of our ongoing analyses of the 2008 systematic surface artefact assessment.

Ceramics

To facilitate the collection of diagnostic pottery and as a means of training Yemeni and foreign archaeology students, we established a standard bilingual reference typology of Himyarite ceramics for the highland region. Using ceramic types generated from pottery recovered in the 2001 excavations at the nearby Himyarite site of DS20 (Lewis 2005) as a baseline, we compiled a catalogue of, and assigned type numbers to, the most commonly recurring ceramic forms of the period. In addition to the DS20 material, we added newly recognized ceramic forms collected from Maṣnaᶜat Māryah to create a comprehensive ceramic field guide. This typology was put to use immediately in the field in 2008 to record the ceramic type distribution across the site. It will also provide the foundation for a standardized ceramic manual for future surveys and excavations in the central Yemeni highlands. During surface collection, ceramic type numbers were recorded in field notes along with sizes and total numbers of sherds. Only unknown types were collected for drawing and documentation in the laboratory. In addition to Himyarite diagnostics, we

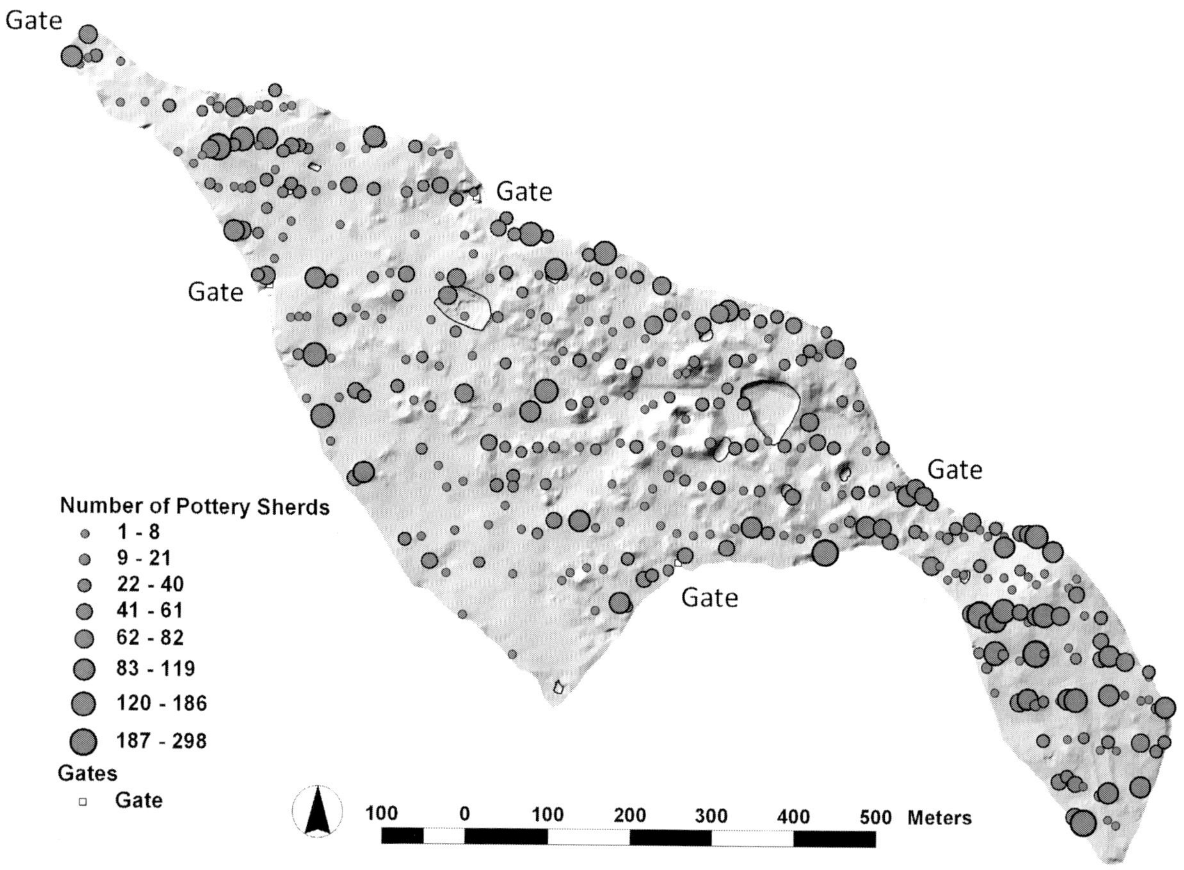

FIGURE 3. *A map of the ceramic sherd distribution across Maṣnaᶜat Māryah, with graduated symbols indicating the total number of sherds collected.*

also recorded and collected sherds from Maṣnaᶜat Māryah that date to the Bronze and Iron Ages.

Looking at map plots of the total number of ceramic sherds across Maṣnaᶜat Māryah (Fig. 3) we note that higher densities are concentrated along the perimeter of the site. This distribution can be explained by two factors. In many locations along the edges of the site, the archaeological deposits are suffering from erosion due to heavy summer rains and water runoff. The likelihood of recovering exposed small artefacts is therefore increased. However, this pattern is not simply a factor of erosion, since a number of these same perimeter areas of the site are also the locations of extensive ancient trash middens. In contrast, surface ceramics are less prevalent in the high-mounded areas of the site, where the sherds are more likely to remain buried in deposits and under structural remains. There is also an interesting pattern of a higher density of pottery sherds in the south-east appendix area of the site.

The effect of erosion patterns becomes even clearer when we plot the sherds according to size categories. We observe that the smaller the sherds, the higher the densities around the edges of the site and in other areas of erosion and water drainage. As the size categories become larger, we generally observe fewer sherds across the site, but those in the "larger than 10 cm^2" category are found as often within enclosed building complexes as they are in areas of acute erosion. The map of all of the diagnostic pottery recorded illustrates a more even density distribution across the site than with the small sherd fragments, although the highest concentrations remain in the areas subject to the most acute erosion. Detailed discussion and analysis of the ceramic types and their distribution patterns is beyond the scope of the current report, and will be published separately at a later date.

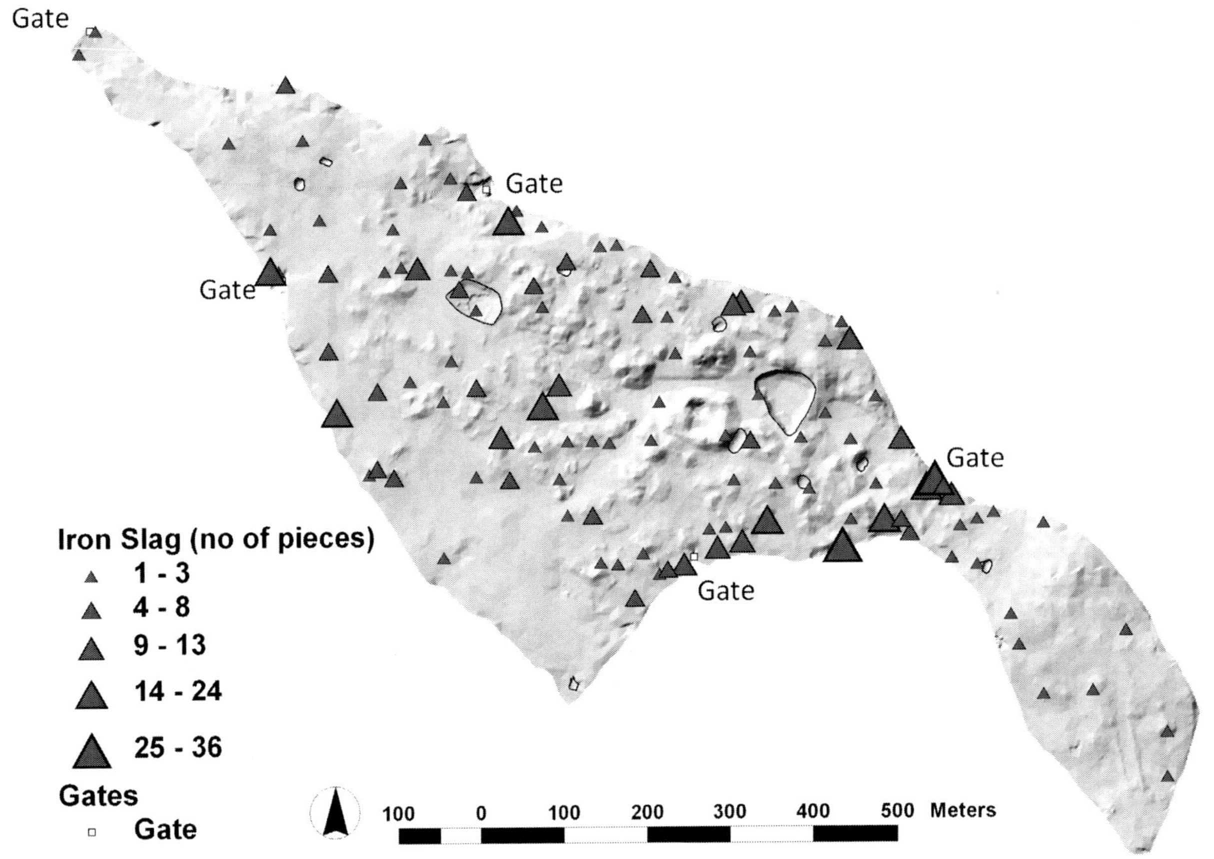

Figure 4. *The distribution of iron slag at Maṣnaᶜat Māryah.*

Bone

Fragments of ancient bone are distributed across the entire site of Maṣnaᶜat Māryah. Bone was recovered more often from deposits that are currently being exposed through erosion. Due to the inherent fragility of bone, once exposed it breaks up and disintegrates quite rapidly on the surface of the plateau.

Unlike bone and ceramics, we observe that other recorded material distributions are more concentrated in certain areas of the site than others, and in patterns that do not appear to be significantly skewed by the forces of erosion. These distributions can indicate where production areas were located, what function different spaces and structures had, which areas of the site were utilized during different chronological periods, and illuminate an array of other important cultural and economic issues.

Worked metal and iron slag

We have previously noted the abundant presence of iron slag at the site of Maṣnaᶜat Māryah (Lewis & Khalidi 2008: 221). Very few sites of ancient Near Eastern metalworking have been identified and documented (Veldhuijzen & Rehren 2007: 189–191), so the clear indications that such activities took place here are extremely significant. When we look at the distribution of the waste product (Fig. 4), we observe that although slag is found in significant quantities over most of the site, the largest concentrations are localized in and around the perimeters of the Himyarite centre of the site. This distribution suggests the presence of iron production, likely both smelting and smithing, on the outskirts of the densely inhabited central zone. Interestingly, worked metal artefacts, although only occasionally found, are also mainly

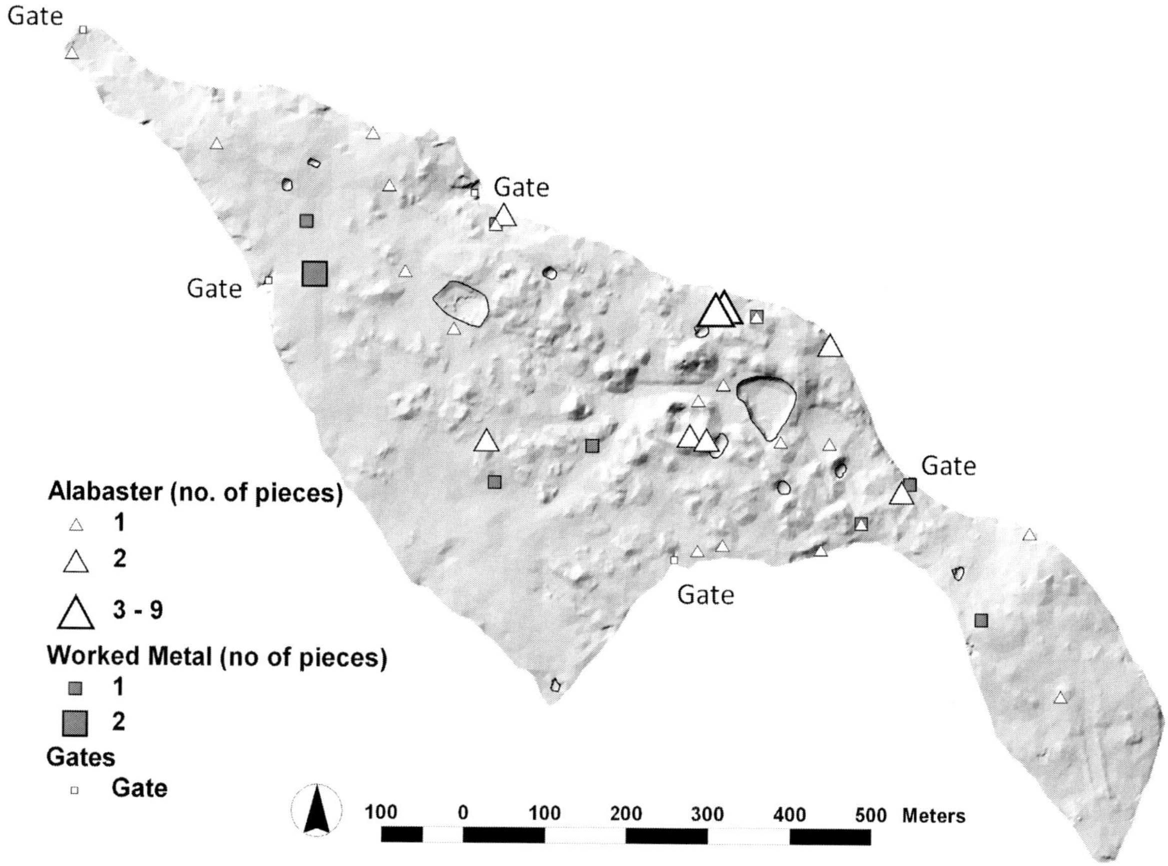

Figure 5. *Worked metal and alabaster distributions concentrate in the Himyarite centre of Maṣnaʿat Māryah.*

restricted to the fringes of the main Himyarite centre of the site.

The mapping of artefact distributions (Fig. 5) has enabled us to confirm previous hypotheses that metalworking was a major production of Maṣnaʿat Māryah during the Himyarite Period, and that production took place in open areas outside the perimeter of the administrative centre. Now that we have identified areas of possible metal production, future work will allow for the elaboration of the nature of production, specialization within the industry, and the relationship between its role as an important iron production centre in south-west Arabia and its growth as a settlement implicated in trade.

Semi-precious stones

Alabaster is another material that was especially valued and utilized in the Himyarite period for the production of elite objects such as bowls, goblets, altars, and architectural embellishments. Its restricted distribution within the Himyarite centre, which is dominated by religious and administrative buildings, reflects this fact.

In contrast, materials that are more commonly associated with earlier periods, especially the Bronze and Iron Ages, are concentrated in but not restricted to the south-east appendix. These include agate, carnelian, and chalcedony (Fig. 6). The majority of samples recorded for these semi-precious stones were used for bead production, judging by the identification of several bead blanks and surface collections of beads made from these materials. Carnelian, commonly found in Bronze and early Iron Age tombs in South Arabia (Caton Thompson 1944; Cleuziou & Tosi 1997; de Maigret 1997; Inizan 1995; Steimer-Herbet 2001), are concentrated in the south-east area and what appears to be a predominantly older part of

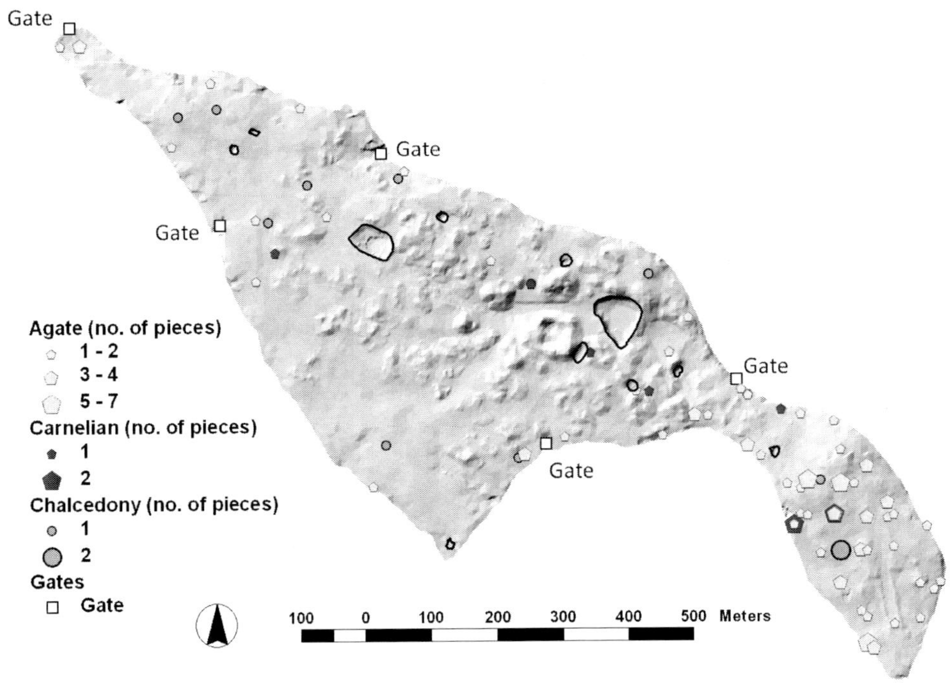

FIGURE 6. *The semi-precious stones, agate, carnelian, and chalcedony, were found primarily in the south-eastern appendix area of Maṣnaᶜat Māryah.*

the site with a ceremonial and even funerary function that persisted into subsequent periods of occupation.

Obsidian

A number of criteria were involved in the analyses of obsidian across the site of Maṣnaᶜat Māryah. Obsidian recovered during the surface collection was classed into three main groups: worked, unworked, and brecciated. Within each type, we recorded the numbers of pieces or nodules, size categories, and the weight of obsidian from each collection unit. Worked obsidian was collected and a typo-technological study of each fragment was carried out.

Brecciated obsidian nodules were particularly dense across the site (Fig. 7). These non-worked nodules that originate in the older, more minor Oligocene sources, are of poor quality and cannot be knapped as they have long been in a process of devitrification. However, they are found in the local ceramics as temper, especially in Bronze and Iron Age pottery and were used in large quantities in Himyarite and early Islamic *qudād* (a lime waterproofing material). This was used as a waterproofing plaster (*qudād*) to line water reservoirs and water channels and also to plaster the walls of public buildings. A number of Himyarite water channels and features that we discovered across the site as a result of exposure from erosion or looting are plastered with thick layers of *qudād* embedded with small to large nodules of brecciated obsidian. While brecciated obsidian is found across the site, the highest concentrations occur in the Himyarite centre and especially in the vicinity of large public buildings where plaster would have been common. It is also dense along the ceremonial walkway in the eastern appendix, suggesting that the large megalithic slabs bounding this massive feature may have been plastered by the Himyarites, perhaps as a renovation long after its original construction.

The highest numbers of unworked obsidian nodules (not including the brecciated obsidian) are found along the south-east appendix and near the gates of the site. However, a map of the weight, rather than the number of pieces of unworked obsidian nodules, reveals a more even distribution of the material, but with somewhat larger concentrations in heavily built areas and primarily across the eastern half of the site.

When we map the distribution of numbers of worked (knapped) obsidian pieces (Fig. 8), we observe that there are high densities in several places; throughout the south-east appendix, around the megalithic elements of the site, and near the city gates, especially the northern and eastern

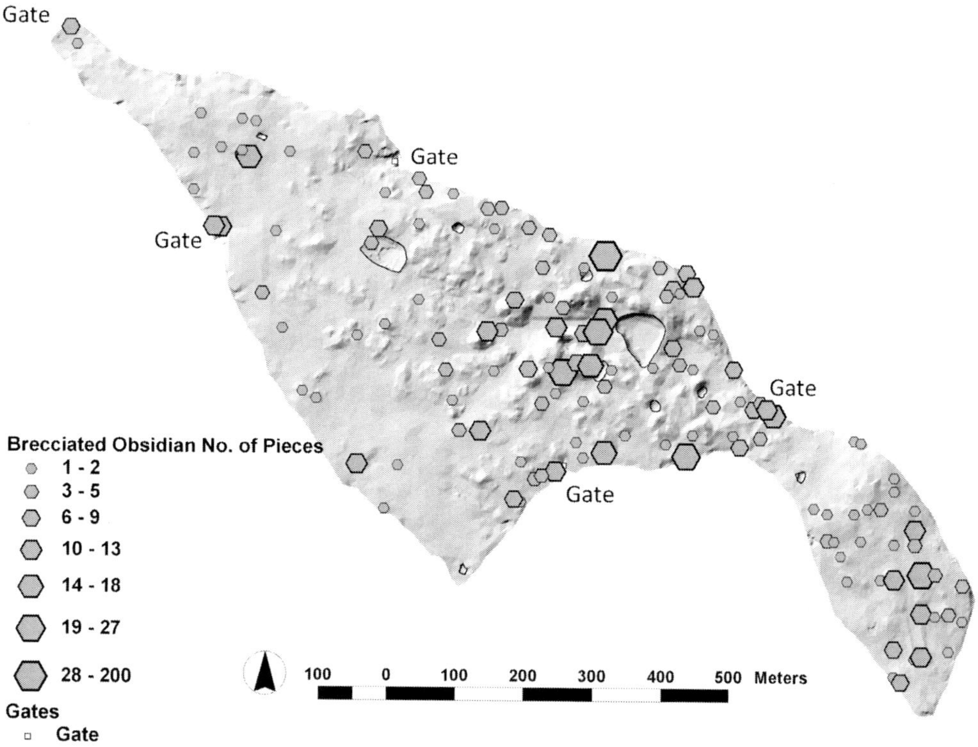

Figure 7. *A map of the distribution of brecciated obsidian at Maṣnaᶜat Māryah, plotted by the number of pieces.*

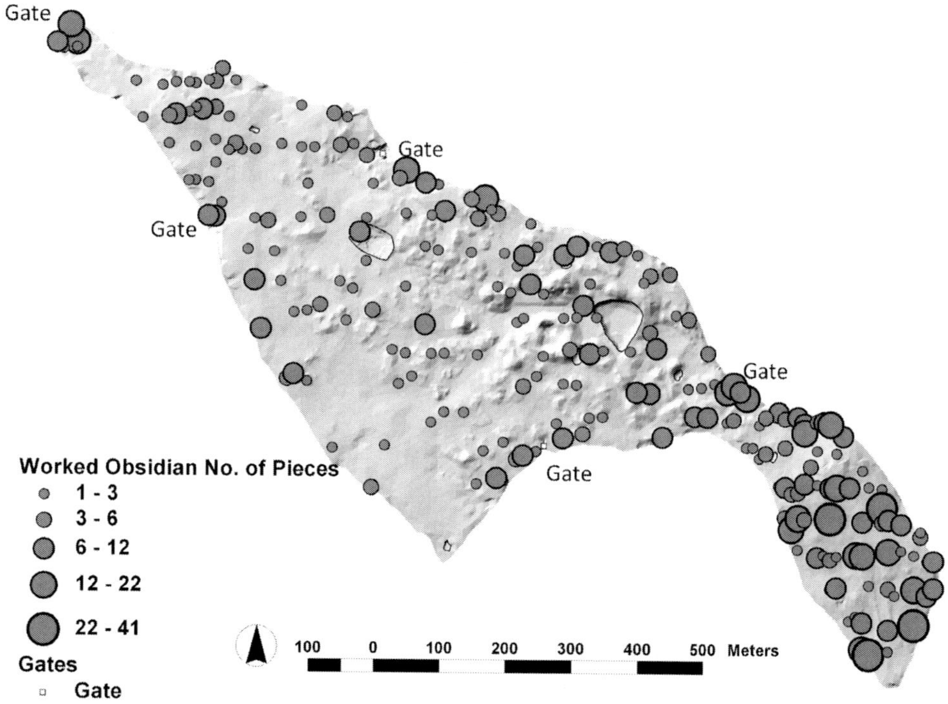

Figure 8. *Worked obsidian distribution at Maṣnaᶜat Māryah, plotted by the number of pieces.*

gates. There is not much difference in the locations of the heavy concentrations of worked obsidian when we plot the distribution by weight rather than number.

Because obsidian was plentiful in the region, and its local production for simple tools like those found at Maṣnaᶜat Māryah could have been carried out on a need to use basis by each household, it is helpful to ascertain areas of higher concentrations of the material. The fact that the highest concentrations of obsidian do appear to be in areas of the site that have older architectural elements, is significant especially in that its production for tool blanks (flakes and bladelets) was most exercised before the introduction of metal, and thus in pre-Himyarite contexts. That higher densities of obsidian are found in the vicinity of the major gates onto the site is also noteworthy, and becomes increasingly interesting when looked at in conjunction with geochemical studies of the origin of the material, which were made in order to understand how certain gates functioned in the trade of goods.

In previous seasons, surveys in the Māryah region provided a window into the local exploitation of obsidian as early as the Neolithic period. Neolithic presence in the area is attested by the typo-technological characteristics of obsidian bifaces found on survey. We have also identified obsidian working on local sites dating to the Bronze Age, Iron Age, and Himyarite periods (Lewis & Khalidi 2008: 222–224). Our systematic survey programmes likewise have given us an opportunity to document and sample natural obsidian sources in the region. For example, the Jirāb al-Souf source is located along the Kowlat Shair (Kawlah Shāᵓib) volcano to the north-west of Māryah. The proximity of this obsidian source to Maṣnaᶜat Māryah and the variability of the quality of the obsidian present along its flows emphasized the need for a more comprehensive look at local exchange patterns of this intensively utilized raw material, as well as the origins of the archaeological specimens.

Through a collaboration between the newly initiated Volcanological and Archaeological Program for Obsidian Research (VAPOR) directed by Khalidi, and the UALR Māryah Archaeological Project directed by Lewis, we are able to report conclusive geochemical data (soon to be published) which we have applied to the distribution of this raw material across the site of Maṣnaᶜat Māryah as well as in its immediate hinterland. In addition to the well-known Quaternary obsidian outcrops of the Jabal Isbīl and Lisi (Lisī) complex which loom on Maṣnaᶜat Māryah's eastern horizon, are the newly sourced outcrops of Jirāb al-Souf and Yafaᵓ Ridge. The relative proximity of these two sources to the Māryah area has enabled us for the first time comprehensively to map out localized patterns of highland obsidian procurement and exchange (Fig. 9).This data shows that the Yafaᵓ source was the major local provider of obsidian to the sites from which obsidian was analysed. In the case of Maṣnaᶜat Māryah, the closer source, Jirāb al Souf, provided the majority of its obsidian, but despite the larger distance to the Yafaᵓ source, Yafaᵓ still remained a major provider. Statistics of the analyses show that DS15, which has Neolithic obsidian bifaces but was also excavated by the DSP and dated to the Iron Age (Wilkinson, Edens & Gibson 1997: 123–127), has a larger percentage of Yafaᵓ obsidian but also exploited the Jirab al-Souf source. The remaining sites appear to have exploited the Yafaᵓ source only. This can partially be explained chronologically with later sites, such as DS15, which were dependent on the large administrative/defensive centre of Maṣnaᶜat Māryah, having been connected with its local access to raw materials. The remaining sites date to earlier periods when obsidian was more intensively used for the manufacture of tools, and the higher quality of the Yafaᵓ source obsidian was a more important factor.

Given this regional perspective on obsidian exchange, we can look at the results of the analyses run on samples from a random selection of archaeological obsidian from the 2008 collection units (Fig. 10). Jirab al-Souf obsidian predominates due to its immediate proximity and is present across the site. However, Yafaᵓ Ridge obsidian appears throughout the south-east appendix and on the northern edge and half of the plateau. Interestingly, the Yafaᵓ Ridge obsidian, located north-west of Maṣnaᶜat Māryah, would have had to arrive to the site from the north gates as, given the topography in the area, they are the closest and only access points onto the Maṣnaᶜat Māryah plateau from the source. Using the multiple overlapping datasets and aided by an active GIS, we are able to offer a glimpse into the life and activity of ancient Maṣnaᶜat Māryah, into the micro socio-economic bustle within its perimeters and in its immediate region, and their transformations through time.

More recent discovery of small local sources of Trap obsidian, which can be found in strata making up the chain of plateaus (Maṣnaᶜat Māryah included) that guard the edge of the escarpment, may reveal more complex local strategies of obsidian exploitation. However, it is now confirmed that Yafaᵓ obsidian supplied most if not all sites in the region, even if minor sources of obsidian lay in closer proximity to them. Minor sources were still exploited but because of their variable quality, were more often used in the Himyarite period, and in building materials and/or for simple tool production.

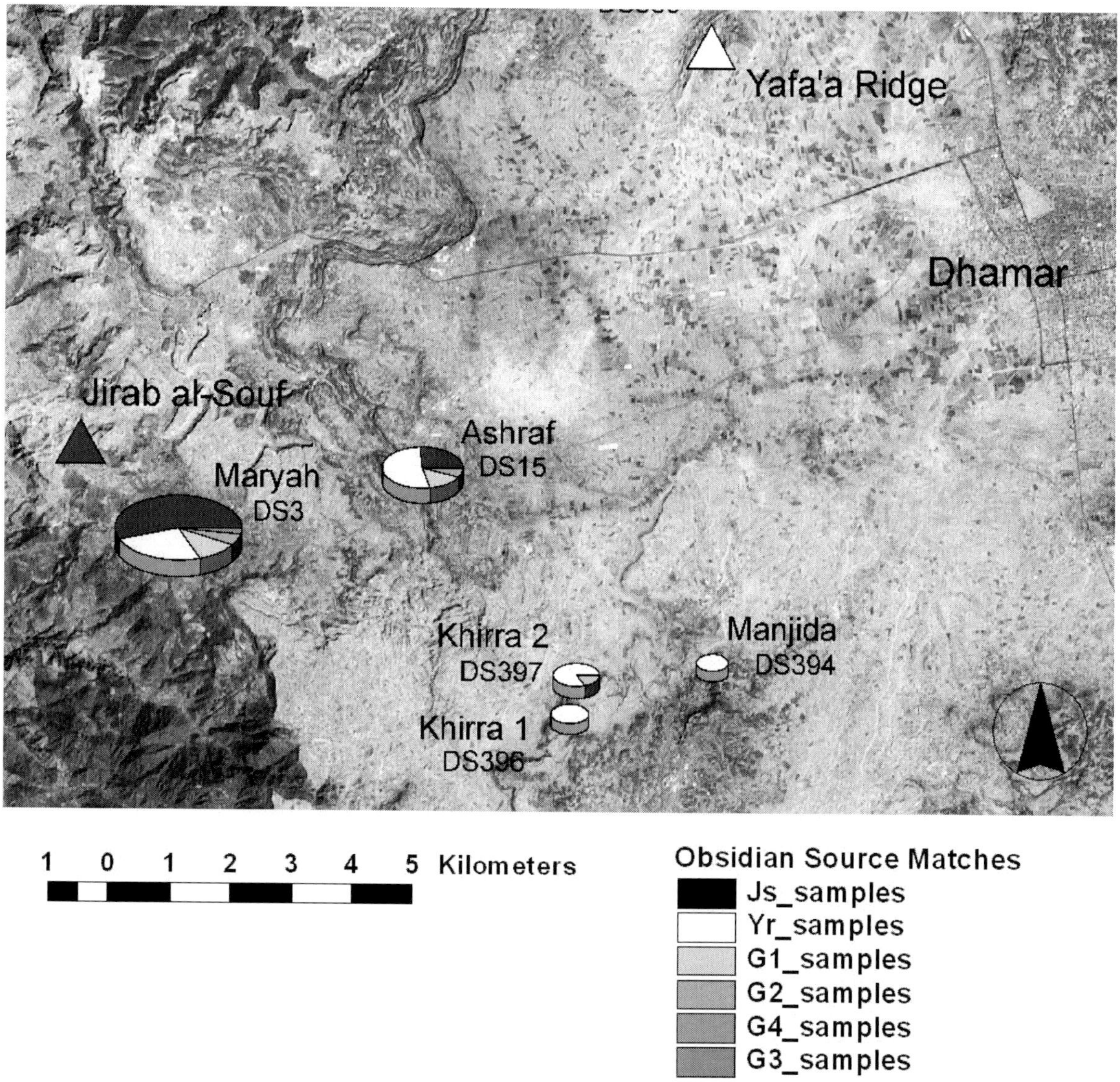

Figure 9. *A satellite image showing the location of local obsidian sources Jirāb al-Souf and Yafaʾ Ridge (triangles), and the percentage of analysed archaeological obsidian originating from these sources (pie charts) at sites in the Maṣnaᶜat Māryah region.*

Implications for site preservation

In addition to recording extant architecture, features, and artefact scatters, we also took care to delimit areas of Maṣnaᶜat Māryah suffering from erosion during the mapping fieldwork. Mapping these areas has not only allowed us better to interpret patterns in the material culture distribution but also to develop an action plan to protect the site. During our summer 2009 field season we applied this data in order to implement an intervention plan to control erosion and protect the archaeological deposits on site. Using traditional highland Yemeni terrace building techniques and together with the co-operation of local villagers, we constructed thirty-nine dry-stone soil-retention walls in critical locations affected by erosion. These walls, stretching in total over 300 m will stabilize critical archaeological deposits in danger of disappearing over the edges of the plateau. Planning for this critical site protection programme would not have been possible without the comprehensive three-

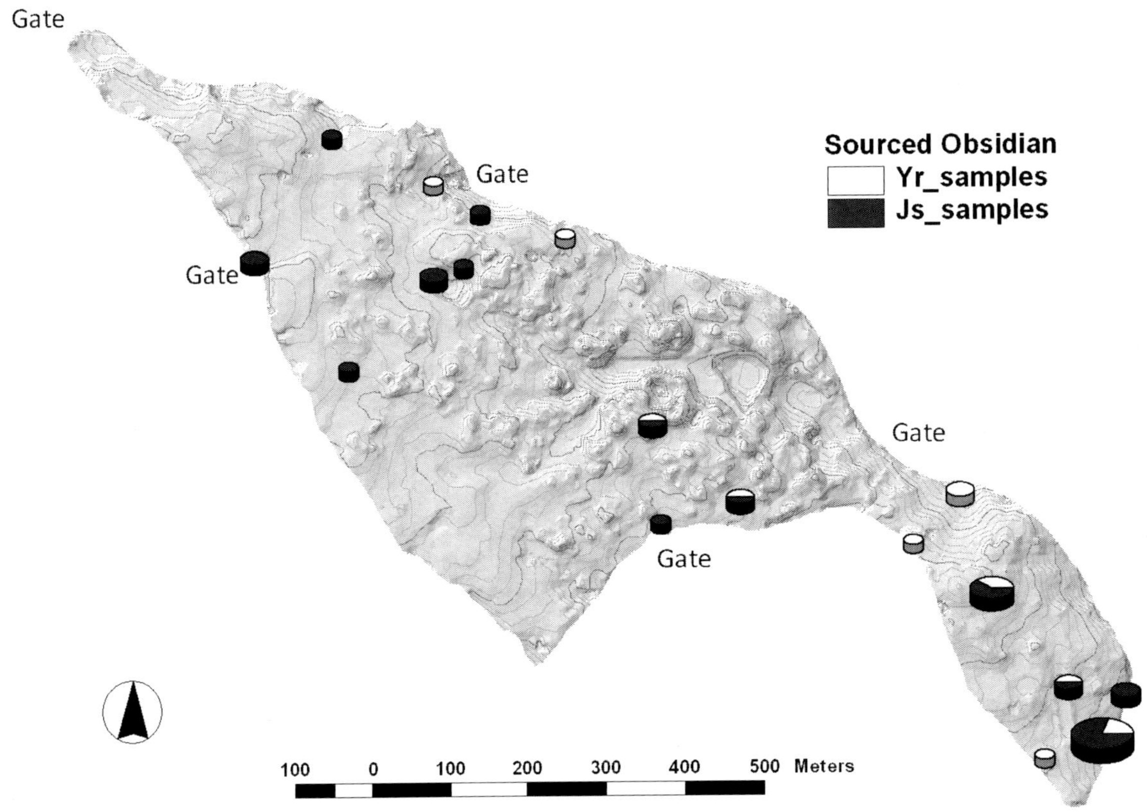

Figure 10. *A map of Maṣnaᶜat Māryah showing the find spots of analysed archaeological obsidian, and the percentage from each of these locations that match the Yafaᵓ and Jirāb al-Souf sources.*

dimensional mapping strategies we implemented at Maṣnaᶜat Māryah. This underlines the importance of such comprehensive mapping strategies for the advancement of effective cultural heritage management in highland Yemen and beyond.

Conclusions

Mapping Maṣnaᶜat Māryah has provided a wealth of information about this complex and very important multi-period highland site. Use of a differential RTK GPS system allowed for rapid and highly accurate recording of topography, structures, spaces, and ancient features. The extensive, systematic surface artefact assessment we undertook is the first study of its kind in Yemen and it has given us an excellent preliminary understanding of cultural processes at Maṣnaᶜat Māryah over time. It enabled us to identify the most promising areas where Himyarite metal smelting and smithing would have occurred, and to lay the framework for a highly accurate spatial reconstruction of the trade, movement, and production of obsidian on and off site. In addition, we were able to confirm certain chronological and spatial trends through the presence of materials indicative of status, function, or period, such as alabaster, primarily used in the Himyarite period in public and religious contexts.

Despite the effects of erosion, bioturbation, and other factors that can cause material culture to shift from its original context on the surface of a site, the multiple layers of data garnered during this project confirm that the Maṣnaᶜat Māryah surface assessment programme has revealed patterns that reflect ancient economic and social forces. Furthermore, systematic precision-mapping projects such as this are of critical importance for cultural heritage management and preservation, particularly in Yemen at this time of increased erosion, looting, and the development-driven destruction of archaeological sites.

Acknowledgements

Maṣnaᶜat Māryah field team members include: Dr Krista Lewis, Director of UALR Māryah Survey; Dr Lamya Khalidi, Assistant Director; Ali Sanabani, Director of the Dhamar Museum; William Isenberger, GIS and mapping specialist; Abdul Basset Qaid Noaman, GOAM; Dan Mahoney, doctoral student, University of Cambridge; Salah al-Komani, University of Dhamar; Ahmad al-Assar, University of Dhamar; Elizabeth Sanders, BA student, UALR; and Basel Khalil, UALR. The 2008 season was sponsored by the University of Arkansas at Little Rock, USA and the General Organization of Antiquities and Museums, Yemen. The erosion protection work in 2009 was funded by the Social Fund for Economic Development in Yemen.

The VAPOR team members include: Dr Khalidi, Director; Bernard Gratuze, Geochemical Analyses, Director of the IRAMAT-CNRS; Sophie Boucetta, IRAMAT; Dr Clive Oppenheimer, Volcanologist, University of Cambridge; Ali Sanabani, Director of the Dhamar Museum; and Ahmed al-Mosabi, Director of the Zabid Museum. The VAPOR 2008 season was financed by a Fyssen Postdoctoral Fellowship. The Geochemical analyses were made possible thanks to a Plan-Pluri Formation between the CEPAM and the IRAMAT – CNRS.

We would like to thank the Buqasha family, the people of the village of Māryah, and the Sanabani family for their hospitality.

References

Caton Thompson G.
1944. *The Tombs and Moon Temple of Hureidha* (Hadhramaut). Oxford: Oxford University Press.

Cleuziou S. & Tosi M.
1997. Evidence for the use of aromatics in the Early Bronze Age of Oman: Period III at RJ-2 (2300–2200 BC). Pages 57–84 in A. Avanzini (ed.), *Profumi d'Arabia.* Rome: L'Erma di Bretschneider.

de Maigret A.
1997. L'âge du Bronze sur les Hautes-Terres. Pages 34–39 in C. Robin (ed.), *Yémen: au pays de la reine de Saba.* Paris: Flammarion Institut du Monde Arabe.

Edens C., Wilkinson T.J. & Barratt G.
2000. Hammat al-Qa and the roots of urbanism in southwest Arabia. *Antiquity* 74: 854–862.

Gibson M. & Wilkinson T.J.
1995. The Dhamar Plain, Yemen: A Preliminary Study of the Archaeological Landscape. *Proceedings of the Seminar for Arabian Studies* 25: 159–183.

Inizan M.-L.
1995. La cornaline de l'Indus et la voie du Golfe au IIIe millénaire. Pages 125–138 in A. Coubet (ed.), *Cornaline et pierres précieuses: La Méditerranée, de l'Antiquité à l'Islam.* Paris: Musée du Louvre.

Lewis K.
2005. The Himyarite site of al-Adhla and its implications for economy and chronology of Early Historic highland Yemen. *Proceedings of the Seminar for Arabian Studies* 35: 129–141.

Lewis K. & Khalidi L.
2008. From Prehistoric Landscapes to Urban Sprawl: The Masna'at Maryah region of highland Yemen. *Proceedings of the Seminar for Arabian Studies* 38: 215–230.

Müller W.W.
1978. Die Sabäische Felsinschrift von Masna'at Māriya. Pages 137–148 in R. Degen, W.W. Müller & W. Röllig (eds), *Neue Ephemeris für semitische Epigraphik.* Wiesbaden: Harrassowitz.

Steimer-Herbet T.
2001. Results of the excavation in Jabal Jidran (February 1999). *Proceedings of the Seminar for Arabian Studies* 31: 221–226.

Veldhuijzen H.A. & Rehren T.
2007. Slags and the City. Early Iron Production at Tell Hammeh, Jordan, and Tel Beth-Shemesh, Israel.

Pages 187–201 in S. Hook, D.R. La Niece & P.T. Craddock (eds), *Metals and Mines — Studies in Archaeometallurgy*. London: Archetype, British Museum.

Wilkinson T.J.

1997. Holocene environments of the high plateau, Yemen, recent geoarchaeological investigations. *Geoarchaeology* 12: 833–864.

2003. The organization of settlement in highland Yemen during the Bronze and Iron Ages. *Proceedings of the Seminar for Arabian Studies* 33: 157–168.

Wilkinson T.J. & Edens C.

1999. Survey and Excavation in the Central Highlands of Yemen: Results of the Dhamar Survey Project, 1996 and 1998. *Arabian archaeology and epigraphy* 10: 1–33.

Wilkinson T.J., Edens C. & Barratt G.

2001. Hammat al-Qa': an early town in southern Arabia. *Proceedings of the Seminar for Arabian Studies* 31: 249–259.

Wilkinson T.J., Edens C. & Gibson M.

1997. "The Archaeology of the Yemen High Plains: A preliminary chronology". *Arabian archaeology and epigraphy* 8: 99–142.

Authors' addresses

Dr Krista Lewis, Assistant Professor of Anthropology, University of Arkansas at Little Rock, 2801 S. University Ave, Little Rock, AR 72204, USA.

e-mail kalewis1@alumni.uchicago.edu

Dr Lamya Khalidi, Associate Researcher, Centre d'Études Préhistoire, Antiquité, Moyen Âge, (CEPAM — UMR 6130 — CNRS), Université de Nice, Sophia Antipolis (UNSA), 250, rue Albert Einstein, Sophia-Antipolis, F–06560 Valbonne, France.

e-mail lamya.khalidi@gmail.com

William Isenberger, Cartographer, Digital Mapping & Graphics, 6346 North Shade Tree Lane, Springfield, MO, 65803, USA.

e-mail billisenberger@yahoo.com

Ali Sanabani, Director of Antiquities for the Dhamar Province, Museum of Archaeology, Dhamar, Yemen.

Proceedings of the Seminar for Arabian Studies 40 (2010): 227–232

Written Mahri, Mahri *fuṣḥā* and their implications for early historical Arabic

Samuel Liebhaber

Summary

As recently as 2004, written poetic texts in the Mahri language of south-east Yemen began to appear at the initiative of native speakers who had a serious interest in preserving and promoting their linguistic heritage. As one of the few surviving non-Arabic languages indigenous to the Arabian Peninsula, the Mahri language remained oral prior to 2004 and is still "inaudible" at the margins of the sociolinguistic framework that characterizes the Arabic-speaking world. However, the emerging oral-literate environment of al-Mahra enables us to draw parallels between the current socio-cultural setting of the Mahri language and that which obtained for Arabic speakers at the cusp of literacy in the late Jāhilī and early Islamic eras. This paper draws on fieldwork that I undertook in al-Mahra between 2003 and 2008, during which time I analysed the impact of writing on the poetic idiom of one of al-Mahra's most prolific poets. Specifically, this paper examines how Mahri-language literacy has forced a reappraisal of native valuations of linguistic quality with close reference to a commonly held, yet far from consensual, notion of an exemplary idiom known locally as Mahri *fuṣḥā*. By examining the shifting valencies of Mahri *fuṣḥā* in recent decades, we can shed some light on the composition and evolution of Arabic *fuṣḥā* in its pre- and early historical guises.

Keywords: Mahri language, orality, literacy, oral poetry, classical Arabic

While collecting data on Mahri poetry between 2003 and 2008, I regularly encountered references to a Mahri "*fuṣḥā*", a linguistic register of the Mahri language deemed by native speakers to be distinct from the more obvious geographic and socio-economic subdivisions of the Mahri language. Thus, alongside the readily recognizable segmentation of the Mahri language, many of the Mahra with whom I spoke proposed an idiom that bears an analogy to Arabic *fuṣḥā*.

Technically speaking, the application of Arabic *fuṣḥā* to the Mahri language ought to be a fraught exercise in cross-linguistic transference. Arabic and Mahri have very divergent sociolinguistic histories. With the exception of a recently produced *dīwān* of lyric poetry, the Mahri language has retained a strictly oral praxis and offers no written models for higher register utterances (Liebhaber, forthcoming, *a*). There is no published corpus of Mahri poetry available to the Mahra or even simple radio broadcasts in the Mahri language that could provide a baseline for a collective, quasi-official linguistic register.[1] There is no such thing as formal education in the Mahri language and therefore there is no institutional motivation to formalize its grammar and lexicon. Finally, there is no case system equivalent to the Arabic *ʾiʿrāb* on which to base a formal definition of Mahri *fuṣḥā*.

Mahri *fuṣḥā* must be based on a different set of principles than Arabic *fuṣḥā*. Attempting to derive a unifying theory of Bedouin sociolinguistics, this paper addresses two questions: what understanding do the Mahra bring to their appellation "Mahri *fuṣḥā*" and what does the concept of a Mahri *fuṣḥā* imply for the evolution of Arabic *fuṣḥā* in its pre-historical and early historical stages?

In addressing the first question, many of my Mahri informants identified Mahri *fuṣḥā* with the Mahri dialect of Qishn and its coastal dependencies. In doing so, they linked the historic centre of Mahri political power under the ʿAfrāri dynasty with linguistic prestige. There is a practical basis for the association of Qishn with Mahri *fuṣḥā*: the mainland administrative apparatus of the ʿAfrāri Sultanate was based in Qishn and the performance of poetry was among its normal functions. Even today, remnants of this active poetic culture can be heard in Qishn where a cluster of respected poets evokes an echo of its vibrant poetic culture.[2]

[1] In a conversation with the director of al-Mahra's only broadcast station, he suggested that while Mahri poetry and language could be spoken about, it would be contrary to station policy and Yemeni law to broadcast in the Mahri language itself.

[2] During a visit to Qishn in 2004, I was provided with a list of poets from Qishn who distinguished themselves in the composition of Mahri

At the same time, many of the most prestigious poets from Qishn were more famous for their compositions in Arabic. Many of the poets that I met felt greater ease composing politically themed or tribal poetry in Arabic than in Mahri. Since much of the poetry to emerge from the daily workings of the ᶜAfrāri administration concerned al-Mahra's relationship with non-Mahri speaking tribes, Arabic poetry formed a significant portion of the total poetic output in Qishn. In fact, it was only after persistent requests that I was able to provoke recitations of Mahri tribal-historical odes in Qishn; Arabic was the preferred and still venerated language of official poetic discourse. In consequence, most of the poets from Qishn with whom I spoke were familiar with the Arabic meta-language for poetry (including the principles of *balāghah*), from whence literary measures of linguistic quality presumably entered into the Mahri poetic meta-language.

The infiltration of an Arabic poetic meta-language into Mahri poetry from Qishn can be detected in a tribal ode by Saᶜīd bir Laᶜṭayṭ, a mid-twentieth-century poet from the hinterlands of Qishn. At the beginning of a long tribal poem, Bir Laᶜṭayṭ describes the act of poetizing along similar lines to those of an educated Arabic-language poet. Bir Laᶜṭayṭ informs his audience that he systematically weighs each phrase for its metrical value in order to construct "a learned melody" (*elēḥen mātlīm*). His choice of words is reflective of Arabic and literary modes of poetic craftsmanship: *mātlīm* ("learned") being derived from the Arabic semantic domain of ᶜ.L.M. (to learn/to know) and not from the Mahri root Ġ.R.B. — which conveys the same meaning and is used more commonly throughout al-Mahra.[3]

On a strictly linguistic level, the equation of the Qishn dialect with *fuṣḥā* flies in the face of phonological innovations in the Qishn dialect that are acknowledged by the Mahra. These are the loss of /ᶜ/, the occlusion of the fricative interdental consonants and palatal /j/, and the articulation of the emphatic phonemes with a creaky voice feature (Lonnet & Simeone-Senelle 1997: 349). The discrepancy between the social prestige that has accrued to the Qishn dialect and its acknowledged lack of phonological conservatism is closely analogous to the status of the dialect of Quraysh within the sociolinguistic hierarchy of Arabic. While the Meccan dialect of the Quraysh provided the immediate linguistic milieu of the Qurʾān, deviations in the Meccan dialect of Quraysh from the trans-local Arabic *fuṣḥā* of that era rendered the association between the two problematic.

Alongside the identification of Mahri *fuṣḥā* with Qishn, the Mahri dialects of the inland Bedouin are also assigned the label of *fuṣḥā*. The inland dialects of al-Mahra are quantifiably more conservative than the coastal dialects since they preserve the laryngeal /ᶜ/, the rare phoneme /ž/ and a stronger articulation of the emphatic series. Moreover, just as medieval Arab lexicographers viewed the language of Arab Bedouin as the communicative medium of an "authentic" Arabian lifestyle, so too the dialects of the inland Bedouin of al-Mahra receive special consideration since they are replete with the pastoralist vocabulary and intimate geographic reckonings of desert nomads.[4]

The two perceptions of Mahri *fuṣḥā* described above have specific tribal and geographical limits. Whether Mahri *fuṣḥā* belongs to the political elite from Qishn or belongs to Bedouin from the inland steppe, the production of Mahri *fuṣḥā* is not accessible to all of the Mahra. However, a broader conception of Mahri *fuṣḥā* was occasionally indicated, one that defies the exclusive sociolinguistic parameters outlined above.

While collecting and transcribing multi-line tribal odes in the tristich *reğzīt* format, certain lines or phrases were pointed out to me as *fuṣḥā*, regardless of the regional provenance of the poet. In particular, a sub-genre of the

poetry: (deceased) Muḥammad ᶜAlī ᶜAfrār, Saᶜīd ᶜAlī ᶜAfrār, Saᶜīd Laᶜṭayṭ al-Gidḥī, Sālim Kābōt al-Gidḥī, Saᶜd ᶜAlī Garwāt al-Gidḥī, Masᶜūd ᶜAshām al-Gidḥī, ᶜAlī ᶜAwḍat al-Gidḥī, Muḥammad ᶜAwḍat al-Gidḥī, Muḥammad Bakhīt Sālim, Saᶜīd Ḥasan bir Ḥaydar, ᶜAnbar al-Ḥrēzī; (living) ʾAḥmad ᶜAlī Saᶜīd ᶜAfrār, ᶜAwḍat ᶜAlī ᶜAwḍat, ʾAḥmad ᶜAlī ᶜAwḍat, Ḥasan Sālim Bā ᶜAbbāt, Sālim Bakhīt Sālim, Muḥammad Saᶜīd al-Ḥrēzī, ᶜAlī Muḥammad Nwēgaᶜ, Saᶜīd Shaᶜrār, Sālim Saᶜd Maᶜnōt, Muḥammad Saᶜd Garwāt, ᶜAbdallāh Saᶜd Zwēdī, Muḥammad Shōlim Qabṭī, ᶜĀmir Sālim Shalmōten and ᶜĪsā Saᶜīd Damōrnak. For evidence of the prestigious poetic culture that once thrived in Qishn, the number of poets is less important than the fact that a list of twenty-four poets could be assembled by the Director of Culture for Qishn, Bakhīt Sālim al-Gidḥī, without hesitation or advance preparation.

[3] According to T.M. Johnstone, the root ᶜ.L.M has two distinct, yet ultimately related, semantic domains: "knowing/learning" and "camel branding" (1987: 22). I suspect that the former meaning is imported from Arabic usage since the unmarked domain for "knowing" in Mahri is covered by the root Ġ.R.B. (1987: 140).

[4] Two lines from the tribal ode by Ṭannāf bir Saᶜd Hamtōt, epitomize the geographical intimacy of *fuṣḥā* Mahri poetry: *yetwīwen l-maġtēk // le-mğebbet 'ālūt* ("They set out for Wādī Maġtēḳ, at the very end of the mountains before the sandy desert" and *yeḥlūl b-hafğūğ //we-mġawteḳ w-ġafθ'ūt* ("They live in the wadis of Hafğūğ, and [its feeder ravines of] Mġawteḳ and Ġafθ'ūt"). For Mahra unfamiliar with the inland steppe, these lines were problematic since it was not self-evident whether the geographical items listed were proper names or descriptions of generic desert features. For the target audience, these names or descriptions are filled with meaning; for my informants from al-Ghaydhah, they were emblematic of the close relationship between the inland Bedouin and the land that they inhabit.

tribal ode called *ʾōdī we-krēm krēm* seemed to attract the most notice as *faṣīḥ*. After collecting a number of these long tribal odes, both the formulaic structure and the lexical formulas of the *ʾōdī we-krēm krēm* genre suggested the outline of a trans-local Mahri *fuṣḥā*.

Poetry labelled as *faṣīḥ* hewed to a formulaic narrative structure. A typical *faṣīḥ* poem begins at dusk with the poet surveying the landscape below him from an elevated vantage point. Standing exposed to the elements, he is buffeted by a strong wind, typically the southerly *mdīt* that blows cold, moist air from the sea. The atmospheric tumult and transition from day to night mirrors the poet's emotional turmoil as he anticipates a shift from social stability to conflict and upheaval. The poet reflects on the cause of his anxiety and narrates the acts of violence that have brought the tribes to the brink of conflict. Raiding vignettes may follow, culminating in a broader war that is described as an indiscriminately destructive rainstorm and flood. While extolling the bravery of his kinsmen, the poet calls for a peaceful resolution to be enacted according to the rules that govern tribal society: responsibility for one's dependants and honest, straightforward speech.[5]

The most readily identifiable lexical formula of *fuṣḥā* Mahri poetry is its characteristic invocation: *ʾōdī we-krēm krēm* ("I begin with the Noble and the Generous [One]").[6] This formula occurs at two possible points in a tribal ode: at the inception of the poem or during the transition to the final theme, when the poet reasserts the strength and magnanimity of his tribe. If the poem begins with *ʾōdī we-krēm krēm*, then the next stage in the programmatic structure of the tribal ode is a reference to the cold, blustery *mdīt* wind. This invocation will appear as a variation of the following formula: *heyya bīš emdīt* ("welcome to you, Sea-breeze"), *we-ṭwōrem emdīt* ("the sea-breeze comes soon afterwards") and *we-mdīt men emṭəlā // emhawǧes enkəśūt* ("then the sea-breeze from the South stirred up strong feelings"). Or, the *mdīt* can be referred to elliptically: *hel mǧawrī ḏ-rīḥeyn* ("where the wind-currents flow"). The breeze finds the poet standing on an elevated position, such as the peak of Karmaym Ḥawrōt for the poets of the Sulaymī tribe or on the peak of Ṭarbūt for the poets of the Gēdeḥ/Gidḥī tribe.

Following the *mdīt*, the dusk is mentioned, often by describing the approach of night-time shadows. Two possible iterations of this formula are *lawb ǧōneš ḥyūm* ("O Sun, you have set") and *šūǧōśen nḥā // berk eśfēḳ*[7] ("We left in the late afternoon, at sunset"). At the beginning of a long battle narrative from the inland steppe, the poet establishes the time frame for his poem in the following fashion:

2) *ke-mǧawnī ḏe-ḥyōm // ġsīreyyen ettəhūt*[8]
3) *we-hlats ṭamḥeyt // sebḥawt ekkerdəfūt*[9]

2) When the sun sets in the evening and its light fades
3) Darkness spreads, swimming over the wadi's edge

The same idea is expressed in the first two lines of an older poem composed by a Ḥrēzī Bedouin from western al-Mahra:

1) *ǧawneš ḥell // yā ġmīḷ yā mġāb*
2) *hōlā medd // θ'eyr eḳā' we-sḥāb*

1) The evening has arrived, O Sunset, O Dusk
2) The shadows spread over the land and flow across [it]

Once the introductory tropes have been covered, the strict ordering of the formulaic motifs breaks down to permit the narration of the particulars of the conflict. Despite the lack of a formulaic progression of themes, the latter sections of a tribal ode still retain their essence of *fuṣḥā* since they detail the duties and rights of the tribesman, the cherished conventions that lie at the heart of the Mahri tribal order.

In traditional Mahri poetics, an aura of *fuṣḥā* accretes around performances of the multi-line, tribal ode. The lexical formulas, narrative structure and tone of the poem

[5] The narrative sequence described for the Mahri tribal ode is immediately recognizable as that which obtains for Arabic *nabaṭī* poetry (Sowayan 1985: *passim*; Kurpershoek 1994; 1999: *passim*). Like *nabaṭī* poetry, the conventional structure of the Mahri tribal ode echoes the van Gennepian paradigm proposed by Suzanne Stetkevych for the pre-Islamic *qaṣīdah* (1993: *passim*). Accordingly, the mythopoetic "stations" of the pre-Islamic *qaṣīdah* examined by Stetkevych (separation/*nasīb* — liminality/*riḥlah* — aggregation/*gharaḍ*) find close analogy in the formulaic narrative outlined above for Mahri poetry.

[6] My translation of *ʾōdī we-krēm krēm* is a periphrasis derived from context; the same formula was also described to me by my informants as a substitute for Arabic *bismillāh* ("In the name of God"). For the most part, the Mahra I spoke with regarded *ʾōdī we-krēm krēm* as an untranslatable, pious formula. In all likelihood, *ōdī* is an imperative form of the verb *wōdī, awōdī,* translated by Alfred Jahn as "die Religionspflichten erfüllen" (1902: 234).

[7] *šūǧōśen* < *W.Ǧ.Ś.*: "*šəwǧūś/yəšəwǧūś:* to go in the early evening (4–7 pm)" (Johnstone 1987: 424); *eśfēḳ* < Ś.F.Ḳ.: Ar. *šafaq* ("twilight, dusk").

[8] *mǧawnī* < Ǧ.N.ʿ.: "*gənō, gənōt/təgōna*: to be nearly set (sun)" (Johnstone 1987: 121); *ġsīreyyen* < Ġ.S.R.W.: "*ġasráwwən*: (in) the early evening" (Johnstone 1987: 143); *ettəhūt*: to disappear from sight, become hidden, Ar. *tawārā*.

[9] *hlats* < H.L.ʿ.: "*hōlaʾ/hīlaʾ*: shade, shadow" (Johnstone 1987: 156) + pos. suffix; *ṭamḥayt* < Ṭ.M.Ḥ.: to spread over sth.; *ekkerdəfūt* < K.R.D.F.(?): the edge of a wadi.

indicate to the Mahri audience that a socially and politically significant performance is under way. On the receiving end, the audience is conditioned to respond to these poems with the *gravitas* appropriate to performances that construct and impart the fundamental values of the Mahri tribal order. The themes of tribal poetry and the attitude of their reception, rather than any linguistic specifics, define Mahri *fuṣḥā*. Conversely, strophic sung poetry and lyric poetry are disqualified from consideration as *faṣīḥ* on the basis of their sentimental content.

In the past five years, this conception of linguistic quality has been challenged by the appearance of the first literary texts in the Mahri language. In the autumn of 2003, one of al-Ghaydhah's more prominent poets, Ḥājj Dākōn, began to write down the texts of his poems in the Mahri language and to circulate them among his friends and colleagues. In addition to being the first models of a popular Mahri literature, the type of strophic sung poetry that Ḥājj composes is also an innovation to Mahri poetics. While written in the Mahri language, the format and tone of these poems are identical to the Ḥaḍramī sung poetry developed by Ḥusayn al-Miḥḍār in the last half of the twentieth century and subsequently popularized by the singer Abū Bakr Sālim.[10] By importing an entirely new genre of poetry into the Mahri language, Ḥājj Dākōn has forced a recalibration of conventional ideas concerning Mahri linguistic quality, and in doing so, has called into question the conventional perception of Mahri *fuṣḥā*.

Pursuant to his dual ambition of achieving national recognition for the Mahri language and fashioning a detribalized, trans-local Mahri identity, Ḥājj purposefully composes his poetry in a pan-Mahri idiom that lies in the broad hollows between the more distinctive topography of the regional dialects. Although Ḥājj is not from al-Mahra's administrative capital, al-Ghaydhah, he purposefully emulates its mixed Arabic-Mahri dialect (known locally as *ghayḍiyyah*) by making ample use of mixed Mahri and Arabic vocabulary and emphasizing obvious Arabic-Mahri cognates rather than uniquely Mahri words.

In Ḥājj's opinion, the accessibility of his poetic idiom is its chief virtue, rather than the traditional Mahri notion of linguistic quality that values a specialized, highly specific lexicon over transparency. In a conversation in the summer of 2008, Ḥājj indicated that he was guided in his choice of idiom by the success of contemporary Arabic *fuṣḥā* (i.e. Modern Standard Arabic) in achieving a linguistic community for the peoples of the Middle East.

Weighing the distinction between the traditional valuation of *fuṣḥā* against his own, newly constituted literary *fuṣḥā*, Ḥājj reckoned that his idiom ought to be described as *rakīk*, loosely translatable as a "knock-off" of *fuṣḥā*. In his own words, Ḥājj described his *rakīk* idiom as a Taiwanese-made product *versus* its better-wrought, Japanese equivalent. In Yemeni terms, Ḥājj's *rakīk* idiom corresponds to the Arabic, semi-vernacular idiom associated with *ḥumaynī* poetry, a literate genre with broad appeal throughout Yemen that lacks the *iʿrāb* case endings of *faṣīḥ* Arabic. Ḥājj's trans-local, Mahri idiom and the Arabic *ḥumaynī* idiom are demotic versions of prestigious linguistic registers. By modelling the accessibility of his poetic idiom after the idiom of contemporary Yemeni sung poetry, Ḥājj demonstrates that Mahri poetics is as flexible as contemporary Arabic poetry and moreover, Mahri sung poetry is a fit constituent for the emergent national culture of the Republic of Yemen.[11]

The following example of one of Ḥājj's strophic, sung poems in Mahri illustrates the precise lineaments of Ḥājj's *fuṣḥā–rakīk* divide. As can be seen below, Ḥājj consciously employs Mahri and Arabic cognates for virtually all nouns and adjectives and eschews the uniquely Mahri vocabulary of traditional poetic formulas. All words with clear Arabic cognates are in boldface.[12]

ẓeyn *w-**kellek** zeyn...we-**ḥlōyet** būk*
*būk **ʻādēb** w-mād* *wel **tkūder** hād*[13]
mawra we-ḳṣāw *lā šūk w-lā fnūk*[14]

zeyn w-kellek zeyn...we-ḥlōyet būk
*heyt ġrūy **ʻāsēl*** ***ḥōlī** we-ḥwēl*
*yehneyh **eḫalḳ*** *kād ettōma lūk*[15]

zeyn w-kellek zeyn...we-ḥlōyet būk
*heyt **ḷeḥketk lūl*** ***bōreḳ** ḏ-īğlūl*[16]
*we-**mθ'ōnī** mēl* ***baḫt** ḏhēh hnūk*[17]

[10] For more on the adoption of Ḥaḍramī sung poetry by Mahri poets, see my article, "The *Ḥumaynī* Pulse Moves East" (forthcoming, *b*).

[11] This argument is made at greater length in my article "The *Ḥumaynī* Pulse Moves East" (Liebhaber, forthcoming, *b*).

[12] This poem can be found in *The Dīwān of Ḥājj Dākōn* (Liebhaber, forthcoming, *a*).

[13] *mād* < M.ᶜ.D.: "*mēd*: intelligence" (Johnstone 1987: 260).

[14] *maẉra* < W.R.[V].: dam, Ar. *sadd,* Mhr. *hawrā, hawrā/yahwōrā, ahwārā*: to lock, Ar. *ʾaqfala; ḳṣaw* < Ḳ.Ṣ.W.: "*ḳəṣō*: (road) to end; to finish; to come to the end" (Johnstone 1987: 241).

[15] *yehneyh* (causative stem) < N.H.Y.: "*náyhi*: to forget, leave (st.) behind" (Johnstone 1987: 291); *ettōma* < H.M.ᶜ.: "*əttōma/yəttáman/yəttōma*: to listen" (Johnstone 1987: 158).

[16] *yeğlūl* < Ğ.L.L.: "*gəl/yəglōl*: to be alight, glow; to boil" (Johnstone 1987: 118).

[17] *mθ'ōnī* < Ť.N.Y.: "*məṯənyēt/məṯōni*: incisor tooth" (Johnstone 1987: 418).

zeyn w-kellek zeyn...we-ḥlōyet būk
hōh men hāl syerk *we-**bḳā** ḳṭerk*[18]
ahnēhek lā *we-**fwōdī** šūk*

zeyn w-kellek zeyn...we-ḥlōyet būk
w-hēt w-lū ḥetġebk *mnī w-ġatyebk*
rawḥī we-fwōd *we-**hǧīs** wdūk*[19]

Beautiful, everything about you is beautiful...and sweetness belongs to you
You've got manners and a good head
You'd never malign anyone
You're the ultimate and the end-point's
There's no one before you or after you

Beautiful, everything about you is beautiful...and sweetness belongs to you
Your speech is honey
Sweet and maddening
He forgets the rest of creation
Whoever listens to you

Beautiful, everything about you is beautiful...and sweetness belongs to you
Your smile is a pearl
Lightning that flashes
Your incisors are complete
Lucky is the man with you!

Beautiful, everything about you is beautiful...and sweetness belongs to you
Wherever I should
I'll never forget you
Since my heart is with you

Beautiful, everything about you is beautiful...and sweetness belongs to you
Even if you are hidden away
And disappear from me
My soul and my heart
And thoughts are with you

Based on the shifting parameters of Mahri *fuṣḥā* observed in the publication of Ḥājj Dākōn's poetic collection, I offer two suggestions concerning the emergence of a written practice for the Arabic language:

a) The first is that *fuṣḥā* as initially conceived by pre-literate Arabs was not a formally definable idiom but an aura of social potency that adhered to the conventional narrative structure of the *Jāhiliyyah*-era *qaṣīdah*. It was not until an unprecedented genre of oral text appeared (the Qurʾān in Arabic and Ḥaḍramī sung poetry in Mahri), that the idea of *fuṣḥā* detached itself from a specific poetic genre and became associated with a grammatically and lexically quantifiable idiom: *iʿrāb* for Arabic and the *g͟hayḍiyyah* idiom for Mahri.

b) The second observation is that Mahri language literacy is linked to the development and preservation of popular sung poetry and not to the more prestigious tribal odes. I propose a greater role for vernacular and semi-vernacular Arabic poetry in the development of a practical Arabic writing system. Even if vernacular texts may have subsequently faded from view, the case of al-Mahra indicates that *rakīk*, rather than *faṣīḥ* poetry, may have played an important role in early Arabic literacy.

Acknowledgements

This article is based on fieldwork conducted with the support of a Fulbright-Hayes Fellowship and a grant from the American Institute for Yemeni Studies. I would like to thank the Yemen Center for Studies and Research in Sana'a and the office of the Ministry of Culture in al-Ghaydhah for their help in the implementation of this project. I would also like to thank Muḥammad ʿAkkūsh, ʿAbd al-Sayf al-Qaḥṭānī and Sālim Luḥaymar al-Qumayrī, for welcoming me to al-Ghaydha and Ḥājj Dākōn and ʿAskarī Ḥujayrān for their invaluable expertise and insight into the Mahri language and poetry. Much of the work in this article can be found in extended form in my doctoral thesis (2007).

[18] *ḳṭerk* < Ḳ.Ṭ.R.: "*ḳəṭáwr/yəḳáwṭər*: to turn round and round (used in children's games); to tire ... to look around, go far and wide" (Johnstone 1987: 245).

[19] *wdūk* (*wdī, wdūk, wdeh, wdēhem*): with you, in your company (Qishn dialect; equivalent to *hnūk* and *twelyek* in other Mahri dialects), Ar. *ʿindaka*.

References

Jahn A.
1902. *Die Mehri-Sprache in Südarabien.* Vienna: Alfred Hölder.
Johnstone T.
1987. *Mehri Lexicon and English-Mehri Word-List.* London: University of London.
Kurpershoek M.
1994. *Oral Poetry & Narratives from Central Arabia.* i. Leiden: E.J. Brill.
1999. *Oral Poetry & Narratives from Central Arabia.* iii. Leiden: E.J. Brill.
Liebhaber S.
2007. Bedouin Without Arabic: Language, Poetry and the Mahra of Southeast Yemen. PhD thesis, University of California, Berkeley. [Unpublished].
(forthcoming, *a*). *The Dīwān of Ḥājj Dākōn.* Ardmore, PA: The American Institute for Yemeni Studies.
(forthcoming, *b*). The *Ḥumaynī* Pulse Moves East: Yemeni Nationalism Meets Mahri Sung-Poetry. *British Journal of Middle Eastern Studies.*
Lonnet A. & Simeone-Senelle M.
1997. La Phonologie des Langues Sudarabiques Modernes. *Phonologies of Asia and Africa.* Winona Lake, IN: Eisenbrauns.
al-Shahri A.A.
2000. *The Language of ᶜAd.* Dhofar Salalah: self-published. [in Arabic.]
Sowayan S.
1985. *Nabaṭi Poetry: The Oral Poetry of Arabia.* Berkeley, CA: University of California Press.
Stetkevych S.
1993. *The Mute Immortals Speak: Pre-Islamic Poetry and Poetics of Ritual.* Ithaca, NY: Cornell University Press.

Author's address
Samuel Liebhaber, Assistant Professor of Arabic and International Studies, Middlebury College, 205 Farrell House, Middlebury, VT 05753, USA.

e-mail slieb@middlebury.edu

Proceedings of the Seminar for Arabian Studies 40 (2010): 233–238

How difficult is it to dedicate a statue? A new approach to some Sabaic inscriptions from Maʾrib

Anne Multhoff

Summary

Although dedicatory inscriptions from Ancient South Arabia normally follow strict formulaic patterns and are thus rather stereotyped, some dedications stand out from the ordinary. This can apply both to context and content. The paper focuses on three rather extraordinary texts from the Maʾrib area, which can help to illustrate the course of events that finally led to a dedication. This includes the rare example of a simultaneous dedication at two different temples, probably ensuring overall protection to the people dedicating them. The second part of the paper deals with the singular case of a subsequent dedication of an object originally conceived as a present from the deity himself. This new approach in interpreting these inscriptions can lead to a better understanding of a number of difficult syntagmata in the texts.

Keywords: Ancient South Arabia, Sabaʾ, inscriptions, dedication, temple

Dedications of objects, normally of statues and statuettes, are certainly one of the best-documented elements of cultic life in Ancient South Arabia, at least in Middle Sabaic times. Although most of these texts follow stereotyped formulaic patterns, one sometimes encounters individual problems and strange situations. In the course of a research project that focused on the Sabaean capital Maʾrib, some interesting parallels between inscriptions originating from different temples were established. Furthermore, new solutions to some problematic texts were found. These results will shed new light on the course of events that eventually led to the dedication of a statue.

Even though these dedications look stereotypic and banal to us, they must have represented an important event in the life of those dedicating them, at least for the common people. Consequently, the inauguration of such a dedication needed some consideration and was often based on some sort of direct or indirect communication between an individual and one or several deities.

Where to place the dedication?

Most importantly, an appropriate temple had to be chosen. In all probability, people normally knew to which temple they should apply with a certain problem, but mistakes could happen. This was obviously the case in Ja 584 B.

Ja 584 B

Text

7.[end of Ja 584 A] *s*^{2}*wf ḏt lnhʾ hqnyt ʾ*
8. *lmqh bʿl-ʾwm ṣlmtn ḏt ḏhbn ḥmd*
9. *m b-ḏt hydʿ-hw bʿl ḥrnm b-ʿbr ʾẖy-h*
10. *w w-rʾ k-hqnyt-hw ḥgn wqh-hw b-ḏ-(b)ṯṯ*
11. *t-hw w-hʾ ẖmr-hw h(nw)l-hw hʾ w-ʾẖy-hw*
12. *b-ʾlmqh*

Translation

(7–8) S^{2}WF of (the clan[?] of) LNHʾ dedicated to ʾLMQH, lord of (the temple) ʾWM, the (present) female statuette in bronze (8–10) in gratitude because (ʾLMQH) the lord of (the temple) ḤRNM informed her 'in the direction of' his brother; (10–11) and indeed, she dedicated to him as he has commanded her in what she had ... him;[1] (11–12) and he granted her to ... her,[2] he and his brother. By ʾLMQH.

Although the text is a dedication to ʾLMQH, the lord of ʾWM, we learn that the person dedicating it originally

[1] Jamme (1962: 90) states that he had read *bḏṭṯṯt* instead of *bḏbṯṯt* but does not have any photograph at his disposal. Since none of the possible readings can be taken for granted, a translation seems rather unpromising.

[2] Jamme (1962: 90) marks the form as an alteration, but does not give his original reading. A translation based on this should thus be omitted.

sought help from the lord of ḪRNM, another manifestation of ʾLMQH. The two different manifestations, both of them venerated in Maʾrib, but situated at different temples, are introduced as brothers and thus clearly conceived as different entities. It would appear that the unknown concern of the person dedicating it did not conform to the scope of the chosen temple, since the deity guided her to another temple, thus guaranteeing that her dedication was not in vain.

Another strategy was to place identical dedications in several temples. This procedure guaranteed overall divine help and protection, but was probably rather expensive. That people nevertheless chose this alternative is illustrated by RES 4150 and Ir 3, a striking example of two stones coming from different temples, but presenting virtually the same text.[3] Diverging passages in both texts are marked in bold face.

RES 4150

Text

1. [symbol$^?$ *s^2rḥᶜ]ṯ{t ʾ}r{y}m w-rṯd{ṯw}n {b}n[y] [... hq]*
2. [symbol$^?$ *ny]{**y** }**ᶜṯtr ḏ-ḏbn bᶜl bḥr ḥṭbm**{ **ḏ**}[n ṣ]*
3. *[lm]n [ḥ]m{d}m b-ḏt hwfy **ᶜṯtr** ᶜbd-hw s^2[rḥᶜṯt]*
4. *{b-}kl ʾ{ml}ʾ s^1tmlʾ w-tḍᶜn b-ᶜm-h{w} w-l-[ḏt yzʾ]*
5. *n **ᶜṯtr** h{w}fyn ᶜbd-hw s^2rḥ{$^{c?}$}ṯt b-k{l} [ʾmlʾ w-]*
6. *{t}ḍᶜ ys^{1}tmlʾn [w-]{t}ḍᶜn b-ᶜm-hw w-{l} s^{1c}{d}[-hw **ᶜṯ**]*
7. ***tr** rḍw {w-}ḥẓy mr{ʾ}-hm{w} {ʾ}ls^{2}rḥ yḥ{ḍ}[b mlk s^1]*
8. *{b}ʾ w-ḏ-rydn w-bn-hw wtrm w-{l s^1}[ᶜd-hw]*

Translation

(1–3) S^2RḤ$^{c?}$ṮT ʾRYM and RṮDṮWN (of the) clan [...] [dedicated (***dual***)] to **ᶜṮTR Ḏ-ḎBN, lord of BḤR ḤṬBM, this**$^?$ [statue$^?$] (3–4) in gratitude because **ᶜṮTR** bestowed on his servant S^2RḤ$^{c?}$ṮT in all fulfilments he asked and requested from him,(4–6) and because **ᶜṮTR** will [continue] to bestow on his servant S^2RḤ$^{c?}$ṮT in all [fulfilments] and elevations he will ask [and] request from him; (6–8) and that **ᶜṮTR** may grant [him$^?$] the goodwill and favour of their lord ʾLS^{2}RḤ YHḌB, [king of] S^1Bʾ and Ḏ-RYDN, and (of) his son WTRM, (8) and that [**ᶜṮTR**] may grant [him$^?$ ...]

Ir 3

Text

*s^2rḥᶜṯt ʾrym w-rṯdṯwn bny ḥlḥlm hqny**w ʾlmqh ṯhwn bᶜl ʾwm ṣlmn ḏ-ḏhbn** ḥmdm b-ḏt hwfy **ʾlmqh** ᶜbd-hw s^2rḥᶜṯt b-kl ʾmlʾ s^1tmlʾ w-tḍᶜn b-ᶜm-hw w-l-ḏt yzʾn **ʾlmqh** hwfyn ᶜbd-hw s^2rḥ$^{c?}$ṯt b-kl ʾmlʾ w-tḍᶜ ys^{1}tmlʾn w-tḍᶜn b-ᶜm-hw w-l-s^{1c}d-hmw **ʾlmqh nᶜmtm** w-rḍw w-ḥẓy mrʾ-hmw ʾls^{2}rḥ yḥḍb mlk s^1bʾ w-ḏ-rydn w-bn-hw wtrm w-l-s^{1c}d-hmw **ʾlmqh*** [(...)]

Translation

S^2RḤ$^{c?}$ṮT ʾRYM and RṮDṮWN (of the) clan ḤLḤLM dedicated [***plural***] to **ʾLMQH ṮHWN, lord of ʾWM, the (present) statue in bronze** in gratitude because **ʾLMQH** bestowed on his servant S^2RḤ$^{c?}$ṮT in all fulfilments he asked and requested from him, and because **ʾLMQH** will continue to bestow on his servant S^2RḤ$^{c?}$ ṮT in all fulfilments and elevations he will ask and request from him; and that **ʾLMQH** may grant them **well-being** and the goodwill and favour of their lord ʾLS^{2}RḤ YHḌB, king of S^1Bʾ and Ḏ-RYDN, and (of) his son WTRM, and that **ʾLMQH** may grant them [...]

The only major difference between the two inscriptions is their reference to two different deities: RES 4150 is a dedication to ᶜṮTR Ḏ-ḎBN, lord of BḤR ḤṬBM, whereas Ir 3 is dedicated to ʾLMQH ṮHWN, lord of ʾWM. Minor variations include the different number of people dedicating the inscriptions (dual in RES 4150, plural in Ir 3) and an extra *nᶜmt* "well-being" in Ir 3; they might, however, result from misreading by the editors. The same may be true for the object of the present dedication, because the relevant passage is almost entirely destroyed in RES 4150 and cannot be restored with any certainty.

Significant parallels include, apart from the overall layout of the text, the noun *tḍᶜ* "elevation".[4] In contrast to both the verb *(n)tḍᶜ* "to ask for elevations" and the noun *nḍᶜ* "elevation" derived from the basic stem, this noun is not attested in any other Sabaic inscription. Another remarkable feature is the name S^2RḤ$^{c?}$ṮT in RES 4150/5. According to Höfner (1938: 26), the letter ᶜ was probably scratched out ("da der Raum für ein ᶜ wohl vorhanden

---

[3] Unfortunately, documentation for both texts is poor. RES 4150 is illustrated only in a summary copy published by Mordtmann & Mittwoch (1932: pl. 11); of the visual appearance of Ir 3 we know nothing, not even the disposition of lines. Note, however, that the exact wording of inscriptions published in the relevant corpus of al-ʾIryānī is not always reliable, the author's interest being mainly focused on historical data and not on philology; see Stein 2002: 447–452.

[4] Mordtmann & Mittwoch (1932: 45) as well as the facsimile in pl. 11 read (the more common) *nḍᶜ*. Nevertheless, Höfner (1938: 27) clearly states that the copy made by Glaser has a sign looking like the left half of a *t* ("etwas, das wie die linke Hälfte eines *t* aussieht").

ist, aber ganz ausgekratzt"). The transcription in al-ʾIryānī (1990: 54) has indeed a form S^2RḤṮT, whereas the facsimile (1990: 53) or rather, transcription in Sabaic lettering, shows S^2RḤʿṮT, but has the ʿ squeezed in between *ḥ* and *ṯ*, thus implying a secondary addition. Since both forms with and without ʿ are attested elsewhere, the correct spelling remains unclear. However, the evidence of RES 4150 might hint at a correction carried out by the stonemason, thus implying a correct form S^2RḤṮT. A third, and probably most important, parallel is the somewhat sudden end of the inscription in the middle of a sentence. This almost certainly implies the original existence of a second block carrying the remaining part of the text. We can thus conclude that not only the text, but also the visual appearance of the two inscriptions must have been quite similar.[5] The only possible explanation for this is that both stones were erected on the same occasion. This is most remarkable, since the text in itself is rather stereotypic and does not state any concrete concern. In theory, at least, the existence of further examples offered to other deities can be imagined.

What to dedicate?

Placing a dedication did not only require finding the right temple. The person who dedicated it also had to provide an adequate object. This object was normally either promised by the person who dedicated it or ordered by the deity and must, in most cases, have been purchased by the person who dedicated it.[6] Dedicated objects could also come from the private property of the person dedicating it. In one extraordinary example, however, the object in question is characterized as a present from the very deity that finally received it.

CIH 581[7]

Text

1. symbol *nʿm{gd} [bnt ʾlt] t{ḥy}[ʿ]z {w-}[h]*
2. symbol *nʾṯ{w}n w-{n}ʿmt bnt ʾlt {t}*
3. *[ḥy]{ʿ}z ʾmh s^1ʿds^2msm kbs^1yn h*
4. *{q}nyy ʾlm{q}h ṯhwn w-ṯ[w]r bʿlm b*
5. *[ʿ]{l}y ḥrwnm ṣlmtn ḏt ḏhbn*
6. *{ḏ}t whb w-ḫmr ʾlmqh ʾmh-hw ʾ*
7. *[l]{t} tḥy{ʿ}z b-ʿmn ʾs^1m ḏ-mẓʾ w-wg*
8. *{r} byt-hmw b-lly s^1dṯm s^3qt btrm*
9. *[w-]yqrʾn-hmw k-hmy ʿkrw< >s^2ʾm hyt*
10. *[ṣ]{l}mtn w-bʿd-hw f-h{b}rrw l-gtzḥ*
11. *[n]b-ʿm ʾs^1n w-nfq bn-hw w-ṣlmtn*
12. *[f-ʾ?]l l-hmw w-[r]{ʾ} k-bhʾt hʾ ʾṯtn*
13. *[n]ʿmgd ʿdy ḥrwnm w-s^1tmlʾt b-ʿm*
14. *[ʾ]lmqh w-hʾ [h]ṯb-hw w-rʾ k-wqh*
15. *[l-]hqnyn-hw hyt ṣlmtn w-ʾlmqh*
16. *[f-]l ys^2rḥn w-s^2wf w-mtʿn grb m{r}*
17. *ʾ-hw m{h}bḍm bn wdm w-bn-hw {l}*
18. *ḥyʿṯt w-ʾmh-hw ʾlt tḥyʿ{z}*
19. *bn bʾs^1tm w-mngt s^1wʾm w-{s^2}[ṣy]*
20. *{s^2}nʾm b-(ʿ)ṯtr w-ʾlmqh*

While both the beginning (ll. 1–5) and the closing section (ll. 15–20) of the text follow well-known patterns and are thus comparatively easy to understand, the central section is far less clear. Not only does it suffer from many lacunae, it is also quite singular in content. Consequently, the text had been interpreted in very different ways in the past. Beeston (1978) suggested that the three women dedicated this statuette because ʾLMQH granted them the conception of a child after a long period of sterility. At some moment within this period of infertility, the deity had summoned them to such a dedication in the event of their pregnancy. During a visit to the temple, the deity repeatedly asked for the statue, which was then duly dedicated. Jamme (1982: 17–28), however, rejected this rendering. In his view, the dedication was related to the visit of a wandering physician.[8] Even though convincing in some individual details, Jamme's translation does not sound very sensible overall and is, unfortunately, more or less incomprehensible.

---

[5] The hypothetical assumption that the text of Ir 3 might be a corrupt copy of RES 4150 can certainly be excluded. According to Mordtmann & Mittwoch (1932: 2), the three fragments constituting the latter inscription have been in Berlin from about 1913 and could thus hardly be accessible to al-ʾIryānī.

[6] Of course, this does not apply when booty was dedicated, as in Ja 635/2–4: *hqny ... ṣlmn ḏ-ḏhbn ḏ-tmly bn qrytm* "dedicated the (present) statue in bronze which he had taken as booty from QRYTM".

[7] Although CIH ii: 374 states that the stone came from ʿAmrān, the deity mentioned indicates that it must have originated in Maʾrib. — The reading of the above transliteration follows the photograph of the inscription as published in CIH ii: pl. 33. Compared with previous treatments of the text, differing reconstructions of some lacunae are proposed: at the beginning of line 12, CIH ii: 375 reconstructs *[f]l*, whereas Rhodokanakis (1926: 468 n. h) prefers a reading *[kf]l*; in line 14, Beeston (1978: 23) has *w-hʾ [f-h]ṯb-hw*, a reading which can be rejected in accordance with Jamme (1982: 18) on palaeographic grounds.

[8] See Jamme 1982: 22: "that entered a man, who had arrived and was a medicine man, (8) their house on the sixth night with a sound contract (9) .. so that He would command that both of them [= Naʿamgad and Hanaʾṭawân] would initiate the buying of this (10) female [st]atue. After that, they [= the women] agreed to get into business (11) with the man and to pay the expenses for her [= Naʿamgad] son and this statue (12) [..] for them [= the women]".

At least part of the problem results from a slightly incorrect reading, or rather, reconstruction, at the beginning of the central passage. Traditionally, this part was restored *hqnyy ... ṣlmtn ḏt ḏhbn* (6) *[b-]ḏt whb w-ḫmr* "they dedicated a statuette in bronze, *for that* he gave and granted etc.". This formula is very common in dedicatory inscriptions and could, in principle, be expected in this place. Close inspection of the photograph published in CIH (ii: pl. 33), however, reveals that all space available at the beginning of line 6 is already filled up with the *ḏ*, leaving no room for an extra letter such as the *b*. Consequently, the traditional reading of this passage can be excluded. Instead, we have to read a relative clause: *ṣlmtn ḏt ḏhbn* (6) *ḏt whb w-ḫmr* "the statuette in bronze, *that* he gave and granted etc.". This sheds new light on the structure of the whole text. Unlike most other texts, it does *not* indicate that a statuette was dedicated because of any divine favour. Rather, we are simply told that the statuette was originally a kind of present from ʾLMQH to the people dedicating it. But how could a supernatural being like the Sabaean god ʾLMQH present somebody with a statue? And why did the three women finally return this present to him?

The present from ʾLMQH obviously masks a more mundane course of events. As we are told (ll. 6–8) ʾLMQH grants the statuette to his maidservants via a man (*b-ʿmn ʾ*s^1*m*) who came (*mẓʾ*) and did something to their house, which is, for the moment, quite impossible to understand.[9] It is, however, beyond doubt that it was that man who actually brought the object. The following part (ll. 9–10) is now easier to understand. Since the lacuna at the beginning can hardly have contained anything but the particle *w-* "and", we can translate the beginning of line 9 as "and he calls [or summons, or similar] them". We can deduce from the content of this call that it is the sudden visitor who is speaking. His request is of a rather worldly nature: he simply asks the women and their relatives[10] whether they want to buy the statuette. As can be deduced from a few other examples, the particle *hmy* is not only used as the conditional particle "if", but can also introduce interrogative sentences.[11] As for the verb *ʿkr*, it is now beyond doubt that it should be translated as "to wish, want".[12]

Of course, being presented with a statuette by a deity and buying (s^2*ʾm*) that very object from a man who can hardly have been anyone other than a pedlar, are not exactly the same thing. But as we shall see, the women did not actually buy it, even though this might have been their original intention. As we are told (ll. 10–11), they came out in the open (*hbrrw*) to enter into some kind of business with the man (*l-gtzḥn b-ʿm ʾ*s^1*n*). On the basis of the Arabic *jazaḥa* "to give, etc." (see *Lisān s.v. jzḥ*), the general meaning of the present verbal stem in Sabaic, and the given context, the verb could either be translated "to give each other" or "to ask to be given".[13] But then, for reasons we do not know, the transaction failed (l. 11). Although a verb *nfq* is otherwise unattested, a related adjective *nfq* appears several times in declarations of annulment where it denotes the invalidity of an older document.[14] The verb can thus be related to Geʿez *nafaqa* "tear off, tear away, (...) divide, (...) separate (...)" (Leslau 1991: 388). This might mean that agreement over prices failed, but might also mean that the man left them, or simply did not keep an appointment.

As for the statuette, we can only guess what precisely happened to it (ll. 11–12) because the predicate of the relevant sentence is damaged. We do, however, know that it must have remained with the three women. As they clearly state that it is a present from ʾLMQH, we can exclude any possibility that the seller simply renounced his claim and gave it as a present. Two possible situations can be imagined. First, the man could have left the statuette with the women, without any explanation. In this case, we would have a verbal predicate in the lacuna

[9] The passage might refer to the statuette, but can also apply to any other activity related to this visit. Apart from this text, a verb *wgr* is only attested in Rob Maš 1/10–11, where Beeston *et al.* (1982: 158) translate "be stoned".

[10] The pronominal suffix *-hmw* as well as the verb *ʿkrw* are masculine plural and thus cannot apply to the three women alone.

[11] See Stein, 2010: 314. Another probable example is Ja 567/10–12: *w-rʾ k-*s^1*tmlʾ<<h>>w b-ʿm ʾlmqh k-* (11) *hmy b-ṣdqm w-hkn hwt ḥlmn w-wkbw b-ʿm* (12) *ʾlmqh k-b-ṣdqm w-hkn hkn hwt ḥlmn* "and behold, they asked ʾLMQH for a fulfilment whether (it is) in good order [= true] and (whether) that (aforementioned) dream was brought into being, and they found with ʾLMQH (the responding fulfilment) that it was in good order and that that dream was in fact brought into being".

[12] This was already shown by Drewes and Ryckmans (1997: 226) for Oost.Inst. 14/5. See also Stein, 2010: 33 n. 107; 720.

[13] That the verb *gtzḥ*, otherwise unattested, denotes some kind of business activity was already supposed by Jamme (1982: 26) on the basis of the Arabic root (see above, note 8). The meaning "?accept bride-gift" as proposed in Beeston *et al.* (1982: 52) does not fit the context.

[14] The adjective forms part of a group of several terms used in receipts and other documents announcing the final settlement of an earlier financial debt, but is never used in inscriptions documenting the existence of such a dept. The interpretation given in Beeston *et al.* (1982: 92) "binding, effective" is thus to be rejected. See e.g. *w-ẓhrn ḏ-hẓhr b-ʿly hlkʾmr w-* (13) *ḥmʿṯt* s^3*ḫlm w-nfqm bn ʿly-hmy* (14) *ḏ-b-hw hẓhry hn blṭn ʾlfn* (CIH 376/12–14) "And the promissory note which was put on record against HLKʾMR and ḤMʿṮT is settled and torn away from them, (namely, the promissory note) in which those (aforementioned) thousand *blṭ*-coins were put on record".

at the beginning of line 12, stating something like "as for the statuette, he has ... it to them". Secondly, the subject for our missing predicate could be the statuette itself. Since the statuette is feminine, although the predicate is not marked as such, it is obvious that, in this case, the predicate cannot be a verb. Given the context and the construction, the most probable reconstruction would be *f-ʾl*, leading to a translation "as for the statuette, it is not to them", i.e. "it did not belong to them".

The account of the acquisition of the statuette ends here. All the remaining part of the section (ll. 12–15) deals with how the women managed to get rid of it again. For reasons we do not know, they must have felt rather uneasy with the situation. It might be that they simply thought that they had not properly acquired the object and feared the sudden reappearance of the dealer, or it might be that they felt slightly embarrassed because the latter showed so little interest in his claims, thus putting a rather bad light on the whole transaction. Perhaps they suspected the statuette was stolen loot and they did not want to be involved in the affair. In the end, they decided to seek help from the deity. One of the women, NᶜMGD, thus entered the temple ḤRWNM and asked ʾLMQH for a fulfilment. The result of this was favourable, because, as we are told (l. 14), "he restored to her". Given the beginning of the section, it must have been during this "restoration" that ʾLMQH declared himself to be the one who "gave and granted" (l. 6) the statuette. This, of course, implies that it now legally belonged to the women, even though the method of acquisition might be rather questionable. Nevertheless, this gift was only temporarily theirs, because in the end, the deity commanded that the statuette should be dedicated, i.e. given back, to him. This command was obeyed by the three women and resulted in the present dedication.

We can thus translate it as follows:

(1–5) NᶜMGD, [daughter of the (women) of] ṮḤYᶜZ, and HNʾṮWN and NᶜMT, daughters of the (women) of ṮḤYᶜZ, maidservants of S¹ᶜDS²MSM, the Kabsite, have dedicated to ʾLMQH ṮHWN and ṮWR BᶜLM, the two lords of (the temple) ḤRWNM, the (present female) statuette in bronze (5–8) that ʾLMQH gave and granted his maidservants, (the women) of ṮḤYᶜZ via a man who came and ... their house ... 'in the night of the sixth'. (9–10) [And] (that man) summoned them whether they wanted to buy that statuette. (10–12) After that, they came into the open in order to engage in (some financial) transaction with the man, (but) he 'separated' from it; and the statuette was not (lawfully) to them (?). (12–14) And that woman NᶜMGD entered (the temple) ḤRWNM and asked ʾLMQH for a fulfilment, and he restored to her. (14–15) And he ordered (them) to dedicate him that statuette. (15–20) And ʾLMQH shall deliver, protect and save the body of her (NᶜMGD's?) lord MHˀBḌM,[15] son of WDM, and her/his son LḤYᶜṮT, and his (ʾLMQH's) maidservants, the (women) of ṮḤYᶜZ, from malice and bad fate, and from the upheaval of an enemy. By ᶜṮTR and ʾLMQH.

CIH 581 is, of course, a rather unusual example of a dedication. While virtually all other texts of this genre can be traced back to some sort of divine favour, be it obtained in the past or expected for the future, which finally resulted in the acquisition and subsequent dedication of an object, this text describes a completely different situation. It does not originate in a divine favour but in the object ultimately being dedicated to the deity. In effect, the whole dedication only took place because the people dedicating it found themselves provided with a statuette without having acquired it properly. Even though traditional formulae seeking divine protection are applied towards the end of the text, what they expected from the deity was probably little more than an opportunity to rid themselves of this dubious property.

Acknowledgements

This paper was written in the framework of a research project entitled "Archäologische und epigraphische Erforschung der sabäischen Hauptstadt Marib (Jemen)" the epigraphic part of which is housed at the Friedrich-Schiller-Universität Jena. This project is generously supported by the Deutsche Forschungsgemeinschaft.

Sigla

CIH	Inscriptions in *Corpus inscriptionum semiticarum*. Pars iv. *Inscriptiones ḥimyariticas et sabaeas continens*. Paris: Reipublicae Typographeo, 1889–1932.
Ir 3	Inscription in al-ʾIryānī 1990.
Ja	Inscriptions in Jamme 1962.
Lisān	Ibn Manẓūr 1997–1998.
Oost.Inst. 14	Inscription in Drewes & Ryckmans 1997.
RES 4150	Inscription in Mordtmann & Mittwoch 1932.
Rob Maš 1	Inscription in Robin & Ryckmans 1978.

[15] The name could be read as either MHBḌM or MḪBḌM.

References

Beeston A.F.L.

1978. Temporary Marriage in Pre-Islamic South Arabia. *Arabian Studies* 4: 21–25.

Beeston A.F.L., Ghul M.A., Müller W.W & Ryckmans J.

1982. *Sabaic Dictionary (English-French-Arabic)*. (Publication of the University of Sanaa, YAR). Louvain-la-Neuve: Peeters/Beirut: Librairie du Liban.

Drewes A.J. & Ryckmans J.

1997. Un pétiole de palme inscrit en sabéen, no. 14 de la collection de l'Oosters Instituut à Leyde. *Proceedings of the Seminar for Arabian Studies* 27: 225–230.

Höfner M.

1938. Die Inschriften aus Glasers Tagebuch XI (Mārib). *Wiener Zeitschrift zur Kunde des Morgenlands* 45: 7–37.

Ibn Manẓūr, Muḥammad b. Mukarram.

1997–1998. *Lisān al-ᶜarab*. (7 volumes) Beirut: Dār Ṣādir.

al-Iryānī M.ᶜA.

1990. *Fī taʾrīh al-Yaman. Nuqūsh musnadiyyah wa-taᶜlīqāt*. (Second edition). Ṣanᶜāʾ: Markaz al-dirāsāt wa 'l-buḥūth al-yamanī.

Jamme A.

1962. *Sabaean Inscriptions from Maḥram Bilqîs (Mârib)*. Baltimore, MD: Johns Hopkins Press.

1982. *Miscellanées d'ancient* (sic) *arabe XII*. Washington. [Published by the author].

Leslau W.

1991. *Comparative Dictionary of Geᶜez (Classical Ethiopic)*. Wiesbaden: Harrassowitz.

Mordtmann J.H. & Mittwoch E.

1932. *Himjarische Inschriften in den Staatlichen Museen zu Berlin*. (Mitteilungen der Vorderasiatische-Aegyptischen Gesellschaft [E.V.] 37.1) Leipzig: J.C. Hinrich'sche Buchhandlung.

Rhodokanakis N.

1926. Altsüdarabische Inschriften. Pages 463–471 in H. Gressmann (ed.), *Altorientalische Texte zum Alten Testament*. (Second edition). Berlin/Leipzig: Walter de Gruyter & Co.

Robin C. & Ryckmans J.

1978. L'attribution d'un bassin à une divinité en Arabie du Sud antique. *Raydān* 1: 39–64.

Stein P.

2002. Schreibfehler im Sabäischen am Beispiel der mittelsabäischen Widmungsinschriften. *Le Muséon* 115: 423–467.

2010. *Die altsüdarabischen Minuskelinschriften aus der Bayerischen Staatsbibliothek in München*. Bd. 1: *Die Inschriften der mittel- und spätsabäischen Periode*. Tübingen/Berlin: Wasmuth.

Author's address

Anne Multhoff, Friedrich-Schiller-Universität Jena, Institut für Sprachen und Kulturen des Vorderen Orients, Löbdergraben 24a, D–07737 Jena, Germany.

e-mail multistein@t-online.de

Proceedings of the Seminar for Arabian Studies 40 (2010): 239–246

The semantic structure of motion verbs in the dialect of Zabīd (Yemen)

Samia Naïm

Summary

This article deals with the basic active motion verbs such as "coming" and "going", in the vernacular Arabic of Zabīd. Primary data reveals the existence of no less than twelve verbs distributed into sub-groups. We first present the semantic components of these verbs, their distribution, and their pragmatic uses. The underlying systems that the study reveals are then considered from a typological point of view. To which typological category of motion verbs attested in the languages of the world does the Arabic vernacular of Zabīd belong? The study reveals the existence of a specific system not previously mentioned for any language, which may provide a useful contribution to the theoretical and typological study of space and the lexicon related to it.

Keywords: Yemen, semantics, motion verbs, lexicalization, temporality

1. Introduction

Spatial relations have been the object of many studies during the last decades. Among the different approaches dealing with the subject, many works took for their object the expression of "location" and "motion". In a large number of languages motion is expressed by verbs, in association with "satellites" (particles, prepositions) — or not, depending on languages and on verbs, cf. verb-framed/satellite-framed system (Talmy 2007). In addition, motion verbs may be divided into two groups: movement verbs such as "to jump, to swim, to crawl" and displacement verbs such as "to leave, to go, to come, to come down". This division is not absolute insofar as the languages of the world do not all identify the two groups of verbs, but it is relevant in the vernacular Arabic of Zabīd (central Yemeni Tihāmah).[1] In this article we will consider displacement verbs and, more specifically, basic active motion verbs such as "coming" and "going", which reveal a specific semantic structure, to our knowledge not yet mentioned in any language description.

2. Basic active motion verbs

Five verbs figure under the general notion of "going", and seven under "coming", as shown in Figure 1.

Going	*Coming*
rāḥ	ʔata
našar	rawwaḥ
bāk	warad
ṣāb	baḥðan
sāfar	ʔaggal
	ðahhar
	dann

These verbs are likely to be set out again in three sub-groups, general, specific, and temporal, according to the complexity of their semantic components. This means that the general sub-system does not correspond here to the one that is most recurrent, but to the least complex one.

General	*Specific*	*Temporal*
rāḥ	našar	ʔaggal
ʔata	warad	baḥḥan
bāk	bāk	ðahhar
rawwaḥ	rawwaḥ	dann
sāfar	ṣāb	

One pair of verbs, *bāk* and *rawwaḥ*, figures in two different sub-systems, the general and the specific (Fig. 2). Depending on the situation of the discourse and the frame of the displacement, these two verbs may incorporate a co-event with the motion event, as we will show later.

[1] The data has been collected during two fieldwork trips conducted in 1993 and 1995 in Zabīd and two other villages, Ḥusaynīyah and Ṣuwayq, less than 18 km from Zabīd. Not all the motion verbs collected in Zabīd are attested in the two other villages. It is interesting to note that neither Greenman (1979) nor Prochazka (1987) mention the existence of this type of verb in Tihāmah or in Zabīd. In this paper, I focus on Zabīd's vernacular because it is in this village that I had the opportunity to undertake all necessary verification, having resided with a Ḥaḍramī family. All thanks are due to them.

2.1. The general system

The general system consists of five verbs; the source, the path, and the goal of the motion being conveyed by directionals.

2.1.1. To go: rāḥ

With *rāḥ* the source of the motion is expressed by the ablative *min* (example 2) and the goal by the allative *sana* (example 3). The verb is also attested as an auxiliary followed by a verb in the imperfect (example 4).

(1)

fēn	*ruḥt?*
Where	go. PFV.2SGM

"Where did you go?"

(2)

qal-l-u	*xlas*	*rəḥ-l-ak*	*min*	*ᵊl-rəggāl*
tell. PFV.3SGM- DAT-3SGM	enough	go. IMP.SGM- DAT-2SGM	ABL	the-man

"He said to him: that is enough, do not annoy this man any more [go from him]"

(3)

rāḥ	*sanā-(ø)*
go. PFV.3SG	ALL- 3SGM

"He went to him"

(4)

ša-rəḥ	*ʔətqarraʔ*
FUT-go. IPFV.1SG	have breakfast. IPFV.1SG

"I will have my breakfast"

2.1.2. To come: ʔata

Like *rāḥ* "to go", *ʔata* does not incorporate in its semantic structure the goal or the source of the motion. In the examples presented below, the goal is introduced by the directionals *ʔind* (example 7) and *sana* (example 9). In example 8, the motion the speaker refers to is deictically anchored in the speaker.

(5)

ša-ʔēt	*m-lēl*
FUT-come. IPFV.1SG	the-night

"I shall come at night"

(6)

ʔata	*biḥīn*
come. PFV.3SGM	early

"He came early"

(7)

ʔata	*l-malik*	*yaxṭəb*	*ʔind-u*
come. PFV.3SGM	the-king	become engaged. IPFV.3SGM	DIR-3SGM

"The king came to him to ask for the hand of his daughter"

(8)

ʔat-an	*təzūr-anī*
come.PFV-3SGF	visit.IPFV.3SGF-1SG

"She came to visit me"

Depending on the context, this verb can take different values, "to go, to come back, to approach". Other examples are presented here, showing the distinct values of *ʔata*, depending on the point of view adopted by the speaker or the narrator, whether he is focusing on the source or on the goal of the motion, or whether he takes this or that person or character as a point of reference. As we have noted for *rāḥ*, *ʔata* has a strong output as an auxiliary of time and aspect (example 12).

(9)

ʔata	*sana*	*zōgt-u*
go. PFV.3SGM	DIR	wife- 3SGM

"He went to his wife"

(10)

ʔat-an	*ʔind*	*bət-he*	*baggar-an*	*f-wagh*	*bət-he*
go. PFV-3SGF	DIR	daughter- 3SGF	look amazed eyes. PFV-3SGF	-face LOC	daughter- 3SGF

"She went to her daughter [and] she looked at her with amazed eyes"

(11)

Lattaf	*kowsara*	*ḥasamu*	*w*	*ʔate*
fill. PFV.3SGM	basket	gravel	and	come. PFV.3SGM

"He filled a basket with stones and came back"

(12)

ʔata	*ykəl*	*l*	*zōgt-u*
go. PFV.3SGM	say. IPFV.3SGM	DAT	wife- 3SGM

"He went to say [something] to his wife"

2.1.3. To go: bāk

The verb *bāk* figures in the specific sub-system as well, where it shows a complex semantic structure. In the general system, *bāk* means "to go" and is usually followed by the allative *sana*. The verb is very productive as an auxiliary of time and aspect, especially for the expression of the durative (a temporally not delimited process): in these constructions, it is followed by a verb in the imperfect (examples 15 & 16). According to native speakers, there is no real difference between *bāk* and *rāḥ*, both mean "to go", but *bāk* is more colloquial and more often employed in everyday speech.

(13)

bāk-an	*sana*	*rāʔi*	*l-ḥalāwi*
go.	ALL	cook	the-pastry
PFV-3SGF			

"She went to see the pastry cook"

(14)

bāk	*yṣobb*	*ʔarūsa*
go.	mould.	doll
PFV.3SGM	IPFV.3SGM	

"He went to make a doll"

(15)

tabūk	*telgaḥ*	*w*	*tēti*
go.	go and come.	and	come.
IPFV.3SGF	IPFV.3SGF		IPFV.3SGF

"She was coming and going through the streets"

(16)

bāk-an	*tamši*	*tše*	*tḥīd*	*bət-he*
go.	walk.	want.	see.	daughter-
PFV-3SGF	IMP.3SGF	IMP.3SGF	IMP.3SGF	3SGF

"She started up, in search of her daughter"

2.1.4. To go (away): rawwaḥ

This verb also figures in the specific sub-system. In the general system, it is most often used intransitively and is shown in the imperative mood. In this context, *rawwaḥ* means "go away". In transitive constructions, the verb is followed by a directional that introduces the source of the motion, such as *min* in example 18.

(17)

qal-l-u	*yalla*	*kəm*	*rawwiḥ*
tell.			go away.
PFV.3SGM-DAT-3SGM	INTRJ	IMP.SGM	IMP.SGM

"He said to him: 'go, go away'"

(18)

rawwaḥ	*ət-tāli*	<u>*min*</u>	*ʔindu-hum*
go.	the-other		
PFV.3SGM		DIR	LOC-3PL

"He [the other] went away from their house"

When *rawwaḥ* is followed by the word "home" in the position of a direct object, it does not mean "to go from" any more, but "to go back home". We will return to this construction under the specific sub-system.

(19)

rawwaḥ-an	*m-bēt*
go.	the-house
PFV-3SGF	

"She went back home"

2.1.5. To travel: sāfar

Sāfar is used whenever somebody goes outside Zabīd, even if it is only to go to a village a few kilometres away, [*lā hū warāʔ l-madīneh, sāfar*] "If it is outside the city, [one employs the word] *sāfar*", whereas in a large variety of vernacular Arabic dialects, *sāfar* means "to go abroad". This verb constitutes a useful introduction to the specific sub-system, which, as we will demonstrate, has for its principal framework of reference the city of Zabīd.

2.2 The specific sub-system

The specific sub-system includes verbs characterized by a complex semantic structure. Five verbs figure in this sub-system; four of them are distributed in pairs, *bāk* and *našar* "to go", on the one hand, and *warad* and *rawwaḥ* "to come back" on the other hand; the last verb is *ṣāb* "to go to".

2.2.1 To go: bāk and našar

As we have seen previously, *bāk* is part of the general system as well (2.1.3). The direction of the displacement is encoded by directionals (see example 13). By contrast, the verb *našar* belongs exclusively to the specific sub-system. These two verbs may be found in the same context, such as in the couple of examples presented below in parallel.

(13)

bāk-an	*sana*	*rāʔi*	*l-ḥalāwi*
go.		cook	the-pastry
PFV-3SGF	DIR		

"She went to see the pastry cook"

(20)

bāk-an	*m-sɔ̄q*
go.	the-market
PFV-3SGF	

"She went to the market."

(20a)

našar	*m-sɔ̄q*
go.	the-market
PFV.3SGM	

"He went to the market"

(21)

fēn	*bāyke?*
where	go.
	PTCP.3SGF

"Where are you going?"

(21a)

fēn	*nāšre?*
where	go.
	PTCP.3SGF

"Where are you going?"

There is, nevertheless, a semantic constraint attached to the usage of each verb. What distinguishes these two verbs is their temporal compatibility: *bāk* is temporally anchored in the period going from the morning, *ṣabḥa*, to the middle of the afternoon, *qarīb al-ʔaṣir*; whereas *našar* relates to the period from the middle of the afternoon to nightfall, *baʔd al-ʔišī*. If the examples (20) and (21a) are both judged acceptable, in the following example (22) only *bāk*, which is temporally compatible with lunchtime, is judged acceptable (i.e. not example 22a).

(22)

bukt	*ʔatġadde*	*bēt*	*fulān*
go.	have lunch.	house	So-and-so
PFV.1SG	IPFV.1SG		

"I went to lunch at someone's place"

(22a) *

našart	*ʔatġadde*	*bēt*	*fulān*

2.2.2 To come/go back: warad and rawwaḥ

These two verbs have the same semantic distribution as *bāk* and *našar*. They can alternate in a neutral temporal context such as in example (23) but they differ on their temporal compatibility, i.e. *warad* is used when the event takes place between the morning and the middle of the afternoon, and *rawwaḥ* when the event takes place between the middle of the afternoon and nightfall. In (24a), *rawwaḥ* is judged unacceptable because school stops at noon.

(23)

ḥīn	*waradtī / rawwaḥtī*
when	come back. / come back.
	PFV.2SGF / PFV.2SGF

"When did you come back?"

(24)

waradu	*min*	*al-madrasah*
come back.		the school
PFV.3PL	ABL	

"They came back from school"

(24a)

rawwaḥu	*min*	*al-madrasah*

Moreover, these two verbs differ with respect to an additional element incorporated to their semantic structure: with *warad* it is the achievement of the motion event that is focalized (stative verb), whereas with *rawwaḥ* it is the trajectory or the path that is focalized (dynamic verb). Thus, a dynamic sentence such as *yalla nūrid* "Let us go home" is judged unacceptable, but it is quite suitable with *rawwaḥ*, if the event takes place in the afternoon (example 25). If the event takes place during the morning, one would have to resort to the verb *bāk* "to go" which also figures in the general system (example 26).

(25)

yalla	*nrawwiḥ*
	go.
EXH	IPFV.1PL

"Let us go home"

(26)

yalla	*nbūk*	*m-bēt*
	go.	the-house
EXH	IPFV.1PL	

"Let us go home"

2.2.3. To visit: ṣāb

The verb *ṣāb* is specific to women's speech. It means "to visit one another repeatedly" and refers to the principal social activity of women in the afternoon. When it is specified, the goal of the displacement is introduced by directionals such as *ʔind* and *la* (example 28).

(27)

yalla	*nṣābi*
	visit.
EXH	IPFV.1PL

"Let us go to visit" [have a round of visits]

(28)

yalla	*nṣābi*	*ʔind*	/	*la*	*maryam*
exh	visit. IPFV.1PL	dir	/	DIR	Mariam

"Let us visit/go to Maryam"

The verb is incompatible with the morning period: it cannot be associated or composed with *bāk* in a verbal phrase (as in example 29).

(29)

fēn	*bāyke?*	(?)	*bāyke*	*ṣābi*
where	go. PTCP. SGF			

"Where are you going?"

(30)

fēn	*nāšre?*	*nāšre*	*ṣābi*
where	go. PTCP.SGF	go. PTCP.SGF	visit. IPFV.1SG

"Where are you going?" "I am going to visit"

2.2.4 The temporal component of the specific sub-system

In the specific sub-system, all the verbs incorporate a temporal dimension into their spatial meaning (motion event), which is revealed by their contextual compatibility. This specificity raises the question of the stability of the temporal element in the core of these verbs: to what extent can temporality be considered as lexicalized?

To answer this question, we will give more information about the specific sub-system first. The data which exposes the sub-system consists of ordinary daily life speeches, conversational discourses, and dialogues recorded on the spot, whereas the data related to the general system consists of real or fictional accounts (stories, tales, etc.). Thus the frame related to motion verbs in each system is not the same: the frame of the specific system relates to the daily displacements within the city of Zabīd.

The verbs *bāk* and *rawwaḥ* figure in both systems, the specific and the general, where the temporal dimension is absent. Moreover, in the general system, *rawwaḥ* means "to go away" (unless it is followed by the word "home", see 2.1.4). Whereas in the specific sub-system this verb means "to go back home", the goal of the displacement ("home") is incorporated to its meaning. Since all the other verbs of the specific system are underlain by temporal constraints, it is reasonable, first, to consider that temporality is lexicalized in all the verbs of the specific system, and second, to conclude that *bāk* and *rawwaḥ* have two lexical entries, with temporality integrated in the core of one of them.[2]

2.3 The temporal sub-system

By temporal sub-system, we refer to motion verbs formed on temporal roots or derived from temporal expressions. These verbs are strongly linked to interlocutory situations.

2.3.1 To come early: *baḥḥan*

The verb *baḥḥan* is derived from the temporal adverb *biḥīn* "early", which is a contraction of *bi* (particle) and *ḥīn* "moment". It expresses the anteriority of an event to another. In example 31 the speaker refers to an invitation for lunch and tells her addressee "come before lunchtime":

(31)

bukra	*baḥḥinī*
tomorrow	come early. IMP.2SGF

"Tomorrow, come early" [before lunchtime]

2.3.2. To come back quickly: *ʔaggal*

The verb's root √ʕʒl expresses the notion of quickness. It is used when one says goodbye at the door: it means "do not be long to come back", an equivalent to the English "see you soon". More often than not, this verb is attested at the imperative mood: /*ʔaggilī*/ "come back (F) quickly". Considering the enunciative situation, the goal of the displacement is deictically anchored in the speaker here.

2.3.3 to come/be late: *ḍahhar* and *dann*

The verb *ḍahhar* is a denominative verb formed from *ḍɔhr* "midday". It is used when somebody is late for an appointment during the morning period. It means "he came late". In the same way, the verb *dann* is used for a delay in the afternoon. The etymology of *dann* is not obvious. The verb could derive from √DNY, which, at the second form of the verb, means "to approach, to come near". The semantic relation with "being late" becomes clear through the answer to the question, "why are you late?" According to my informants, this answer is always:

[2] In previous work I suggested that, from a diachronic point of view, the temporality of the verb *bāk* has emerged by default, in parallel with the temporality integrated to the verb *našar* "to go in the afternoon" (Naïm 2006).

[*əl-lēl dannēnī*] "It is because of the night" (literally: the night came near to me). So a metaphoric use of the verb *dann* seems acceptable here: I am late because the night fell on me and I couldn't hasten any more.

(32)

mā-l-ik	*ð̣ahharti*	*mā-l-ik*	*dannēti*
why- DAT-2SGF	be late. PFV.2SGF	why -DAT-2SGF	be late. PFV.2SGF
Why are you late? (a.m.)		Why are you late? (p.m.)	

3. The semantic components of motion verbs

Going	*Motion*	*Path*	*Temporality*	*Manner*	*Purpose*
rāḥ	+	+	-		
našar	+	+	+		
bāk	+	+	-		
ṣāb	+	+	+		+
sāfar	+	+	-		
ʔata	+	+	-		
rawwaḥ	+	+	-		
warad	+	+	-		
baḥḥan	+	+	+		
ʔaggal	+	+		+	
ð̣ahhar	+	+	+		
dann	+	+	+		

In a recent study, Leonard Talmy (2007) proposed three typological categories for motion verbs, based on the examination of their components in many languages of the world. This work reveals three principal components lexicalized in the verb root: 1. The co-event (the manner or the cause of the motion); 2. the path (the vector, the conformation, and the deictic); and 3. the figure (the moving object). Semitic is among languages that conflate motion + path.

In the vernacular Arabic of Zabīd, all motion verbs presented here conflate the motion event and the path (Fig. 3). Two verbs of the specific system, *ʔaggal* and *ṣāb*, conflate an additional element: *ʔaggal* > motion + path + manner; *ṣāb* > motion + path + purpose. Yet the temporal element persists, a pattern which does not fit with the patterns proposed by Talmy, and which is central to the dialect of Zabīd since it underlies a major system, the specific.

Indeed, under co-event, Talmy (2007: 85-87), besides manner and cause, distinguishes other kinds of relation between a co-event and the motion event, attested in the languages of the world, i.e. precursion, enablement, concomitance, and subsequence (including consequence/purpose). None of these relations, which at different degrees convey a temporal relation (or rather an aspectual relation) with the motion event, corresponds to the temporality of motion verbs in the dialect of Zabīd. In fact, temporality operates here as the reference par excellence for the specific system, i.e. it establishes a relation between the linguistic expression (motion verbs) and the extra-linguistic reality to which the expression refers (the daily life in Zabīd). We may consider temporality as an equivalent to what Talmy calls "Ground", an abstract equivalent nevertheless because, in the terminology of Talmy, "Ground" is closely associated with a concrete object:

The basic Motion event consists of one object (the "Figure") moving or located with respect to another object (the reference-object or "Ground"). It is analysed as having four components: besides "Figure" and "Ground", there are "Path" and "Motion". The "Path" is the path followed or site occupied by the Figure object with respect to the Ground object. (Talmy 2007: 70)

Moreover, all the examples given by Talmy to illustrate the Ground component confirm this formal definition: English "emplane" (verb root — plane) "move with respect to an airplane" (2007: 99). In this respect, two verbs of the temporal system, *baḥḥan* "to come early" and *ð̣ahhar* "to come late" may be categorized under verbs which conflate motion-event and ground: *ð̣ahhar* (verb root "midday"), *baḥḥan* (verb root "early").

Furthermore, it seems that in the languages of the world, "the Ground does not by itself conflate with the Motion verb to form any language's core system for expressing Motion. Conflations of this sort may not even form any minor systems" (2007: 99). Talmy proposes different explanations to that in terms of economy (being the most unvarying component, the Ground does not need specification), saliency (the Ground is the component the least salient or least accessible to identification) or hierarchy. On the basis of the concept of hierarchy he concludes:

The different conflation types seem to be ranked in their prevalence among the world's languages, with conflation of Path apparently as the most extensively represented, of Co-event next, and of Figure least so. It may therefore be the case that Ground conflation is also a possibility, but one so unlikely that it has not yet been instantiated in any language that has come to attention (2007: 100).

If we admit the existence of an abstract ground, as defined above, we may say that for the specific system temporality constitutes the ground. Besides, such an alternative to a concrete, formally expressed Ground, still remains in agreement with the economy, saliency, and hierarchy to which Talmy refers to define the Ground: the temporality of the motion verbs has been revealed by the examination of their compatibility (i.e. the constraints attached to each verb) and not just by looking into their lexical components. Thus, the vernacular Arabic of Zabīd may be that language which testifies to the existence of a language core system with the conflation motion verb + Ground.[3]

Abbreviations

1	first person	IMP	imperative
2	second person	INTRJ	interjection
3	third person	IPFV	imperfective
ABL	ablative	LOC	locative
ALL	allative	M	masculine
DAT	dative	PFV	perfective
DIR	directional	PL	plural
EXH	exhortative	PTCP	participle
F	feminine	SG	singular
FUT	future		

References

Behnstedt P.
1985. *Die nordjemenitischen Dialecte*. i. *Atlas*. Wiesbaden: DR. Ludwig Reichert.
1987. *Die Dialecte der gegend von Ṣaʿah (Nord-Jemen)*. Wiesbaden: Harrassowitz.

Greenman J.
1979. A sketch of the Arabic dialect of the Central Yamani Tihāmah. *Zeitschrift für arabische Linguistik* 3: 47–61.

Landberg L.C.
1901. *Études sur les dialectes de l'Arabie méridionale. Hadramoût.* i. Leiden: Brill.

Naïm S.
2006. Les cadres temporels du déplacement (parlers yéménites de la mer Rouge). Pages 81–103 in S. Naïm (ed.), *La rencontre du Temps et de l'Espace. Approches linguistique et anthropologique.* Leuven/Paris: Peeters.

Piamenta M.
1990–1991. *Dictionary of Post-Classical Yemeni Arabic.* (2 volumes). Leiden: Brill.

Prochazka S.
1987. Remarks on the spoken Arabic of Zabīd. *Zeitschrift für arabische Linguistik* 17: 58–68.

Talmy L.
2007. Lexical typologies. Pages 66–168 in T. Shopen (ed.), *Language Typology and Syntaxic Description.* Cambridge: Cambridge University Press.

Author's address
Dr Samia Naïm, CNRS — LACITO, 33 avenue des Gobelins, 75013 Paris, France.
e-mail snaim@vjf.cnrs.fr

[3] Such systems are not so common in Arabic dialects. There is no equivalent to these verbs in the vernacular of Ṣanʕā, for example. In other Yemenite dialects (Piamenta 1990–1991; Behnstedt 1985; Landberg 1901), we can find one or other of these verbs (mainly *našar*), but on the basis of these scattered and incomplete data, it is impossible to know if such a temporal system actually exists in other Yemenite dialects. However, it seems that the vernacular of Ṣaʕdah presents similar data (Behnstedt 1987), as well as Mehri, a modern South Arabian language spoken in Yemen and Oman (Janet Watson, personal communication).

Proceedings of the Seminar for Arabian Studies 40 (2010): 247–266

Preliminary results of the Dhofar archaeological survey

LYNNE S. NEWTON & JURIS ZARINS

Summary
A general archaeological survey of the Governorate of Dhofar, Sultanate of Oman, conducted under the auspices of the Office of the Advisor to H.M. the Sultan for Cultural Affairs, was carried out from 2008 to 2009. Over 300 new sites have been identified, adding to the 800 previously known sites. Identification covers the lower Palaeolithic through to the Islamic period. Geographically, sites have been identified from the Rub^{c} al-Khālī, Nejd (Najd), the Dhofar hills, and the coastal plains. The most outstanding results of the survey to date include:
1) the prolific nature of the Upper Palaeolithic in the fore Nejd;
2) the Neolithic occupation of the Nejd and Dhofar hills (8500–3500 BCE);
3) the expansion of cattle and ovicaprid domestication in the Bronze Age of the Dhofar hills and Salalah plain (3500–1000 BCE);
4) Iron Age rock shelters in the Dhofar hills with associated stratigraphical debris and rock paintings;
5) the recognition of early Islamic seaports on the Dhofar coast;
6) the integration of archaeological sites into the medieval al-Baleed (al-Balīd) horizon (1000–1500 CE).

Keywords: Dhofar, Oman, archaeological survey, prehistoric archaeology, historic archaeology

Introduction

An archaeological survey of Dhofar, the southern region of Oman that stretches from Sharbithāt up to Muqshin in the east to Dalqut up to al-Hashman in the west, was conducted by the authors from May 2008 to June 2009. A total of 310 new sites were registered during this survey covering the Palaeolithic to the medieval Islamic periods.

The ecology of Dhofar

Archaeological survey was conducted in at least four major ecological zones of Dhofar, including the coastal plain, uplands, Nejd and Rub^{c} al Khālī.

Dhofar has an environment unique to the rest of Arabia, as it is quenched by the mists, and sometimes rain, of the south-west monsoon each summer. From approximately mid-June to mid-September upwelling in the ocean pounds the coast, while the coastal plain and mountains become a sea of green. In combination with the ecological zones mentioned above and the south-west monsoon, a particularly distinctive and diverse flora has evolved (Miller & Morris 1998; Ghazanfar 1994; Pickering & Patzelt 2008: 1). Perhaps the bridge through all periods of occupation in Dhofar is frankincense (*Boswellia sacra*), the most prized variety growing on the back slopes of the Dhofar mountains in the Nejd. Thus, Dhofar's unique environment is important when considering the archaeology of the region as it has influenced human occupation here since the Palaeolithic (Parker & Rose 2008).

In the early Holocene the monsoon was much stronger than it is today, as evidenced by lakes in the Rub^{c} al-Khālī. The Neolithic sites in this area attest to contemporary human occupation. With the weakening of monsoonal flows, human occupation retreated to regions bordering the desert. The Bronze Age occupation of the Dhofar mountains and upland Nejd attest to these adaptations as human occupation becomes more complex with the establishment of hierarchical chiefdoms.

Environmental considerations are equally important when discussing historical and current inhabitants and their traditional territories in the Iron Age. For example, Bedouin, who first appear in the ESA inscriptions of the Ḥaḍramawt by the third century CE as 'ARB (Newton 2009: 16 and refs), are usually associated with the more arid Nejd and desert environs, while Modern South Arabic Language (MSAL) speakers (often quoted generically as "jebbali") are customarily transhumant cattle pastoralists who seasonally inhabit the mountains and coastal plains

(Janzen 1986). The archaeology of the region reflects this type of transhumant lifestyle at least since the Bronze Age (see below).

Settled sections of Bedouin tribes became the dominant element of the urban landscape and over time they have become distinct from their nomadic counterparts. Urbanization in Dhofar began in the late Iron Age (*c.* fifth century CE, as distinct from the Khor Rori colony). The creation of towns in Dhofar is largely restricted to the littoral. Our surveys, and the work of others, have located a large number of such sites stretching from Ḥāsik to Raysūt. Such settlements originated in the Late Iron Age and continued to blossom throughout the succeeding Abbasid period (eighth–tenth centuries CE). These settlements participated in Abbasid period international trade as local wares are found in conjunction with diagnostic imports. Noteworthy, however, is the fact that Abbasid-period imports are virtually absent both in the mountains and in the Nejd.

By the eleventh century CE, small-scale Abbasid-period ports underwent consolidation in the medieval period at al-Balīd (al-Baleed), Mirbāt, and Ḥāsik. Our investigation of these sites has concluded that international trade, which linked East Africa to China, did not require natural harbours. Instead, fresh water was a key source, which allowed these settlements to grow and as suggested by historic texts, ocean-going ships anchored offshore in the roadsteads. Similar sites to the west include Kidmet Eurob (Rougeulle 2001), Qishn, and al-Shiḥr (Hardy-Guilbert 2001; 2004). Our work at these sites has again defined a ceramic assemblage composed of imported diagnostic wares (Indian Red Polished Ware, Yemen Yellow, porcelains, and stonewares) as opposed to local ceramic production, which perhaps originated both on the coastal plain and in the mountains. Note the presence of a particular ceramic type known from contexts at Zabid in the Tihīmah, the likely region of production of "Yemen Yellow" (Kennet 2004: 41–42; also referred to as mustard ware, Ciuk & Keall 1996: 4–5). This distinctive powdery yellow glazed ware with black and/or green line underglaze designs can almost exclusively be associated with the expansion of the Rasulid dynasty at Taᶜizz, Yemen (Vallet 2006). Yemen Yellow has a wide distribution as these wares have been found in East Africa (Horton 1996: 291, figs 215, 216/a–f), southern Arabia, e.g. al-Balīd and al-Shisr (Zarins, personal communication), Sharmah (Rougeulle 2003), and the UAE (Kennet 2004: 41–42).

Of course, the historical and current inter- and intra-group relationships of Dhofar's inhabitants are far more complex than presented here (e.g. Newton 2009; Peterson 2004; Janzen 1986; Carter 1982). On the whole, however, it is important to recognize the social and historical dynamics that have influenced the cultural history of Dhofar. This is particularly important when considering the development of trade and interaction in the region as the three major groups (the Bedouin, MSAL speakers, and settled Arabs) depended on each other for access to resources (e.g. milk, meat, frankincense, sardines, etc.) and devised the various socio-political institutions that facilitated safe passage along trade routes (Newton, in press).

Previous archaeological surveys in Dhofar

The American Foundation for the Study of Man (AFSM) conducted the first archaeological survey and excavations in the region from 1952–1960 (Albright 1982; Phillips 1972; Jamme 1967, 1982; Cleveland 1960). The first intensive archaeological field surveys were conducted by J. Pullar and K. Frifelt in the early 1970s and focused primarily on the Palaeolithic and Neolithic of the Nejd (Pullar & Jäckli 1978). In the late 1970s P. Costa headed survey and excavation of al-Balīd (1982). He conducted regional architectural surveys (Costa 2001; Costa & Kite 1985) and, along with G. Oman's work on the medieval Islamic cemeteries of al-Balīd and greater Salalah (1983; 1989), the more recent history of Dhofar was highlighted. J. Zarins Trans-Arabia expedition (1991–1995) excavated at al-Shisr, ᶜAyn Humran, and Tāqah and also conducted an archaeological survey with limited soundings at sites in the Nejd and the coastal plain (Zarins 2001). From 1993 to 1995 J. Owen, as part of the Trans-Arabian expedition, conducted underwater surveys around Mirbāt and Ḥāsik (1997). Similar underwater survey was continued by the Italian Mission to Oman (IMtO) by Davidde and Petriaggi (1996).

IMtO, along with its intensive excavation and restoration project at Khor Rori (Avanzini 2002; 2008) has conducted survey restricted to the Nejd, mountains, and coastal plain around Wādī Darbāt (Cremaschi & Negrino 2002; Cremaschi & Perego 2008; Dini & Tozzi 2008). Meanwhile, S. Cleuziou and M. Tosi conducted a series of small-scale surveys of shell middens along the coast around Ḥāsik (1999) while Putzolu investigated the al-Hallaniyat islands (1999). N. Whalen and K. Schatte found Lower Palaeolithic sites in Wādī ᶜAydim, Wādī Ḥalūf, and Wādī Iztah (1997), while J. Rose recently conducted survey and test excavations in Dhofar on mostly Upper

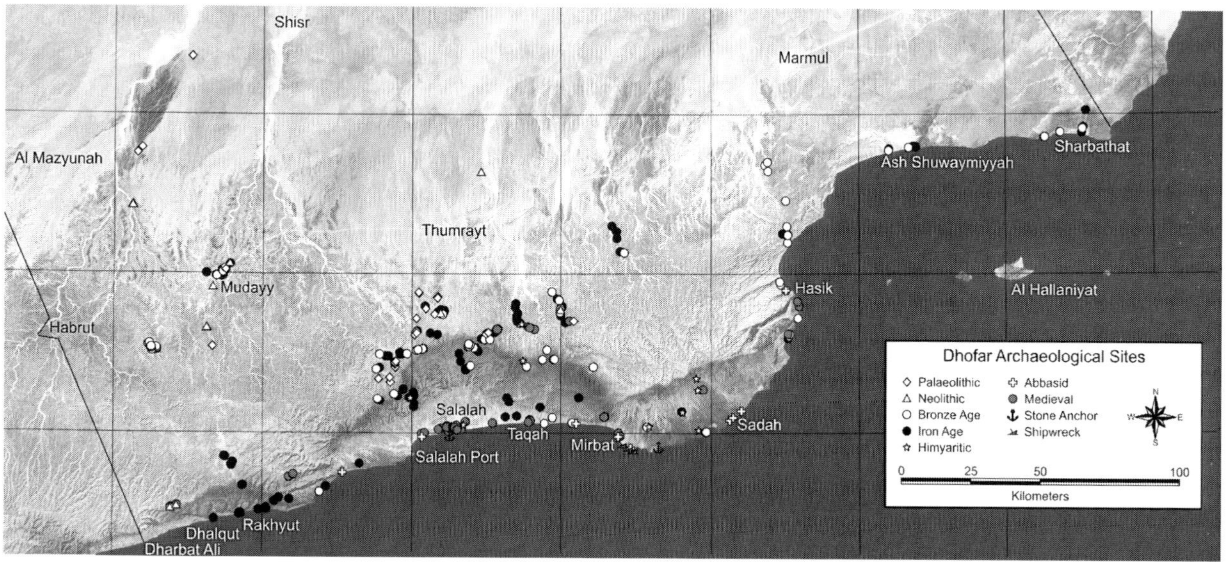

Figure 1. *The Dhofar Survey sites 2008–2009.*

Palaeolithic sites located in the Nejd between Thumrait and Marmūl (2004; 2007; Rose *et al.* 2008). More recently, a team from Brigham Young University, headed by K. Johnson, has conducted three seasons of excavation and survey in the vicinity of Mughsayl (Johnson *et al.* 2007; 2008; Johnson 2009; Glanzman, Robertson & Robertson 2009). J. McCorriston's team completed its second field season in the Nejd in early 2010.

Methodology

The objective of the current Dhofar Survey was to sample the cultural resources available in the entire Dhofar Governorate from all time periods. Based on previous surveys, certain areas were targeted for examination; for example, more time was spent in the mountains, as they had not been systematically surveyed before. These areas cross-cut ecological, geological, and historical time frames. All archaeological sites were given a Dhofar Survey (DS) number, the position was recorded with GPS, and a general collection of surface materials was made, if available. Exemplary sites were mapped and all sites were photographed and plotted on Oman topographical 1:100,000 sheets geo-rectified and loaded in Google Earth. The information and photographs of all sites were archived into a database on file at the Office of the Advisor to H.M. the Sultan for Cultural Affairs, Salalah.

Preliminary results of the Dhofar Survey (2008–2009)

A total of 310 sites dating from the Palaeolithic to the medieval Islamic periods were recorded (Fig. 1). The results of the survey are provided in brief by period below, highlighting a number of outstanding sites and their significance.

Palaeolithic (1.5 million–13,000 BP)

Nearly 10% of survey sites date to the Palaeolithic period. The Lower Palaeolithic is represented by the appearance of Lower and Middle Acheulean as defined by the presence of bifaces, cores, and retouched large flakes (Fig. 2/1–4; Whalen 2002; 2004; Rose 2004; 2007). Sites classified as Middle Palaeolithic (i.e. defined by the presence of the Levallois technique, see Fig. 2/4) are exceedingly rare and most likely represent the continuation of the preceding Acheulean period. However, within our survey the Upper Palaeolithic is extremely well represented at the immediate back-slope of the northern face of the mountains. Here, along a series of slow moving streams, Upper Palaeolithic lithic procurement sites are characteristic. Based on the work of J. Rose (2006) and others (Petraglia & Rose 2010), it appears that these sites span a time horizon of over 50,000 years, as defined by blade production (Fig. 2/6–18). Some of these sites are defined by the presence of collapsed rock shelters. Test

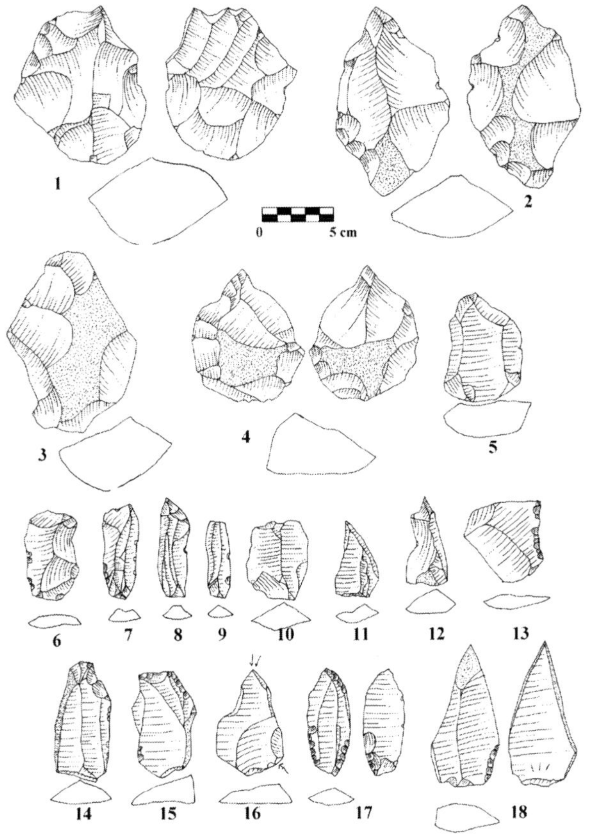

Figure 2. *Palaeolithic:* **1.** *DS-08-127 Al-Rahat;* **2.** *DS-09-281 Mudayy;* **3–4.** *DS-09-262 Tudho;* **5–18.** *DS-09-310 Hanun.*
1–4. *Lower Palaeolithic choppers and bifaces;* **5.** *Middle Palaeolithic Levallois;* **6–18.** *Upper Palaeolithic blades, burins, and flakes.*

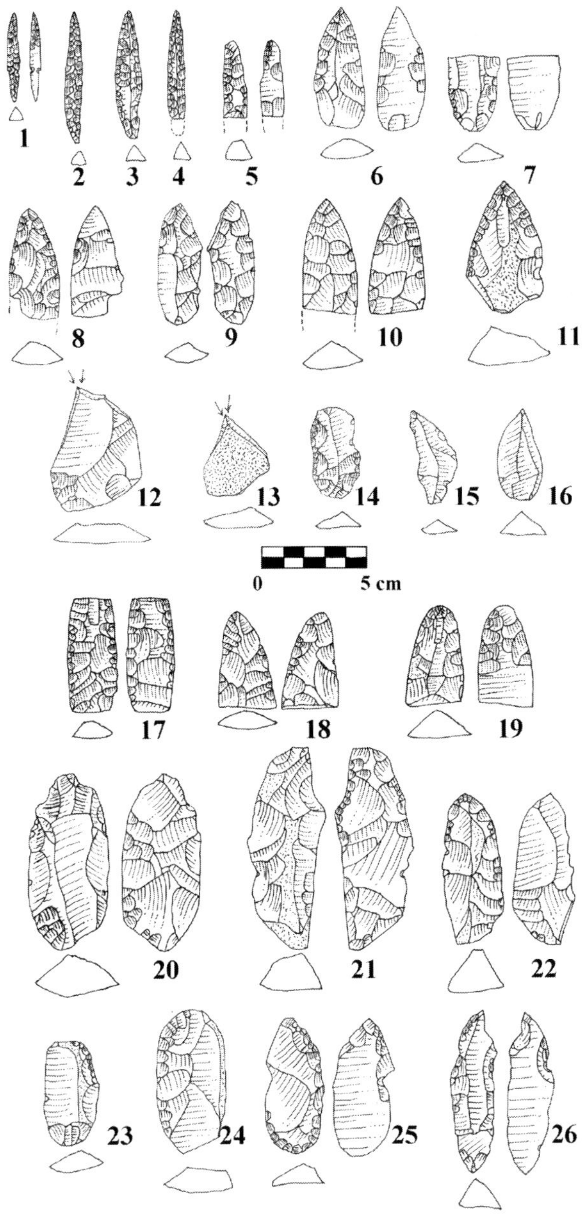

Figure 3. *Neolithic:* **1–16.** *DS-09-88 Wādī Dhahabūn;* **17–26.** *DS-09-253 Harun village.*
1–10. *trihedral rods and bifaces;* **11–16.** *flakes, burins, and blades;* **17–26.** *bifaces, scrapers, and piercers.*

excavations at several of these sites suggest that the Fasad lithic tradition begins in the late Epipalaeolithic, beginning 16,000 years ago, and continues well into the early Neolithic (see below; Rose *et al.* 2008; Cremaschi & Negrino 2002: 328–333).

While no one particular Upper Palaeolithic site of the Dhofar Survey stands out, they are all equally important, as it is evident that lithic evidence for occupation during this period nearly blankets the entire landscape of the Dhofari Nejd. These sites are a treasure for Oman and the world, and future fieldwork will likely lead to some very important discoveries not only about the peopling of Arabia (Rose 2007; see also Marks 2008), but also the ways of life, resource procurement, and land-use patterns of the people who lived here, particularly in the Upper Palaeolithic period.

Our survey indicates that there is a hint of Upper Palaeolithic in the mountains of Dhofar, particularly in the very western section. However, little Palaeolithic material has been found on the Salalah plain, suggesting that evidence of this period is likely far offshore or has been covered by post-Pleistocene deposits.

Neolithic (8000–3000 BP)

Neolithic period sites comprise about 6% of total survey sites. The Neolithic of the Nejd follows the periodization as established by Charpentier and defined by the presence of finely retouched tools (Fig. 3). Neolithic I (Fasad) is defined by blade projectile points, which may be tied to the Waᶜshah technique as defined by Crassard (2008*a*: 81–86; 2008*b*). The distribution of such material is widespread throughout our survey area, but is defined by these projectile points. Stratified material in several shelters suggests the onset of this period by 10,000 years ago and it may be possible that the tradition stretches back to the late Palaeolithic period (see above). It is possible that the so-called tethering stones found throughout Dhofar belong to this period. The following period is defined by the presence of bifacially flaked and notched arrowheads (ABT of Edens 1988). The outstanding features of this period include "trihedral rods", which demonstrate the basal fluting method (Zarins 2001: 48; Crassard *et al.* 2006: 158–165). Such diagnostic material was found in a stratified sequence at the open-air lake site of Hailat Araka, which we tested in March 2009. Based on similar work in both northern Oman and eastern Yemen, it seems clear that domestication of animals (and probably plants) took place during this period (Crassard *et al.* 2006; McCorriston & Martin 2010).

The last phase of the Neolithic, beginning perhaps by 4000 BCE, gradually integrates itself with the succeeding Bronze Age period in Dhofar. Neolithic III sites, defined by blade and retouched flack tools, were found in the Nejd, as well as in the drier northern slopes (*qaṭn*) of the Dhofar mountains.

Neolithic survey sites were found in a wide variety of locales in the Nejd. These consist of both lithic scatters and formal settlements with stone-circle houses, ceremonial centres, and tombs. The Neolithic presence had been documented for the first time in a number of wadi cave shelters located in the southern foothills of the mountains from Mughsayl to Ḥāsik.

Harūn Neolithic village: DS-09-253–DS-09-257

As noted above, most Neolithic period sites in the Nejd are located near wadis and along the fringes of the Rubᶜ al-Khālī near lake deposits. One particular area near Harūn yielded an exceptional complex, which includes houses, ceremonial structures that are substantially larger, and tombs. This complex covers at least 0.5 km^2 and is located on both sides of a wadi near a relic waterfall. For the most part, it is pristine with *in situ* lithic material (Fig. 3/17–26). Most of the surface lithics include chunky bifacials and retouched tools and debitage (Fig. 3).

Bronze Age (3000–1100 BP)

The Bronze Age, as a focus of this survey, is extremely well represented in Dhofar and nearly 25% of all DS sites can be assigned to this period. Major settlement sites were located in the Dhofar hills and in the immediate western hinterland. The coastal sites of this period are primarily shell middens. Many of these sites are deflated, such as the one at al-Fazyiḥ, while others near Ḥāsik and Wādī Sunayk have very promising stratigraphy. ^{14}C dates (Zarins 2001: 67) suggest a third-millennium BC occupation, if not earlier. The so-called "tombs with tails" (or "tombes des traîns", see Steimer-Herbet 2004: 95) are present, particularly around Muḍayy. Also noteworthy are mortuary sites associated with large outcrops of geodes and crypto-crystalline rock near Muḍayy and Tudho.

The Bronze Age in Dhofar is characterized by the introduction of metallurgy, but it remains to be seen whether materials are made from true bronze or from copper alone. Note that Yule's analysis of metal implements from Aztah suggests the presence of true bronze in the region by *c.*2000 BCE (1999). Settlement sites tend to be extremely large with characteristic round structures with double pebble in-filled walls, water diversion channels, ceremonial centres, and tombs. Unifacial flake tools dominate lithic assemblages of this period, perhaps demonstrating the replacement of fine lithic workmanship of the earlier Neolithic with the introduction of metal tools. Charpentier's al-Suwayh facies likely has some overlap with these types of lithics (2008: 110).

Clearly the interface between the end of the Neolithic and the beginning of the Bronze Age is complex; however, in terms of ecology Bronze Age populations were gradually forced out of the Nejd into the highlands, or adapted to a more mobile pastoralism. By at least 2500 BCE, domesticated cattle appear in the area, a hallmark in the hills to the present (Warman & Clutton-Brock 1996). Shell-midden occupation along the coast may reflect an early pattern of transhumance with the highlands, a pattern already known in the Iron Age to the present.

A major find was the discovery of pre-Iron Age painted rock art at a number of locales. In one instance, a number of figures are using re-curved and/or compound bows (Fig. 4). These depictions may be Bronze Age in date and have significant parallels to similar figures

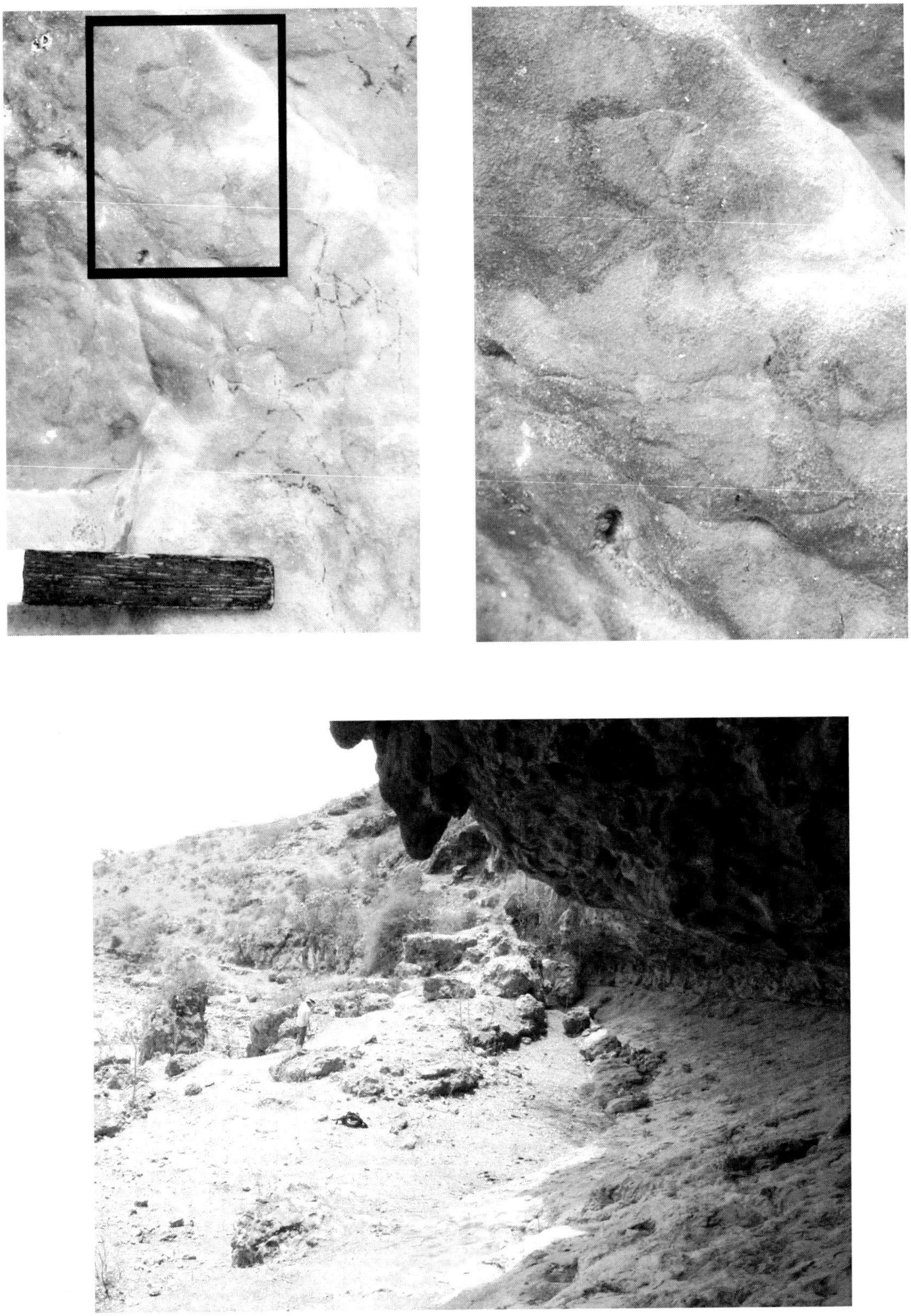

FIGURE 4. *DS-08-42: a rock shelter with associated rock art.*

in both Central Arabia (Anati 1968*a*; 1968*b*) and Egypt's Eastern Desert, particularly with the so-called Hunter's Palette.

The Hodor Bronze Age tomb complex: DS-09-149 and DS-09-264–DS-09-267

The most outstanding Bronze Age sites of the Dhofar Survey are the tomb/ceremonial complexes found at Hodor (al-Ḥudūr). The site is currently situated in a typical *jol* (highland arid tableland) environment, approximately 100 km from the mountain front along Wādī Jarayt. A large-scale formal Bronze Age rectangular tomb, measuring 15×18 m, was discovered first. Built with drywall construction out of large orthostatic stones, many over 1 m high and nearly 2 m wide, this tomb was unfortunately bulldozed from the south-south-east and 75% of the structure is missing. The building appears to be oriented to the cardinal directions. The remaining fill has both limestone slabs and deliberate highly patinated iron quartzite fill. This tomb is associated with two stone troughs with large limestone slabs at both ends. To the north-west is another smaller tomb similar in construction. Looking farther afield on the ridgeline to the east is a series of three discreet tombs and to the north-east of these a pillbox construction with two attached tombs, again with deliberately placed highly patinated ferruginous quartzite fill. The outer edges of these features are clearly outlined with larger limestone slabs. Nearby are at least fifteen round stone fireplaces that appear to be contemporary to the structures. The entire complex is surrounded, particularly on the north-east side, with lithic debris. The vast percentage of these lithics is finely made side-scrapers suggesting a late Neolithic to early Bronze Age date (*c.*3500–3000 BC; see Fig. 5). Further to the north is a third formal rectangular tomb with an extremely large orthostat, approximately 3.2×1 m in size. It has fallen down and has broken into three pieces, similar in size and function to the one found earlier at Hagif. To the north on the western T2 terrace of the wadi, interspersed with a very large lithic scatter and dark quartzite, are four possible fire-pits aligned in a north–south row.

A revisit to the area proved fruitful as it became clear that the mountain just to the west of this site with its peculiar black stone paving, was part of this larger complex. Like the black stone paving mentioned above, two large areas on the east side and one to the north of this mountain were deliberately covered with the same type of black stones (many of which appear to be struck and

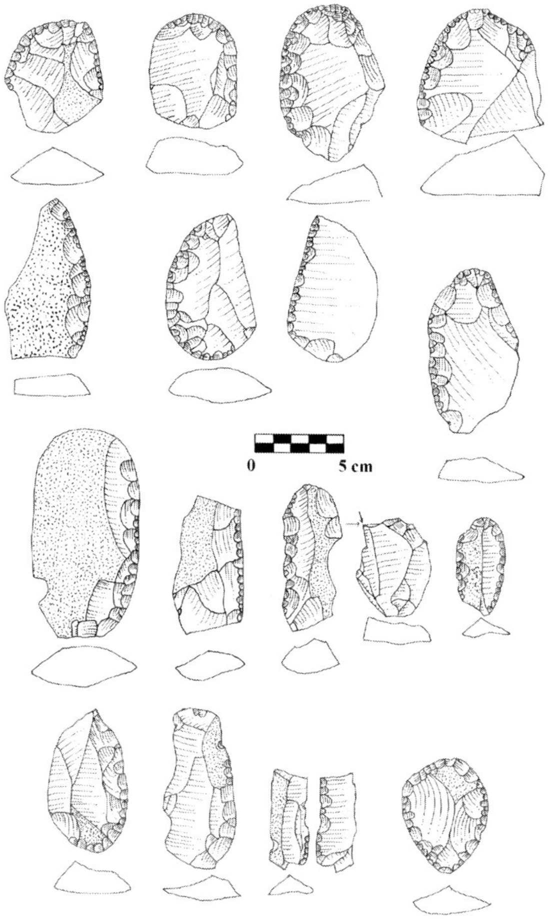

Figure 5. *Bronze Age: DS-09-149 Hodor; tabular flint scrapers and blades.*

are similar to the ever-present Upper Palaeolithic material throughout the entire Dhofari Nejd). There is a tomb on top of the mountain from where the pavements emanate. Also, to the north of DS-09-149 is another large tomb that is still intact, which has similar peculiar black stone paving associated with it. There are a number of smaller stone alignments and more typical Bronze Age stone cairns nearby, suggesting that this area as a whole was an important ceremonial centre for Bronze Age populations in Dhofar. A number of more common round Neolithic-Bronze Age tombs on the outskirts of these larger tomb complexes appear to be part of this larger site complex.

The impressive complex at Hodor is not unique to Dhofar as late in the survey a similar set of graves was located on top of a hill near Hanūn. Like the tombs at Hodor, these tombs are also associated with heavily patinated stone paving. Further survey will shed light on the distribution of these types of tombs, while future excavation will provide the data to date them more precisely.

Outstanding contemporary Bronze Age monuments have been found by us at Sarif springs and the ring of Nahrit in the western Mahrah Governate of Yemen. While orthostats and carved blocks are characteristic of the Dhofari Bronze Age, the statue-menhirs, so characteristic of the Yemen *jol* (*jawl*) have to date not been located in Dhofar (Newton & Zarins 2000).

Iron Age (1100 BCE–600 CE)

The Iron Age is probably one of the most problematic time horizons currently in the archaeological history of Dhofar because no stratified sites have been excavated which date to the Bronze–Iron Age transition (*c.*1100 BC). Early microliths characteristic of the period, have been dated to as early as 800 BCE in Yemen at Wādī Jawf (Rahimi 1987: 139–143), but the earliest ^{14}C dated Iron Age site at Tāqah 60 is dated to *c.*400 BCE (Zarins 2001: 73, fig. 30, 2340±100 BP, BA-83797). The appearance of triliths most likely reflects much earlier monuments of similar type, which ultimately derived from Bronze Age examples (Vogt & Sedov 1994). At 37% of total sites, Iron Age sites form the majority of the Dhofar Survey.

No older than approximately 500 BC, the earliest ceramics known to date in Dhofar derive from this period and are found at sites primarily on the coastal plain. Many sites located in the Dhofar hills and their southern fore-slopes, once excavated, promise to fill this gap of materials identified as Iron Age, characterized by the presence of stone-circle houses (differentiated from earlier Bronze Age counterparts by the use of much smaller stones). These houses are often found in compounds and have associated lithics (microliths) and distinctive local ceramics, which include grit-tempered, often highly burnished, hard-fired red wares. These Iron Age local wares are often incised with a distinctive pattern of dots and short lines and often have what have been described as pendentive triangles (this ware is referred to as "riceware" by Sedov 2002: 47, 69, pl. 14/6–7; 2008: 248, pls 12/13, 14/1–3; Glanzman, Robertson & Robertson 2009). A local ceramic typology and chronology is now emerging. Probably dating to the late centuries BC, "ricewares" are likely to be the antecedents to the so-called "dot and circle" wares, which, based upon survey and excavation at al-Balīd, Shisr, and al-Qisha, date from approximately 400–1200 CE (Zarins 2007; Newton 2009: 64; see Fig. 6). Excavated examples from al-Balīd with the overlap in design of dot-and-circle and red paint suggest that it is likely that dot-and-circle ceramics represent the local antecedent to the later red painted wares produced in medieval Dhofar.

Coastal settlement sites

One of our conclusions after completing this survey is that water catchment systems and dams appear to be a hallmark of Iron Age settlements along the coastal plain of Dhofar, particularly to the west of Raysūt where coastal areas tend to be enclosed by sheer cliffs. Four sites stand out as examples: Rakhyūt North, Kherfut, al-Hawta (al-Ḥawtah), and al-Hawta East. While each of these sites has its own characteristics, the presence of water channels and deflectors, check and diversion dams, and water retention basins demonstrates the importance of water, particularly to these, until very recently, isolated communities. There are examples of similar sites to the east of Salalah, including Wādī Ḥinnā (Zarins 2001: 83, fig. 33/b). Here small stone-wall catchment dams are found high on the mountain slope. Iron Age lithics and ceramics, as well as seashells were collected from a terrace just above the dam. In conclusion, local coastal Iron Age populations created sophisticated water diversion systems to take advantage of flash floods to irrigate subsistence and cash crops, a method similar to the flash flood (*seil*) irrigation that was the impetus for the rise of the contemporary South Arabic city-states further to the west.

Triliths

The Iron Age of Dhofar is perhaps most famously characterized by the development of monuments known as triliths, whose distribution has been already documented and spans much of eastern Yemen to northern Oman (Fig. 7; de Cardi *et al.* 1977; al-Shahri 1991; Cremaschi & Negrino 2002: 340–343; Newton 2009: 18–19). At least ten such trilith monuments have been ^{14}C dated directly, and they have a known span of 300 BCE–200 CE. While there are undoubtedly more triliths to be recorded, they comprise 20% of all DS sites and 53% of Iron Age DS sites. In Dhofar, they are almost exclusively located in the near Nejd at the northern base of the Dhofar hills. They are probably associated with the trade of incense throughout the region. Trilith complexes usually consist of a stone collar outlined with stones, with sets of three stones standing upright forming a line down the middle. The number of these three stones, hence "triliths", varies but it is usually an odd number. Often there are sets of four boulders nearby

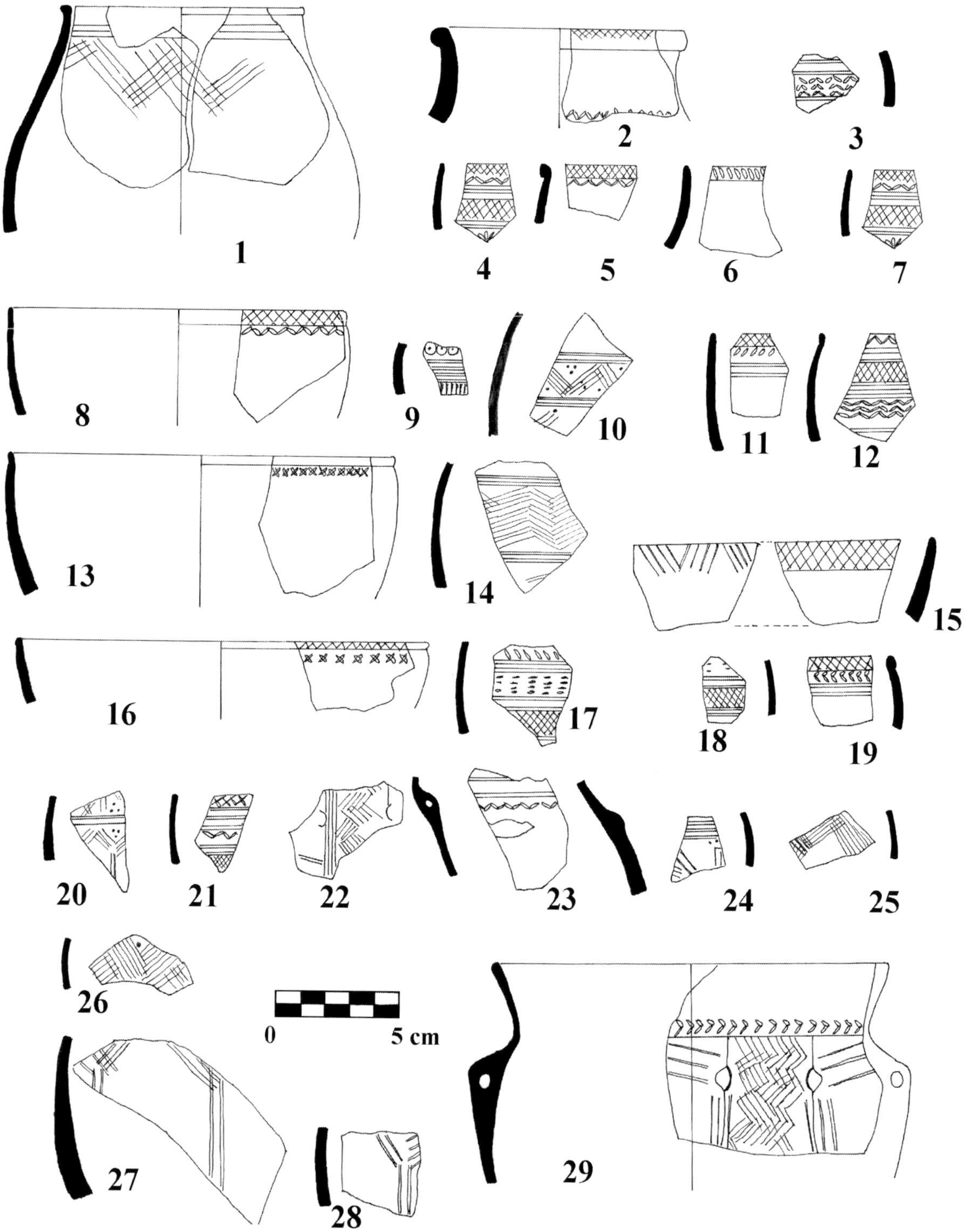

Figure 6. *Iron Age:* **1.** *TA-95-60, level 2, BA-83797 2340±100 BP (Zarins 2001: 73, fig. 30);* **2–29.** *DS-08-67 al-Hawta. All examples are grit buffware, handmade with incised and impressed decoration.*

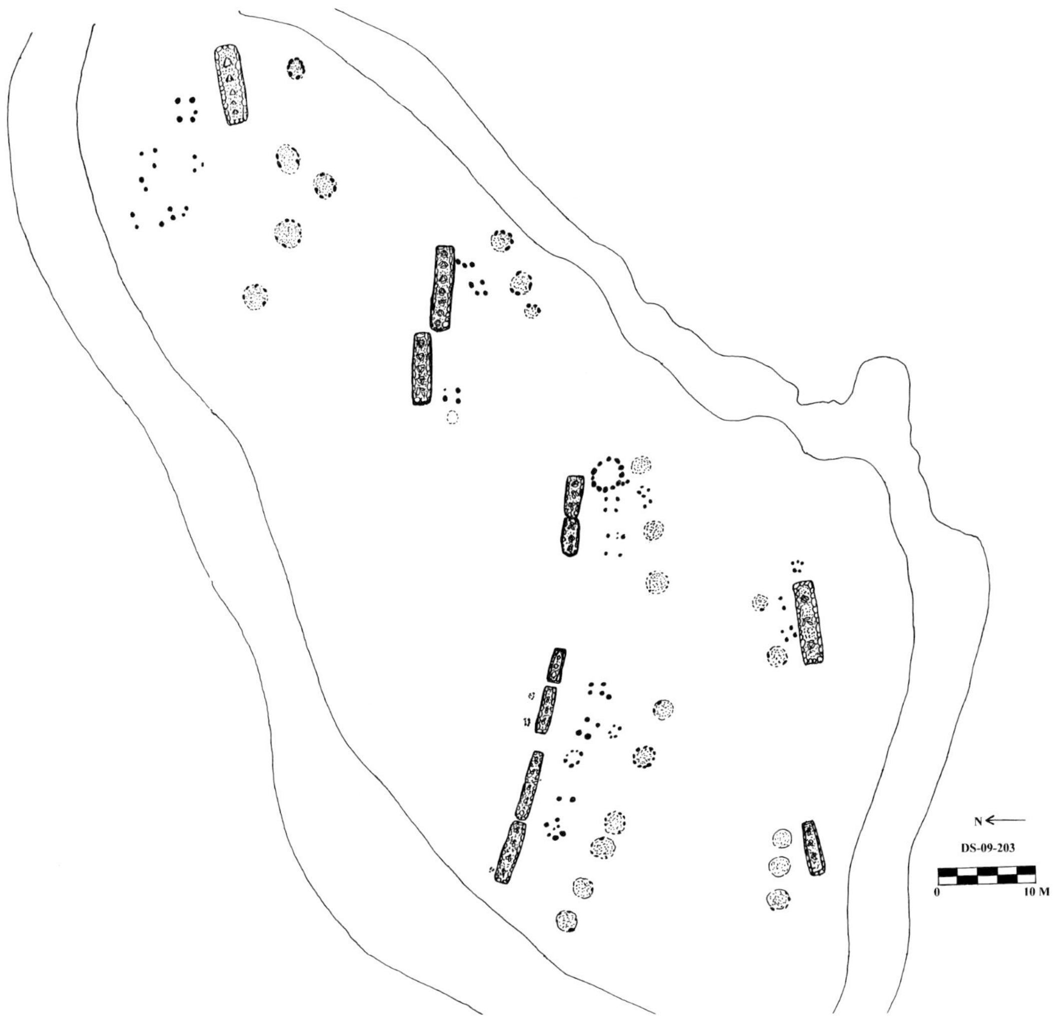

Figure 7. *Triliths DS-09-203, Ayun area.*

along with a series of stone fire-pits. Two DS sites have pecked stone ESA inscriptions.

The appearance of the Sumhuram (Khawr al-Rawrī) colony and its satellite at Hanūn, are the only known "classical" period sites on the Dhofar coast. Their establishment by the third century BCE is obviously predicated upon the knowledge that local populations had been producing and trading incense long before 300 BCE, as indicated by the distribution of early triliths. As noted by B. Thomas (1932), al-Shahri (1991*a*; 1991*b*) and others, what then is the script associated with triliths and cave paintings of Dhofar? There are two possible scenarios: 1) the ESA script borrowed from the Sumhuram colony or other earlier contacts with South Arabic states; and/or 2) an alphabetic script derived from northern Arabian sources ("Thamudic"). The latter possibility is favoured by Macdonald (2009) and Beeston (personal communication).

Himyarite (350–700 CE)

The Himyarites, as a political power that succeeded the earlier South Arabic city-states of Yemen, have provided some evidence of their presence in Dhofar. These include fourth-century coinage found at Sumhuram (Sedov 2002: 255–256; 2008: 282–283), as well as inscriptional material from the Wādī Jawf dated to 489 CE, mentioning the land of Sakalan (Bafaqih 1979; Robin 1986). Of course, Dhofar was already known as Sakalan on the second-century CE gate inscription at Sumhuram (Avanzini 2002: 125–140 and refs). Himyarite pottery, dated to the third to sixth centuries CE has been found at al-Shisr with ^{14}C dates of 400–600 CE (Zarins 2001: fig. 42).

The narrative of *Cosmos Indicopleustes* of Aksum, dated to the early sixth century CE, also clearly demonstrates that Dhofar continued to play a role in the international maritime trade of the Indian Ocean. This idea is also supported by the random discoveries of Byzantine coinage of Justinian at Raysūt (Phillips 1972: 175–176b), and the Gaza-type amphorae found both at Khawr Rawrī (A. Pavan, personal communication) and Maṣīrah Island (al-Shanfari 1987). Undoubtedly, a large number of Dhofar hill sites will belong to this period as well. Our survey of boat-shaped graves (Zarins, in press) and excavations at Khawr Rawrī (Bonacossi 2002: 43–45) and Mughsayl (Glanzman, Robertson & Robertson 2009) suggest their location in the Nejd, the mountains, and the coastal plain probably belong to this period.

To summarize, our survey of the Iron Age period illustrates a much greater complexity to the term than previously realized. Future survey and excavation at sites of this period must recognize an earlier indigenous Iron Age followed by later trilith and inscriptional sites contemporary to the colony of Sumhuram. The late Iron Age in reality is a continuation of the earlier materials without significant gaps in the record. Note that the Dhofar Iron Age is restricted to small-scale sites and settlements without the benefit of large towns so characteristic of South Arabic city-states and the Iron Age of northern Oman.

Early medieval (750–1150 CE)

The early medieval period in Dhofar, commonly referred to as the Abbasid or Early Islamic period, is characterized by the presence of many small-scale coastal trading centres. Well-dated glazed ceramic imports, such as barbotine blue, opaque white glazed ware, and sgraffiatos comprise the means for identifying and dating these sites. These sites also have a distinct type of associated architecture. The walls are all "square" (unlike local architecture which tends to be round up to the very recent past) and are probably warehouses (perhaps similar to the warehouses mapped by Rougeulle at Sharma [2004; 2005]). Note that the majority of wares from these coastal sites, however, are local wares, which can be clearly dated by association with the well-established so-called "Abbasid" corpus.

Ḥāsik is the farthest east of these sites, while Mughsayl represents the westernmost settlement. Between these extremes are Jin Jali, Sadḥ, Hinu, Mirbāt, Juweana (Jawaynah), Inqiṭā᾿ al-Mirbāt, al-Balīd, and Raysūt. Our limited soundings at Hinw and Sadḥ, Rougeulle's excavations at Inqiṭā᾿ al-Mirbāt (2008: 645–656), and the BYU excavations at Mughsayl (Johnson *et al.* 2007; 2008; Glanzman, Robertson & Robertson 2009) provide considerable evidence for stratification extending from the late Iron Age to the Abbasid period.

These coastal sites represent non-centralized points of trade linking East Africa, southern Arabia, the Gulf, India, Southeast Asia, and China during this period. Needless to say, these modest ports are tied to formal trade networks linking them to the vast Dhofari interior (e.g. Newton 2009; Cremaschi & Negrino 2002: 346). These sites, as well as Sumhuram (Inqiṭā᾿ al-Mirbāt, Rougeulle 2008), represent a continuum of trade from the Iron Age directly into the Abbasid period. The shift from Gulf-centred trade to that of the Red Sea begins in this period, perhaps associated with the destruction of Sirāf, the decline of the Abbasids, and the rise of the Fatimids. Local sites of this period found in the Dhofar hills undoubtedly represent the continued development of local populations. The inland site of Shisr revealed the presence of Abbasid period barbotine blues, dot-and-circle ceramics, and sgraffiatos, providing support for the continuation of inland trade linking the Rubᶜ al-Khālī to eastern Arabia. This time horizon is supported by a number of ^{14}C dates from Shisr (Zarins & Newton, in preparation).

International trade from the South Arabian period onwards was defined archaeologically by the presence of amphorae that began to flood the market by the third century BC. Many of these amphorae can be identified as originating in the Aegean Islands, Alexandria, and Italy (Sedov & Benvenuti 2002: 180). These amphorae continue to be traded through the Late Iron Age as exemplified by the "Gaza-type" ceramic vessels. One of the major discoveries of our survey was the recognition that such amphorae continued to be manufactured in a distinctive shape throughout the Iron Age and Abbasid periods (Fig. 8). These red-bodied and yellow-slipped wheel-made vessels, over 1.5 m tall, have provided evidence of large-scale international trade. They were found at a number of Abbasid-period ports, underwater, from shipwrecks as well as from the Abbasid-period component at al-Balīd, Sharma, Socotra, and Saqar (Rougeulle 1999: 125–126, fig. 3). Complete examples of these vessels have remarkably survived in Salalah houses, the tomb of Saleh bin Ḥud, and the largest number from Maḥawt and Filim near Maṣirah. A second type consists of a greyish/black body with incised necks and no handles. Again, this ceramic evidence suggests an unbroken historical record linking the "classical" period to the "Abbasid" period in Dhofar.

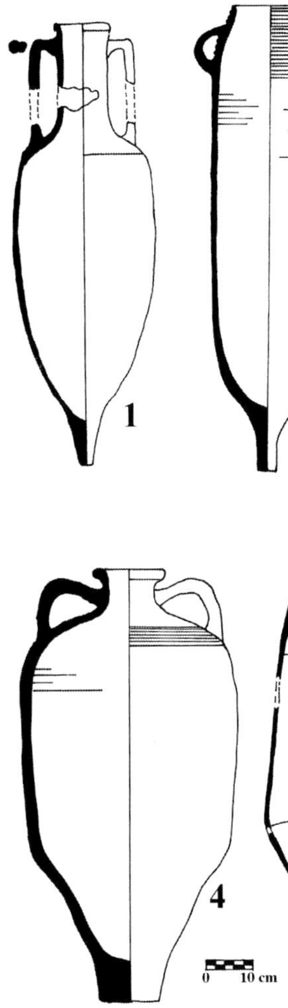

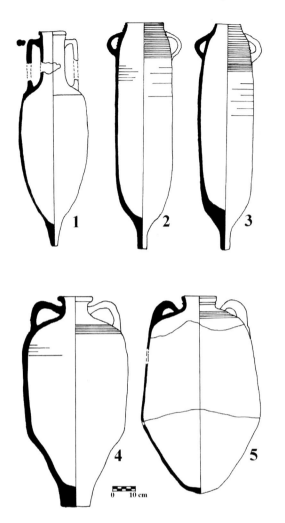

Figure 8. *Amphorae:* **1.** *Qana, first century BC–third century AD (Sedov 1996: 15, fig. 3);* **2–3.** *Masirah, fifth–seventh century AD (Shanfari 1987: pl. 7/3 Site 64);* **4.** *Mahawt;* **5.** *Alto Bay (east of Mirbat), found at a depth of 11 m.*

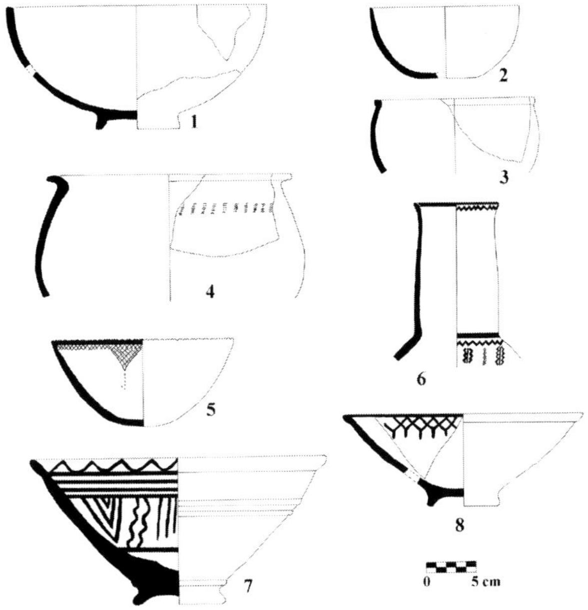

Figure 9. *Medieval wares from al-Balīd:* **1–3.** *grit buffware, level 1 Great Mosque ablution area;* **4.** *punctate grit buffware, level 1 Great Mosque ablution area;* **5.** *red-painted grit buffware, north city wall (570/403);* **6.** *red-painted highly polished gritware, level 1 Great Mosque;* **7.** *"Yemen Yellow" (wheel-made red mica tempered body with yellow slip and black painted lines), north wall* husn *(enclosure) square 229;* **8.** *red-painted grit buffware, L.930 Merchant's House.*

Medieval period (1000–1500 CE)

By 1000 CE al-Balīd exploded in size to form the first major urban centre on the Dhofar coast (Albright 1982; Costa 1982). Similar, but smaller towns are found at Ḥāsik and Mirbāt. Wādī Garziz being the largest source of fresh water along the Dhofar coast, it resurfaces near al-Balīd and forms the largest lagoon in the region. Between 1000 CE and its demise in the late sixteenth century, the town dominates both international trade and access to the interior and becomes the centre of power on the Salalah plain. Excavations of al-Balīd (Zarins 2007) are complimented by the historical description of the town and its international trade (Ibn Mujāwir 1220, see Smith 2008; Ibn Baṭṭūṭah 1340 and 1360, see Gibb 1929; Marco Polo 1290, see Penzer 1929; Ma Huan 1420, see Mills 1970; Hirth & Rockhill 1966; Dreyer 2007) and tax base revenue (Smith 2006; al-Shamrookh 1996; al-Jâzim 2003).

Three major phases of the city's development between 1000–1500 CE are attested by ceramic evidence. Local red grit and shell-tempered wares are found throughout the sequence, as well as diagnostic materials from India, East Africa, South-east Asia, and China. Red painted and incised grit tempered wares from the previous Abbasid period continue to be manufactured in the medieval period. Such ceramic material is abundant at al-Balīd (Fig. 9), but otherwise has only been found at Mirbāt and Ḥāsik in Dhofar. Shisr represents the historically documented route into the interior. Identical contemporary ceramic materials are known from excavations supported by accompanying radiocarbon dates (Zarins & Newton, in preparation). For ship timbers found at al-Balīd, see Belfioretti and Vosmer (this volume). The gradual decline

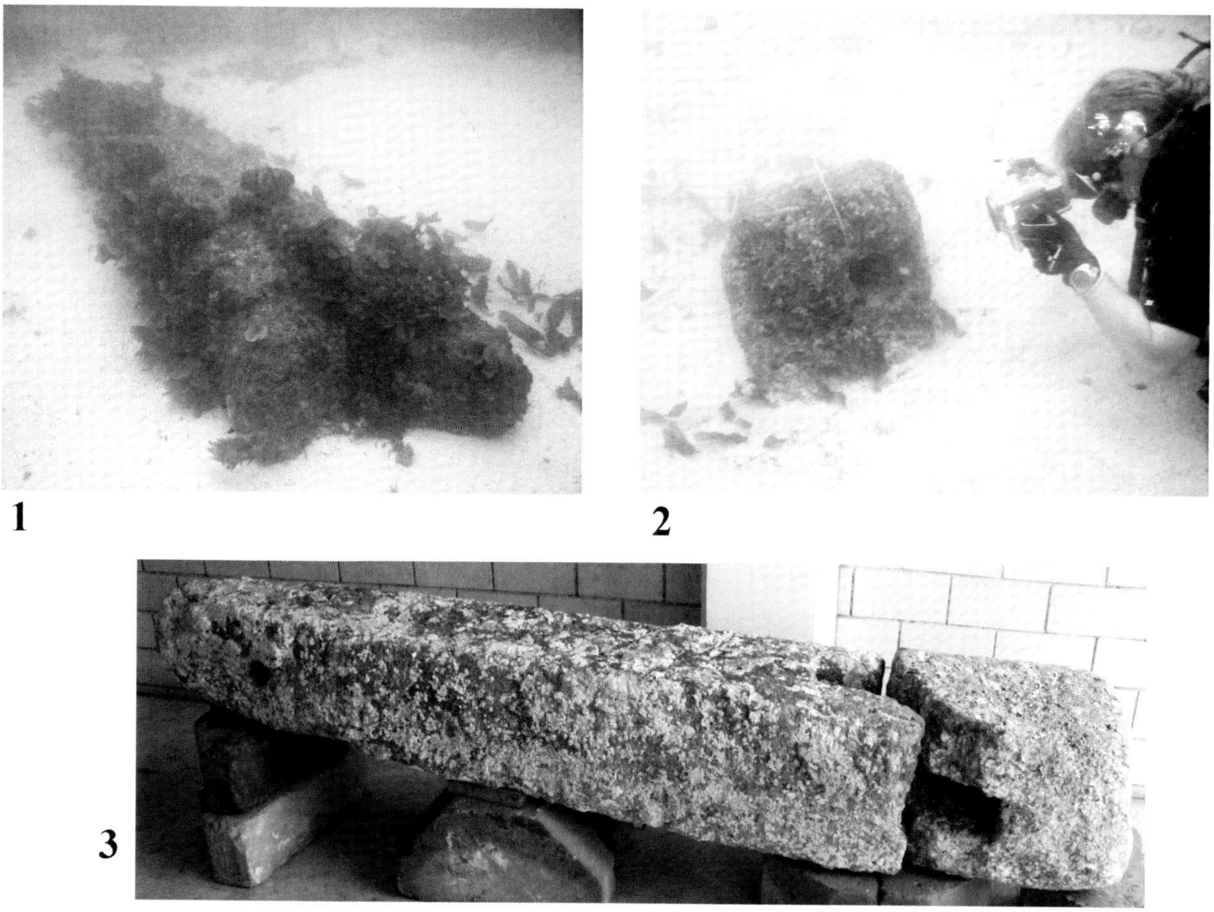

Figure 10. *al-Balīd stone anchor:* **1–2.** *the anchor in two pieces underwater;* **3.** *the anchor as it is currently displayed at the Museum of the Frankincense Land in Salalah, Oman.*

and end of the medieval trade at al-Balīd was caused by a number of converging factors, such as the arrival of the Portuguese and Turks (Serjeant 1963; Costa 1982), as well as possible ecological disasters (Reinhardt 2000).

Underwater survey

A two-week preliminary underwater survey was conducted in April 2008 at al-Balīd, Khawr Rawrī, and Juweana (Jawaynah) Island. While no new finds were discovered offshore at Khawr Rawrī, cut stone blocks were found between the mainland and Juweana Island. These blocks may lend credence to the local stories that mention a bridge or causeway that once connected the island to the mainland. Ceramic material from the island and mainland belongs primarily to the Abbasid period.

An even more impressive find was discovered about 1.5 km offshore of al-Balīd at a depth of 11 m. Here a finely shaped stone anchor was found (Fig. 10). Broken in two pieces, this anchor weighs 860 kg and measures 2.6 m in total length. Of a non-local conglomerate stone, this finely shaped anchor has a rope hole near the top. In the lower end, now broken, two square transverse holes were cut to contain wooden flukes. This arrangement was designed to hold the ship in place in deep water and prevent drifting. Anchorage at these locations offshore is supported by Ibn Baṭṭūṭah who in 1347 mentions that ships anchored a considerable distance offshore at al-Balīd and that goods were transferred to the town via smaller *sanābīk* (sg. *sambūk*) (Gibb 1929).

Anchors such as this one have been found at many sites in the Indian Ocean, Persian Gulf, and the Red Sea (Owen 1997 and refs). Locally similar anchors have been found concentrated offshore along the rugged Mirbāt–Sadḥ coast (Owen 1997; Davidde & Petriaggi 1996). Several examples were recovered from the dredging of

Raysūt harbour in 1980 and are now on display in the Maritime Hall of the Museum of the Frankincense Land in Salalah. Stone anchors were produced and utilized from the Bronze Age (2500 BCE) to the late first millennium CE when iron/wood composite grapple anchors were first introduced to the region. Therefore, while one cannot dismiss the residual use of stone anchors after the late first millennium CE, it is more likely that their heyday is earlier.

Conclusions

1) The Upper Palaeolithic of Dhofar is extremely rich, from both a surface scatter and a stratigraphic perspective.

2) Neolithic sites are extremely large in number, particularly in the Nejd. Several open-air sites have clear stratigraphy and the largely un-surveyed west Dhofar region has provided documentation of villages promising future intra-site variation studies. The Fasad horizon should in the future help to understand the transition from the Late Upper Palaeolithic to the Early Neolithic.

3) The survey has provided evidence of an extremely large distribution of Bronze Age sites in the uplands. The sites at Hodor with its orthostats, large rectangular tombs, and platforms suggest the presence of a highly stratified society in the region.

4) The Iron Age is the least understood of the periods and we must emphasize that future excavations are necessary to better define a local chronology.

5) Based on limited excavation, survey, and historical analysis, it is clear that there is no break in the Dhofar archaeological record from the Bronze Age (*c.*2500 BCE) to the present. Periodization is strictly an archaeological tool to categorize survey sites, but many overlap and do not fit solely into one period.

6) Our discovery of numerous Abbasid period small seaports is clearly indicative of a very interesting trade pattern that involves both international trade primarily from the Persian Gulf and the Dhofar interior. The identification of large amphorae connects this trade to its earlier antecedents in the Iron Age.

7) Survey and excavations at medieval al-Balīd have shown that populations along the coastal plain concentrated in key cities. These large-scale urban centres were attractive for international maritime trade, as well as specialized labour opportunities. Excavations at al-Shiḥr have shown that al-Balīd continued to dominate the interior trade, particularly in horses.

Acknowledgements

This archaeological survey was conducted at the request of H.E. Abdul Aziz bin Mohammad al-Rowas, Advisor to H.M. the Sultan for Cultural Affairs in Oman. We would like to acknowledge Ghanim al-Shanfari, Ahmed al-Awaid, Mohammad al-Jahfali, and Said al-Mashani of the Office of the Advisor to H.M. the Sultan for Cultural Affairs who facilitated the fieldwork. In addition, we would like to thank Ali Ahmed Mahash al-Shahri and Robert Jackson. All specific site information from this survey is on file at the Office of the Advisor to H.M. the Sultan for Cultural Affairs, Muscat, Oman.

References

Albright F.P.

1982. *The American Archaeological Expedition in Dhofar, Oman, 1952–1953*. Washington, DC: American Foundation for the Study of Man 7.

Anati E.

1968*a*. *Rock Art in Central Arabia*, ii/ii. *"The Realistic-Dynamic" Style of Rock Art in the Jebel Qara*. Louvain: Bibliothèque du Muséon.

1968*b*. *Rock Art in Central Arabia*, i. *The "Oval-Headed" People of Arabia*. Louvain: Bibliothèque du Muséon.

Avanzini A.

2002. The Construction Inscriptions on the Gate Complex. Pages 125–140 in A. Avanzini (ed.), *Khor Rori Report I*. Pisa: Edizione Plus.

2008. Notes for a History of Sumhuram and a New Inscription of Yashhurḥil. Pages 609–641 in A. Avanzini (ed.), *A Port in Ancient Arabia Between Rome and the Indian Ocean (3rd century BC–5th century AD). Khor Rori Report 2*. Rome: "L'Erma" di Bretschneider.

Bafaqi M.
1979. New light on the Yazanite dynasty. *Proceedings of the Seminar for Arabian Studies* 9: 5–9.
Belfioretti L. & Vosmer T.
(in this volume). Al-Balīd ship timbers: preliminary overview and comparisons. *Proceedings of the Seminar for Arabian Studies* 40.
Bonacossi D.M.
2002. Excavations at Khor Rori: the 1997 and 1998 campaigns. Pages 29–69 in A. Avanzini (ed.), *Khor Rori Report 1*. Pisa: Edizione Plus.
Carter J.R.L.
1982. *Tribes in Oman*. London: Peninsular Publishing.
Charpentier V.
2008. Hunter-gatherers of the "empty quarter of the early Holocene" to the last Neolithic societies: chronology of the late prehistory of south-eastern Arabia (8000–3100 BC). *Proceedings of the Seminar for Arabian Studies* 38: 59–82.
Ciuk C. & E. Keall E.
1996. *Zabid project pottery manual 1995: pre-Islamic and Islamic ceramics from the Zabid area, North Yemen*. (BAR International Series, 655). Archaeopress: Oxford.
Cleuziou S. & Tosi M.
1999. Preliminary Report. Archaeological Reconnaissance in the Jabal Samhan-Hasek Region of Dhofar, Sultanate of Oman, 30 January–3 February 1999. Muscat: Ministry of Heritage and Culture. [Unpublished report].
Cleveland R.L.
1960. The 1960 American Expedition to Dhofar. *Bulletin of the American Schools of Oriental Research* 159: 14–26.
Costa P.
1982. The Study of the City of Zafar (al-Baleed). *Journal of Oman Studies* 5: 111–150.
2001. *Historic Mosques and Shrines of Oman*. (BAR International Series, 938). Oxford: Archaeopress.
Costa P. & Kite S.
1985. The Architecture of Salalah and the Dhofar Littoral. *Journal of Oman Studies* 7: 131–158.
Crassard R.
2008*a*. *La Préhistoire du Yémen*. (BAR International Series, 1842). Oxford: Archaeopress.
2008*b*. The "Wa'shah method": an original laminar debitage from Hadramawt, Yemen. *Proceedings of the Seminar for Arabian Studies* 38: 3–14.
Crassard R., McCorriston J., Oches E., ᶜAqil, ᶜA. bin, Espagne J. & Sinnah M.
2006. Manayzah, early to mid-Holocene occupations in Wādī Ṣanā (Ḥaḍramawt, Yemen). *Proceedings of the Seminar for Arabian Studies* 36: 151–173.
Cremaschi M. & Negrino F.
2002. The Frankincense Road of Sumhuram: Palaeoenvironmental and Prehistorical Background. Pages 325–364 in A. Avanzini (ed.), *Khor Rori Report I*. Pisa: Edizione Plus.
Cremaschi M. & Perego A.
2008. Patterns of Land Use and Settlements in the Surroundings of Sumhuram. An Intensive Geo-Archaeological Survey at Khor Rori: Report of Field Season February 2006. Pages 563–607 in A. Avanzini (eds), *A Port in Ancient Arabia Between Rome and the Indian Ocean (3rd century BC–5th century AD). Khor Rori Report 2*. Rome: "L'Erma" di Bretschneider.
Davidde B. & Petriaggi R.
1996. Prospenzioni Subacquee nella Regione del Dhofar. *Egitto E Vicino Oriente* 19: 212–216.
de Cardi B., Doe D.B. & Roskams S.P.
1977. Excavation and survey in the Sharqiyah, Oman, 1976. *Journal of Oman studies* 3/1: 17–33.
Dini M. & Tozzi C.
2008. Prehistoric Archaeological Prospecting in Dhofar. Pages 703–708 in A. Avanzini (ed.), *A Port in*

Ancient Arabia Between Rome and the Indian Ocean (3rd century BC–5th century AD). Khor Rori Report 2. Rome: "L'Erma" di Bretschneider.

Dreyer E.L.
2007. *Zheng-He, China and the Oceans in the Early Ming Dynasty, 1405–1433*. New York: Pearson/Longman.

Edens C.
1988. The Rub al-Khali 'Neolithic' Revisited: the View from Naqdan. Pages 15–43 in D.T. Potts (ed.), *Araby the Blest*. Copenhagen: Museum Tusculanum Press.

Ghazanfar S.A.
1994. *Handbook of Arabian Medicinal Plants*. Boca Raton: CRC Press.

Gibb H.
1929. *The Travels of Ibn Battuta*. London: The Hakluyt Society.

Glanzman W., Robertson J. & Robertson W.
2009. BYU Dhofar Project 2009: Site 5E Report. Office of the Advisor to H.M. the Sultan for Cultural Affairs, Muscat. [Unpublished report].

Hardy-Guilbert C.
2001. Archaeological research at al-Shihr, the Islamic port of Hadramawt, Yemen (1996–1999). *Proceedings of the Seminar for Arabian Studies* 31: 69–79.
2004. Al-Šihr, Porte du Hadramawt sur l'Océan Indien. *Annales Islamologiques* 38/1: 95–136.

Hirth F. & Rockhill W.W.
1966. *Chau Ju-Kua: His Work on the Chinese and Arab Trade in the Twelfth and Thirteenth Centuries, entitled Chu-fan-chi* [1255]. New York: Paragon.

Horton, M.C.
1996. *Shanga. The archaeology of a Muslim trading community on the coast of East Africa*. (The British Institute of East Africa Memoir, 14). London: The British Institute of East Africa.

Jamme A.
1967. Two New Hadrami Inscriptions from Zofar. *Biblioteca Orientalis* 24: 146–148.
1982. *The Inscriptions*. Pages 41–48 in F. Albright, *The American Archaeological Expedition in Dhofar, Oman, 1952–1953*. Washington, DC: American Foundation for the Study of Man 7.

Janzen J.
1986. *Nomads in the Sultanate of Oman. Tradition and Development in Dhofar.* Boulder, CO: Westview Press.

Al-Jâzim M.A.
2003. *Lumière de la connaissance. Règles, lois et coutumes du Yémen sous le règne du Sultan Rasoulide al-Muzaffar.* Sanaa: Centre Français d'Archéologie et de Sciences Sociales de Sanaa.

Johnson D.
2009. Archaeological Preliminary Report. Brigham Young University Excavations at Khor Mughsayl, 2009. Office of the Advisor to H.M. the Sultan for Cultural Affairs, Muscat. [Unpublished report].

Johnson D., Brown S.K., Phillips W.R. & Rempel S.
2007. Excavations at Khor Mughsayl. Brigham Young University, July 2007. Office of the Advisor to H.M. the Sultan for Cultural Affairs, Muscat. [Unpublished report].

Johnson D., Brown S.K., Glanzman W., Rempel S. & Gudrian G.
2008. Excavations and Survey around Khor Mughsayl. Brigham Young University, 28 June–25 July, 2008. Office of the Advisor to H.M. the Sultan for Cultural Affairs, Muscat. [Unpublished report].

Kennet D.
2004. *Sasanian and Islamic Pottery from Ras al-Khaimah. Classification, Chronology and Analysis of Trade in the Western Indian Ocean*. (BAR International Series, 1248). Oxford: Archaeopress.

McCorriston J. & Martin L.
2010. Southern Arabia's Early Pastoral Population History: Some Recent Evidence. Pages 237–250 in M.D. Petraglia & J.I. Rose (eds), *The Evolution of Human Populations in Arabia*. Heidelberg/London: Springer.

Macdonald M.C.A.
2009. *Literacy and Identity in Pre-Islamic Arabia.* Oxford: Ashgate.

Marks A.E.
2008. Into Arabia, perhaps, but if so, from where? *Proceedings of the Seminar for Arabian Studies* 38: 15–24.

Miller A.G. & Morris M.
1988. *Plants of Dhofar: The Southern Region of Oman. Traditional, Economic and Medicinal Uses.* Edinburgh: Holmes McDougall/Muscat: Diwan of the Royal Court.

Mills J.V.G.
1970. *Ma Huan: Ying-Yai Sheng-Lan. The Overall Survey of the Ocean's Shores*. London: The Hakluyt Society.

Newton L.S.
2009. *A Landscape of Pilgrimage and Trade in Wadi Masila, Yemen. Al-Qisha and Qabr Hud in the Islamic Period.* (BAR International Series, 1899). Oxford: Archaeopress.
(in press). Shrines in Dhofar. *Proceedings of the death, burial and the transition to the afterlife in Arabia and adjacent regions biennial conference.* L. Weeks (ed.). Oxford: Archaeopress.

Newton L.S. & Zarins J.
2000. Aspects of Bronze Age Art of Southern Arabia: the Pictorial Landscape and its Relation to Economic and Socio-Political Status. *Arabian archaeology and epigraphy* 11: 154–179.

Oman G.
1983. Preliminary Epigraphic Survey of Islamic Material in Dhofar. *Journal of Oman Studies* 6/2: 277–289.
1989. Arabic-Islamic Epigraphy in Dhofar in the Sultanate of Oman. Pages 193–198 in P. Costa & M. Tosi (eds), *Oman Studies.* Rome: IsMEO.

Owen J.
1997. Do Anchors Mean Ships? Underwater Evidence for Maritime Trade Along the Dhofar Coast, Northern Indian Ocean. Pages 351–364 in A. Avanzini (ed.), *Profumi D'Arabia.* Rome: "L'Erma" Bretschneider.

Parker A.G. &. Rose J.I.
2008. Climate change and human origins in southern Arabia. *Proceedings of the Seminar for Arabian Studies* 38: 25–42.

Penzer N.M.
1929. *The Most Noble and Famous Travels of Marco Polo.* London: Argonaut Press.

Peterson J.E.
2004. Oman's Diverse Society: Southern Oman. *Middle East Journal* 58/2: 254–269.

Petraglia M.D. & Rose J.I. (eds)
2010. *The Evolution of Human Populations in Arabia.* Heidelberg/London: Springer.

Phillips W.
1972. History and Archaeology of Dhofar. PhD thesis, University of Brussels. [Unpublished].

Pickering H. & Patzelt A.
2008. *Field Guide to the Wild Plants of Oman.* Richmond: Royal Botanic Gardens, Kew.

Pullar J. & Jäckli B.
1978. Some Aceramic Sites in Oman. *Journal of Oman Studies* 4: 53–74.

Putzolu C.
1999. Preliminary Report. A Brief Survey in Masirah, Hallaniyat and Hasik Sultanate of Oman, November 15–25, 1999. Muscat: Ministry of Heritage and Culture. [Unpublished report].

Rahimi, D.
1987. Lithics. Pages 139–143 in W. Glanzman & A. Ghaleb (eds), *The Wadi al-Jubah project.* iii. *The stratigraphic probe at Hajar ar-Rayhan.* Washington DC: American Foundation for the Study of Man.

Reinhardt E.G.
2000. Al-Balid harbor site formation. Hamilton, Ontario: McMaster University. [Unpublished manuscript].

Robin, C.
1986. Du Nouveau sur les Yaz'anides. *Proceedings of the Seminar for Arabian Studies* 16: 181–197.

Rose J.I.

2004. The Question of Upper Pleistocene Connections between East Africa and South Arabia. *Current Anthropology* 45/4: 551–555.

2006. Origins of Early Man in Oman During the Middle and Upper Pleistocene. Pages 31–51 in H.M. al-Lawati, B. al-Sabri, R. al-Farsi & K. al-Rahbi (eds), *Proceedings of the International Symposium, Archaeology of the Arabian Peninsula Through the Ages*. Muscat: Ministry of Heritage and Culture.

2007. The Arabian Corridor Migration Model: Archaeological Evidence for Hominin Dispersals into Oman during the Middle and Upper Pleistocene. *Proceedings of the Seminar for Arabian Studies* 37: 219–237.

Rose J., Usik V., Parker A., Schwenninger J-L., Clark-Balzan L., Oppenheimer S.J., Parton A., Underdown S., Petraglia M., Lahr M. & Foley R.

2008. Archaeological Evidence for Modern Humans in Arabia during the Last Glacial Maximum. [Unpublished manuscript].

Rougeulle A.

1999. Coastal settlements in southern Yemen: the 1996–1997 survey expeditions on the Hadramawt and Mahra coasts. *Proceedings of the Seminar for Arabian Studies* 29: 123–136.

2001. Notes on Pre-Islamic and Early Islamic Harbours of Hadramawt (Yemen). *Proceedings of the Seminar for Arabian* Studies 31: 203–214.

2003. Excavations at Sharmah, Hadhramawt: the 2001 and 2002 Seasons. *Proceedings of the Seminar for Arabian Studies* 33: 287–307.

2004. Le Yémen entre Orient et Afrique: Sharma, un entrepôt du commerce médiéval sur la Côte Sud de l'Arabie. *Annales Islamologiques* 38: 201–253.

2005. The Sharma Horizon: Sgraffiato Wares and other Glazed Ceramics of the Indian Ocean Trade (*c.* AD 980–1140). *Proceedings of the Seminar for Arabian Studies* 35: 223–246.

2008. A medieval trade entrepôt at Khor Rori? The Study of the Islamic Ceramics from Hamr al-Sharqiya. Pages 645–667 in A. Avanzini (ed.), *A Port in Ancient Arabia Between Rome and the Indian Ocean (3rd century BC–5th century AD). Khor Rori Report 2*. Rome: "L'Erma" di Bretschneider.

Sedov A.

1996. Qana^c (Yemen) and the Indian Ocean: the Archaeological Evidence. Pages 11–35 in H.P. Ray & J-F. Salles (eds), *Tradition and Archaeology, Early Maritime Contacts in the Indian Ocean*. New Delhi: Manohar.

2002. The Coins from Sumhuram: the 1997–2000 Seasons. Pages 249–270 in A. Avanzini (ed.), *Khor Rori Report I*. Pisa: Edizione Plus.

2008. The Coins from Sumhuram: the 2001A–2004A Seasons. Pages 277–316 in A. Avanzini (ed.), *A Port in Ancient Arabia Between Rome and the Indian Ocean (3rd century BC–5th century AD). Khor Rori Report 2*. Rome: "L'Erma" di Bretschneider.

Sedov A. & Bienvenuti C.

2002. The pottery of Sumhuram: general typology. Pages 177–248 in A. Avanzini (ed.), *Khor Rori Report 1*. Pisa: Edizione Plus.

Serjeant R.B.

1963. *The Portuguese off the South Arabian coast. Hadrami Chronicles*. Oxford: Clarendon Press.

al-Shahri, A.A.M.

1991*a*. Recent epigraphic discoveries in Dhofar. *Proceedings of the Seminar for Arabian Studies* 21: 173–191.

1991*b*. Grave types and triliths in Dhofar. *Arabian archaeology and epigraphy* 2: 182–195.

al-Shamrookh N.A.

1996. *The Commerce and Trade of the Rasulids in the Yemen 630–858/1231–1454*. Kuwait.

al-Shanfari A.B.

1987. The Archaeology of Masirah Island, Sultanate of Oman. PhD thesis, University of Naples. [Unpublished].

Smith G.R.
2006. *A Medieval Administrative and Fiscal Treatise from the Yemen.* (Journal of Semitic Studies Supplement, 20). Oxford: Oxford University Press.
2008. *A Traveller in Thirteenth-Century Arabia. Ibn al-Mujawir's Tārīkh al-Mustabsir.* London: The Hakluyt Society.
Steimer-Herbet T.
2004. *Classification des sépultures à superstructure lithique dans le Levant et l'Arabie occidentale.* (BAR International Series, 1246). Oxford: Archaeopress.
Thomas B.
1932. *Arabia felix. Across the Empty Quarter of Arabia.* New York: Charles Scribner's Sons.
Vallet E.
2006. Yemeni "oceanic policy" at the end of the thirteenth century. *Proceedings of the Seminar for Arabian Studies* 36: 289–296.
Vogt B. & Sedov A.
1994. Surveys and Rescue Excavations in the Hadhramawt Governorate, Republic of Yemen. Sanaa. [Unpublished manuscript].
Warman S. & Clutton-Brock J.
1996. Preliminary Report for Dr Juris Zarins on the Animal Remains from the Trans Arabia Expedition. [Unpublished manuscript].
Whalen N.
2002. The Lower Palaeolithic in Southwestern Oman. *Adumatu* 5: 27–34.
2004. Lower Palaeolithic Sites in the Huqf Area of Central Oman. *Journal of Oman Studies* 13: 175–182.
Whalen N. & Schatte K.
1997. Pleistocene sites in southern Yemen. *Arabian archaeology and epigraphy* 8: 1–10.
Yule P.
1999. A Prehistoric Grave Inventory from Aztah, Zufar. Pages 91–96 in P. Yule (ed.), *Studies in the Archaeology of the Sultanate of Oman.* Rahden: Marie Leidorf.
Zarins J.
2001. *The Land of Incense.* (Sultan Qaboos University Publications, Archaeology & Cultural Heritage Series, 1). Muscat: Al Nahda Printing Press.
2007. Aspects of recent archaeological work at al-Baleed (Zafar), Sultanate of Oman. *Proceedings of the Seminar for Arabian Studies* 37: 309–324.
(in press). Funerary Monuments of Southern Arabia: the Iron Age-Early Islamic Traditions. In L. Weeks (ed.), *Proceedings of the Death, Burial and the Transition to the Afterlife in Arabia and Adjacent Regions Seminar.*
Zarins J. & Newton L.S.
(in preparation). *Ancient Zafar (al-Baleed): an Historical and Archaeological Assessment.* (2 volumes).

Authors' addresses
Lynne Newton, Office of the Advisor to H.M. the Sultan for Cultural Affairs, P.O. Box 1, Al Hafa, Al Baleed, PC 216, Salalah, Oman.

e-mail lynnesnewton@gmail.com

Juris Zarins, Office of the Advisor to H.M. the Sultan for Cultural Affairs, P.O. Box 1, Al Hafa, Al Baleed, PC 216, Salalah, Oman.

e-mail dr.zarins@gmail.com

Proceedings of the Seminar for Arabian Studies 40 (2010): 267–276

An early MIS3 wet phase at palaeolake ᶜAqabah: preliminary interpretation of the multi-proxy record

Ash Parton, Adrian G. Parker, Andrew R. Farrant, Melanie J. Leng, Hans-Peter Uerpmann, Jean-Luc Schwenninger, Chris Galletti & Jon Wells

Summary
South-east Arabia is uniquely positioned with respect to both palaeoclimate and archaeological studies. While its role in the migration and dispersal of early modern humans continues to generate debate, its location at the critical interface between two of the world's major climate systems, the Indian Ocean Monsoon (IOM) and the mid-latitude westerlies (MLW), has prompted a wide variety of palaeoclimatic studies to be conducted. A continually expanding body of work now indicates that Arabia has experienced significant climatic and environmental changes since the last interglacial around 135–120,000 years BP (Before Present), largely as a result of monsoon variability, but the timing of such changes remains unresolved. In particular, the occurrence of a pluvial phase during Marine Isotope Stage 3 (MIS3) continues to generate debate, with a variety of records often providing conflicting evidence as to its timing. To address this issue, we present a high-resolution multi-proxy terrestrial record of an early MIS3 wet phase within the Arabian interior at approximately 56,000 years BP. Geomorphological and multi-proxy evidence indicates that during this period, the northward migration and incursion of the IOM into Arabia caused large-scale alluvial fan and wadi networks to become active, issuing from the Ḥajar Mountains towards the Gulf. Of these, a large alluvial fan and its associated drainage network became heavily constrained around the Jabal al-Fāyah anticline. This led to the significant ponding of surface water, which subsequently formed a large overbank palaeolake deposit. Isotopic, geochemical, and bulk physical evidence are also presented which provide important information regarding hydrological and catchment stability processes, thereby helping to reconstruct the landscape of Arabia during this period. The evidence presented here, therefore, not only provides important information regarding the timing and intensity of low-latitude climatic excursions, but also provides substantial support for the ability of Arabia to support autochthonous human occupation and development during the Late Pleistocene.

Keywords: Arabia, monsoon, MIS3, Palaeoclimate, human dispersal

Introduction

Climatic and environmental evidence from palaeolake ᶜAqabah indicates that Arabia may have experienced pluvial conditions significantly earlier during MIS3 than has been previously suggested. Northward migration of the ITCZ and the associated IOM rainfall belt activated extensive wadi and alluvial fan systems, which issued from the Ḥajar Mountains, flowing north-west towards the Gulf. Lake formation, initiated by wadi overbanking, was short-lived, however, and the water body itself was at times considerably saline. While the regional climate around Jabal ᶜAqabah may have remained semi-arid/arid, geomorphological and multi-proxy evidence, nonetheless, suggests that the volume of fresh water available within the area would have been considerable. While evidence for an early MIS3 humid period within Arabia remains scarce, correlations are clearly seen between ᶜAqabah and both regional (Arabian Sea, Socotra, and Saudi Arabia) and global records of climate change. In particular, global climatic events such as D-O Event 12 (Dansgaard-Oeschger Event 12) are detectable within the terrestrial record at ᶜAqabah, highlighting the sensitivity of the monsoon to Northern Hemisphere climatic excursions and insolation variability. The palaeoclimatic record from ᶜAqabah, therefore, not only provides important information regarding the timing and intensity of monsoon variability, but also gives substantial support to the ability of Arabia to support autochthonous human occupation and development during the Late Pleistocene.

Background

The south-west Indian Ocean Monsoon (IOM) represents

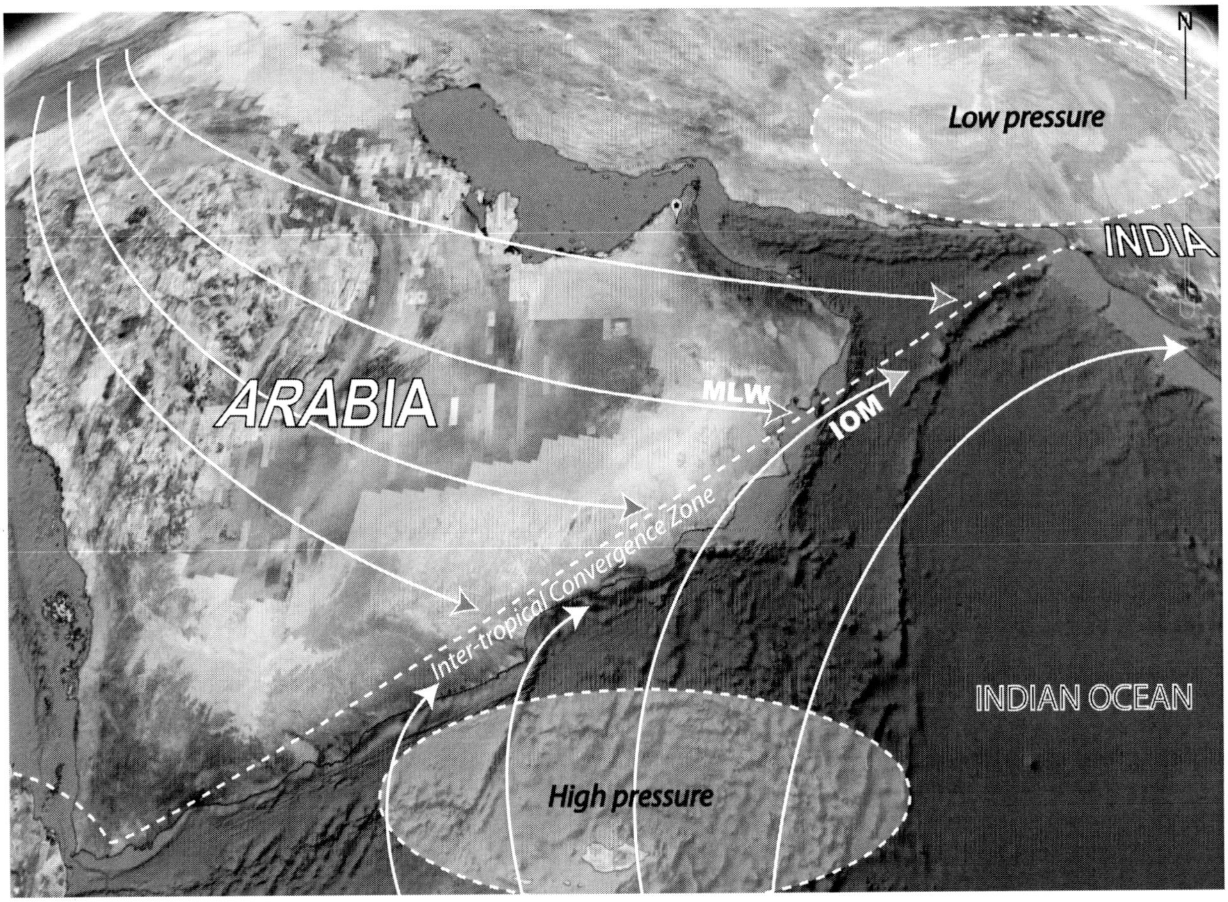

FIGURE 1. *Generalized modern, summer surface-wind patterns of the Mid-latitude Westerlies (MLW) and the Indian Ocean Monsoon (IOM). The approximate position of the Inter-tropical Convergence Zone (ITCZ) is shown, which today roughly marks the northern limit of the summer monsoon rainfall (Burns* et al. *2001). During pluvial episodes (i.e. MIS5e, MIS3, and the early Holocene), the IOM/ITCZ migrated further north to penetrate the interior of Arabia.*

one of the most dynamic inter-hemispheric interactions between atmosphere, oceans, and continents, driving a wide variety of both morphological and climatological changes throughout Arabia. Although the present-day latitudinal extent of the monsoon does not penetrate the desert interior (Fig. 1), periodic incursions of the IOM into Arabia transformed its arid interior into an ameliorated landscape capable of supporting a variety of flora and fauna (e.g. Parker *et al.* 2006; Parker 2009). Such intermittent pluvial phases are inexorably linked to periodic changes in Northern Hemisphere insolation and glacial boundary conditions (Clemens *et al.* 1991; 1996; Sirocko *et al.* 1993; Neff *et al.* 2001; Fleitmann & Matter 2009), however, the timing of these pluvials and the degree to which the monsoon varies in response to orbital forcing, remain unresolved (e.g. Kutzbach 1981; Ruddiman 2006; Clemens & Prell 2007). Furthermore, the lack of clarity regarding the timing of northward IOM migration means that issues surrounding the ability of Arabia to support continual autochthonous human occupation following the last interglacial, also remain unclear.

While substantial evidence now indicates the presence of earlier pluvials during Marine Isotope Stage 5 (MIS5), *c.*135–120,000 years BP (e.g. Maizels 1987; Sanlaville 1992; Burns *et al.* 1998; 2001; Fleitmann & Matter 2009; Blechschmidt *et al.* 2009), the issue of a later pluvial phase during MIS3 (*c.*60–30,000 years BP) is less clear. Many palaeoclimatic investigations from south-east Arabia reveal a landscape that remained arid and inhospitable following the last interglacial, only becoming humid by around 35 kyr BP. This is supported by numerous palaeolake, wadi terrace, and calcite deposits (e.g.

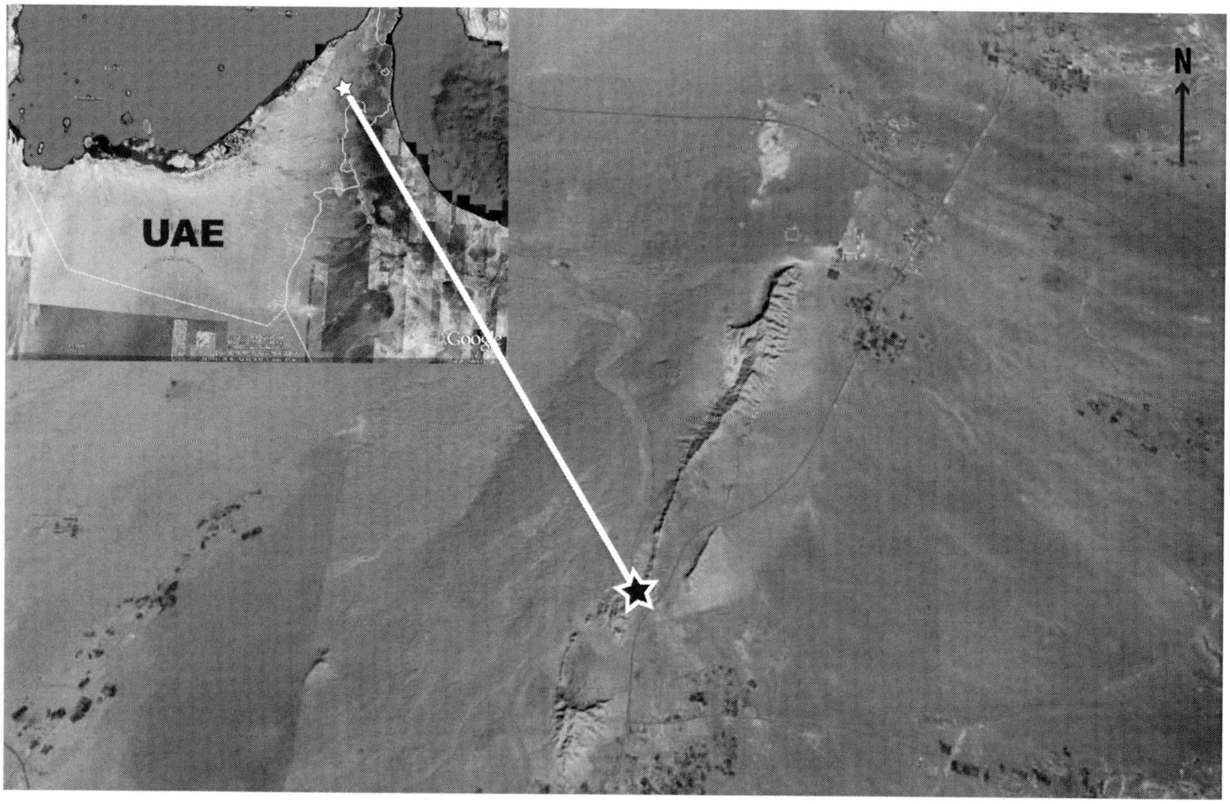

Figure 2. *An aerial map of the study site and its position within the UAE. The relict lake sequence at Jabal ᶜAqabah is situated at the lower end of the Jabal al-Fāyah anticline, which separates the deflated alluvial fan surfaces to the east, and the dune fields to the west.*

McClure 1976; Garrard *et al.* 1981; Schulz & Whitney 1986; Clark & Fontes 1990; Sanlaville 1992; Lézine *et al.* 1998; 2007). To date, little evidence exists for an *early* MIS3 pluvial phase within Arabia; however, recent evidence is beginning to challenge this assumption (e.g. Burns *et al.* 2003; McLaren *et al.* 2008), with research showing that humid phases may have occurred as early as 55,000 years BP. The paucity of data regarding the Arabian climate during MIS3 has meant that our understanding of monsoon variability and its correlation with high latitude climatic excursions (i.e. D-O Event 12) during this important period remains unclear. Furthermore, Arabia lies at a critical location with regards to human migration and dispersal out of Africa, with many theories suggesting that the movements of early humans during and following the last interglacial would be intrinsically linked to, if not driven by, climatic fluctuations across the peninsula (e.g. Mellars 2006; Rose 2006; 2009). Therefore, if the ability of Arabia to support autochthonous human development during this period is to be validated, confirmation of the environmental conditions within the peninsula during this time is also essential.

To address these important issues, a study has been conducted on sediments retrieved from an interstratified aeolian-fluvial palaeolake sequence situated at the base of Jabal ᶜAqabah, Mleiha, Sharjah, UAE. A multi-proxy approach has been adopted utilizing bulk physical, mineral magnetic, Digital Elevation Mapping (DEM), geochemical and isotopic analyses, while a chronology based upon a series of six OSL dates is also being determined. Here we present a brief overview of the key findings and implications of this ongoing project.

Study site and results

Jabal ᶜAqabah (Fig. 2) lies approximately 10 km south-south-west of Jabal al-Fāyah, where an ongoing excavation has uncovered numerous stratified assemblages of Late Palaeolithic origin (Uerpmann, personal communication). A pilot archaeological study of

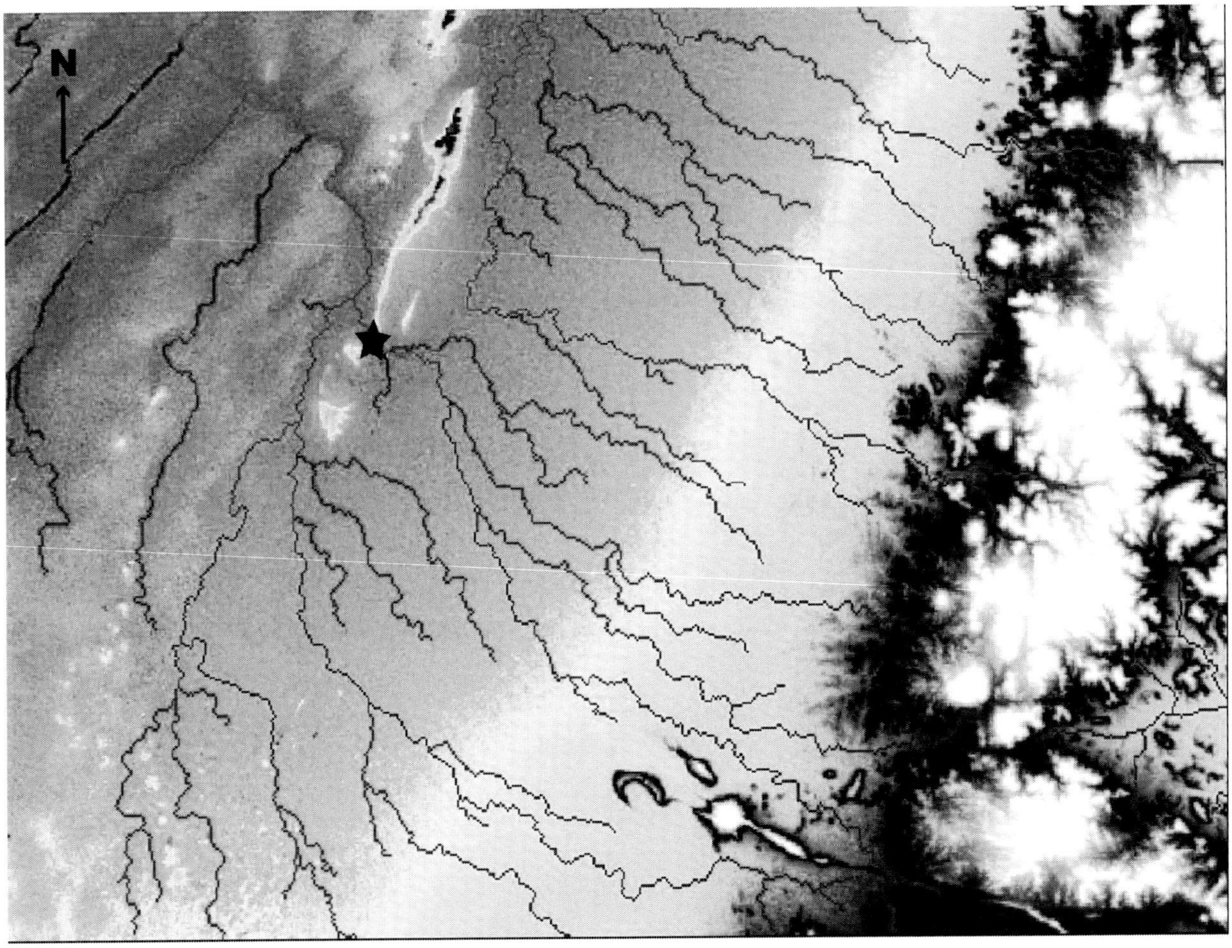

FIGURE 3. *A DEM image featuring modelled hydrology of the area surrounding the study site. The drainage channels shown are those calculated to have greater than 10,000 fluvial inputs. A convergence of channels is clearly seen at the site location, where flow became restricted, leading to the ponding of surface water (USGS 2006).*

surface lithic scatters approximately 150 m west of the palaeolake also indicates that at some point local chert outcrops had been used as a source of raw material, further highlighting the presence of early human communities within the region. The sequence at Jabal ᶜAqabah is comprised of interstratified aeolian-fluvial deposits overlain by limestone colluvium, of Holocene (depositional) age. Periods of fluvial sedimentation are marked by the deposition of calcareous, laminated material with significant manganese staining and root impressions between laminae, while aeolian sedimentation is marked by the deposition of homogeneous, iron-rich sand with no bedding structures and the formation of small *nabkhah* dunes (formed from sediment accumulations around shrubs) within aeolian strata.

Geomorphological and DEM data (Fig. 3) suggest that lake formation occurred along the distal edge of a former alluvial fan that had been triggered by IOM incursion into Arabia. Lake formation occurred as alluvial fan and wadi flow, initiated from the Ḥajar Mountains to the east, debouched westwards towards the Gulf before becoming severely constrained as it reached the narrow gap between Jabal ᶜAqabah and Jabal al-Fāyah. The subsequent "backing-up" of stream flow would have then led to episodes of overbank flooding and lake formation as fluvial input ceased.

OSL age estimates suggest that intermittent pulses of wadi/alluvial fan flow and subsequent overbank flooding occurred within the region between ~56±6.2 and ~52.4±5.1 kyr BP, therefore indicating the presence

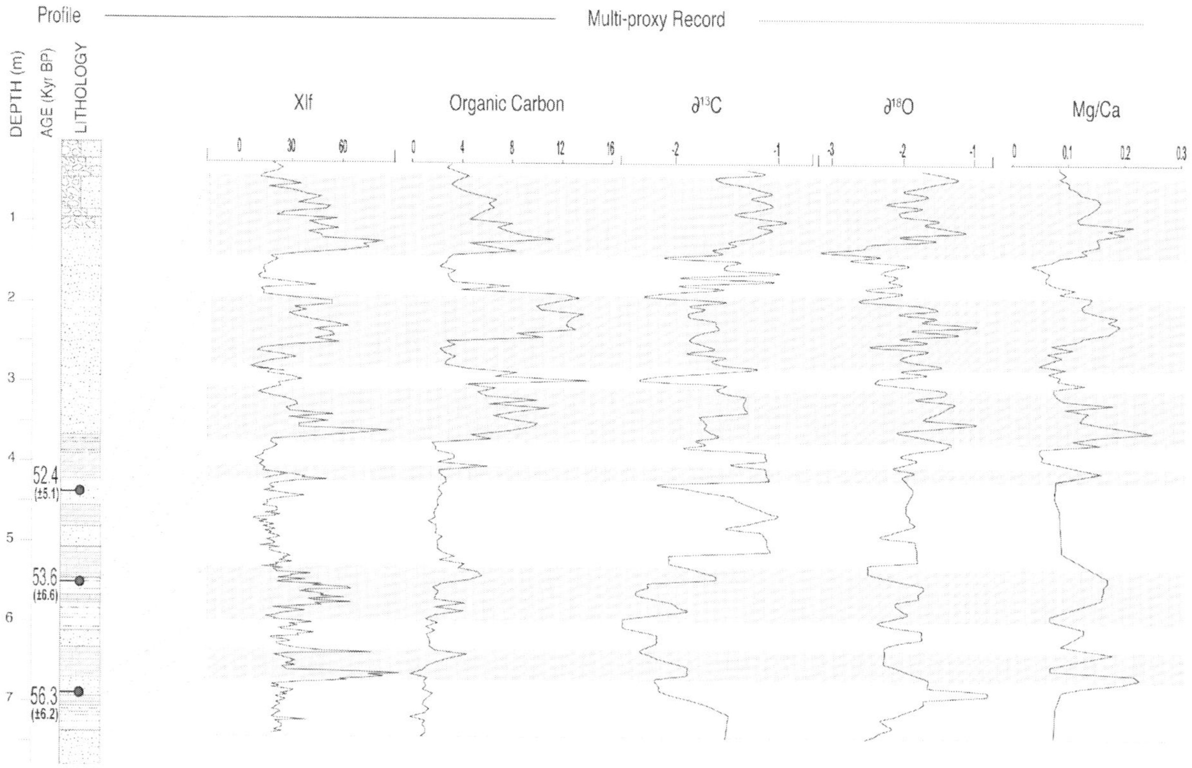

FIGURE 4. *A sedimentary profile of palaeolake ᶜAqabah alongside key palaeo-environmental indicators: magnetic susceptibility (Xlf, values expressed in SI), organic carbon content (given as loss-on-ignition percentage), $\delta^{18}O$ and $\delta^{13}C$ (carbonate) values (reported as per mil (‰) deviations of the isotopic ratios ($^{13}C/^{12}C$, $^{18}O/^{16}O$) from laboratory standards V-PDB) and Mg/Ca (%) ratios.*

of an early MIS3 humid phase within the region. These short-lived pluvial episodes are detectable within the mineral magnetic and geochemical record, which reflect the deposition of mineragenic detritus, fluvially eroded from the Ḥajar Mountains and the surrounding watershed, and subsequently transported as sustained stream-flow to Jabal ᶜAqabah (Fig. 4). Variations in lake hydrology and catchment productivity are also detectable through carbonate isotope analysis ($\delta^{18}O$ and $\delta^{13}C$) (Leng & Marshall 2004). The transition from arid to humid conditions is clearly indicated by a marked decline in $\delta^{18}O$ values due to the freshening of the lake waters, but down-profile interpretation is, at this stage, problematic. Due to the depositional nature of palaeolake ᶜAqabah, values are facies dependent as each successive phase of aeolian and lacustrine sedimentation produces values relative to their depositional environment. Furthermore, as lake formation is surface-water driven at ᶜAqabah, the absence of a continual water supply into the basin following an initial flood event, disrupts the evaporation/precipitation balance of the lake and reduces the dilution effect, producing apparent increases in $\delta^{18}O$ values during pluvials. In addition, in such depositional environments the authigenic carbonate isotope signal can be contaminated by the influx of detrital carbonate from the catchment (Leng & Marshall 2004), and therefore forthcoming scanning electron microscope (SEM) analysis will help to determine the potential influence of detrital carbonate (e.g. calcite, dolomite).

Sedimentological evidence from palaeolake ᶜAqabah also indicates that while extensive alluvial fan and wadi networks may have been widespread, local precipitation may have been minimal. The lack of large clasts within the profile, which are indicative of the distance from the source (intersection point) from which the mineragenic material has travelled, simultaneously discount Jabal ᶜAqabah itself as a source of such material. It is therefore possible to infer that little precipitation fell directly within the study area during early MIS3, as any such rainfall would have undoubtedly activated localized alluvial fan

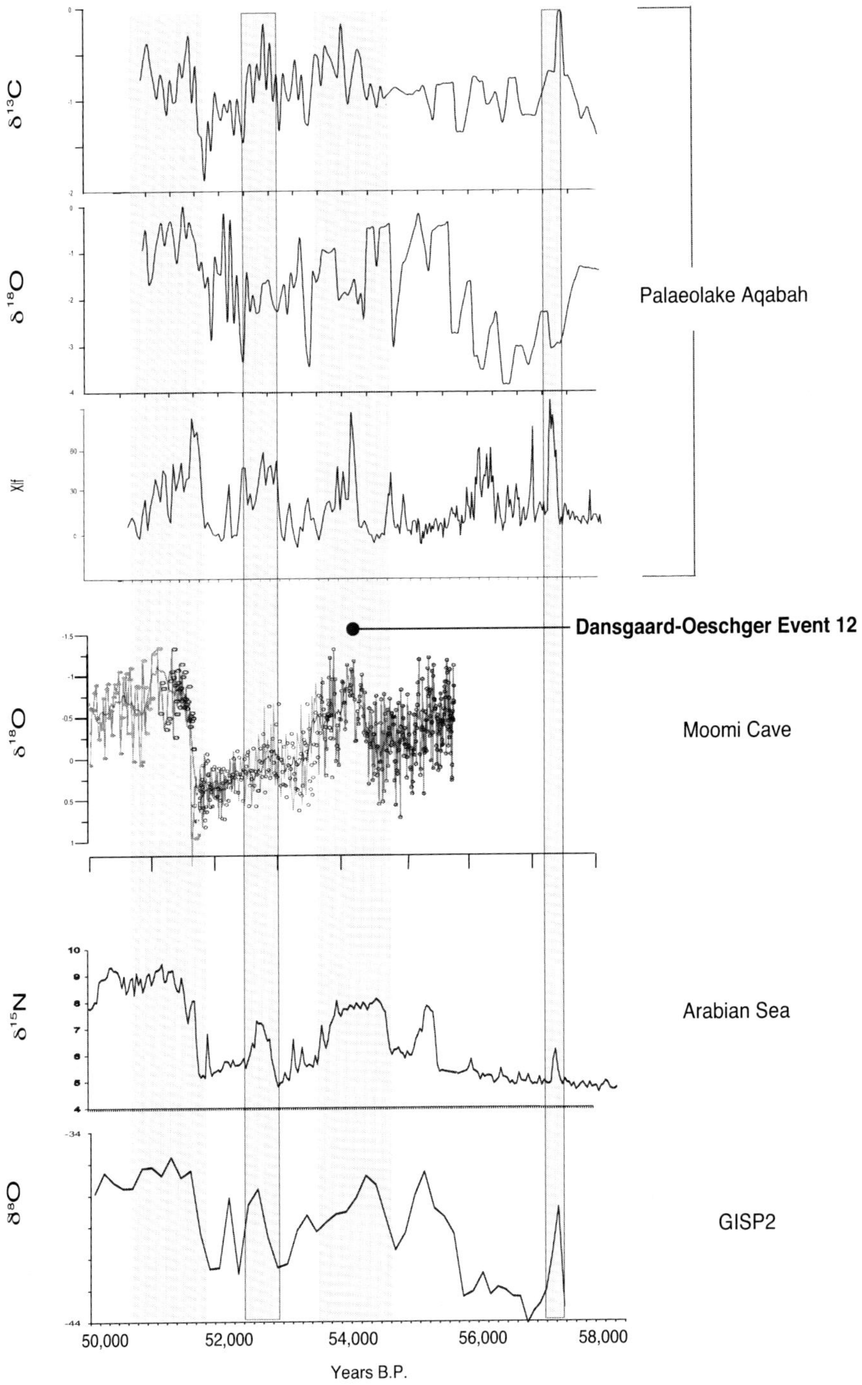

Figure 5. *A comparison of palaeolake ʿAqabah with regional and global palaeoclimate records. Susceptibility (Xlf) measurements and $\delta^{18}O$ and $\delta^{13}C$ (carb) values are given from ʿAqabah, alongside denitrification data from the Arabian Sea (Altabet* et al. *2002), values from Moomi Cave, Socotra (Burns* et al. *2003) and $\delta^{18}O$ values from GISP2 ice-core record (Bender* et al. *1994). Good correlation is observed between the records; in particular, D-O Event 12 is detectable in both high latitude (GISP2) and low latitude (Arabian) records.*

systems, enabling the inclusion of colluvium within the profile. Such colluvial deposits are evident at the surface of the sequence, suggesting that at some point following MIS3, possibly the early Holocene, regional rainfall led to the activation of local alluvial fans. The notion that wadi flow and lake formation took place within arid surroundings, is further supported by the $\delta^{18}O$ signature (Fig. 4), which also suggests that lacustrine conditions may have been short-lived, with rapid increases in $\delta^{18}O$ values during pluvials, indicating an abrupt imbalance between inputs and outputs as stream-input ceased. This is further supported by Mg/Ca ratios within the geochemical record, which are used to reflect salinity changes, and indicate that shortly after lake formation, the water body may have become increasingly saline and brackish.

The palaeoclimatic record from ᶜAqabah therefore depicts a predominantly arid, early MIS3 environment, briefly punctuated by the intermittent, large-scale activation of extensive wadi and alluvial fan networks into the interior of Arabia. Al-Fāyah fan is a relatively modest example of such alluvial fans; geomorphological evidence suggests that many larger fans, extending from the northern limit of the Ḥajar Mountains down to the Umm al-Samīm, may have also been active at this time (e.g. Farrant *et al.* 2006), alongside those active within Saudi Arabia (McLaren *et al.* 2008). These expansive corridors of fresh surface water would have no doubt proved essential to human and animal communities such as those around al-Fāyah region, who occupied the Arabian interior during the Late Pleistocene.

Similarities are also detectable between both regional and global palaeoclimatic records, and those retrieved from ᶜAqabah. A comparison of the proxy records from ᶜAqabah with those from Socotra, the Arabian Sea, and Greenland (Fig. 5), indicates a strong correspondence in frequency and pattern, with all palaeoclimatic records depicting climatic excursions between 50–60 kyr BP, in particular during Dansgaard-Oeschger Event 12 (Fig. 5). This period of high-latitude warming is associated with enhanced humidity within low-latitude regions such as Arabia, demonstrating a possible millennial-scale mechanistic linkage between the two regions. The apparent near-zero phase relationship between the Arabian records and the North Atlantic, also suggests that monsoonal variability is closely tied to Northern Hemisphere insolation, such that abrupt radiative changes would have an instantaneous expression within Arabian palaeoclimatic records. The ability to correlate records in this way therefore provides important information regarding the sensitivity of the monsoon to various forcing mechanisms, and indicates that fluvial sequences such as ᶜAqabah are just as sensitive as other palaeoclimatic archives.

Acknowledgements

The authors would like to acknowledge the following people, without whom this study would have proved far more difficult, if not impossible: Jeff Rose, Richard Ellison (and all other members of the BGS Mapping Project), Emma Tomlinson, Nick Walsh, David Peat, Gareth Preston, Helen Walkington, Daniel Parslow, Isis Jones, Yusef Ibrahim, and of course, all of our collective families for their enduring patience.

References

Altabet M.A., Higginson M.J. & Murray D.W.
2002. The effect of millennial scale changes in Arabian Sea denitrification on atmospheric CO2. *Nature* 415: 159–162.

Bender M., Sowers T., Dickson M-L., Orchado J., Grootes P., Mayewski P.A. & Meese D.A.
1994. Climate Correlations Between Freenland and Antarctica During the Past 100,000 Years. *Nature* 372: 663–666.

Blechschmidt I., Matter A., Preusser F. & Rieke-Zapp D.
2009. Monsoon triggered formation of Quaternary alluvial megafans in the interior of Oman. *Geomorphology* 110: 128–139.

Burns S.J., Matter A., Frank N. & Mangini A.
1998. Speleothem-based palaeoclimate Record from Northern Oman. *Geology* 26: 499–502.

Burns S.J., Fleitmann D., Matter A., Kramers J. & Al-Subbary A.A.
2003. Indian Ocean Climate and an Absolute Chronology Over Dansgaard/Oeschger Events 9 to 13. *Science* 301: 1365.
Burns S.J., Fleitmann D., Matter A., Neff U. & Mangini A.
2001. Speleothem evidence from Oman for continental pluvial events during interglacial periods. *Geology* 29/7: 623–626.
Clark I. & Fontes J-C.
1990. Paleoclimatic Reconstruction of Northern Oman Based on Carbonates from Hyperalkaline Groundwaters. *Quaternary Research* 33: 320–336.
Clemens S.C. & Prell W.L.
2007. The Timing of Orbital-scale Indian Monsoon Changes. *Quaternary Science Reviews* 26: 275–278.
Clemens S.C., Murray D. & Prell W.L.
1996. Nonstationary Phase of the Plio-Pleistocene Asian Monsoon. *Science* 274: 943–948.
Clemens S., Prell W., Murray D., Shimmield G. & Weedon G.
1991. Forcing Mechanisms of the Indian Ocean Monsoon. *Nature* 353: 720–725.
Farrant A.R., Arkley S.L.B., Ellison R.A., Styles M.T. & Phillips E.R.
2006. Geology of the Al Dhaid. UAE Ministry of Energy, *Map Sheet 100–2*, British Geological Survey.
Fleitmann D. & Matter A.
2009. The speleothem record of climate variability in Southern Arabia, *Comptes Rendus Geoscience* 341: 633–642.
Garrard A.N., Harvey C.P.D. & Switsur V.R.
1981. Environment and Settlement During the Upper Pleistocene and Holocene at Jubbah in the Great Nafud, Northern Arabia. *Atlal* 5: 137–148.
Kutzbach J.E.
1981. Monsoon Climate of the Early Holocene: Climate Experiment with the Earth's Orbital Parameters for 9000 Years Ago. *Science* 214: 59–61.
Leng M.J. & Marshall J.D.
2004. Palaeoclimate interpretation of stable isotope data from the lake sediment archives. *Quaternary Science Reviews* 23: 811–831.
Lézine A., Saliège J., Robert C., Wertz F. & Inizan M.
1998. Holocene lakes from Ramlat as-Sabʾatayn (Yemen) illustrate the impact of monsoon activity in southern Arabia. *Quaternary Research* 50: 290–299.
Lézine A., Tiercelin J-J., Robert C., Saliège J-F., Cleuziou S., Inizan M-L. & Braemer F.
2007. Centennial to millennial-scale variability of the Indian monsoon during the early Holocene from a sediment, pollen and isotope record from the desert of Yemen. *Palaeogeography, Palaeoclimatology, Palaeoecology* 243: 235–249.
McClure H.A.
1976. Radiocarbon chronology of Late Quaternary Lakes in the Arabian Desert. *Nature* 263: 755–756.
McLaren S.J., Al-Juaidi F., Bateman M.D. & Millington A.C.
2008. First evidence for episodic flooding events in the arid interior of central Saudi Arabia over the last 60 ka. *Journal of Quaternary Science* 24: 198–207.
Maizels J.K.
1987. Plio-Pleistocene raised channel systems of the western Sharqiya (Wahiba), Oman. Pages 31–50 in L. Frostick & I. Reid (eds), *Desert Sediments: Ancient and Modern* (Geological Society Special Publications, 35). London: Geological Society.
Mellars P.
2006. Going East: New Genetic and Archaeological Perspectives on the Modern Human Colonization of Eurasia. *Science* 313: 796–800.
Neff U., Burns S.J., Mangini A., Mudelsee M., Fleitman D. & Matter A.
2001. Strong coherence between solar variability and the monsoon in Oman between 9 and 6 kyr ago. *Nature* 411: 290–293.

Parker A.G.

2009. Pleistocene Climate Change in Arabia—Developing a Framework for Hominin Dispersal Over the Last 350kyr. Pages 39–51 in M.D. Petraglia & J.I. Rose (eds), *The Evolution of Human Populations in Arabia: Palaeo-environments, Prehistory and Genetics*. Heidelberg/London: Springer.

Parker A.G., Preston G., Walkington H. & Hodson M.J.

2006. Developing a framework of Holocene climatic change and landscape archaeology for southeastern Arabia. *Arabian archaeology and epigraphy* 17: 125–130.

Rose J.I.

2006. Among Arabian Sands: defining the Palaeolithic of southern Arabia. PhD thesis, Southern Methodist University, Dallas. [Unpublished].

2007. The Arabian Corridor Migration Model: archaeological evidence for hominin dispersals into Oman during the Middle and Upper Pleistocene. *Proceedings of the Seminar for Arabian Studies* 37: 219–237.

2009. Tracking the Origin and Evolution of Human Populations in Arabia. Pages 1–15 in M.D. Petraglia & J.I. Rose (eds), *The Evolution of Human Populations in Arabia: Palaeo-environments, Prehistory and Genetics*. Heidelberg/London: Springer.

Ruddiman W.F.

2006. What is the Timing of Orbital-scale Monsoon Changes? *Quaternary Science Reviews* 25: 657–658.

Sanlaville P.

1992. Changements Climatiques dans la Péninsule Arabique durant le Pléistocène Supérieur et l'Holocène. *Paléorient* 18: 5–25.

Schulz E. & Whitney J.W.

1986. Upper Pleistocene and Holocene lakes in the An Nafud, Saudi Arabia. *Hydrobiologia* 143: 175–190.

Sirocko F., Sarthein M., Erlenkeuser H., Lange H., Arnold M. & Duplessy J.C.

1993. Century-scale events in monsoonal climate over the past 24,000 years. *Nature* 364: 322–324.

United States Geological Survey (USGS)

2006. Shuttle Radar Topography Mission, 3 Arc Second scene SRTM_f03_n025e056, Unified Finished 2.0, Global Land Cover Facility, University of Maryland, February 2000.

Authors' addresses

Ash Parton, Department of Anthropology and Geography, Oxford Brookes University, Oxford, OX3 0BP, UK.

e-mail ashparton@btinternet.com

Professor Adrian Parker, Department of Anthropology and Geography, Oxford Brookes University, Oxford, OX3 0BP, UK.

e-mail agparker@brookes.ac.uk

Dr Andrew Farrant, British Geological Survey, Keyworth, Nottingham, NG12 5GG, UK.

e-mail arf@bgs.ac.uk

Professor Melanie Leng, NERC Isotope Geosciences Laboratory, British Geological Survey, Keyworth, Nottingham, NG12 5GG, UK.

e-mail mjl@nigl.nerc.ac.uk

Professor Hans-Peter Uerpmann, Eberhard-Karls-Universität Tübingen, Rümelinstr. 23, 72076 Tübingen, Germany.

e-mail hans-peter.uerpmann@uni-tuebingen.de

Dr Jean-Luc Schwenninger, Research Laboratory for Archaeology and the History of Art, University of Oxford, Oxford, OX1 3QY, UK.

e-mail jean-luc.schwenninger@rlaha.ac.uk

Chris Galletti, School of Geographical Sciences, Arizona State University, 975 S. Myrtle Avenue, P.O. Box 875302, Temple, AZ 85287-5302, USA.

e-mail chris.galletti@gmail.com

Jon Wells, Department of Anthropology and Geography, Oxford Brookes University, Oxford, OX3 0BP, UK.

e-mail jrwells@brookes.ac.uk

Proceedings of the Seminar for Arabian Studies 40 (2010): 277–282

South Arabian inscriptions from the Farasān Islands (Saudi Arabia) (poster)

Solène Marion de Procé & Carl Phillips

Summary
A few years ago the study of a Latin inscription found on Farasān Island was published in *Proceedings of the Seminar for Arabian Studies* (2004). Prior to this, the only inscription known from Farasān was a fragmentary South Arabian inscription published in the journal *Atlal* (1981). As a result of further surveys of the island several more South Arabian inscriptions have now been recorded. All of the inscriptions are very short, or incomplete, and often heavily eroded. The legible inscriptions appear to show mainly personal names. The inscriptions and suggested readings are presented along with a description of the sites where they were found, where such evidence is available. The possible dates for the inscriptions are considered alongside supporting archaeological evidence. Finally, the evidence that the inscriptions provide for South Arabians on Farasān will be discussed in relation to historical developments on the adjacent mainland and southern Red Sea coast from the early first millennium BC to the first few centuries AD.

Keywords: Farasān Islands, epigraphy, South Arabian, Latin, inscriptions

Introduction

A few years ago a Latin inscription found on Farasān Island was published in *PSAS* (Phillips, Villeneuve & Facey 2004: 239–250). Prior to this a fragmentary South Arabian inscription published in *Atlal* (Zarins, Murad & Al-Yish 1981: 9–42) was the only inscription known from Farasān. A second Latin inscription has since been found and, as a result of further surveys of the islands (Nehmé & Villeneuve [n.d.]), more South Arabian inscriptions have been recorded, some of which had only been mentioned previously by Miftāḥ (1990; 2003). The inscriptions are short, incomplete, or heavily eroded. The legible content of the inscriptions appears to be personal names as well as the name of the South Arabian deity, Athtar, in one of them.

The inscriptions and preliminary readings are presented below with a description of the contexts (where such evidence is available). The possible dates for the inscriptions are considered alongside supporting archaeological and epigraphic evidence. Finally, the evidence that the inscriptions provide for South Arabians on Farasān is discussed in relation to historical developments on the adjacent mainland and southern Red Sea coast from the early first millennium BC to the first few centuries AD. The Farasān Islands (Fig. 1) are located approximately 60 km west of Jizān off the southern Red Sea coast of Arabia.

One of the Latin inscriptions found on Farasān commemorates the dedication of a monument to the Emperor Antoninus Pius, built on Farasān (*Ferresan*), probably in AD 144/145, by a detachment of the *II Traiana Fortis* and its auxiliaries. The dedicator is a prefect of the *Portus Ferresan* and of the "Sea of Hercules" (much more likely than "the Bridge of Hercules").

The second Latin inscription is fragmentary and probably comprised four lines with the end of lines 3 and 4 being all that has survived. This fragment of text possibly mentions a *Legio VI Ferrata*, which would date the inscription to *c.* AD 120, thus approximately a quarter of a century earlier than the first inscription.

Prior to the discovery of these Latin inscriptions the earliest historical references to Farasān date from the sixth century AD.

Once again, the strategic location of Farasān is implied in the Greek *Martyrium Arethae* where it is reported how Farasān (*Farsan*) contributed seven ships to the Ethiopian fleet sent in a bid to halt the persecution of Christians in Najrān ("The Martyrs of Najrān") in about 525. Incidentally, around this time, Nannosos, the Byzantine ambassador sent by Justinian (527–565) to the King of Axum, also visited Farasān and provided a description of its inhabitants (Photius/ed. Henry 1959). There is also a South Arabian inscription (Ja 1028, see Robin 1995: 230) mentioning both Farasānites (*Frs^{1}nyt-m*) and Farasān

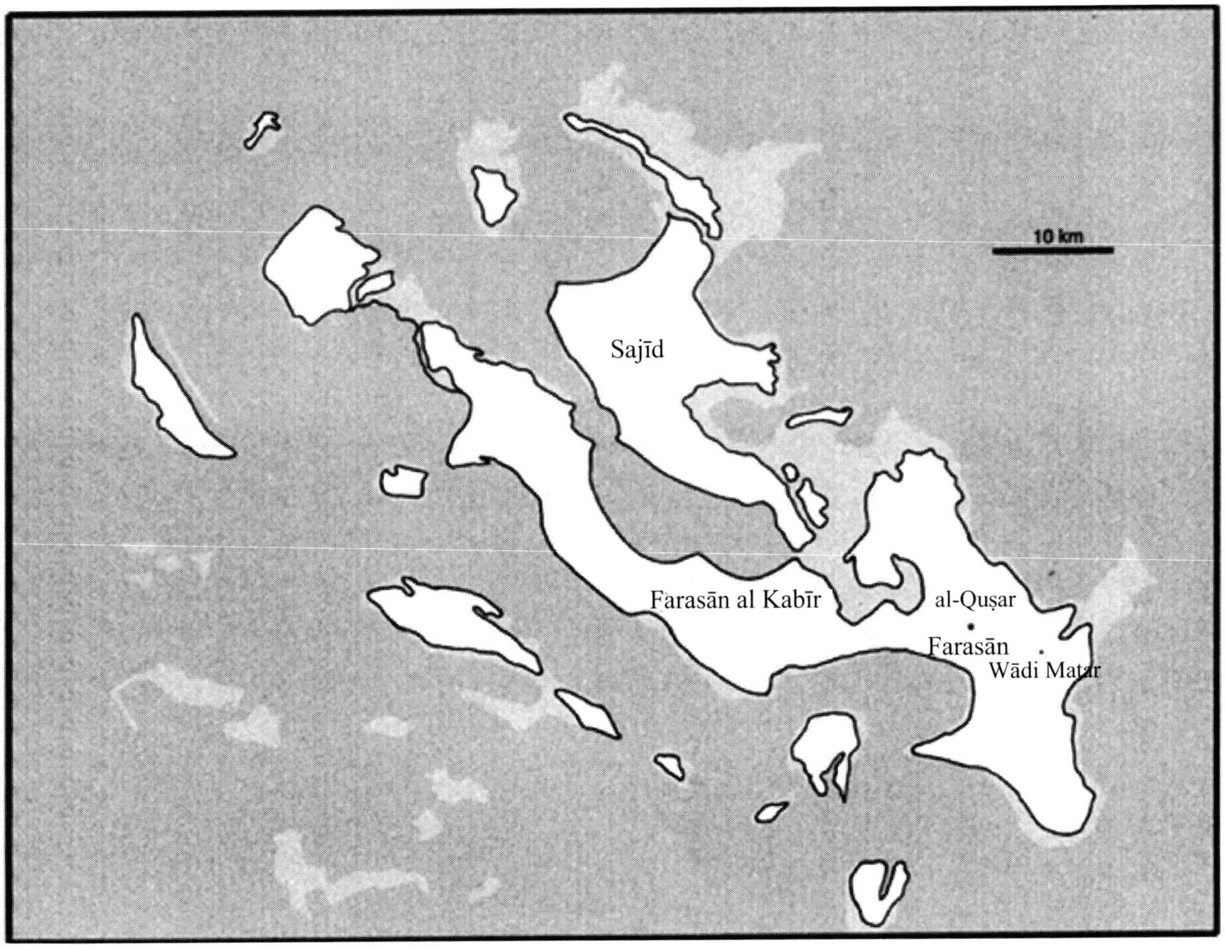

FIGURE 1. *Main map of the Farasān archipelago (Saudi Arabia).*

(*Frs¹n*) when describing events in the neighbourhood of al-Mukhā.

Farasān seems to have occasionally played an important role in the history of this part of the Red Sea. It is hoped the inscriptions presented here and consideration of their contexts will provide further insight into the history of Farasān and its connections with South Arabia.

Qusār

One of the two Latin inscriptions (the smallest) was found at Qusār, approximately 5 km south-east of Farasān city on the main island. This site was previously occupied by a village that was abandoned in 1975. Many limestone blocks were reused in the recent building including capitals and columns. An ashlar block was reused and cut to form a semi-circular arch, which bears a South Arabian inscription (Fig. 2/a).

There were possibly two inscriptions: the upper inscription comprising four lines, and beneath this is a two-line inscription. The letters in the lower inscription are noticeably larger than the upper one but the style of the letters is similar.

The inscription is eroded and the remodelling of the block has cut away a large part of the text. It is possible, however, to identify a number of personal names. The suggested reading of the inscription is as follows:

1. */yhz*
2. */lḥy*
3. */'*
4. */bn*

SPACE

5. */bn/m*
6. *ywm*

Figure 2. *Ancient South Arabian inscriptions from the Farasān Islands.*

It is possible that *yhz* in line 1 represents the beginning of a name such as *Yhzhm* (Harding 1971: 689). Likewise, *lḥy* in line 2 might be the beginning of a common name or simply the name *Lḥy* which is known from a Sabaic inscription (Wāqir 1) found at Wāqir, a site in Wādī Sihām, on the Yemeni Tihāmah (Beeston 2005: 48–49).

It should be noted that the South Arabian inscription published by Zarins, Murad and Al-Yish (photographed by W. Facey) was also found at Qusār. This fragmentary inscription is also eroded. It is, however, possible that the name *'dn* occurs in the lower line of the inscription (Fig. 2/b).

Khutūb (Khaṭīb)

On Sajīd Island is the village of Khutūb. There is no clear pre-Islamic site there but there is a cemetery, to the north-west of the village, where ancient carved blocks have been reused. Among these reused blocks an almost complete South Arabian inscription was found some years ago by Ibrahim Miftāḥ (Fig. 2/c). The inscription comprises four lines, the first three of which are completely legible. Most of the fourth line is missing. The inscription comprises a list of names:

1. *gldm/w'ls*^{2}
2. *rh/w'n'm/*
3. *wdlwn/wmr*
4. *hr*

Alternatives that have been suggested for the first name in line 1 are *Mgdm* and *Mldm*. The value of the first letter is misleading because of a small fissure in the stone, which gives the appearance of it being an M. On closer inspection, it appears more likely to be G. The horizontal line of the letter that follows is definitely sloping and is most likely L. The name is, therefore, *Gldm*.

The second name on lines 1 and 2, *'ls*^{2}*rh*, is well known throughout South Arabia. The second name on line 2 appears to be *'n'm*. This name is common in Safaitic (also known from Minaic and Sabaic inscriptions, Harding 1971: 80).

The first name on line 3 is clearly *Dlwn*. This name is also known from a Sabaic inscription (1971: 242). Unfortunately, the other names are partially missing.

Wādī Maṭar

In the south-western part of Farasān al-Kabīr, in Wādī Maṭar, there are several archaeological sites close to one another. They were first surveyed by a team led by J. Zarins in 1980 (Zarins, Murad & Al-Yish 1981: 9–42).

The foundations of buildings are visible and it was also observed that some of the monolithic door jambs have short South Arabian inscriptions on them (Fig. 2/d).

An early publication by Miftāḥ (1990) includes a photograph of an inscription which it appears safe to conclude was found in the vicinity of the Wādī Maṭar sites (Wādī Maṭar 1 & Wādī Maṭar 2). In this inscription two lines are visible (Fig. 2/e). In the upper line the only word that can be read is the verb *hqny* — to dedicate. On the second line it is possible to read *bn/qwdm/'ṯtr*. The inscription appears, therefore, to record a dedication to the South Arabian deity Athtar. It is also important to note that this inscription is written boustrophedon unlike the inscriptions found at Qusār and Khutūb.

The date of the inscriptions

The inscriptions from Wādī Maṭar provide a baseline for dating the South Arabian inscriptions from Farasān. The palaeography of the inscription mentioning Athtar, written boustrophedon, is clearly archaic. The inscription can be dated, therefore, to the first half of the first millennium BC and the "*mukarrib* period", and could even be dated to the fifth or fourth century BC, at the very end of the archaic period. It is worth mentioning that there is only one other inscription from the Tihāmah, which mentions Athtar (from Wāqir, also boustrophedon and similar letters forms, see Beeston 2005: 49–50). We obviously cannot relate them to one another and settle on a date based on palaeography but we can, nevertheless, acknowledge the similarities between the two inscriptions. Moreover, the pottery from the Wādī Maṭar sites can also be compared with pottery from sites located on the Tihāmah such as Salīf, al-Ḥāmid, and Wāqir that has been dated to the first half of the first millennium BC (Philips 2005).

The inscriptions from Qusār and Khutūb are clearly much later. It is tempting to say that they could be contemporary with the second century AD Roman occupation of the site, thus representing the local component of the island's occupants at this time. It is possible, however, that these inscriptions are slightly earlier (not later) in date and that some of the inscribed characters were reworked and reused during the Roman presence.

Historical and geographical contexts

The early South Arabian presence on Farasān during the first half of the first millennium BC is not surprising: the islands probably provided a point of embarkation to the

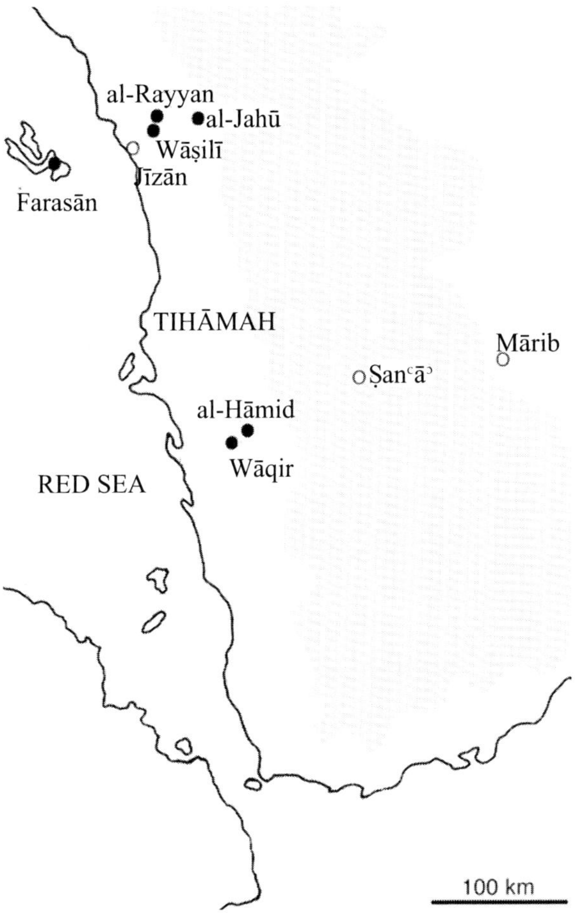

Figure 3. *A map of ancient sites mentioned in the Tihāmah (Saudi Arabia).*

other side of the Red Sea where comparable South Arabian inscriptions are known from sites in Eritrea and Ethiopia. The evidence thus complements the information gathered from further south on the Tihāmah at sites such as al-Ḥāmid and Wāqir (Fig. 3). Archaic inscriptions reported from that region have content and letter forms that are comparable with those found elsewhere in South Arabia, and the synchronisms are based not just on palaeography but also on dated contexts, inclusion of royal names, etc.

Similarly, given what is known of Roman and local trade in the Red Sea at this time, a South Arabian presence is to be expected on the Farasān Islands during the first and second centuries AD — as described, for example, in the *Periplus of the Erythraean Sea* — although no mention is made of Farasān itself. Moreover, the names mentioned in the inscriptions from Qusār and Khutūb are well-known South Arabian names. There is not yet, however, any conclusive archaeological or epigraphic evidence for occupation of the Farasān Islands during the latter half of the first millennium BC.

Finally, alongside the Farasān Islands, it is appropriate to mention the South Arabian inscriptions found on the adjacent mainland, in the hinterland of Jizān. At al-Wāsilī, a village located 18 km east of Jizān, a short funerary inscription was reported. The text (Ry 518 = Philby 391) comprises only a personal name, *Lb n bn | Wdd l̲*, inscribed on a coral block that forms part of a tomb. H.St J. Philby communicated details about it to G. Ryckmans. It is interesting to note the close proximity of al-Wāsilī to al-Rayyan where Zarins, Murad and Al-Yish have since recorded a pre-Islamic site, site 217–103, which they consider to be characteristic of "formal South Arabic sites" (1981: 26). Unfortunately, nothing more precise is mentioned in the text about the dates or characteristics of the sites. More recently, rock inscriptions have been reported in the foothills of Wādī Ḍamad, near al-Juhū, at a site known as al-Maktūb. The site is said to have "Southern Musnad inscriptions" but, unfortunately, none have been illustrated.

Conclusion

The South Arabian inscriptions from Farasān are only tantalising fragments of its past. However, viewed as archaeological objects as well as written sources, they provide some indication of when the islands were occupied and by whom. The evidence provided by them also enables Farasān to be integrated into the broader picture of pre-Islamic occupation along the southern shores of the Red Sea.

Acknowledgements

We would like to thank Laila Nehmé and François Villeneuve for the information and photographs they provided.

References

Beeston A.F.L./eds Macdonald M.C.A. & Phillips C.S.
2005. *A.F.L. Beeston at the Arabian Seminar and other papers, including a personal reminiscence by W.W. Müller*. Oxford: Archaeopress.

Harding G.L.
1971. *An Index and Concordance of pre-Islamic Arabian names and inscriptions*. Toronto: University of Toronto Press.

Miftāḥ I.A.
1990. *Farasān, al-nās wa ʾl-baḥr wa ʾl-taʾrīkh*. Jizān.
2003. *Farasān bayna ʾl-jiyūlūjiyā wa ʾl-taʾrīkh*. Jizān.

Nehmé L. & Villeneuve F.
[n.d.] Report on two surveys in the Farasan Islands (2005–2006). [Unpublished].

Phillips C.
2005. A preliminary description of the pottery from al-Hamid and its significance in relation to other pre-Islamic sites on the Tihamah. *Proceedings of the Seminar for Arabian Studies* 35: 177–193.

Phillips C., Villeneuve F. & Facey W.
2004. A Latin Inscription from South Arabia. *Proceedings of the Seminar for Arabian Studies* 34: 239–250.

Photius/ed. Henry R.
1959. *La Bibliothèque (tome I, codex 3)*. Paris : Les Belles Lettres.

Robin C.
1995. La Tihâma yéménite avant l'Islam: notes d'histoire et de géographie historique. *Arabian archaeology and epigraphy* 6: 222–235.

Zarins J., Murad A. El-J. & Al-Yish K.S.
1981. The second preliminary report on the South-western province. *Atlal* 5: 9–42.

Authors' addresses
Solène Marion de Procé, CNRS UMR 7041 (ArcScAn) Maison René Ginouvès de l'Archéologie et de L'Ethnologie, 21 allée de l'Université, 92023 Nanterre cedex, France; Université Paris 1 Panthéon-Sorbonne, 1, place du Panthéon, 75005, Paris, France.

e-mail solenemarion@gmail.com

Carl Phillips, Associate Researcher, CNRS UMR 7041, Maison René Ginouvès de l'Archéologie et de L'Ethnologie, 21 allée de l'Université, 92023 Nanterre cedex, France.

e-mail carl.phillips@mae.u-paris10.fr

Proceedings of the Seminar for Arabian Studies 40 (2010): 283–292

The Wādī Sūq pottery: a typological study of the pottery assemblage at Hili 8 (UAE)

Sabrina Righetti & †Serge Cleuziou

Summary
At the beginning of the second millennium BC, a new set of pottery appears in the Oman peninsula, reflecting a new society: the Wādī Sūq culture. Hili 8 (Ḥilī) was the first settlement site discovered for this period and was excavated by a French team under the direction of Serge Cleuziou from 1977 to 1984. The present paper is the result of work carried out on the archives of the Hili 8 excavations. Its aim is a typological study of the pottery assemblage, based on material from the period III levels, which is published (to a large extent) for the first time in this paper. An inter-site study compares Hili 8 pottery with other contemporary sites, in order to define the pottery characteristics of the former settlement and to establish if the pottery assemblage is common to other contemporary sites.

Keywords: UAE, Hili 8, Wādī Sūq, pottery, typology

Introduction

Hili 8 (Ḥilī) is located in the region of al-ᶜAyn, Emirate of Abu Dhabi. Several campaigns of excavations were conducted from 1977 to 1984 under the direction of Serge Cleuziou. During the second campaign, levels dated to the Wādī Sūq Period (2000–1600 BC) were identified; they were, at first, called "phase H" and then afterwards renamed "period III". This was because the architectural remains and the artefacts discovered were very different from those of "period II" which corresponded to the Umm an-Nar period (2700–2000 BC) (Cleuziou 1979: 23; 1989: 71). They are the first domestic remains identified for the Wādī Sūq period, which was first recognized by K. Frifelt in a funerary context at Wādī Sūq (1975: 377–378).

Period III at Hili 8 shows evidence for a continuous use of building I and its well, both constructed during the Umm an-Nar period. Several stone wall bases, 80 cm wide, were discovered, built in the so-called "double wall" technique, typical of Wādī Sūq domestic and funerary architecture (two walls made of slabs with a filling of small stones and sand). They probably acted as a surrounding wall pressed against building I. The building materials of their upper courses are not known, but they could have been mud bricks. Several layers were associated with these walls, as well as several hearths and kilns (Cleuziou 1979: 23–24).

In this paper we will present the pottery found in the period III levels. The corpus is made up of 868 diagnostic sherds but our study is limited to the 233 sherds or shapes, all drawn by P. Gouin. The macroscopic and microscopic studies have already been undertaken by S. Méry (2000). We present here an inter-site typological analysis, outlining the main characteristics of the fabric.

Two types of pottery were found in the levels under study: coarse ware which was not known for the earlier period, and semi-fine ware which was dominant on the site: in fact, it accounts for 90% of the registered material. Coarse ware is represented by vessels with flaring sides and a rounded rim (Fig. 1/25, 28) (Méry 2000: 250).

Both wares are light brown-orange to red-buff with a red or buff-cream slip, sometimes with no slip. The decoration is painted in black or dark brown and situated in the upper two-thirds of the pottery.

Open forms

Beakers (type 1) (Fig. 1)

Beakers are the most common shape found in period III levels. They are now found with a low carination with an everted rim or vertical sides.

Beakers with vertical upper part (type 1a) (Fig. 1/1–6, 22, 24)

Some non-carinated beakers with a vertical upper part,

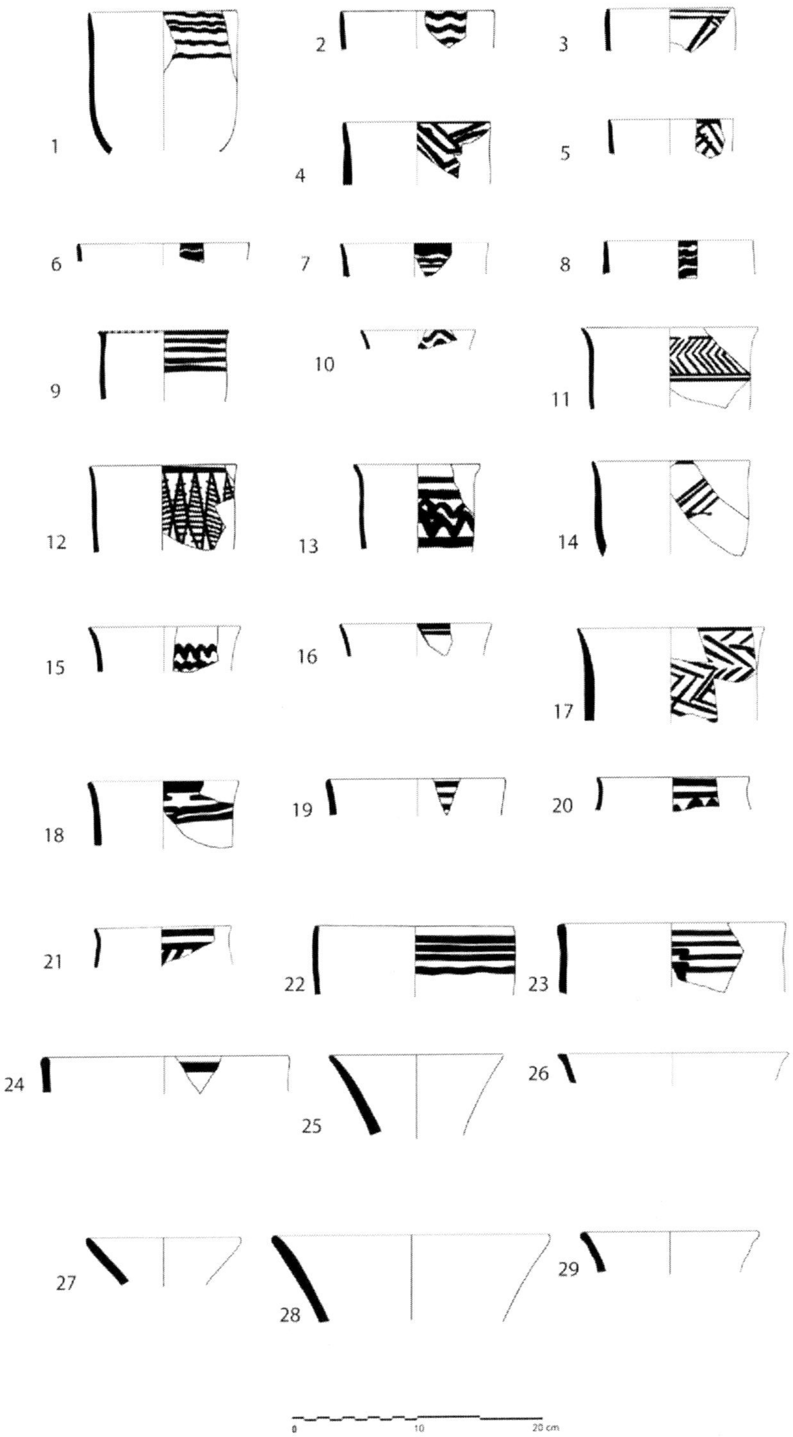

FIGURE 1. *Beakers and coarse ware (type 1):* **1.** *2620/UF1217;* **2.** *1032/UF789;* **3.** *2359/UF722;* **4.** *1272/UF125;* **5.** *81/UF3;* **6.** *847/UF60;* **7.** *1360/UF401;* **8.** *1275/UF125;* **9.** *725/UF66;* **10.** *2313/UF901;* **11.** *2091/UF603;* **12.** *1057/UF76;* **13.** *850/UF60;* **14.** *2585/UF1201;* **15.** *862/UF60;* **16.** *2330/UF753;* **17.** *2310/UF901;* **18.** *858/UF60;* **19.** *865/UF60;* **20.** *1313/UF300;* **21.** *2337/UF732;* **22.** *845/UF60;* **23.** *1271/UF125;* **24.** *783/UF59;* **25.** *397/UF12;* **26.** *651/UF55;* **27.** *396/UF12;* **28.** *700/UF62;* **29.** *2489/UF754.*

and a vertical or a slightly everted rim, were also found. Their decoration consists of several wavy lines under the rim (Fig.1/1–2). Parallels can be found at the Wādī Sūq site (Frifelt 1975: fig. 23/e) and Kalba 4 (Carter 1997: fig. 20/5).

Beakers with low carination (type 1b) (Fig. 1/7–21)

These beakers have vertical sides or a slightly divergent body and a slightly tapering and everted rim with a rounded bottom.

The beakers with a carinated upper body have different decorative patterns: horizontal or double lines under the rim framing a decoration of wavy or oblique lines (Fig.1/13–14, 20), chevron or rhombic patterns (Fig.1/11–12, 17), or parallel wavy lines (Fig.1/15). This shape is common for the period in the whole of the Oman peninsula; several parallels can be found in different settlement sites at Kalba 4 (Carter 1997: fig. 20/2–3), Bidyā (Al-Tikriti 1989: pl. 64/A), or Tell Abraq (Potts 1990: fig. 50/3) but also in funerary contexts, as at Shimal. The combination of shape and decoration of these beakers clearly indicates an early and middle Wādī Sūq date (Velde 2003: 104).

Globular and open bowls (types 2a and 2b) (Fig. 2)

The globular bowls with a flat base and a slightly thickened rim (type 2a) (Fig. 2/6–8) and the open bowls (type 2b) (Fig. 2/1–5) are also representative of the period. Both of these types (types 2a and 2b) have the same kind of decoration consisting of horizontal lines (Fig. 2/2) that sometimes frame oblique lines (Fig. 2/3), chevrons (Fig. 2/6), and wavy lines (Fig. 2/4–5). They can be undecorated.

Parallels for type 2a can be found at Kalba 4 (Carter 1997: fig. 23/3), Wādī Sunaysl (Frifelt 1975: fig. 27/e), and Raʾs al-Jinz 1 (Monchablon *et al.* 2003: fig. 3/4); for type 2b a parallel has been found at the Wādī Sūq site (Frifelt 1975: fig. 22/b).

Bowls (type 3) (Fig. 3)

Type 3a (Fig. 3/1–16)

Bowls with very divergent sides are very numerous; they may have a rounded rim and do not appear to have been decorated.

Type 3b (Fig. 3/17–18)

Within the settlement of Hili 8, one shape was found with several examples: large vessels of brown ware with a mineral temper (Cleuziou 1989: 87), without slip, and a horizontally everted rim.

Type 3c (Fig. 3/19–20)

This type of vessel of buff ware, with extremely carinated sides and slightly everted and thickened rim, was found with a few examples.

Closed forms

Jars (type 4) (Fig. 4/1–15)

Some jars with different types of neck and rim have been identified. Some have a beaded rim, more or less everted; they seem to have black painted decoration at the top of the body. They are part of the settlement assemblage, and probably had a storage function. These types of jars are also represented at Tell Abraq (Potts 1990: fig. 98; 1991: fig. 53).

Miniature flasks or jars (type 5) (Fig. 4/17–19)

A small number of miniature flasks or jars were also found and are similar to examples found in the Shimal tombs (Velde 2003: fig. 2/2). They have a short flared rim and are decorated with wavy (Fig. 4/19) or horizontal lines (Fig. 4/17–18).

Teapots or spouted jars (type 6) (Fig. 5/1–6)

One of the most characteristic shapes of the Wādī Sūq period is the teapot, also called the spouted jar (Fig. 5/1). These spouted jars are globular with a flat base, and have an open spout under the rim. Parallels with this shape are found at Wādī Sūq (Frifelt 1975: fig. 20/a) and Shimal (Velde 2003: fig. 2/11). The typical zoomorphological motif of birds with a long neck or a horned animal found at Wādī Sūq (Frifelt 1975: fig. 20/b), for example, is not present at Hili 8 where the decoration consists of zigzag lines framed by a double horizontal line. According to Velde's chronological typology of the Wādī Sūq pottery (2003: 104), the shape of the rim in period III-level vessels seems to belong to the early or middle Wādī Sūq phase. Teapots with double lines under the rim framing a

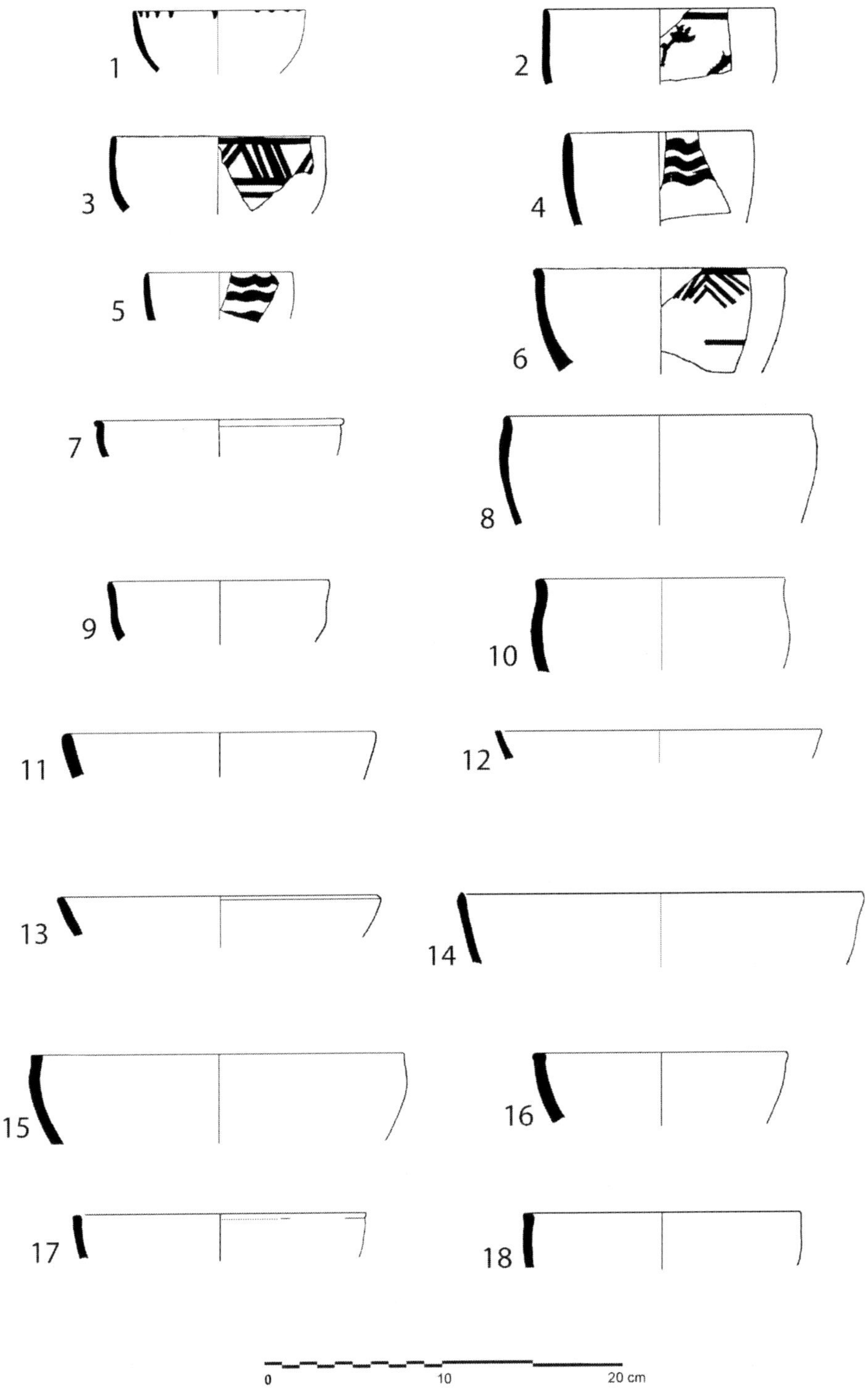

Figure 2. *Globular and open bowls (type 2):* **1.** *2367/UF734;* **2.** *2118/UF606;* **3.** *1031/UF79;* **4.** *1088/UF46;* **5.** *2502/UF743;* **6.** *756/UF59;* **7.** *1327/UF131;* **8.** *721/UF66;* **9.** *870/UF 606;* **10.** *1378/UF130;* **11.** *866/UF60;* **12.** *2586/UF1203;* **13.** *1093/UF46;* **14.** *2581/UF1201;* **15.** *2233/UF612;* **16.** *964/UF54;* **17.** *2626/UF1226;* **18.** *1994/UF505.*

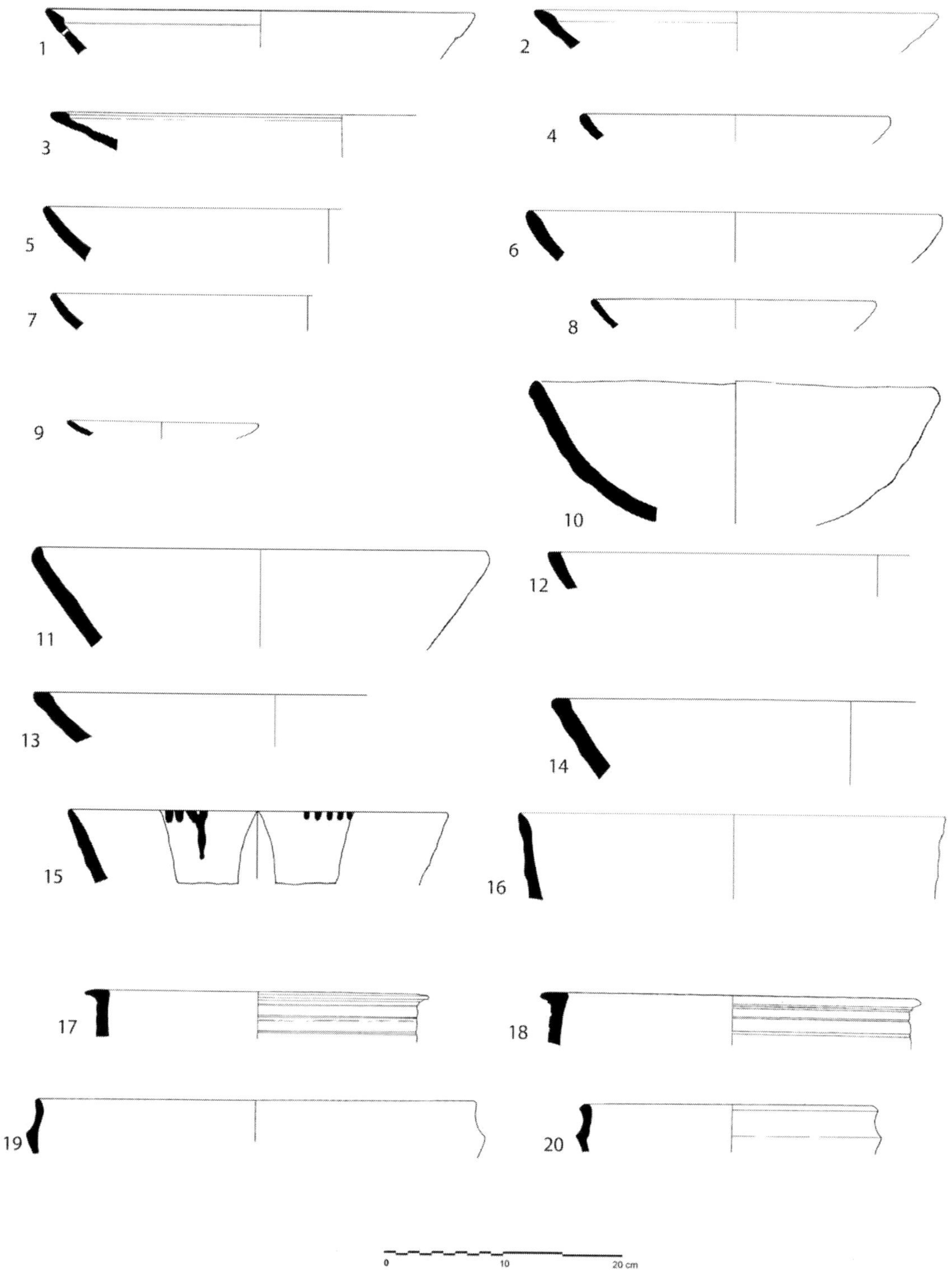

FIGURE 3. *Bowls with divergent side and large vessels (type 3):* **1.** *1974/UF 501;* **2.** *2513/UF907;* **3.** *2536/UF 728;* **4.** *788/UF 53;* **5.** *2335/UF 732;* **6.** *2533/UF747;* **7.** *495/UF24;* **8.** *2347/UF728;* **9.** *496/UF24;* **10.** *V27/UF1203;* **11.** *893/UF60;* **12.** *1990/UF505;* **13.** *2064/UF603;* **14.** *2065/UF603;* **15.** *1132/UF93;* **16.** *2530/UF732;* **17.** *1347/UF132;* **18.** *1980/UF501;* **19.** *82;* **20.** *2076/UF603*

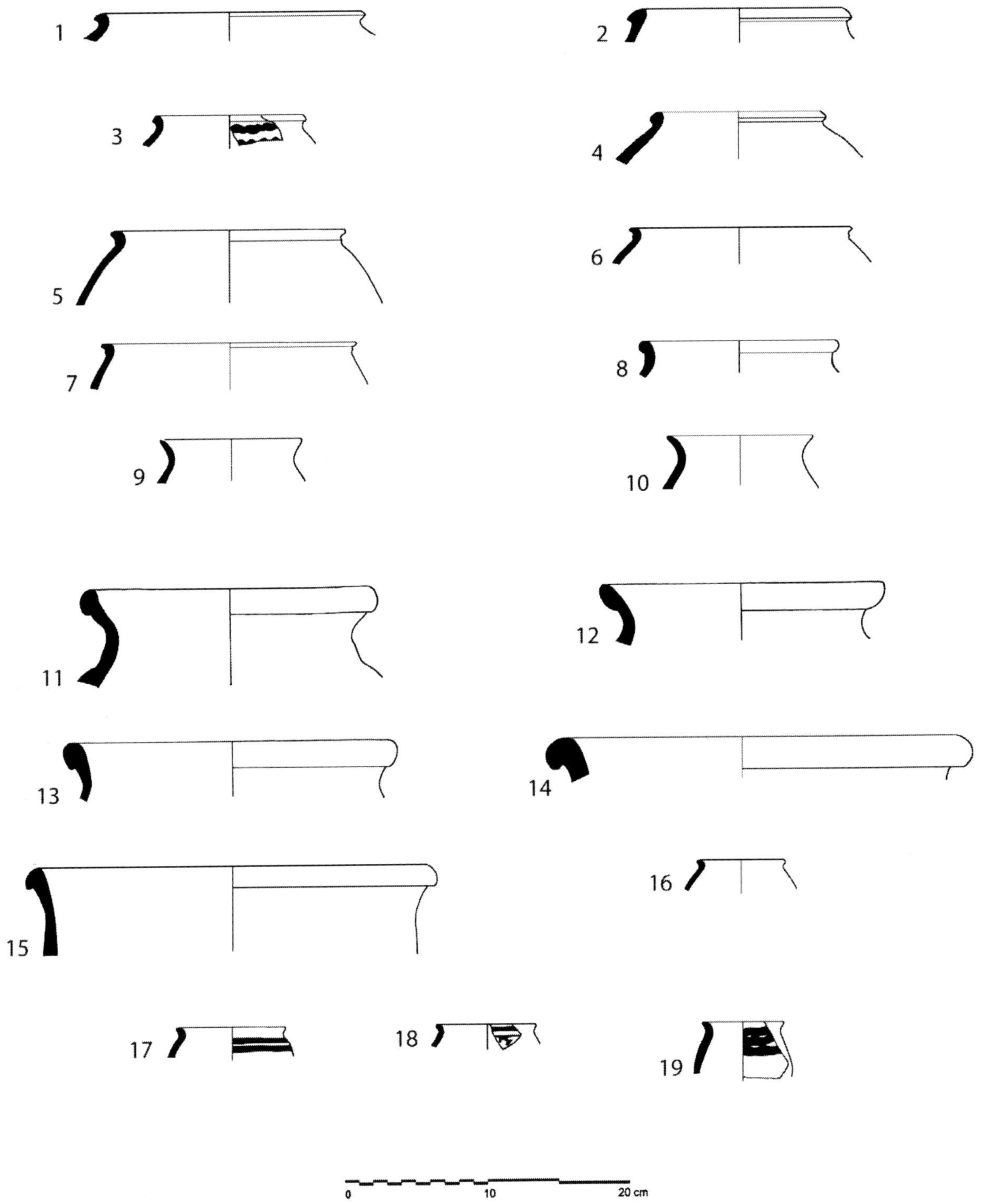

FIGURE 4. *Jars and miniature jars (types 4 and 5):* **1.** *1448/UF303;* **2.** *782/UF59;* **3.** *1971/UF247;* **4.** *1395/UF203;* **5.** *2074/UF603;* **6.** *1580/UF405;* **7.** *1363/UF401;* **8.** *828/UF60;* **9.** *1976/UF501;* **10.** *2582/UF1201;* **11.** *2062/603;* **12.** *1310/300;* **13.** *418;* **14.** *1973/UF 501;* **15.** *65/UF3;* **16.** *2501/UF743;* **17.** *857/UF60;* **18.** *773/UF59;* **19.** *945/UF86.*

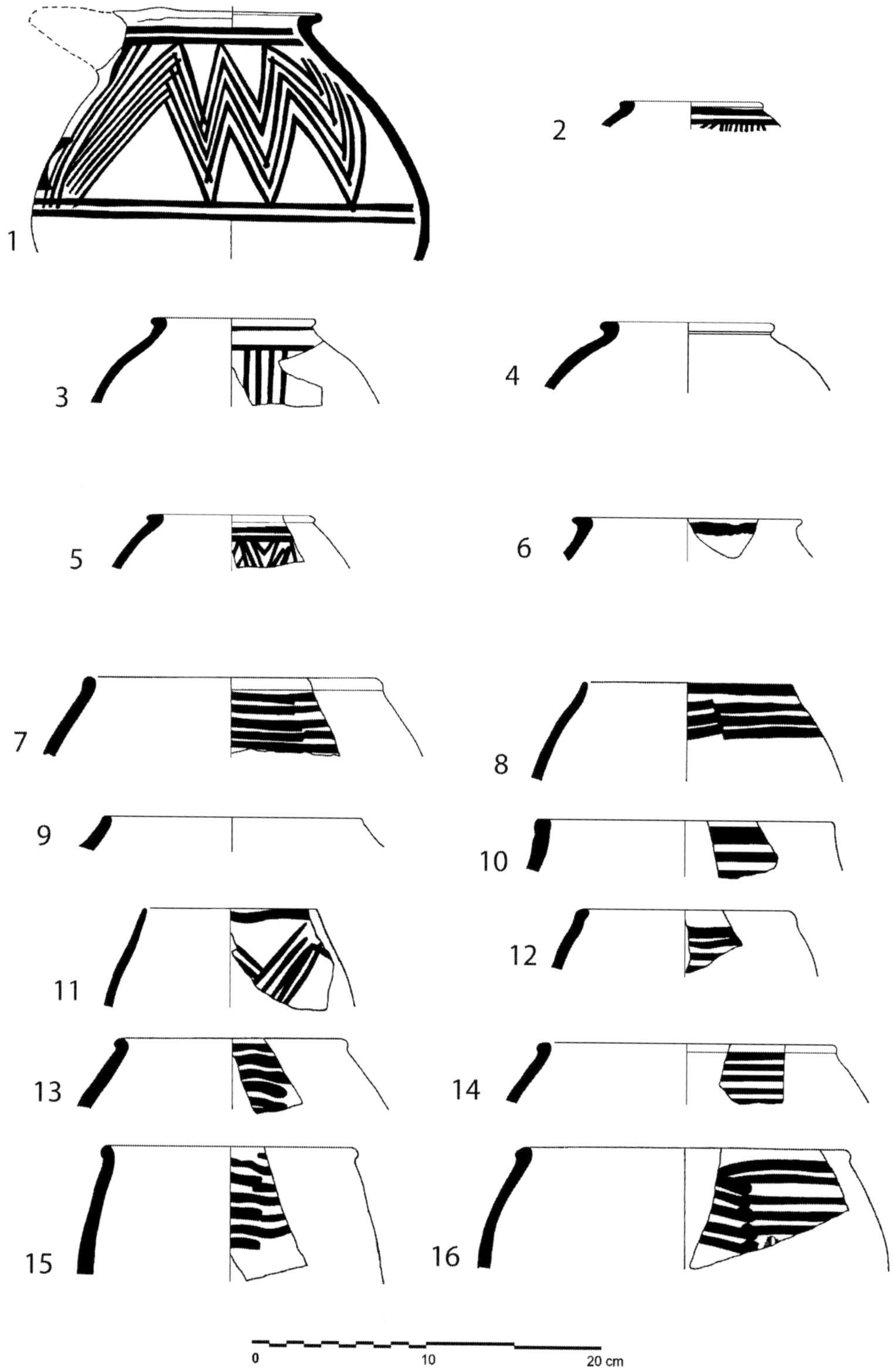

Figure 5. *Spouted jars (teapots) and globular pots (types 6 and 7):* **1.** *1141/UF93;* **2.** *1266/UF125;* **3.** *1977/UF501;* **4.** *916/UF47;* **5.** *1267a/UF125;* **6.** *2346/UF728;* **7.** *2525/UF762;* **8.** *2633–2634/UF1222;* **9.** *2345/UF728;* **10.** *769/UF59;* **11.** *2625/UF1222;* **12.** *2300/UF711;* **13.** *1249/UF125;* **14.** *2587/UF1203;* **15.** *1127/UF95;* **16.** *2089/UF603.*

vertical (Fig. 5/3) or oblique lines pattern (Fig. 5/2, 5) are also found in several examples.

Globular pots or cooking pots (type 7) (Fig. 5/716)

Some globular pots with a decoration of horizontal (Fig. 5/10, 14) or slightly wavy lines (Fig. 5/13, 15) were also found in period III levels. Their rim could be vertical and tapering (Fig. 5/8, 11) or slightly everted (Fig. 5/12–16).

Conclusive remarks

The pottery from period III levels at Hili 8 exhibits typical fabrics, surface treatment, shapes, and decoration as found in the Wādī Sūq pottery assemblage in the Oman peninsula. Based on a petrographic study of several samples, it appears that this pottery was made with raw materials found in the Wādī Jizī, 40 km east of the site (Méry 2000: 257). The same pottery assemblage is found throughout the peninsula although there are differences between funerary and settlement contexts. As outlined above, open flat bowls, storage jars, and (cooking) pots are typical settlement shapes, while beakers, bowls, spouted jars, and miniature jars or small pots are found in both funerary and settlement contexts.

Acknowledgements

I would like to thank Serge Cleuziou for his support, for allowing me to study the typology of this pottery assemblage, and for letting me have access to the Hili 8 archives for this work. I am also very grateful to the French Archaeological Mission in Adam (Sultanate of Oman) for their encouragement and constant support. I would also like to thank J.P. Thalmann for his help.

References

Carter R.
1997. Defining the Late Bronze Age in Southeast Arabia: ceramic evolution and settlement during the second millennium BC. PhD thesis, Institute of Archaeology, University College, London. [Unpublished].

Cleuziou S.
1979. Les deuxième et troisième campagnes de fouilles à Hili 8. *Archéologie aux Émirats Arabes Unis* 2/3: 19–69.
1989. Excavations at Hili 8: a preliminary report on the 4th to 7th campaigns. *Archaeology in the United Arab Emirates* 5: 61–87.

Frifelt K.
1975. On prehistoric Settlement and Chronology of the Oman Peninsula. *East and West* 25: 359–423.

Méry S.
2000. *Les Céramiques d'Oman et d'Asie moyenne: une archéologie des échanges à l'Age du Bronze.* Paris: CNRS Éditions.

Monchablon C., Crassard R., Munoz O., Guy H., Bruley-Chabot G. & Cleuziou S.
2003. Excavations at Ras al-Jinz RJ–1: stratigraphy without tells. *Proceedings of the Seminar for Arabian Studies* 33: 31–47.

Potts D.T.
1990. *A prehistoric mound in the Emirates of Umm al Qaiwain UAE. Excavations at Tell Abraq in 1989.* Copenhagen: Munksgaard.
1991. *Further excavations at Tell Abraq. The 1990 Season.* Copenhagen: Munksgaard.

Al-Tikriti W. Y.
1989. The excavations at Bidya, Fujairah: the 3rd and 2nd millennia BC culture. *Archaeology in the United Arab Emirates* 5: 101–114.

Velde C.
2003. Wādī Sūq and Late Bronze Age in the Oman Peninsula. Pages 102–113 in D.T. Potts, H. Al Naboodah & P. Hellyer (eds), *Archaeology of the United Arab Emirates.* London: Trident Press.

Author's address
Sabrina Righetti, Université Paris 1 Panthéon-Sorbonne, UMR 7041 CNRS, Maison de l'Archéologie et de l'Ethnologie, R. Ginouvès, 21 allée de l'Université, 92023 Nanterre Cedex, France.

e-mail sabrina.righetti@gmail.com

Proceedings of the Seminar for Arabian Studies 40 (2010): 293–302

A *ṣarf* talisman from Ghayl Bā Wazīr, Ḥaḍramawt

Mikhail Rodionov

Summary

This article addresses the written and functional aspects of magic practices in South Arabia. Based on new data collected by the author during his field season in Ḥaḍramawt in 2008, it provides a case study of a talisman called *ṣarf* (literally "pebble"). The most effective magic texts have to be written on a robust substance with a durable paint (e.g. saffron, dragon-blood resin, etc.) in the belief that the integrity of the letters and material guards the power of a talisman. The *ṣarf* under examination (from about the first half of the twentieth century), however, was written on paper, according to modern practice. It was kept between two layers of leather in the dagger sheath of a Bedouin ᶜAwaḍ b. Ṭiflah (in *ṣarf* talismans only maternal names are mentioned). Analysis of the written text and discussions with local informants demonstrates that the old Arabian tradition, articulated in the famous *Shams al-maᶜārif* of Aḥmad b. ᶜAlī al-Būnī (d. 1225), of trying to keep the delicate balance between "white" and "black" magic is still alive in Ghayl Bā Wazīr, al-Shiḥr, Shibām, Tarīm, and elsewhere in Ḥaḍramawt.

Keywords: magic, talisman, South Arabia, Ḥaḍramawt, *ṣarf*

In 2008, during my field season in Ḥaḍramawt, I was engaged in ethnographic research in Ghayl Bā Wazīr, an important agricultural centre with a wide network of underground irrigation channels (*maᶜāyin*, sg. *maᶜyān*, lit. "spring") (Bin Shaykhan 2005: 24–338) (Fig. 1).

After independence, the renowned middle school, al-Madrasah al-Wusṭā, established under British patronage in the al-Quᶜayṭī Sultanate, was turned into a cultural centre with a permanent memorial exhibition, archives, and a local ethnographical museum. With the courteous permission of the head of the centre, al-Sayyid Muḥammad Saᶜīd Mudayḥij (*b.* 1930), a former *mudīr* of the school from 1961 to 1965 (see Mudayḥij 2005: 172–251), and the custodian of the museum ᶜUmar ᶜAwaḍ Bā Karūn, I took photographs of a talisman (*ṣarf*, pl. *ṣurūf*), exhibited in the museum along with the shabby and dry leather sheath (Fig. 2) exhibited under a caption with the explanation *Al-jafīr alladhī wujida fīhi al-ṣarf al-ṭilsam*, i.e. "The sheath in which a *ṣarf* (talisman) was found". The last word is repeated in English.

For many Ḥaḍramīs the word *ṭilsam* is connected with the British, as is reflected in a well-known quatrain by the greatest local singer of the twentieth century Saᶜīd Marzūq:

laqū ᵓl-firḍah ḥawālī ḥayd qāsim
rayt ᶜād al-baḥr bā yiqtasim
bā yiqsimūnu ᶜamid ahl al-ṭalāsim
kull min takallim bā yaqūl al-baḥr maqsūm

They made a seaport custom-house near Qāsim Hill
[in the main wadi near Tarīm].
Perhaps they will divide the sea;
no doubt, it will be divided by the people of talismans
[i.e. by Englishmen];
Everyone who talks will say, "The sea is divided".

According to Ḥadramī tradition, various kinds of written talismans (*khuṭab*, sg. *kaṭbah*) can be kept either in a rich silver scabbard of the renowned Bā Qaṭiyān work — *jambiyyah quṣbīyyah* — or in a simple leather sheath of a *qudaymī*, a shorter tribal *jambiyyah*, typical, for example, of the Saybān tribe (Fig. 3).

The talisman under examination belongs to a *ṣarf* category very popular in Ḥaḍramawt, but mentioned only obliquely by Carlo Landberg in his *Glossaire Daṯinois*, as "Liebeszauber" or "Zaubermittel", among other meanings (1942: 2127). Informants from the Ḥumūm tribe refer to three main local centres of *taṣrīf*, or *ṣarf*-making: Shibām, Tarīm, and al-Shiḥr. The last-mentioned town, where *ṣarf*-making has been practised for at least five centuries, seems to be the origin of the *ṣarf* as well as of many other rituals and customs of Ghayl Bā Wazīr. The word *ṣarf* is interpreted here as a flat sea stone — a

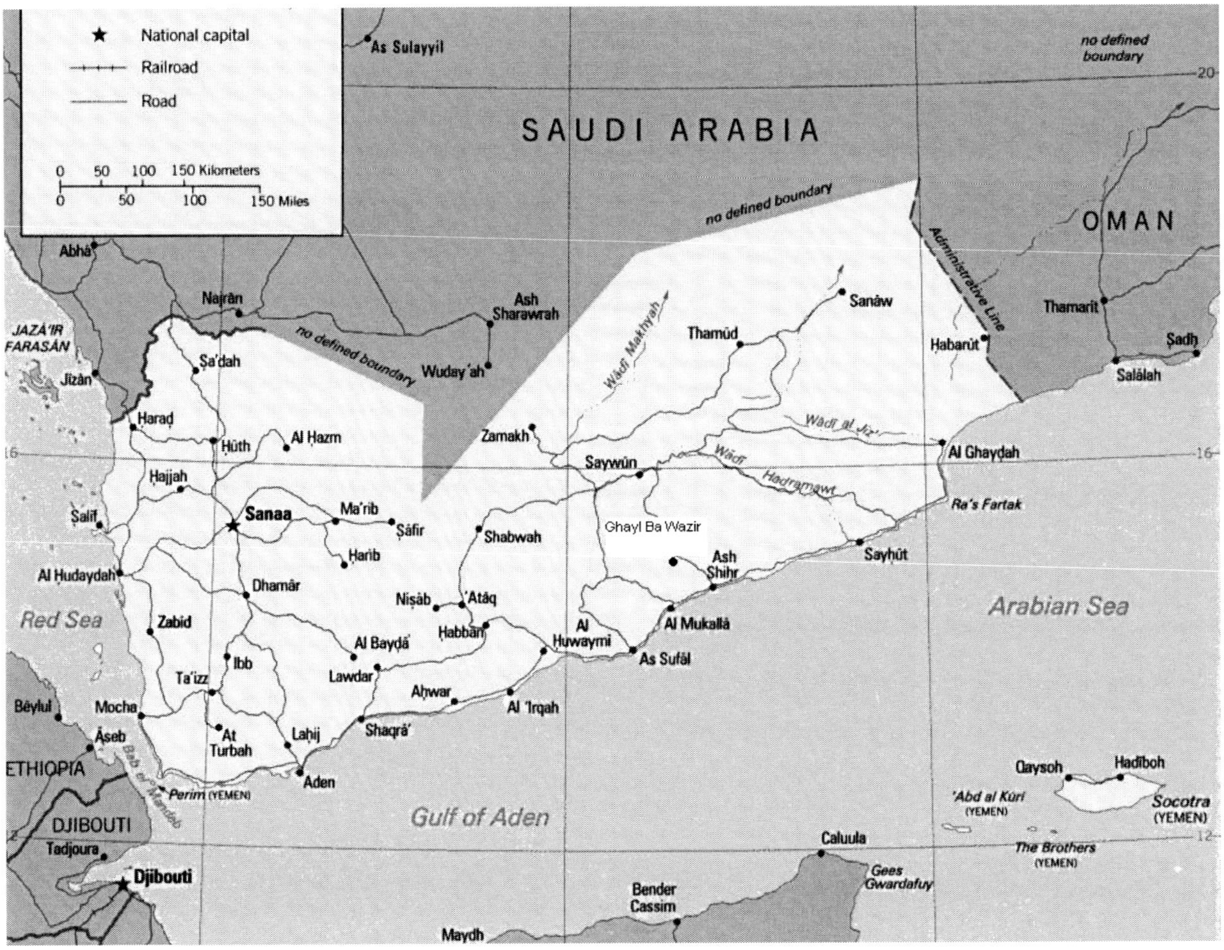

FIGURE 1. *A map of Yemen.*

FIGURE 2. *The sheath of the Ghayl Bā Wazīr* ṣarf *talisman. (Courtesy of the Ghayl Bā Wazīr Cultural Centre.)*

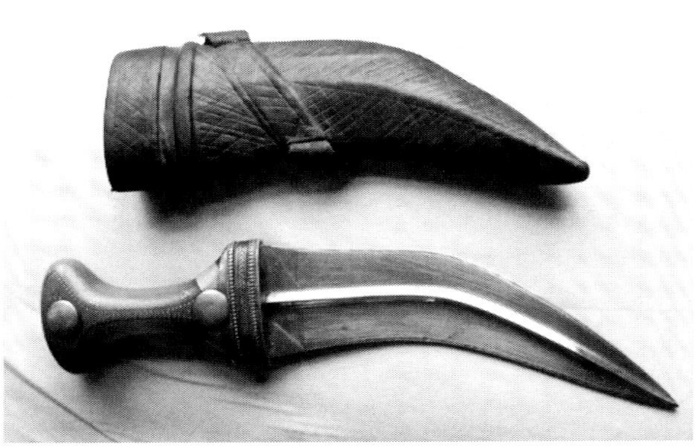

FIGURE 3. *A* qudaymī *(a shorter tribal* jambiyyah*) with its sheath. (Photograph by the author.)*

pebble — according to the belief that a talisman keeps its strength as long as the integrity of the inscription and material is unaffected. Therefore the most effective magic texts are written on flat stones with a durable paint, either dragon-blood resin or saffron, both of which have a reddish colour — hence the idea that these kinds of inscriptions are painted with human blood. Most of the talismans of this category are malevolent and should be kept in a safe place, such as a rubbish dump. The best way is to throw a *ṣarf* into the sea where it will work forever. If one desires to cancel its effect, one can extract the *ṣarf* from the depository and bring it back to its maker (*ṣāḥib al-ṣurūf*) saying "*fakk al-ṣarf*" ("undo the *ṣarf*").

This *ṣarf* (Figs 4 and 5) dates back to the first half of the twentieth century and is written with ink on paper, according to modern practice. Folded into a tiny rectangle, the sheet of paper was kept between two layers of leather in a dagger sheath.

The main text of the *ṣarf* is comprised of twenty-two lines. It starts with invocations to Allāh, "His Most Beautiful Names" and at the same time to specific jinn — a practice condemned by Islam (Figs 6 and 7):

1. *Allahuma*, by truth of these [= His] Names and by truth of Budūḥ and by truth of Ahab, Ashrāhī, Anūkh

Of these four names of the jinn, or satans as they are called in Ḥaḍramawt, the most important for South Arabia is Budūḥ. According to E. Graefe (2001, ii: 369b), *budūḥ* is a talismanic word derived from the four corners of the threefold magic square (*wifq*) and used in South Arabian as a feminine proper name (meaning "fat"); this word is personified in Egypt (and also in Ḥaḍramawt) as a *jinnī* who runs various errands if his name is written down — mostly to ensure the exchange of correspondence and packages.

In the next few lines we find some of the "Most Beautiful Names of God" and a pair of rhymed names of the jinn:

2. Life-giving, Mighty, Allah give strength to Maʿrūsh Ṭālūsh and by the truth of one thousand [sayings] There is no power and no strength

3. save in God, the Most High, Superb (…)

Then come four Qurʾanic *suwar* (sg. *sūrah*) — *al-Fātiḥah* (ll. 3–5 of the *ṣarf*), *sūrat al-ikhlāṣ* (112, ll. 6–7), *sūrat al-falaq* (113, ll. 7–8), and *sūrat al-nās* (114, ll. 9–10). Qurʾanic passages are recorded with two minor mistakes: (l. 3) *wa lam* [*ya*]*kun*, (l. 4) *min sharrihā wa min* [*sharr*].

The last three *suwar* (sg. *sūrah*), early Meccan ones, are intended to fight popular superstitions according to an authoritative Islamic commentary. Thus, *sūrah* 112 (*al-Ikhlāṣ*) condemns polytheism; *sūrah* 113 (*al-Falaq*) "provides the antidote to superstition and fear by teaching us to seek refuge in Allāh [*taʿwīz*, which is also a synonym for talisman] from every kind of ill arising from outer nature and from dark and evil plotting and envy on the part of others"; *sūrah* 114 (*al-Nās*) "warns us especially against the secret whispers of evil within our own hearts" (Holy Qurʾān [1989]: 2027–2034). In fact, *sūrat al-nās* concludes the Qurʾān by warning the jinn and men against insinuations of Satan — *al-Waswās al-Khannās* (114: 4–6), or the whisperer who withdraws (when the Name of God is mentioned) — again using a rhymed pair of names of a spirit. Frequently used in magic practices, *suwar* 113–114 are known as *al-muʿawwiḍatāni*, or *suwar al-muʿawwiḍitayn*, the "Protective two" or the "verses of refuge".

11. And guide us in that to them and that is their nourishment from which they eat. Take care of

12. and be submissive, Oh Slūmah bint Ṭiflah and Ṭiflah bint

13. Slūmah to ʿAwaḍ ibn Ṭiflah by truth of Your Names, so that they lowered

14. their necks to them [= God's Names], both submissive to him [to ʿAwaḍ ibn Ṭiflah], to him [twelve times].

It is noteworthy that the names above are spelled with separated (non-legated) letters apparently in order to stress their numerical value, and in all cases the maternal name is given instead of the paternal one.

15. To him [*Lahu* — eighteen times; total = 30]. [Letter] *ʿAyn* [five times].

16. [Letter] *ʿAyn* [four times, total = 9, the figure being written under the line, followed by "To him" [fifteen times and fifteen more times continued at l. 17, the magic figure "30" is written after the twelfth ligature and repeated between the seventeenth and eighteenth lines].

17. [The rest of] To him [are followed by Qurʾanic letters] *Alam* [six times, the figure is underlined],

18. *Ṭāsīn* [seven times, the figure is underlined]

19. Perfect Beauty [mentioned nine times, the figure being written below].

20. Verily, it is from Sulaymān and verily it is in the Name of God, the Merciful, the Compassionate.

21. They can't rise higher to lofty heights and endow [obedient] Muslims.

22. *Allāh* [is followed by eight crossed-out letters] *ḥāʾ* [which, as I am told by my informants, means "*Allāh ḥayy*" or "God Alive"].

The other side of the text (Fig. 8) exemplifies a typical Arabic *jadwal* ("table"). For example, as in the *Shams al-*

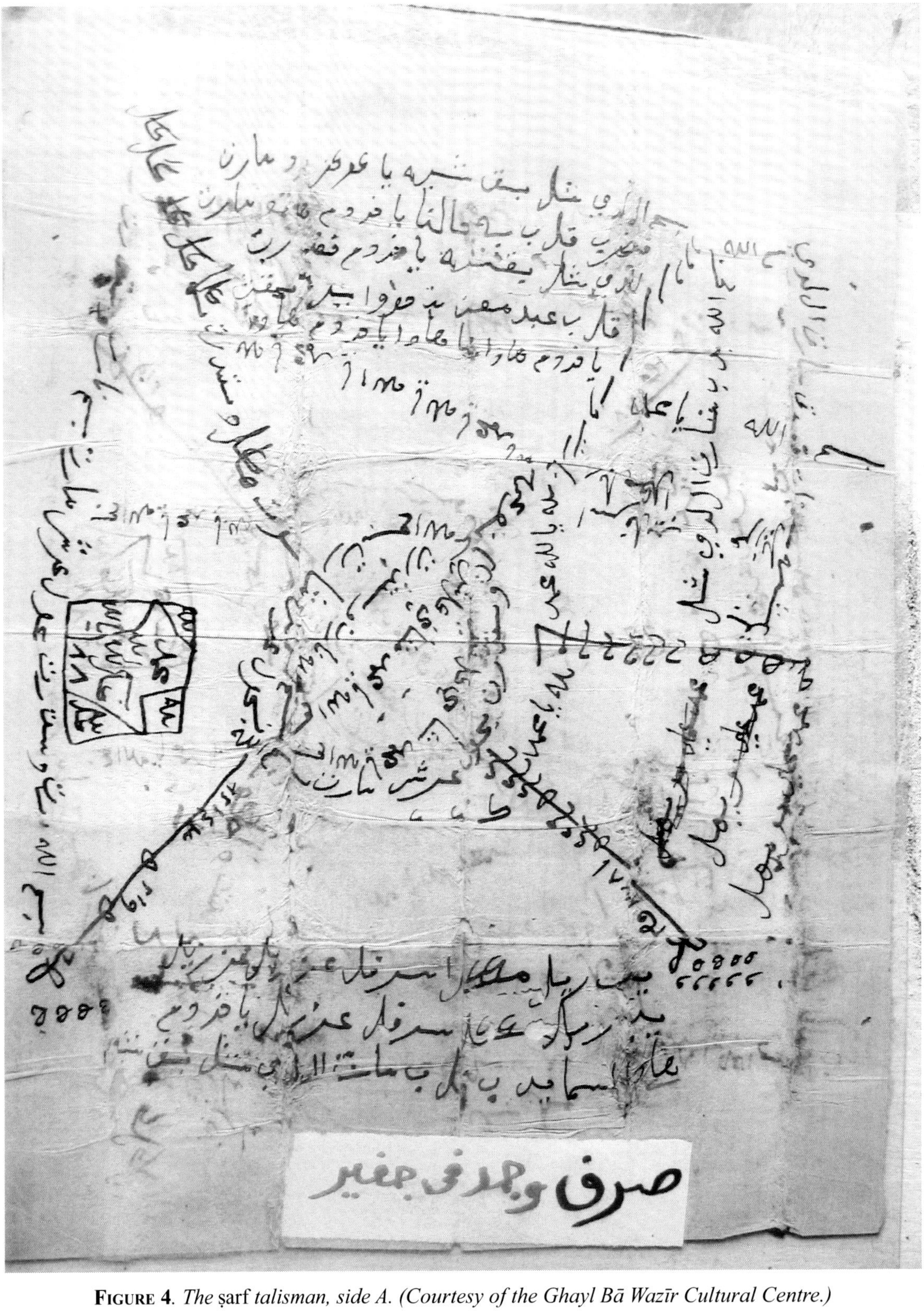

FIGURE 4. *The* ṣarf *talisman, side A. (Courtesy of the Ghayl Bā Wazīr Cultural Centre.)*

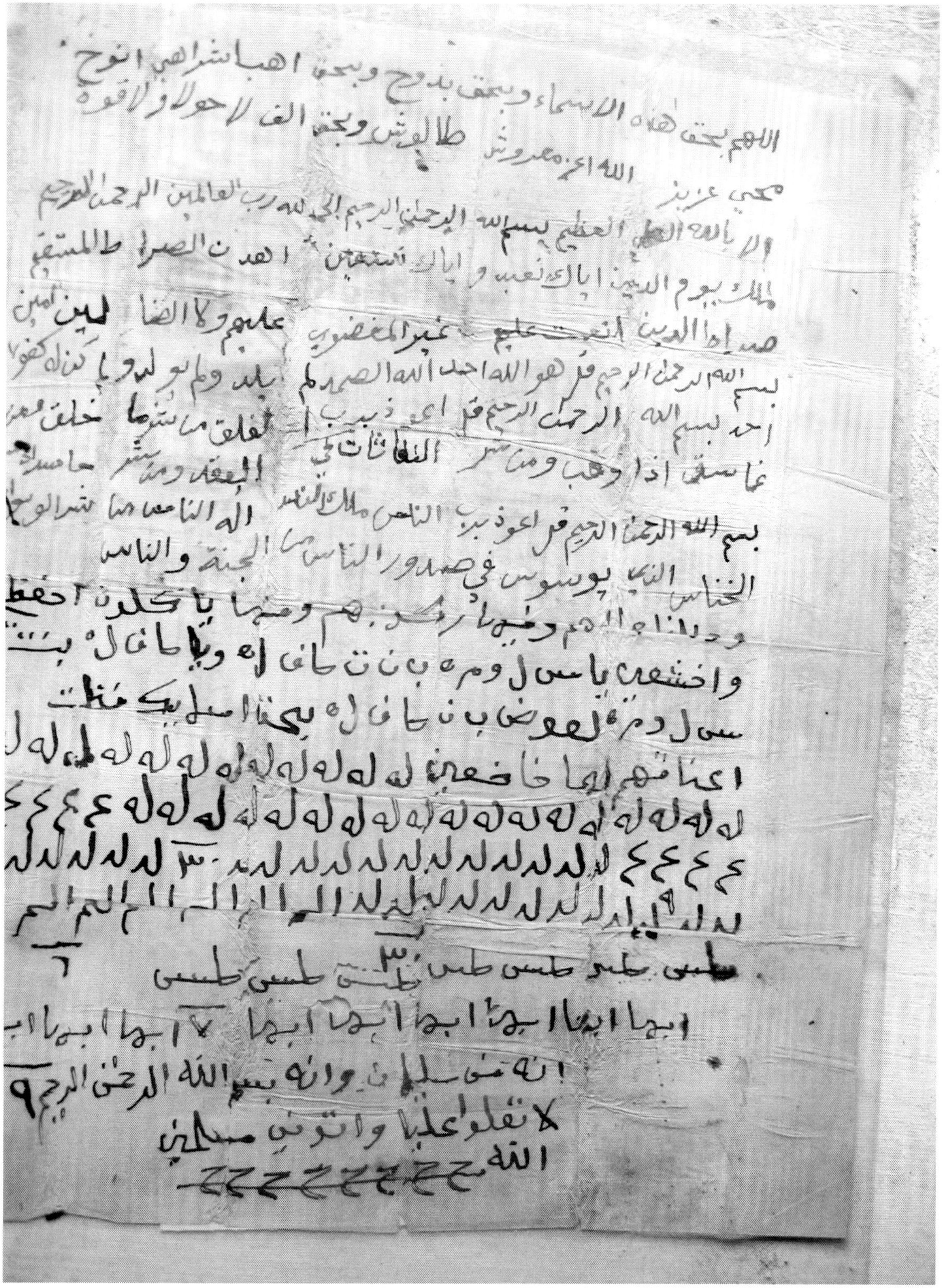

FIGURE 5. *The* ṣarf *talisman, side B. (Courtesy of the Ghayl Bā Wazīr Cultural Centre.)*

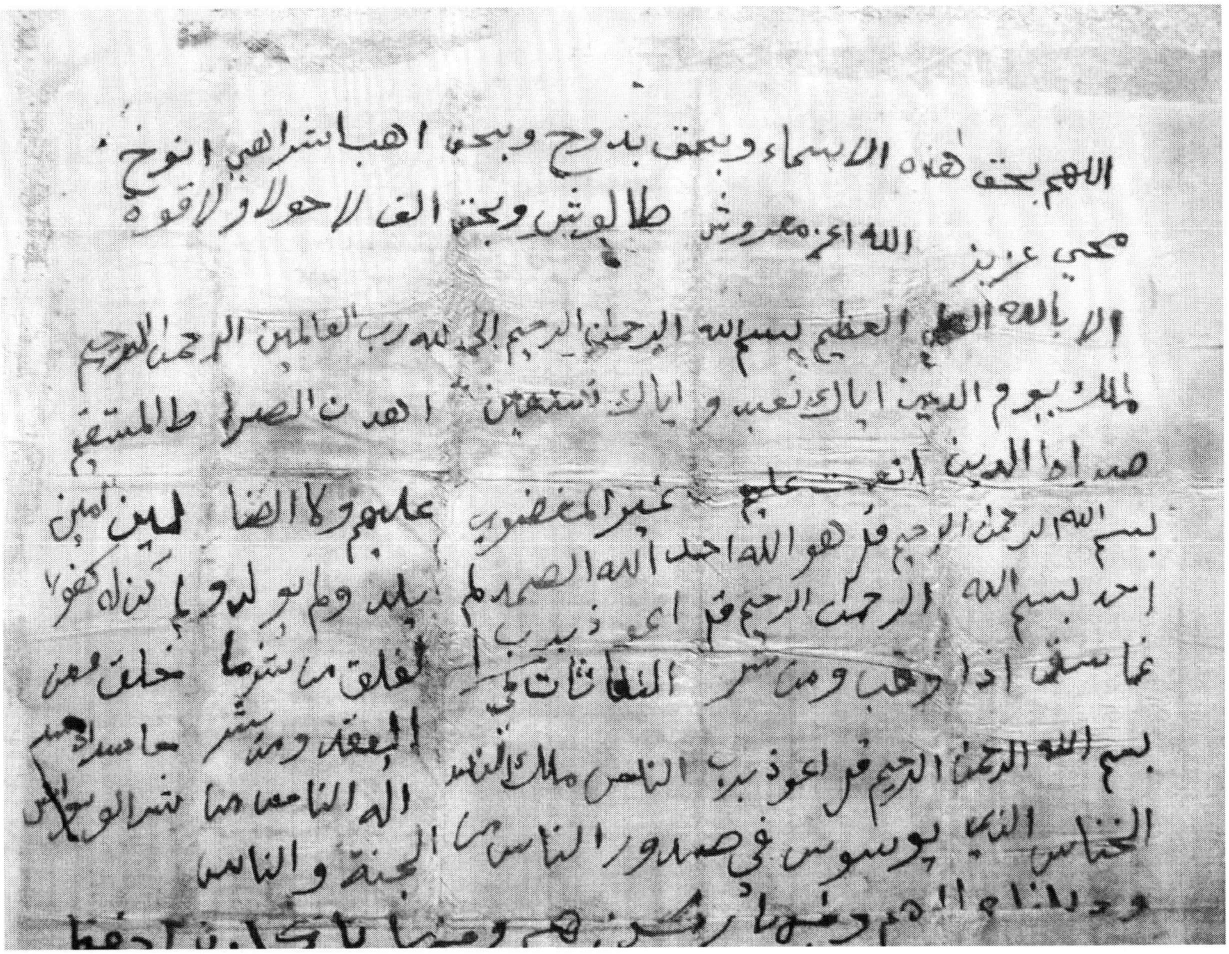

Figure 6. *The* ṣarf *talisman, side B, lines 1–11.*

*ma*ᶜ*ārif* by a famous medieval author, Aḥmad b. ᶜAlī al-Būnī (*d.* 1225), whose book is known in Ḥaḍramawt, and by international scholars, including Russians (e.g. MS C 963, fols. 1a–168b etc.) in the St Petersburg Institute for Oriental Manuscripts, Russian Academy of Sciences (Khalidov 1986, Pt 1: 470–471).

The rectangular area on the sheet is divided up diagonally into four isosceles triangles by various inscriptions (e.g. *huwa*, etc.) and figures, centred on a circle formed by several formulaic clichés, mostly *Bismillāhi yā Muḥammad mashāfī kullu shay* ("In the Name of God, Oh Muḥammad, the cure for everything"). *Ayyāt al-*ᶜ*Arsh*, or "Verses of the Throne" (9: 129) are mentioned, as well as the names of the four angels (Mīkhāʾīl, Jabrāʾīl, ᶜAzrāʾīl, ʾIsrāʾfīl) and other obligatory attributes of a regular talisman. To read the entire text one must turn the paper clockwise and anti-clockwise like the Yemeni spiral documents studied by B. Messick (1996: 231–250).

The square in the left triangle bears the words *yā Allāh*, *Muḥammad* and a figure "88", which roughly equals to the numerical value of the name ᶜAwaḍ bin Ṭiflah, divided into 12, the number of months: (70 + 6 + 800) + (2 + 50) + (9 + 80 + 30 + 5) = 1052, which divided by 12 is 87 and two thirds (2/3). According to my informants, this is a common way to write down the name of those who commissioned a talisman.

Conclusions

The study of a *ṣarf* talisman from Ghayl Bā Wazīr allows us to draw some conclusions.

The ordering and making of written talismans, both malevolent and benevolent, is still practised in Ghayl

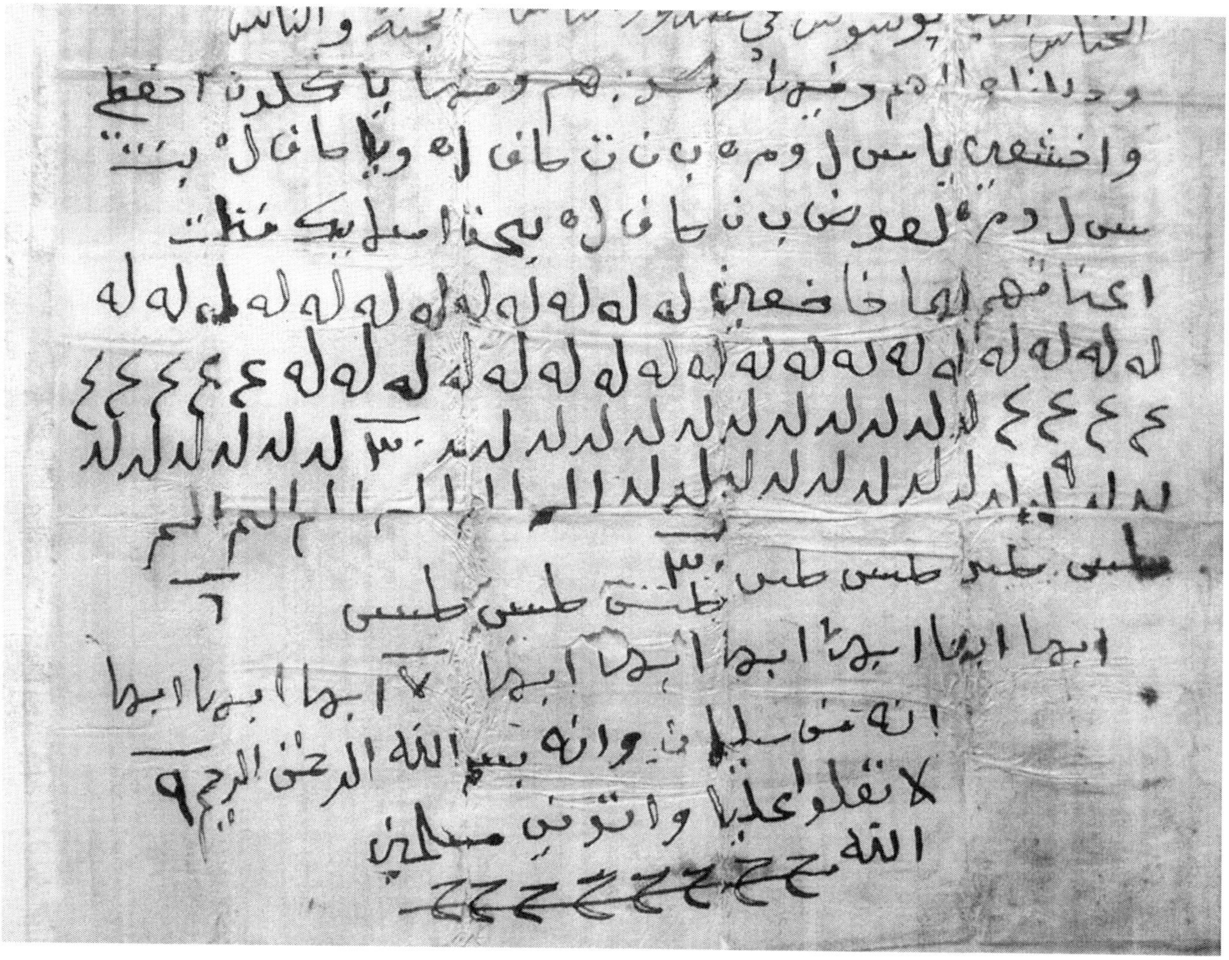

Figure 7. *The* ṣarf *talisman, side B, lines 10–21.*

Bā Wazīr and elsewhere in Ḥaḍramawt, mainly in such centres as Shibām, Tarīm, and al-Shiḥr where the talismans are produced primarily by the Mashāyikh and Sādah social classes and according to standard medieval Arab tradition.

Radical Islamists, in particular, overtly disapprove of this tradition under the pretext that talismans seek protection not only from God alone but also, as we have seen in the text of the examined talisman, from angels, the jinn, King Sulaymān, magic numbers, etc.

Local malevolent talismans are called *ṣarf* (pl. *ṣurūf*), stressing the significance of durable material on which a magic text is written; the name remains in use even in the twenty-first century, although solid pebbles have been replaced by fragile paper. Hence the word *katbah* is gradually ousting the previous one, *ṣarf*, but bearing the same negative meaning. People in the Ghayl say, "*fulān ᶜamal li-fulān katbah*" ("so-and-so made for so-and-so a written talisman"). The Ḥaḍramīs also believe that people of different religious denominations cannot use malevolent magic against one another, for example a Christian cannot use magic against a Muslim and vice versa.

The benevolent talisman, as opposed to *ṣarf*, is referred to by the common Arabic word *ḥirz*. A person comes to a shaykh and says, "So-and-so wants to make a *ṣarf* against me!" The shaykh replies, "I'll make you a *ḥirz* with pork meat (*laḥm khinzīr*)", and this person will wear it him- or herself. This is an example of the custom of using prohibited food as a homeopathic and magical cure.

The majority of those who commission talismans are women. In our case it is a man, a Bedouin ᶜAwaḍ b. Ṭiflah. However, women play an important role in local talismanic culture. It has already been emphasized that the names of

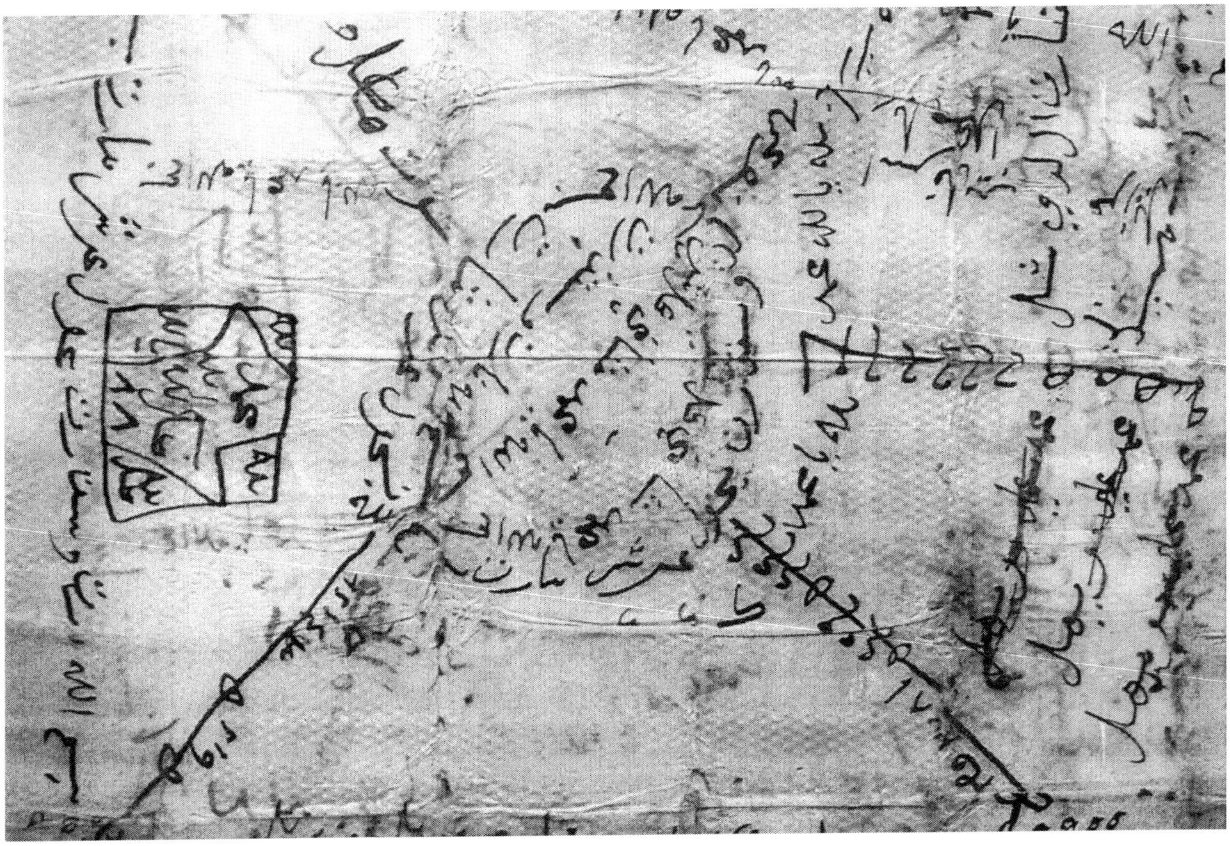

Figure 8. *The* ṣarf *talisman, side A, enlarged.*

people mentioned in a talisman are given with the name of one's mother instead of one's father, so only the matrilineal kinship is relevant. Feminine magic is vaguely referred to in the Qurʾanic quotation from *sūrah* 113, *al-Falaq* (ll. 7–8 of the *ṣarf*) which says: "I seek refuge with the Lord of the Dawn (…) from the mischief of those [women] who blow on knots" (*al-naffāthāti fīʾl-ʿuqadi*).

Finally, I should stress that the one who commissioned our talisman asked for peace and the obedience of his sister Slūmah and her daughter, a rather benevolent intention. However, the talisman is classified as malevolent (*ṣarf*), thus showing that there is still much to be done in studying local magic practices in South Arabia notwithstanding all the difficulties of the relevant fieldwork.

References

Bin Shaykhān S.
2005. *Nafaḥāt wa ʿabīr min taʾrīkh ghayl bāwazīr.* (Second edition). Ghayl Bā Wazīr.

Graefe E.
2001. Djadwal. Page 369b in *The Encyclopaedia of Islam* (New edition). ii. Leiden: Brill.

Holy Qurʾān
[1989]. *The Holy Qurʾān. English translation of the meanings and Commentary.* Medina: King Fahd Holy Qurʾān printing complex.

Khalidov A. (ed.)
1986. *Arabic Manuscripts of the Institute of Oriental Studies, USSR Academy of Sciences. Brief Catalogue.* Parts 1–2. Moscow: Nauka. [In Russian].

Landberg C.
1942. *Glossaire Daṯinois*. iii. Leiden: E.J. Brill.
Messick B.
1996. *The Calligraphic State. Textual Domination and History in a Moslem Society*. Berkeley, CA: University of California Press.
Mudayḥij M.
2005. *Al-madrasat al-ᶜumm, al-madrasah al-wusṭā bi-ghayl bā wazīr [19]40–[19]44, [19]64–1965*. (Third edition). Aden: Jāmiᶜat ᶜadan.

Author's address
Mikhail Rodionov, Tul'skaya Street 8, app. 2, St Petersburg, 191124, Russia.
e-mail mrodio@yandex.ru

Proceedings of the Seminar for Arabian Studies 40 (2010): 303–320

The Qalhāt Project: new research at the medieval harbour site of Qalhāt, Oman (2008)

Axelle Rougeulle

Summary
One of the most impressive archaeological sites of Oman, Qalhāt was a key harbour in southern Arabia during the Middle Ages. It was the twin city of Hormūz during the thirteenth to fifteenth centuries, but was abandoned in the middle of the sixteenth century and never reoccupied. Despite its importance, the site has rarely been studied except for one season of excavations in 2003, but the Ministry of Heritage and Culture of the Sultanate of Oman recently decided to start a major research and development project at the site, in co-operation with French and Iranian teams.

The first season of the French mission took place in November to December 2008. A Digital Elevation Model (DEM) was created and a preliminary analysis of the urbanism of the city was achieved: its different quarters and main buildings were identified and the chronology of the fortifications and city gates was studied. The Friday mosque was discovered. Its last two architectural periods, both having glazed tile decoration, were recognized and dated to about the fourteenth and fifteenth centuries. A ceramic kiln was also discovered and excavated, producing valuable information on the local ceramics of the fourteenth century, with unglazed, glazed, and painted wares. A large house and a small terrace mosque within a settlement unit in the north-west quarter of the city were excavated and cleared for further restoration. Finally, a stratigraphic sounding against the qiblah wall of the Friday mosque yielded occupation layers dating from around the twelfth to sixteenth centuries. The history of Qalhāt, its urbanism, and the trade networks of this strategic Omani harbour of the Hormuzī period are now, therefore, emerging out of obscurity.

Keywords: Qalhāt, harbour city, Indian Ocean, Middle Ages, Hormūz

Qalhāt (22° 41' 40" N 59° 22' 30" E) is one of the most impressive archaeological sites of Oman, a huge area of ruins of about 35 ha, all that is left of a medieval harbour city which was destroyed at the beginning of the sixteenth century and never reoccupied. It is located on the coast of al-Sharqiyyah province, 20 km north of the city of Ṣūr (Fig. 1).

A brief history of Qalhāt

According to an Omani tradition, Qalhāt already existed at the beginning of the Christian era, when Mālik bin Fahm, the mythical king of the Yemeni al-Azd tribe, is reported to have migrated from Ḥaḍramawt to Oman. The country was at that time under Persian occupation and al-Azd left their baggage at Qalhāt before defeating the Persians in a battle at Salūt near Nizwah. Mālik then founded one of his capital cities at Qalhāt (Bhacker & Bhacker 2004: 25–26). Another tradition, reported by Tūrānshāh in his history of Hormūz, mentions that a later Yemeni migration, headed by Muḥammad Dirhem Kuh, sailed from Qalhāt in the eleventh century to Iran where it founded the Hormuzī kingdom. Dirhem Kuh built "in that port a city, inasmuch as it was a place suitable for those of the country to trade with the ships that passed that way", leaving his son as governor (Teixeira & Sinclair 1902: 153–155, 256–257).

This last tradition is more in accordance with Yāqūt al-Rūmī al-Ḥamawī (1179–1229), who visited Oman at the beginning of the thirteenth century and reports that Qalhāt was a rather new city founded around the beginning of the twelfth century (Yāqūt 1868, iv: 393).[1] In any case, Qalhāt is first mentioned in texts around the middle of the twelfth century and the harbour became famous in the thirteenth to fifteenth centuries, when it became the second capital of the kingdom of Hormūz which, at that time, dominated most of the trade routes in the western Indian Ocean. It was one of the main ports of the Islamic world, an emporium for Indian goods and the principal centre for the export of Arab horses, as well as a checkpoint on the maritime routes of the Gulf of Oman (Polo 1980, ii: 498–499).

[1] This reference was kindly provided by Guy Ducatez (CNRS, Umr 8167).

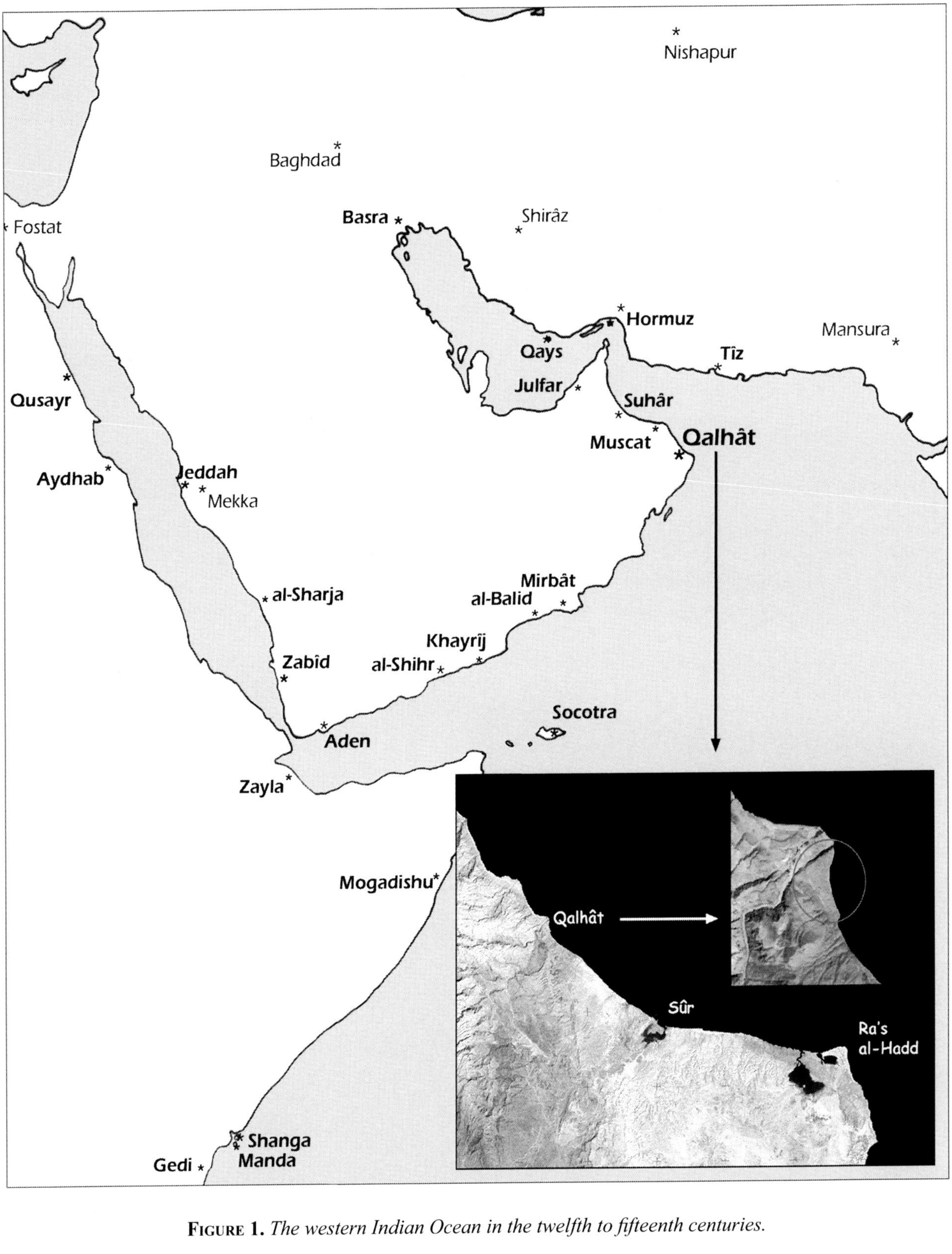

Figure 1. *The western Indian Ocean in the twelfth to fifteenth centuries.*

Qalhāt played a major part in the battles between Hormūz and its enemies, as well as in the internal struggles for power between members of the dynasty. One of its most famous historical characters was ᶜAyāz, a governor of the city, who became the ruler of the kingdom at the end of the thirteenth century. He conducted many naval battles and in 1300 moved Hormūz from the Mīnāb mainland (Old Hormūz) to Jarun island (New Hormūz), a stroke of genius that made the fortune of Hormūz. His wife Maryam, who ruled Qalhāt in his absence, built a mausoleum which is the only edifice still standing on the site and is one of the most famous tourist attractions in the region.

The harbour was supplanted by Muscat as the chief port of Oman in the fifteenth century and was probably destroyed by an earthquake at the end of the century (Bhacker & Bhacker 2004: n. 44). However, it was still one of the main coastal cities of Oman when the Portuguese sacked it in 1508 (de Albuquerque 1874, i: 64–66, 221). It subsequently became a station for the Portuguese fleet and was then permanently abandoned (Bhacker & Bhacker 2004: 19, 39).

The Qalhāt Project

Despite its importance, Qalhāt has rarely been studied. The site was described by Miles in 1874 (Miles 1919: 521) but, except for limited surveys, the only research was carried out by the Oman Maritime Heritage Project directed by Tom Vosmer, who conducted a detailed survey in 1998 and then excavations in 2003. A hammam (bathhouse) was excavated, two soundings were dug in the north-eastern part of the city, and underwater surveys were conducted beyond the site (Vosmer 2004).[2]

The area of Ṣūr is currently undergoing major development, including the construction of a coastal highway between Muscat and Ṣūr, which approaches the edge of the site of Qalhāt. In this context, the Ministry of Heritage and Culture of the Sultanate decided to start an important research and development project, in collaboration with French and Iranian missions.[3]

The objectives of the Qalhāt Project are manifold. First, to provide information on the history of Qalhāt itself, its foundation, rise and decline, and on the local economy, exchange networks of the harbour, and the part it played in the Indian Ocean trade, especially during the Hormuzī period which is still poorly documented. Secondly, to provide information on the layout of a medieval Omani city, as Qalhāt is a unique example of an ancient settlement completely preserved under its ruins. Although virtually nothing is visible on the surface, the plan of the city appears quite clearly on aerial views, and it may be possible to reconstruct it rather precisely. Finally, the project must also provide a scientific basis for the development of the site. Following a short exploratory mission in spring, the first expedition of the French team took place from November to December 2008 and has already produced a substantial amount of data under these headings.

Town planning

Thanks to a special grant from the Total Foundation in Paris, a GIS project was undertaken and a Digital Elevation Model (DEM) was completed in 2008. A kite photography survey was also undertaken by the Ministry of Heritage and Culture (MHC) of the Sultanate of Oman. Based on that documentation and a detailed survey of the surface, a preliminary study of the layout of the city was achieved and its different quarters and main buildings identified.

Qalhāt is located on the lower slopes of the Jabal al-Ḥajar al-Sharqī, between the mountain to the south-west, the sea to the east, and the steep bank of the Wādī Ḥilm to the north-west, one of the best-defended positions on the coast (Figs 1–2). The city was further protected by fortifications with many towers. These fortifications were in the shape of an equilateral triangle with sides measuring *c.* 900 m, the western corner separated from the main intramural area by an intermediate rampart. In addition, another wall some 700 m south of the city cut the coastal plain between the sea and the mountains. Qalhāt was therefore entirely in control of movement along the coastal road.

The city gates

It is probable that the ancient coastal road was on the same line as the modern track, following the foot of the mountain and crossing the western corner of the walled area, which could therefore have served as a checkpoint. The track has destroyed all traces of ancient gates, but the northern access, at least, was certainly situated in the same place, as it is the only breach in the wadi bank where descent is possible. Indeed, it is on this slope along the

[2] Our deepest thanks are due to Tom Vosmer for his friendly and efficient help when starting this new excavation project at Qalhāt.

[3] The Iranian team is directed by Dr Mohsen Javeri, from the Iranian Centre for Archaeological Research, Iranian Cultural Heritage, Handicrafts and Tourism Organization.

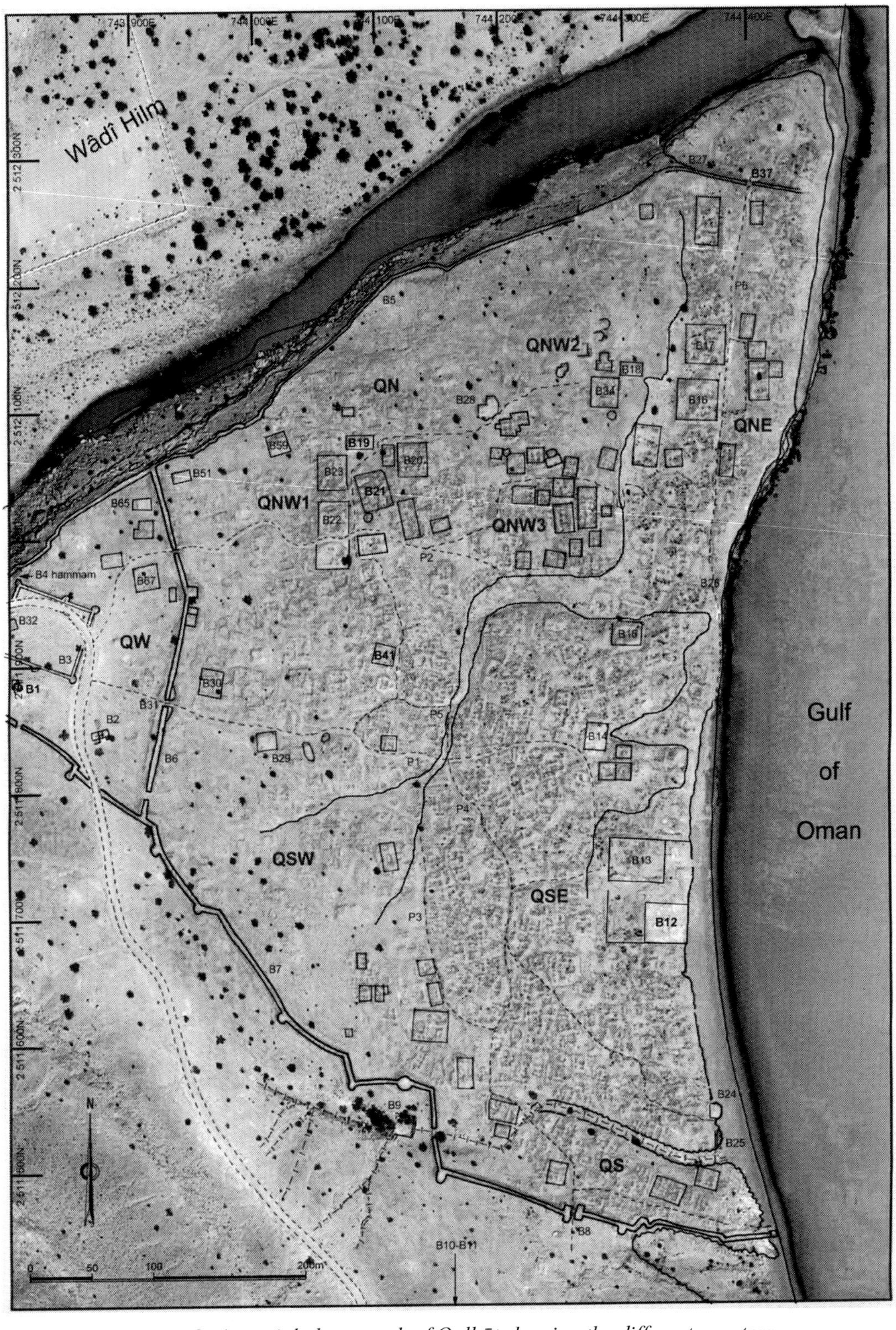

FIGURE 2. *An aerial photograph of Qalhāt showing the different quarters and main buildings of the medieval city.*

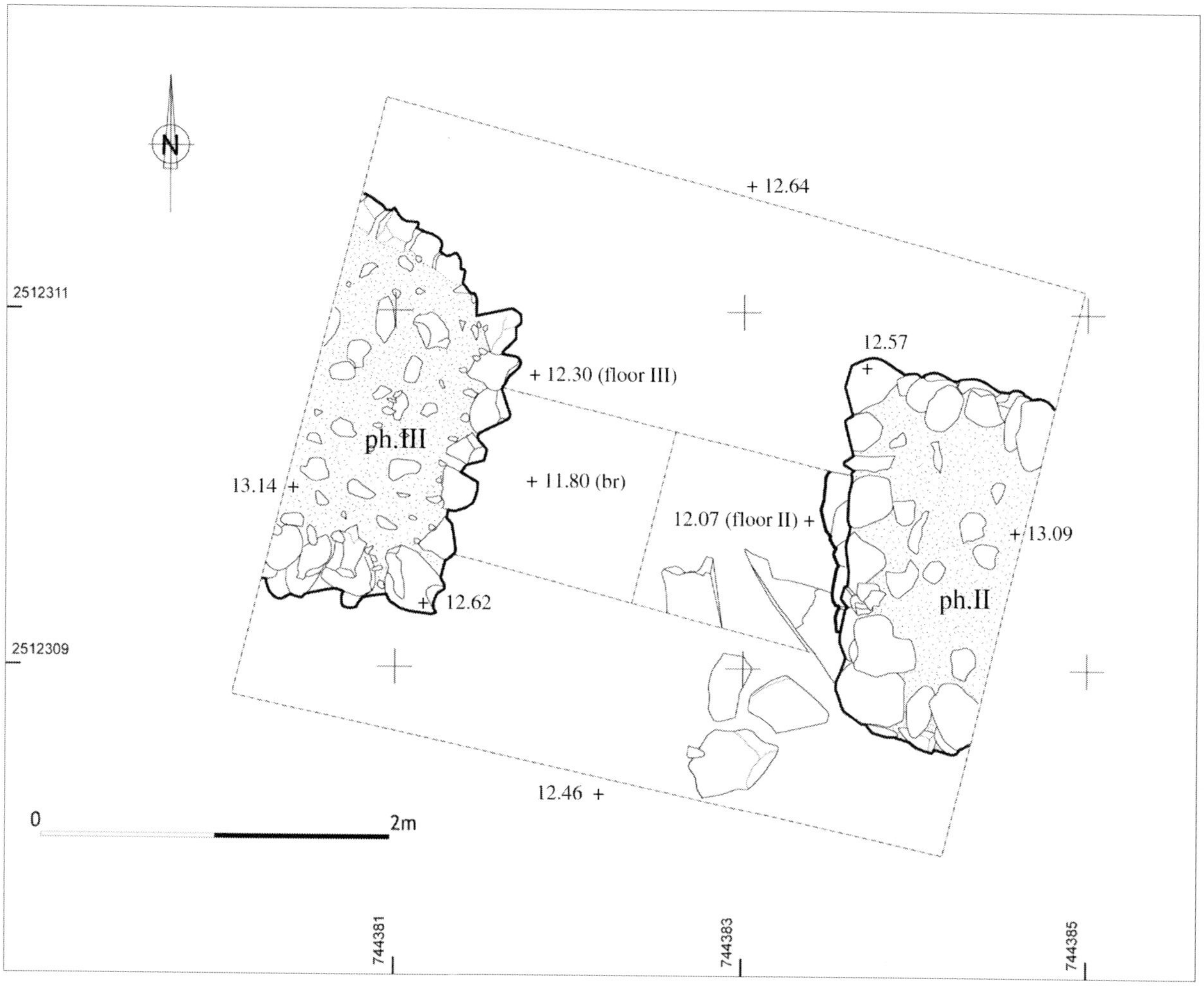

FIGURE 3. *A plan of the gate in the northern wall B37 (planning and topography B. Hollemaert & T. Creissen, geo-referencing E. Régagnon, computer graphics B. Hollemaert).*

track that the hammam, excavated in 2003, was located (Vosmer 2004: 396). From there, at least one gate in the intermediary rampart (B31) gave access eastwards to the main settled area along the shore, but the main entry to the city itself was located near the eastern extremity of the southern wall, an impressive gate protected by bastions (B8).

The Portuguese mention several gates leading to the mountains and one, at least, on the coastal side (de Albuquerque 1874, i: 216–219). No sea wall is visible today but a sketch plan of Qalhāt drawn by Ibn al-Mujāwir around 1230 clearly shows the presence of a sea wall, with several towers (Ibn al-Mujāwir [n.d.]: 215). In fact, traces of a tower were discovered along the beach south of the city. In this location was a massive basement, 10×9.6 m and *c.*2 m high, built on an elevation of the bedrock (B24). The tower itself was erected on the western part of this basement, a rectangular structure 10×6.7 m, now almost totally destroyed. Ruins of a sea wall were found south of this tower (B25), with a narrow gate leading to a small street. According to al-Mujāwir this rampart was built in 1218, in stone and plaster (Löfgren 1986: 274).

The last gate (B37) was at the northern extremity of the city, leading to the northern coastal plain through the mouth of Wādī Ḥilm, and excavations there revealed three chronological phases (Fig. 3). The first one is earlier than the construction of the fortification, so possibly earlier than 1218 according to Ibn al-Mujāwir, a dating in accordance with the associated material, which includes sgraffitiatos of the polychrome and champlevé types, dated to the eleventh to thirteenth centuries. The fortification was erected in phase II, with walls of limestone blocks that were quite well built and a wide gate slightly narrowing from the inside to the outside. The associated material includes Mustard-ware pieces, a frit bowl, and some moulded fragments from Mīnāb, and this phase could be dated to the thirteenth and fourteenth centuries. The western jamb of the gate was rebuilt during phase III, a much coarser construction reducing the width of the gate to 2 m. The material is here mostly undiagnostic.

The city quarters

The main quarter of the city, certainly the most ancient part, is located near the coast in the south-eastern part of the walled area (see Fig. 2, south-east quarter [QSE]). The beach in front of this quarter is the only place where landing is possible and it is from this area that many anchors were found underwater during the 2003 expedition (Vosmer 2004: 399–401). This quarter is very densely built, with clusters of small structures served by narrow streets, but several large buildings are also visible. One of them (B14) was recently excavated by the Iranian team and interpreted as a possible *khān* (caravanserai) or *madrasah* (religious school) (Mohsen Javeri, personal communication). Further down near the beach is another large edifice (B12), which was identified as the Friday mosque (see below).

The north-east quarter (QNE) is located on a terrace between the shore, which here resembles a small cliff, and a steep slope in the ground. It is mainly composed of large buildings, up to 1000 m², on both sides of a street running from the beach and harbour to the northern gate of the city. It could be a residential quarter or an entrepôt quarter with warehouses. Up the slope, the north-western quarter (QNW) is mainly composed of rather large buildings, most of them grouped in clusters around a square and often associated with a small terrace mosque (QNW1–3, see below). It is probably a residential quarter. The central quarter (QC) has not yet been well defined but it included a ceramic kiln (B41, see below).

The settled area was surrounded by wide cemeteries stretching north (QN), west (QW), and south-west (QSW) of the city, both inside and outside the walled area. These cemeteries include terrace mosques, simple graves, small mausoleums, and funerary terraces.

The Friday mosque

The most famous building of the city of Qalhāt was the Friday mosque, which was described by Ibn Baṭṭūṭah and Bras de Albuquerque. Ibn Baṭṭūṭah says that the mosque he visited in 1330 was built by Bībī Maryam in a position overlooking the sea and harbour and that its walls were covered with Kāshān glazed tiles (Ibn Baṭṭūṭah 1982, ii: 110–113). Nearly two centuries later, de Albuquerque gives a much more detailed description of the mosque destroyed by the Portuguese, a large building with seven aisles including a very large one with arcading in front of the entrance, all decorated with tiles. De Albuquerque adds that Afonso ordered a look-out to be placed in the tower of the mosque, which indicates that it had a minaret (1874, i: 219, 221).

The location of the Friday mosque has been a main focus of interest in Qalhāt and was tentatively identified with the Bībī Maryam complex (Ibrahim & ElMahi 2000: 131), with the wide enclosure nearby (Costa 2002: 58), or with one of the large buildings in the north-eastern quarter of the site (Vosmer *et al.* 1998: fig. 2; Agius 1999: n. 9). However, the description by the Portuguese of their attack against Qalhāt does not support any of the above-mentioned locations and states that, "as soon as they disembarked they were to proceed at once to attack the city on the side near the mosque, which was close to the sea" (de Albuquerque 1874, i: 217). This clearly means that the mosque was located on the coast at a place where disembarkation was possible, which must mean near the beach in the south-east quarter of the city.

In fact, a wide architectural complex with two units is visible along the beach in the middle of this quarter (Fig. 2, 4/a). In its north-west corner is a rectangular building (B13), *c.*40×30 m, which, given the mass of collapsed blocks, was certainly an impressive construction. In the south-east corner is another building (B12), about 30×20 m. The surface here is generally even, and contains many plaster fragments together with many architectonic elements such as cut limestone blocks, remains of columns, and fragments of glazed tiles. Two open areas, resembling courtyards, are located in the north-east and south-west corners of the complex.

The stratigraphic sounding

A sounding was opened in the south-west courtyard against the western wall of B12 down to the bedrock (level 11.90), and six chronological phases were identified within more than 5 m of deposits (Fig. 4/b).

The two earliest phases show thin successive layers of occupation, which were classified according to the associated material. The lowest ones (layers 1–9, 11.90–12.90) are characterized by the presence of sgraffiatiatos

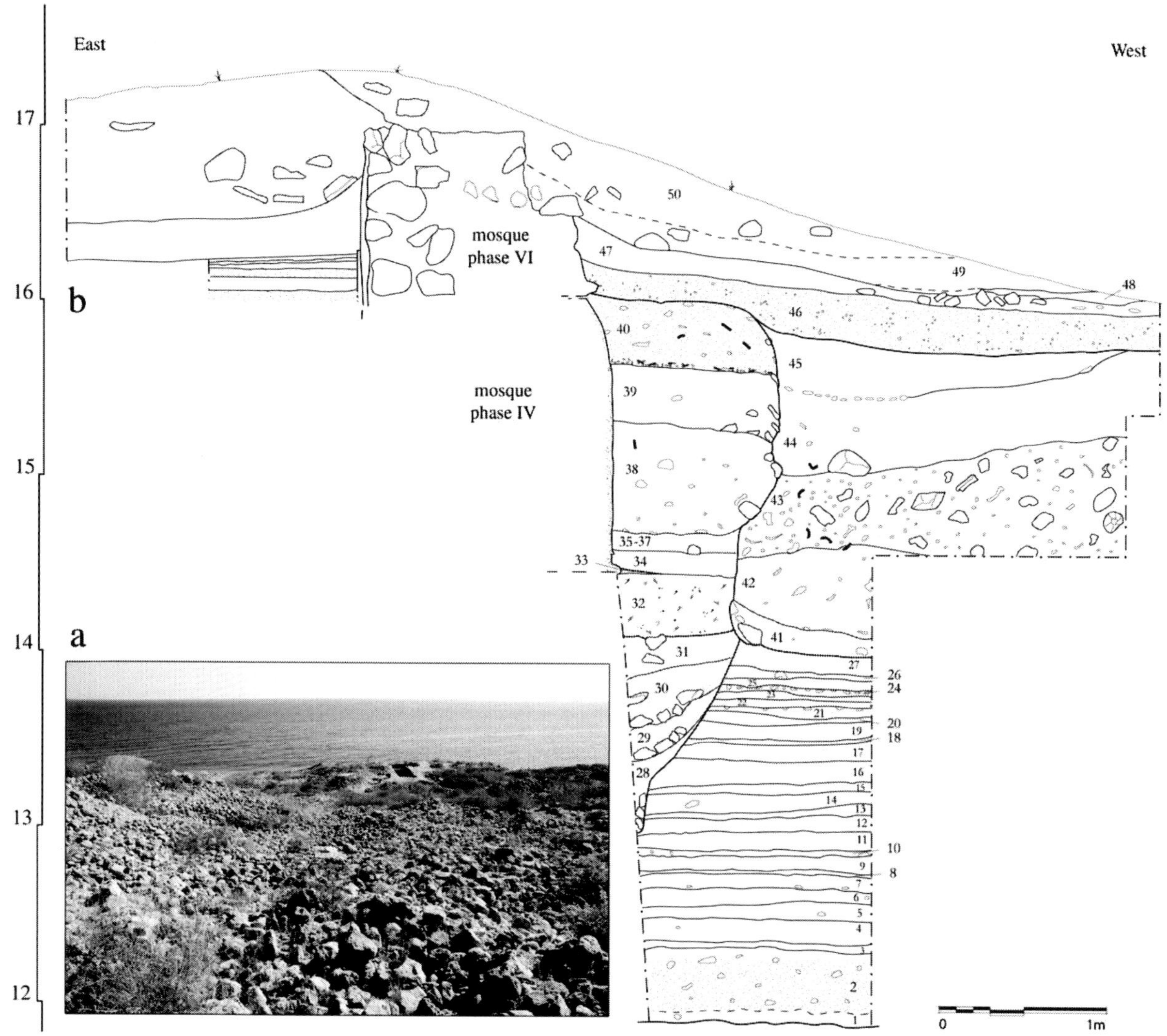

FIGURE 4. *The Friday mosque:* **a.** *a general view from the west;* **b.** *the southern section of the stratigraphic sounding outside the qiblah wall (drawing and topography T. Creissen, computer graphics S. Eliès).*

with hatched, champlevé, and green monochrome styles that can be dated to around the twelfth century; Indian imports amount to 35% of the assemblage. The upper layers (10–27, 12.90–14.10) are characterized by the appearance of Mustard ware, a Yemeni production commonly dated to around 1250–1350.

In phase III a trench about 1 m deep was cut in phases I–II layers, partly visible under the eastern section of the sounding. It contained some stones and pieces of masonry (IIIa, layers 28–31) and was sealed by a thick occupation layer (IIIb, 32, 14.10–14.50), which is probably associated with a building nearby. The Mustard ware is still characteristic of this level and some Chinese imports appear in level 32, a sample being dated to the end of the thirteenth or the beginning of the fourteenth century.[4]

During phase IV a building was erected, its western wall covered with a fine coating. It is associated with

[4] The dating of a selection of some Chinese sherds imported to France for study was provided by Zhao Bing (CNRS, Umr 7133).

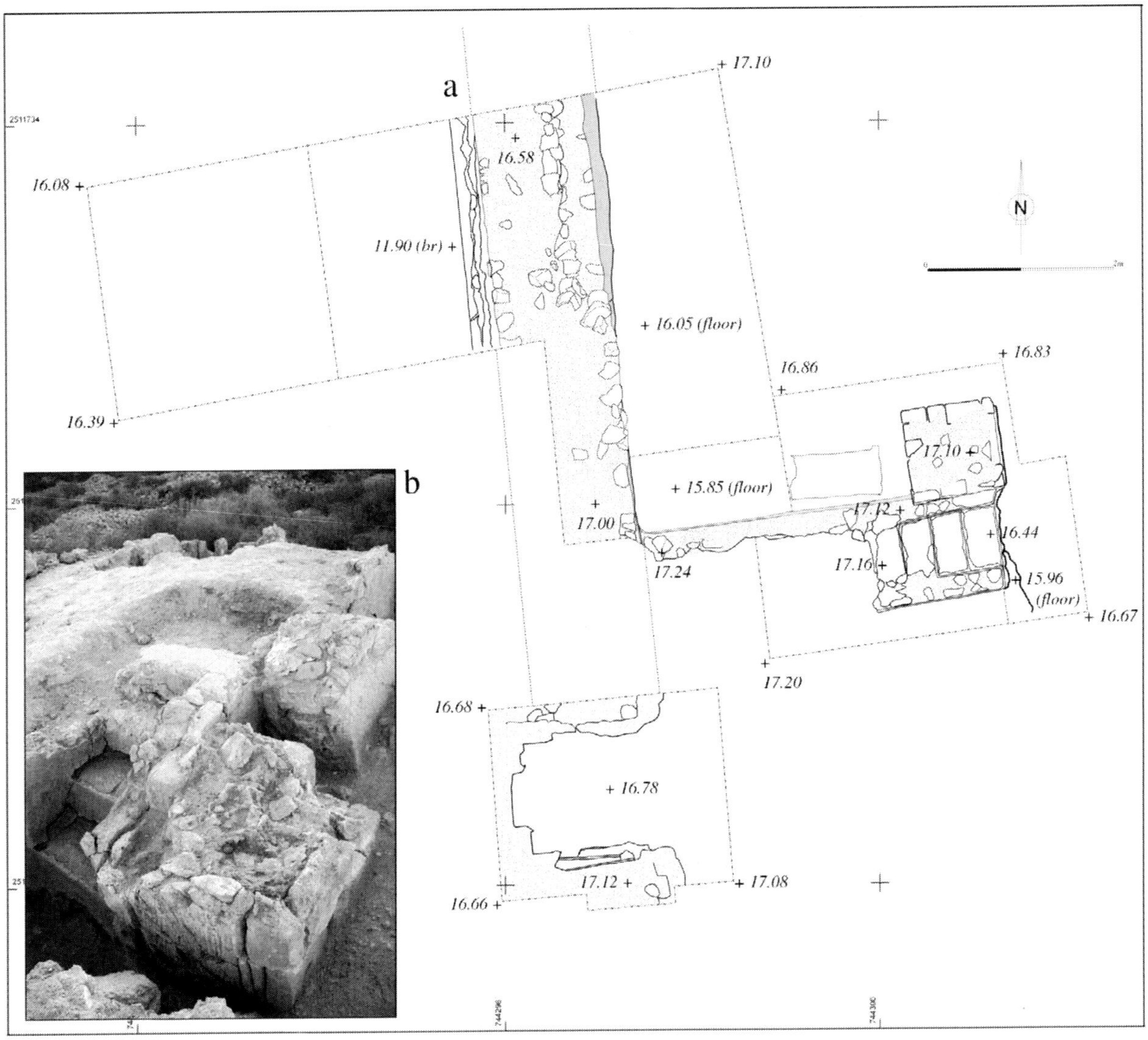

FIGURE 5. *The Friday mosque:* **a.** *a plan of the excavated structures (planning T. Creissen, geo-referencing E. Régagnon, topography and computer graphics B. Hollemaert);* **b.** *the pillar and the* minbar.

a substantial outer floor and several occupation layers (IVa, layers 33–37, 14.50–14.90/15.20), surmounted by what seems to be a thick backfill (IVb, 38–40, 14.90/15.20–16.05) which contained quite a few Chinese pieces, all the samples of which have been dated to the fourteenth century.

Deposits of phases III and IV were then cut through during phase V by a large pit nearly 2 m deep which yielded many charcoal and organic remains, with a very specific ceramic assemblage including blue speckled glaze, painted Julfār and Textile wares (layers 41–45), and Chinese imports that could also be dated to the fourteenth century. During phase VI, a new wall was erected on top of the wall of phase IV, associated outside with an occupation layer (46, 16.05–16.20).

The mosque

Excavations on the inner side of that wall proved that this phase VI building was a mosque, and the mihrab, the *minbar*, and one pillar of the central aisle were cleared (Fig. 5/a). Their respective positions allow the reconstruction of a central aisle 5.20 m wide, with a rear arcade *c.*3 m deep. Given that the building measures

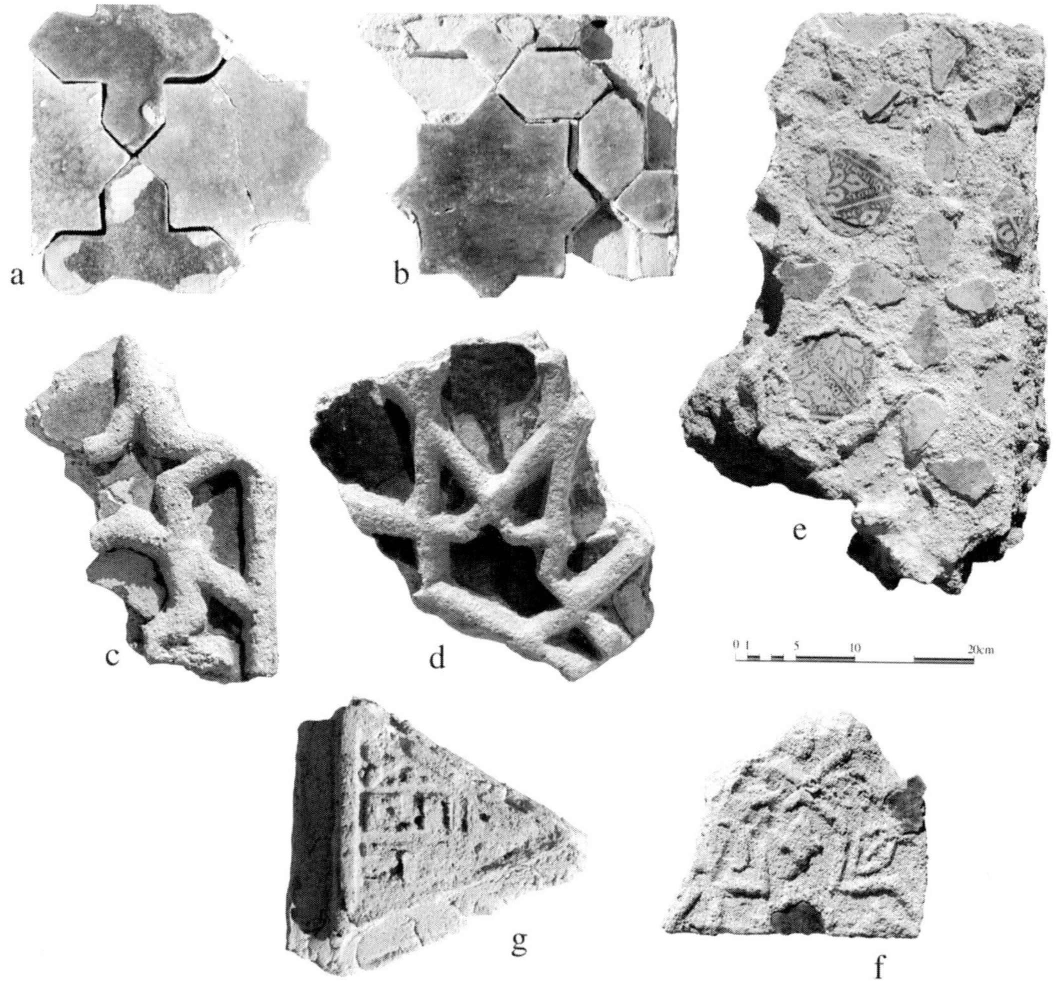

Figure 6. *Elements of decoration of the Friday mosque, phase VI:* **a–b.** *from the qiblah area;* **c–d.** *the* minbar *and pillar sounding;* **e–g.** *the mihrab.*

approximately 30×20 m and that the pillar is *c.*1×1 m, it is possible to recreate a prayer hall with five arcades 3 m deep and five aisles about 5 m wide, or three aisles *c.*3 m wide on both sides of a central aisle 5.20 m wide.

The mihrab is a niche 1.40 m wide and 1.60 m deep, decorated with small pilasters and recesses.[5] The pillar is built in square and rectangular limestone blocks 20 cm high and up to 40 cm long. Its eastern side, facing the entrance, was decorated with a vertical panel flanked by two small contiguous half-rounded pilasters carved on a square block (Fig. 4/b). The *minbar* is a plastered staircase 1 m wide and 3.80 m long, with stairs protected by a parapet. Four stairs are now preserved, each one *c.*25 cm high and 30 cm deep, and up to four more stairs could be reconstructed, the total elevation of the platform being estimated at *c.*2 m. Attached to the pillar and leaning against the plaster of the *qiblah* wall, this *minbar* is dated later than the original floor of the mosque (phase VI/a, level 15.85) but is associated with two later floors (phase VI/b, 15.95 and 16.05), all laid in strong mortar.

The most recent Friday mosque of Qalhāt was built in small coral blocks set in a thick mortar, the walls being covered with white plaster and decorated with glazed tiles. Three different types of decoration were found: panels of blue- and green-glazed tiles in the shapes of stars and crosses in the *qiblah* area (Fig. 6/a–b), fragments of similar tiles set in plaster under thick interlacing stucco lines to produce stars in the *minbar* and pillar sounding

[5] The upper part of the mihrab area only was excavated this year (2008) to avoid further destruction.

(Fig. 6/c–d), and stucco panels and fragments of lustre Kashān tiles inlaid in a thick plaster to produce sketchy motifs of flowers in the mihrab (Fig. 6/e–g). Most of these elements were probably reused from the former mosque of phase IV.

Dating

The dating of the two mosques from phases IV and VI is not absolutely certain as the chronology of most of the associated ceramic wares is not yet well established, but the original building, with its decoration of blue glazed and Kashān tiles, fits in well with the description given by Ibn Baṭṭūṭah of the mosque built by Bībī Maryam. This mosque was probably erected around 1300 or the early part of the fourteenth century, a dating that accords with the associated Chinese imports, all samples having been dated to that century.

The mosque was later ruined or badly damaged (phase V) and then rebuilt or restored reusing fragments of decoration from the former building. This phase VI mosque would therefore be the one destroyed by the Portuguese in 1508. The reconstructed plan with a central aisle 5.20 m wide and three aisles *c.*3 m wide on each side, the *qiblah*, mihrab, and pillars decorated with tiles, fits the description by de Albuquerque. It must, nevertheless, be noted that no trace was found in the soundings of the fire that reputedly destroyed that building.

The ceramic workshop

Surveys of the site led to the discovery of much kiln waste and slag on the surface of the central quarter. These were mostly concentrated in a rather flat area in the middle of the usual heaps of collapsed stones; excavations there led to the discovery of a ceramic kiln.

The total area of the ceramic workshop is not known, but may be 15×20 m. It is limited by a boundary wall, at least to the south and east sides, and a street ran parallel to the eastern wall (Fig. 7/a–b). The kiln is a roughly circular structure, 2.30 m in diameter, built against a partition wall in the south-eastern part of the area. The furnace is completely preserved, the hearth being only a few centimetres under the present surface. It comprises a 20 cm-thick baked clay floor with one central and twelve peripheral ventilation holes. The door was located to the east, and the area east and north of the kiln was filled with kiln refuse — ashes, burnt fish bones, slag, wasters, and tripods — that was probably discharged here from another kiln when this one was already out of use. In fact, more than 2 m of deposits have accumulated against the eastern wall, with three main phases visible. To the south, the small space between the kiln and the southern wall was entirely filled with small limestone blocks, maybe a stock of material for the production of lime.

This kiln was built on top of an earlier layer about 30 cm thick, which lies on the bedrock and is associated with the base of the surrounding walls, as well as with another curving wall in the northern section of the excavated area. This layer also contained some kiln elements and the curving wall could therefore be part of a former kiln. A door in the partition wall next to the kiln led to the western part of the complex, possibly the workshop itself.

Excavations at B41 yielded huge amounts of local ceramics, which are still being studied. The fabric is buff-pinkish to red depending on the firing temperature, with green-coloured wasters, with a grog and lime temper. The pottery is wheel-turned, of medium quality, and shapes are varied. There are various types of jars (Fig. 8), all unglazed except for a type with a very typical thickened, grooved rim and incised decoration (Fig. 8/1–8), some basins and plates and many bowls, more or less globular or conical, glazed and unglazed or painted (Fig. 9). The glaze is greenish blue, degrading to whitish or blackish. The stars and crosses tiles of the mosque were possibly produced here as the fabric and glaze are similar and several fragments of tiles were found in the kiln area. Ceramics produced in workshop B41 were found in all excavated areas, together with ceramics of similar fabric and glaze but different in shape, which were probably made at some other kilns in Qalhāt.

The associated material includes some sgraffiatiatos, Mustard-ware pieces, and Chinese imports, which are dated to around the fourteenth century.

The north-western quarter, mosque B19, and building B21

The last area excavated was located in the north-west quarter of the city (QNW1). Here, several structures are arranged around a rectangular square *c.*25×15 m, with large buildings (B20–23) on the east, south, and west sides, and a small mosque (B19) on the north side, at the edge of the funerary quarter QN (Fig. 10/a). Mosque B19 and part of building B21 were excavated in 2008.

The small mosque (B19)

Mosque B19 is a simple construction with a room fronted by a courtyard. It was erected on a terrace *c.*1.50 m high,

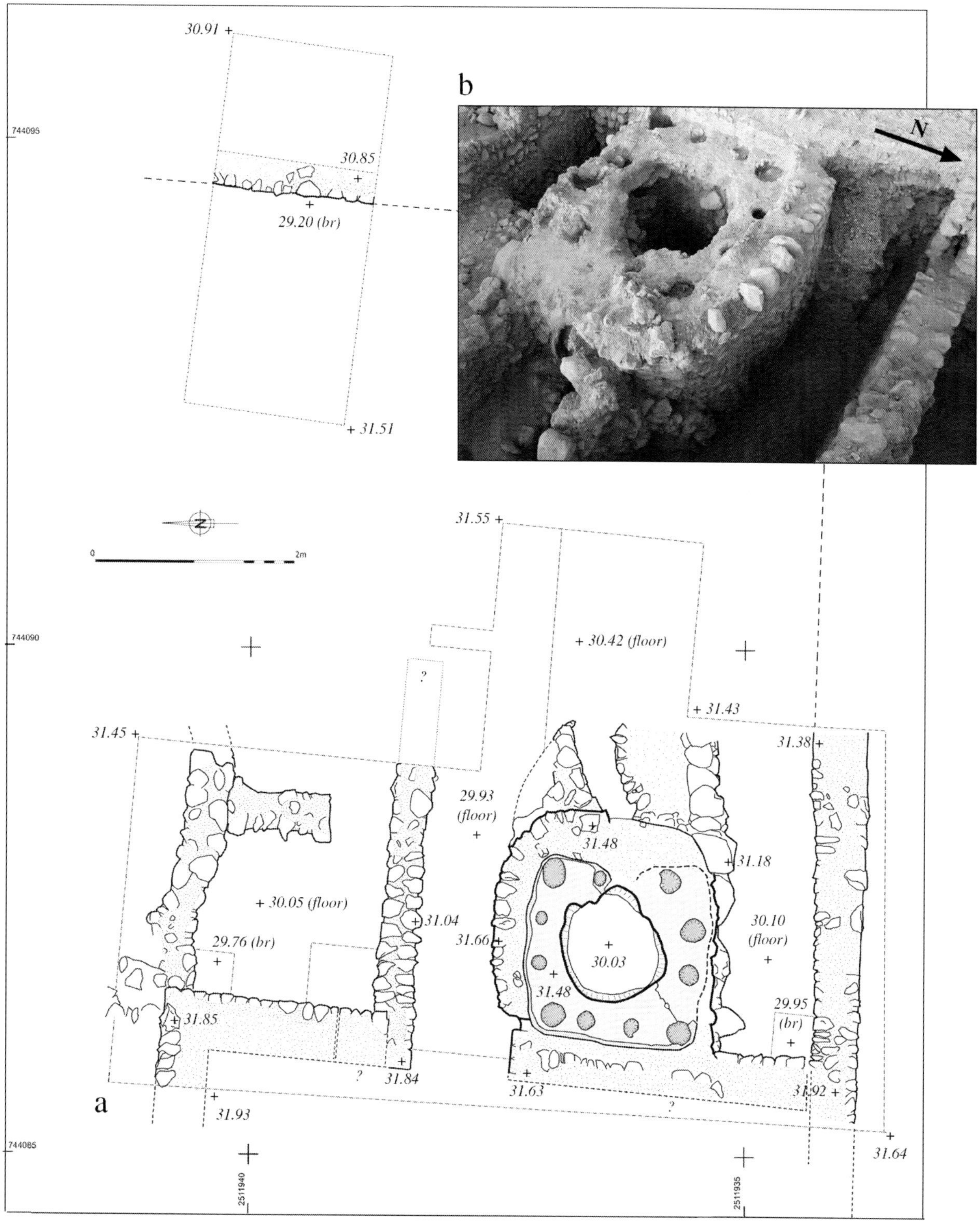

Figure 7. a. *A plan of the ceramic workshop B41 (planning and topography A. Joyard & A. Ihr, geo-referencing E. Régagnon, computer graphics B. Hollemaert);* **b.** *the kiln.*

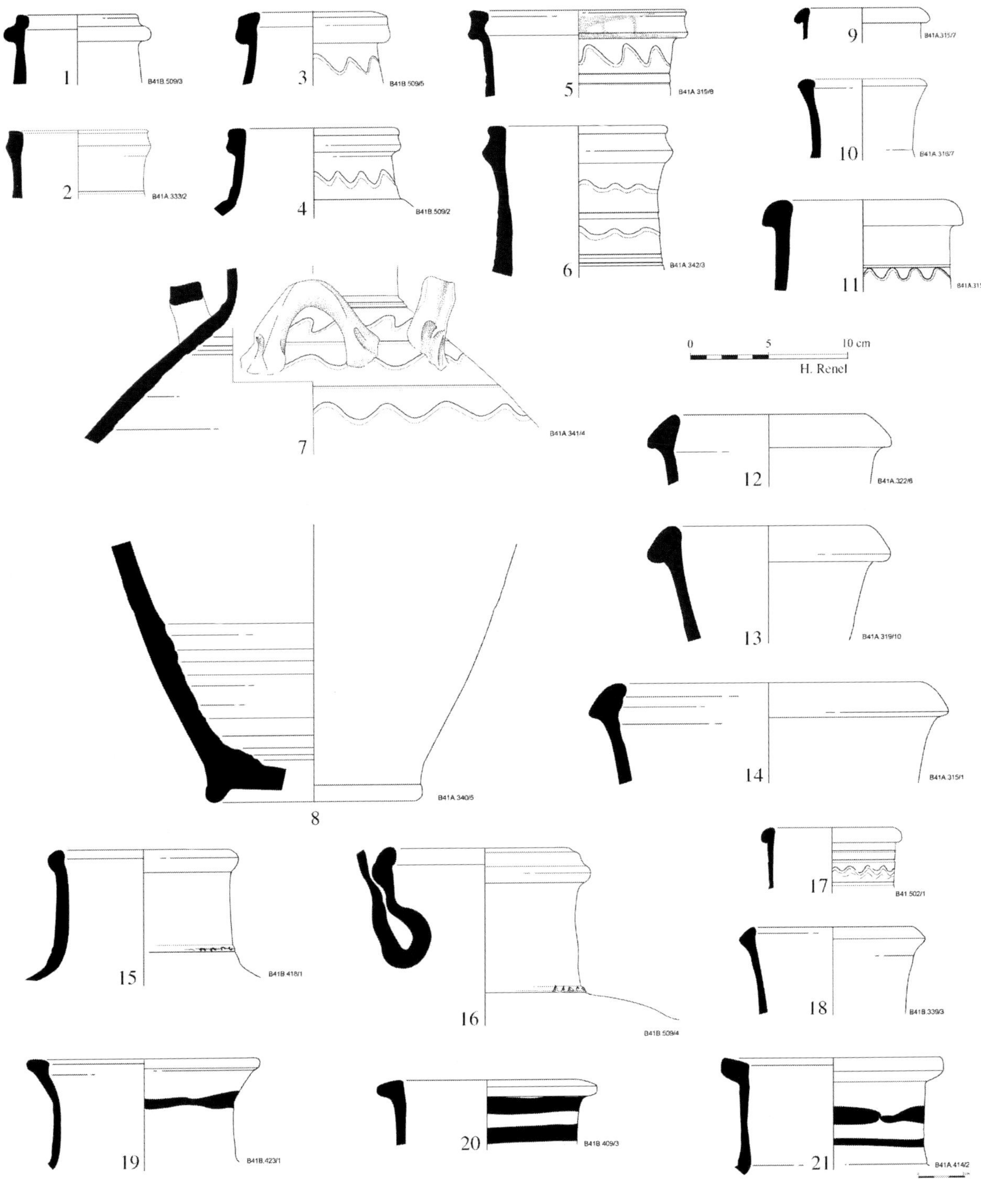

Figure 8. *Ceramics from workshop B41, closed shapes:* **1–11.** *glazed;* **12–18.** *unglazed;* **19–21.** *painted (drawings H. Renel).*

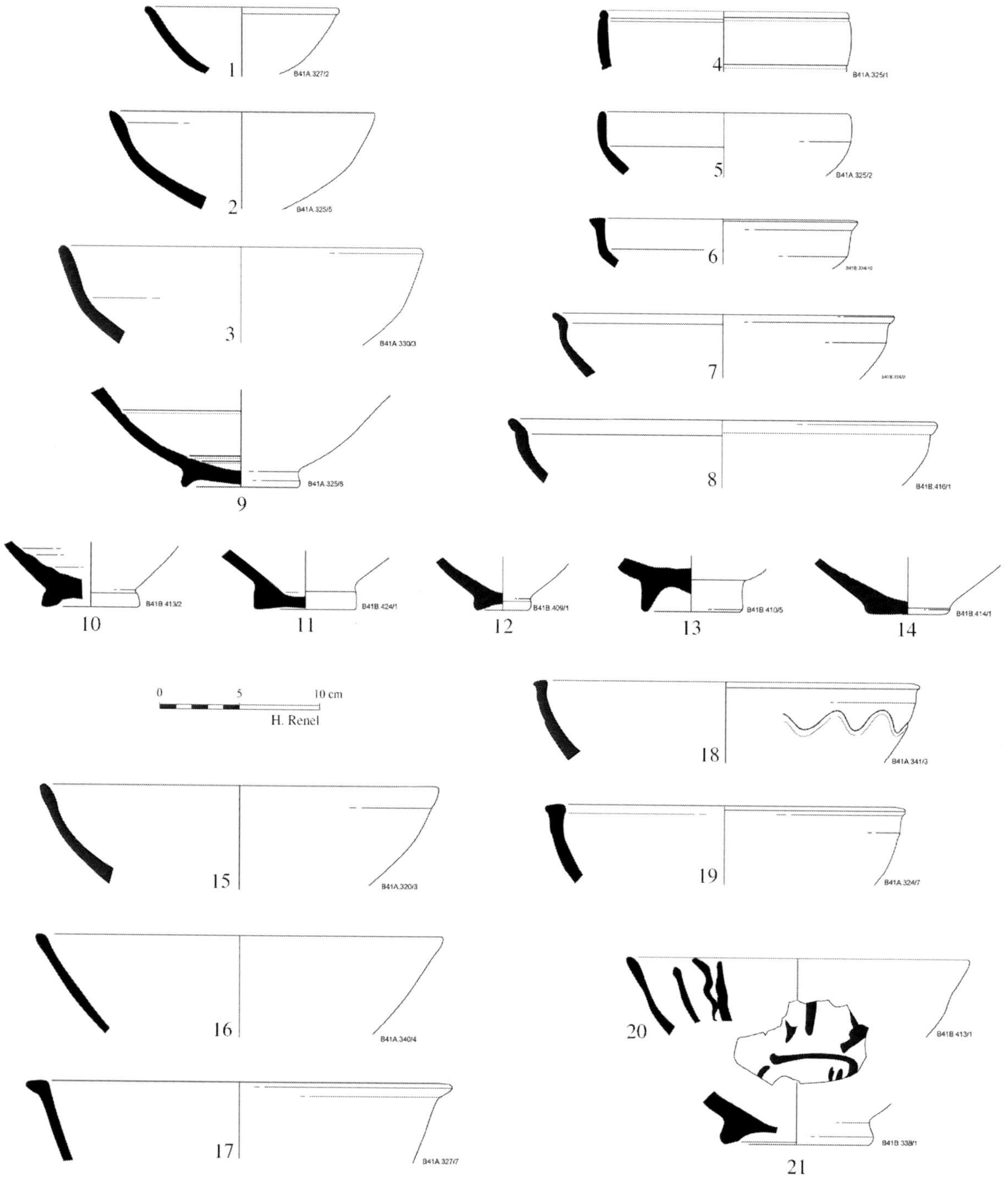

FIGURE 9. *Ceramics from workshop B41, open shapes:* **1–14.** *glazed;* **15–19.** *unglazed;* **20–21.** *painted (drawings H. Renel).*

which is composed of two contiguous platforms together measuring 16.30 m east–west and 8.20 m north–south. It was built directly on the bedrock (level *c*.29.50), except at its south-western corner where a fragment of an earlier wall was reused as the base of the southern wall.

Against the eastern facade of the terrace, a staircase 1.20 m wide led to a courtyard located on the eastern platform, 7.90×8.20 m, around level 31.00. This courtyard was covered with small gravel pieces and was probably surrounded by a low wall, now eroded. A shallow ablution basin, *c*.2×2 m, with three successive coatings, was located in the north-east corner.

The *muṣallā* is located on the western platform (8.40×8.20 m), and opens onto the courtyard with three bays, one central bay 2.10 m wide, and two lateral bays 1 m wide. The north and south walls are now totally eroded but were probably of the same thickness as the facade, 0.65 m. In contrast, the *qiblah* wall is more than 1 m thick, with a mihrab in the form of a shallow niche decorated with thin pillars and flanked by lateral bays. Traces of a substantial plastered floor are still preserved in some places, around level 31.20. Contrasting with the retaining walls of the terrace, which are made of limestone blocks and pebbles, the superstructures were almost exclusively constructed of coral blocks set in a strong dark pink mortar.

No occupation layer was found in B19, the collapse debris of the mosque lying directly on the floor inside and on the bedrock outside. Archaeological material is therefore unstratified and rather limited, the identified pieces, such as a fragment of Mustard ware, Chinese celadon and Dehua porcelain bowls, and blue and white porcelains, being dated to the fourteenth to fifteenth centuries. It seems reasonable to assume that mosque B19 is probably contemporary with the other buildings around the square and, in particular, B21.

Building B21

Building B21 is located south of the square, opposite the mosque. It is a large structure, *c*.27×28.50 m, and only its western half was excavated (Fig. 10/b).

As with B19, B21 was built on the bedrock. The walls are generally 70 cm thick, with facades made of angular limestone blocks roughly set in a thick red clay mortar. The general layout of the building does not seem to have been consistently planned from the beginning, as walls are not precisely orthogonal, some of them are not even aligned, and several others are not bonded and could be later additions.

The main entrance to B21 was located in the middle of the southern wall through a corridor 1.20 m wide and 6.85 m long (B21I), which gave access to the south-east corner of 21H. This space in the centre of the building, 4.70×11.40 m, could be a courtyard although it is not connected with most of the surrounding rooms. In fact, the only other opening to 21H in the area excavated is located in its south-west corner, where a doorway gives access to rooms 21F and 21G. To the east, the central space H could also be connected with the unexcavated half of the building. Rooms 21A–B and 21D–E, in the south-west and north-west corners of B21 respectively, open to the outside of the building but no doorway was found to room 21C.

The floors are made of a compacted mortar that has been used to level the surface of the bedrock; two superimposed floors were found in room F, and three in room E. A shallow basin 40×65 cm was located in the south-east corner of room H. The occupation of B21 is otherwise only attested by fireplaces, small shallow pits full of ashes and charcoal. The collapse layer lies directly on the floors but traces of a squatter reoccupation were found in several places.

The construction layers delivered a mixed assemblage from the twelfth to the fourteenth centuries. The occupation yielded few diagnostic pieces apart from a Dehua porcelain bowl, some Textile ware, and local productions from kiln B41, and can therefore probably be dated to around the fourteenth century. The destruction/squatter layers yielded an assemblage dated to the fifteenth to sixteenth centuries, including blue and brown speckled sherds, frit ware, blue and white porcelain, Martaban jars, Thai stoneware, and many Indian imports.

Conclusions

The first season of excavations at Qalhāt has already provided interesting information on the history of the city. Initially, it seems possible that Qalhāt was not settled before the eleventh or twelfth centuries, at least not on a large scale. In fact, an important Early Islamic harbour site is known at Raʾs al-Ḥadd, about 50 km to the south, which has provided much Abbasid pottery together with many Tang and Sung Chinese porcelain and stoneware pieces, as well as a complete assemblage of ceramics traded in the Indian Ocean during the eleventh century (Whitcomb 1975: 126, Reade 1989, and personal documentation). It is therefore probable that Qalhāt succeeded Raʾs al-Ḥadd as the international port of the region around 1100. Excavations at gate B37

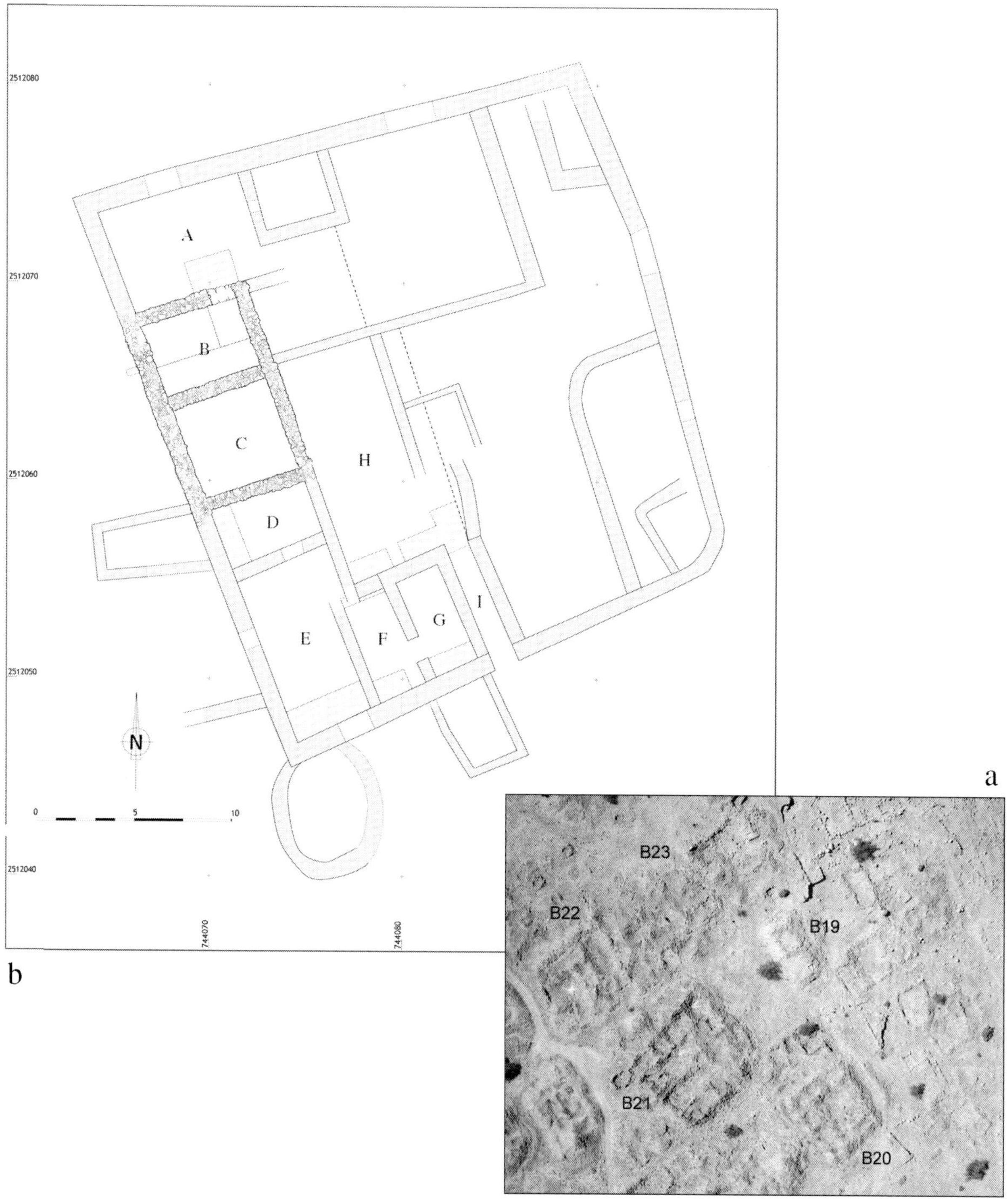

Figure 10. *A kite photograph of* **a.** *the north-west 1 quarter;* **b.** *a plan of building B21 (planning and topography B. Hollemaert & A. Rougeulle, geo-referencing E. Régagnon, computer graphics B. Hollemaert).*

also indicate that the city was possibly not walled in the beginning phases — perhaps not before 1218 according to Ibn al-Mujāwir. The ancient town was located around the great mosque, fronting the beach and harbour and surrounded by suburbs and cemeteries, the period of maximum extension of the city most probably dating to the fourteenth century. As described by chroniclers, the Friday mosque was a beautiful edifice that underwent at least two reconstructions. The discovery of the ceramic kiln will allow us to establish a typology of ceramics of local production, thus clearly identifying the imports, exports, and the exchange networks of the harbour.

Acknowledgements

The Qalhāt Project is held under the authority of the Ministry of Heritage and Culture (MHC) of the Sultanate of Oman, with the financial support of the MHC on the Omani side and of the Ministry of Foreign Affairs and National Centre for Scientific Research (Umr 8167) on the French side. Our deepest gratitude is due to the Department of Excavations and Archaeological Studies of the MHC, to its Director Mrs Biubwa Ali al-Sabri and all the staff, for their constant and friendly help and support. Special thanks are also due to the Total Foundation, who provided the necessary funds for the GIS project at the site, and to Eveha, a French archaeological consulting agency that put two of its members at the disposal of the mission.

Data presented here are the result of the collaborative efforts by all the members of the 2008 expedition: Thomas Creissen (Eveha, Limoges — archaeologist, excavations at B12 and B37), Boris Hollemaert (Eveha, Limoges — archaeologist, excavations at B21), Anna Ihr (University of Göteborg, Sweden — archaeologist, excavations at B41), and Anne Joyard (archaeologist, excavations at B41); Emmanuelle Regagnon (Géofil, Lyon — topographer, GIS project); Hélène Renel (CNRS Umr 8167, Paris — ceramologist, registration and study of the material). The spring exploratory mission was held thanks to the collaboration of Mr Patrick Anselm, architect at Abako Arkitektkontor (Göteborg, Sweden).

References

Agius D.

1999. Medieval Qalhat: travellers, dhows and stone anchors in south-east Oman. Pages 173–220 in H.P. Ray (ed.), *Archaeology of Seafaring. The Indian Ocean in the ancient period.* Delhi: Pragati Publications.

Bhacker M.R. & Bhacker B.

2004. Qalhât in Arabian History: Context and Chronicles. *Journal of Oman Studies* 13: 11–55.

Costa P.M.

2002. The Great Mosque of Qalhāt. *Journal of Oman Studies* 12: 55–70.

de Albuquerque B.

1874. *The commentaries of the Great Afonso Dalboquerque, second viceroy of India.* (4 volumes). London: Hakluyt Society.

Ibn Baṭṭūṭah

1982. *Voyages.* (2 volumes). (FM La Découverte nos 51–52). Paris: Librairie François Maspéro.

Ibn al-Mujāwir

[n.d.]. Taʿrīkh al-mustabṣir. MS Aya Sofia 3080, Istanbul. [Unpublished.]

Ibrahim M. & ElMahi A.T.

2000. A survey between Quriyat and Sur in the Sultanate of Oman (1997). *Proceedings of the Seminar for Arabian Studies* 30: 119–136.

Löfgren O.

1986. *Ṣifat bilād al-Yaman. Al-musammāt Taʾrīkh al-mustabṣir li Ibn al-Mujāwir.* Sanaa: Manshūrāt al-Madīnah.

Miles S.B.

1919. *The Countries and Tribes of the Persian Gulf.* London: Frank Cass.

Polo M.
1980. *Le Devisement du monde.* (2 volumes). (FM La Découverte nos 21–22). Paris: Librairie François Maspéro.

Reade J.
1989. Excavations at Ras al-Hadd, 1989: preliminary report. [Unpublished report to the MHC].

Teixeira P. & Sinclair W.F.
1902. *The travels of Pedro Teixeira; with his "Kings of Harmuz" and extracts from his "Kings of Persia".* London: Hakluyt Society.

Vosmer T.
2004. Qalhât, an ancient port of Oman: results of the first mission. *Proceedings of the Seminar for Arabian Studies* 34: 389–404.

Vosmer T., Agius D., Baker P., Carpenter J. & Cave S.
1998. Oman Maritime Heritage Project. Field Report 1998. [Unpublished report].

Whitcomb D.S.
1975. The archaeology of Oman: a preliminary discussion of the Islamic period. *The Journal of Oman Studies* 1: 123–137.

Yāqūt al-Rūmī al-Ḥamawī/ed. F. Wüstenfeld
1866–1873. *Kitāb muʿjam al-buldān. Jacut's Geographisches Wörterbuch* (6 volumes). Leipzig: In Commission bei F.A. Brockhaus.

Author's address
Dr Axelle Rougeulle, CNRS — Umr 8167, Laboratoire islam médiéval, 27 rue Paul Bert, 94200 Ivry sur Seine, France.
e-mail arougeulle@aol.com

Proceedings of the Seminar for Arabian Studies 40 (2010): 321–336

The "River Aftan": an old caravan/trade route along Wādī al-Sahbā᾽?

Nabiel Y. Al Shaikh & Claire Reeler

Summary

Wādī al-Sahbā᾽ (Wādī ᾽l-Sahbā᾽) originates in the al-Kharj region in central Saudi Arabia and is formed by the confluence of several wadis; these ancient drainage systems were originally formed by rain falling on the Najd plateau during the Quaternary period. Wādī al-Sahbā᾽ runs west–east to Sabkhat Muṭṭī on the Saudi/UAE border. Several historical sources and old maps of Arabia give the names "River Aftan" or "Wadi Aftan" and these possibly refer to the Wādī al-Sahbā᾽. It is probable that these mark an old caravan route. In order to test this hypothesis we traced the course of the wadi and conducted an archaeological investigation. This paper will assess the likelihood that Wādī al-Sahbā᾽ is the "River/Wādī Aftan" and part of an old caravan/trade route. Important considerations in this regard include the geomorphology of the wadi, the presence of vegetation, wildlife, and water sources, and the nature of the archaeological sites found there. The relationship between Wādī al-Sahbā᾽ and surrounding areas with significant archaeological sites, such as al Kharj, Yabrīn, Wādī Ḥanīfah, and Wādī Nisāḥ is also examined in this paper. Similarly, the relationship with other, well-documented trade and caravan routes in the area has been investigated.

Keywords: Aftan, Wādī al-Sahbā᾽, al-Yamāmah, trade, route

Introduction

In a previous study of old maps of Arabia, we noticed that many of the maps contain a reference to "River" or "Wadi" Aftan (Reeler, Al Shaikh & Potts 2009). The "River Aftan" is depicted on early maps of Arabia in two ways. In maps of the early eighteenth century, it is usually shown as a river running roughly from south to north, from the area of al-Yamāmah (also called "Iemene" or "Ḥaḍrama") to debouch in the Arabian Gulf somewhere north of al-Qaṭīf ("El Catif") (see Fig. 1) (al-Qasimi 1996; 1999). Occasionally this river is shown connecting to a southwards-flowing branch of the Shaṭṭ al-ᶜArab, sometimes marked as "an artificial river" (map "Arabia" 1734) (Al Shaikh 2004). In maps of the nineteenth century, however, the River Aftan is marked as a river flowing from west to east, debouching into the Gulf south of al-Qaṭīf, usually on the coast opposite al-Hofuf (al-Hufūf) (see Fig. 2). This "river" was marked as flowing from the area of ancient al-Yamāmah in central Arabia (near modern al-Kharj), eastwards to the Gulf. In most maps, the river is shown as having three feeder tributaries at its source south of Riyadh and then flowing east to an area south of al-Hofuf, at which point it turns north towards al-Hofuf and then east again, until reaching the coast of the Gulf somewhere opposite the island of Bahrain.

The consistency with which this river was drawn on many different maps, as well as the consistency with which towns are marked relative to it, suggests that it refers to some actual geographic feature. Clearly not an actual river, as these have not flowed regularly through this area in millennia, it must refer to some other natural geographic feature. There are several possible explanations as to why it was drawn as a river and these will be examined below. Finally, the evidence will be assessed to support the assertion that the geographic feature actually being depicted is the Wādī al-Sahbā᾽. It is possible that Wādī al-Sahbā᾽ formed part of an east–west caravan and trade route, linking the Arabian Gulf coast with the Najd heartland in central Arabia and beyond (Fig. 3). These routes allowed for the transport of goods in both directions — from the Arabian Gulf Coast into the interior and further to the Red Sea and even the Mediterranean — and also allowed for goods to flow back from these areas to the Gulf.

Old trade routes through Arabia

The land of Arabia has always been a busy network of trade, both within the region and beyond, even to other continents. These routes covered both land and sea. We know that the maritime trade routes extend back as far

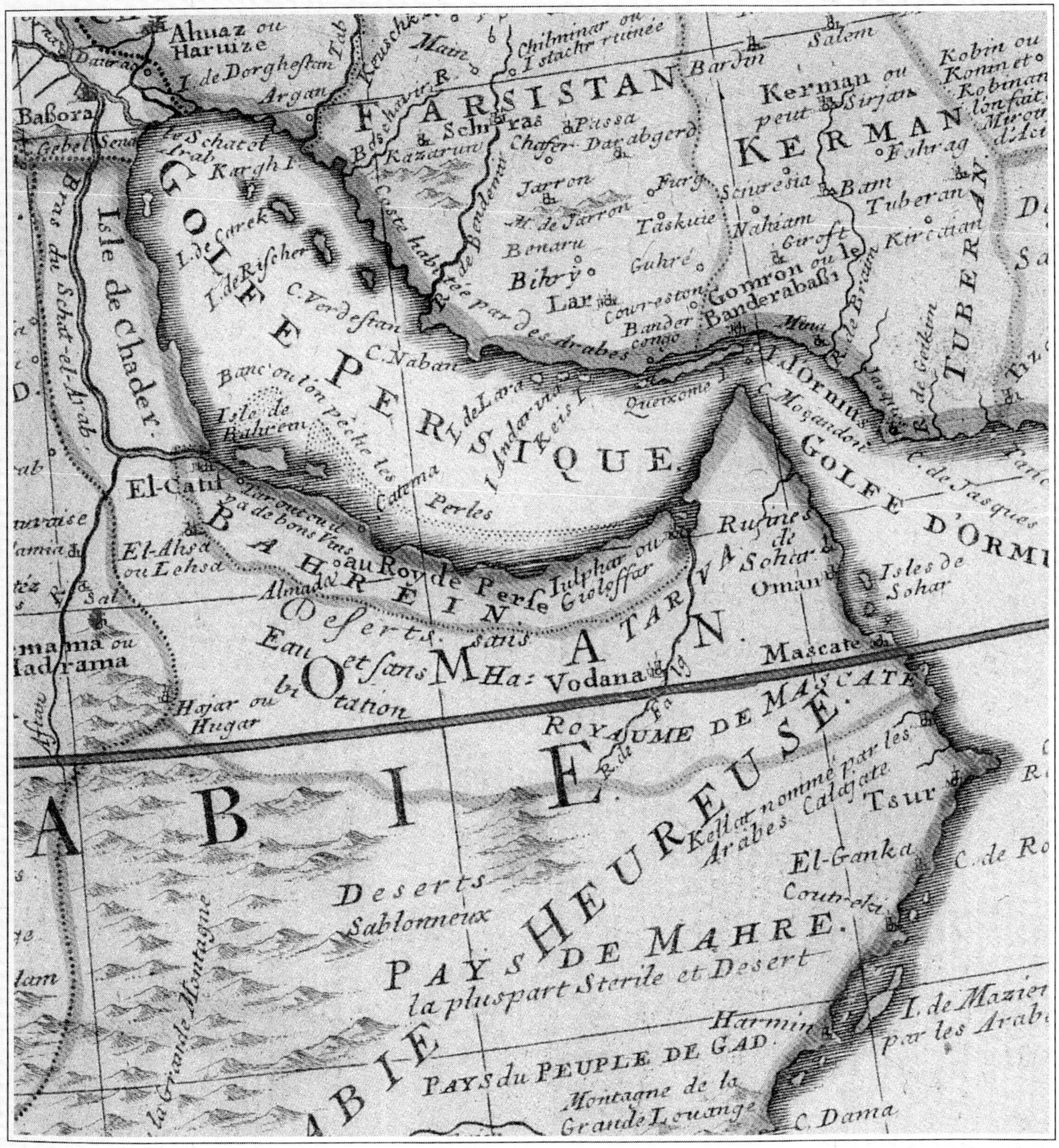

FIGURE 1. *The river Aftan, "1701, Carte de la Turquie de l'Arabie et de la Perse, Guillaume de l'Ilse, Paris" (al-Qasimi 1996: 113).*

as the fifth and sixth millennia BC in the Arabian Gulf, because of the transport of Ubaid pottery and bitumen along the coast (Potts 1990; McClure & Al Shaikh 1993; Carter 2006). We know that inland trade routes were very active during the first millennium BC, when incense was transported overland from South Arabia (Potts 1988; 1990; al-Saud 1996), but we do not yet fully understand the origins of these overland trade routes. This discussion has usually been linked to the question of the date of the domestication of camels, with evidence being assessed from eastern Arabia (Potts 1993; 2001; Uerpmann 2001; Uerpmann & Uerpmann 2002). However, we know that

FIGURE 2. *Detail of the river Aftan, "1822, Carte Générale de la Turquie d'Asie, de la Perse, de l'Arabie, du Caboul et du Turkestan Indépendant, A. Brue, Paris" (al-Qasimi 1999: 264).*

certain items such as bronze, steatite, and obsidian were making their way across inland parts of Arabia, at least as early as the second and third millennia BC, possibly even earlier. The origins of these trade routes need to be analysed by sourcing some of these items that were traded at an early date.

An example of this trade is indicated by the presence of bronze weapons at archaeological sites in Yabrīn on the northern edge of the Rubᶜ al-Khālī desert. There is no local source of copper or tin for the production of bronze at Yabrīn, or anywhere close by. Some of the bronze weapons are of a form dated to the second millennium BC. The bronze must have come either from Oman or south-west Saudi Arabia. Even if the bronze was transported from Oman by sea, the closest coast is 270 km away, requiring a substantial desert crossing in order to reach Yabrīn. If there were no domestic camels at this time (although there have been suggestions that there might have been, see e.g. al-Saud 1996; 1997), then the bronze must have been transported by another animal, such as donkeys. It is therefore necessary to broaden the analysis of the origins of inland trade and look at the possible uses of other animals besides camels, and also to examine the evidence for domestic camels within Saudi Arabia.

There have been several attempts to reconstruct the ancient trade routes across Arabia from early maps. Place names given by Pliny have been analysed for recognisable toponyms from which suggested routes

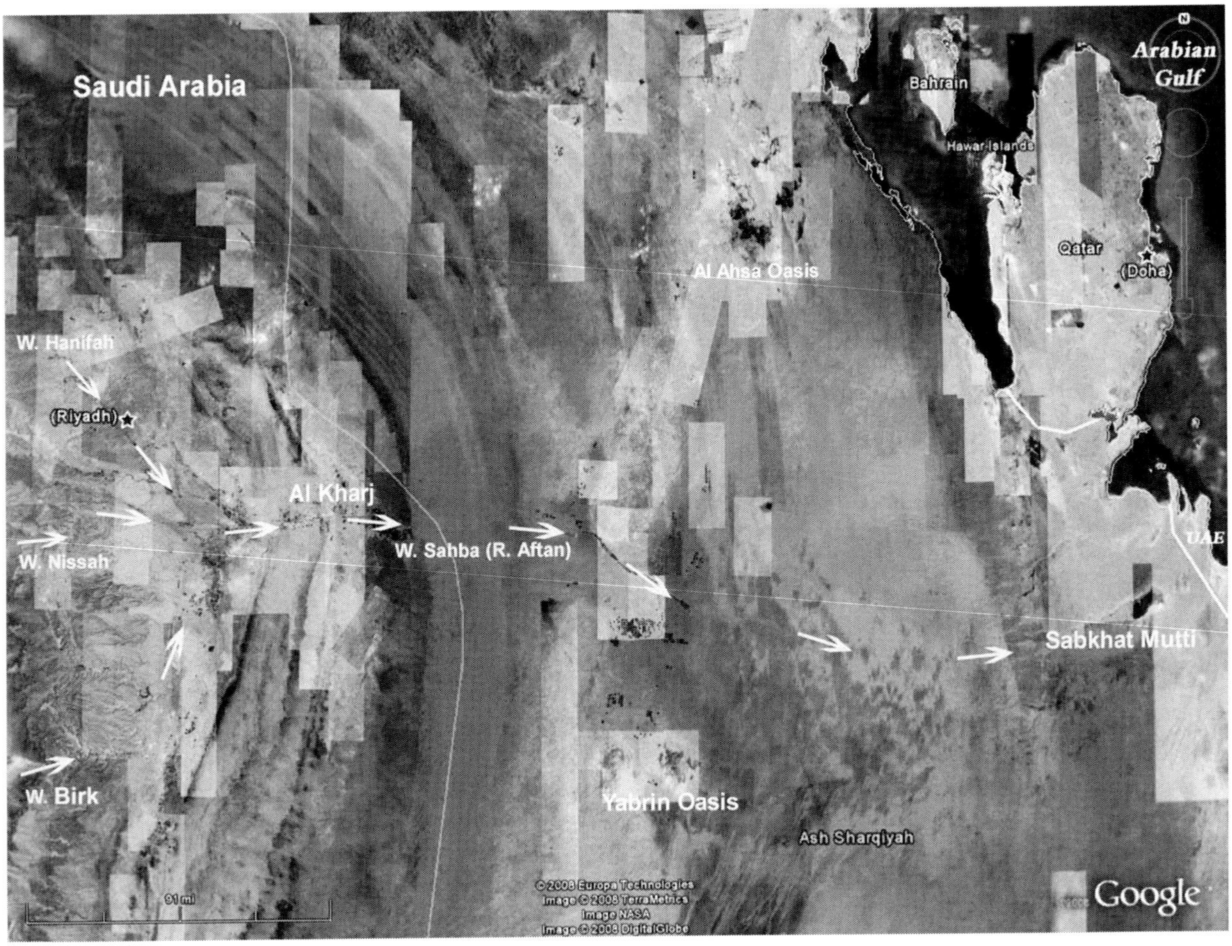

FIGURE 3. *The course of Wādī al-Sahbāʾ and its origin from Wādī Ḥanīfaḥ, Wādī Nisāḥ, and Wādī Birk. (Base map courtesy of Google Earth, 2008).*

could be reconstructed. Pliny described places along the trade routes for incense and there seems to be general agreement that there were at least two main routes, which diverged from each other at Qaryat al-Fāw in southern Saudi Arabia. One ran northwards and passed through Madāʾin Ṣāliḥ on its way to Petra. The other was bound for "Gerrha" and on to Babylonia. Potts (1988) argues for the latter route to run from Qaryat al-Fāw to al-Sulayyil, al-Aflāj, and al-Kharj (al-Yamāmah) before heading towards Gerrha and the Arabian Gulf coast. This is of direct relevance to this paper, as will be seen below.

The study of al-Aflāj by al-Saud (1997) amply demonstrates the importance of this centre on a trade route connecting to both southern Arabia and the Mediterranean. Archaeological survey and excavations at al-Aflāj revealed the presence of tetradrachmae bearing the name of Alexander, as well as coins with Heracles and Zeus depicted. Ceramic incense burners and a South Arabian seal attest to the site's location on an incense trade route to South Arabia. Both Hellenistic and South Arabian items date the site to about the second or third century BC (al-Saud 1997). Hellenistic pottery has also been found at several sites in the area of al-Kharj (al-Ghazzi 1990).

On the western side of Saudi Arabia, we know that Darb al-fīl ("The Elephant Way", also known as Darb al-Bakhūr, "The Incense Route") between Yemen and Mecca was established during the pre-Islamic period. Inscriptions along the route show that it can be dated to this period. Furthermore, the name "Incense Route" implies that it probably dates back to at least the first millennium BC. This route is also known as "The Yemeni Pilgrim Route" as it runs between Ṣanʿāʾ and Mecca and was used by pilgrims during the Islamic period (al-Thenayian 1999).

Many of the major hajj routes crossing Arabia probably originated as earlier trade and pre-Islamic pilgrim routes. However, we do not know exactly how early these routes originated. While the first millennium BC is usually given as the period during which inland trade opened up throughout the Arabian Peninsula (Magee 2004; Uerpmann & Uerpmann 2002; Potts 2001), it is possible that some of these routes may go back further to the second or even third millennium BC.

There is some evidence that there was a hajj route running across Arabia from Oman to Mecca. This route is marked on several old maps of Arabia (al-Qasimi 1996: 278; 1999: 306, 308). It is possible that this route ran through Yabrīn at some time (Reeler, Al Shaikh & Potts 2009). This would be the inland version of the more common route for pilgrims, which brought them by sea to the Gulf coast and the eastern side of Saudi Arabia and then across land to Mecca. Ibn Baṭṭuṭah mentions travelling for hajj through al-Aḥsāʾ (modern al-Hofuf) to al-Yamāmah (modern al-Kharj) in 1331, on his way to Mecca. He also mentions a route from Oman to al-Bahrain (which included the east coast of Saudi Arabia), which had been abandoned because of shifting sand, and that people in the fourteenth century travelled by sea (Ibn Baṭṭuṭah 1992: 280).

The River Aftan in old maps

Many old maps of Arabia show a river running through part of north-eastern Arabia. This river is usually marked as running from the inland area of al-Yamāmah (often called "Iemene" or even "Ḥaḍrama") to the coast. In several of these old maps, the river is marked as the "River Aftan", occasionally called the "River Astan" or even the "River Iemama", "River Ard", or "River Efnan". At least thirty maps in the al-Qasimi Collection contain references to the River Aftan by these names (al-Qasimi 1996; 1999). Almost all of the others show a river marked in the approximate position of the River Aftan, most with two or three tributaries at the source, usually in the mountains of central Arabia. This clearly refers to a natural feature of some definite geographical significance, some landmark by which people defined their country.

Palaeoclimate and Wādī al-Sahbāʾ: geography

During the Quaternary period, which started about 2.5 million years ago, there was more rainfall on the Arabian Peninsula than today. Rivers flowed across the Peninsula and drained into what is now the Arabian Gulf. These rivers flowed through what are today the major wadis such as Wādī Dawāsir, Wādī Sarḥān, and Wādī al-Bāṭin. Wādī al-Sahbāʾ is one of these old river drainage systems and has three tributaries — Wādī Ḥanīfah, Wādī Nisāḥ, and Wādī Birk. These tributaries join to form Wādī al-Sahbāʾ in the area of modern al-Kharj. The river ran from here eastwards all the way to the basin of the modern Arabian Gulf. There was a shifting delta near modern Ḥaraḍ, where there is a wide alluvial plain. South-east of Ḥaraḍ, the wadi continues into the Jāfūrah Desert to longitude *c.*51° E. The slope of Wādī al-Sahbāʾ varies between 1.02 m to 0.88 m per kilometre (al-Welaie 1997: 349). The old river pebbles of water-smoothed rocks from the western side of Saudi Arabia (the Arabian Shield) that washed down these rivers, can still be seen in Wādī al-Sahbāʾ today (observed by the authors in 2008). The climate is now very arid with very occasional heavy rain on high ground. Storms bring downfalls of heavy rainfall onto the Ṭuwayq Escarpment in central Arabia. This rare rainfall causes flash floods down the wadis, demonstrating the ancient drainage systems.

In several places across the Arabian Peninsula, underground aquifers used to provide so much water that it overflowed and in some places formed lakes (such as the lakes at Laylah in al-Aflāj) or even streams (such as "River Muhallim" at al-Hofuf in al-Aḥsāʾ). These oases came to support large areas of agricultural land. The area of al-Kharj is well known as one of these agricultural areas, because of the presence of significant amounts of water just below the surface of the ground. Unfortunately in modern times, most of these aquifers have been drained and the water no longer flows to the surface spontaneously. The arid climate means that there is very little rain to replenish the aquifers.

Wādī al-Sahbāʾ would at times have experienced both of these phenomena. Flash floods from rain on the Ṭuwayq Escarpment would have washed down the wadi, possibly even as far as Sabkhat Muṭṭī, between Saudi Arabia and the UAE, south of Qatar. Wādī al-Sahbāʾ also sits on a large aquifer, which still provides water to farms, although today this water is pumped up from below the ground. There are also old wells in certain places along the wadi.

Wādī al-Sahbāʾ: archaeology

In autumn and winter 2008 we conducted an archaeological survey of Wādī Ḥanīfah, Wādī Nisāḥ, al-Kharj district, and Wādī al-Sahbāʾ. The third tributary, Wādī Birk, runs west to east through the Ṭuwayq

Escarpment some distance south of Wādī Nisāḥ and then turns north towards al-Kharj. It was not surveyed. However, examination of the wadi online on Google Earth suggests that it contains many burial mounds and stone structures on elevated ground, similar to Wādī Nisāḥ. Sites were sampled for recording from Wādī Ḥanīfah, Wādī Nisāḥ, and al-Kharj district, where the survey methodology was to gain an understanding of the types of archaeological sites present in those areas and their approximate density, rather than to conduct a comprehensive archaeological survey. These areas have been comprehensively surveyed by the Antiquities Department of Saudi Arabia and King Saud University and reports on these surveys have been published in *Atlal: The Journal of Saudi Arabian Archaeology*. However, all the archaeological sites found in our survey of Wādī al-Sahbāʾ were recorded in detail, since this area forms the core of the research for this paper.

Wādī Ḥanīfah

Wādī Ḥanīfah runs in a roughly north-west to south-east direction from north of Riyadh, through the western edge of the city and joins Wādī Nisāḥ just west of the city of al-Kharj. It has been subjected to extensive development in recent decades and more than 100 km through the city of Riyadh are currently being landscaped to develop it as a recreational park for the city's inhabitants. As a result, many of the archaeological sites have been damaged and/or destroyed. About half of the sites recorded in the wadi in the surveys of the Riyadh region in 1994 (al-Hamud 2000) and 1997 (al-Shuwaish *et al.* 2001) could not be located or had been extensively damaged in 2008. The majority of sites in this wadi date from the Islamic period, and are either settlements or watchtowers. Some of the ubiquitous stone structures found on elevated ground in many parts of Saudi Arabia were noted on the high ground on either side of the wadi. These are predominantly burial mounds and "tails" (stone features either stand alone or attached to a mound of stone, resembling a wall or wedge of varying length and height) and probably are mostly pre-Islamic in date. The stone structures are scattered and appear in small numbers over a wide area. No large concentrations of mounds were noted from Wādī Ḥanīfah.

Wādī Nisāḥ

Wādī Nisāḥ is a large wadi running mostly west to east about 50 km south of the city of Riyadh. The majority of sites recorded in this wadi are stone structures such as burial mounds and "tails". These are scattered on the mountains to the north and south of the wadi, but they also occur in large numbers on certain hills in the wadi. Most of the mounds are carefully constructed of slabs of the local, brown, weathered limestone laid in layered courses, while some are more jumbled piles of rock. There are also ring walls around some structures. The mounds vary in size from about 2 m in diameter and about 80 cm high, to 11 m in diameter with a height of up to 2 m (see Fig. 4). "Tails" in this area seem to have been used for burials and contain chambers, usually at one end. They are often wedge-shaped. Mounds and tails often occur in the same areas. In one place we found a mound placed over the end of a tail, overlapping it and slightly off to one side. This implies that here the tail is earlier than the mound, although this may not necessarily apply to other mounds and tails (Fig. 5).

We also found one rock painting in a rock shelter, depicting a palm tree and an ibex (Fig 6). Rock art is rare in this area because the type of rock is not good for engraving, hence the use of some kind of paint. Rock paintings are also fairly rare in Saudi Arabia. The cave itself shows evidence of human activity and excavation of this site might provide useful information. Wādī Nisāḥ debouches into the western area of al-Kharj. It provides a wide east–west corridor that was in the past clearly used as a route to the west from al-Kharj. The presence of watchtowers at regular intervals along Wādī Nisāḥ indicates this use during the Islamic period. The archaeological evidence therefore suggests that Wādī Nisāḥ was widely used during both the Islamic and pre-Islamic periods.

Al-Kharj district

Al-Kharj district has been a centre of settlement for thousands of years because of the availability of water. In al-Kharj this water is mostly available from solutional-collapse holes in the limestone and other sediments, which used to be filled with water coming up to the surface from the underlying aquifer at a depth of about 450 m. It was the centre of the historic kingdom of al-Yamāmah, but before that, there is evidence of settlement in the Hellenistic period and even earlier (Zarins *et al.* 1979). There is evidence of extensive mound fields in this area, situated on particular hills. Zarins *et al.* (1979: 23) recorded over 700 mounds "scattered along a prominent ridgeline, slopes and interior of a plateau overlooking Wadi Kharj", as well as several other mound fields. We

Wadi	GPS Site#	Site type	Dimensions (m)	Elevation (m)	Northing (deg., min., sec.)	Easting (deg., min., sec.)
Kharj	207	1 burial mound		451.1	24°12' 31.968"	47°11'46.860"
Kharj	208	1 burial mound, 1 tail		479.1	24°12'28.728"	47°11'37.428"
Kharj	209	3 burial mounds	1×0.8×0.9, 0.8×0.6×0.9, 1×0.7×0.9	474.9	24°12'48.384"	47°11'26.340"
Kharj	210	1 burial mound	5×5×2	488.6	24°12'47.700"	47°11'24.576"
Kharj	211	1 burial mound	2 m high	516	24°12'52.344"	47°10'53.040"
Kharj	212	1 tail	27×1.5	519.7	24°12'52.560"	47°10'44.580"
Kharj	214	1 burial mound		529.7	24°12'55.152"	47°10'42.888"
Kharj	215	1 burial mound		522.1	24°12'54.684"	47°10'43.608"
Sahba	224	?hearth		229.5	23°51'56.16"	49°26'57.804"
Sahba	224	?grave	1.5×2 m	229.5	23°51'56.16"	49°26'57.804"
Sahba	224	?grave	1.5×2 m	229.5	23°51'56.16"	49°26'57.804"
Sahba	225	Islamic grave	1.5×2 m	236.8	23°52'58.62"	49°20'36.78"
Sahba	225	mihrab		236.8	23°52'58.62"	49°20'36.78"
Nisah	245	4 burial mounds, 1 tail	5×5×2, 8×1	677.9	24°12'45.648"	46°28'46.128"
Nisah	247	1 burial mound, 1 tail	5×5×0.5, 15×1	675.1	24°13'46.92"	46°28'40.584"
Nisah	248	1 burial mound, 1 tail	4×4×1, 12×0.8	691.3	24°14'57.696"	46°29'17.016"
Nisah	249	1 burial mound	2×2×1	674.8	24°14'57.012"	46°29'18.528"
Nisah	250	1 burial mound	5×5×1.5	677.3	24°14'57.12"	46°29'21.516"
Nisah	254	1 burial mound		714.1	24°14'59.172"	46°29'25.656"
Nisah	255	1 burial mound	2.5×2.5×1	686.7	24°14'58.956"	46°29'29.292"
Nisah	258	2 burial mounds	7×7×1, 4.5×4.5×1	662.3	24°14'47.328"	46°36'23.004"
Nisah	259	1 burial mound	5×5×1	667.5	24°14'46.176"	46°36'21.384"
Nisah	260	1 burial mound, 1 tail	5×5×0.8, 3	660.5	24°14'46.68"	46°36'13.428"
Nisah	261	1 burial mound	5×5×2	680	24°14'52.26"	46°36'9.396"
Nisah	262	1 burial mound	2.5×2.5×1	682.8	24°14'57.048"	46°36'13.212"
Nisah	263	1 tail	44×0.3	654.1	24°15'1.512"	46°36'7.704"
Nisah	265	2 burial mounds		676.4	24°14'51.144"	46°36'10.8
Nisah	266	1 burial mound	3×3×1.5	664.2	24°14'46.032"	46°36'27.432"
Nisah	267	1 burial mound, 1 tail	10 m long	667.2	24°14'46.176"	46°36'27.792"
Nisah	268	1 burial mound	6×6×1	689.8	24°14'41.928"	46°36'39.996"
Nisah	274	1 burial mound		703.2	24°14'44.988"	46°36'51.264"
Nisah	275	2 tails	4.5 m long	677.3	24°14'47.616"	46°36'55.008"
Nisah	277	1 burial mound		664.8	24°14'48.048"	46°36'55.584"
Nisah	278	1 burial mound		658.1	24°14'48.84"	46°36'56.664"
Nisah	279	1 burial mound		660.5	24°14'49.02"	46°36'56.808"
Nisah	280	2 burial mounds, 1 tail	5×5×0.7, 2×2×1.2, 5 m long	658.7	24°14'31.632"	46°37'11.64"
Nisah	282	1 burial mound	11×11×1	638.3	24°15'17.46"	46°41'8.52"
Nisah	283	1 burial mound	3×3×0.9	636.7	24°15'13.716"	46°41'11.616"
Nisah	284	1 tail	5.5×1.2	630.9	24°15'13.284"	46°41'13.776"
Nisah	285	1 burial mound	6×6×0.8	632.2	24°15'13.104"	46°41'13.92"

FIGURE 4. *Sites surveyed in 2008.*

Figure 5. *Burial mounds and "tail" overlooking Wādī Nisāḥ.*

were able to relocate two of these mound fields, one of which is protected by an Antiquities Department fence, the other is not. The mounds in these mound fields are very similar to those in Wādī Nisāḥ. Tails are also found among the mounds. Zarins *et al.* (1979) also identified Hellenistic settlements and irrigation systems (sing. *qanāt* pl. *qanawāt*). Some of these can still be seen in satellite images and we were able to find some still existing on the ground, and even a few sherds of Hellenistic pottery. This archaeological evidence suggests that the area of al-Kharj was an important agricultural and settlement centre from at least the Hellenistic period and probably earlier, right through into the Islamic period.

Wādī al-Sahbāʾ

Wādī al-Sahbāʾ (Fig. 7) originates in the al-Kharj area, at the confluence of Wādī Ḥanīfaḥ, Wādī Nisāḥ, and Wādī Birk. The western half of Wādī al-Sahbāʾ is under extensive agriculture today, irrigated by water pumped up from the underlying aquifer. The wadi disappears beneath the sands to the south-east of Ḥaraḍ, but originally ran east down to Sabkhat Muṭṭī (a salt flat) and then into what is now the Arabian Gulf. The wadi is low and flat with slightly raised terraces along its banks, marked by water-rolled cobblestones, many of exotic raw materials from the Arabian Shield to the west. The course of the wadi is marked by relatively significant amounts of vegetation, mostly in the form of low bushes of hardy plants. When compared to the arid sand dunes and gravel plains around the wadi, this is a significant source of vegetation. Thomas (1932), in his account of crossing the Rubᶜ al-Khālī (Empty Quarter) in 1930–1931, refers to the critical importance of grazing for the camels when crossing large tracts of desert. He stresses that vegetation was more important than water for the camels. The line of vegetation between low banks also provides an easy marked trail through the barren desert, which would have greatly aided navigation through the desert. The wadi was also a source of water from the frequent wells situated along it. Although we did not find any archaeological evidence of these wells, they are marked on old maps.

Figure 6. *A rock shelter with a rock painting showing a detail of a palm tree and an ibex, Wādī Nisāḥ.*

Figure 7. *The southern bank of Wādī al-Sahbāʾ, looking east.*

Figure 8. *Wādī al-Sahbāʾ, GPS Site 225, with a possible Islamic grave.*

Due to difficulties of access and the size of the area (Wādī al-Sahbāʾ is over 400 km long), only a basic survey was conducted of Wādī al-Sahbāʾ and the surrounding area. Sample areas were surveyed from both banks and the course of the wadi. The presence of farms and settlements in the western half of the wadi restricted access. The confluence of Wādī Nisāḥ, Wādī Ḥanīfaḥ, and Wādī Birk and the first part of Wādī al-Sahbāʾ, lie under the city of al-Kharj, and the main road east from al-Kharj, towards Ḥaraḍ and the UAE, follows the Wādī al-Sahbāʾ for the first 100 km or so through the Dahnāʾ dunes. These factors have affected the presence of possible archaeological sites and also our ability to survey in these areas. In the eastern part of the wadi, the movement of barchan dunes may have covered archaeological sites within the wadi. The survey conducted was therefore not a comprehensive survey and other archaeological evidence may exist. However, the sample areas surveyed and the impression gained by travelling along most of the length of the wadi, gave us an idea of the nature of the archaeological sites in this wadi.

There is relatively little archaeological evidence within Wādī al-Sahbāʾ itself and there is nothing like the density of sites in Wādī Ḥanīfaḥ, Wādī Nisāḥ, and the al-Kharj region. We did not find any burial mounds or mound fields. Some arrangements of cobblestones suggest graves or hearths, but they are few. Two arrangements of stones were found, about 1.5 to 2 m long, oriented north–south. These are possibly graves (Fig. 8). Another possibly Islamic grave was found, oriented north-east, near a stone alignment marking the direction of Mecca. This marks the direction in a place for prayer (mihrab) for a small group of people (Fig. 9). A couple of possible hearths were found, and near them a very few, scrappy worked chert flakes were also found. One would not expect large amounts of archaeological material on caravan routes between settlements. People were travelling through, camping overnight (or during the day, depending on the season) and continuing on their way immediately. They would have made hearths for cooking or warmth in the winter months (when overnight, desert temperatures can drop below 0°C) and occasionally someone might

Figure 9. *Wādī al-Sahbāʾ, GPS Site 225,* mihrab.

die and need burial. Someone might lose an item or opportunistically make a flake or two for immediate use for cutting. The sparse archaeological evidence that we found is therefore not incompatible with the use of Wādī al-Sahbāʾ as a caravan route between the Gulf coast to the east and the important centre of al-Kharj, which linked on in turn to the west and Mecca.

Wādī al-Sahbāʾ in historical sources

The route between al-Yamāmah and the coast of the Arabian Gulf, usually passing through al-Aḥsāʾ or al-Hofuf, is well known and mentioned in many historical sources. Ibn Baṭṭuṭah travelled this route in 1331 on his way to perform hajj in Mecca. Hamadānī mentions walking through al-Sahbāʾ to reach Ḥaḍrama (al-Yamāmah) (Bin Khamees 1980). However, detailed descriptions of the routes were seldom given. As Potts (1988) has argued, in many areas of Arabia, trade routes did not follow clearly defined paths, like roads, but generally passed through an area. Different stopping places might be used, perhaps due to differences in the availability of water or vegetation for the camels at different times of the year. However, in some places the nature of the terrain meant that one route was used more frequently than others. The crossing of the Dahnāʾ dunes provides one such obstacle. Wādī al-Sahbāʾ provides one of the best and shortest east–west crossing points through the Dahnāʾ dunes in this barren and harsh landscape.

Palgrave (1908) emphasized that there was only one safe way to cross the Dahnāʾ in his account of his own journey through this area on his way to al-Qaṭīf in 1862–1863. It is clear from Palgrave's map and from clues in his description of the journey, that he and his companions travelled along Wādī al-Sahbāʾ as far as "El Shabeh", which they made a detour to reach, before turning north to al-Hofuf (Fig. 10). Later communications between Palgrave (1864*a*; 1864*b*) and Badger (1864) concerning Palgrave's route and the "River Aftan" refer to descriptions by the twelfth-century geographer and cartographer, al-Idrīsī, concerning the "El-ᶜArdh" or "Wadi Aftan", which "divides El-Yemamah from top to bottom" (Badger 1864: 100), although al-Idrīsī seems to have been describing a region of villages and plantations rather than a watercourse or route. No other Arabic sources seem to have used the name "Aftan".

Why a river?

Although it has not flowed as a river in human times, Wādī al-Sahbā᾽ was a source of water. In places this water actually ran on the surface of the ground. In al-Kharj, Lorimer (1976) describes a stream running from one of the solutional-collapse holes, which actually continued for several miles. Although not part of Wādī al-Sahbā᾽, the section of the "River Aftan", drawn between al-Hofuf and the Arabian Gulf, probably recalls the streams of overflow water ("River Muhallim") from the aquifer under al-Hofuf that ran above the ground through this area until the recent past (Al Shaikh 2004). According to Lorimer (1976), in the early twentieth century people stated that, during times of flash flooding, water would sometimes run down Wādī Ḥanīfah to Wādī Nisāḥ and reach as far as the Dahnā᾽ desert (Wādī al-Sahbā᾽). Heavy rain, causing flash floods, can make the wadis run like rivers, sometimes for several days. Wādī al-Sahbā᾽ may have been drawn on old maps as a river after an account by someone who had seen a flash flood running through it like a river.

However, even during times without rain, Wādī al-Sahbā᾽ was an area where aquifer water was available not very far below the surface. It was relatively easy to reach this water by digging wells, and the water at no great distance below the surface meant that vegetation grew along the course of the wadi. Wādī al-Sahbā᾽ might have been marked as a river because people stated that there was water there, along the whole course of the wadi. This might be interpreted in Europe as a river.

The wadi also sheltered the vegetation that grew there and being the lowest land, was where water lingered longest after the infrequent rains. As Thomas (1932) stressed, it was vegetation that was critical for the camels when crossing desert. They could go without water for several days, as could the people with them, by drinking milk from the camels and carrying stores of water, but the camels could not go without grazing. In Thomas's (1932) account of his crossing of the Rubᶜ al-Khālī in 1931–1932 (the first recorded crossing by a European), he eloquently describes how it was grazing for the camels that determined their route and how desperate the search for adequate grazing was in those barren lands. The major wadis with their relatively plentiful vegetation were, therefore, critical to people crossing the desert

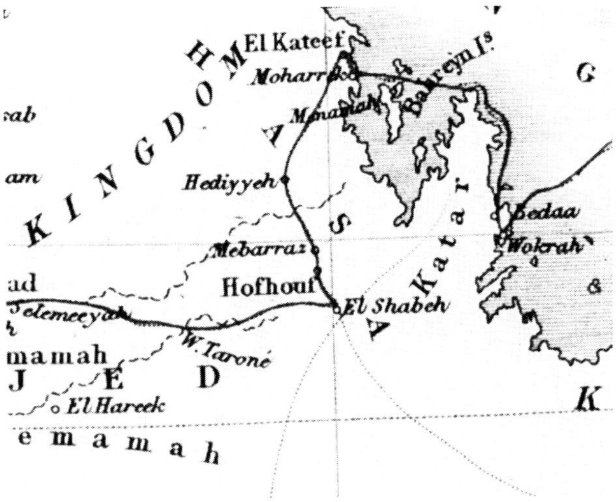

Figure 10. *Detail of Palgrave's route, "1865, Map of Arabia shewing the routes of W.G. Palgrave Esq. in 1862–3, Royal Geographical Society, London" (al-Qasimi 1999: 272).*

with camels. The vegetation would also have attracted other animals to graze, and these animals would have provided a welcome source of meat to supplement the diet of the people travelling with the caravans. Wādī al-Sahbā᾽ not only has vegetation, it also runs in exactly the right direction to facilitate travel from the east towards central Arabia and the west. It is therefore also possible that Wādī al-Sahbā᾽ was drawn as a river because it was a passage for transport and a communication route across the eastern part of Arabia. In Europe those functions were often borne by rivers, and thus a valley used for transport and as a line of communication might be interpreted as a river by Europeans who had not seen it.

One further clue to the use of the term "river" is provided by a debate held in the Proceedings of the Royal Geographical Society of London in 1864. On 22 February 1864, Palgrave presented a paper to the Royal Geographical Society in which he described his journeys though Arabia in 1862–1823 (1864*a*). One of the gentlemen in the audience was the Reverend G.P. Badger (who later travelled through Arabia). Badger asked a series of questions of Palgrave concerning the "Wadi Aftan" (Badger 1864). Palgrave replied that the name was almost unknown, referring to "the valleys known as the Wadi Farouk, Ghour, Ghöweir, and part of the Dahna" (Palgrave 1864*b*: 103). Badger (1864: 100) had suggested that, according to al-Idrīsī, the "Wadi Aftan" was "synonymous with "El-ᶜArdh". This is supported by a map of Arabia dated 1734, which marks the "al Ard or Aftan River" running north–south past al-Yamāmah. Badger (1864: 100) includes a footnote stating that the Latin translation of al-Idrīsī by Gabriel Sionita included a marginal note concerning the "El-ᶜArdh" that read "i.e. Flumen". It is therefore possible that the Latin word *flumen,* meaning river, perhaps the closest approximation the translator could achieve for the Arabic term, *wadi*, may have led later scholars and map-makers to refer to the "River Aftan". The use of the word "river" may therefore be purely a problem resulting from translation. Nevertheless, the importance of the "Aftan" (or "al-ᶜArdh") as a landmark in historic times, whether it is a river or wadi, cannot be disputed.

Conclusion

We can therefore conclude that the Wādī al-Sahbāʾ lies in approximately the right area and orientation to be the geographic feature marked as the "River Aftan" on old maps of Arabia, between the Gulf coast and the area of al-Kharj. It is probable that trade and hajj routes through this part of Arabia used this wadi, or part of it, for travel, particularly as an easy route of access through the desolate Dahnāʾ dunes and a corridor opening up travel between the East and the West. The archaeology of the wadi, while relatively sparse in itself, is not incompatible with use of this wadi as a caravan route. The significant amount of archaeological material in the area of al-Kharj and its surrounding wadis shows that this area was important, with sizeable populations over thousands of years. It seems likely that trade routes between this important region and the Gulf stretch back to at least the second or third millennium BC, given the number and nature of the burial mounds in the region. We should therefore re-examine the origins of overland trade within the Arabian Peninsula, which was clearly not confined to the first millennium BC and later periods.

Acknowledgements

We would like to acknowledge the assistance of the Committee of the Seminar of Arabian Studies in helping us to attend the Seminar at the British Museum in July 2009 in order to present this paper. We would also like to thank H.H. Sheikh Dr Sultan bin Muhammad al-Qasimi and the Centre for Gulf Studies in Sharjah, United Arab Emirates; Dr A.S. al-Ghazzi for providing us with a copy of his PhD thesis; Dr A.A. al-Majed, Director of Research, Center for Petroleum and Minerals; King Fahd University of Petroleum and Minerals and staff of the Remote Sensing Laboratory for help with maps; and our friends who accompanied us on surveying trips into the desert.

References

Badger G.P.
1864. Communication on Mr. Palgrave's Paper. *Proceedings of the Royal Geographical Society of London* 8/3: 97–103.

Bin Khamees A.M.
1980. *Dictionary of al-Yamāmah, The Geographic Dictionary of the Kingdom of Saudi Arabia*. i. (Second edition). Riyadh: Maṭbaᶜat al-Farazdaq al-Tijāriyyah [in Arabic].

Carter R.
2006. Boat remains and maritime trade in the Persian Gulf during the sixth and fifth millennia BC. *Antiquity* 80: 52–63.

al-Ghazzi A.S.
1990. A Comparative Study of Pottery from a Site in the Al-Kharj Valley, central Arabia. PhD thesis, Institute of Archaeology, University College, London. [Unpublished].

al-Hamud M.S.
2000. A Preliminary Report on the Archaeological and Historical Sites Survey in the City of Riyadh and its Vicinity 1414 H, 1994 A.D. *Atlal* 15: 116–176 [English Section]; 125–185 [Arabic Section].

Ibn Baṭṭūṭah
1992. *The Journey of Ibn Baṭṭūṭah*. Beirut: Dar Sader Press. [In Arabic].

Lorimer J.G.
1976. *Gazetteer of the Persian Gulf, Oman and Central Arabia*. ii. *Geography*. Parts 2 and 3 (Second edition). Doha: Ali Bin Ali Press. [In Arabic].

McClure H.A. & Al Shaikh N.Y.
1993. Paleogeography of an Ubaid archaeological site, Saudi Arabia. *Arabian archaeology and epigraphy* 4: 107–125.
Magee P.
2004. The impact of southeast Arabian intra-regional trade on settlement location and organization during the Iron Age II period. *Arabian archaeology and epigraphy* 15: 24–42.
Palgrave W.G.
1864*a*. Notes of a Journey from Gaza, through the interior of Arabia, to El Khatif on the Persian Gulf, and thence to Oman, in 1862–63. *Proceedings of the Royal Geographical Society of London* 8/3: 63–82.
1864*b*. Reply to Queries of the Rev. G.P. Badger. *Proceedings of the Royal Geographical Society of London* 8/3: 103–105.
1908. *Personal Narrative of a Year's Journey Through Central and Eastern Arabia (1862–1863)*. ii. London: Macmillan.
Potts D.T.
1988. Trans-Arabian Routes of the Pre-Islamic Period. Pages 127–162 in J.F. Salles (ed.), *L'Arabie et ses mers bordières*. Lyon: Travaux de la Maison de l'Orient.
1990. *The Arabian Gulf in Antiquity*. (2 volumes). Oxford: Clarendon Press.
1993. Rethinking Some Aspects of Trade in the Arabian Gulf. *World Archaeology* 24: 423–440.
2001. Before the Emirates: An Archaeological and Historical Account of Developments in the Region *c.*5000 BC to 676 AD. Pages 28–69 in E.I. Al Abed & P. Hellyer (eds), *United Arab Emirates: A new perspective*. London: Trident Press.
al-Qasimi, (Sheikh Sultan) bin M.
1996. *The Gulf in Historic Maps 1478–1931*. United Arab Emirates: H.H. Sultan bin Muhammad al-Qasimi.
1999. *The Gulf in Historic Maps 1478–1861*. (Second edition). United Arab Emirates: H.H. Sultan bin Muhammad al-Qasimi.
Reeler C.N., Al Shaikh N.Y & Potts D.T.
2009. An Historical cartographic study of the Yabrīn Oasis (Saudi Arabia). *Proceedings of the Seminar for Arabian Studies* 39: 353–360.
al-Saud A.S.
1996. The Domestication of Camels and Inland Trading Routes in Arabia. *Atlal* 14: 129–136 [English Section]; 99–104 [Arabic Section].
1997. *Central Arabia during the Hellenistic period*. Riyadh: King Fahd National Library.
Al Shaikh N.Y.
2004. The Eastern Province in Prehistoric Times. *Al-Waha* 33: 6–21. [In Arabic].

al-Shuwaish S.F., al-Salook M.A., Eskoubi K.M., al-Hamoud M.S., al-Hammad A., al-Showaiti M. & al-Helwa S.
2001. Report on the Archaeological Survey of Ar-Riyadh Region. Second Season 1417 AH/1997 AD. *Atlal* 16: 29–49 [English Section]; 75–98 [Arabic Section].
al-Thenayian M.A.R.
1999. *An Archaeological Study of the Yemen Highland Pilgrim Route between Sana'a and Mecca*. Riyadh: Deputy Ministry of Antiquities and Museums.
Thomas B.
1932. *Arabia Felix. Across the Empty Quarter of Arabia*. London: Jonathan Cape.
Uerpmann M.
2001. Remarks on the animal economy of Tell Abraq (Emirates of Sharjah and Umm al-Qaywayn, UAE). *Proceedings of the Seminar for Arabian Studies* 31: 227–233.
Uerpmann H-P. & Uerpmann M.
2002. The Appearance of the Domesticated Camel in South-East Arabia. *Journal of Oman Studies* 12: 235–260.

al-Welaie A.N.
1997. *Geology and Geomorphology of the Kingdom of Saudi Arabia (the shape of the landforms of the Earth)*. Riyadh: King Fahd Library Press. [In Arabic].

Zarins J., Ibrahim M., Potts D. & Edens C.
1979. Saudi Arabian Archaeological Reconnaissance 1978. The Preliminary Report on the Third Phase of the Comprehensive Archaeological Survey Program — The Central Province. *Atlal* 3: 9–42 [English Section]; 9–47 [Arabic Section].

Authors' addresses

Nabiel Y. Al Shaikh, Saudi Commission for Tourism & Antiquities, Dammam Regional Museum, Saudi Arabia, PO Box 40227, Hamad Town, Bahrain.

e-mail nabielalshaikh@gmail.com

Claire N. Reeler, Saudi Commission for Tourism & Antiquities, Riyadh, PO Box 250305, Riyadh, 11391, Saudi Arabia.

e-mail cl.reeler@gmail.com

Proceedings of the Seminar for Arabian Studies 40 (2010): 337–344

Irrigation management in pre-Islamic South Arabia according to the epigraphic evidence

Peter Stein

Summary
Within the huge irrigation systems in Ancient South Arabia, the correct allocation of water to each single field was a task of great responsibility. A number of Sabaic inscriptions from the Jawf provide us with some details of the duties of water management in the irrigation system of a water flow (*ġyl*) named Hirrān in the vicinity of the ancient cities of Nas²qum and Nas²s²an. As we learn from these texts, this task was performed by a special office called *qdmt* (approx. "supervision"). The holders of this office, named *ʾqdmt* "chief managers, supervisors", were recruited from several Sabaean clans by rotation. Even though its mode of operation, duration of tenure, and appointing authority still remain obscure, the main character and duties of this office can already be established with the present epigraphic evidence.

Keywords: Ancient South Arabian inscriptions, irrigation management, water allocation, dealing with water, supervisor

Introduction

Flood-water or *sayl* irrigation using dams, canals and distribution devices is one of the basic features of agriculture in pre-Islamic Yemen. As is well known, this type of agriculture helped form the basis of the flourishing civilization in the oases along the desert fringe in northern and eastern Yemen. Remains of sedimented fields as well as irrigation devices have survived up to the present, testifying to the immense efforts that were undertaken in the past to keep these systems alive. By far the most impressive remains of such an irrigation system are certainly those of Maʾrib, covering an area of almost 10,000 ha. Another means of irrigation in Yemen, ancient and modern, includes using spring flow (Arabic *ghayl*, cf. Sabaic *ġyl* "water-course; conduit, covered channel, ghayl", Beeston *et al.* 1982: 54f.). One characteristic of this method is that the water is not led directly from the source onto the fields but rather stored in basins first, in order to allow a well-balanced distribution to the land of each participant in the system.[1]

One of the main characteristics of both systems is the fact that many, if not all, participants in the system are dependent on one and the same source, namely the main canal that leads the water out of the source, be it a cistern or the bed of a wadi. From this main canal, a complicated system of subsequent canals is needed to distribute the water onto each individual field. The important issue is to ensure that even the last, most remote field in this succession will be provided with a sufficient amount of water, even in the rather large and complicated structure that is the extended oasis of Maʾrib. This task requires not only a highly elaborate technology but also a strictly organized management.[2] In short, there must be reliable personnel who are responsible for the correct allocation of each portion of water to the appropriate field. The office of chief administrator of irrigation is mentioned in a number of Sabaic inscriptions, not from Maʾrib but from the oasis of Nas²s²ān in the western part of the Wādī al-Jawf. Some of these texts have already been known for some time; their particular relevance to the context in question has, however, been identified only recently with the help of two Sabaic letters in minuscule script.

Discussion of the epigraphic evidence

These two letters are found among the collection of minuscule inscriptions in the Bavarian State library in Munich (X.BSB 121 and 122) and thus originate from the presumed archive in the city of Nas²s²ān (present-day

[1] For a general evaluation of both types of irrigation, see Varisco 1983. I am very much indebted to Janet Starkey for having drawn my attention to this paper.

[2] This can also be concluded from the well-documented Islamic history of Yemen up to the present, where different institutions of supervision can be observed, see also Varisco 1983.

al-Sawdāʾ).[3] On the basis of palaeographic and historical comparison, both texts may be dated to about the late second or early third century AD.[4] Since their contents are more or less similar, we may confine our investigation on the first-mentioned X.BSB 121 which is, in contrast to the latter, almost completely preserved.

X.BSB 121 = Mon.script.sab. 557[5]

Text

Recto:

1. *l-ʾqdmt / ġyln / hrn / ḏ-ḫrf / w-*
2. *b$^{?}$n / s^{1}ʿdm$^{?}$ / ʿm-n / whbʾwm / bn / s^{2}*
3. *llm / w-ʾntmw / f-htlynn$^{?}$ / w-h*
4. *qdḥ$^{?}$n / s^{1}ʿdṯwn / bn / gdnm / s^{1}*
5. *dṯy$^{?}$ / (m)frʿtm / tlym / bn / mw*
6. *y / bn / s^{2}llm / b-s^{2}tyn / w-ʾl / th*
7. *ʿlmnn-hw / b-s^{2}ʾmn / w-bḍʿn / k-*

Verso:

8. *ʿ$^{?}$l$^{?}$hn / hʿl$^{?}$m$^{?}$-hw / w-kwnt / ḏt / ṭ*
9. *bytn / b-wrḫ / ḏ-ʾlʾlt / ḏ-ḫrf*
10. *wddʾ[l / bn / ns^{2}ʾk]rb / bn / ḥḏ*
11. *mt / ṯny<<ṯ>>n / whbṯwn* signature

Translation

1. To the supervisors of the canal Hirrān (in the time) of autumn and
2. (to) the Banū S^{1}ʿDM from WHBʾWM of (the clan)
3. S^{2}LLM. As for you, let
4. S^{1}ʿDṮWN of (the clan) GDNM continue and
5. drain off[6] 60 continuing *mfrʿ* (=unit of measure)[7] of the water
6. of the Banū S^{2}LLM during the winter season! Don't have him
7. certify the purchase and the (resulting?)[8] obligation (of this water) since
8. ʿLHN has had him certify already. This message was created
9. in the month Ḏ-ʾLʾLT of the second year
10. of (the eponym) WDDʾL, son of NS^{2}ʾKRB, of (the clan)
11. ḤḎMT. WHBṮWN (has signed).

According to the common letter formulae, we would expect the addressee at the beginning, followed, after the preposition *ʿm-n* "from", by the sender. Consequently, the noun *ʾqdmt* must represent some person here and may easily be read as a plural form of the well-known *qdm* "leader, commander"[9] or another etymologically related noun.[10] These *ʾqdmt* are the chief managers of a canal named Hirrān which is already mentioned in a monumental inscription from the neighbouring city of Nas^{2}qum (present-day al-Bayḍāʾ). This toponym has been identified by C. Robin (1994: 231) with the actual Wādī Hirrān, the lower course of which flows exactly through the oasis where the inscriptions were found, the cities of Nas^{2}qum and Nas^{2}s^{2}ān (Robin & Brunner 1997: E4).[11]

[3] For details on the Sabaic minuscule inscriptions in general, and the collection of the Bavarian State Library in particular, see the introductory chapters in Stein, (2010). An extensive commentary on the two texts in question is given there (2010: 419–426).

[4] From the palaeographic perspective, the two letters are quite close to the legal document X.BSB 58, the date of which can be synchronized with that of the Sabaean king S^{2}ʿRM ʾWTR, and which is perhaps also contemporary to X.BSB 57 and YM 11726 (Stein, 2010: 222, 226). The other important text discussed here, MAFRAY-al-Bayḍāʾ 100, was also written at the same time as this king. There seems to be no argument that would contradict a close historical connection of all the texts discussed in this paper.

[5] A palm-leaf stalk of 13.9×3.0 cm with 11 lines of inscription, dated according to an eponym about AD 200 (see n. 4). The document has been annulled by three diagonal strokes carved into the surface of the inscription. For details of the text and its support see Stein, 2010: 419–423.

[6] Translation according to the basic meaning of the roots *TLW/Y* and *QDḤ* in Arabic; for a more detailed explanation of these and other terms, see the German edition of the text (Stein, 2010: 419–421).

[7] See Ryckmans, Müller and Abdallah (1994: 60) for an interpretation of this term, the correct reading of which is affirmed by YM 11726/1 and X.BSB 122/5. According to Yemeni-Arabic *mafraʿ*, pl. *mafāriʿ*, this unit designates the amount of water which flows through a canal during a certain time span.

[8] Perhaps the water was purchased on condition that a comparable amount would be returned to the owner in a later season.

[9] See Beeston *et al.* (1982: 103) who give a plural *ʾqdm*, which is established as designating someone "responsible" or "overseers" in a definitely non-irrigational context in at least two Sabaic texts: Ko 3/1 (*ʾqdm mḥrmn* ^{2} *w-mḥfdn* "Die Vorsteher des Tempels und der Türme", thus Müller 1978: 122–123) and Rob Maš 1/13–14 (*w-ḏ-yʾs^{1}yn b-hw qn[ym]*^{13} *f-ʾw ḏ-ydrmn-hw w-ʾl yḥdṯn ʾ*^{14}*qdmn l-yhnkrn ḫms^{1} blṭm* "Whosoever finds in it (sc. the cistern) a (piece of) livestock, or knows of it, and does not tell the overseers, shall be punished by (a fine of) five *blṭt*-coins", interpreted by Anne Multhoff in a personal communication). Other instances of both *qdm* and *ʾqdm* point to a tribal or even military leadership (Müller 1978: 122–123, "Anführer") so that we have to proceed with the idea that there were two or more different offices, which may well be represented partly by a homograph, but are nevertheless morphologically distinct titles. The plural pattern *ʾfʿlt* for a singular *fʿl* in Sabaic is established by other examples, see Stein 2003: 80.

[10] Derivates of the root *QDM* are in use for designating responsible personnel up to modern times, such as the *muqaddim al-maʿyān*, the supervisor of a tunnel system, who was responsible for timing the water allocation in the town of Ghayl Bā Wazīr near al-Mukallā, as described by Hehmeyer 2005.

[11] The identification of the whole wadi with the toponym *ġyln* "der Fluß" derives from H. von Wissmann who had no knowledge of the inscriptions under discussion above (von Wissmann 1976: 316, fig. 2, and 401–402: "Ghayl von Hirrān", see also von Wissmann 1964: 347 and fig. 17: "Hirrān Ġayl Wadd").

The actual letter consists merely of one order, a request to the irrigation managers to allow a particular person named S^{1}ʿDṮWN to drain off a certain amount of water from the main canal of the irrigation system. The supervisors, or *ʾqdmt*, of that canal can thus clearly be identified with the authority that is responsible for distributing the water onto the different fields. The owner of the irrigation device, or the particular fields that are normally watered by it, is apparently not personally involved in the practical handling of this matter. Rather, he may be identified as the sender of our letter, giving orders by mail from abroad.

As the nouns *s^{2}ʾm* and *bḍʿ* in l. 7 prove, the water in question was purchased by the beneficiary S^{1}ʿDṮWN. An official document about this purchase had already been set up in the past (ll. 7–8). That water for irrigation was generally a subject for negotiation in Ancient South Arabia is known from other inscriptions as well. A legal document on wood assumed to be from the same provenance and more or less of the same date as our letter (see above, n. 4), preserved in the collection of the Yemeni National Museum in Ṣanʿāʾ and published fifteen years ago, contains exactly the required information in the context above. The text reads as follows:

YM 11726 = TYA 11[12]

Text

Recto:

1. *bḍʿ / s^{1}bʿt / w-ʾrbʿy / mfrʿtm / tlym / b*
2. *n / mwy / s^{2}tyn / ḏ-yts^{1}ynn / ʾqdmtn / bn / ʿṯk*
3. *ln / w-bn / ḥlḥlm / l-whbʾwm / bn / ʾws^{1}m / bn / bḍ*
4. *ʿ / b-ʿly-hw / l-twfy / b-hw / tʿlm / l-mlʾn / b-hyt*

Verso:

5. *qdmtn / bḍʿ / yhs^{1}bʾn / b-qdmt / bn / ʿṯkln / w-b*
6. *[n / ḥlḥl]m / b-[wr]ẖ / ḏ-s^{1}ḥr / ḏ-ẖrf / yʿqbn / ẖrf / ʾbkrb / b*
7. *n / ḥywm / bn / ḥzfrm / w-kwn / ḏn / ʾs^{1}m[ʿn] / b-wrẖ / ḏ-hwbs^1 / ḏ-m-ḏ*
8. *n / ẖ[r]fn*

Translation

1. The amount of 47 continuing *mfrʿ* (=unit of measure)
2. of the water of the winter season, which the supervisors, (namely) the Banū ʿṮKLN
3. and the Banū ḤLḤLM, guarantee[13] to WHBʾWM of (the clan) ʾWS^{1}M, (i.e. part) of the total
4. which is (encumbering) upon him due to the (obligation of) fulfilment that he has signed to fulfil in that
5. (turn of the) *qdmt*-office, the total he is going to contribute (lit.: to let flow) in the *qdmt*-office of the Banū ʿṮKLN and
6. the Banū ḤLḤLM in the month Ḏ-S^{1}ḤR of the year which follows the year of (the eponym) ʾBKRB, son
7. of ḤYWM, of (the clan) ḤZFRM. This attestation was created in the month Ḏ-HWBS^1 of the very same year.

This legal document states that a certain individual (named WHBʾWM) had signed an obligation to contribute a certain amount of water during the running irrigation season (ll. 3–6). It should be emphasized that this obligation must have been certified on another document some time in the past. With the present document, the supervisors of the irrigation system gave this person due rights to make use of the same amount of water in the winter season (*s^{2}tyn*) in a subsequent year (ll. 1–3). The office of these supervisors, which is called *qdmt* according to l. 5 of the present text,[14] was without doubt endowed with a high responsibility.

The considerable burden that rested on the shoulders of a supervisor becomes evident in the third inscription to be presented here. This text, a dedication to ʾLMQH, lord of S^{2}BʿN, the main deity of the city of Nas^{2}qum, was written during the reign of the Sabaean kings S^{2}ʿRM ʾWTR and his brother ḤYWʿṮTR YḌʿ (as mentioned in ll. 17–18) and is thus more or less contemporary with the texts mentioned above. In view of what we have already discussed, the relevant passages of this text may be read and translated as follows:

[12] Published in Ryckmans, Müller and Abdallah (1994: 59–61, 94–95 pl. 11/A–B). The following interpretation, however, differs somewhat from that given in the publication.

[13] The verb form in line 2, read *ytsʿnn* "(ils) accordent libéralement" by the editors, is surely to be identified as the verb *wsy* T_1 meaning "to guarantee" (in the sense of promising a [re]payment in future), as is attested in quite a number of legal documents (e.g. X.BSB 58 / 1, see Stein, 2010: 225–226).

[14] Ryckmans, Müller and Abdallah (1994: 60) translate the word as "allocation (d'eau)"; they mix, however, the form *qdmt* with the plural *ʾqdmt* in line 2 which is, as we have seen, the plural of another noun designating the holder of this office.

MAFRAY-al-Bayḏāʾ 100[15]

Text

1. *ḥywm / ʾ$^?$[ẖ]ṭr / bn / ʿṯ[k]*
2. *ln / w-glwm / hqny / ʾlm*
3. *[q]h / bʿl / s^2bʿn / ḏn / ṯwrn / ḥmdm / b-*
4. *[ḏ]t / s^1twfy / qdmt / ġyln / hrn*
5. *b$^?$-qdmt [/] t$^?$qdm / l-byt-hmw / b-ʿm / [b]*
6. *n / ḥlḥl$^?$m / b-ḫrf / mʿdkrb / bn / ʾ*
7. *bkrb / bn / kbr-ḫl[l] / ṯnyn / w-ẖ*
8. *[m]r / bʿl / s^2bʿn / s^1tʿḏ$^?$b$^?$n / ġyln [/ h]*
9. *[r]n / w-s^1twfyn / kl / ʾṯmr / hwt / s^2*
10. *[t]yn / bn / kl / qmlt<<x>>m / w-ʾtw / hʾ*
11. *nʾdm / … …*

Translation

1. ḤYWM ʾẖṬR of (the clan) ʿṮKLN
2. and GLWM has dedicated to ʾLMQH,
3. lord of S^2BʿN, this bull in praise for (the fact)
4. that he was preserved (from misfortune in) the *qdmt*-office[16] of the canal Hirrān,
5. (namely) in (the turn of) the *qdmt*-office he was in charge of on behalf of their house (i.e. the Banū ʿṮKLN) together with
6. the Banū ḤLḤLM in the second year of (the eponym) MʿDKRB, son of
7. ʾBKRB, of (the clan) KBR ḪLL. And
8. the lord of S^2BʿN has vouchsafed the canal Hirrān being repaired,[17]
9. all the fruits of that winter[18] being preserved
10. from any louse attack, and it (i.e. that winter flood) coming
11. abundantly. … …

[15] The text was published by Robin (1994: 230–232) with a photograph on p. 247. Based on a different interpretation of the keyword *qdmt* in line 4 (see the following note), his interpretation of the whole matter is therefore quite different from ours.

[16] This interpretation was already proposed by C. Robin in a preliminary commentary on the inscription referred to by Beeston (1988: 33 "office of overseer"). In the actual publication of the text, however, Robin had recourse to the translation "conflit, affrontement" or even "procès", obviously drawn from the verb *tqdm* "confront, do battle with someone" (thus Beeston *et al.* 1982: 103), without any further discussion (Robin 1994: 231).

[17] The infinitive *s^1tʿḏb* is interpreted as a passive of the verb *hʿḏb* "to repair, put in order" (thus Beeston *et al.* 1982: 12), as attested in C 338/14=Gr 173/11 and J 542/2.

[18] The reading *s^2*[10]*[t]yn* "winter" in ll. 9–10, already suggested by Sima (2000: 130 with n. 460), is confirmed by the parallel YM 11726/2.

In this inscription, the author expresses his gratitude for having successfully accomplished his duty as the canal's supervisor. Set up at the end of his turn of office, the text reveals the author's unconcealed sigh of relief that his tenure of office passed by without any trouble. As the depicted situations show, the supervisor's duty was not just restricted to the appropriate allocation of water to the different users. He also had to ensure the function and efficiency of the irrigation system, including maintenance and repair work, if necessary. Perhaps it is not by chance that such an important and extensive task was not shouldered by one single person or family, but rather by the members of two clans, the Banū ʿṮKLN and ḤLḤLM, together. Interestingly, the same constellation is reflected in the contract YM 11726/2–3 mentioned before, where the supervisors (*ʾqdmtn*) are also identified as Banū ʿṮKLN and ḤLḤLM. Likewise the letter discussed at the beginning is addressed, as we have seen, not to a certain individual, but rather to a clan.[19]

Furthermore, the connection of the *qdmt*-office with a certain clan or "house" (*byt*) is found in two other inscriptions of more or less the same historical period. The authors of the first inscription state that their fruits were again preserved during the rainy season in the *qdmt*-office of the Banū ʿṮKLN and Banū ḤLḤLM. As the following passages (lines 10–13) show, these fruits were cultivated in fields in the immediate vicinity of the cities of Nas²qum and Nas²s²ān:

DhM 208[20]

Text

1. *rbbm / ʾḥrs^1 / w-ʾẖy-hw / [h]*
2. *wfʿṯt / ʾs^2wʿ / bny / g[dn]*
3. *m / hqnyw / mrʾ–hmw / ʾlmqh / [b]*
4. *ʿl-s^2bʿn / ṣlmn / ḏ-ḏhbn / ḏ-b-hw*
5. *ḥmdw / ẖyl / w-mqm / ʾlmqh / b-ḏ*
6. *t / ẖmr / ʿbdy-hw / rbbm / ʾḥr*
7. *[s^1 / w-]hwfʿṯt / ʾs^2wʿ / s^1twfy*
8. *[n /]kl / ʾṯmr-hmw / b-brqn / ḏ-qd*
9. *mt / ḏ-ʿṯkln / w-bn / ḥlḥlm / w-*
10. *l-wzʾ / ʾlmqh / hwfyn / kl*

[19] One might argue whether the apposition *w-bn s^1ʿdm* in X.BSB 121/1–2 must be considered explicative to the initial addressee, thus "To the supervisors (...), namely the Banū S^1ʿDM".

[20] The stone is preserved in the Dhamār Regional Museum and may be found on http://csai.humnet.unipi.it (viewed 6 July 2009). A photograph is also published by Avanzini (2009: 18 fig. 4). The inscription was written under King NS²ʾKRB YʾMN YHRḤB (ll. 15–18), hence about AD 260.

11. *ʾṯmr / w-ʾfql / ᶜbdy-hw / rbb*
12. *m / w-hwfᶜṯt / kl / ḏ-ytfrnn*
13. *[b-]hgrnhn / ns^{2}qm / w-ns^{2}n / w-ʾs^1*
14. *rr-hmy … …*

Translation

1. RBBM ʾḤRS^1 and his brother
2. HWFᶜṮT ʾS^{2}Wᶜ, of (the clan) GDNM,
3. have dedicated to their lord ʾLMQH,
4. lord of S^{2}BᶜN, the statuette of bronze by which
5. they praised the power and might of ʾLMQH for that
6. he has vouchsafed his two servants RBBM ʾḤRS^1
7. and HWFᶜṮT ʾS^{2}Wᶜ
8. all their fruits being preserved during the rain of the
9. *qdmt*-office of the one of ᶜṮKLN and the Banū ḤLḤLM, and
10. in order that ʾLMQH may continue to preserve all
11. the fruits of his two servants RBBM
12. and HWFᶜṮT, (namely) all that they will cultivate
13. in the cities of Nas^{2}qum and Nas^{2}s^{2}ān and
14. their valleys (in future) … …

The relevant passage of the second inscription, though fragmentary, may be reconstructed as follows:

Cullen 2[21]

Text

1'. xxxx[xxxxxxxxxxxxxxxxxxxxxx]
2'. *ẖlfn ḥmdm b-ḏt s$^{1?}$[twfy hyt qd]*
3'. *mtn w-l-wzʾ bᶜl s^{2}bᶜn hwfy[n-hw]*
4'. *qdmt yzʾn qdm l-byt-hmw* [xxxx]
5'. ʾ … …

Translation

1'. […]
2'. ẈLFN[22] in praise for (the fact) that he was [preserved (from misfortune in) that]
3'. *qdmt*-office,[23] and in order that the lord of S^{2}BᶜN may continue to preserve [him]
4'. (in all) *qdmt*-office(s) he is going to take over on behalf of their house […] (in future)
5'. … …

It is remarkable that both texts, despite the uncertain provenance of the actual stone, are also addressed to the god ʾLMQH, lord of S^{2}BᶜN and thus probably originate from the same context as MAFRAY-al-Bayḍāʾ 100. A third though less secure instance is found in a dedication to ʾLMQH that was probably set up in Maʾrib. Referring to the parallels discussed above, the first part of this text could be restored as follows:

C 365[24]

Text

1'. [xxxx]*l$^?$m*x[xxxxxxxxxxxxx / *w$^?$-ḥm*]
2'. *[d]m / b-ḏt[/ ẖ]mr / w-hws^{2c}[n / w-s^{1c}d / ᶜ]*
3'. *bd-hw / tbᶜkrb / s^{1}twfyn / q$^?$[dmt]*
4'. *tqdm / tbᶜkrb / b-(ᶜ)m / bn / ḥzfr*
5'. *m / w-hrḍ-hw / b-kn / twṣᶜt / ḏt / mẖ$^?$*
6'. *ṭrn / b-hyt / q$^?$d$^?$m$^?$tn … …*

Translation

1'. […, and(?)[25] in]

[21] This text, published by Beeston (1988: 33–35), was written in the mid-third century AD (ʾLS^{2}RḤ YḤḌB and YʾZL BYN, ll. 6'–7'). The beginning of the inscription is broken off; there are only traces of a few signs to the right of a line that may be counted as line 1' (in the Beeston 1988 edition, this being ignored, his first line corresponds to line 2' in our transliteration).

[22] In MAFRAY-al-Bayḍāʾ 100/4, the noun *qdmt* is grammatically determined by the particular canal for which the office is intended. In the present inscription, the determination of that noun in ll. 2'–3' is simply the article *-n*, thus referring to a specification of the term earlier in the text. Unlike the restoration by Beeston, there must have been some narrative passages before the preserved text currently starting with l. 2'. The noun *ẖlfn* at the beginning of this line is therefore probably not the votive object of the dedicatory formula (thus Beeston 1988) but something else, perhaps the name of one of the subjects in this sentence.

[23] The restoration of the noun *qdmtn* in the lacuna at the end of l. 2' was already suggested by Beeston (1988), the additions before that follow parallels in MAFRAY-al-Bayḍāʾ 100/4.

[24] See also the most recent interpretation by Calvet and Robin (1997: 148–151). As in all previous treatments, that passage is understood to refer to a (military) conflict between the author (TBᶜKRB) and the Banū ḤZFRM, relating the verb in line 4' with *tqdm* "confront, do battle with someone" (see above, n. 16). The text was written under the Himyarite king ḎMRᶜLY YHBR son of YSRM YHṢDQ, hence in the second half of the second century AD (1997: 150).

[25] Even though a restoration of the few preserved signs of this line to *[ṣ]lmn* "the statuette" seems quite enticing, the space before *ḥmdm* is too large just to be filled up with the expected apposition *ḏ-ḏhbn* "of bronze". The suggestion that the divine name ʾLMQH as the addressed deity was in this position, as proposed in CIH II 1911: 7, is even less convincing for similar reasons, since we would have to put the required epithet "lord of (the temple) NN" *and* the dedicatory object in the

2'. praise for (the fact) that he has vouchsafed, granted [and bestowed]
3'. his servant TBᶜKRB to be preserved (from misfortune in) the [*qdmt*-office]
4'. TBᶜKRB was in charge of together with the Banū ḤZFRM.
5'. And he (sc. ʾLMQH) has pleased him when this danger[26] had been overcome
6'. during that *qdmt*-office[27] ... ...

The (however restored) term *qdmt* in combination with the verb *tqdm*, and the statement that this duty was executed together with the members of another clan[28] are effectively in parallel with the other texts in question. As the keyword *qdmt* cannot be established with certainty, however, the relevance of this inscription for our purpose remains speculative.

Conclusions

Taking into account the evidence of the presented inscriptions, we can establish the particular office of a supervisor who was responsible for the function of a certain canal within the irrigation systems in the oases of Ancient South Arabia. This office, called *qdmt*, was occupied in rotation by one or two clans, the members of which were called *ʾqdmt*. These supervisors had to allocate a particular amount of water to each plot of land, especially when water was leased or sold. The practice of leasing water is illustrated in YM 11726: one participant in the irrigation system could lease his allocation of water to another participant in one season, and get it back in another season. As the presented documents show, these transactions were arranged by written contract. Finally, the supervisors of the irrigation system were instructed (for example, by letter as in the case of the above-mentioned X.BSB 121 and 122) to allocate the particular quantities accordingly.

At present, as far as we can see the office of water supervisor was restricted to the oasis of Nas²qum and Nas²s²ān in the Wādī al-Jawf around the (late) second to third centuries AD, a fact that raises some further questions about the actual character of the irrigation system referred to in the text discussed above. As we have seen, the terminology used in these texts seems to point to the presence of a perennial watercourse fed by groundwater, rather than a periodically flooded wadi. The term *ġyl* used for the canal in question in X.BSB 121/1 and MAFRAY-al-Bayḍāʾ 100/4 clearly corresponds to the Arabic *ghayl* which is characteristic of water flowing from springs, especially in the Yemeni highlands (Varisco 1983: 371). In the case of the canals which are part of flood-water irrigation systems, other terms such as *ḏhb*, *fnwt*, and *ḥrt*, are used in the inscriptions. Furthermore, the term *s²ty* stands for the dry winter season between mid-September and mid-December ("la saison sèche en hiver, entre le 13 septembre et le 12 décembre", Ryckmans, Müller & Abdallah 1994: 60), i.e. a time when no substantial flood water was expected. On the other hand, the actual Wādī Hirrān, which is feeding the site of the ancient oasis of Nas²qum and Nas²s²ān, can hardly be considered a perennial watercourse. Could the evidence of our inscriptions be taken as an indication of a different ecological environment in pre-Islamic times? Indeed H. von Wissmann (1964: 253, n. 126; 347) proposes that the lower course of that wadi was a perennial rivulet in the past. And finally, the relationship between the *ʾqdmt* and other offices like *mdrr* "controller of irrigation" (thus Beeston *et al.* 1982: 36, still with question mark)[29] must be cleared up in future research.[30]

---

following lacuna. Moreover, the demonstrative pronoun in l. 5' strongly suggests that the topic there was discussed previously in the text. Thus *ḥmdm b-ḏt* in ll. 1'–2' does not seem to be the first adverbial phrase of the dedicatory clause. For a syntactic parallel, see the dedicatory inscription F 71.

[26] This interpretation follows that given in Calvet and Robin (1997: 148–151). Nevertheless, the reading of the letter *ḫ* is far from being definite. If correctly defined, the word must refer to a pernicious situation, mentioned earlier in the text (see n. 25), which probably affected the irrigation system when it was under the supervision of the author of our inscription.

[27] Even though the reconstruction of the word *qdmtn* here is not definite, all earlier suggestions (CIH II 1911: 8: *ḫ..n* "expedition", rejecting a previous reading *mkntn*; similarly Höfner [1938: 19–20] *sbʾtn* "Feldzug"; Calvet and Robin [1997: 149–151] *s³ᶜʾtn* "occasion", stating "la lecture n'est pas sûre") are not definite either.

[28] As is shown later in the text, the author belongs to the clan ʾS¹LM (l. 14').

[29] See Mazzini & Porter 2009: 289 with n. 27. To the only reference for this term quoted there (Gl 1563/8), three other texts may be added: MAFRAY-Ḥuṣn Āl Ṣāliḥ 1/11 (Robin 1987: 167–169), Y.90.DA 2/7 (Gnoli & Robin 1992: 95–97), and YM 18352/12 (Arbach & Audouin 2007: 84 no. 53).

[30] Perhaps the various titles focus on the different duties of particular persons: the person with overall responsibility (*ʾqdmt*) being in charge of the entire irrigation system, in contrast to subordinate inspectors (*mdrr*) who are directed by the manager to work in one or other part of that particular system. It has been observed that in MAFRAY-Ḥuṣn Āl Ṣāliḥ 1 and Y.90.DA 2, both originating from the vicinity of Yatill/Barāqiš and written in the eighth century BC, the person in question (*mdrr*) is, again, a member of one and the same clan (namely KBR YṮL).

Sigla

Note: Sigla of inscriptions are quoted according to the list given in Stein 2003: 274–290.

CIH 1889–1932. *Corpus inscriptionum semiticarum. Pars quarta. Inscriptiones ḥimyariticas et sabæas continens*. Paris: Reipublicae Typographeo.

References

Arbach M. & Audouin R.

2007. *Ṣanᶜāᵓ National Museum. Collections of Epigraphic and Archaeological Artifacts from al-Jawf Sites. Part II*. Ṣanᶜāᵓ: National Museum.

Avanzini A.

2009. CASIS "Cataloguing and Fruition of South Arabian Inscriptions through an Informatic Support". Pages 15–25 in *Art and technique in Yemen. The bronzes from the museum of Baynun*. Pontedera: Bandecchi & Vivaldi.

Beeston A.F.L.

1988. Two Sabaic texts. *Raydān* 5: 33–38.

Beeston A.F.L., Ghul M.A., Müller W.W. & Ryckmans J.

1982. *Sabaic Dictionary (English–French–Arabic)*. (Publication of the University of Sanaa, YAR). Louvain-la-Neuve/Beirut: Peeters/Librairie du Liban.

Calvet Y. & Robin C.

1997. *Arabie heureuse — Arabie déserte. Les Antiquités arabiques du musée du Louvre*. (Notes et documents des musées de France, 31). Paris: Réunion des musées nationaux.

Gnoli G. & Robin C.

1992. Nouveaux documents sabéens de Barāqish. *Yemen* 1: 93–98.

Hehmeyer I.

2005. Diurnal time measurement for water allocation in southern Yemen. *Proceedings of the Seminar for Arabian Studies* 35: 87–96.

Höfner M.

1938. Die Inschriften aus Glasers Tagebuch XI (Mārib). *Wiener Zeitschrift für die Kunde des Morgenlandes* 45: 7–37.

Mazzini G. & Porter A.

2009. Stela BM 102600=CIH 611 in the British Museum: water regulation between two bordering estates. *Proceedings of the Seminar for Arabian Studies* 39: 283–294.

Müller W.W.

1978. Sabäische Felsinschriften von der jemenitischen Grenze zur Rubᶜ al-Ḫālī. *Neue Ephemeris für semitische Epigraphik* 3: 113–136.

Robin C.

1987. Trois inscriptions sabéennes découvertes près de Barāqish (République Arabe du Yémen). *Proceedings of the Seminar for Arabian Studies* 17: 165–177.

1994. À propos d'une nouvelle inscription du règne de Shaᶜrᵘᵐ Awtar, un réexamen de l'éponymat sabéen à l'époque des rois de Sabaᵓ et de dhū-Raydān. Pages 230–249 in N. Nebes (ed.), *Arabia Felix. Beiträge zur Sprache und Kultur des vorislamischen Arabien. Festschrift Walter W. Müller zum 60. Geburtstag*. Wiesbaden: Harrassowitz.

Robin C. & Brunner U.

1997. *Map of Ancient Yemen 1:1 000 000*. Munich: Staatliches Museum für Völkerkunde.

Ryckmans J., Müller W.W. & Abdallah Y.M.
1994. *Textes du Yémen antique inscrits sur bois (with an English Summary)*. (Publications de l'Institut Orientaliste de Louvain, 43). Louvain-la-Neuve: Institut Orientaliste.

Sima A.
2000. *Tiere, Pflanzen, Steine und Metalle in den altsüdarabischen Inschriften. Eine lexikalische und realienkundliche Untersuchung*. (Veröffentlichungen der Orientalischen Kommission der Akademie der Wissenschaften und der Literatur Mainz, 46). Wiesbaden: Harrassowitz.

Stein P.
2003. *Untersuchungen zur Phonologie und Morphologie des Sabäischen*. (Epigraphische Forschungen auf der Arabischen Halbinsel, 3). Rahden/Westf.: Marie Leidorf.
2010. *Die altsüdarabischen Minuskelinschriften auf Holzstäbchen aus der Bayerischen Staatsbibliothek in München*. Bd. 1: *Die Inschriften der mittel- und spätsabäischen Periode*. (Epigraphische Forschungen auf der Arabischen Halbinsel, 5). Tübingen/Berlin: Wasmuth.

Varisco D.M.
1983. *Sayl* and *Ghayl*. The Ecology of Water Allocation in Yemen. *Human Ecology* 11, 365–383.

Wissmann H. von
1964. *Zur Geschichte und Landeskunde von Alt-Südarabien*. (Sammlung Eduard Glaser, 3). Vienna: H. Böhlaus Nachf.
1976. Die Geschichte des Sabäerreichs und der Feldzug des Aelius Gallus. Pages 308–544 in H. Temporini & W. Haase (eds.), *Aufstieg und Niedergang der Römischen Welt* 2/9. Berlin/New York: de Gruyter.

Author's address
PD Dr. Peter Stein, Friedrich-Schiller-Universität Jena, Lehrstuhl für Semitische Philologie und Islamwissenschaft, Löbdergraben 24a, D–07737 Jena, Germany.

e-mail multistein@t-online.de

Proceedings of the Seminar for Arabian Studies 40 (2010): 345–356

A detective story: emphatics in Mehri

Janet C.E. Watson & Alex Bellem

Summary
Until 1970, Ethio-Semitic was believed to be the only Semitic language sub-family in which the main correlate of "emphasis" is glottalization, a feature said at the time to be due to Cushitic influence. Since the work of T.M. Johnstone, however, it has been argued that glottalization is a South Semitic feature, attested not only in Ethio-Semitic, but also in the Modern South Arabian languages. Two statements in the literature on Modern South Arabian, however, suggested to us that the original evidence needed to be re-investigated: first, some of the "ejectives" are described as at least partially voiced, not a phonetic impossibility, but so far unheard of in the phonological system of any language; and secondly, the degree of glottalization is frequently described as dependent on the phonological environment, although details of the environment in which emphatics are always realized as ejectives are not given. In this paper, we consider acoustic data from Mahriyōt (a Mehri dialect spoken in the easternmost province of Yemen), we examine descriptions of emphatics in other dialects of Mehri and other Modern South Arabian languages, we look at phonological environments in which emphatics are realized as ejectives and those in which they are not, and we conclude that the file on emphasis in these languages needs to be re-opened to fresh judgement.

Keywords: Modern South Arabian, Mehri, emphasis, phonetics, phonology

1. Introduction

Until 1970, Ethio-Semitic was believed to be the only Semitic language sub-family in which the emphatic consonants are predominantly glottalic pressure consonants, i.e. ejectives, a feature said at the time to be due to Cushitic influence. Since the work of T.M. Johnstone, however, it has been argued that glottalic pressure is a South Semitic feature, attested not only in Ethio-Semitic, but also in the Modern South Arabian languages.

There were, however, two statements in the literature that attracted our attention: first, some of the "ejectives" are said to be at least partially voiced, not a phonetic impossibility, but so far unheard of in the phonological system of any language; and secondly, the degree of glottalization is sometimes described as dependent on the phonological environment (e.g. Simeone-Senelle 1997: 382), although details of the environment in which emphatics are always realized as ejectives are not given.

Our data come from Mahriyōt, a dialect of the Modern South Arabian language Mehri, spoken in the Sharqiyyah province of Yemen bordering Oman. Watson had initially worked on pre-pausal phenomena in this dialect with the late Alexander Sima. She then conducted fieldwork in al-Ghayḍah between January and March 2008, working with Askari Saad Hujayran and his extended family. Askari had moved to al-Ghayḍah from Sharqiyyah with his immediate family nine years previously, and has since been joined by members of his extended family. Since summer 2008, Watson has been working with Bellem on the phonetics and phonology of Mehri emphatics.

In this paper, we begin by presenting the consonantal inventory of Mahriyōt. We then briefly consider the phonological patterning of the emphatics, which in Mehri pattern on the one hand with voiced consonants and on the other with pharyngeals and uvulars. We then consider the history of work on the emphatic system in Modern South Arabian in general, and in Mehri in particular. This section is followed by an acoustic analysis of Watson's data, which shows that only one of the emphatics is realized in all syllabic positions as an ejective. Although this study is based on data from a single dialect region, written descriptions and our initial listenings to archived Modern South Arabian sound files indicate that the phonetic correlates of emphasis in Mehri in general have been misanalysed, a fact due partly to the assumption that all emphatics share a single main correlate of emphasis, and partly to a failure to recognize the importance of the phonological environment.

		labial	*dental*	*alveolar*	*palato-alveolar*	*palatal*	*velar*	*uvular*	*pharyngeal*	*glottal*
PLOSIVE	voiced	b		d						
	voiceless			t			k			’
	emphatic			ṭ			ḳ			
affricate					j					
FRICATIVE	voiced		ḏ	z				ġ	ʕ	
	voiceless	f	ṯ	s	š			x	ḥ	h
	emphatic		ṯ̣	ṣ	č̣					
LATERAL	voiced			l						
	voiceless				ś					
	emphatic				ź					
nasal		m		n						
rhotic				r						
glide						y	w			

Figure 1. *The consonantal inventory of Mahriyōt.*

2. Consonants

The consonantal inventory of Mahriyōt is given above. The transcription system adopted is that used in Sima (2009). The emphatics, and the pharyngeal fricative /ḥ/, are transcribed with subscript dots. There is another emphatic, /ź/, the counterpart of the voiceless lateral /ś/.[1]

3. Patterning of emphatics with voiced consonants

Gemination of root-initial consonants affects obstruents that are neither phonologically voiced nor fall into the set of emphatics: /ḳ/, /ṣ/, /ṭ/, /č̣/, /ź/ (but not /ṯ̣/). Thus, certain particles may geminate nominal-initial voiceless consonants for pragmatic or stylistic emphasis. These include *w-* of focus, *la-, k-, ḏ-* and, occasionally *b-*.[2] Examples from the texts include: *ka-śśētu* "in winter", *śaḥnā̃t ḏa-ssīyaryat* "the load of the car", *ba-ḥḥays* "with energy", *ba-ffaʕmah* "with his foot", *ka-xxarf* "in the monsoon period", *ka-ṯṯuhr* "at noon", *wa-xxadyīt* "and the *xadyīt* [fish type]", *wa-hhāxā̃r* "and the old man", *wa-ttiwyah* "and its meat". Gemination appears to be a remnant of the definite article, which no longer has a phonological exponent in this dialect.[3] Of the voiceless consonants subject to gemination, a larger percentage of the tokens of /ḥ/ fail to be geminated than, for example, /k/, /t/, /x/, /f/, /s/, /ś/ or /š/.[4]

[1] /ź/ is transcribed as such by Johnstone (1975) and Lonnet (2009), but phonologically more accurately as *ṡ́* by Simeone-Senelle (e.g. 1997).

[2] The affricate, originally *g*, as it is in other dialects of Mehri, forms a phonological voiced — voiceless — emphatic triad with /ḳ/ and /k/.

[3] In comparison to the Mehri of Oman where definite nominals beginning with non-voiceless (voiced or emphatic) consonants take initial *a-* (Johnstone 1970; 1987: xiii; cf. Simeone-Senelle 1997: 412; Sima 2002).

[4] Gemination of one of the voiceless coronal consonants following *ḏ-*

In a number of verb types, including the intensive-conative[5] verb, *afōʕal*, and the basic quadrilateral verb, a root-initial voiceless non-emphatic consonant is geminated in the inflected verb and in the participles, as in: *affōkar* "to think", participle m.s. *maffakrā*, *attōfaġ* "to wash one's face with water", participle m.s. *mattafġā*, *aḥḥōd̲ar* "to be embarrassed", participle m.s. *maḥḥad̲īrōna, aśśarḳāʕ* "to take a large step", *attartūr* "to take something violently", *aššarxūf* "to take/put sth. down"; in h-stem verbs, /h/ is often deleted. Omission of *h-* is usually accompanied by gemination of the initial root consonant, where this latter is voiceless. Examples include:

aśśanūh ~ *haśnūh*	"he showed"
axxanūf ~ *haxnūf*	"he took out"
axxalūf ~ *haxlūf*	"he left behind"
attamūm ~ *hatmūm*	"he finished"

By contrast, initial emphatic and voiced root consonants remain ungeminated in all these verb forms, as in: *ajōrab* "to try", *awōd̲an* "to make the call to prayer", participle m.s. *mawid̲nōna, aṣōfi* "to cleanse", *aḳūnūm* "to gather green fodder", *aṭaḳṭūḳ* "to clatter", *adaġdāġ* "to tickle", *abartūm* "to amuse o.s.".

In dialects in which a vestige of the definite article remains (the Mehri of Oman), the article *a-* is realized before voiced consonants and emphatics, but not before voiceless consonants, as in the following examples from Johnstone (1975: 98):

a-gɛ:d	"the skin"
a-ḳa:b	"the heart"
kawb	"a/the wolf"

In these dialects, /a/ is prefixed to the intensive-conative verbal pattern before voiced consonants and emphatics, but not before voiceless consonants, as in the following examples from Johnstone (1975: 99):

ago:rəb	"to try"
aḳo:bəl	"to point at"
ko:rəm	"to be generous"

rules out the otherwise common progressive assimilation of the particle *d̲-* to a following coronal obstruent (e.g. Sima 2005: 6, 11, 16), as in: *aš-šäʕjūl* < **š-šaʕjūl* < **d̲-šaʕjūl* "he who hurries" (2005: 14) and *as-säbōṭ* < **s-sbōṭ* < **d̲ä-sbōṭ* "he who hits" (2005: 16).

[5] Terminology adopted from Johnstone (1975: 98).

4. Patterning of emphatics with pharyngeals and uvulars

The emphatics pattern with the pharyngeals and the uvulars in terms of the vowel allophones they attract. Thus, in Mahriyōt *ay* and *aw* may occur to the exclusion of *ī* and *ū* after the emphatics, pharyngeals and uvulars.[6] Examples from Watson's data include: *ba-ḥḥays* "with energy", *ḳayṭ* "hot/pre-monsoon period", *ʕayd* "sardines", *ʕaylūj* "camel calf", *ḥayd̲ān* "ear", *ʕayś* "sorghum", *ḥamźawt* "yoghurt dish", *mṣawġat* "jewellery shop", *źayjaʕ* "hut". The diphthong also may be separated from the trigger by another consonant, as in *śaṭrayr* "cloth" and *śaʕṭayt* "three". The feminine nominal, adjectival, and numeral ending *-īt* is realized as *-ayt* in the following words:

ṣarʕayt	"smell under the armpits" (cf. *šabdīt* "liver")
bīźayt	"egg" (cf. *rēśīt* "snake")
habʕayt	"seven" (cf. *ṯamnīt* "eight")
ṣalḥayt	"fat (f.s.)" (cf. *xaṭmīt* "thin [f.s.]")

Less commonly, the feminine nominal and 3 f.s. perfect verbal ending *-ōt* is realized as *-awt* in the environment of gutturals:

malḥawt	"salt; salt water" (also *malḥōt*)
wasʕawt	"it (f.) held" (cf. *barwōt* "she gave birth")

No examples of /ṱ/ followed by a diphthong are attested in Watson's data; at this stage, it is not certain whether this is because diphthongization does not occur in the environment of /ṱ/ or whether the database is too small — /ṱ/ occurs rarely, and the only possible examples in the texts are *aṱ-ṱīr* + pronoun suffix, such as *aṱ-ṱīras* "on it (f.)", and *ṱīrōb* "sticks", and in this latter case /ī/ does not fall in a stressed syllable.

The low vowel /a/ is realized as a low central-ish vowel [a] in the environment of emphatics, pharyngeals, and uvulars; long /ā/ is realized as low central-ish [a:] after emphatics, pharyngeals, and uvulars. By contrast, where the context does not contain a backing consonant (emphatic, pharyngeal, or uvular), this vowel is fronted and raised ([ɛ]/[ɛ:]).[7] Compare the height of the second

[6] In Omani Mehri, this appears to be invariably the case (cf. Johnstone 1987: xiii).

[7] In the literature on Modern South Arabian languages (MSAL), there

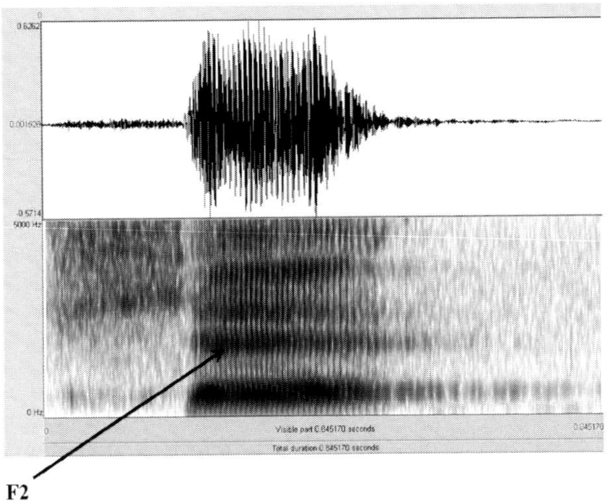

Figure 2. *Spectrogram and waveform of a token of* śā [ɬɛː] *(name of the letter* ś*) — the spectrogram shows comparatively higher F2 of the low vowel* ā*, which is raised to* [ɛː] *in this (non-backing) environment; the speaker of all the data used for this paper is an adult male from Ḥawf, in the province of Mahra.*

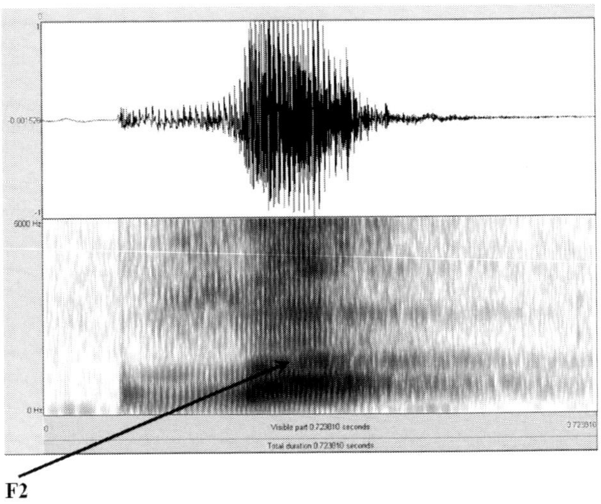

Figure 3. *Spectrogram and waveform of a token of* źā [ɮ̴aː] *(name of the letter* ź*) — the spectrogram shows comparatively lower F2 of the low vowel* ā*, which is realized as low central-ish* [aː] *in this (backing) environment.*

formant, F2, in the names of the palato-alveolar lateral fricative *śā*[8] and its emphatic counterpart *źā* in the spectrograms in Figures 2 and 3, above.

Thus, with few exceptions, the nominal feminine ending /āt/ is realized as *-āt* after emphatics, pharyngeals, or uvulars, as in *ḳaṣṣāt* "story", *mṭarḳāt* "hammer", *ṣafḥāt* "hinge"; as *-ā̃t* after nasals, as in *raḥmā̃t* "rain", *ʕadmā̃t* "lack of means", *snā̃t* "year", *maḥnā̃t* "problem", *mḳalmā̃t* "pruning shears"; and as *-ēt* in all other environments, as in: *barzēt* "small hole at back of boat to let water out", *raḥbēt* "village; town", *mbaxrēt* "iron frame for incensing clothes", *xabzēt* "piece of bread", *ḳaśrēt* "naughtiness".

5. The description of the emphatics in Mehri

In works based on the fieldwork of the Viennese expedition in the early twentieth century (e.g. Jahn 1902; Müller 1909; Bittner 1909) and of Bertram Thomas (Thomas 1937; Leslau 1947), emphasis in Modern South Arabian appears to be considered similar to, but also less salient than, emphasis in Arabic. Thomas (1937: 14), for example, describes the differences in the respective sound values of the pairs *q* and *k*; *g* and *ġ* and the triads *t*, *ṭ*, and *d*; *s*, *ṣ*, and *z* as "not unmistakably evident to the listener like their familiar Arabic equivalents". This lack of unmistakability is evident in the (inconsistent) transcription of the Viennese expedition; thus Hein (edited by Müller 1909) transcribes /ḳ/ in his Mehri texts as *g*, as in *ġalgōt* "she saw" for *ġalḳōt*, and occasionally as *k*, as in *tekefôd* "she goes down" (1909: 1), but *ugofôd* "and he went down" (1909: 6); he frequently transcribes /ṣ/ as voiced *z*, as in *zóṭer* "basket" for *ṣōṭar* and *zayd* "fish" for *ṣayd*, but also as *ṣ* and *s*, particularly in the word for "morning", as in *kṣôbaḥ* and *hesôbaḥ* "am Morgen" (1909: 3). It is not until literature based on the fieldwork of Johnstone and Lonnet and Simeone-Senelle that emphasis in Mehri is described as (post-) glottalization (Johnstone 1975; 1987; Simeone-Senelle 1997: 382–383). These descriptions are accompanied by the proviso, by Johnstone, that the strength of the glottalic release in Modern South Arabian as a whole is less than that in the Ethio-Semitic languages (e.g. Amharic, Johnstone 1975: 98), and that the degree of glottalization varies according to phonological context and dialect (e.g. Simeone-Senelle 1997: 382): glottalization in some Soqotri dialects is described as "weaker" (1997: 382), and for the western Mehri dialect of Qishn, glottal closure is said to be incomplete, provoking "a laryngealization or creaky voice" (1997: 382; see also Lonnet & Simeone-Senelle 1983; 1997).

is no clear consensus on vowel inventories. However, in Mahriyōt, the vowel often transcribed as "ē" seems pretty clearly to be the raised and fronted variant of /ā/ (i.e. "ā" and "ē" are in complementary distribution: "ē" appears in non-guttural environments, and is thus an allophone).

[8] Described by Watson's informant as *aš-šīn al-jānibiyyah* "the lateral šīn".

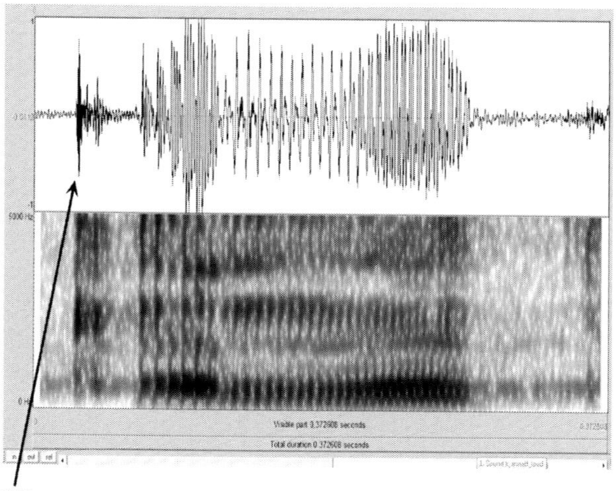

[k']

Figure 4, *Spectrogram and waveform showing the sharp "spike" typical of glottalic initiation in the (ejective) emphatic* ḳ *in this token of* ḳannatt [k'an:ət^{h}:] *"small (f.s.)".*

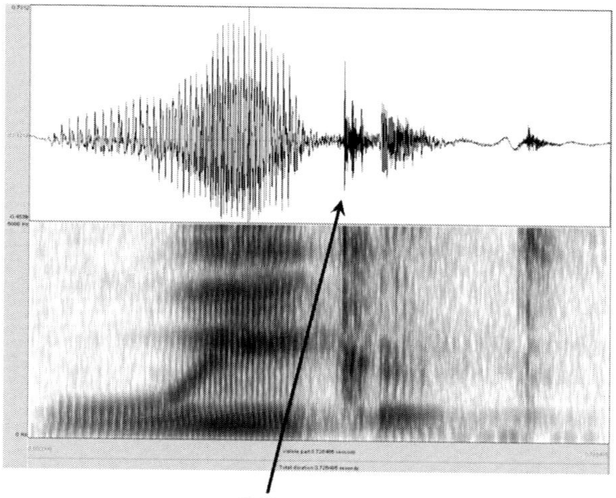

[k']

Figure 5. *Spectrogram and waveform showing the sharp "spike" typical of glottalic initiation in the (ejective) emphatic* ḳ *in this token of* w-wīḳad [w wi:k'at'] *"and* wīḳad *(a type of fish)"; the final* d *is prepausal and thus also devoiced and ejective.*

For some dialects of the languages, glottalization is said to be increasingly restricted to a sub-set of the emphatics (Lonnet 2009). Significantly, Johnstone and Simeone-Senelle and Lonnet describe some of the "ejective" emphatics as at least partially voiced.

6. The phonetic correlates of the emphatic feature in Mahriyōt

In the field, Watson was aware of ejective articulations invariably only in the case of /ḳ/. Furthermore, any attempts on Watson's part to produce ejective tokens of the other emphatics in any position other than pre-pausal were rejected by her informants. Acoustic analysis later confirmed that /ḳ/ was the only consonant to exhibit in waveforms the spike typical of glottalic pressure consonants in all phonological environments. This is seen in initial position in the waveform for the word *ḳannatt* "small (f.s.)", and in medial position in the word *w-wīḳad* "and *wīḳad* (type of fish)" (Figs 4 & 5).

By contrast, no spike is visible on waveforms of tokens of any other emphatic in non-pre-pausal position. This is exemplified below in [ṣ] in *ṣwārāb* "harvest period [diminutive]" (Fig. 6), in [č̣] in *č̣aʕrīr* "back of the neck" (Fig. 7), in [ṭ] in *ṭayr* "bird" (Fig. 8), or in [ẓ́] in *ẓ́ā* (sound name) (Fig. 9). (The arrows on the waveforms indicate the onset of [ṭ] and the mid-positions of [ṣ], [č̣], and [ẓ́].)

However, the phonemes /ṣ/, /č̣/, /ṭ/, /ẓ́/ and (less so) /ṯ̣/, as we have seen, pattern with /ḳ/ phonologically in that they have a "backing" effect on surrounding vowels (seen spectrographically in a lowered second formant), tend to take diphthong allophones of /ī/ and /ō/, and fail to geminate after geminating particles or as the initial root consonant of certain verb patterns. The question is therefore: what are the correlates of "emphasis" in these cases?

Watson's main informant describes the two dorsal emphatic stops — /ḳ/ and /č̣/ — in terms of combinations of articulations: /k/ plus *ʕayn* for /ḳ/, and the "heavy Egyptian *jīm*" plus *ʕayn* for /č̣/, suggesting an awareness of a similar phonological element in both these sounds. The reference to Egyptian *jīm* probably reflects the retracted place of articulation in comparison to /š/. The heaviness and *ʕayn* element associated with /č̣/ is most probably tongue retraction/pharyngealization. In men's speech in particular, creak accompanies some tokens of /č̣/, which may be nevertheless totally or predominantly voiceless. Acoustic analysis carried out by Barry Heselwood (personal communication) showed tokens of initial /č̣/ to be similar to the devoiced voiced affricates of English and Persian — no voice during the closure period, but no aspiration after the frication and shorter frication than usually found in phonemically voiceless affricates. In intervocalic position, /č̣/ often lacks the initial occlusive element and is realized as a partially or fully voiced pharyngealized palato-alveolar fricative, as in *ač̣ōbaʕ* "fingers", realized as *aẓ̌ōbaʕ,* in

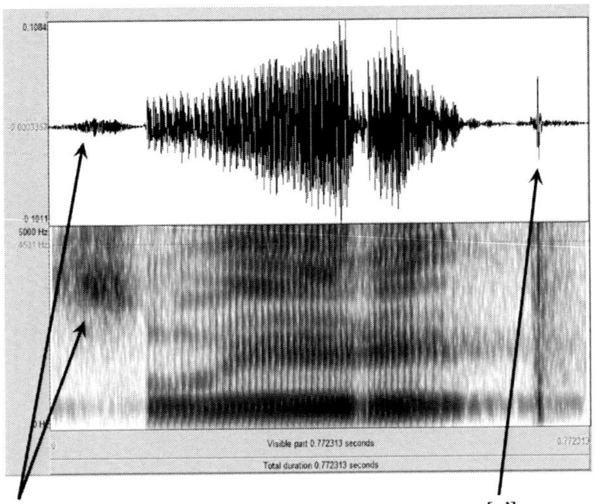

FIGURE 6. *Spectrogram and waveform showing that the emphatic* ṣ *of* ṣwārāb [ṣwɛ:rɛ:p’] *“harvest period (diminutive)” is not ejective; in this token, the final* b *is prepausal and thus devoiced and produced on a glottalic airstream — the sharp spike is visible on the waveform.*

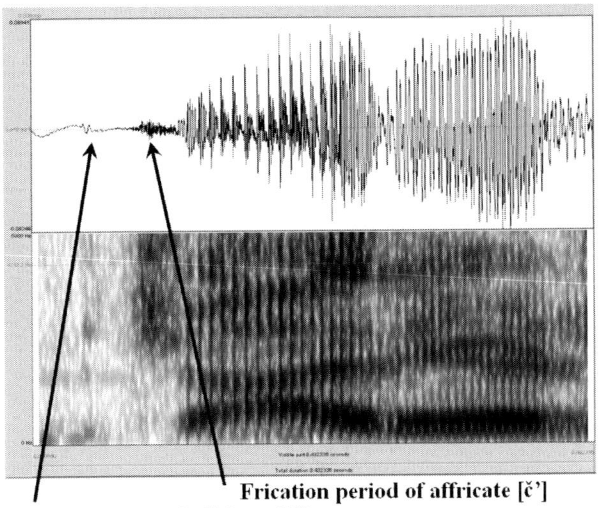

FIGURE 7. *Spectrogram and waveform showing that the emphatic* č̣ *of* č̣aʕrīr [ʧaʕri:r] *“back of the neck” is not ejective (note, however, that it is an affricate in this position, cf.* FIGURE *10 below).*

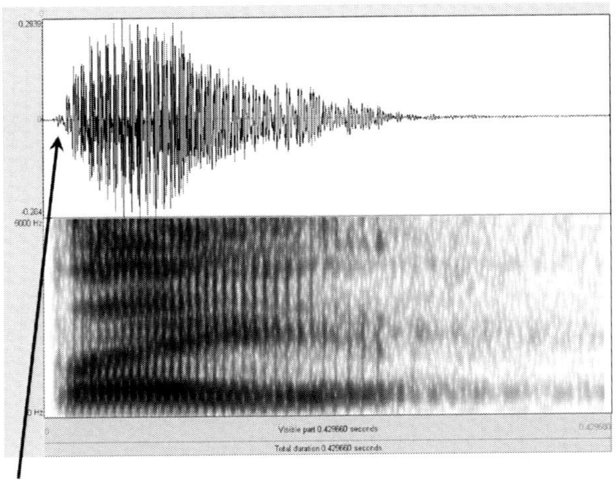

FIGURE 8. *Spectrogram and waveform showing that the emphatic* ṭ *of* ṭayr [ṭajr] *“bird” is not ejective.*

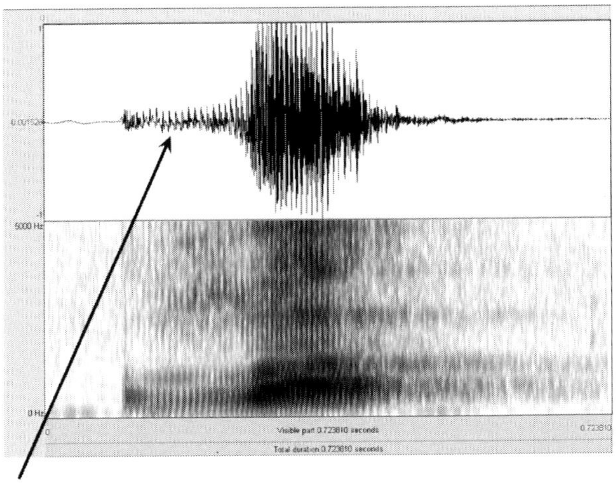

FIGURE 9. *Spectrogram and waveform showing that the emphatic* ẓ́ *of* ẓ́ā [ɮa:] *(name of the letter* ẓ́*) is not ejective.*

the spectrogram in Figure 10. (The arrow indicates the mid-position of /č̣/.)

The emphatic sibilant /ṣ/ is most often considerably more voiced than the typical Arabic *ṣād*, with tokens varying from predominantly voiced to, less commonly, fully unvoiced. The onset of word-initial /ṣ/, however, tends to be voiceless and sharply sibilant. Johnstone describes /ṣ/ in the Mehri of Oman as partially voiced (1987: xiii); in his article on Modern South Arabian, he claims that on account of the voicing of “glottalized consonants”, “[n]ative speakers seem to have difficulty on occasions in distinguishing between ... the contrasting pair *s’/z...*” (1975: 98). Indeed, as we have seen above, in Hein’s texts from Qishn there often appears to be

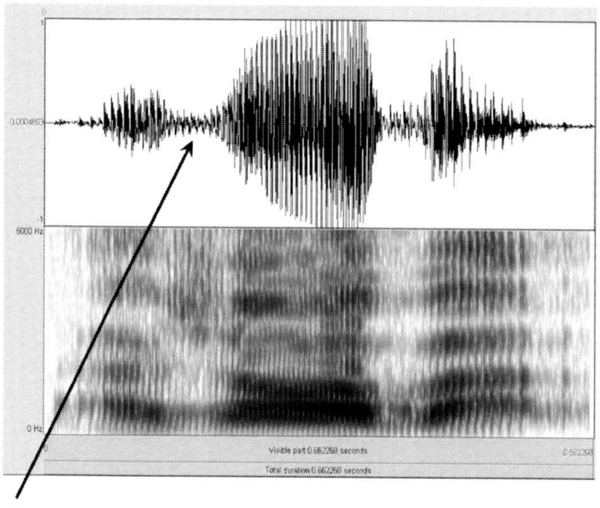

[ẓ̌]

Figure 10. *Spectrogram and waveform of a token of* ač̣ōbaʕ [aẓ̌o:baʕ] *"fingers" showing that* č̣ *is both voiced and continuant (no initial occlusion).*

confusion between /z/ and /ṣ/, such that *zayd* is given for what in Mahriyōt would be *ṣayd* "fish" (e.g. Müller 1909: 185). However, /ṣ/ exhibits considerably more tenseness in both Omani Mehri (Johnstone 1987) and in Mahriyōt than /z/, a tenseness which is probably due to tongue retraction/pharyngealization or laryngealization, and no confusion between the two sounds was evident among Watson's informants.

For Omani Mehri /ṭ/ has been described by Johnstone as glottalized; Watson's impressions in the field agreed with those of her informants that /ṭ/ was most often pharyngealized rather than glottalized[9] — informants described this sound as "the same as" or "like" Arabic /ṭ/. Apart from the pre-pausal examples, none of the spectrograms of /ṭ/ examined both by us and by Heselwood exhibited the spike indicative of glottalic release. One main distinction between /ṭ/ and /t/ in Mahriyōt appears to be the lack of aspiration in the former, a distinction also noted by several researchers independently for some (but not all) Arabic dialects (Khattab, Al-Tamimi & Heselwood 2006; Bellem 2007).

The lateral fricative /ź/[10] is, like /č̣/, slightly affricated in word-initial and word-final position,[11] at least partially voiced — as compared with the fully voiceless lateral fricative /ś/ — and lowers the formants of surrounding vowels, suggesting that a combination of affrication and pharyngeal contraction are the correlates of emphasis in this case. Impressionistic and acoustic analyses also suggest it has a retracted, pre-velar, place of articulation, with the tongue making contact with the back molars. The relative saliency of the affrication is still unclear, since both affricated and non-affricated tokens are attested. In isolated dialects of Arabic spoken either side of the Saudi–Yemeni border, affrication or abfrication is a correlate of emphasis in the sibilant emphatics, as in the (plain–emphatic) /s/–/st/ opposition in Faifi dialect (Yahya Asiri, personal communication) and Minabbih dialect (Behnstedt 1987), and in Jabal Rāziḥ where a lateralized palato-alveolar affricate is the emphatic counterpart of a slightly lateralized palato-alveolar fricative (Watson *et al.* 2006).[12]

The emphatic interdental fricative is transcribed here, as in Sima (2009), as /ṯ̣/. It is a more appropriate symbol than /ḏ̣/: /ṯ̣/ is similar in place and manner to the voiced interdental pharyngealized /ḏ̣/ of many Yemeni Arabic dialects, but exhibits substantially less voicing; Johnstone describes what he transcribes as /ḏ̣/ as "partially voiceless" for Omani Mehri (1987: xiii). Phonologically /ṯ̣/ behaves like the other emphatics insofar as it attracts a low central-ish allophone of /a/ and /ā/ ([a] and [a:]). Alone of the emphatics, however, it patterns with the voiceless consonants in its tendency to geminate after geminating particles (see above), and, from the data available, appears to pattern with non-emphatics insofar as it does not induce diphthongization of /ī/ or /ō/.

Voicing is phonologically immaterial in the emphatics, and although /ḳ/, by virtue of being released on a glottalic airstream, is invariably produced without any vocal fold activity, the remaining emphatics exhibit variable degrees of voicing, with the more voiced tokens particularly evident in intervocalic position. On this point the data from Mahriyōt agree with that discussed by Johnstone, Simeone-Senelle, and Simeone-Senelle and Lonnet. In all cases, the emphatics lack aspiration (hence lack any significant voicing lag), and thus contrast on the one hand with voiced counterparts in which voicing is evident throughout, and on the other hand with voiceless counterparts in which there is significant voicing lag and aspiration after release (see Bellem 2007). Since, as we have seen, the emphatic consonants in all three main dialect groups of Mehri pattern in various environments with the voiced rather than the voiceless obstruents, one of the main distinctions between the emphatics and the

[9] Significantly, /ṭ/ is not grouped by Askari with the five consonants that are either not attested in Arabic, or that differ perceptually from similar sounds in Arabic.

[10] Transcribed by Simeone-Senelle (1997: 382) as *ṣ́*.

[11] Women are more likely to produce affricated, voiceless tokens of /ź/ than men.

[12] See also Steiner (1982) on the affricated *ṣāde* in Semitic.

voiceless obstruents appears to be the phonologized voicing lag associated with aspiration. The lowering of formants of surrounding vowels suggests a degree of tongue retraction and pharyngeal contraction, placing the emphatics together with pharyngeals and uvulars in a class that we describe here for convenience as “guttural”.[13]

7. Conclusion

In Mahriyōt, the articulatory correlates of emphasis differ according to the primary place and the manner of articulation of the consonant concerned. The main correlates of emphasis are glottalic initiation in the case of /ḳ/, and tongue retraction and pharyngeal contraction in the case of /ṭ/ and the continuant emphatics. Affrication appears to be a contributory or enhancing feature in the case of the sibilant emphatics /č̣/ and /ẓ́/, but not in the case of /ṣ/.

This paper is based on the impressionistic and acoustic analysis of data from one dialect of Mehri; however, descriptions of the emphatics in the literature and preliminary auditory and acoustic analysis of recordings from Jibbali (in Oman) and Soqotri by Bellem suggest that Mahriyōt is not unique in exhibiting differing articulatory correlates of emphasis. The key lies in descriptions of the non-plosive emphatics in the Modern South Arabian languages as at least partially voiced. These descriptions are supported by the transcriptions of the Viennese expedition at the beginning of the twentieth century. Voiced ejectives may be physiologically possible (Laver 1994: 369); however, due to the difficulty in acquiring the required pressure differential to cause vibration of the upward-moving glottis, they are not used contrastively in any known language (Ladefoged & Maddieson 1996: 79–80). In the one language for which a voiced ejective has been reported, Zhuǀ’hõasi, the sound in question has been found to be *pre*-voiced (Maddieson 1984: 216, based on Snyman 1970; 1975). It is highly doubtful, therefore, that the voiced or partially voiced allophones of the emphatics are ejective in any dialect of Mehri.

The description of emphatic consonants as invariably ejective in the literature on Mehri is due, we believe, to two combined reasons. First, the influence of the phonological environment on the phonetic realization of segments has not always been fully recognized. In pre-pausal position, all consonants are realized without voice (final devoicing in Modern South Arabian was already observed by Leslau [1947] on the basis of Bertram Thomas’s material), and all voiced consonants (including sonorants) may be pre-glottalized particularly, but not exclusively, following a long vowel, as in: *syōr* > *syō’r̥* # “he went”, *mōnaġ* > *mōna’x*# (place name), *b-ḥāwēl* > *b-ḥāwē’l̥* # “firstly” (cf. Simeone-Senelle 1997: 385; Watson & Asiri 2007).[14] In this position, phonologically voiceless consonants are heavily aspirated, while phonologically non-voiceless non-continuant obstruents (i.e. emphatic stops and voiced obstruent stops) are frequently released on a glottalic airstream, with neutralization of the distinction between emphatics and their plain voiced counterparts, but maintenance of the distinction between emphatics and voiced stops, on the one hand, and voiceless stops, on the other: *ġayj* > *ġayč’*# “man”, *yanhōč̣* > *yanhōč’*# “he shouts to s.o.”, *ṭād* > *ṭāt’* # “one”, *śīwōṭ* > *śīwōt’* “fire”, *ṣwārāb* > *ṣwārāp’*# “harvest period [diminutive]” (see Fig. 6), but *šīt* > *šīt*^{h} # “genitals” and *yaṣkūk* > *yaṣkūk*^{h}# “he closes”.

The perception of ejective emphatics in one position (i.e. pre-pausal) combined with the fact that one of the emphatics — /ḳ/ — is released on a glottalic airstream in all phonological environments presumably then led researchers to the assumption that emphatics as a class were ejectives. This second part of the equation appears to be based on an (unwritten) belief that all emphatic consonants within a language share one main articulatory correlate. In this case, if /ḳ/ is indubitably an ejective, then the other emphatics must be too. In many cases this is so, as in the ejective emphatics in Amharic and Tigrinya and the pharyngealized emphatics in the majority of non-peripheral Arabic dialects. However, this is not necessarily the case, and Mehri is not unique in exhibiting differing articulatory correlates of emphatics. A few dialects of Arabic, including Yemeni Zabīd (Naïm 2008), ilXarga (Kharga) in Middle Egypt (Behnstedt & Woidich 1985), and (variably) some Northern Sinai Bedouin (de Jong 2000), have ejective plosives /t’/ and/or /k’/, but pharyngealized fricatives /ṣ/ (and /ḍ/ in Zabīd). Faifi and Minabbih, South Arabian dialects spoken on either side of the western Saudi–Yemeni border, have

[13] Note that this is a term used for convenience, since the class of gutturals is usually said in Semitic to include the laryngeals /h/ and /’/ (Hayward & Hayward 1989; McCarthy 1991), sounds which do not pattern with pharyngeals, uvulars, and emphatics in Mahriyōt.

[14] It appears to be lack of recognition of pre-pausal glottalization that led Johnstone (1975: 99) to postulate the pre-glottalized phonemes /’r/ and /’l/ in Mehri, and possibly also /’ḍ/. Pre-glottalized (note also concomitantly devoiced) [’r̥] and [’l̥] are restricted to pre-pausal position: the examples given by Johnstone of these phones follow long vowels in word-final position — *səyo:’r* “to go” and *məyo:’l* “to turn aside” (1975: 99).

a non-pharyngealized abfricated reflex of **ṣ*, namely /st/, but all other emphatics are pharyngealized. And in several dialects of Arabic, the pharyngealization in /ṣ/ has weakened to the degree that any former distinction between **ṣ* and **s* has broken down (Watson 2002: 279).

The different articulatory correlates of emphasis in Mahriyōt are at least partially phonetically motivated: crucially, the place and stricture of a segment are responsible for the phonetic interpretation of a phonological feature in a particular context. The most common pharyngealized consonants are those sounds with a primary articulation at a distance to the secondary (pharyngeal) articulation — namely dentals, alveolars, and bilabials. In a system in which the main correlate of emphasis is pharyngealization, velar consonants are rarely pharyngealized due to the proximity of the primary oral stricture to the secondary pharyngeal stricture — pharyngealization is either reflected principally in a lowering and retraction of adjacent vowels, or results in a retraction of the place of articulation from velar to uvular (see Delattre 1971; Zemánek 1996). Both cases are found in different dialects of Arabic. In a system in which the main correlate of emphasis is glottalization, the problem is reversed: the most favoured place for ejectives is velar (Ladefoged & Maddieson 1996: 78), since it is easy to raise the necessary pressure in the relatively smaller pharyngeal cavity used to produce [k']. In terms of manner of articulation, ejective fricatives are rare because of the physical difficulty in building up the requisite pressure while air is escaping from the oral stricture. Sibilants may be realized as affricates or abfricates, to aid or partially mimic the glottalic release of ejectives. The behaviour of Mahriyōt is therefore fully comprehensible — the only invariable glottalic pressure consonant is at the velar place, all other emphatics are realized with at least partial pharyngeal contraction, and two of the sibilant emphatics are affricated.

Acknowledgements

The authors thank Barry Heselwood for his original help with the spectrograms, and the Leverhulme Trust for a research fellowship for Janet Watson during which time much of the research for this paper was carried out.

References

Behnstedt P.
1987. *Die Dialekte der Gegend von Ṣaʕdah (Nord-Jemen).* Wiesbaden: Harrassowitz.

Behnstedt P. & Woidich M.
1985. *Die ägyptisch-arabischen Dialekte.* i. Wiesbaden: Dr. Ludwig Reichert.

Bellem A.
2007. Towards a Comparative Typology of Emphatics: Across Semitic and into Arabic dialect phonology. PhD thesis, School of Oriental and African Studies, University of London. [Unpublished].

Bittner M.
1909. *Studien zur Laut- und Formenlehre der Mehri-Sprache in Südarabien.* i. *Zum Nomen im engeren Sinn.* Vienna: Alfred Hölder.

De Jong R.
2000. *A Grammar of the Bedouin Dialects of the Northern Sinai Littoral: Bridging the linguistic gap between the eastern and western Arab world.* Leiden: Brill.

Delattre P.
1971. Pharyngeal features in the consonants of Arabic, German, French, Spanish and American English. *Phonetica* 23: 129–155.

Hayward K.M. & Hayward R.J.
1989. "Guttural": Arguments for a new distinctive feature. *Transactions of the Philological Society* 87: 179–193.

Jahn A.
1902. *Südarabische Expedition.* iii. *Die Mehri-Sprache in Südarabien.* Vienna: Alfred Hölder.

Johnstone T.M.
1970. A definite article in the Modern South Arabian Languages. *Bulletin of the School of Oriental and African Studies* 33: 295–307.
1975. The Modern South Arabian languages. *Afroasiatic Linguistics* 1/5: 93–121.
1987. *Mehri Lexicon and English-Mehri Word-list.* London: School of Oriental and African Studies.
Khattab G., Al-Tamimi F. & Heselwood B.
2006. Acoustic and auditory differences in the /t/-/ṭ/ opposition in male and female speakers of Jordanian Arabic. Pages 131–160 in S. Boudelaa (ed.), *Perspectives on Arabic Linguistics.* xvi. Amsterdam: John Benjamins.
Ladefoged P. & Maddieson I.
1996. *The Sounds of the World's Languages*. Oxford: Blackwell.
Laver J.
1994. *Principles of Phonetics*. Cambridge: Cambridge University Press.
Leslau W.
1947. Four Modern South Arabian languages. *Word* 3: 180–203.
Lonnet A.
2009. South Arabian, Modern. Pages 297–300 in K. Versteegh *et al.* (eds), *Encyclopedia of Arabic Language and Linguistics.* iv. Leiden: Brill.
Lonnet A. & Simeone-Senelle M-C.
1983. Observations phonétiques et phonologiques sur les consonnes d'un dialecte mehri. *Matériaux Arabes et Sudarabique (MAS-GELLAS)* 1: 187–218.
1997. La phonologie des langues sudarabiques modernes. Pages 337–371 in A.S. Kaye (ed.), *Phonologies of Asia and Africa.* i. Indiana: Eisenbrauns.
McCarthy J.
1991. Guttural phonology. Pages 63–92 in B. Comrie & M. Eid (eds), *Perspectives on Arabic Linguistics.* iii. Amsterdam: John Benjamins.
Maddieson I.
1984. *Patterns of Sounds*. Cambridge: Cambridge University Press.
Müller D.H. (ed.).
1909. *Südarabische Expedition.* ix. *Mehri- und Ḥaḍrami-Texte gesammelt im Jahre 1902 in Gischin von Dr. Wilhelm Hein, bearbeitet und herausgegeben von Dav. Heinr. Müller.* Vienna: Alfred Hölder.
Naïm S.
2008. Compléments à "Remarks on the spoken Arabic of Zabid". Paper delivered at the 8th AIDA Conference (Association internationale de dialectologie arabe), University of Essex, England, 28–31 August 2008. [Unpublished].
Sima A.
2002. Der bestimmte Artikel im Mehri. Pages 647–667 in W. Arnold & H. Bobzin (eds), *Festschrift für Otto Jastrow zum 60. Geburtstag.* Wiesbaden: Harrassowitz.
2005. 101 Sprichwörter und Redensarten im Mehri-Dialekt von Ḥawf. *Zeitschrift für Arabische Linguistik* 44: 71–93.
2009. *Mehri-Texte aus der jemenitischen Šarqiyyah*. Edited, introduced, and annotated by J.C.E. Watson & W. Arnold. Wiesbaden: Harrassowitz.
Simeone-Senelle M-C.
1997. The Modern South Arabian languages. Pages 378–423 in R. Hetztron (ed.), *The Semitic Languages*. London: Routledge.
Snyman J.W.
1970. *An Introduction to the !Xũ Language*. Cape Town: Balkema.
1975. *Žu|'hoasi fonologie en woordeboek*. Cape Town: Balkema.
Steiner R.C.
1982. *Affricated Ṣade in the Semitic Languages*. New York: American Academy for Jewish Research.

Thomas B.
1937. *Four Strange Tongues from Central South Arabia — the Hadara group.* London: Proceedings of the British Academy.

Watson J.C.E.
2002. *The Phonology and Morphology of Arabic*. Oxford: Oxford University Press.

Watson J.C.E. & Asiri Y.
2007. Pre-pausal devoicing and glottalisation in varieties of the south-western Arabian peninsula. *International Congress of Phonetic Sciences, Saarbrücken, Aug. 2007*. http://www.icphs2007.de/conference/Papers/1738/1738.pdf

Watson J.C.E., Glover Stalls B., al-Razihi K. & Weir S.
2006. The language of Jabal Rāziḥ: Arabic or something else? *Proceedings of the Seminar for Arabian Studies* 36: 35–41.

Zemánek P.
1996. *The Origins of Pharyngealization in Semitic*. Prague: Enigma Corporation.

Authors' addresses
Professor Janet C.E. Watson, School of Languages, University of Salford, Salford, Greater Manchester, M5 4WT, UK.
e-mail j.c.e.watson@salford.ac.uk

Dr Alex Bellem, Research Director (Syria), British Institute, PO Box 519, Jubaiha 11941, Amman, Jordan.
e-mail alex.bellem@bi-amman.org.uk

Proceedings of the Seminar for Arabian Studies 40 (2010): 357–366

Shell mounds of the Farasān Islands, Saudi Arabia

M.G.M. Williams

Summary
The Farasān Islands lie in the southern Red Sea in Saudi Arabian waters. Recent work has detected the presence of over 1000 shell mounds dated to between 7000–2000 BP (Bailey *et al.* 2007), many of which are under threat of destruction as the islands become a focus for development driven by the tourist industry. The sites have been unprecedentedly preserved due to the aridity of the region. Work to investigate these unprovenanced deposits began with reconnaissance fieldwork in 2006 that first identified the mounds as having anthropogenic origins. Full-scale investigations followed in 2008 and 2009; these employed a number of techniques ranging from satellite image interpretation to geo-archaeology. Two key sites were chosen for excavation and detailed survey, revealing two contrasting site histories and differing modes of evolution. Efforts to disentangle the environmental and cultural signals between the sites have followed a number of lines of enquiry, including survey and excavation, geo-archaeology, a landscape survey, and laboratory analysis. Preliminary results reveal an intriguing story of temporal and spatial shell-mound evolution at both an inter- and intra-site scale. These research methods are being followed up with a comprehensive dating programme using a variety of dating techniques, a method that has rarely been attempted on this type of site. In this paper we present the preliminary results of this work.

Keywords: shell mound, shell midden, site evolution, Farasān Islands, coastal archaeology

Introduction

This paper deals with the shell mounds of the Farasān Islands (Jazāʾir Farāsan) — one element of the archaeological diversity on the archipelago — which were only recently recognized as having anthropogenic origins (Bailey *et al.* 2007). Until this time, their provenance was almost completely unknown, save for three radiocarbon dates (ranging between 5400 and 2410 cal BP) that had been obtained by separate projects whose focus was not always archaeological (Zarins, Al-Jawad Murad & Al-Yish 1981; Dabbagh, Hotzl & Schnier 1984; Bantan 1999). As a result, the locations from which the dating materials were obtained are vague, detailing only that they came from a "shell mound" in a broad geographic area. Shell sites have been found throughout the Red Sea and Arabian Peninsula (e.g. Biagi 1994; 2006; Edens & Wilkinson 1998; Durrani 2005; Vermeersch *et al.* 2005), but these deposits are often restricted, both in terms of size and concentration of sites. The Farasān Islands stand out because of the number and density of sites, and their state of preservation, which has benefited both from the arid environment and the low population density of the islands.

The Farasān Islands were formed as a result of the dynamic tectonic forces at work in the region: the islands are a collection of uplifted coral terracing overlying salt domes (Bantan 1999). Where the salt has withdrawn, the overlying rock has subsided forming deep depressions, which are often circular, forming wide arcing bays on the islands (Fig. 1). The Farasān Islands are composed of nearly 250 islands of uplifted coral pavement, underlain by limestone, which has been uplifted and deformed.

During the mid-Holocene shell mounds start increasing in numbers across the globe (e.g. Bailey & Parkington 2009). In the broad majority of areas, sites were initiated around 6000 BP. However, there is some degree of variability and the first appearance of shell sites can be earlier or later (e.g. Milner, Craig & Bailey 2007). This would seem to reflect the stabilization in global sea levels at *c.*6000 BP, with earlier dates apparently corresponding to areas where local tectonic, eustatic, and isostatic influences have resulted in the raising of local shorelines at a greater rate than sea levels rise, thus preserving earlier sites. There is much debate surrounding this discrepancy, and whether shell mounds started accumulating as a response to changing climatic conditions, whereby coastal and marine resources became more intensively exploited, or whether their appearance is due to better archaeological visibility of the sites once sea levels had stabilized. In addition to this last point,

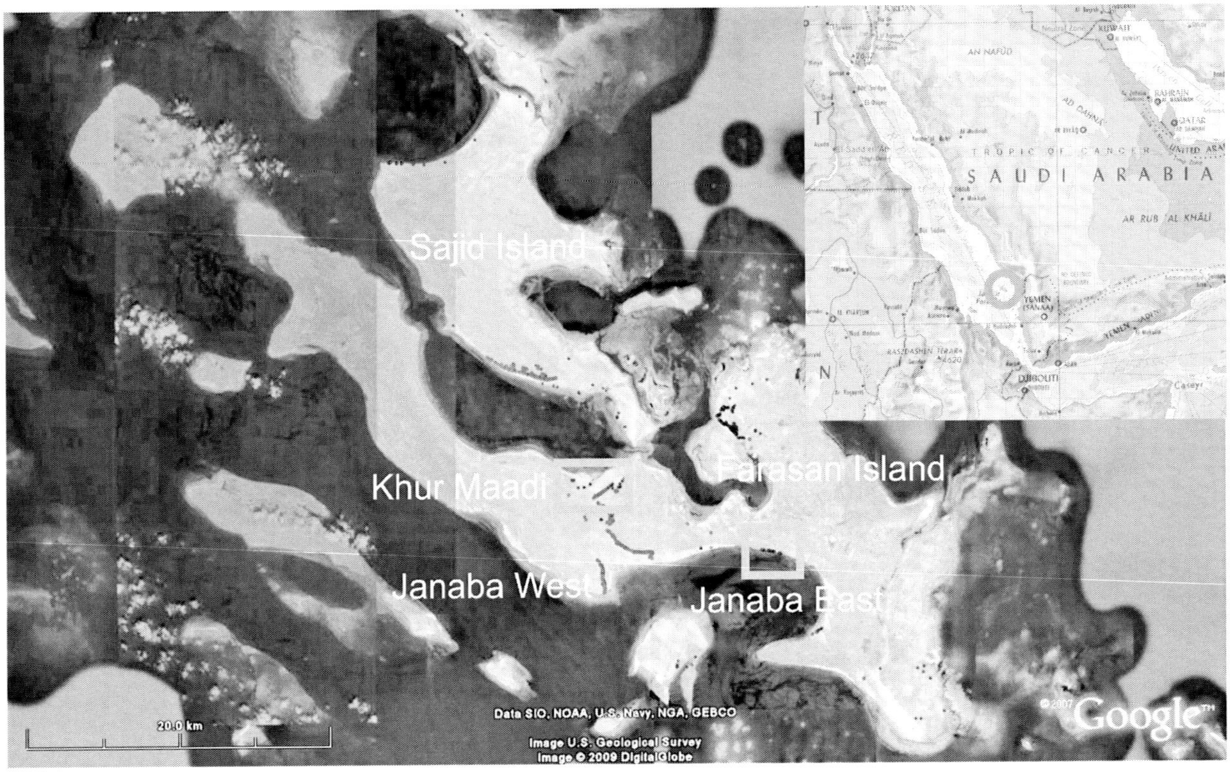

FIGURE 1. *The location of the Farasān Islands, and the location of sites across the islands indicated by dots. Case study areas are shown by boxes.*

as sea levels stabilized conditions may have been more conducive for the accumulation of larger mounds, since the shorelines would have been stable for longer. Shell sites persisted in many parts of the world for several thousand years, and indeed still accumulate today in some locations, for example the Saloum Delta, Senegal.

Aims and objectives

The aim of the project is to investigate the spatial and temporal evolution of shell sites on the Farasān Islands, both at an inter- and intra-site scale. This translates into the basic research questions: "How do individual shell mounds grow?" and "What are the relationships between shell mounds in a group, and more widely between groups?" A key consideration for the study is why shell sites are of different sizes. A group of shell sites can be dominated by a large centrally located shell mound or mounds, which can be many times larger than the surrounding sites (e.g. Bailey & Parkington 2009; Gaspar 1998). This is a common phenomenon that occurs globally and various hypotheses have been proposed to explain the emergence of these large central mounds: 1. that larger sites are an amalgamation of smaller sites; 2. that mounds of different sizes have different functions; and 3. that mounds of different size originate from different phases of mound building. This project will test these hypotheses at two sites on the islands, using a variety of methods detailed below.

Methods of investigation

Data from previous research on the islands was consulted to determine areas of known archaeological potential (e.g. Zarins, Al-Jawad Murad & Al-Yish 1981; Dabbagh, Hotzl & Schnier 1984; Bantan 1999; Bailey *et al.* 2007). Of particular use were the GPS points collected by Bailey *et al.* (2007). When these were used in conjunction with high-resolution satellite images taken from Google Earth, they provided an excellent indication of the location of clusters of sites. The satellite images are of sufficiently high resolution to enable individual sites, as small as individual shell scatters, to be identified. Satellite image interpretation was a primary method for locating new sites and assessing archaeological potential. The sites could easily be picked out as white stains (shell material) on a darker background (fossil coral terraces).

The fieldwork was broken down into three activities, survey, excavation, and geo-archaeological investigation. Initial work focused on surveying sites identified from the satellite images, first verifying and then surveying them. This included recording the dimensions and surface composition (shellfish species present) at each site, and allocating a GPS point. Certain groups of sites were deemed higher priority, and extra time was taken to survey accurately each individual mound using a differential GPS, which takes a sequence of closely spaced GPS points at 10 cm accuracy, to record the site in three dimensions.

Excavation formed the bulk of fieldwork activities, with two key sites being targeted for full-scale excavation. Where possible, transverse trenches were cut and excavated through the mounds to the full depth of the archaeological material. Several test-pitting programmes were also undertaken, both on sites surrounding the excavations and on other groups of shell mounds. These produced datable material, and recorded a snapshot of the internal structure of the sites in question. Test pitting involved excavating a trench of 50 cm^3 into a shell mound, from which a bulk sample of 15 cm^3 could be extracted and dating samples obtained. Finally geo-archaeological investigations were conducted to determine whether environmental and/or geo-morphological changes had influenced the formation of the adjacent shell mounds.

Two methods of dating have been utilized for this project: radiocarbon dating and amino-acid racemization dating (AAR). Radiocarbon dating was used to assess the time-depth of the two excavated sites, while AAR was employed both to assess further the stratigraphy of the two excavated sites and to assess the age of surrounding sites. AAR methodology followed that of Penkman *et al.* (2008) using the shellfish species *Strombus fasciatus*. This project demonstrated that the method works in this region, and could be used to distinguish between sites of different periods of shell-mound building activity (Demarchi *et al.*, in preparation). Radiocarbon dates were obtained from charcoal where possible, but due to the lack of appropriate dating material in the sites shell was often used. The most recent literature (and several experts) was consulted in order to select the best candidates for dating to minimize errors. *Chama reflexa*, which is a siphon feeder and grows at a depth of *c.*5 m, was chosen.

Case studies

Fieldwork focused on the largest and most central islands of the Farasān archipelago, these being Farasān al-Kabīr (the largest island), Saquid (Sajīd), Qumah (Qumāʾ), and Zufāf, although no shell sites were located on Zufāf. This paper will focus on two case studies: Janābah East and Khawr al-Maᶜādī, both located on the main island, where the largest shell mound of the group was excavated in each study area (Fig. 1). The two areas were selected because of their vulnerability to destruction. The Khawr al-Maᶜādī sites have been extensively destroyed by extraction of material for the building industry. The Janābah East site is at high risk both of falling into the sea as a result of cliff undercutting, and also because of its location between a growing power station and water desalination plant, and a harbour. Excavating both sites allows a broader spectrum of the island's sites to be investigated, as well as ensuring that preservation by record can be accomplished. Investigating "at risk" sites also minimizes destruction and damage to sites where there is no imminent threat, preserving them for future generations.

Case study 1

The first case study reviewed here is the Khawr al-Maᶜādī group of sites (Fig. 2), located in the centre of Farasān Island. Initial observations of the distribution of shell sites for this area show that there are sites extending from the Khawr al-Maᶜādī right across the centre of the island to Janābah Bay West. This indicates that both the Khawr al-Maᶜādī and Janābah Bay West inlets were once joined by a narrow channel that divided the island into two. Both bays (and channel) have since been uplifted and in-filled with sediments; evidence for uplift comes from large fault lines visible in the coral platforms in addition to the raised topography in the centre of the island.

The study area is located at the mouth of the former Khawr al-Maᶜādī bay, on the transition from the former open coastline to the inner bay (Fig. 2). In-filling and uplift have resulted in the coastline prograding (or building up with sediment) to approximately 400 m further out from the palaeo-shoreline. The group of sites is dominated by two very close 3 m-high shell mounds at the junction of the former open coastline and the mouth of the bay. These two mounds are surrounded by a number of smaller shell mounds and scatters. There are two distinct shell-site distribution patterns: to the north-west the mounds form a linear pattern following the palaeo-shoreline. To the south, the mounds are apparently randomly distributed

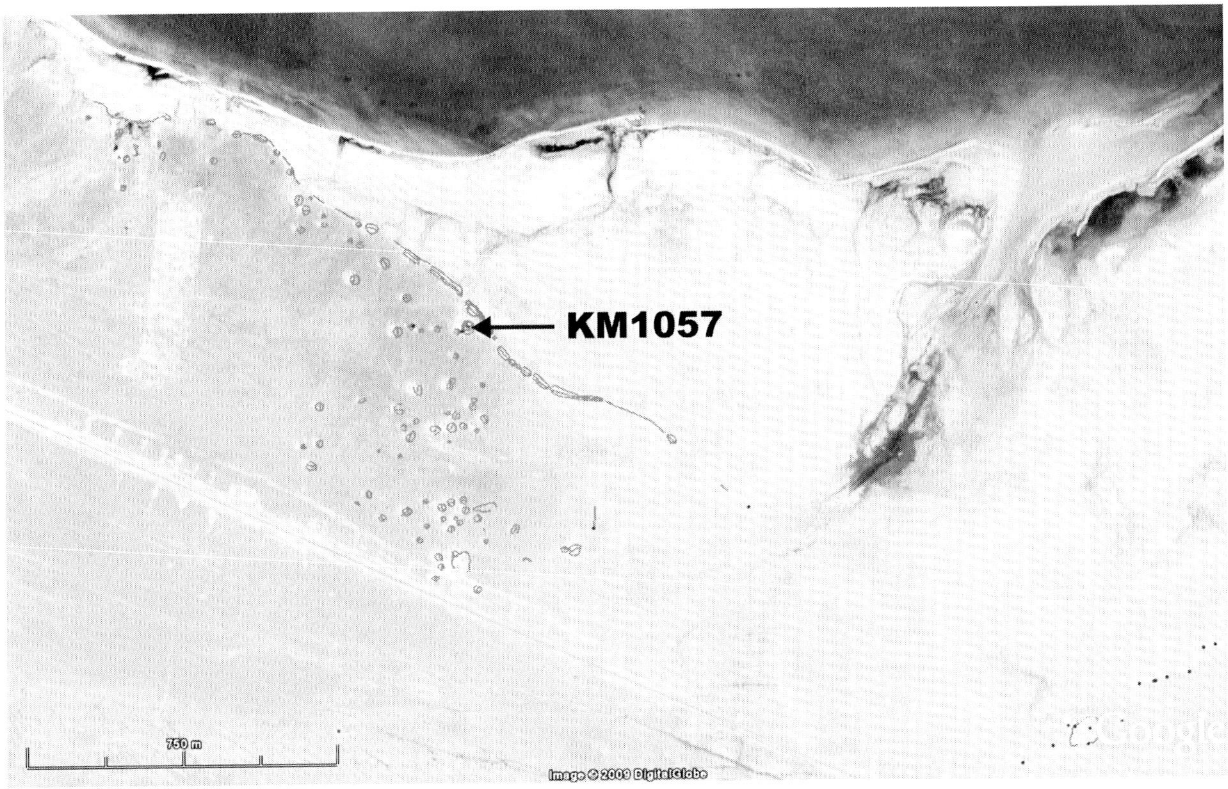

Figure 2. *The location of sites in the Khawr al-Maᶜādī group (circles denote the sites). The excavated mound designated KM1057.*

within a broad north–south band. This band appears to represent the edge of the former bay, where a highly transitional shallow-water environment existed, reaching various levels in different years. Sites accumulating at the water's edge during lower stands would eventually form self-selecting dry sites when the water level was higher (e.g. Bailey, Chappell & Cribb 1994).

The large mound chosen for excavation was designated KM1057; the destruction to the site allowed a 3 m-deep section to be exposed through the centre of the unstable mound (Fig. 3). This section revealed an assemblage largely dominated by the shellfish *Strombus fasciatus* (Born, 1778, common name: Lineated conch), a species that today thrives in shallow sandy sub-tidal environments, where it grazes on seagrass. The large Khawr al-Maᶜādī bay would have provided the required habitat for this species; geo-archaeological investigations in this area have uncovered *in situ* fossil shell beds with a diverse range of species, including large numbers of *Strombus fasciatus*. The profile of the mound is interrupted in only two places, near the top and base by two discreet horizons dominated by the shellfish *Chama reflexa* (Reeve, 1846, common name: Reflexed jewel box). This species grows on coral reefs, at depths of *c.*5 m, where it cements itself onto the coral; at present this habitat is found *c.*100 m off the present shoreline. Small quantities of fishbone were also found in the uppermost layer associated with the ash.

Two dates were obtained from the mound, both from the *Chama* layers. These were 4770±60 cal BP (BETA–255385) for the top and 4900±60 cal BP (BETA–255383) for the base (Fig. 4). These dates clearly show that the mound accumulated very rapidly, indeed the dates are so close together that they are within the margins of error of radiocarbon dating. No other features were found in the mound and there was a distinct absence of finds, those present being restricted to the limited numbers of fishbone.

Case study 2

The second case study is from Janābah East (Fig. 1), where the coastal setting is in contrast to the Khawr al-Maᶜādī (Fig. 5). The coastline is open, and appears to have been stable since at least the initiation of shell-

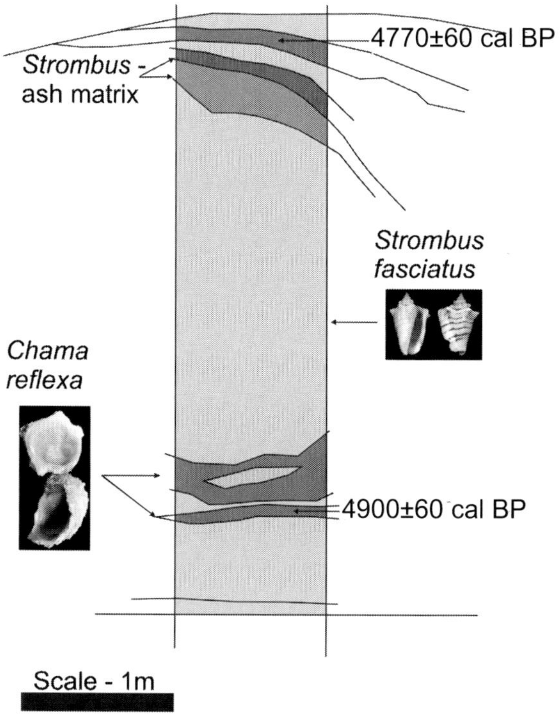

FIGURE 3. *An annotated section drawing for site KM1057, excavated in the Khawr al-Maʿādī group.*

mound building activities, as evidenced by a well-developed undercutting of the cliff. There are eight sites in the group, all of which are located on the cliff top, and the majority of which are low mounds and scatters. The site chosen for excavation, designated JE0004, is the largest and most centrally located mound of the group, at *c.*1.5 m high, and 20 m across (Fig. 6); it is located on a small but prominent headland that offers excellent visibility across the surrounding bay. This part of the cliff has also experienced the most undercutting, in places reaching up to *c.*4 m. Offshore is a *c.*150 m-wide sub-tidal shelf with an average depth of *c.*1 m; there are patches of sand on which seagrass grows and *Strombus fasciatus* can be found. After this the depth drops off in a series of short shelves to a depth of *c.*12 m.

A transverse trench was opened up across the centre of the site, exposing a 20 m-long section, to a maximum depth of 1.5 m at the deepest point. The mound presents a complex stratigraphy, and is split into two distinct depositional units, to the north (inland) and south (seaward) (Fig. 6). The northern side was dominated by inter-fingering layers of larger shells with layers of clean *Strombus*, which would seem to represent dumping activities. The species composition of large shell layers varies, with some layers being almost exclusively made up of *Chicoreus virgineus* (Röding, 1798, common name: Virgin murex) and *Pleuroploca gigantea* (Kiener, 1840, common name: Horse conch), while others are composed predominantly of *Spondylus marisrubri* (Röding, 1798, common name: thorny/spiny oysters) and *Chama reflexa*. Sparsely interspersed in these are layers that contain a mixture of the above species, and some layers that contain an abundance of ash or ash and clean *Strombus*. On the south side were alternating layers of hearth deposits and clean *Strombus*, which may represent the occupation (or processing) side of the site. In addition, several small but steep-sided cuts were observed in this area of the mound, which might tentatively be interpreted as post holes.

When this configuration is compared to the characteristics of some of the shell scatters, a similar pattern can be seen, which can be interpreted in terms

Site	*Horizon*	*Lab Code*	*Material*	^{14}C *(‰)*	*Age (yr BP)*	*Adjusted for local Marine Reservoir Effect*	*Age Cal. BC (yr) 2 σ*
JE0004	Top	OxA–19587	Charcoal	-24.53	4709±31		3632–3561
JE0004	Base	BETA–255384	Shell (*Chama reflexa*)	1.3	4850±50	4740±60	3270–2880
KM1057	Top	BETA–255385	Shell (*Chama reflexa*)	2.4	4880±50	4770±60	3300–2900
KM1057	Base	BETA–255383	Shell (*Chama reflexa*)	1.6	5010±50	4900±60	3380–3080

FIGURE 4. *Radiocarbon dates.*

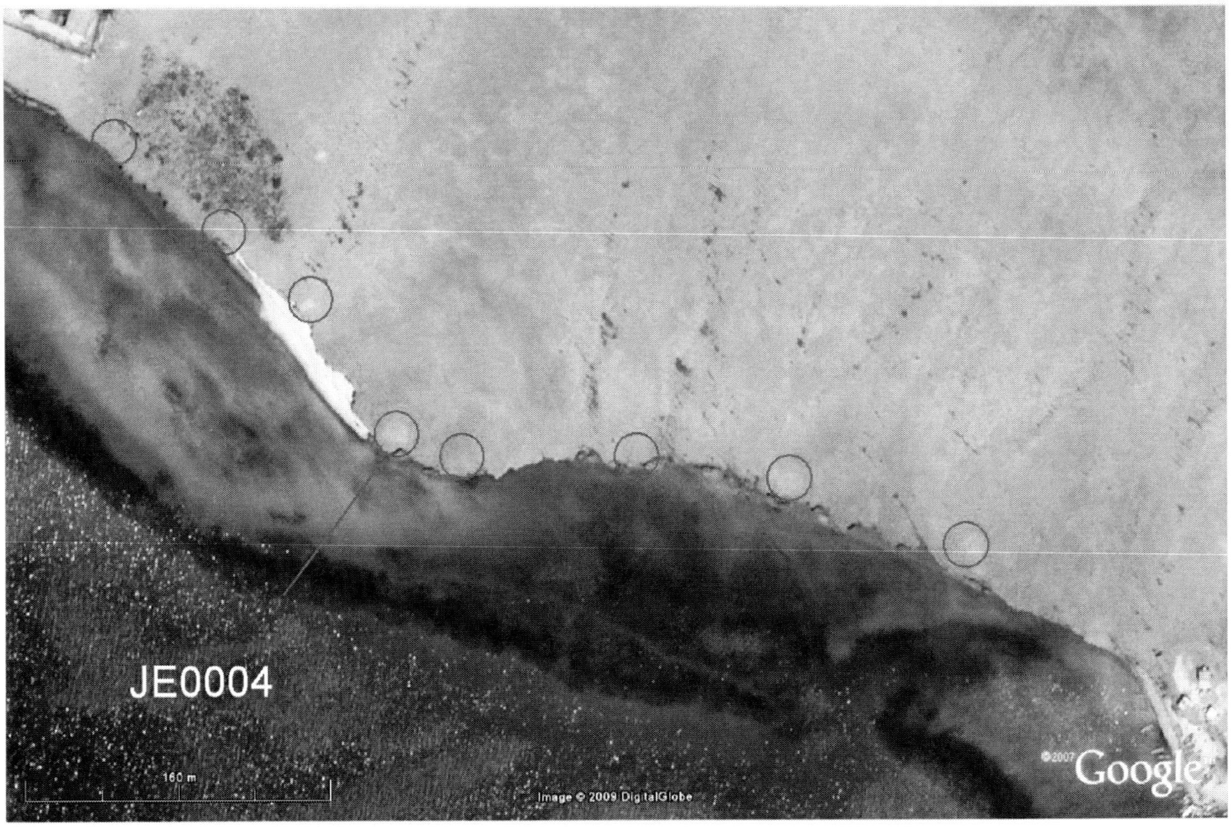

Figure 5. *The location of the Janābah East group (circles denote the sites). The excavated mound designated JE0004.*

of the "drop" and "toss" zone model (Binford 1978). This model describes how a group might sit about a focal point, normally a hearth, while eating or performing other activities, disposing of waste products in a manner whereby larger items (in this case the larger shells) are discarded by throwing them a certain distance over the camp fire, or over the shoulder. Smaller waste items (such as smaller shells) are dropped around the immediate area in which the group is sitting. This results in a very distinctive pattern of deposition (Fig. 7).

Two dates were obtained from the deepest part of the site, 4740±60 cal BP (BETA–255384) from the base, and 4709±31 cal BP (OxA–19587) from the top (Fig. 4). These dates show a rapid accumulation rate for the site, being within the margin of error for radiocarbon dating, indicating that the site was used intensively over a relatively short period of time. There is also evidence for erosion at the site, and loss of material from the uppermost part of the mound; this evidence comes both from the coastal erosion and the steep nature of the coastal side of the mound, indicating that sections have been lost to the sea. Here a number of layers within the mound end abruptly at the surface mound where they appear to have been truncated.

Discussion

The two case studies make for an interesting comparative study, both because of their contrasting coastal settings, and because of the difference of internal features. From the distribution of sites, it is clear that the coastal setting influences where shell sites are situated. Where there is an open, straight coastline, mounds accumulate along the edge of the shore in a linear distribution. There is some variation on this, where some smaller sites, mainly scatters, are set back a little from the main distribution, but the largest sites are situated at the water's edge. This pattern is clearly seen at both sites, to the north-west of the Khawr al-Maᶜādī and over the entirety of Janābah East. The transitory nature of the interior of the Khawr al-Maᶜādī bay has resulted in an apparently random distribution of sites, with both mounds and scatters densely packed into a

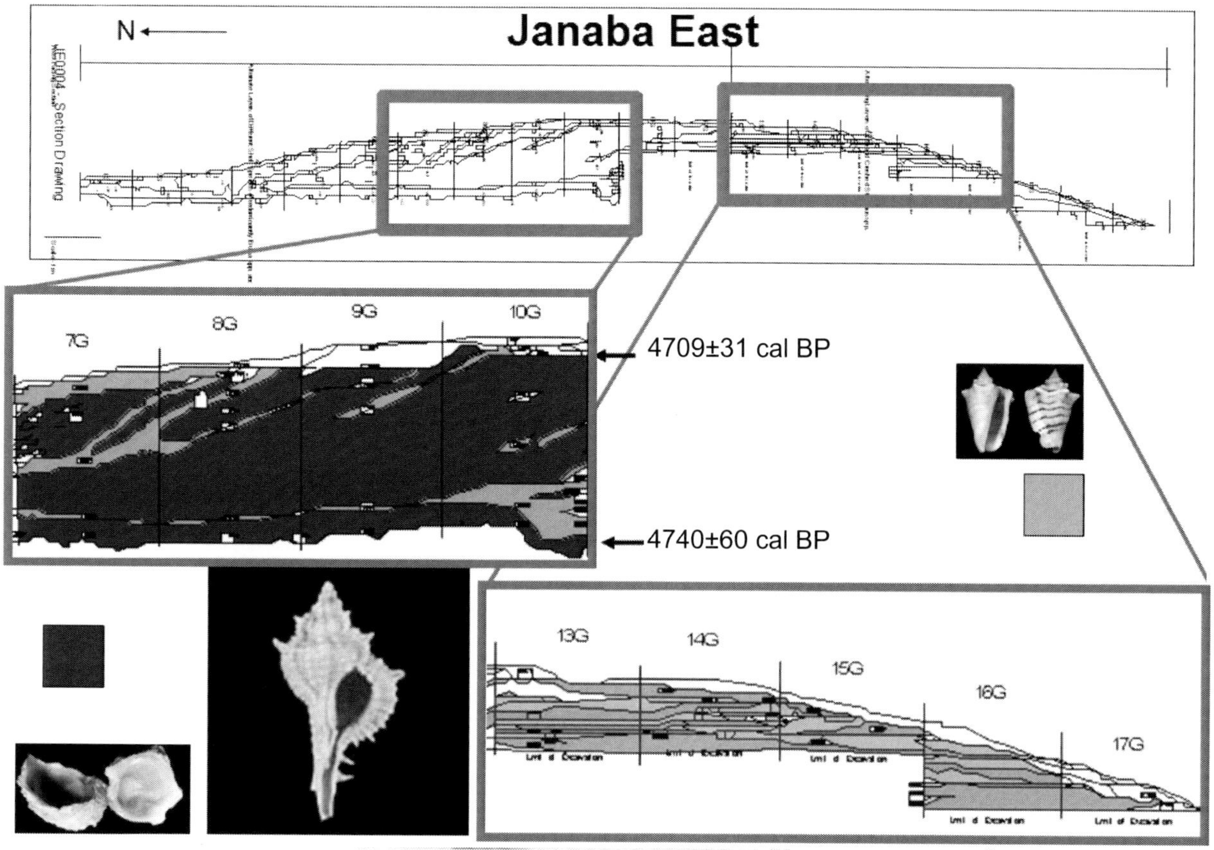

Figure 6. *An annotated section drawing of site JE0004, excavated in the Janābah East group.*

wide band between what were presumably the upper and lower limits of seasonal fluctuations in the water level of the bay. The larger sites are likely to have become self-selecting sites (e.g. Bailey, Chappell & Cribb 1994) during higher stands of water, since they would have presented dry islands on which to process and presumably consume the gathered food. Ethnographic studies have shown that shell mounds often accumulate at the nearest convenient location to the shell beds where the shells are gathered (e.g. Bird *et al.* 2002; Meehan 1982; Thomas 2007). This is primarily due to the bulky nature of shellfish, which acts as a limiting factor on the distance people are likely to carry the unshelled molluscs. Once the meat is removed from the bulky shells, it is often transported over longer distances, but the need to gather more food in the near future often results in camps being located at these sites with the incorporation of other non-shell (often terrestrial) material into the site. The differences in composition between the two sites might be related to this aspect, and reflect the activities taking place. The Khawr al-Maᶜādī site contained very little other material apart from the *Strombus*, *Chama*, and the restricted ash matrix. However the Janābah East site contained concentrations of fish and mammal bone, indicating a wider variety of activities. This might indicate that the Khawr al-Maᶜādī site was used almost exclusively for processing the shells, either before transport or before consumption, as there is evidence only for a limited range of activities at the site. In contrast the Janābah East site might well have been a "home base", being used for a much wider variety of activities, in addition to the processing of shellfish. The presence of possible post holes would strengthen this theory.

The question of why these two sites grew to become the largest sites in their respective groups is multifaceted. They have markedly different patterns of development, although both seem to have originated from a single point, and not from an amalgamation of smaller sites as one hypothesis suggests. The activities at each site have had a large influence on their formation and the size of the sites relative to each other is perhaps a reflection of this. It may be that changing resource exploitation strategies over time are responsible, since the Khawr al-Maᶜādī site

FIGURE 7. *A shell scatter showing the "toss and drop zone" pattern.*

closely predates Janābah East (if the radiocarbon dates are taken at face value). This difference in timings might also be indicative of changing environmental factors having ecological implications, with more accessible shell beds becoming unproductive, forcing the exploitation of harder-to-access resources. The primary reason for their dominant size would seem to be location, which would appear to be primarily responsible for their large size. It may be that the locations lent themselves to longer occupation, whether a larger area could be accessed using the sites as a base, or whether the better visibility and transport opportunities resulted in more frequent visits to the sites. Janābah East offers a good potential for fishing, and displays a greater diversity of activities taking place at the site. It is uncertain what opportunities would have been available in the Khawr al-Maᶜādī. The more limited assemblage found at the Khawr al-Maᶜādī site may well be specific to the activities carried out on the excavated mound, rather than a representation of the available resources. Analysis of material from the surrounding mounds obtained during test pitting may well uncover a broader assemblage in these surrounding sites.

Conclusions

The most obvious difference between the sites is their internal structure and composition. This can be interpreted as a reflection of the activities taking place on each mound. It can therefore be said with some confidence that the formation of a mound is linked both to the exploitation strategies and the activities associated with each site. That different activities were taking place at both sites might be linked to the age of the mounds and the fact that they come from two different phases of mound-building activity. However, it might also be a product of different exploitation strategies being employed to deal with the different coastal settings of each site. Perhaps it is a result of both, or of environmental change impacting on shell-bed productivity and forcing the exploitation of more inaccessible coastline. Certainly at Janābah East there is no obvious sign of environmental change, yet the site went out of use. Could this be indicative of over-exploitation? The dates of the two sites are (within the uncertainties of radiocarbon dating) very close, and may even overlap. This suggests that both sites result from the same phase of shell-mound building activity, or at least two phases which closely follow one another.

These sites do stand out because of their positioning in prominent locations on the coastline. Location is likely to be influential in the emergence of large centrally located shell mounds, at least in this area. Any conclusions regarding a link between mound composition and mound size will have to wait for the analysis of test pit material from the surrounding mounds, together with information from the dating programme.

The dating of the sites falls within the broad chronology of shell-bearing sites as outlined by Bailey *et al.* (2007). On a broader timescale these sites fall close to the onset of more arid conditions in the region (e.g. Arz *et al.* 2003), which occurred between 6000–5500 BP. These sites might represent an intensification of coastal resource exploitation, as aridity forced people to find alternative food sources. It is also around this time (*c.*6000 BP) that sea levels stabilized at their present levels, which might also have influenced the degree to which coastal resources were exploited. Certainly the location of the sites over 40 km from the mainland suggests that these people were already coastally adapted, and capable of making voyages far out to sea. Broadly contemporaneous shell-bearing sites demonstrating similar qualities to the Janābah East site have been found on the adjacent mainland near Jizān (e.g. Zarins, Al-Jawad Murad & Al-Yish 1981). How much contact they had with the mainland is debatable, but seasonal movements between the Farasān Islands and the mainland cannot be ruled out.

Acknowledgements

My thanks are due to Geoff Bailey, Abdullah Alsharekh, Kirsty Penkman, Nicky Milner, Kevin Walsh, Mark Beech, Bea Demarchi, Graham Oliver, Harry Robson, the Field Team, the British Academy, and the Supreme Commission for Tourism and Antiquities of Saudi Arabia. In addition, my thanks to the reviewers for their invaluable comments.

References

Arz H.W., Lamy F., Patzold J., Muller P.J. & Prins M.
2003. Mediterranean Moisture Source for an Early-Holocene Humid Period in the Northern Red Sea. *Science* 300: 118–121.
Bailey G.N. & Parkington J.
2009. *The Archaeology of Prehistoric Coastlines*. Cambridge: Cambridge University Press.
Bailey G.N., Chappell J. & Cribb R.
1994. The origin of Anadara shell mounds at Weipa, North Queensland, Australia. *Archaeology in Oceania* 29: 22, 69–80.
Bailey G.N., AlSharekh A., Flemming N., Lambeck K., Momber G., Sinclair A. & Vita-Finzi C.
2007. Coastal prehistory in the southern Red Sea Basin: underwater archaeology and the Farasan Islands. *Proceedings of the Seminar for Arabian Studies* 37: 1–16.
Bantan R.A.
1999. Geology and sedimentary environments of Farasan Bank (Saudi Arabia) southern Red Sea: A combined remote sensing and field study. PhD thesis, University of London. [Unpublished].
Biagi P.
1994. A radiocarbon chronology for the aceramic shell-middens of coastal Oman. *Arabian archaeology and epigraphy* 5/1: 17–31.
2006. The shell-middens of the Arabian Sea and Persian Gulf: Maritime connections in the seventh millennium BP? *Adumatu* 14: 7–16.
Binford L.R.
1978. Dimensional Analysis of Behavior and Site Structure: Learning from an Eskimo Hunting Stand. *American Antiquity* 43/3: 330–361.
Bird D.W., Richardson J.L., Veth P.M. & Barham A.J.
2002. Explaining Shellfish Variability in Middens on the Meriam Islands, Torres Strait, Australia. *Journal of Archaeological Science* 29/5: 457–469.

Dabbagh A., Hotzl H. & Schnier H.
1984. Farasan Islands. General considerations and geological structure. Pages 212–220 in A.R. Jado & J.G. Zotl (eds), *Quaternary Period in Saudi Arabia*. ii. Vienna/New York: Springer.

Demarchi B., Williams M.G.M, Milner N., Russell N., Bailey B. & Penkman K.
(in preparation). Amino acid racemisation dating of marine shells: a mound of possibilities. *Quaternary International.*

Durrani N.
2005. *The Tihamah Coastal Plain of South-West Arabia in its Regional Context c.6000 BC– AD 600.* (British Archaeological Reports, International Series, 1456). Oxford: Archaeopress.

Edens C. & Wilkinson T.
1998. Southwest Arabia during the Holocene: Recent archaeological developments. *Journal of World Prehistory* 12/1: 55–119.

Gaspar M.D.
1998. Considerations of the sambaquis of the Brazilian coast. *Antiquity* 72/277: 592.

Meehan B.
1982. *Shell bed to shell midden.* Canberra: Australian Institute of Aboriginal Studies.

Milner N., Craig O.E. & Bailey G.N.
2007. *Shell Middens in Atlantic Europe.* Oxford: Oxbow Books.

Penkman K.E.H., Kaufman D.S., Maddy D. & Collins M.J.
2008. Closed-system behaviour of the intra-crystalline fraction of amino acids in mollusc shells. *Quaternary Geochronology* 3: 2–25.

Thomas F.
2007. The Behavioral Ecology of Shellfish Gathering in Western Kiribati, Micronesia. 2: Patch Choice, Patch Sampling, and Risk. *Human Ecology* 35/5: 515–526.

Vermeersch P.M., Van Philip P., Veerle R. & Van Wim N.
2005. The Middle Holocene Shell Mound of E1 Gouna on the Red Sea (Egypt). *Journal of Field Archaeology* 30/4: 435–442.

Zarins J., Al-Jawad Murad A. & Al-Yish K.S.
1981. The Comprehensive Archaeological Survey Program, a. The second preliminary report on the southwestern province. *Atlal* 5: 9–42.

Author's address
Matt G.M. Williams, Archaeology Department, University of York, The King's Manor, York YO1 7EP, UK.

e-mail mgmw500@york.ac.uk

Proceedings of the Seminar for Arabian Studies 40 (2010): 367–380

The Almaqah temple of Meqaber Ga^cewa near Wuqro (Tigray, Ethiopia)

PAWEL WOLF & ULRIKE NOWOTNICK

Summary

Meqaber Gaᶜewa is a recently discovered site that indicates Sabaean cultural contacts with the Ethiopian highlands. Its main temple, dedicated to Almaqah, was unearthed under the auspices of a joint Ethiopian-German co-operation established in 2008. The single-roomed temple with a porticus and a tripartite sanctuary, situated within a large temenos, clearly resembles South Arabian prototypes and represents the southernmost architectural evidence of Sabaean influence hitherto discovered in Ethiopia. A number of well-preserved cult objects of outstanding quality — among them a completely preserved libation altar and a seated female statue — were found *in situ* at their original places in the temple. Their Ethio-Sabaic inscriptions, palaeographically dated to the early first millennium BC, mention the ancient name of Yeha for the first time and refer to a hitherto unknown king. At the same time, they reflect an African aspect by mentioning the king's mother in his affiliation. A *baityl* cult installation in the central sanctuary, pottery and votive objects such as incense burners, miniature vessels, and female figurines, illuminate liturgical practices predominating in that particular region and period. A surface field survey acquired initial information on the archaeological topography of the area and yielded seven further sites of that period.

Keywords: Ethio-Sabaean, epigraphy, architecture, Yeha, *baityl*

Introduction

In the early first millennium BC new features indicative of complex socio-economic structures appeared in the northern Horn of Africa. A number of these features, for example the emergence of a distinctive sacral architecture, characteristic sculptures, and inscriptions indicating religious beliefs related to the Sabaean pantheon, resulted from cultural interchange with South Arabia, especially with the flourishing kingdom of Saba. After excavations in the 1950s and 1960s at prominent sites with apparently strong Sabaean contact, such as Yeha, Hawlti, Melazo, and Matara, that period was labelled "Ethio-Sabaean" and a "Pre-Aksumite" kingdom of *DᶜMT* was assumed basically on very poor epigraphic evidence and characterized as a strongly South Arabian stimulated polity.[1] However, archaeological evidence of that polity and its Sabaean traits — especially in the sense of monumental objects like architecture — remained limited to a few core sites concentrated in the south of the central highlands of Eritrea and in the northern part of Tigray, especially around Aksum and Yeha, which is considered to be the ceremonial centre of that kingdom (Fig. 1). As a result, the approach to the spatial extent of that period and a polity of *DᶜMT*, as well as towards generalizing and ambiguous terms like "Pre-Aksumite" or "Ethio-Sabaean", is now being reviewed rather critically (Finneran 2007: 110f., 117–122, 143–145; Phillipson, in press). While the social impact of the Sabaean contact is regarded as being largely confined to the elite only, the rarity of sites indicative of the polity of *DᶜMT* caused it to be seen as a somewhat local phenomenon. For example, the area of Wuqro and ᶜAddi Akaweh, just about 80 km as the crow flies south-east of Yeha, was recently designated as being "beyond its conventionally recognised south-eastern borders".[2] Beside this reasonable critical approach, however, the question arises as to whether such statements are justified as regards the still inadequate coverage of data on archaeological sites beyond the prominent centres and especially south of the Aksum-Yeha region.

[1] For overviews of the period see de Contenson 1981: 341–361; Anfray 1990: 17–57; Phillipson 1998: 42–49; Finneran 2007: 109–144. For a site-gazetteer with commentary and bibliography, see Godet 1977; 1983.

[2] Finneran (2007: 118); nevertheless this source (inappropriately) recommends *DᶜMT* as a synonym for "Pre-Aksumite".

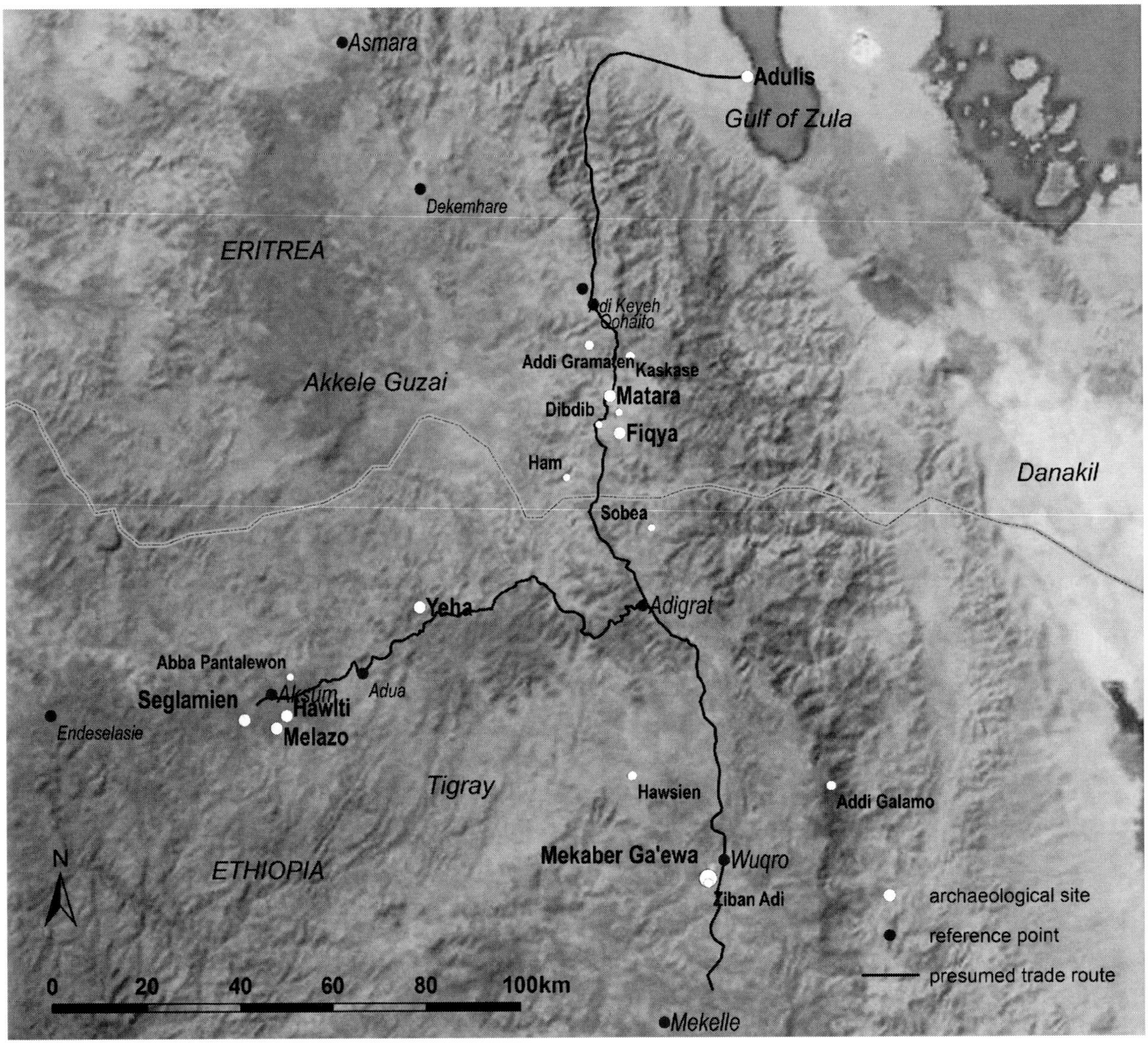

FIGURE 1. *Significant sites with archaeological evidence of South Arabian cultural influence during the early first millennium BC in the Ethiopian and Eritrean highlands. Map: P. Wolf, © DAI; underlying satelite-data: © GoogleEarth 2009.*

In view of that situation, rescue excavations under the auspices of the Tigray Tourism and Culture Commission (TCC) have led in 2007 to the discovery of a site of more than local significance: Meqaber Ga^cewa,[3] just a short distance away from the church of Abuna Garima which houses three incense burners with Ethio-Sabaic inscriptions found in the vicinity of ^cAddi Akaweh (RIE 9–10, see also Godet 1977: 35). The TCC rescue excavations[4] revealed several cult objects: a perfectly preserved libation altar with a royal dedication, a seated female statue, architectural blocks, and limestone incense burners. Their Ethio-Sabaic inscriptions, which are palaeographically dated to the eighth–sixth centuries BC,[5] include references to Almaqah and to a hitherto

[3] Situated about 5 km south-west of Wuqro; co-ordinates: 39.566908 E, 13.761824 N (Datum Adindan); it was announced to the TCC by Yohannes Gebre Selassie.

[4] Directed by Hiluf Berhe.

[5] All information on the inscriptions was provided by N. Nebes (personal communication, July 2009; see also Nebes, forthcoming). The dating of

Figure 2. *The temple and the northern part of the precinct at the end of the excavations in June 2009. P. Wolf, © DAI.*

unknown king, and they mention the ancient name of Yeha for the first time. However, it remained unclear how these objects of high craftsmanship and artistic quality were associated to walls unearthed in nearby test trenches, and especially whether these objects, large yet portable, were secondarily deposited at the site or whether they signified a sacral centre of that period. To solve these questions was one of the main tasks of the first two seasons of the joint Ethiopian-German excavations conducted in autumn 2008 and spring 2009. They led to the discovery of an Almaqah temple and its sacral precinct. The cult objects were part of its temple furnishing, some being still *in situ*.

The temple and its cult inventory

The temple represents a regional example of a "Sabaean-style" temple comprising many structural elements and the cult inventory of South Arabian temples (see below), but in a rather modest execution. It was a single-roomed temple with a hypaethral naos and pronaos, probably in the form of a porticus, all arranged along an east–west axis (Figs 2–3).[6] Occupying the rear part of a rectangular temenos located on the eastern edge of a limestone plateau, it represented an impressive landscape marker overlooking the plains to the north-east of ᶜAddi Akaweh. The western half of the temenos, with a main gate indicated by a 6 m-broad gap at its western face, formed a transverse oriented forecourt in front of the temple. Several subsidiary rooms were arranged along the northern side of the court; a small open yard and two further rooms have been located between the temple and the northern temenos wall.

The temple walls, about 100 cm thick, as well as the slightly thinner walls of the temenos buildings were executed in limestone masonry set in earthen

the inscriptions into the earlier part of this date range, i.e. the eighth century BC, was confirmed in December 2009 by ^{14}C datings of the first building stage of the Almaqah temple described in this article.

[6] The temple and precinct have been designated as MG 100 (which stands for Meqaber Gaᶜewa 100) with serial room numbers starting with MG 101, 102 etc.

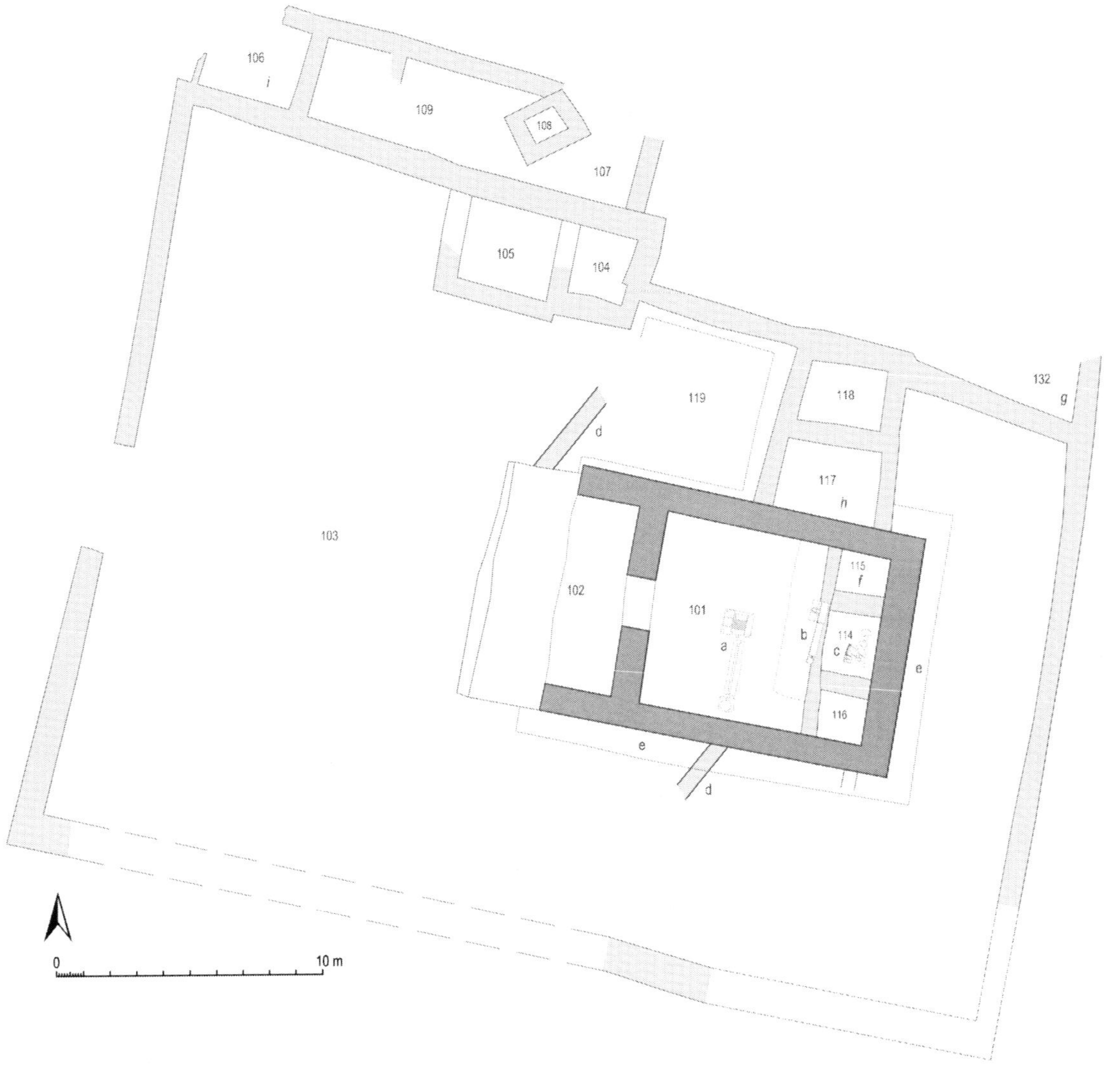

FIGURE 3. *A general plan of the Almaqah temple and its precinct at Meqaber Gaᶜewa during its initial building stage. Room numbers:* **[101]** *naos;* **[102]** *pronaos/porticus and staircase;* **[103]** *forecourt;* **[104–107, 109]** *side rooms;* **[108]** *later building;* **[114–116]** *tripartite sanctuary;* **[117–118]** *side rooms;* **[119]** *small open yard;* **[132]** *side room with votive objects. Find spots:* **(a)** *libation installation;* **(b)** *stone pavement, sanctuary facing, female statue, and incense burner;* **(c)** *elevated central sanctuary with* baityl *cult place;* **(d)** *remains of earlier building structures;* **(e)** *banquette of temple;* **(f)** *pottery incense burners;* **(g)** *votive objects;* **(h)** *miniature altar;* **(i)** *Type-4100 vessel. P. Wolf, © DAI.*

mortar. Their outer faces consist of roughly cut but carefully laid limestone slabs up to 40×30×10 cm in size. No solid foundations have been found in the test trenches. However, a *krepis*-like banquette of one- or two-stone courses supports the bases of the walls (Fig. 3/e). It is almost 1 m wide along the temple's eastern and southern walls, indicating a flat podium erected on a low mound. A broad flight of steps leads up to the temple's pronaos, stretching over the entire width of the western facade. That porticus, elevated about 1 m above the surrounding temple precinct, might have had a propylon of four supports, which were possibly made of wood.[7]

[7] Indicated by large but broken stone slabs at the western side of the porticus, which might have served as pillar foundations.

FIGURE 4. *The libation altar after its conservation, with the drain and basin. P. Wolf, © DAI.*

The naos, measuring *c.*8.5×7 m, was an elevated hypaethral room with a libation altar placed on its main axis (Fig. 3/a). In later building stages it was most likely provided with a peristasis (see below). The temple's tripartite sanctuary, with a podium-like elevated central room, was situated in the rear part of the naos opposite its entrance.

Throughout the history of the temple, its centre was dominated by a libation altar (Fig. 4; cf. Fig. 3/a).[8] It consists of several separate parts, perfectly dressed and assembled with great precision. Its body is faced by five limestone slabs, decorated with a facade of "false windows" resting on four steps. The slabs hide an asymmetrically worked limestone offering tablet, with a spout in the shape of a bull's head protruding from the altar's southern face. The altar is covered by four inscribed top stones with a denticulated frieze. A shallow square depression in the surface of the western block served as the actual offering spot. A tauro-cephaloid spout at its inner face led the offered liquid onto the offering tablet. It was then conducted down to a 2 m-long monolithic limestone drain in the temple floor and was finally collected in a concave basin at the end of it. The inscription running around the top stones dedicates the altar to Almaqah. It was commissioned by a king called *WR'N*, son of *RD'M*, on the occasion of his inauguration as master of the temple of Yeha. According to its palaeography, the inscription can be dated to the eighth–sixth centuries BC, while ^{14}C datings of the first building stage, to which the altar very probably belongs, indicate a date in the same period.

The lower part of the elevated central sanctuary room in the rear part of the naos was faced by perfectly dressed limestone masonry (Fig. 5; cf. Fig. 3/b–c). Three of its ashlar blocks were still resting *in situ*. One block protrudes into the naos indicating that the facing had a step. The block resting on top of it bears a short text, palaeographically contemporaneous with the altar's inscription, dedicating the facade to Almaqah. The name of the donating stonemason is known from South

[8] It was partially unearthed during the TCC excavations in December 2007, and fully excavated and moderately preserved in spring 2009.

FIGURE 5. *The tripartite sanctuary in the rear part of the naos with its facing blocks, the seated female statue, the incense burners, and the* baityl *in the central room, as well as the remains of the supports of the second building stage in front of the sanctuary. P. Wolf, © DAI.*

Arabian inscriptions, suggesting that his clan was based in the north of the central Yemenite highlands.

While the libation altar and the facing blocks were evidently found *in situ*, the find spot of the seated female statue on top of one of these blocks cannot have been its original place. Its base was found on top of the pedestal near the rear wall of the central sanctuary, next to a number of smooth stones and the fragment of a large inscribed limestone incense burner (Figs 3/c, 5). Very likely that arrangement represents a *baityl* (arrangement of cult stones) of naturally worn stones (*al-anṣāb*) and votive objects. The statue and the large incense burner fragment might have been part of it. As the central sanctuary has not yet been fully excavated, it is not clear whether this arrangement of cult objects belongs to the original temple inventory or whether it was installed in this place during a later period of the temple's history.

The artistic quality of the statue[9] and its striking stylistic similarity to the statue from ᶜAddi Galamo[10] are remarkable (Fig. 6). As both statues are similar in size, shape, and iconography, representing a seated woman wearing a similar coat with a pattern of drilled rosettes, one might assume that they have been produced by one and the same workshop or sculptor. The text on its base, asking for healthy offspring, is likewise almost identical to the inscription on the base of the statue from ᶜAddi Galamo. The only difference is that it mentions Almaqah. Thus, there is no reason to doubt that the statue was part of the original temple inventory as well.

Building history

The temple is not the most ancient building structure on the site. It has been erected on top of ruins of an earlier occupation horizon, which consists of a series of archaeological strata lying directly on bedrock. The preserved wall, up to 40 cm high, forms the remains of that horizon and runs in a north-east/south-west direction,

[9] Unfortunately its head and hands are missing.

[10] Addis Ababa, Nat. Mus. JE 3 (Caquot & Drewes 1955: 17–26; for its inscription see RIE 52). Cf. the statues from Hawlti: JE 1657 and JE 1555 (de Contenson 1963: pls 31, 34).

Figure 6. *The female statue on its inscribed base. P. Wolf, © DAI.*

clearly different from the orientation of the temple (Fig. 3/d).[11] While it is clear that the walls of the Almaqah temple and its porticus have been partially built on top of these ruins, it remains unclear by how long the horizon predates the temple's construction period. According to our ^{14}C datings, however, these ruins are to be dated to the eighth century BC as well.

After the construction of the main walls, the substructure of the naos and the porticus was filled up with stone debris. As a result, the temple's floor level is elevated about 100 cm above the bedrock. The initial temple building was provided with a tripartite sanctuary; its central room might have been emphasized by a podium-like elevation by that stage (Figs 5, 7/a). The entire naos was covered by a packed mud floor that abutted the base of the libation altar, the drain, and its basin. No features indicating the support of a roof have been found associated with that early stage. A 1 m-wide area in front of the central and northern sanctuaries was paved with stone slabs, perhaps as a basement for the facing blocks of its central room (Fig. 3/b). It is not yet entirely clear whether the libation altar and that facing it were installed directly after the temple's initial construction or during a slightly later building stage. In any case, both date before the later alterations of the naos.

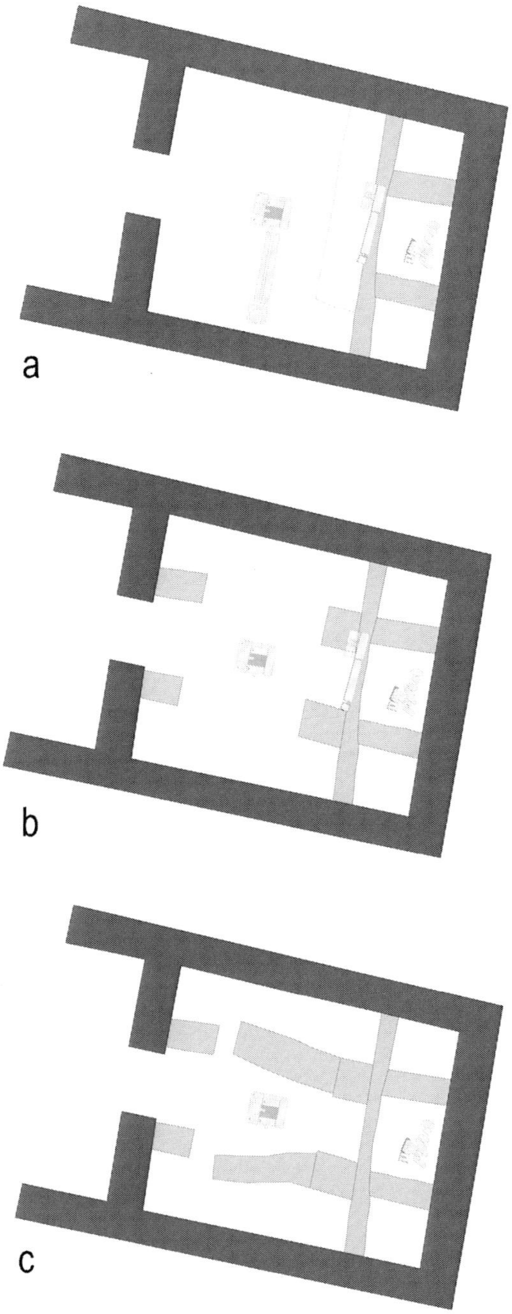

Figure 7. *A schematic plan indicating the building stages of the temple:* **(a)** *initial stage;* **(b)** *second stage;* **(c)** *last preserved stage. P. Wolf, © DAI.*

[11] An orientation that is, interestingly, more frequent in Sabaean sacral architecture than the east–west orientation of the temple (M. Schnelle, personal communication).

Figure 8. *A view into the naos with the walls and the floor of the third building stage. P. Wolf, © DAI.*

According to our ^{14}C dates, the temple underwent a first larger modification with the erection of four rectangular supports between the middle of the eighth century and the end of the fifth century BC. During this period the floor level of the naos had risen slightly (Fig. 7/b). Two rectangular supports were set to the left and right of its entrance in the west, forming a kind of inner porticus. The other two were erected in front of the partition walls of the tripartite sanctuary (Fig. 5). They might have supported the wooden entablature of a roof. However, given the large distance between them, a solid roof cannot have covered the central part of the naos. Remarkably, the north-eastern support was set up directly in front of the inscribed facing block, covering its dedication text. Additionally, the raised floor must have sealed the drain of the libation altar, causing the loss of a basic part of its original libation function.

According to our ^{14}C dates, the third and probably last building stage[12], during the fourth and third centuries BC is characterized by two new walls that divide the naos into three aisles (Figs 7/c, 8). They were built without any sound foundation onto a floor level established about 30 cm above the original temple floor, and they covered the ruined rectangular supports of the former building stage. In the central aisle of the naos, the new floor was paved with stone slabs, abutting the libation altar about 25 cm above its base. In the rear part of the naos, the floor covered parts of the former temple furniture almost completely, especially the lower facing blocks of the sanctuary and one of the incense burners next to them, which was cut off exactly at the height of that floor level.

The two longitudinal walls probably served as low

[12] There are no substantial remains of later occupation periods evident in our trenches in the temple.

foundation walls for the wooden posts of a peristasis that supported a roof of slate slabs along the side walls of the temple. Several such slabs, up to 80 cm in length, have been found in the debris. The roof probably did not cover the central part of the naos, as indicated by the small number of slate slabs and by the fact that only the floor of the central aisle was paved with stone slabs.

Thus, the temple's principal features apparently did not change during these building stages. Its initial design as a hypaethral temple was probably kept and just modified by the addition of a peristasis. The libation altar, probably open to the sky, continued to be the liturgical focus. It was not removed and was thus obviously still in use or at least respected. The sealing of its drain by the later floors and walls might, however, indicate a shift in ritual practice.

Pottery and small finds

Most of the site's pottery assemblage is basically contemporaneous with the Almaqah temple and has a rather homogeneous character. The clays used for the production of pottery vessels were tempered with fine inorganic and organic particles, sometimes also with very large inclusions. All vessels were handmade with mostly untreated surfaces. Only a few specimens were roughly smoothed with straw or grass or had decorations of incised patterns or figural applications. The fabrics range between bright red and light brown colours; a few grey and black wares are also present; black-topped vessels are rather infrequent. A division of the corpus into distinctively coloured wares, such as red, brown, or black could not be observed. By contrast, similar clays of the same provenance were fired red, grey, or black, depending on the firing process.

In the field, the pottery was grouped on the basis of macroscopic observation according to paste and temper inclusions, density, firing behaviour, and colour. These wares were later assessed by laboratory analysis, sampling 118 ceramic fragments from the Wuqro area by refiring (MGR) and chemical analysis (XRF).[13] The examination resulted in the definition of fabric groups and production

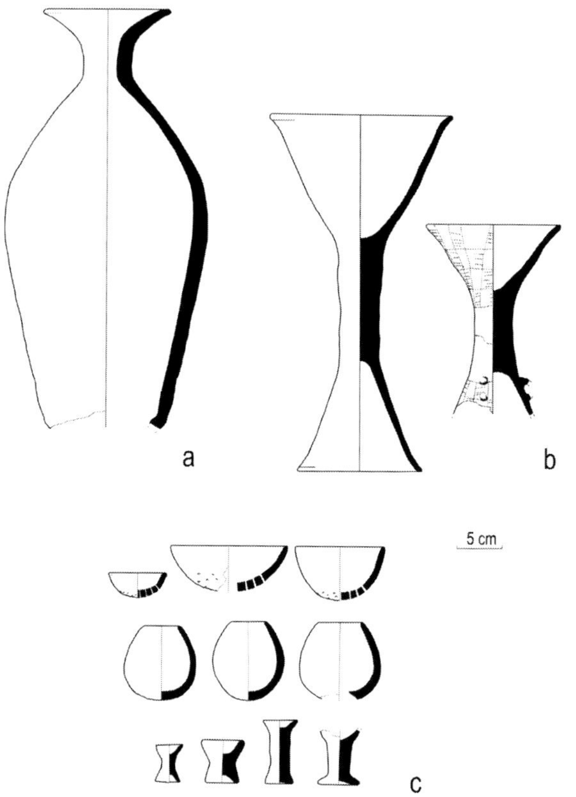

Figure 9. *Pottery from the Almaqah temple:* **(a)** *"torpedo-shaped" Type-4100 jar;* **(b)** *incense burners found on the initial floor level of the northern sanctuary;* **(c)** *examples of miniature vessels from the assemblage in room 132. U. Nowotnick, © DAI.*

centres, classifying the pottery of the temple precinct into twenty-three different groups of clay sources belonging to six production centres. The pinkish wares of production centre "A" are geochemically different to the other clays and might have been imported from another region.

Among the pottery of production centre "A", there is one example of a typical seventh–fourth centuries BC "torpedo-shaped" Type-4100 jar (van Beek 1969: 170; see Fig. 9/a), recovered near the western temenos wall inside the temple forecourt (Fig. 3/i). Such vessels are known from other sites in the highlands and from South Arabia (Porter 2004: 262–264). However, the fabric of the Wuqro specimen does not resemble the sand-tempered wares of Type-4100 jars hitherto published. It was made of a very light, distinctively pink ware with a few temper inclusions and fired at high temperatures in an oxidizing atmosphere. The fabrics of production centre "A" were

[13] The archaeometric analysis was conducted by M. Daszkiewicz (ARCHEA — Archaeometric Analysis and Research, Warsaw), E. Bobryk (Faculty of Chemistry, Warsaw University of Technology), and G. Schneider (Arbeitsgruppe Archäometrie, Freie Universität, Berlin). Matrix group by refiring classifies the clays according to their composition, while X-ray fluorescence spectroscopy determines the composition of elements within a sample and classifies them into provenance groups (Daszkiewicz & Schneider 2001).

only used for a few other vessel forms at the temple site; otherwise this ware is unmatched to and incompatible with all other clays in the assemblage.

The relatively small sample of pottery produced only a few preserved vessel forms. The spectrum ranges from cups, small dishes, and fine jars to big bowls and deep pots similar to examples from Yeha (Robin & de Maigret 1998: fig. 47) and Kidane Mehret (Phillips JS 2000: 304–309). Vessels with rounded or footed bases are quite frequent. A type of red ware bottle with a globular body and long cylindrical neck probably from the second building period of the temple is only rarely known from other sites.

The northern room 115 of the tripartite sanctuary was most likely used for incense offerings. Three burners were found in an ash accumulation on the floor level of the first phase (Fig. 3/f). One of the bi-conical shaped vessels was 38 cm high; the other was decorated with incised lines (Fig. 9/b); the third one was a four-legged rectangular pottery box or stove with incised triangles, most likely serving the same function as a burner. In addition, several fragments of copper alloy implements were found among the artefacts in the tripartite sanctuary.

A remarkable collection of miniature vessels and votive objects was discovered in room 132 in the north-eastern corner of the temenos (Fig. 3/g). The thirty recovered pottery vessels comprise mainly miniatures of small bowls, strainers, globular jars, and incense burners (Fig. 9/c). In addition, several clay figurines of humans and animals were found there. The dense assemblage, its good state of preservation, and the symbolic size of the objects suggest either a workshop or storage of the temple's liturgical inventory or a place where people without access to the inner parts of the precinct could sacrifice votive objects. Such an assemblage of miniatures can be compared to similar collections found at different sacral and funerary sites in Tigray and Eritrea.[14] A masterpiece, a miniature shrine bearing the sculptured image of a tiny female figure and decorated with the Almaqah symbol of the moon crescent and disc, was found in the debris directly north of the temple (Fig. 10, cf. Fig. 3/h).

FIGURE 10. *A miniature shrine with a female effigy. P. Wolf, © DAI.*

The "Sabaean style" of the Wuqro temple

In addition to the temples of Yeha (Krencker 1913: 78–84; Robin & de Maigret 1998) and Melazo (Leclant 1959), the temple under discussion in this paper is the third one dedicated to Almaqah discovered in the Tigrean highlands.[15] The temples of Wuqro and Melazo are almost identical in size, while the Yeha temple is larger but has similar proportions.[16] The three temples have several structural features in common: their western orientation; a rectangular, symmetrical layout; and an axial arrangement of their basic components of pronaos, naos with a centrally placed libation altar,[17] and a separate sanctuary in the rear part, which was divided in Wuqro and Yeha into three compartments.[18] In addition, the Wuqro and Yeha temples represent temples with an elevated inner floor level.

Many of these features are common in South Arabian sacral architecture. The architectural concept of the Wuqro temple is, in particular, related to a specific prototype in the

[14] At Hawlti (de Contenson 1963: 44, 48–60), Matara (Anfray 1963*a*: pl. 86; Anfray & Annequin 1965: pl. 58–61; Anfray 1965: pl. 18), in the graves at Yeha (Anfray 1963*b*: pls 136–138), and later at Aksum (Wilding 1989: 242–243).

[15] For the dedication of both other temples to Almaqah, see Robin & de Maigret (1998: 794–796) and Leclant (1959: 45).

[16] Wuqro: *c*.8.5×7 m; Melazo: 8.90×6.75 m (Leclant 1959: 44); Yeha: 18.6×15 m (Robin & de Maigret 1998: 745).

[17] In Yeha, the actual location of the altar is still indicated in the temple floor (Robin & de Maigret 1998: 758, figs 7, 22, 25); fragments of the inscribed libation altar top stones are kept in the small "museum" in the precinct. In Melazo, fragments of a libation altar were found in the main sanctuary (Leclant 1959: 50, doc. 15, pl. 38/b).

[18] In Melazo this can only be assumed.

sacral architecture of the early Sabaean period, which is basically characterized by its symmetrical, axis-oriented rectangular layout, usually provided with a hypaethral naos and a tripartite sanctuary (Schmidt 1982*a*: 161–165; 1997–1998: 14–20). It is common not only in the centre of the Sabaean kingdom around Māʾrib and Ṣirwāḥ, but also known from examples in the neighbouring Minean or Tiḥāmah regions (e.g. Phillips C 1997). The initial building stage of the Wuqro temple closely resembles early prototypes of Sabaean hypaethral temples without peristasis, such as the temple of Ǧabal Balaq al-Ausaṭ near Māʾrib (Schmidt 1982*a*: 162; 1997–1998: 14). Its latest preserved state, which provided the longitudinal walls that supported a peristasis, corresponds to a more elaborate form of this schema, represented by temples like the Waddum ḏū-Masmaᶜim temple at Wādī Quṭūṭah, which is epigraphically dated to *c*.700 BC (Schmidt 1982*b*; 2007), the contemporaneous Almaqah temple in al-Masāǧid (Schmidt 1982*c*), or the ᶜAṭtar temple near Maᶜīn (Schmidt 1982*d*). The resemblance concerns not only components of the naos but also the layout of the entire precinct. Similar to these temples, the Wuqro temple occupies the rear part of a rectangular-shaped temenos surrounded by a wall, while the space in front of the elevated building represents a large forecourt, in its architectural concept comparable to the Barʾān temple of Almaqah in the southern oasis of Māʾrib (Vogt 1998). Without large-scale prospection of the area around the temple precinct, it is not yet possible to establish whether the Wuqro temple was situated *intra* or *extra muros*.

By comparison, the temple of Yeha has specific features in common with a different line of sacral architecture in South Arabia, the so-called "hypostyle temples", prevalent in the Minean region and the Ḥaḍramawt (see e.g. Schmidt 1982*a*: 166–169; 1997–1998: 26–32; Jung 1988: 196f.), and represented for example by the Minean Nakraḥ temple in Barāqish, which in many of its features it closely resembles (Robin & de Maigret 1998: 775–780).

Finally, the basic architectural concept of these three Almaqah temples contrasts with other structures of attributed sacral function in Tigray, such as the two eastward-oriented, square-shaped sanctuaries at Hawlti (de Contenson 1963: 41–45, pls 26–29), with which, according to Finneran (2007: 135) and Michels (1979: 13), the monuments at Seglamien near Aksum and Fiqya near Matara in Eritrea are broadly compatible (see Anfray 1965: 6, pl. 3/A–B; Curtis & Habtemichael 2008: 325).

The rarity of sites with sacral architecture indicative of South Arabian influence in Tigray led recently to the statement that "the temple architecture of the *DᶜMT* polity does not faithfully reflect South Arabian designs" (Finneran 2007: 136). With regard to our discoveries we can, as in Yeha, undoubtedly challenge this statement. The Tigrean sacral architecture of the early first millennium BC was evidently not uniform. A variety of religious attitudes were certainly present in the Ethiopio-Eritrean highlands as they were in contemporaneous South Arabia, which must have resulted in different architectural concepts. The temple of Wuqro reflects a concept that is clearly attested in the sacral architecture of the Sabaean kingdom.

Concluding remarks

Apart from its significance for the study of religious architecture, the site of Meqaber Gaᶜewa has further important implications. First of all, it shows that the political and religious network of that period extended much farther into the south than hitherto assumed, probably along an ancient trade route linking the Red Sea and the northern centres with southern regions of Tigray.[19] This conclusion is supported not only by the discovery of the Almaqah temple. The field survey started in autumn 2008 revealed twenty-seven sites within a 2.5 km range around Meqaber Gaᶜewa. By comparing pottery fabrics we were able to identify at least seven further sites that can be dated to the period of the temple. Most interesting is a small mound called Ziban Adi. It resembles the site of Meqaber Gaᶜewa in size and shape, and is the find spot of one of the incense burners stored in the church of Abuna Garima. Large amounts of surface pottery and obsidian flakes are distributed at the foot of this mound.

The cult objects of the Wuqro temple are of a remarkable preservation and quality. The libation installation found *in situ* and completely preserved with altar, drain, and collecting basin, is not only singular in the northern Horn of Africa but also comparable to the finest examples of its kind in South Arabia, where such libation installations are essential components of temples of that type.

The temple's components — the altar, the dedication inscriptions, the female statue, as well as various incense burners found in its northern sanctuary — shed light on the temple cult and liturgical practices and thus the religious beliefs predominating in that particular region and period. The large number of pottery and votive objects found mainly in the rear part of the precinct indicate that

[19] It is attested in later periods by an Arabic inscription of the tenth century AD (Smidt, forthcoming).

the temple was an important and frequented centre of religious activities — apparently not only for the local elite. It was the place where the god was invoked for help and favour by offering liquids, incense, and symbolic objects. A particular aspect of Almaqah is eminent in several of these artefacts. The god's nature as a creator, granting health and fertility, is not only attested by the epigraphic evidence on the base of the female statue but is, furthermore, indicated by the numerous female effigies: the miniature shrine and several clay figurines. Another significant feature is the *baityl* cult installation in the central sanctuary. Such cult places played an important role in pre-Islamic (South) Arabian ritual practice and are regarded as being archetypes of Sabaean sacral shrines (e.g. Schmidt 1997–1998: 14).

In addition, the inscriptions of the Wuqro temple confirm the significance of Yeha as a super-regional sacral and ceremonial centre of that period, since Yeha was epigraphically hitherto not confirmed. At the same time they shed some light on the indigenous African substratum. According to Norbert Nebes, the inscriptions are palaeographically and orthographically clearly Sabaic. The affiliation of king *WR'N* mentions, however, the name of his mother beside the name of his father. This is very unusual in South Arabian inscriptions and reflects an African concept, comparable to the inscriptions of the contemporaneous Egyptianized kings of Napata in the middle Nile Valley, which use Egyptian language and titles, but refer to their matrilineal ancestry in their texts and depict their female ancestors in royal reliefs and stelae.[20] Finally, the inscriptions help to clarify the kind of contacts between the northern Horn and South Arabia, showing that Sabaean craftsmen were active at different places in Tigray, not only in centres such as Yeha.

The interaction of an indigenous culture with a dominant civilization is of major interest in the current research. During the first millennium BC, interesting parallels of the Ethiopian highlands can be drawn with similar processes in the middle Nile Valley.[21] During the Napatan period in the seventh to fourth centuries BC, the Kushite elite similarly adopted cultural elements from its northern neighbour Egypt, including religious attitudes, burial customs, as well as sacral and funerary architecture. Egyptian craftsmen from Memphis were active in the building and furnishing of Napatan temples that were closely reminiscent of their Egyptian counterparts; the Egyptian language was used for royal inscriptions. At the same time, clear indications of local African traits can be perceived in titles, inscriptions, artistic iconography, and styles. During the Meroitic period in the following centuries, Egyptian cultural influence declined and the indigenous traditions became stronger — similar to contemporary periods in Tigray. Thus, a comparative look at neighbouring regions in Eastern Africa might contribute to the understanding of the Ethio-Sabaean contacts in the Ethiopian highlands.

Acknowledgements

Both preliminary excavations conducted in autumn 2008 and spring 2009 are based on scholarly co-operation, established in 2008, between the Tigray Tourism & Culture Commission (TCC, Mekelle), the Institut für Sprachen und Kulturen des Vorderen Orients, Friedrich-Schiller-Universität (FSU Jena), and the Oriental Department, German Archaeological Institute (DAI, Berlin). Both seasons were financially supported by funds from the FSU and the DAI. Initial preservation work at the site and the construction of stores and working rooms suitable for a future on-site museum, were funded by the German Ministry of Foreign Affairs in spring 2009.

The authors would like to express their gratitude to these institutions and especially to their directors, Kebede Amare, Norbert Nebes, and Ricardo Eichmann, as well as to the Authority for Research & Conservation of Cultural Heritage, Ministry of Culture & Tourism (Addis Ababa) and its director, Jara Haile Mariam, for enabling the project and the excavations to take place within a very short period. In addition, we wish to thank all those who have taken part in the actual fieldwork, the local workforce, our Ethiopian-German team of scholars and students, and especially Bereket Gebretsadik, the TCC representative in Wuqro.

Sigla

FHN *Fontes Historiae Nubiorum*, see Eide *et al.* 1994.

JE Registration *siglum* in the National Museum in Addis Ababa (Ethiopia).

RIE *Recueil des inscriptions de l'Éthiopie,* see Bernand, Drewes & Schneider 1991–2000.

[20] See, for example, the stelae of King Taharqo from Kawa (FHN 22 and 24) or of King Aspelta from the great Amun temple at Napata (FHN 37 and 39).

[21] However, the Egyptian impact on Nubia was much more intense and extensive. In the second millennium BC, Nubia had been part of the Egyptian empire for many centuries. During the 25th Dynasty, Nubian kings ruled over Egypt for several decades.

References

Anfray F.

1963*a*. Première campagne de fouilles à Matara (Nov 1959–Jan 1960). *Annales d'Éthiopie* 5: 87–166.

1963*b*. Une campagne de fouilles à Yeha (Février–Mars 1960). *Annales d'Éthiopie* 5: 171–192.

1965. Chronique Archéologique (1960–1964). *Annales d'Éthiopie* 6: 3–26.

1990. *Les Anciens Éthiopiens.* Paris: Colin.

Anfray F. & Annequin G.

1965. Matara: deuxième, troisième et quatrième campagnes de fouilles. *Annales d'Éthiopie* 6: 49–142.

Bernand E., Drewes A.J. & Schneider R.

1991–2000. *Recueil des inscriptions de l'Éthiopie des périodes pré-axoumite et axoumite.* Paris: Académie des Inscriptions et Belles Lettres.

Caquot A. & Drewes J.

1955. Les Monuments recueillis à Magallé. *Annales d'Éthiopie* 1: 17–26.

Contenson H. de

1963. Les fouilles à Haoulti en 1959: rapport préliminaire. *Annales d'Éthiopie* 5: 41–86.

1981. Pre-Aksumite culture. Pages 341–361 in G. Mokhtar (ed.), *UNESCO General History of Africa.* ii. London: Heinemann.

Curtis M.C. & Habtemichael D.

2008. Matara, Keskese and the "Classical Period" archaeology of the Akkele Guzay highlands: a brief overview. Pages 311–327 in P.R. Schmidt, M.C. Curtis & Z. Teka (eds), *The Archaeology of Ancient Eritrea.* Trenton/Asmara: Red Sea Press.

Daszkiewicz M. & Schneider G.

2001. Klassifizierung von Keramik durch Nachbrennen von Scherben. *Zeitschrift für Schweizerische Archäologie und Kunstgeschichte* 58: 25–32.

Eide T., Hägg T., Pierce R.H. & Török L. (eds)

1994. *Fontes Historiae Nubiorum. Textual Sources for the History of the Middle Nile Region between the Eighth Century BC and the Sixth Century AD.* i. *From the eighth to the mid-fifth century BC.* Bergen: John Grieg AS.

Finneran N.

2007. *The Archaeology of Ethiopia.* Abingdon: Routledge.

Godet E.

1977. Répertoire des sites pré-axoumites et axoumites de Tigré (Éthiopie). *Abbay* 8: 19–58.

1983. Répertoire des sites pré-axoumites et axoumites d'Éthiopie du nord, IIe partie: Erythrée. *Abbay* 11: 73–113.

Jung M.

1988. The Religious Monuments of Ancient Southern Arabia. A Preliminary Typological Classification. *Annali dell'istituto universitario orientale di Napoli* 48: 177–218.

Krencker D.

1913. *Ältere Denkmäler Nordabessiniens, Deutsche Aksum-Expedition.* ii. Berlin: Reimer.

Leclant J.

1959. Haoulti-Melazo (1955–1956). *Annales d'Éthiopie* 3: 43–57.

Michels J.W.

1979. Axumite Archaeology: an introductory essay. Page 13 in Y.M. Kobishchanov, *Axum.* London: The Pennsylvania State University Press.

Nebes N.

(forthcoming). Neue äthio-sabäische Inschriften aus Addi Akaweh. *Zeitschrift für Orientarchäologie.*

Phillips C.

1997. Al-Hamid — A Route to the Red Sea? Pages 287–295 in A. Avanzini (ed.), *Profumi d'Arabia.* Rome: "L'Erma" di Bretschneider.

Phillips J.S.
2000. Pottery and clay objects. Pages 303–337 in D.W. Phillipson (ed.), *Archaeology at Aksum, Ethiopia, 1993–97*. London: British Institute in Eastern Africa and Society of Antiquaries.

Phillipson D.W.
1998. *Ancient Ethiopia: Aksum, its antecedents and successors*. London: The British Museum Press.
(in press). The first millennium BC in the highlands of northern Ethiopia and south-central Eritrea: a reassessment of cultural and political development. *African Archaeological Review* 26/4.

Porter A.
2004. Amphora trade between South Arabia and East Africa in the first millennium BC: a re-examination of the evidence. *Proceedings of the Seminar for Arabian Studies* 34: 261–275.

Robin C.J. & de Maigret M.A.
1998. Le grand temple de Yéha (Tigray, Éthiopie), après la première campagne de fouilles de la mission française (1998). *Académie des Inscriptions et Belles-Lettres, comptes rendus* 142: 737–798.

Schmidt J.
1982*a*. Zur altsüdarabischen Tempelarchitektur. *Archäologische Berichte aus dem Yemen* 1: 161–169.
1982*b*. Der Tempel des Waddum ḏū-Masmaᶜim. *Archäologische Berichte aus dem Yemen* 1: 91–99.
1982*c*. Tempel und Heiligtum von al-Masāǧid. *Archäologische Berichte aus dem Yemen* 1: 135–141.
1982*d*. Der ᶜAṯtar -Tempel bei Maᶜīn. *Archäologische Berichte aus dem Yemen* 1: 143–155.
1997–1998. Tempel und Heiligtümer in Südarabien. Zu den materiellen und formalen Strukturen der Sakralbaukunst. *Nürnberger Blätter zur Archäologie* 14: 10–40.
2007. Der Tempel des Waddum ḏū-Masmaᶜim am Wādī Quṭūṭa. *Archäologische Berichte aus dem Yemen* 11: 3–15.

Smidt W.
(forthcoming). "Weqro". In S. Uhlig (ed.), *Encyclopaedia Aethiopica*. iv. Wiesbaden: Harrassowitz.

van Beek G.W.
1969. *Hajar Bin Ḥumeid. Investigations at a pre-Islamic Site in South Arabia.* (Publications of the American Foundation of the Study of Man, 5). Baltimore, MD: The Johns Hopkins Press.

Vogt B.
1998. Der Almaqah-Tempel von Barᵓān (ᶜArsh Bilqīs). Pages 219–222 in W. Seipel (ed.), *Jemen. Kunst und Archäologie im Land der Königin von Sabaᵓ*. Vienna: Kunshistorisches Museum/Milan: Skira.

Wilding R.F.
1989. The Pottery. Pages 235–316 in S.C. Munro-Hay, *Excavations at Aksum. An account of research at the ancient Ethiopian capital directed in 1972–4 by the late Dr Neville Chittick*. London: The British Institute in Eastern Africa.

Authors' addresses
Dr Pawel Wolf, Deutsches Archäologisches Institut, Orient Abteilung (Projekt Wuqro) & Zentrale (Projekt Meroe-Hamadab), Podbielskiallee 69–71, D–14195 Berlin, Germany.

e-mail pwolf@skydsl.de

Mag. Ulrike Nowotnick, Deutsches Archäologisches Institut, Zentrale (Projekt Meroe-Hamadab), Podbielskiallee 69–71, D-14195 Berlin, Germany.

e-mail un@dainst.de

Papers read at the Seminar for Arabian Studies held at the British Museum, London on 23–25 July 2009

NB All papers published in this volume of PSAS or in its Supplement are in *italics.*

Papers from the "Special Session: The development of Arabic as a written language" are published in a Supplement to this volume which is edited by Michael Macdonald.

FOCUS SESSION: CURRENT FIELDWORK IN QATAR

Rebecca Beardmore, Richard Cuttler, Eleanor Ramsey, Faisal Abdulla Al-Naimi, Simon Fitch & Heiko Kallweit	*Reconstruction of the Late Pleistocene and Holocene palaeogeography of Qatar using remotely sensed datasets, and the implications for the integration of such data into the National Monument Record for Qatar*
Juergen Schreiber	Excavations at Umm al-Mā', Qatar: preliminary report on the first two campaigns
Alexandrine Guérin & Faisal Abdulla Al-Naimi	*Using pottery to understand a district in the Abbasid village of Murwab (ninth century, Qatar)*
Andrew Petersen, Tony Grey & Catherine Rees	*Qalᶜat al-Ruwayḍah, Qatar*
Alan Walmsley, Hugh Barnes & Phillip Macumber	*Al-Zubārah and its hinterland: archaeology and heritage*

SPECIAL SESSION: THE DEVELOPMENT OF ARABIC AS A WRITTEN LANGUAGE

Christian Julien Robin	*Introduction to the Special Session: the development of Arabic as a written language*
Michael Macdonald	Why did Arabic remain a purely spoken language for so long?
Laïla Nehmé	*A glimpse of the development of the Nabataean script into Arabic based on old and new epigraphic material*
ᶜAlī Ibrāhīm Al-Ghabbān	*The evolution of the Arabic script in the period of the Prophet Muḥammad and the Orthodox Caliphs in the light of new inscriptions discovered in the Kingdom of Saudi Arabia*
Robert Hoyland	*Power, patronage and Arabic inscriptions*
Pierre Larcher	*In search of a standard: dialect choices in the development of Classical Arabic*
François Déroche	*The Codex Parisino-petropolitanus and the Ḥijāzī scripts*
Alain George	On the roots and context of the Ḥijāzī corpus
Venetia Porter	*The use of writing in magic*
Gregor Schoeler	*The relationship of literacy and memory in the second/eighth century*
Marcus Fraser	Qur'āns in 'Ḥijāzī' scripts: marshalling the evidence

THE MBI AL JABER PUBLIC LECTURE

Michael C.A. Macdonald	*Ancient Arabia and the written word*

ARCHITECTURE, LANDSCAPE & FOOD RESOURCES

Christian Darles	*La généralisation du bois chez les bâtisseurs du Yémen antique*
Soumyen Bandyopadhyay	*Topographic conceptions in Omani architecture*

ARABIC & MODERN SOUTH ARABIAN

Samia Naïm	*The semantic structure of motion verbs in the dialect of Zabīd (Tihāmah, Yemen)*

Janet C.E. Watson & Alex Bellem	*A detective story: emphatics in Mehri*
Samuel Liebhaber	*Written Mahri, Mahri* fuṣḥā *and their implications for early historical Arabic*

ANCIENT WEST & SOUTH ARABIA

Anne Multhoff	*How difficult is it to dedicate a statuette? A new approach to some Sabaic inscriptions from Maʾrib*
Serge A. Frantsouzoff	*Once more on the interpretation of* mṯl *in Epigraphic South Arabian (a new expiatory inscription on irrigation from Kamna)*
Peter Stein	*Irrigation management in pre-Islamic South Arabia according to the epigraphic evidence*
Alessio Agostini	*Building materials in South Arabian construction inscriptions*
Stephen Buckley, Katherine Worthington, Joann Fletcher, Kirsty Penkman, Michael Buckley & Hanna Koon	Study of leather involved in ancient Yemeni burial practices
Paul Yule	Fieldwork in Ẓafār, capital of Ḥimyar (Yemen)
Krista Lewis, Lamya Khalidi, William Eisenberger & Ali Sanabani	*Mapping Maṣnaʿat Māryah: using GIS to reconstruct the development of a multi-period site in the highlands of Yemen*
Pawel Wolf & Ulrike Nowotnick	*The Almaqah temple of Mekaber Gaʿewa near Wuqro (Tigray, Ethiopia)*

SOUTH ARABIAN ETHNOGRAPHY

Dionisius Agius, John Cooper, Julian Jansen Van Rensburg & Chiara Zazzaro	*Wooden boatbuilding in Yemen: Arabia's last redoubt (The MARES Project)*
Mikhail Rodionov	*A* ṣarf *talisman from Ghayl Bā Wazīr, Ḥaḍramawt*

POSTER PRESENTATIONS

Luca Belfioretti & Tom Vosmer	Jawharat Muscat Project
Ora Berger	Fishes (*Hūtī*)
Ora Berger	Sanaa and Aden: Arabic writing in "carpet pages" of Hebrew illuminated Bibles
Manfred Böhme	*Wādī al-ʿAyn: first investigations at Qubur Juhal, Oman*
Paul Breeze	Cultural mapping and signature landscape characterization in Qatar using Remote Sensing
Philipp Drechsler, Dhaifallah al-Talhi & Abdulhamid al-Hashash	Dosariyah revisited — new archaeological investigations in the Eastern Province of the Kingdom of Saudi Arabia
Jessica Giraud, Ali Hamood Saif al-Mahrooqi, Guillaume Gernez, Sabrina Righetti, Émilie Portat, Christophe Sévin-Allouet, Marion Lemée & †Serge Cleuziou	*First three campaigns of survey to Ādam from 2007 to 2009*

Moawiyah M. Ibrahim	Arabic epigraphy and writing materials in Oman
Bill Isenberger	The west wall of the Peristyle Hall, Awam Temple (Mahram Bilqis)
Ali Hamood Saif al-Mahrooqi	Documentation of old township (*ḥarat*) in the Sultanate of Oman
Faisal Abdulla Al-Naimi, Richard Cuttler, Hatem Arrock & Howell Roberts	*An Upper Palaeolithic and Early Holocene flint scatter at Raʾs ʿUshayriq, western Qatar*
Khudooma Said al-Naʾimi	Estimation of body height of old Omani *aflāj* builders from hands impressions on *sarooj* disks
Ash Parton, Adrian G. Parker, Andrew R. Farrant, Melanie J. Leng, Hans-Peter Uerpmann, Jean-Luc Schwenninger, Chris Galletti & Jon Wells	*Evidence for an early MIS3 wet phase from within south-east Arabia*
Abdulla el Reyes	The National Centre for Documentation and Research (NCDR) "Memory of the Nation"
Sabrina Righetti & †Serge Cleuziou	*The Wadi Suq pottery: typological study of the pottery assemblage at Hili 8 (UAE)*
Janet C.E. Watson & Alex Bellem	The changing role of Semitic emphatics? Evidence from Arabic and beyond
Paul Yule	Relative chronology of the stone building at Ẓafār, capital of the Ḥimyarite Confederation
Zaydoon Zaid	Awam Temple (Mahram Bilqis)